BY THE EDITORS OF
CONSUMER GUIDE®

THE ILLUSTRATED DO·IT·YOURSELF MANUAL

PUBLICATIONS INTERNATIONAL, LTD.

Written by James Hufnagle
Illustrations: Clarence A. Moberg
Cover photos courtesy of:
The Hirsh Company, Skokie, IL
Skil Corporation, Chicago, IL
Stanley Tools, Division of The Stanley Works, New
   Britain, CT

CONTENTS

INTERIOR PAINTING AND PAPERING
8

FURNITURE
41

OTHER INSIDE JOBS
96

INTRODUCTION

Congratulations! By purchasing *The Illustrated Do-It-Yourself Manual*, you've taken the first step to becoming an accomplished home handyperson. There is a lot to learn, but this book can be your guide.

Perhaps you're eager to flip the pages and tackle a do-it-yourself project that urgently needs doing at your house. Please go ahead and do this, but first take a few minutes to learn how *The Illustrated Do-It-Yourself Manual* is organized, and why it's organized the way it is. By familiarizing yourself with the contents of each chapter, you can quickly turn to the right place when you need help.

We started with two of the most popular do-it-yourself activities: painting and papering. Even if you've already successfully painted or papered a room, Chapter 1 can help you accomplish faster, neater, and more professional-looking decorating projects. You'll learn about different paint and paper choices, how accurately to estimate the amounts of materials you'll need, and which tools and supplies produce the best results. New paint or wall covering can give a room an entirely different look, but neither removes surface defects in walls and ceilings. Chapter 1 guides you through the all-important prepping process, then shows you, step by step, how to paint and paper like a pro. You'll even find time-saving tips about cleaning up.

Every household has some furniture that needs repair or refinishing. Chapter 2 explains the way in which furniture is put together, then presents techniques you can use to remedy surface defects and minor blemishes. Do you have a piece of furniture with a finish that has grown shabby with age? Maybe you can revive it with a thorough cleaning or by reamalgamating the original finish. Maybe you would be better off to strip away the old finish and put on a new one. Chapter 2 tells how to evaluate what has to be done and shows you how to do it. If you have furniture that is wobbly, weak, split, or broken, you'll be especially interested in learning how to make structural repairs.

Look around the interior of your home or apartment. Chances are you'll find a few things that need repairing. There also may be places you would like to decorate or improve. Chapter 3 covers a wide range of inside jobs. We arranged it according to the major elements of your home: walls and ceilings, stairs and floors, windows and doors. Here you'll find information about how to hang things, how to repair moldings, and how to install ceramic tile. We also discuss flooring and ceiling tiles, how to put up paneling, lay carpeting, build a partition, and hang a door. None of these tasks is too difficult to do yourself. All it takes is know-how.

Chapter 4 deals with work that needs to be done outside your home. It starts with landscaping and tells about ways to simplify yard work. Masonry and fence projects come next; there is everything from patching concrete to constructing a new fence and railroad-tie retaining wall. Then we turn to your home's exterior components: siding, garage doors, roofs, and gutters. If you are planning to paint your house, our instructions take you, step by step, through the job. This chapter also focuses on foundation work that can be vital to your home's comfort and structural integrity.

Drains that don't drain, toilets that gurgle, and faucets that drip haunt every household from time to time. Chapter 5 takes the mystery out of plumbing. Here you'll learn exactly how plumbing works and what to do when it doesn't. Most plumbing repairs are easy once you have a few special tools and a working knowledge of what you need to do. Master the basics in Chapter 5, and you need never again be vexed by a clogged drain or toilet; a leaky faucet; or dripping, frozen, or banging pipes. There is even a section that explains how private septic systems work and how to maintain them.

Learning to work safely with electricity is easy. Chapter 6 examines the principles and precautions you need to know about your home's electrical system, then shows how you can apply them to many electrical repairs. The chapter also demonstrates electrical installations you can do yourself.

Once you've mastered the principles of electricity, you'll be ready to learn about some of your home's major electric appliances. Refrigerators and freezers, dishwashers, clothes washers, and dryers respond to the same basic repair procedures: You systematically locate the cause of a problem, then fix or replace the faulty components. As with other chapters, Chapter 7 begins by explaining how appliances work and acquaints you with the few special tools you need to track down appliance problems. Next it tells how to repair or replace components basic to all appliances, such as cords and plugs, gaskets, switches, and thermostats. Then you'll find an appliance-by-appliance guide.

Heating and cooling systems are responsible for our comfort. In many households, they also consume more energy than all the other appli-ances put together. Chapter 8 treats heating and cooling systems by presenting the basics first and then giving a component-by-component run-down of maintenance and repair procedures and troubleshooting techniques. Although you may take them for granted, your home's insulation, ventilation, and weather stripping are as important to your family's comfort and budget as the machinery that supplies heating and cooling. Chapter 8 concludes with information about conserving costly heating and cooling energy.

Chapters 9 and 10 lead you, one step at a time, through two complex do-it-yourself projects: remodeling your kitchen and your bathroom. Painstaking planning is critical to the success of any remodeling project, especially in spaces as tight as baths and kitchens. You'll find detailed plans here. Most construction procedures involve techniques covered in earlier chapters, such as framing a wall, installing drywall and flooring, hanging doors, painting, and papering. Cabinet, countertop, appliance, and fixture installations also are covered in Chapters 9 and 10.

An appendix of helpful information about basic tools, abrasives, fasteners, and adhesives completes this do-it-yourself reference guide. Refer to these pages before you set out for the hardware store or lumberyard.

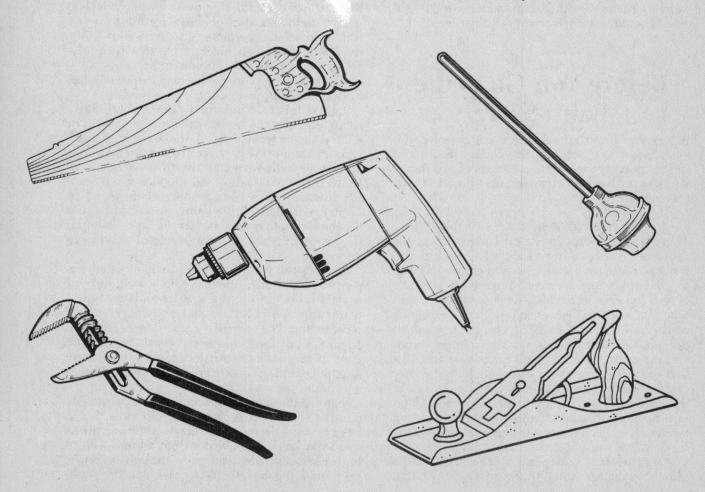

INTERIOR PAINTING AND PAPERING

At one time or another, just about everyone, owners and renters alike, has a room that needs painting or papering. These are the most popular do-it-yourself activities and the ones most frequently botched. Painting and papering are easy but neither is as easy as it seems. You need the right materials, the right tools, and the right techniques to do the job right. Invest a little time in doing your homework before you get down to work, and you'll find yourself painting and papering like a pro the first time out. Because paint is the more popular decorating material, we'll begin with it, and then move on to wall coverings.

Before You Go to the Paint Store

Before you pop the top on a fresh can of paint, even before you venture out to your local paint dealer to pore over color chips, there are things you should know about paint and how to use it successfully.

SELECTING THE RIGHT PAINT

There are paints for every possible surface, but there is no such thing as an all-surface paint. Because the wrong paint can sometimes damage a wall surface and often will not adhere well, it's crucial to know in advance what goes where and when. Modern paint technology has taken much of the risk out of choosing the proper paint. Formulas for latex paints have been improved to withstand dirt, moisture, and daily wear and tear, and are no longer reserved exclusively for low traffic areas. They are now as washable and durable as the old oil-base paints. This means that you no longer have to think in terms of latex paints for walls and oil-base enamels for woodwork, windows, and doors.

An important factor in paint selection is its gloss. No matter which coating you choose (the two major categories are latex and alkyd), the gloss of the paint you buy affects both its appearance and its durability. Generally, high-gloss paints are the most durable because they contain more resin than either semigloss or flat paints. Resin is an ingredient that solidifies and hardens as the paint dries. The more resin, the harder the surface. For kitchens, bathrooms, utility rooms, doors, windows, and trim, high-gloss paints are ideal. Semigloss paints, with less resin and a reduced surface shine, are less wear resistant, but they are still suitable for most woodwork. Flat paints are the coatings of choice for most interior walls and ceilings because they provide an attractive low-glare finish for surfaces that take little abuse and require only infrequent washings.

The following paint primer will help you select the kind of paint you need for your project.

Latex Paints. The word "latex" originally stemmed from the use of rubber in one form or another as the resin, or solid, in the paint. The solvent, or thinner, was water. Today, many paints are made with water as the thinner but with resins that are not latex, and the industry is leaning toward terms such as "water-thinned" or "water-reducible." If the paints are called latex at all, the term often used is "acrylic latex" because they contain a plastic resin made of acrylics or polyvinyls.

Besides the speed of drying, which usually is just over an hour, opacity, and washability of acrylic latex paints, the greatest advantage of water-thinned paints is that you can clean up with water. The expense and the potential fire hazard of volatile thinners and brush cleaners are gone. If you wash the brush or roller immediately after the painting session is over, it comes clean in a few minutes.

Latex paint works well on surfaces previously painted with latex or flat oil-base paints. It can even be used on unprimed drywall or unpainted masonry. Latex usually does not adhere well to high-gloss finishes, and even though it can be used on wallpaper, there is a risk that the water

HOW MUCH PAINT AND TIME WILL YOU NEED?

Standing in line at the counter at the paint store is no time to try to estimate how much paint your project requires. Take a few minutes at home to measure the area to be painted.

According to the manufacturer's calculations, a gallon of paint will cover 450 square feet. Don't even think about "stretching it." If you do, you'll sacrifice overall performance. Worse, especially if you're buying custom-colored paint, you may have to go back to the store for more paint that, despite the dealer's best effort, may not be a perfect match. If you're buying two or more gallons of the same color, it's a good idea to mix them together at home so that color variations don't show up in the middle of a wall. For estimating purposes, do yourself a favor and figure 400 square feet of coverage per gallon of paint.

To determine the amount of paint required to cover a wall, multiply the height of the wall by its length, then divide by 400. This means a gallon of paint will cover a 10-by-15-foot room with one coat. Two coats will take two gallons.

When a wall is textured or rough-troweled, it takes more paint than a smooth wall. This is because the texture represents added surface to be covered, although it does not contribute to the size of the area. How much more depends on how textured the surface is, but, for medium-rough, porous, or previously unpainted walls, don't expect to get more than 350 square feet of coverage from a gallon of paint.

Most walls have doors or windows or other areas that are not painted. If the nonpaint area is small, such as a single window or door, ignore it. Two or three windows, a door and a window, multiple sliding doors, or a fireplace offer a little savings in materials, if not labor. You can multiply the lengths by the widths of these nonpaint areas to get the total square footage that you can subtract from your surface figures, or you can subtract about 15 square feet for typical windows and 21 square feet for typical doors. (These figures also can be used to estimate the paint you'll need for each if you plan to use a different color or surface finish.) If you're also painting the ceiling, figure its square foot area at width times length.

Estimating the time you'll have to put in on any given paint project is significantly less precise. Obviously, some people work faster than others, so there is no way to account for individual differences in speed. On the average, you should be able to cover about 120 square feet of flat surface in about an hour. For bare wood or plaster, figure about 100 square feet. In a typical 12-by-15-foot room, you're likely to spend four or five hours on the job, trim work included for the first coat. The second coat will go faster, but you'll have to wait for the first coat to dry, from 2 to 36 hours.

---

in the paint may cause the paper to peel away from the wall. Because of its water content, latex causes iron and steel to rust and raises the grain on raw wood.

Alkyd Resin Paints. The use of synthetic alkyd resin for solvent-thinned (oil-base) paints has several advantages. One of the most useful is a special formulation that makes the paint the consistency of yogurt. A brush dipped in it carries many times as much paint to the surface as older formulas. Under the friction of stroking, the paint spreads and smoothes readily.

Gloss and semigloss (or satin) alkyd materials are preferred by many painters for trim, doors, and even heavy-traffic hallways. Many homeowners use alkyd paint for bathrooms and kitchens, where they feel more confident of washability despite the availability of water-thinned enamels in satin or gloss that can be safely cleaned with standard household cleaners.

The opacity of alkyd paints (the ability completely to cover one color with another) has been improved through the addition of an entirely new ingredient. When the paint is manufactured, a portion of the white pigment particles (titanium dioxide) is replaced with a material that diffuses and evaporates, leaving minute bubbles. These "microvids" reflect and scatter light, giving the paint the effect of more thickness than it really has. With paints of this formula, one coat of white will cover black completely.

While alkyds should not be used on unprimed drywall (they can raise the nap of its paper coating) or unprimed masonry, they are suitable for raw wood and almost any previously painted or papered surface. Alkyds are dry enough for a second coat within four to six hours. Solvents must be used for thinning and cleanup. Check the label to find out which solvent is recommended by the manufacturer. While solvents may be almost odorless, they are toxic and flammable, so work in a well-ventilated room.

Rubber-Base Paints. Containing a liquified rubber, this paint is available only in a few colors and in flat or low-gloss finishes. It's also expensive and has a potent aroma. Because rubber-base paint is waterproof and durable, it's an excellent coating for concrete. It can be applied directly to unprimed masonry. When it's used on brick, it should be preceded by a sealing coat of clear varnish. Before putting it on new concrete, wash the concrete with a 10 percent solution of muriatic acid, rinse thoroughly, and allow it to dry completely. Always wear goggles and gloves when working with muriatic acid and use it only in a well-ventilated space. Like alkyds, rubber-base paints require special solvents; check the label for specifications.

Masonry Paints. While most of the water-thinned paints can be used over brick, concrete, concrete block, and other masonry walls, there are situations where the special features of cement-base paint are ideal. This paint, made by stirring a cement powder into water, is pancake-batter thick. As you brush it on masonry surfaces, it fills in depressions, reducing the amount of texture. Some paint even obscures the mortar joints in concrete block walls, yielding a wall that is uniform in surface texture. These paints can be tinted with special colorants sold by masonry or paint outlets, or you can simply paint over cement paint with ordinary latex paint to get the color you want.

Plastic Paints. Also known as epoxy and urethane paints, these coatings are incredibly durable, but they can be tricky to use and expensive to purchase. If you need extreme durability on steps, floors, woodwork, or kitchen or bathroom walls, plastic paints may be worth the price because they stand up to grease, dirt, alcohol, abrasions, and chemicals.

There are some differences between the two versions. Epoxy paints can be used on ceramic tile, fiberglass, porcelain, metal, and wood or concrete floors. But they won't stick to surfaces previously painted with latex, alkyd, or oil-base paints. Urethanes can be applied to unprimed wood or over most other paint coatings. The toughest urethanes and epoxies are two-part solutions. You have to mix two ingredients together and then be prepared to work rapidly because they dry fast and harden quickly.

Textured Paints. If you're after a stuccolike finish on walls or ceilings, or if you simply want an effective cover-up for flawed surfaces, textured-surface paint will do the job. Some varieties come premixed with sandlike particles suspended in the paint. Because of their grittiness, their use is usually reserved for ceilings. With others, you have to add the particles and stir thoroughly. Another form of textured paint has no granules. Thick and smooth, it's applied to the surface then textured with special tools. Textured paints are available in either flat-finish latex or alkyd formulations. Latex versions are frequently used on bare drywall ceilings because they can be used without a primer and they help to camouflage the seams between sheets of drywall.

One special problem with textured paint becomes evident when the time comes to paint over it. All those peaks and valleys created by the texturing increase the surface area of the wall. The rough surface will require from 15 to 25 percent more paint the second time around.

Dripless Paints. Considerably more expensive than conventional alkyd paint, dripless paint is ideal for ceilings because it's so thick it won't run off a roller or a brush. It will usually cover in a single coat. Because of its consistency, it won't go as far as more spreadable paints.

One-Coat Paints. With additional pigment to improve their covering capabilities, one-coat paints are just more expensive versions of ordinary latex or alkyd paints. For best results, reserve them for use on flawless, same-color surfaces that have been previously sealed.

Acoustic Paints. Designed for use on acoustic ceiling tile, it covers without impairing the tile's acoustic qualities. It can be applied with a roller, but a paint sprayer is more efficient and less likely to affect the sound-deadening properties of the tile.

Primers. These inexpensive undercoatings smooth out uneven surfaces, provide a barrier between porous surfaces and certain finishing coats, and allow you to use an otherwise incompatible paint on a bare or previously painted surface. For flat paint finishes, the primer can be a thinned-out version of the paint itself. But that is often more expensive than using a premixed primer that contains less expensive pigment, dries quickly, and provides a firm foundation or "tooth" for the final coat of paint. Latex primer has all the advantages of latex paint: It is almost odor-free and quick drying, and it cleans up easily. It is the best undercoat for drywall, plaster, and concrete. Don't use it on bare wood because the water in it will raise the grain. For raw wood, it's best to use an alkyd primer. It won't raise the grain on wood, and it creates a good base for most other paints, including latex.

SELECTING THE RIGHT EQUIPMENT

A good interior paint job depends as much on selecting the right tools as on selecting the right paint. With the proper equipment, even amateurs can pull off a professional-looking job. At the paint store, you may be confronted with a huge assortment of paintbrushes. With very few exceptions, paintbrushes fall into two categories: natural-bristle brushes, made of animal hair, and synthetic-bristle brushes, usually made of nylon. The naturals used to be considered the best brushes, but today the synthetics are just as good. Besides, you can't use a natural-bristle brush with water-base latex paints. Water makes the bristles limp and moplike. If you're painting with a water-thinned paint, your brush selection must be a synthetic.

As for price, there are two schools of thought. Among purists, expensive brushes are the only choice. Even in the hands of an experienced professional, they argue, a bad brush will produce a bad paint job. Other professionals feel that top-of-the-line brushes are less than crucial. You'll have to decide for yourself. An expensive brush will last for years and see you through dozens of painting projects if you clean it after each use and store it properly. If you're not meticulous or if you're not planning another painting project, you may as well buy a medium- or low-priced brush that you can simply discard when the job is finished.

Try to get the best brush for your money. Regardless of price, you can distinguish between a good brush and a bad one by examining it closely at the store. Here is what to look for:

Split ends, called "flags," on the ends of the bristles. Spread the bristles and inspect the tips. The more flags the better the brush and its paint-spreading capabilities.

Tapered bristles. With square-cut bristles you won't be able to paint as fine a line or as smooth a finish.

Shedding. Rap the brush on the edge of a counter. A good brush may lose a few bristles, but a bad one will lose more. A brush that sheds in the store will shed even more when you load it with paint and drag it across your wall at home.

Long bristles, particularly on narrow brushes. Short bristles will be stiff and difficult to paint with. As a rule of thumb, the bristles should be about one and a half times as long as the width of the brush. For example, a 1 1/2-inch-wide brush should have bristles about 2 1/4 inches long. Bristle length gives you flexibility to paint into corners and around trim. The exception is with wider brushes, often called wall brushes. A wall brush that is 4 inches wide and has 4-inch bristles will produce a good painted finish.

Smooth, well-shaped handles of wood or plastic that fit in your hand comfortably. There are four basic handle types. Beaver-tail handles, common on wide brushes, allow you to cradle the handle in the palm of your hand for wide-stroke spreading. Pencil- and flat-handled varieties are usually found on narrow brushes and promote fine-line accuracy. The kaiser handle gives you an easy-to-hold grip and good control.

How many different brushes do you need? This depends on what kind of painter you are, what kind of paint you're using, and on how many different colors you'll be using. Unless you're meticulous about cleaning a brush, you run the risk of contaminating a second color with residue of the first color or with water or paint cleaner. To avoid color contamination (which sometimes doesn't show up until the paint dries), it's best to buy one brush of several basic types for each color of paint you'll be using. The three basic brushes for most interior jobs are:

Wall brush. This is the workhorse among brushes, the one that spreads the most paint over

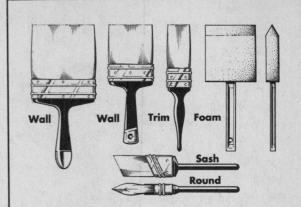

With a wall brush, a trim brush, and a sash brush you can handle most interior painting jobs. Use the wall brush for wide open areas; the trim brush is ideal for "cutting in" at corners and around doors and windows; the sash brush, with its angled bristles, makes close work easier.

the most surface. For ordinary purposes, a 4-inch-wide brush will do nicely, although 3 1/2- and 3-inch wall brushes may be easier to use, especially for people with small hands. If you're doing a big masonry job, you may want to move up to a 6-inch-wide wall brush.

Trim brush. Just 2 inches wide, it's ideal for woodwork and for "cutting in" around windows and doors before painting walls with a roller.

Sash brush with an angled bristle end. Available in 1-, 1½-, or 2-inch widths, the angled sash brush makes close work easier, especially when you're painting around windows. Used carefully, it practically eliminates the need to scrape dried paint off windowpanes.

The same size brushes are also available in foamed urethane. Instead of bristles, they have spongelike heads and are increasingly popular among do-it-yourselfers, particularly in smaller sizes used for interior or exterior trim painting. Disposable foam brushes come in widths up to 3 inches, and they are cheap enough to toss out after one use.

For large flat surface areas like walls and ceilings, paint rollers will help you get the job done in about half the time it would take using a paintbrush. Most painters use brushes for trim work and for cutting in around windows and doors and use rollers to fill in the big blank spaces. Rollers for painting flat areas come in varying widths from 4 to 18 inches, but the two most common sizes for interior jobs are 9 inches and 7 inches wide. For trim work and small spaces, there are specially designed rollers: miniature versions of the basic wall roller and cone- or doughnut-shaped rollers that range in width from 1 to 4 inches.

Paint rollers intended for wall or ceiling painting have handles made of plastic or wood that

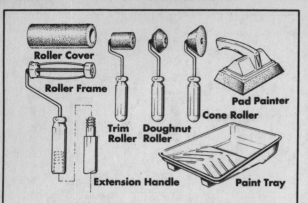

For large flat areas, choose a 7- or 9-inch-wide roller. Trim, doughnut-, and cone-shaped rollers range in width from 1 to 4 inches; these work well for trim and in tight spots. Pad painters are flat-surface applicators with replaceable pads.

may have been hollowed out and machined to accept an extension handle. They also have a cylindrical frame, either a solid metal tube or a series of metal ribs, that is slipped inside a roller cover. Of the two types, the metal-rib version (also known as a "bird cage" or spring-metal frame) is better because it's easier to clean and is less likely to stick to the inside of the roller cover.

The kind of roller cover you should buy is largely determined by the kind of paint you'll be using, but they are all fiber- or urethane foam-covered cylinders that soak up paint from a tray and then release it when rolled over a flat surface. The rolling action creates a vacuum that pulls the paint off the roller. Made of lamb's wool, mohair, Dynel, acetate, or polyurethane foam, most rollers have been labeled with the kind of paint for which they are intended to be used. Lamb's wool is reserved for solvent-thinned paints, and mohair for high-gloss paints and varnishes. The other materials may be used with any kind of paint.

The roller package is also likely to list the length of the roller cover's nap, or pile, which can vary from 1/16 to 1 1/2 inches. For rough surfaces, use the long naps. For smooth surfaces, choose the short ones. The pile is attached to a tube, which slips over the roller's frame. It is made of plastic or cardboard. Unless you intend to use the cover just once and then toss it out, go for the plastic type because it'll stand up to repeated cleanings with solvents or water.

Paint trays, some with hooks that let you attach them to ladders, are made of metal (usually aluminum) or plastic and come in standard 7- and 9-inch versions. The 9-inch is better because you can then use either a 7- or 9-inch roller. The trays are washable and durable, but to make cleanup even easier, buy disposable plastic tray liners.

Some paint applicators that are neither brushes nor rollers might better be called daubers. They include pad painters and painting mitts, both of which effectively smear paint on surfaces. A painting mitt is a woolly mitten that fits over your hand; you dip it in a tray of paint and then smear paint where you want it to go. Mitts are particularly good for painting stair rail columns, lamp posts, and other tubular surfaces. Pad painters are flat-surface applicators with replaceable pads that fit into plastic handles. If you're already accustomed to painting with brushes, it may take some practice to get the hang of pad painters. But adept users claim that pads apply paint faster than brushes of equivalent size. They're especially good for painting shakes, shingles, siding, fences, and shutters.

LADDER AND SCAFFOLD BASICS

If you don't already own a stepladder, get one. Maybe you can change light bulbs and hang curtains by teetering on a stool or an old chair, but you can't safely paint a room without a ladder. Invest in a good one and use it for all those out-of-reach projects.

Most home-use ladders are made of aluminum or wood. Depending on quality, both are reliable. Aluminum weighs 20 to 50 percent as much as wood, which means you don't have to be a body builder to take it in and out of storage or move it around. On most good ladders, you'll find labels that state a rated strength. A Type I industrial

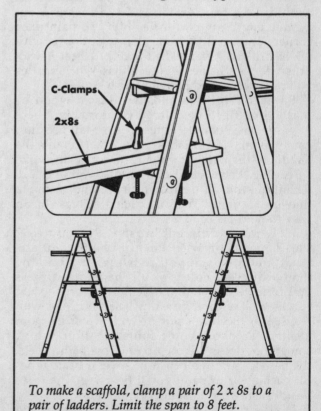

To make a scaffold, clamp a pair of 2 x 8s to a pair of ladders. Limit the span to 8 feet.

LADDER SAFETY

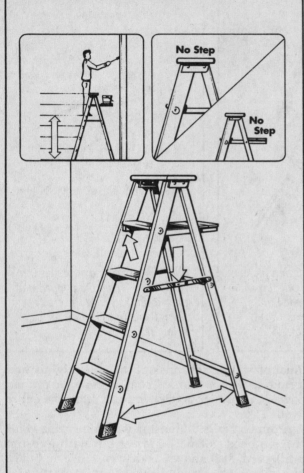

There is no such thing as an absolutely safe ladder. Gravity is an unrelenting enemy, but there are ways greatly to reduce your risks of accidents and injury:

• Inspect a rented, borrowed, or old ladder for defects, including loose rungs, rivets, or screws, cracks or splits in the rails.

• For stability, always open a stepladder to its fullest position, lock the spreader braces on each side in place and pull down the bucket shelf.

• Going up or coming down, always face the ladder head on and use both hands to hold on to the side rails or rungs.

• Don't climb higher than two rungs from the top; don't sit or stand on the top or the bucket shelf.

• To keep yourself from overreaching and getting off balance, never let your navel go beyond either of the ladder's side rails.

• If you have to work on a ladder in front of a door, lock the door.

• Put the paint can or tray on the bucket shelf before you climb the ladder. Don't go up with tools in hand or in your pockets.

grade, rated at 250 pounds, is the strongest. A Type II commercial grade is rated at 225 pounds. A Type III household grade is rated at 200 pounds. Each type has been successfully tested at four times its rated load. For around-the-house purposes, invest in security and durability and buy a Type II ladder. One that is 6 feet tall will do for most homeowners, but taller ladders of 8, 10, 12, and all the way up to 16 feet are available. For extra safety, get one with rubber feet so your ladder won't skid on hard floors.

If you're painting a ceiling from a single stepladder, you'll find yourself going up and down constantly, moving the ladder to reach unpainted areas. This isn't the safest way to do the job. Buy a second ladder of the same size, and place a pair of 2 x 8 boards between them to make a scaffold, a platform from which you can paint for longer periods by moving from one end of the bridge to the other. For stability, don't make your scaffold one rung higher than is absolutely necessary, nor longer than 6 to 8 feet. Use C-clamps to fasten each end of the 2 x 8s to a rung of each ladder. Your platform is only 15 inches wide, so unless you have good balance, stick to the one-ladder method of painting high-altitude spaces.

Prep Work

Even the best paints, applied with the best tools by the best painter, won't result in a job well done if you fail to fix the flaws in surfaces that are to be painted. Paint, when used properly, is a marvelous material, but don't expect it to hide a multitude of defects. Chances are, it will make them even more noticeable. Peeling or "alligatored" old paint, cracks in plaster, dents and popped nail heads in drywall, and splits in woodwork have to be dealt with before you put brush to wall.

First you've got to find the problems. To make this easier (you'll have to do it before you paint anyway), remove all the furniture, if possible. If not, cluster it in one area, and cover it and the floors with drop cloths. Take down the draperies and the drapery hardware. Loosen the light fixtures; let them hang and wrap them with plastic bags. Remove the wall plates from electrical outlets and switches. If you intend to paint them the same color as the wall, do so while they're off the wall.

Now is the time to fix the flaws. Don't feel compelled to take care of the whole project in one weekend. Make the surface mends and otherwise prepare the to-be-painted surfaces one weekend, paint the next.

PATCHING PLASTER AND DRYWALL
Two of the most common defects you'll find are damaged plaster and drywall. Age, settling, temperature swings, variations in humidity, and

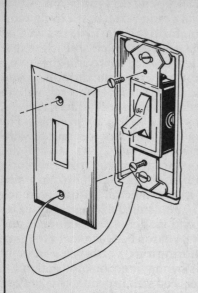

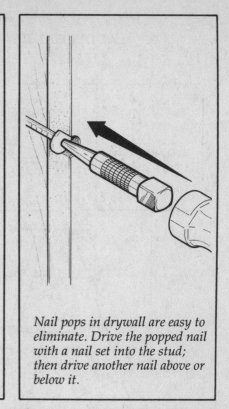

Remove the wall plates from electrical outlets and switches. Paint them separately, even if you intend to paint them the same color as the wall.

To fill a large crack in a plaster wall, remove loose plaster; then wet the crack and pack in plaster of paris. Smooth the surface with a scraper.

Nail pops in drywall are easy to eliminate. Drive the popped nail with a nail set into the stud; then drive another nail above or below it.

everyday wear and tear take their toll on walls. Cosmetic surgery can correct these problems in short order.

Cracked Plaster. Paint can hide hairline cracks in plaster, at least temporarily. The cover-up may last only a few hours or a few months. Small plaster cracks have an annoying way of showing up again and again. It may be smarter to enlarge them and repair them properly. Making a small flaw bigger may sound like reverse logic, but it's easier to fix big cracks in plaster than small ones. The trick is to use patching plaster, which doesn't shrink as it dries.

Before you can fill a large crack, you'll have to clean it out. Use the pointed end of a can opener to cut out the loose plaster; turn the opener to undercut and widen the opening. Use steady but gentle pressure; the idea is to remove debris while preserving the structural integrity of the surface around it. Clean the loose plaster and dust from the crack with a vacuum cleaner. Wet the crack thoroughly with a paint brush dipped in water. Pack the plaster into the wet crack to its full depth and smooth the surface with a scraper or trowel. Let the filled crack dry until the plaster turns bright white—at least 24 hours.

Sand the patch lightly when the plaster is dry, using medium- or fine-grade sandpaper wrapped around a wood block. If the crack was a wide one, you'll probably have to replaster it at least once more to make the surface smooth. If so, wet the plastered area again with a wet paintbrush and then smooth more patching plaster over the patch. Let it dry for at least 24 hours after the

final plastering. Then, sand the patch lightly and prime it with a thinned coat of paint or primer. When the primer is dry, you can paint the entire wall.

Popped Nails. In most newer homes, the walls are surfaced not with plaster but with gypsum wallboard, also known as drywall. Like all building materials, drywall has its own particular problems. One of the most common results from shrinking or warping in the framing behind the drywall. As the wood studs age and shrink, nails loosen and pop out, producing an unsightly bump or hole in the surface of the drywall. No matter how many times you drive the nails back in, the problem is likely to recur. Better to fix them permanently before you paint.

The first step is to eliminate the popped nails. If the nail is sticking out far enough to get the claw of a hammer around, pull it out. To redrive popped nails, hold a nail set over the nail head and hammer the nail as far as you can into the stud. The nail head will punch through the drywall's outside layer of paper and into the drywall itself. To make sure the nail stays in the stud and to take the pressure off it, drive another drywall nail through the wall into the stud; set the new nail about 2 inches above or below the old one. Don't use a nail set on the new nail. Just pound it flush with the wall and then give it one more light hammer whack to "dimple" the drywall surface around the nail head. Using a putty knife, cover the new nail head and fill the hole over the old one with spackling compound. Let it dry then sand it lightly. If necessary, repeat the process once or twice more. Touch up the patches with paint or primer.

Holes in Drywall. Tough as it is, drywall can only withstand so much abuse. A door flung open with too much force can produce a neat doorknob-size hole in the wall. This kind of damage looks bad, but even large holes are easy to repair. For small holes, use a tin can lid to back a plaster patch. For large ones, cut a patch from scrap drywall of the same thickness.

To fix a small hole, remove any loose paper or plaster around the edges. Use a clean tin can lid, at least 1 1/2 inches larger in diameter than the hole. Measure across the lid and cut out a narrow slit from each side of the hole with a keyhole saw, so that you can insert the lid sideways into the hole. Punch two holes in the center of the lid and thread a 12-inch piece of string or thin wire through them. Then, holding the ends of the string or wire, slide the lid through the slit. Pull the lid flat against the inside of the wall. To hold it in place, set a stick of scrap wood over the hole on the outside of the wall and tie the string or twist the wire tightly over the stick. The tin can lid should be firmly held against the inside of the wall.

Pack plaster into the hole against the backer and behind the stick. Spackling compound doesn't work as well as patching plaster because it shrinks as it dries. Keep the plaster inside the hole, cover the backer, and fill the slits, but don't spread the plaster on the wall surface. Leave the patch slightly low. Don't try to level it yet. Let the patch dry until the plaster turns bright white—at least 24 hours.

When the plaster is dry, cut the string or wire and remove the stick. You may be able to pull the string out of the wall, but don't force it. If it won't come out, cut the ends flush with the patch surface. If you used wire, also cut it flush with the patch. To finish the patch, fill it completely with plaster to cover the string or wire ends and make the patch level with the wall surface. Let it dry, sand it lightly, and prime.

If the wallboard is badly broken, it requires a different repair procedure. Instead of filling the hole with plaster, it's better to cut a scrap piece of wallboard to rebuild the damaged area. Cut a scrap piece of drywall into a square or rectangle a little bigger than the hole or damaged area. Set the patch against the damaged area and trace around it lightly with a pencil. Cut out the out-

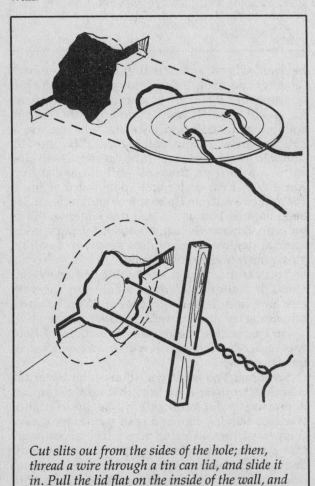

Cut slits out from the sides of the hole; then, thread a wire through a tin can lid, and slide it in. Pull the lid flat on the inside of the wall, and hold it in place with a stick.

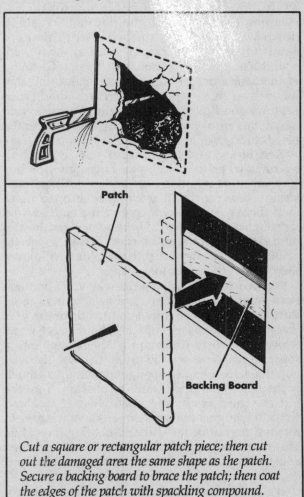

Cut a square or rectangular patch piece; then cut out the damaged area the same shape as the patch. Secure a backing board to brace the patch; then coat the edges of the patch with spackling compound.

lined area with a keyhole saw. Keep your saw cut on the inside the traced line so that the hole will be the same size as the patch.

To hold the wallboard patch in place, you'll need a backing board that is about 6 inches longer than the long dimension of the hole. Insert the board into the hole and hold it firmly against the inside of the wallboard. To keep it there, fasten the ends of the board to the drywall with flathead screws driven through the wall at the sides of the hole; countersink the screws below the surface of the drywall.

Use spackling compound or wallboard joint compound as a glue to hold the patch in place. Spread compound on the back of the drywall patch and around its edges. Set the patch into the hole and adjust it so that it's exactly even with the surrounding wall. Hold it in place until the compound starts to set. Let the compound dry at least overnight. Then fill the patch outline and cover the exposed screw heads with spackling or joint compound. Let it dry, sand it lightly, and prime.

READYING A ROOM FOR A PAINT JOB

Now that the major repairs are out of the way, the worst preparation work is behind you. What's left requires less skill, but just as much patience: cleaning the surfaces to be painted. Washing down walls, ceilings, and woodwork that are about to get a new coat of paint anyway may sound like a waste of time, but it's not. Cleaning is another assurance that the new paint will stay where you put it and look terrific. Good paint needs a good, clean surface foundation to bite into. Otherwise, you risk peeling, chipping, or the bleed-through of grease spots.

Scrubbing and Sanding. If you're painting over a new, primed wall, you can safely skip this step. If you're painting over a previously painted surface, look for rough, peeling, or chipped areas, sand them smooth and then give the entire wall a thorough washing with warm water and household detergent to remove soot, grease, cigarette smoke, and airborne dirt. New paint will cover these soils, but not for long.

Approach wall washing the way you approach floor washing, with a sponge or a sponge mop. With the mop just slightly less than dripping wet, go over a vertical strip of wall about 2 feet wide. Squeeze the dirty water out of the sponge into a separate pail or down the drain. Go over the wall with the squeezed out sponge to pick up as much of the remaining dirty water as possible. Squeeze out the mop again and then rinse it in clean water. Then give the same area one more pass to remove the last of the dirt and detergent residue. This routine sounds tedious, but it goes fairly fast and you'll end up with a wall that is clean and provides a good "tooth" for a new coat of paint.

It's not a good idea to attempt to paint over a surface that already has a glossy finish, even if it

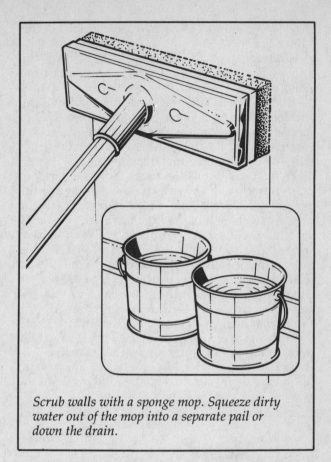

Scrub walls with a sponge mop. Squeeze dirty water out of the mop into a separate pail or down the drain.

is clean. Glossy surfaces don't provide enough "tooth," and even if the paint goes on, which is questionable, it's likely to smear. To cut the gloss on an entire wall, wash it down with a strong solution of trisodium phosphate, which is available at hardware and paint stores. Mix the TSP powder into hot water until no more will dissolve. Swab it on the wall and sponge it dry. Rinse with clear water and sponge dry again. If TSP is not available (in many communities it has been banned because it pollutes water sources), you can achieve the same ends by using a commercial deglosser, a solution that you swab on glossy surfaces before painting.

You can use deglossing solutions on woodwork, or you can give them a light sanding with medium- and fine-grit sandpaper. Wipe or vacuum off the resulting powder before you paint.

On baseboards remove accumulations of floor wax or acrylic floor finish with a wax remover or finish remover.

Scraping. The older your house, the better the chances that there is an area that needs scraping. A previous paint job may have begun to peel or crack, or windowsills and sash frames may have chipped or the old paint may have "alligatored" into a maze of cracks. If you find these conditions, scrape them gently to remove the loose particles and then sand them smooth to blend with the area around them. If you get down to bare wood on woodwork, prime the spots before you

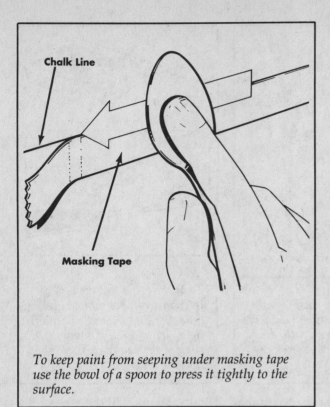

To keep paint from seeping under masking tape use the bowl of a spoon to press it tightly to the surface.

apply the final coat of paint. If it's impossible to blend the scraped areas with the nonscraped areas on walls, go over them with a light coat of drywall joint compound. When it dries, sand the area smooth, prime, and paint.

Masking Basics. Where two new paint colors come together on a single surface, such as a simple stripe or a wall one color half way up, another up to the ceiling, it's practically impossible to keep a straight line between them while painting freehand with either a brush or a roller. To get a straight line in the first place, use a carpenter's level and a pencil to draw a faint line on the wall. Then align masking tape with the line across the wall. Peel the tape off the roll a little at a time and press it to the wall with your thumb. Don't pull the tape too tightly as you go or it may stretch and retract once it's in place. To keep the paint from seeping under the masking tape, use the bowl of a spoon to press it tightly to the surface.

Don't leave the tape on until the paint is dry. If you do, it may pull the paint away from the surface. With latex paint, wait only a half hour before peeling off the tape. With alkyds, two or three hours are enough. Don't apply masking tape to a freshly painted wall until you're absolutely sure the finish is dry and hard. The label on the paint can will tell you how long it takes for the paint to set up completely.

Masking tape is especially useful for protecting trim around doors, windows, built-ins, baseboards, or bookshelves. When you're brushing or rolling new paint on the wall, you won't have to slow down or worry about sideswiping the trim.

Brush and Roller Basics

Now that the materials have been assembled and prep work completed, you're ready, at long last, to resuscitate those old, drab walls with new paint. You'll soon discover that using brushes and rollers competently comes almost naturally, but there are a few techniques that will help postpone fatigue and provide a neater job.

HOW TO HOLD A BRUSH

The grip you get is partly dependent on the brush you're using. With trim and sash brushes with pencil handles, you grasp them much as you would a pencil, with the thumb and the first two fingers of the hand. This technique gives you excellent control for intricate painting. With beaver-tail handles on larger brushes, you'll need a stronger grip because the brushes are wider and heavier. Hold a beaver-tail handle with the entire hand, letting the handle span the width of your palm, much as you would grip the handle of a frying pan or a tennis racket. This technique works best when you are painting large, flat surfaces.

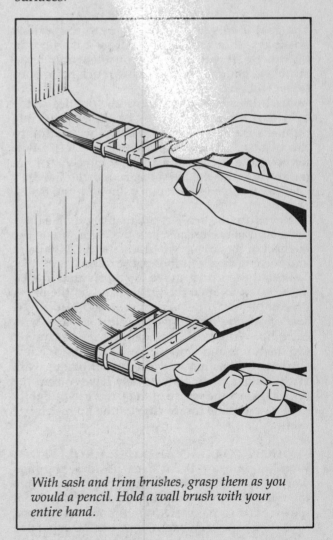

With sash and trim brushes, grasp them as you would a pencil. Hold a wall brush with your entire hand.

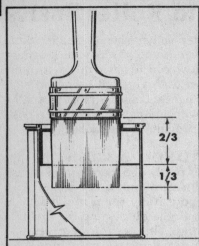

2/3

1/3

Never dip a brush more than about one third the length of the bristles into the paint. If you do, the brush will become next to impossible to clean.

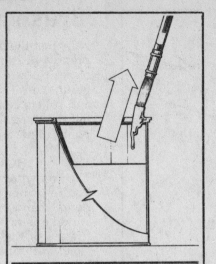

To remove excess paint, gently slap the brush against the inside of the paint can or lightly drag it across the inside edge of the can's lip.

To load a roller, fill the well of the pan about half full and set the roller into the well. Then lift the roller and roll it down the slope of the pan to work paint into the roller.

HOW TO LOAD A BRUSH

The goal is to get as much paint to the wall as possible without dribbling it all over the floor in the process. It will only take you a few minutes to be able to gauge accurately how much paint your brush will hold.

Start the job by dampening the bristles of the brush with water for latex or the appropriate thinner for other types of paint. This conditions the bristles and makes them more efficient. Remove the excess moisture by gently striking the ferrule (the metal band around the handle's base) over the edge of your palm and into a sink or pail.

Never dip the brush more than about one third the length of the bristles into the paint. If you do, the heel of the brush will gradually fill with paint and become next to impossible to clean.

With the first dip, move the brush around a bit in the paint to open the bristles and let the brush fill completely. It helps pick up a full load if you sort of jab the brush gently into the paint with each dip. With most latex paints, you can simply dip the brush and let the excess drip off for a few seconds before moving the brush to the wall. With thinner coatings, you may have to slap the brush against the inside of the paint can or lightly drag it across the inside edge of the lip to remove excess.

HOW TO LOAD AND USE A ROLLER

Working with a roller is even less exacting than working with a brush. As with brushes, moisten the roller first in the appropriate thinner. Roll out the excess on a piece of scrap lumber, craft paper, or a paper grocery bag. Don't use newspapers;

the roller may pick up the ink. Fill the well of the roller pan about half full and set the roller into the middle of the well. Lift the roller and roll it down the slope of the pan, stopping just short of the well. Do this two or three times to allow the paint to work into the roller. Then dip the roller into the well once more and roll it on the slope until the pile is well saturated. You'll know immediately when you've overloaded the roller. It will drip en route to the wall and have a tendency to slide and smear instead of roll across the surface.

When you get to the wall or ceiling, the most effective way to paint with a roller is to work on one 2- or 3-square-foot area at a time. Roll on the paint in a zigzag pattern without lifting the roller from the wall, as if you're painting a large M, W, or a backward N. Still without lifting the roller, fill in the blanks of the letters with more horizontal or vertical zigzag strokes. Finish the area with light strokes that start in the unpainted area and roll into the paint. At the end of the stroke, raise the roller slowly so that it leaves no mark. Go to the next unpainted area and repeat the zigzag technique, ending it just below or next to the first painted patch. Finally, smooth the new application and blend it into the previously finished area.

Two basic roller techniques are important. First, always start with a roller stroke away from you. On walls, that means the first stroke should be up. If you roll down on the first stroke, the paint may puddle under the roller and run down the wall. Second, be careful not to run the roller so rapidly across the wall that centrifugal force causes it to spray droplets of paint.

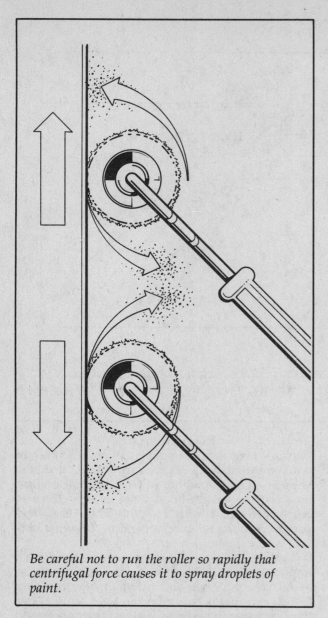

Be careful not to run the roller so rapidly that centrifugal force causes it to spray droplets of paint.

Painting Ceilings and Walls

Whether you're using one, two, or more colors of paint in a single room, paint the ceiling before painting the walls. This approach not only eliminates the risk of spattering ceiling paint on newly painted walls, but it gets the most arduous overhead work out of the way first.

CUTTING IN

Rollers make quick work of vast expanses of flat surfaces, but they are not effective for painting in wall-to-wall or wall-to-ceiling corners or even around woodwork. At these junctions you'll need a trim brush to paint a 2-inch-wide border around the ceiling, the walls, windows, doors, and baseboards. This border painting technique is called "cutting in," and there are two ways to do it.

To cut in at a corner, paint out from the corner for five or six strokes, then smooth over them with a single, long vertical stroke.

Where Same-Color Surfaces Meet. Using a trim brush with beveled bristles, paint five or six strokes perpendicular to the edge of the ceiling or the wall. Next smooth over these strokes with a single, long stroke. Where two walls meet, this means painting out from the corner first, then vertically. Where the wall and ceiling come together, you'll be using downward strokes on the wall first, followed by smoothing horizontal strokes. On the ceiling itself, your first cutting in

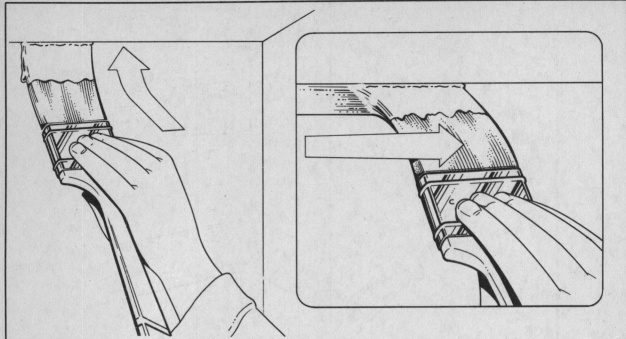

Where different-color surfaces meet, use a technique called beading. Press the brush lightly against the surface, then as you move the brush, add enough pressure to bend the bristles away from the direction of your brush stroke.

strokes will be toward the center of the room, away from the wall. Then you'll paint a smoothing horizontal stroke on the ceiling that follows the direction of the wall. What you're doing is painting 2-inch-wide borders around each flat surface or opening. Even if you're using the same color of paint on adjoining surfaces, follow this method of cutting in; resist the temptation to plop a loaded brush directly into a corner or you'll end up with drips, sags, and runs.

Where Different-Color Surfaces Meet. This cutting-in approach is also known as "beading," and if you get good enough at it, you can practically eliminate the need to use masking tape to protect one painted area from another. Use a beveled trim brush with long bristles. Hold the brush so that your thumb is on one side of the metal ferrule and your fingers on the other. Press the brush lightly against the surface, then, as you move the brush, add just enough pressure to make the bristles bend away from the direction of your brush stroke. Keep the brush about 1/16 inch away from the other colored surface. The bent bristles and the pressure will release a fine bead of paint that will spread into the gap. With both methods of cutting in, but especially when you're dealing with two colors, it's better to have a brush that's too dry than one that's too wet. This is detail work and to do it effectively, go slowly and only cut in 4 or 5 inches at a time. It will seem tedious at first, but your speed and accuracy will improve with practice. Even one ordinary size room will give you lots of practice.

ROLLER WORK

This is where the going gets easy and the pace of your painting project picks up speed. If this is your first venture with a roller, you'll be amazed how fast the job goes and what an amazing and efficient device a roller really is. There are a few variations in technique, depending on what surface you're dealing with.

Ceilings. When rolling paint on the ceiling, it's important to maintain a wet edge at all times to avoid creating lines and ridges. If you're using fast-drying paint, you may have to work faster than you anticipated and without taking a break. Both speed and ease can be achieved by using an extension handle so you can paint from the floor rather than from a stepladder. Many roller handles are made to accept a screw-in extension that you can buy at the paint store, but you may want to see if the threaded end of your broom or mop handle will work.

You can paint in a series of strips or by using the zigzag technique to put the paint on the ceiling. In either case, fill in the blanks with a crisscross motion and paint from the dry areas into the wet areas, smoothing as you go. Don't worry about keeping your roller strokes the same length. The lines won't show when the paint dries. If you paint in strips, do so across the narrow dimension of the room to maintain the wet edges. If you choose to use the zigzag method, start about 3 feet out from one corner and paint toward the corner. Make a W pattern about 3 feet square and fill it in. Then, working across the nar-

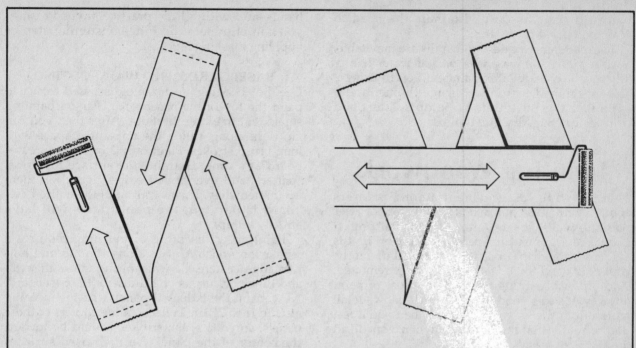

With a roller, begin by making an M, backward N, or W pattern about 3 feet square. Always start with an upstroke so paint won't run down the wall. Next fill in the pattern with crosswise strokes. You should be able to paint each 3-square-foot area with one dip of the roller.

row dimension of the room again, roll on another 3-square-foot area. You should be able to paint each 3-square-foot area with one dip of the roller in the paint pan.

Walls. As with the ceiling, paint an entire wall before taking a break so that the painted portions won't lose their wet edges. Then stand back, scan the wall, and cover any missed spots or smears. Whether you paint in sections from top to bottom or from side to side across the room is up to you, but if you're using an extension handle, you may well find it more convenient to start at one high corner and go all the way across the room with a series of completed zigzag patterns. That way you won't have constantly to change the handle on your roller as you would if you painted in sections from the ceiling down to the floor. If you're right-handed, start in the wall's left corner; if you're left-handed, start in the wall's right corner.

Tight Spots. Over and under windows and above doors and doorways, you probably won't have enough room to use the zigzag technique. Just roll the paint on horizontally. For areas that are narrower than the roller you're using, such as between windows and around doors near a corner, use a 4-inch roller or a paintbrush. The little roller is best because it will give you the same surface finish as the rest of the wall. Brushes apply paint less evenly and tend to leave telltale trails.

Minimizing Drips and Spatters. Even if you have already cut in around the room, avoid bumping the roller into the walls as you paint the ceiling or into the ceiling as you paint the walls, even if you're using the same color paint on both surfaces. The roller may deposit a visible ridge of paint each time it touches the ceiling or the wall. The reason for going through the time and trouble to cut in is to avoid having to get the roller too close to an adjacent surface.

Also you should know that no matter how slowly and steadily you move the roller across a surface it will emit a fine spray of paint. Wear a scarf or inexpensive painters' cap and make sure the floor and furniture are covered completely with drop cloths. Canvas drop cloths are best because they're durable, washable, and reusable. Plastic drop cloths are less expensive, and if you tape them down so they won't slide around, just as effective. Buying roller covers with beveled edges prevents another roller-painting problem: paint buildup on roller ends that leaves tracks. If they're not available, use scissors to bevel the pile at each end of the roller.

If you chose not to mask around windows, doors, and woodwork, minimize the risk of spatters by using a paint shield. Store-bought shields come in several sizes and are made of plastic or aluminum. Do-it-yourself shields can be made from shirt cardboard or the slats of an old venetian blind. The paint shield works like a moving masker. Holding the shield in one hand, place it perpendicular to the surface being painted and over the woodwork. With your other hand, apply the paint. Paint shields are ideal for painting window frames because they can be used to keep paint off the glass and eliminate the need to scrape off dried paint later.

Because some spatters and spills are inevitable, keep a moist sponge and a pail of water handy when you're using latex paints. If you're using a solvent-thinned paint, keep some thinner and a supply of rags nearby to wipe up spatters and drips before they dry into bumps.

Painting Woodwork

There is wide disagreement among painters about whether to paint woodwork before or after painting walls. It's a matter of personal preference. The argument for painting the trim first is that any stray drips or spatters that end up on the wall only need to be feathered out, not removed, since the wall's going to get a new coat of paint anyway. It's also good to get all of the slow, detail work out of the way first because then you'll feel you're really making progress when you fill in the big, flat areas.

Since rollers always emit a fine spray of paint, no matter how careful you are, some of it is going to end up on the woodwork. If you paint the trim first, you should mask it. You may want to tape plastic drop cloths over entire windows and doors when you paint the ceiling and walls.

A third option, if you're using only one color and one finish on all surfaces, is to paint the trim as you come to it while painting the walls. You'll have to keep alternating between brush and roller this way, but in most rooms there are only a couple of windows and a single door.

No matter when you decide to paint it, inspect all the woodwork in the room for defects and make the necessary repairs before you start painting. If you'll be painting over glossy woodwork, sand it lightly with sandpaper or steel wool first to give it "tooth." Or give it a coat of deglosser.

Painting trim progresses even more slowly than cutting in walls and ceilings, and there is more room for error. If you learn to paint free-

hand—and with a little practice anybody can— you can eliminate the time-consuming step of applying masking tape.

BASEBOARDS AND WAINSCOTING

Use the "beading" technique discussed earlier to paint the top of the baseboard. Using a painting shield, cut in along the floor. After that, you can zip right along, filling the unpainted space with long brush strokes. Paint only 2 or 3 feet of baseboard at a time. Examine the surface for drips, spatters, and overlapped edges, and clean them up immediately. If you wait until the entire baseboard is painted, the paint flaws will have already set up.

Painting wainscoting or paneling requires a similar approach. Cut in along the top and bottom edges where the wainscoting meets the wall and the floor, just as you did with the baseboard. Next, paint the indented panels and the molding around them. Paint collects in the corners of these panels, so your brush strokes should be toward the center of the panel. On the raised surfaces around and between panels, work from the top down and use up-and-down strokes on the verticals, back-and-forth strokes on the horizontals.

WINDOWS, DOORS, AND SHUTTERS

If you practiced painting freehand on the baseboards, here is where you'll get your reward. You won't have to scrape dried paint off the glass, nor will you have to apply masking tape, a savings in time and energy in either case.

Flush doors, those with smooth, flat surfaces are easy to paint with either a brush or a roller, but doors with inset panels can be tricky. No matter what type of door you're painting, finish the entire door without stopping. Otherwise the lap marks may show. If possible remove the doorknobs, the plates behind them, and the latch plate on the edge of the door.

Start by painting the inset panels at the top of the door. As with wainscoting, paint all the panels and the molding around them. Then work

PAUSING FOR A BREAK

Although not difficult, painting can be tiring. It's worth taking a break while painting a room to rest your muscles, especially those in the shoulder, neck, arms, and back. Try not to stop in the middle of a wall or the ceiling, or you'll lose the wet edge and risk visible lap marks when the paint dries. When you do stop for a few minutes or even a few hours, take steps to protect the paint and your equipment.

• For breaks of less than half an hour, you can leave your brush on a flat surface, such as a piece of scrap wood, or lying across the top of the paint can. Do not leave it standing up in

the can. The bristles may bend or paint may be drawn up into the top of the brush.

• If you have to suspend painting for several hours, wrap a plastic sheet or aluminum foil around brushes and rollers, just tight enough to keep the air out. Try not the mash the bristles on brushes or the pile on rollers.

• Leftover paint in trays should be returned to paint cans and the cans should be resealed. Wipe out the rim of the can first with the tip of the brush, then with a paper towel or a cotton swab. Drape a cloth over the lid and lightly hammer it down.

Paint double-hung windows in the sequence shown, moving the top and bottom sashes for access to all surfaces.

your way down from the top to the bottom, painting the top rail, middle rail, and bottom rail (the horizontals) with back-and-forth strokes. Next, paint the stiles (the verticals) with up-and-down strokes. If you're painting both sides of the door, repeat this procedure. If you're painting only one side, now paint the top edge of the door, but give it only a light coat. Over time, paint can build up on the top edge and cause the door to stick. Finally, paint the door's hinge edge and latch edge.

The job of painting windows will go faster if you purchase a 2- or 2 1/2-inch sash-trim brush, one angled slightly across the bottom that makes getting into 90-degree corners and tight spaces easier.

Brush in hand, follow these steps for window painting: Raise the bottom sash more than half way up and lower the top sash until its bottom rail is several inches below the bottom sash. Paint the bottom rail of the top sash and on up the stiles (or sides) as far as you can go. Paint all the surfaces of the bottom sash except the top edge. Now reverse the position of the sashes: top sash up to within an inch of the window frame, bottom sash down to within an inch of the sill. Now

paint the formerly obstructed surfaces of the top sash and the top edges of both sashes.

Don't paint the jambs (the channels in which the sashes move up and down) next, and don't paint them at all if they're metal. Instead, paint the window frame, working from top to bottom, including the sill. When the paint on the sashes is dry to the touch, move them both down as far as they will go. Now, paint the exposed jambs. Let the paint dry, raise both sashes all the way and paint the lower jambs. To keep the sashes from sticking in the jambs, put on only as much paint as necessary to cover the old coat. Again, wait for the paint to dry, then lubricate the channels with paraffin or a silicone spray.

The best way to paint shutters, both interior and exterior types, is to spray them, using either canned spray paint or a power sprayer. If this isn't possible, you can still get a quality finish on old shutters by using a brush. First, take them down and scrape, sand, and clean as needed. If you can then hang them up from a ceiling joist in the garage or from the top of a swing set, you can paint both sides at the same time. Otherwise, stand them upright or lay them out on a table and paint one side at a time. Don't load your brush with paint; a too-wet brush will result in runs and sags, and if the louvers are adjustable, sticking problems. Paint the window side of the shutter first. That way, if you do miss a sag or run, it won't show. On adjustable shutters, put a wooden matchstick or a little wood wedge between the adjusting rod and one or two of its staples to keep the rod away from the louvers, making both of them easier to paint. Paint the louvers first with a 1/2- or 1-inch trim brush. Then paint the frame with a 2-inch brush. Leave the shutter edges until last so you can periodically turn the shutter over to check for runs. If you find any, smooth them out with an almost-dry brush before they set. When the front is dry, paint the back.

CABINETS

As with windows, doors, walls, and ceilings, painting cabinets and cupboards will be easier if you remove all obstructions first, including handles, pulls, knobs, and latches. If the hinges on the doors have pins that you can remove easily, you may even want to take off the doors until the cabinet and cupboard interiors and surfaces have been painted. Take out all the drawers, too.

The trickiest part of the project is trying to paint barely accessible interior surfaces. You may want to saw off the handles on your trim brushes to make things easier. Then paint in this order: inside back walls, inside top, side walls, bottoms, tops, and edges of shelves. Now paint all the exterior surfaces, working from the top down. If the doors are still in place, swing them open and paint the inside surfaces. Then close them part way and paint the outsides. Finally, stand the

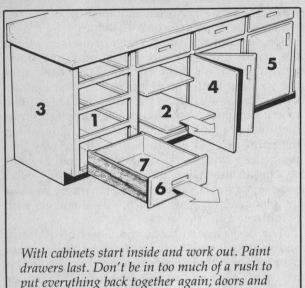

With cabinets start inside and work out. Paint drawers last. Don't be in too much of a rush to put everything back together again; doors and drawers can stick to tacky surfaces.

drawers up on newspapers and paint only their fronts. Do not paint the exterior sides or bottoms of the drawers.

Don't be in too much of a rush to put the cabinets and cupboards back together again. Doors and drawers have an annoying tendency to stick to still-tacky surfaces.

FLOORS

The techniques for painting floors are the same as for painting any other large flat surface. Just be sure to remove all traces of wax and sand the floor lightly to roughen its surface and improve its ability to hold paint. You can use porch and deck paint, but the color selections are limited. You also can use a good-quality oil-base enamel. In either case, plan to follow up with two to four coats of clear polyurethane to protect the painted finish.

To begin, remove all the furniture and cut in the paint around the baseboards with a brush. Then you can use either a wide wall brush or a medium-pile roller for the rest of the floor. Use an extension handle on a roller and you can do the job standing up. Remember to paint your way out of the room. On most wood floors, you probably can plan on having to apply at least two coats of paint, then two to four coats of polyurethane. Let each coat dry to absolute hardness before reentering the room and wear rubber-soled shoes until the last coat has dried to avoid marring the surface.

Painting masonry floors is much easier, much faster, and much less expensive than painting wood floors. Moisture is a major cause of masonry painting problems. Most masonry is porous, and water that comes through it pushes at the paint, causing small particles to come off. The alkalinity of masonry affects the adhesiveness of

some paints and attacks the pigments in others. Paint that goes on masonry surfaces designed for rough treatment, especially floors, must be tough to withstand abuse. Paint selection is crucial and preparation must be thorough.

There are many latex-base masonry paints, which offer the advantages of easy application and easy cleanup. They can be used in damp conditions without adhesion problems. Cement-base paints are frequently used on previously unpainted concrete where low-pressure moisture is a problem. Epoxy paints are often applied where a hard finish that resists moisture and chemicals is needed. Make sure that the paint you use is compatible with any existing paint and with the type of masonry. Tell the paint dealer your plans and ask for the appropriate coating.

Before you get down to painting, repair and patch all cracks and holes and allow the patch compounds to cure fully. Then, wearing rubber gloves and goggles, use a 10 percent muriatic acid solution to remove efflorescence, the whitish powder that appears in spots on concrete. Mop up the solution, let the area dry, rinse it thoroughly, and let it dry again. Next, wash the entire floor with a strong detergent or a concrete degreaser. Just before you paint, vacuum the floor.

On most masonry floors you can paint with a long-napped roller fitted with an extension handle so you can paint standing up, but you may need a brush for very rough areas. Depending on the surface conditions and the kind of paint you use, you may have to apply a second coat. If so, read the label on the paint can to find out how long you should wait between coats.

Cleaning Up

If you used drop cloths and maskers, mastered the art of freehand painting, and wiped up drips and spatters during the paint job, then most of your cleanup has already been taken care of. All you have to do is clean your tools, track down and remove any stray paint, and put the room back together.

EQUIPMENT

This includes not only brushes and rollers but also reusable drop cloths, paint cans, containers, and roller pans. Don't delay cleaning your equipment one minute longer than necessary. Fresh paint comes out of brushes, rollers, and pans easily; let paint dry for a while and you'll have to put a lot more time and effort into getting it out.

Rollers don't respond well to even thorough cleaning. Some paint residue usually remains in the nap of the roller cover. When the roller is later exposed to fresh paint, the dried-in paint can soften and cause streaks in the new finish. Since they're inexpensive, buy a new roller cover for each new job and save yourself the time and effort of trying to clean them. If the ones you bought are too costly to toss out, clean them as best you can, but use them only on projects that involve almost the same colors and watch for streaks.

If you used latex paint, drag the brushes across the lip of the paint can to remove most of the paint. Then rinse the brushes and rollers under warm tap water and wash with dishwashing detergent. A paintbrush comb helps remove paint residue from the bristles. To get out the excess water, gently squeeze the bristles or take the brush outside and give it a few vigorous flicks. Squeeze the water out of roller covers. Then, use paper towels to soak up the remaining water in both brushes and rollers.

With solvent-thinned paints, you'll have to use the appropriate solvent (check the label on the paint can). Agitate brushes and rollers in a container of the solvent. To get out all the paint, you'll probably have to do this two or three times, replacing the solvent when it becomes cloudy and until the brush or roller barely tints it. To clean brushes, pour the solvent into an old coffee can. For rollers, use an inexpensive aluminum foil loaf pan or a clean roller pan. Solvents, remember, are toxic and flammable, so don't smoke or work near a water heater or furnace. Make sure there is plenty of ventilation. Use paper towels to blot out the excess solvent from brushes and rollers, then wash everything in warm, soapy water. Hang brushes until they're dry; set roller covers on end.

Wipe out, wash, and dry roller pans and paint containers. Wipe off the lips of paint cans and hammer down the lids to preserve leftover paint. Then, store the cans (preferably upside down, to prevent "skinning over") away from extreme heat or cold and out of the reach of children. The same goes for solvents. If you have less than a quart of paint left, store it in a tightly capped glass jar and save it for touch-ups. Brushes and rollers that have been cleaned and dried should be wrapped up before they're stored away. Brushes can go back in the plastic or paper packages they came in or you can wrap them in aluminum foil or kraft paper (grocery bags). Rollers can be wrapped in kraft paper, foil, or perforated plastic sandwich bags.

For reusable canvas or plastic drop cloths, wipe off major paint splotches with soap and water and paper towels. Don't use solvents on drop cloths. The solvent may dissolve plastic ones or the rubber backing on canvas ones. Let them dry thoroughly, fold them up, and store them with your other equipment for the next project.

WINDOWPANES, SPATTERS, AND DRIPS

One major difference between the professional painter and the amateur is that the pro doesn't wait until the end of the job to go after drips and spatters. When they're still wet is the best time to clean them up. You're bound to overlook a few mistakes that you'll have to deal with later.

If you used masking tape around windows, it's best to peel it off right after painting. Later, it may pull off some paint. If you painted with a painting shield or freehand, you're almost certain to encounter a few errant drops or smudges on the glass. A razor-blade scraper (available at paint and hardware stores) will easily scrape the paint off the glass, but try to avoid breaking the seal between the new paint and the windowpane when you're cleaning up around the sash.

Cleaning up drips and spatters on most other surfaces is easier and less time consuming. With latex paint, a soft cloth, household detergent, warm water, and a little elbow grease should do the trick. Don't scrub a freshly painted finish, even if it is dry to the touch. Many paints don't cure for 30 days or more. If you're dealing with solvent-thinned paints, use a soft cloth and thinner (usually turpentine or mineral spirits) to soften and remove dried-on paint droplets. Go over the area with warm water and detergent.

To get paint drips off hardwood, ceramic tile, or resilient flooring, wrap a cloth around a putty knife and gently scrape them up. Then wash the

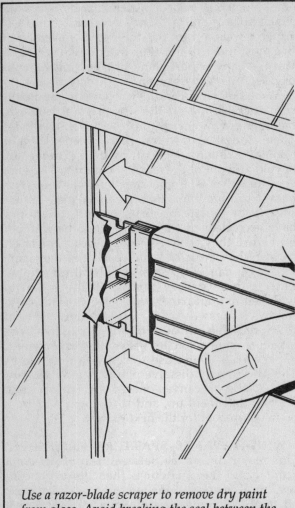

Use a razor-blade scraper to remove dry paint from glass. Avoid breaking the seal between the paint and windowpane.

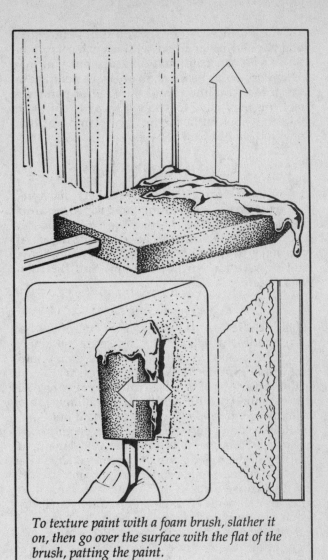

To texture paint with a foam brush, slather it on, then go over the surface with the flat of the brush, patting the paint.

areas with warm soapy water. Don't use solvent if you can avoid it. It can damage the finish on the floor. Now restore order to your freshly painted room. Replace the caps on ceiling fixtures and rehang drapery hardware and the draperies and/or blinds. Put the electrical outlet and switch plates back on. Remount doorknobs and latch plates on doors. Slide the drawers back into the cabinets and replace the pulls, handles, and knobs. Restore and arrange the furniture.

Special Effects

Sometimes, extraordinary measures are required to deal with extraordinary conditions, such as a seriously marred wall surface. Other times, you may want to produce a painted finish that is more decorative than can be achieved with just a new coat of paint. In either case, several popular special techniques can fulfill your requirements. The materials and tools are readily available at most retail paint stores.

TEXTURE PAINTING

If you have a wall with flaws so serious that ordinary paint won't cover them up, want a surface with a more tactile quality, or want a weathered or stucco look, go with texturing. Paints specifically designed for texture work are as thick as pancake batter or wet plaster. Some are gritty and best reserved for ceilings, and some are not. All are ideal for flawed surfaces and for creating a rustic look. You should wash the surface, scrape off flaking paint and patch major holes, but you don't need to make the surface perfectly smooth. Texture paints will camouflage most surface blemishes.

Texture paint without granules in it can be applied with special texturing rollers, a wide brush, a urethane foam brush, or even a trowel. Whatever tool you use, just smear the paint onto the surface about 1/16 inch thick. As with regular wall paint, work with sections approximately 3 feet square.

Now, create your surface design in one section at a time. A long-napped texturing roller will give you a uniform stippled effect all over. Similar but less regular stippling can be achieved with a foam brush. Slather on the paint, then go over the surface with the flat of the brush, patting the paint to create little peaks and valleys. Once the paint is on the wall, you also can use less conventional texturing tools, such as crumpled wax paper or a big sponge. With a coarse brush you can create circles or swirls in the paint. Whatever tool you rely on, try to keep the thickness and the texture uniform from one section to another, overlapping their borders as you go.

For applying grit-textured paint to ceilings, buy a special long-napped roller or use a synthetic-bristle brush. Instructions on the can explain how to do it.

STRIPING

Want to paint a chair-rail stripe around your dining room, a wide stripe up one wall, or a series of very thin stripes? All would be difficult to do freehand, but there are other methods that make it simple.

For medium-wide stripes of 1 to 4 inches, use a carpenter's level to draw two parallel lines on the wall. Follow the lines with masking tape, pressing it down carefully with your thumb or the bowl of a spoon so that paint doesn't seep under its edges. Use a trim brush to paint between the tape lines. Wait until the paint is just barely dry to the touch, then slowly peel the tape away from the wall.

A series of thin, parallel stripes can be painted all at one time if you use the special striping tape that is used to paint racing stripes on cars. It is available at automobile supply stores. The tape is 1 inch wide overall, but it has up to eight 1/16-inch peel-off strips down its length. Use a carpenter's level to create a straight line. Follow the line with striping tape. Then peel off as many removable strips as you like, automatically exposing what will soon be stripes. Because you're dealing with several tape edges, go back over the tape again, pressing down all the edges to keep the paint from seeping under them. Finally, working with a dry brush (a 1/2-inch trim brush is best for delicate work), paint over the tape. Let the paint dry to the touch, then slowly peel away the tape.

STENCILING

Stenciling is one of the oldest and easiest decorative painting techniques. Use it to create borders of various patterns on walls, ceilings, floors, and around windows and doors. Stencils look like the reverse of a coloring-book page, with spaces where the pattern would ordinarily be. About the size of a sheet of typewriter paper, reusable stencils are made of thin plastic or heavy paper. They're available at art supply stores or retail paint outlets.

You can make your own stencils, using thin cardboard. Sketch a design, transfer it to tracing paper, and then cut it out with scissors or an art knife. Lay the pattern on a piece of cardboard slightly larger than the pattern itself, trace around it, then cut it out.

To transfer your design to the wall, tape up the stencil at all four corners. Use a special stenciling brush (round in shape but flat across the bristles) to apply latex or alkyd paint to the cutout. Pour the paint into an old saucer or pie tin. Dab the brush lightly into the paint, then dab it lightly on kraft paper to remove excess paint. You should be working with an almost dry brush. Don't stroke the paint on the stencil; if you do, you'll force the paint under its edges. Instead, use a light up-and-down dabbing motion. Let the paint dry to the touch, peel the stencil slowly away from the wall, and move on to the next area. If you want to create a border using the same pattern over and over again, it makes sense to buy or make extra stencils so you can continue to work

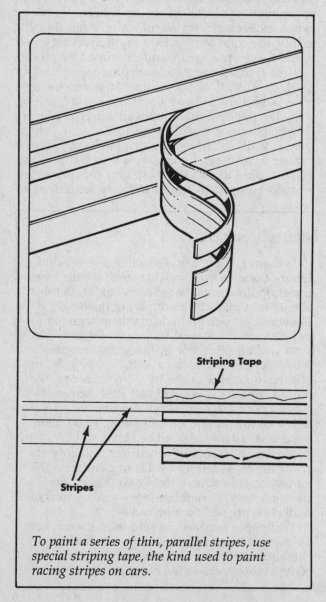

Striping Tape

Stripes

To paint a series of thin, parallel stripes, use special striping tape, the kind used to paint racing stripes on cars.

on other areas as the paint dries on the first ones. If your stencil requires two or more colors, do only one color at a time and let the first dry to the touch before adding the second.

Plastic ready-made stencils are washable and reusable. Those made of heavy paper or cardboard will only last until paint saturates the fibers and weakens the stencil. When that happens, buy or make new ones so that the stencil stays flat against the wall as you paint.

Selecting the Right Wall Covering

With a dozen kinds of wall covering to choose from, selecting the right one can be as challenging as putting them up. Notice that we called them wall coverings not wallpaper. In addition to regular printed paper, you'll find coverings made of fabric, fiber, plastic, or a combination of several materials.

Wall coverings have several important advantages over old-fashioned wallpaper. Besides being easier to handle and less likely to rip, they're also more durable. Many are prepasted at the factory and come with pretrimmed edges. These features make installing wall coverings easier than ever before.

Although color, pattern, and texture will undoubtedly influence your choice of which covering to buy, durability is also a crucial factor. Some wall coverings, like some paints, are tougher than others; this characteristic makes

them particularly suitable for areas like a child's room, bath, or kitchen. Among commonly used wall coverings, fabric-backed vinyls tolerate the most abuse. Not only are they more washable than painted surfaces, they're also more resistant to scuffs and scratches. Next on the scale of durability comes unbacked vinyls, followed by vinyl-coated paper. Other wall coverings that are not as strong are more suited for rooms that are subjected to little wear and tear. Among them are regular printed papers, flocked papers, foils, and grass cloths.

Different wall coverings require special handling. Some should be preceded by lining paper, which is the paper equivalent of paint primer. Even on rough walls, it yields a smooth surface and absorbs moisture; these characteristics assure success with foil papers and grass cloth, among several others.

Adhesives vary widely as well. Many wall coverings are available prepasted. The dry, factory-applied adhesive on the back becomes sticky when moistened with warm water. After that, it's ready to hang. With other wall coverings you should use an appropriate premixed or mix-it-yourself adhesive. For example, paper-backed burlaps, flocks, hand prints, foils, murals, and vinyls should be hung with vinyl adhesive. Regular papers and unbacked burlaps require wheat paste or stainless adhesive. For "strippable" wall coverings, use strippable adhesive or wheat paste. Some adhesives, especially wheat paste, come in mildew-resistant formulas that should be used in high-humidity situations or

---

HOW MANY ROLLS WILL YOU NEED?

As mentioned previously, to avoid color variations in wall coverings it's a good idea to calculate precisely how much you'll need and then buy it all at once.

Wall coverings are sold in rolls that are 15 to 54 inches wide. Regardless of the width, a single roll contains about 36 square feet; with trimming and waste, figure on getting only about 30 square feet of coverage per roll.

To calculate how many rolls you'll need for a given room, find its perimeter by measuring the length of each wall and adding all four measurements together. For example, in a 9-by-12-foot room, the perimeter equals 42 feet (9 + 9 + 12 + 12). Measure the room's height, 8 feet, for example, and multiply your first figure (42) by the second (8) to get the total square footage of the walls (336 square feet). Divide this figure by 30, which is the average usable number of square feet in a typical roll of wall covering, to find out how many rolls you'll need. In this case, 11 rolls will do the job.

If there is only one door and one window, ignore them in your calculations; if you have multiple doors and windows, calculate their square foot totals by multiplying the height by the width of each and adding them together to get a square foot total you can subtract from your overall total. For instance, if there was a 3-by-7-foot entrance door and two 3-by-7-foot sliding doors in our 9-by-12-foot room, we would subtract 63 square feet from our previous total of 336 square feet, giving us a final figure of 273 square feet. Divided by 30, then, we'd need 10 rolls instead of 11.

If you're papering a ceiling, multiply its width by its length (9 by 12) to determine the surface area in square feet (108). Again, divide the total by 30 to determine how many rolls of wall covering will be required (4).

Wallpaper borders are sold by the yard, not by the roll. If you plan to put a border around the room, add up the distance around the room in feet, then divide by three.

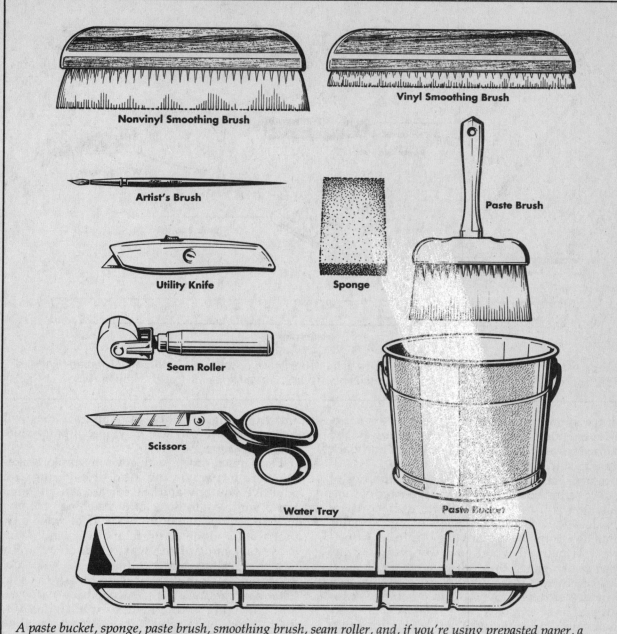

Nonvinyl Smoothing Brush

Vinyl Smoothing Brush

Artist's Brush

Paste Brush

Utility Knife

Sponge

Seam Roller

Scissors

Water Tray

Paste Bucket

A paste bucket, sponge, paste brush, smoothing brush, seam roller, and, if you're using prepasted paper, a water tray are some accessories you will need to wallpaper a room.

with any vinyl-coated paper. Vinyl can trap moisture behind the covering and promote the growth of mildew.

Another factor that may influence your choice of coverings is the pattern and whether it was produced by machine (printed) or by hand (silkscreened). Of the two, machine prints are less expensive. Intricate patterns will be more difficult to hang than large patterns because you'll have to take the time to make sure the patterns from one strip are perfectly matched with the strip that follows it.

In silk-screened or hand-printed papers, color can vary from roll to roll. Instead of cutting off a strip and pasting it to the wall, you should try to minimize variations in shading by matching strips from the same or different rolls as closely as possible before hanging them.

Color is uniform on machine-printed rolls cut from one continuous run, but it may differ from previous or subsequent runs. Because of this, wallpaper manufacturers assign lot or run numbers to each roll. When you buy machine-printed paper, make sure to get rolls that have the same lot number on them.

To a lesser extent, color variations can be found in certain fabric wall coverings and in grass cloth. Fibers in these wall coverings don't always absorb dyes evenly. The shadings can contribute to the appeal of fabric wall coverings,

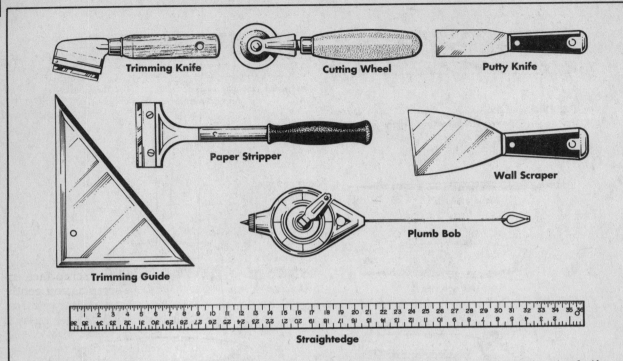

Paper-hanging tools are often sold prepackaged. If an entire kit isn't available, plan to buy a trimming knife, a cutting wheel, a paper stripper, a triangular trimming guide, a metal straightedge, and a plumb bob.

but try to prevent abrupt color changes by hanging every other strip upside down. That way, the light edges will be next to light edges and dark edges next to dark edges.

Many retail dealers have lending libraries of wall covering books, with page after page of samples, that you can take home for a day or two. This lets you compare the colors of a prospective purchase to the colors of your furniture, carpeting, and painted woodwork. By propping the open book against the wall, you can get a good idea of how a covering will look in the room. If your dealer doesn't lend sample books, ask for cuttings of several coverings that you can take home and tape to the wall before making a purchase.

If you plan to paint the ceiling or the woodwork in a room, do it before hanging your new paper. Although it's not absolutely necessary, before papering a previously painted wall give it a coat of wall sizing, a solution that will roughen the surface. Sizing, which you can apply with a paint roller, makes sliding a strip of wall covering into position on the wall easier and aids in removing the wall covering the next time around.

All the tools you'll need often come prepackaged. If not, plan to buy a trimming knife, cutting wheel, paper stripper, plumb bob, paste bucket (unless the adhesive comes premixed), sponge, paste brush, smoothing brush (there is one for vinyls, one for nonvinyls), seam roller, triangular trimming guide, metal straightedge, and if you're using prepasted paper, a water tray. For cutting

and trimming, a utility knife and scissors will come in handy. You also may need a putty knife and wall scraper.

How much time a wall-covering project takes depends in part on the kind of covering and adhesive you buy and the surface it's intended for. If you have to do a lot of patching or if you have to remove one or more layers of wallpaper, preparation alone could take a weekend. With those tasks out of the way, even an amateur paperhanger can expect to finish a 12-by-15-foot bedroom in a single day. Don't rush the job. Establishing straight lines, matching patterns, and trimming and cutting around windows, doors, woodwork, and light switches are time consuming, but doing those things slowly and carefully makes the difference between a professional-looking job and a botched one. Who says you have to finish the job in one day or even a weekend? You can stop whenever you have to and pick up hours or even days later without jeopardizing a successful job.

Repairing and Removing Wallpaper

Despite the remarkable durability of most wall coverings, they are not indestructible. When damage occurs or flaws turn up, it's best to fix them as soon as possible. Defects have an annoying way of enlarging themselves. The longer you wait, the larger they get, and the tougher the repair job.

REPAIRING BLISTERS, SEAMS, AND TORN SECTIONS

Blisters, which result from excess adhesive or air trapped in bubbles between the wall and the backside of the wall covering, can show up within minutes, days, weeks, or even years after the project is finished. The easiest way to deal with them is to prevent them in the first place. Be sure to smooth out a just-applied strip of paper as thoroughly as possible with a smoothing brush, straightedge, or a sponge. If you encounter blisters, work them toward the nearest edge of the strip to release trapped air or excess adhesive. Blisters located in inconspicuous places won't be noticed and can be ignored. If you're using an untreated printed paper, small blisters might go away by themselves as the paste dries and the paper contracts. If a blister is still there an hour after the strip has been applied to the wall, it's not likely that it will disappear on its own.

Blisters that are only an hour or two old can often be repaired with a pin prick. Use a sewing needle or a straight pin to puncture the blister. Then, with your thumbs, gently squeeze out the trapped blob of still-wet adhesive or trapped air through the hole. If that doesn't work, use a single-edge razor blade or utility knife to slit a small X in the wall covering and peel back the tips of the slit. If there is a lump of adhesive underneath, gently scrape it out. If air was the villain, use an artist's brush to apply a tiny bit of adhesive behind the flaps, then press the flaps back down.

To repair a blister in the paper, slit it twice to form an X. Peel back the tips of the slit, brush paste into the blister, and smooth.

The edges may overlap a little, but this overlapping is seldom detectable.

Loose seams are even easier to repair. Save a small container of adhesive for this purpose. Lift the seam, use an artist's brush to work the paste under the seam, then press it back down and go over it with a seam roller. If the seam starts to pull away again, tack it in place with two or three straight pins stuck through the paper and into the wall until the adhesive is dry. The tiny holes won't show. If you find a loose seam in overlapped vinyl wall covering, use a vinyl-to-vinyl adhesive to stick it back down.

Holes and tears in wall coverings are more difficult to repair, but if done with care, the repairs will be all but invisible. Use a single-edge razor blade to trim off any ragged edges around the damaged area. From a scrap of wall covering, tear out a bigger patch. Hold the scrap face up with one hand, and rotate the scrap as you gently tear out a round patch. It may take some practice, but when you do it correctly you'll have a patch with an intact design on the printed side of the paper and a feathered edge on the backside. Spread a thin coating of adhesive on the back of the patch and place it over the damaged area. Line up the pattern on the patch with the pattern on the wall. A perfect pattern alignment may not be possible, but the match will be close enough to escape detection. If you're patching vinyl wall covering, use a vinyl-to-vinyl adhesive.

Another technique for repairing holes is called double cutting. With this method you create a patch that is perfectly sized to fit the damaged area.

Cut a square scrap of wall covering about an inch larger than the damaged section. Place the scrap over the hole and align the pattern of the scrap with the pattern on the wall. Hold it in place with masking tape or thumbtacks, whichever is less likely to damage the wall covering.

Using a metal ruler held firmly against the wall over the scrap, take a very sharp utility knife and cut a square bigger than the hole itself through both layers of wall covering. Remove the scrap and the square patch and set them aside. Use the end of the utility knife to lift one corner of the square you've cut around the hole and peel this square off the wall.

Paste the back of the new patch and press it into the cleaned-out area on the wall, making sure the patterns are aligned.

REMOVING WALLPAPER

You can successfully paper over old wall coverings, but it's not always a good idea because the moisture in adhesives can cause both the old and new coverings to peel away from the wall. If strips of the old wall covering have been lapped at the seams, there is a good chance these lap marks will show through the new covering. At

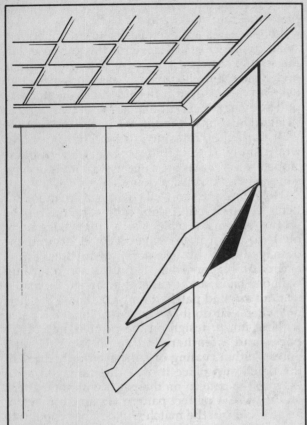

To remove strippable paper, lift up one corner and pull the paper down the wall, keeping it as close to the wall as possible to minimize the possibility of tearing.

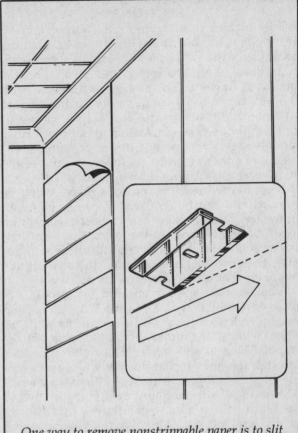

One way to remove nonstrippable paper is to slit and soak it. Make slits at 8- or 10-inch intervals; allow soapy water or a liquid paper remover to get behind the paper and soften the adhesive.

the very least, sand the seams smooth before applying the new covering, tear away any loose strips, and repaste loose edges around butt seams or defects. If you're papering over foil or vinyl wall coverings, go over the shiny areas lightly with coarse sandpaper and then vacuum or wipe the sanding dust off the wall.

It takes more work of course, but stripping off the old wall covering is usually wiser than leaving it on. New coverings adhere better to stripped-down surfaces. Depending on the wall covering and the kind of wall it is on, there are several ways to approach the job.

Strippable Papers. Although most strippable wall coverings have smooth, plasticlike textures (including vinyl, fabric-backed vinyl, or fabric-backed paper), the only way to find out if a covering is really strippable is to try peeling it off the wall. Pry up a corner in an inconspicuous location at the top of a wall with the tip of a utility knife. Grasp the tip of the corner, and keeping it as close to the wall as possible, try to pull it down the surface of the wall. Pulling it toward you and away from the wall increases the likelihood of tearing it. If a covering is strippable, it should peel away from the wall when you apply steady,

moderate pressure. If not, you're probably dealing with a nonstrippable paper that you must soak, steam, or dry strip off the wall. Do not soak or use steam stripping methods on drywall. The moisture can soften its kraft-paper surface and its gypsum core. Instead, use a dry-strip method.

Slitting and Soaking. With this technique, you make horizontal slits in the surface of the old wall covering with a razor blade or a special tool called a paper stripper (available at wall covering stores). The slits, made 8 or 10 inches apart, allow warm soapy water or a liquid paper remover to get behind the paper and soften the adhesive so you can pull or scrape the paper off plaster walls. You can apply either solution with a sponge or a spray bottle. If you spray on a liquid paper remover, use a painter's mask to keep from inhaling chemical vapors.

Work on one strip at a time and from the top of the wall to the bottom. Apply the water or the paper remover and let it soak in for a few minutes. Do the same thing on the next strip, then go back to the first and rewet it top to bottom. Then use a 3 1/2-inch-wide wall scraper with a flexible blade to begin stripping. Slide the blade under the top edge of one of the horizontal slits, and holding it at a 30-degree angle, push up on the wet paper. A scraper-width section should rip along the sides of the blade and wrinkle up above it as you push. If it does, continue pushing as long as the paper comes off. If the strip of scraped paper breaks, resoak that area and start scraping at another slit. After repeated soaking and scraping attempts, if the adhesive is clearly not yielding, you'll have to use another method.

On walls made of drywall, use a paper stripper to make the horizontal slits as before, but this time don't wet it. Slowly scrape or peel the paper away from the wall.

Steaming. Many tool rental and wallpaper outlets rent electrical steamers to do-it-yourselfers. These appliances typically consist of an electrically heated water tank connected by a long hose to a steamer plate with a perforated face. All you have to do, once the water is hot, is hold the plate against the wall until you see the wall covering darken with moisture around the edges of the plate. Start on a single strip and work from the top down. After about half the strip has been steamed, lift a top corner with a fingernail or a utility knife and attempt to peel the paper downward. If that doesn't work, resort to a wall scraper. You may have to steam the same areas two or three times to loosen the adhesive behind the paper.

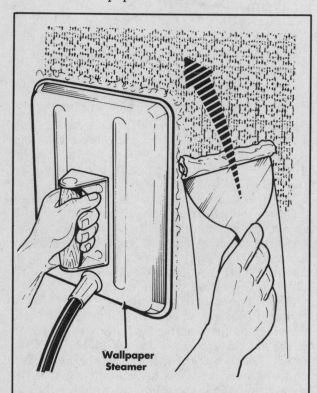

Wallpaper Steamer

Removing old wallpaper is no easy job. You can rent a steamer but you still have to scrape off most of the covering with a wide-blade putty knife.

Papering Walls

Putting up wall covering is something you can master within a very short time. In effect, once you've hung one strip, you've hung them all because, with a few exceptions, the materials and techniques are simply repeated all the way around the room. After the first strip is up, you'll be amazed how fast the job goes.

Cut the first strip of wall covering 4 to 6 inches longer than the height of the room. Place it pattern side up on the pasting table. Cut the second piece and all subsequent pieces for the same wall to match the pattern and length of the first strip. Then paste and hang them in order.

APPLYING PASTE TO PAPER

Applying paste to wallpaper can be very messy, so keep a container of clean water close by, along with clean rags and a sponge. To keep the paste off the patterned side of the paper, wash your hands frequently and wipe off the handles of brushes, seam rollers, and cutting tools as you go along.

Knowing how to paste a strip of wallpaper properly will keep the paste in its place. Follow this guide and you'll have a lot less cleaning up to do both during and after the job.

First cut a strip of paper to length and place it pattern side down on the table. Let the top edge hang over the edge of the table. The bottom edge and one side of the paper should hang over the tabletop by only about 1/4 inch.

Brush paste on the bottom quarter of the strip, the quarter that extends beyond the tabletop. Still working from the bottom, slide the strip over the other edge of the table and again let the bottom and the edge of the paper go beyond the tabletop by 1/4 inch.

Paste the other bottom quarter of the strip. Fold the pasted portion of the strip (less than half the length of the strip should have been pasted by now) on top of itself so that paste meets paste. Pull the strip toward you so that the top of the strip is in the position the bottom was when you began. Paste one top quarter of the strip, shift the paper to the other edge of the table and paste the last quarter.

As before, fold the strip so that paste meets paste and the top edge of the strip meets the bottom edge. When you fold the strip over on itself, do not crease either of the folds. The strip is pattern-side up and the pasted surfaces are inside. Better yet, there is no paste on the table to be wiped off before pasting another strip.

PLACING THE FIRST STRIP

Success here depends less on skill than on patience. It's vital to establish a straight, vertical line down the wall and to align the outside edge of the first strip of wall covering with that line.

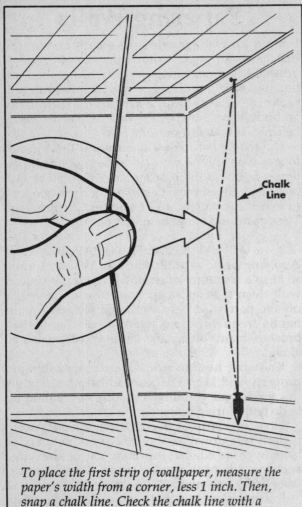

To place the first strip of wallpaper, measure the paper's width from a corner, less 1 inch. Then, snap a chalk line. Check the chalk line with a level to make sure it's accurate.

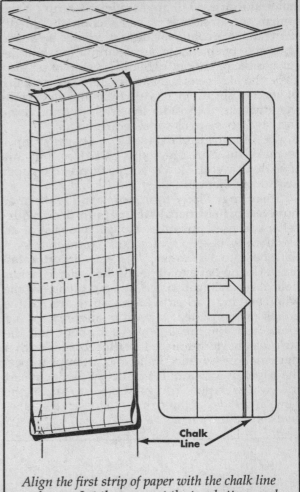

Align the first strip of paper with the chalk line and press. Let the excess at the top, bottom, and side lap onto adjacent surfaces.

That way, all the following strips (and the pattern on them) will fall into line almost automatically. Start with a tilt here, and the problem will compound itself with each successive strip that you put up.

Because there is no such thing as a perfectly plumb wall or a perfectly level floor or ceiling, you can't align the edge of the paper with a corner of the room and keep going. By the time you work your way around to the starting point, the last strip may be seriously out of whack. Therefore, you must establish a plumb line for the first strip.

To do this, start in an inconspicuous corner behind a door, and mount a stepladder to measure out the width of a roll of wall covering minus 1 inch. At this point, and as near to the ceiling as you can get, drive a nail into the wall (but just barely). On the nail, hang the looped end of the plumb bob, unreel the chalked string and let the bob hang to within about an inch of the floor. When the bob stops swinging, pull the string taut, hold it against the bottom of the wall with the thumb of one hand, reach up and pinch

the string with the other. Pull it out from the wall an inch or so and let it snap back. The chalk from the string will give you a perfectly plumb line on the wall. Take down the plumb bob, reel in the chalked string, and remove the nail.

Align the outside edge of the first strip of pasted paper with your chalk line and, with a smoothing brush or a sponge and your hands, press the paper to the wall. Let the excess at the top and bottom of the strip lap onto the ceiling or the baseboard. You can trim them off later with a utility knife or trimming knife.

The inside edge of your first strip will turn the corner, lapping onto the adjoining wall. Smooth the overlap down on the adjoining wall. Move on to the second strip, then come back and trim the top and bottom of the first one. Whenever a strip of wall covering turns an inside corner of the room, you can pound it into place with light jabs of the bristles on the smoothing brush.

Place the second strip of wall covering as near as possible to the outside edge of the first strip. Slide it toward the edge of the first strip until the edges of both strips butt. Slide it up or down to match the pattern. Smooth it with a brush or a sponge, working air bubbles and excess adhesive out from the middle of the strip toward the edges. Put up the third strip before trimming the top and bottom of the second one.

Except for papering around corners or doors or windows, the procedure remains the same for the rest of the project.

SEAMING

A seam is the joint between any two strips of wall covering and there are three basic kinds of seams: lapped, wire-edge, and butt. Years ago, the lap seam was the most common. It's rarely used anymore except in corners where pattern and vertical alignment must be corrected, because it leaves an unsightly ridge.

The wire-edge seam is also a lap seam, but it is about 1/16 inch smaller. It's still used with some wall coverings, those that don't butt smoothly and those that have a tendency to shrink and leave a gap between strips. The butt seam is by far the most popular today because it produces a joint between strips of wall covering that is all but invisible.

To make a butt seam, lightly stick up the second strip about 1/4 inch from the first and align

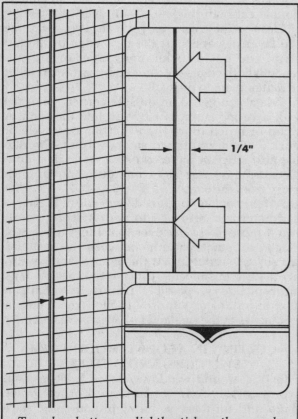

To make a butt seam, lightly stick up the second strip about 1/4 inch from the first, align the pattern, and slide the second strip until it bumps into the first and buckles both strips.

the patterns. Slide the second strip of paper over until it bumps into the first. The edges of both strips should buckle when this collision occurs. You can put up several strips of paper in this manner before finishing off the first seam because as the adhesive dries, the paper will contract enough to make the buckle in the joint flatten out against the wall. Fifteen or 20 minutes after you've made a butt joint, go over it with a seam roller to press the edges together and to the wall. Don't use a seam roller on flocked, foil, or textured wall coverings, because it can damage the paper. Instead use a sponge to finish the seams.

If you must lap the seams, make the laps as small as possible to create a wire-edge joint. To do this, lap the edge of the second strip over the first by 1/2 inch. Then slide the second strip away from the first until the lap measures only about 1/16 inch. If the wall covering is patterned, be sure the patterns match from strip to strip.

Because vinyl wall covering will not stick to itself, its seams should be butted if possible. Where that is not possible, the second-best solution is to double-cut them. First overlap the first strip with the second by 1/2 inch. Smooth the lap seam down lightly. Then, with a metal straightedge to guide your utility knife, cut through both layers of the lap, slicing downward through the middle of the overlap. Peel off the top layer of the overlap. Next, peel back the edge of the strip of wall covering you've just put up, and peel off the cut-through edge of the first strip. Finally, press both new edges together with a sponge and seam roller.

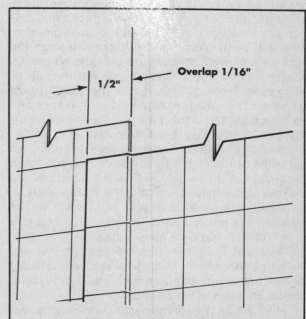

If you must lap seams, lap the edge of the second strip over the first by 1/2 inch, then slide the second strip away from the first until the lap measures about 1/16 inch.

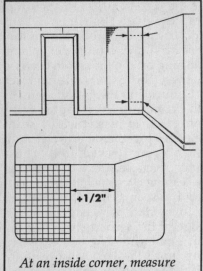

At an inside corner, measure both top and bottom from the edge of the last strip of paper. Take the wider of these measurements, add 1/2 inch, and cut to this dimension.

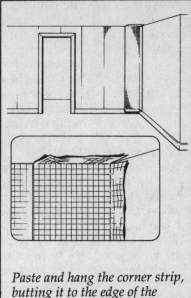

Paste and hang the corner strip, butting it to the edge of the previous strip and running it into and out of the corner. Trim at top and bottom as necessary.

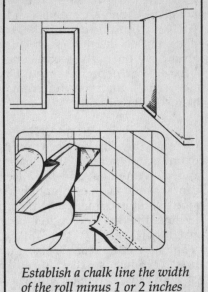

Establish a chalk line the width of the roll minus 1 or 2 inches from the corner. Align a strip with the chalk line, then double cut at the corner.

No matter what kind of wall covering you use, handle it as carefully as you can. To avoid jeopardizing seams, don't stretch the paper and try not to crease it.

PAPERING AROUND CORNERS

The last strip of paper you put up on a wall should be made to turn any inside or outside corner that it encounters. Because perfectly straight walls and perfectly plumb corners are a rarity, never start or stop a strip of paper at or in a corner. If you do, you will find that there is a noticeable gap in the seam when you try to align the first strip of wall covering on the adjoining wall. Either that or you'll throw your pattern out of alignment. Instead, plan to run the final strip of paper on the wall into or around the corner and then master the double-cutting technique outlined before. Here is how to negotiate a turn.

On inside corners, measure the distance from the edge of the last strip of paper you put up to the corner of the room. Do this at the top and the bottom of the strip. Then take the widest of those two measurements and add 1/2 inch. Cut the next strip of paper vertically to make a strip that is as wide as your final measurement.

Paste and hang this strip, butting it to the edge of the previous strip and running it into and out of the corner. Smooth it on both walls and trim at top and bottom as necessary.

Working on the adjacent and as-yet-unpapered wall, establish a plumb line as you did when you put up the first strip. From the width of the roll, subtract 1 or 2 inches, measure out from the corner of the room this distance and snap a chalk line from ceiling to floor. As you did before, align the outside edge of the first strip on the unpapered wall with the chalk line.

Using a sharp utility knife and a straightedge, double cut both thicknesses on one wall, getting as close to the corner as you can. Peel away the top layer of paper, lift the new edge of the top strip, and peel off the inner layer of the cut. Smooth both edges together and use a seam roller to flatten them to the wall.

When you get to an outside corner, wrap the wall covering an inch or two around the bend. A wrap of much more than that may wrinkle or buckle when you try to smooth it out. Overlap the next strip on the unpapered wall. Then double cut the overlap as before, but about an inch away from the corner.

After you've papered the room's entire perimeter and returned to your starting point, you'll most likely discover that there is no way exactly to match patterns between the first and last strips you put up. At this point you'll have to live with a mismatch. To make the mismatch as inconspicuous as possible, plan for it to happen next to a door or window frame, where only a few inches of the first and last strips will touch.

CUTTING IN AROUND WOODWORK, SWITCHES, AND OUTLETS

Papering around windows, doors, built-ins, and woodwork is time consuming, but not much more difficult than papering around corners. To make the job easier, work with a sharp utility knife and change the blade when it shows any signs of pulling or tearing the wall covering.

Depending on the kind of wall covering you're working with, use a smoothing brush or a sponge

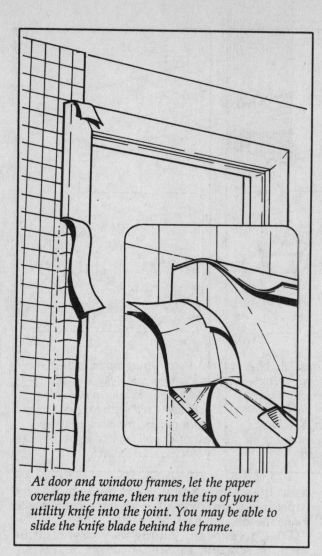

At door and window frames, let the paper overlap the frame, then run the tip of your utility knife into the joint. You may be able to slide the knife blade behind the frame.

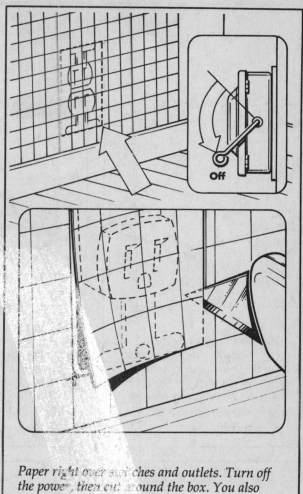

Paper right over switches and outlets. Turn off the power, then cut around the box. You also can paper the faceplates.

to make a snug fit around obstacles, pounding lightly against the paper with the bristles of the brush. Let the paper overlap the window or door frame and then run the tip of your utility knife into the joint. Around windows and doors, you may be able to slide the blade of the knife behind the frame while trimming the paper to fit.

Around large openings or obstacles, make the longest cuts first. At a door, for example, slice the paper from the top of the frame to the baseboard and discard or set aside this strip. Next, crease the flap of paper at the top of the frame and make a horizontal cut, using the frame as a guide.

When it comes to electrical switches and outlets, remember this: Wall covering paste is a superb conductor of electricity, so plan to cut off the power to the circuits you're working on at the circuit breaker box. If you need additional light, run an extension cord to a "live" outlet in another room.

For outlets and switches, remove the faceplates and paper right over the recessed electrical boxes. With your utility knife, trim away the overlap, cutting a rectangle in the paper the same size as the box itself.

If you like, you also can paper the faceplates. Remount the plate on the wall, but use only two or three turns of the screws to do so. Cut a rectangle of wallpaper larger than the plate. Place the paper over the plate and fold the top edge over the top edge of the plate so that the pattern on the plate will match the pattern on the wall. Once you've matched the pattern at the top, make a crease in the paper and repeat the procedure to get a match at the sides. Remove the creased paper and the plate. Using the creases as your guide, position the plate face down on the pasted side of the paper. With scissors, trim off the corners of the paper diagonally, so that you can then fold the four edges over the back of the plate without overlapping them. Cut an X in the plate where the toggle switch will go through, pull the flaps through the hole and paste them down. Make paper covers for outlets the same way.

To get the best results around both wall- and ceiling-mounted light fixtures, it's better to take them down completely. Then you can paper right over the electrical box. Afterward, use the inside of the box as a guide for your knife and cut away the paper covering the opening.

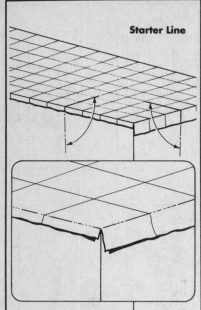

Starter Line

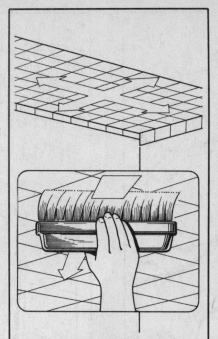

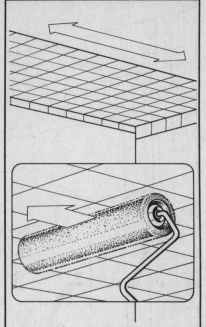

After you've established a starter line for the ceiling, cut and paste up a strip that is 4 to 6 inches longer than the width of the room. You can trim off the overlap or lap over it when you paper the walls.

Put up ceiling strips 2 or 3 feet at a time, first patting them into place with a smoothing brush. After each strip is in place, go over the whole length with the smoothing brush, searching out wrinkles and blisters.

After putting up each strip, use a clean paint roller with an extension handle to roll out bubbles and secure the paper to the ceiling. Working from the center, roll left and right toward the edges of the strip.

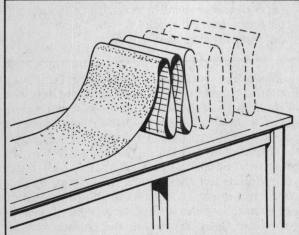

Ceiling strips will be easier to handle if you fold them accordion-fashion, pasted side to pasted side in small, regular folds. Don't let the pasted side touch the patterned side and try not to crease the paper.

Papering Ceilings

Once you've papered a ceiling, you'll realize why most are painted. Juggling and balancing strips of wet, fragile paper on a scaffold and working with your arms over your head for long periods of time is real labor. Simply stated, it's far easier to paint the ceiling. Still, if your preference is for paper, there are some labor-saving techniques to make the job easier.

First prepare the ceiling as you would the walls, by scraping, sanding, patching, and washing. Turn off the power and disconnect the ceiling fixtures, too. If you're papering both the walls and the ceiling, do the ceiling first.

The equipment needed to paper a ceiling is the same as that required for walls, with one exception. If you don't already have one, recruit a helper.

Setting Up Scaffolding. Unless you're a professional basketball player, you're going to need something to stand on that will get you and the paper up to within easy reach of the ceiling. Homemade scaffolding will do the job, but you also can rent scaffolding. Ideally, your scaffold should span the width of the ceiling so you can paper all the way across without having constantly to climb down and move your equipment. At the very least, you'll need two stepladders to support each end of a bridge. For the bridge itself, use a pair of 2 x 8s, set on the second rungs of the ladders, as explained at the beginning of this chapter. You can buy the lumber in 8-, 10-, 12-, or even 14-foot lengths, but a span of more than 8 feet will sag dangerously between the ladders. You can overcome this problem by keeping your bridge on the short side and using a sawhorse, a stool, or a third stepladder as a middle support for the scaffolding. Place one ladder on one side of the room, a second on the other side, a third in the middle. Run one plank from the second ladder (or sawhorse, etc.) to the third.

Establishing a Starter Line. Because no room is a perfect square or rectangle, you'll need to snap a chalk line across the narrow width of the ceiling as a point of departure for the first strip of paper. Measure the width of the roll, subtract 1 inch, and then measure this distance out from both ends of the wall. Tack a chalk line across the ceiling from these two points, pinch it in the middle, pull it down an inch or so, and let it snap against the ceiling. Cut and paste a strip of paper that is 4 to 6 inches longer than the width of the ceiling to allow for pattern matching with subsequent strips. Align the first strip with the chalk line and pat it into place. The opposite edge will lap down on the wall about an inch. You can trim off the overlap later or lap over it when you put paper on the walls.

Pasting and Folding. Cut all the strips of paper you'll need to cover the entire ceiling at one time. As before, make the strips 4 to 6 inches longer than the width of the ceiling to facilitate pattern matching. On a rented wallpaper table or a long cafeteria table, place a strip of paper face down and apply the adhesive to the back. The strip will be easier to handle if you fold it accordion-fashion, pasted side to pasted side in small, regular folds. Don't let the pasted side touch the patterned side and try not to crease the paper.

Brushing. It helps to have an assistant hold the folded strip while you pat the end of it into place on the ceiling, starting at the wall. Put up the strip 2 or 3 feet at a time, first patting it into place and then using short strokes of a smoothing brush to flatten it against the ceiling. Your helper can unfold the paper a little at a time, fold by fold, as you need it. Work excess paste and air bubbles toward the nearest edge of the strip as you go. When the entire strip is in place, go over the whole length with the smoothing brush, checking the alignment and searching out wrinkles and blisters.

Notching Corners. With both the first strip and the last, the paper will lap down on three walls. To make it fit tightly into the corners, you'll have to cut notches, which are 1-by-2-inch rectangles, in the paper where the strip encounters an inside corner.

First, push the paper into the corner by gently pounding the paper with the bristles of the smoothing brush. This should give you a 90-degree crease that duplicates the position of the corner. Peel down a foot or so of the paper from the ceiling and use scissors to cut out the notch, following the lines of the crease (if the creasing technique doesn't work, use chalk to mark the notch first). Smooth the paper into the corner.

Smoothing. After putting up each strip, use a clean paint roller with an extension handle to roll out bubbles and secure the paper to the ceiling. Working from the center, roll left and right toward the edges of the strip. Finish the process by rolling lengthwise from wall to wall. Use a seam roller to flatten the butt seams between strips of paper.

If you are not papering the walls as well, trim off the overlap at each end of the strip with a sharp utility knife. If the walls are going to be papered too, and you are working with a non-vinyl paper, leave a 1/2-inch overlap and paper over it. With vinyl paper, leave an overlap of 1 or 2 inches to be double cut when the paper goes on the walls.

Putting Up Specialty Coverings

There are two reasons to use an out-of-the-ordinary wall covering: Either the surface, such as a rough wall, demands it or your taste in decoration dictates something special.

Vinyl. Washable, durable, and heavier than regular printed paper, vinyl wall coverings often come in extra-wide rolls that can reduce the number of seams and trims. They are usually more strippable than ordinary papers. Perhaps their greatest value is that vinyl wall coverings are particularly good at covering up defects that paint or thinner wall coverings can't begin to hide.

Because vinyl is not nearly as fragile as printed paper, you don't have to worry so much about punctures or ripped edges. Still, do try to avoid stretching it unnecessarily.

Whenever possible, try to butt and roll the seams, even if you have to double cut them. Remember that vinyl will not stick to itself, so if

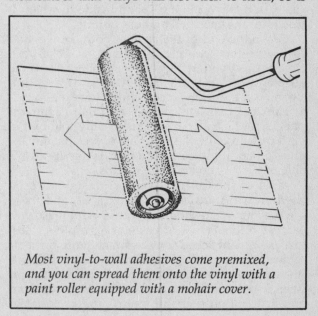

Most vinyl-to-wall adhesives come premixed, and you can spread them onto the vinyl with a paint roller equipped with a mohair cover.

you have to resort to a lap seam you'll need to have some vinyl-to-vinyl adhesive on hand.

Most vinyl-to-wall adhesives come premixed, another advantage over paper and mix-it-yourself wheat pastes. You can spread the adhesive on the vinyl with a paint roller equipped with a mohair roller cover. Afterward, apply the vinyl strips to the wall as you would any other wall covering, but use a smoothing brush with 3/4-inch bristles, which are shorter and sturdier than the longer-bristled brushes used on paper. With really heavyweight vinyl, even a short-bristle brush may not do an adequate job of smoothing. If that is the case, use a straight edge, such as a strip of hardboard or a yardstick.

Smooth three or four vinyl strips on the wall and then go back to make the trims and look for blisters. Puncture blisters with a needle or the tip of a single-edge razor blade and then squeeze out the trapped air or excess adhesive.

Prepasted Paper. The advantages of this type of wall covering should be evident from the name. Because the water-activated adhesive is applied at the factory, you don't have to bother with paste brushes, rollers, or adhesive mixes. You can paper a room faster than with other wall coverings, but you still have a choice between paper, vinyl, foils, even flocked surfaces.

To activate the adhesive on prepasted wall coverings, all you have to do is soak them briefly in a special water tray available from the wallpaper store. Place the tray on the floor directly next to the wall where the paper will go. Pour water into the tray until it is about two-thirds full. Position a stepladder in front of the tray. Cut a strip of paper to length, reroll it loosely so the pattern is on the inside, and dunk it in the water-filled tray. The manufacturer's directions will tell you how long to let the paper soak, anywhere from 10 seconds to a minute. If the roll floats in the water, slip a mixing spoon inside to weigh it down for the specified amount of time.

Grasp the end of the strip at both corners and let it unroll as you climb the ladder. Take your time at this point, letting the water cascade off the strip and back into the tray. After that, smooth it down, roll the seams, and trim off the excess.

Fabric. Expensive compared to more common papers, fabric wall covering is usually sold by the yard instead of by the roll. One of its chief advantages, in addition to strippability, is that it's available in 45-, 54-, and 60-inch widths.

Most of the fabric coverings designed to be used on walls are backed with paper, and these are the kinds you should look for. With these you can use ordinary wheat paste or a stainless cellulose paste. Unbacked vinyl is much more difficult to deal with and not recommended, especially for novice paperhangers. If you purchase an unbacked fabric, use a powdered vinyl adhesive and brush it on the wall, not on the back of the

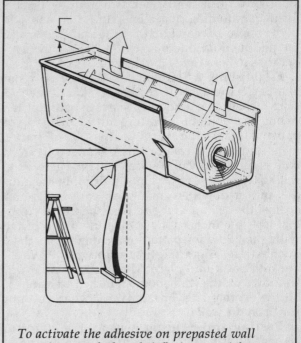

To activate the adhesive on prepasted wall coverings, soak them briefly in a special water tray. Grasp the strip at both corners and let it unroll as you climb the ladder.

fabric. No matter which kind you use, be sure to put lining paper on the walls first so that you get a good bond between wall and fabric.

Paper-backed fabric can be smoothed with your hands or a smoothing brush (be sure the bristles don't snag or fray the fibers). Unbacked fabric is much trickier. For one thing, you'll have to trim off the selvages with scissors before pasting the fabric to the wall. Another disadvantage is that fabric can absorb moisture from the adhesive on the wall. The extra weight makes it heavy and gives it a tendency to droop. Moisture also may allow the fabric to stretch and that can be hazardous because, as the adhesive dries and the moisture evaporates, the fabric may shrink, opening seams in the process. If possible, pat and smooth the fabric on the wall with your hands, pulling it taut, but not out of shape. Try to buy a nonshrinkable fabric in the first place.

Foil. Also expensive and delicate, foil coverings can add dramatic sparkle to entire rooms, entries, or alcoves. Most are backed with either paper or fabric and should be used with a vinyl adhesive (water in wheat paste can't evaporate through the foil).

Because of its reflective surface, foil wall covering emphasizes the tiniest bumps or pockmarks in a wall, so plan to use it over a lining paper. Also be extremely careful to avoid creasing or wrinkling it when you put it up. Instead of a smoothing brush, which may scratch the foil, smooth it on the wall with a sponge or a folded towel. Bond the seams the same way.

FURNITURE

Unlike most of the other components that make up your home, your furniture goes with you when you move, it's rearranged or shifted periodically, and it may be handed down for generations. You add to your furniture collection gradually, and you may end up with more old pieces than new. Because it gets moved around and takes a lot of abuse over years of service, your furniture needs regular care to keep it looking good. When it needs repairing, whether the problem is in the finish or the wood, in the surface or the structure, you should know how to do the job yourself. Many people are afraid to do more to a finished wood surface than polish it, but this is a groundless fear. Once you know how your furniture is put together, you're equipped for anything. With patience and a little know-how, you can repair the finish, remove it and apply a new one, and then go on to repair the structure.

How Furniture Is Made

Like all the other components of your home, furniture is easy to work with when you know how it is put together. Furniture is made to provide comfort and convenience, and judged on how well it succeeds in providing them. To function well, furniture must be sturdy, steady, and securely joined. There is more to good furniture than sturdy legs. Good wood and workmanship make good furniture; age enhances its value; and style is, if not essential, at least important.

THE FINISH

The most common furniture problems involve the finish (the coating that protects the wood and gives it its glossy surface). Most furniture finishes are surface coatings; they protect the wood by forming a solid layer on top of it. Shellac, lacquer, and varnish, the most common furniture finishes, are all surface coatings. Other finishes, such as oil and penetrating resin, sink into the wood; they don't form a surface coating, but protect the wood by hardening inside the fibers. A damaged finish coating can be repaired easily when the damage doesn't extend into the wood underneath it. When the damage goes through the finish and into the wood, repairs will involve spot refinishing—an unpredictable technique and not always a successful one, especially when the wood is stained. Whenever you work on the finish, remember that the less finish you remove, the better your results are likely to be.

Many repair jobs and most restoration projects require a knowledge of the finish with which you're working. If you don't know what the finish is, you could damage a perfectly good finish, or you could waste your time on a technique that won't work. This knowledge is also essential when you have to match one finish to another.

The only distinction that matters is the difference among the three basic natural, or clear, finishes: shellac, lacquer, and varnish. The pigmented finishes, such as paint or enamel, are easy to identify. The only other finishes you may encounter are oil, wax, and penetrating sealers, which are identifiable by touch and by the absence of a high gloss. On most furniture a clear finish is shellac, lacquer, or varnish. Modern furniture is often lacquered, but the finish on a piece made before about 1860 is usually shellac; lacquer and varnish were not developed until the mid 1800s. A varnish finish is rare on factory-finished pieces, because varnish is hard to apply and requires a long drying period in a dust-free environment. Very old furniture may be finished with oil, wax, or milk paint, and many fine furniture pieces are French polished, which is a kind of shellac finish. Old finishes are natural products; brand-new finishes, such as the polyurethanes, may be synthetics.

Before you make any extensive repairs to a finish, take a minute to identify it. First, test the finish with denatured alcohol; rub a little alcohol onto an inconspicuous finished area. If the finish dissolves, it's shellac. If it partially dissolves, it's probably a combination of shellac and lacquer. Test it again with a mixture of denatured alcohol and lacquer thinner; this should completely dissolve the finish.

If alcohol doesn't affect the finish, rub a little lacquer thinner on an inconspicuous finished spot. If the area turns rough and then smooth again, the finish is lacquer; if the finish crinkles and doesn't get smooth again, it's some type of varnish. If neither alcohol nor lacquer thinner affects it, the finish is varnish.

If the piece of furniture is painted, test the finish with ammonia; very old pieces may be finished with milk paint, which is dissolved only by ammonia. If the piece of furniture is very dirty or encrusted with wax, clean it first with a mixture of denatured alcohol, white vinegar, and kerosene, in equal parts. Then test it with the various solvents.

THE STRUCTURE: BASIC JOINERY

All furniture is put together in a series of joints, and structural problems often involve joint weakening or failure. Some joints are simple, some complicated; some joints are stronger than others. The joints used in good furniture are usually stronger than those in cheap pieces, but age and abuse take their toll even when the original construction was good. To prevent more serious damage, all joints should be repaired as soon as possible when they loosen or separate.

Old furniture is often made with mortise-and-tenon joints, which consist of a prong held in a hole. The dovetail joint is used in good-quality furniture; butt and lapped joints, the weakest kind, are also the easiest to make and are often used in cheap pieces. Other joints used in furniture manufacturing include blank, or stopped, mortise-and-tenon joints, dadoes, and stopped or dovetailed dadoes, miters, and doweled, rabbeted, or splined joints.

Mortise-and-Tenon Joints. In this kind of joint, a prong, or tongue, of wood—the tenon—is secured in a hole—the mortise—in the joining piece. If the joint is blank, or stopped, the mortise doesn't extend completely through the joining piece, and the end of the tenon is not visible on the outside of the joint. Mortise-and-tenon joints are strong; they're used chiefly in chairs and tables.

Dovetail Joints. Dovetail joints consist of wedge-shaped openings—the dovetails—holding matching pins cut in the joining piece. These joints are the pride of cabinetmakers in both old and new furniture. The through dovetail is the early version; in this joint, the dovetail goes completely through both pieces of wood. The pins in handmade dovetails are usually narrower than

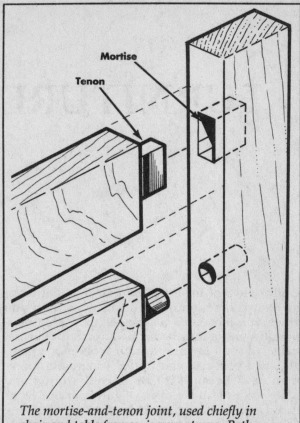

The mortise-and-tenon joint, used chiefly in chair and table frames, is very strong. Both square and round tenons are used in furniture.

The dovetail is a strong, precision-cut joint. On some antiques and hand-built furniture, dovetails were cut by hand; these dovetails are less even than machine-cut joints.

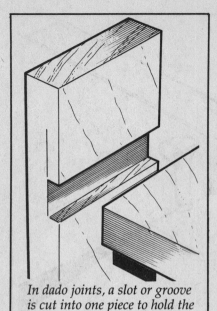

In dado joints, a slot or groove is cut into one piece to hold the end of the joining piece.

The groove of a stopped or blind dado does not extend completely across the wood.

The dovetail dado is cut with a dovetail for extra strength.

In butt joints the two joining pieces are butted together. Nails or metal mending plates are used for reinforcement.

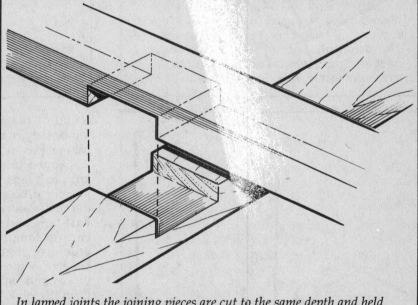

In lapped joints the joining pieces are cut to the same depth and held with glue. The cross-lap joint joins crossing pieces.

the spaces between the pins. On some antique pieces, only a few dovetails are used, and the tails and pins don't match exactly. With woodworking machines and jigs, the tails and the pins are the same width and more dovetails are used in each joint. Some dovetail joints are blind: The pins don't extend completely through the joining piece and only the top or face of the joint is visible.

Dado Joints. A dado is a slot cut into the face or end of a piece of wood; the joining piece fits into this slot. In a simple dado joint, the slot goes completely across the wood, and the edges of the joining piece are visible along the edges of the base piece. In a stopped, or blind, dado, the joint does not extend completely across the face of the wood and is not visible from the edges. Dadoes and stopped dadoes have considerable shear strength and are used for shelving. The dovetail dado is a dado with a dovetail at the bottom. It's a fancy cabinet joint, which is strong and especially good looking.

Butt Joints. In this kind of joint, the joining pieces are simply butted together—face to face, edge to edge, or face to edge—with no integral fastener. Butt joints are weak and are sometimes fastened or held with metal surface plates. Butt joints held with a metal fastener, such as a nail, screw, or mending plate, or a specially machined

The miter joint, used for frames and molding, consists of two pieces cut at a 45-degree angle and joined in a right angle.

In the rabbet joint one or both joining members are notched. Screws or nails are usually used for reinforcement.

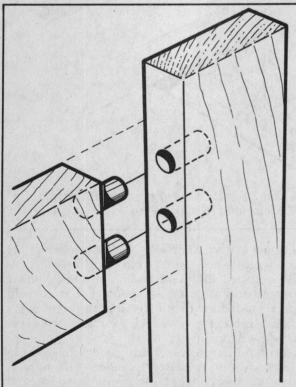

The doweled joint is a variation of the mortise-and-tenon, with dowels holding the pieces together.

metal or plastic fitting, are called mechanical joints; they're used in chairs, tables, dressers, and cabinet pieces.

Lapped Joints. Lapped joints, including cross-laps, half-laps, and sloped-laps, are cut with both joining pieces notched or slanted to the same depth. Cross-laps are used to join crossing pieces; half-laps and sloped-laps are used to join the ends of long pieces. Lapped joints offer a large glue area, but they aren't particularly strong; they're often used in drawer guide framing pieces and may be pinned with nails or screws from the back. To strengthen lap joints, some cabinetmakers cut them with a dovetail.

Miter Joints. In a miter the joining pieces are cut at a 45-degree angle and joined to form a right angle. Miters are used for decorative molding and for frames. They are weak and are often reinforced with dowels, splines, or mechanical fasteners. Many cabinets have mitered corner joints, which usually are reinforced by dowels or by a plywood spline running the length of each joint. In less expensive furniture, miter joints may be supported with a strip of wood nailed or screwed to the inside corner of the joint. Sometimes triangular glue blocks are used for strength; the blocks may be reinforced by screws.

Doweled Joints. The doweled joint is a simple variation of the mortise-and-tenon joint, with dowels instead of a cut tenon holding the joining

The splined joint is held together by a reinforcing spline, fitted into matching grooves in the joining members.

pieces together. Doweled joints are strong, and are common in chairs, tables, and cabinets, usually on stretchers and other framing pieces.

Rabbet Joints. The rabbet is a reinforced butt joint, with one or both joining members notched to fit together. It is usually reinforced with screws or nails. Rabbet joints are easy to make and strong. They are used chiefly for shelving and at the corners of cabinet pieces. A stopped rabbet extends only partway through the wood.

Splined Joints. In a splined joint, the edges of the joining pieces are grooved to match each other and a reinforcing spline—usually plywood or hardboard—is inserted into the grooves to hold the pieces together. Splined joints are used chiefly to join boards.

Surface Repairs

Old and new furniture often shows evidence of hard service: stains, scratches, burns, and other signs of use and abuse. Veneer may be loose or broken, hardware may be missing, or the wood may be discolored. Unless the damage is severe or extensive, most of these problems are easy to fix. Surface repairs aren't difficult, but it can be hard to tell what you're getting into. If only the surface is affected, the damage is usually easy to repair; if the wood is damaged too, you may have to refinish part or all of the piece.

STAINS AND DISCOLORATION

White Spots. Shellac and lacquer finishes are not resistant to water and alcohol; spills and condensation from glasses can leave permanent white spots or rings on these finishes. To remove these white spots, polish the surface with liquid furniture polish, and buff the surface firmly. If this doesn't work, lightly wipe the stained surface with denatured alcohol. Use as little alcohol as possible; too much will damage the finish.

If neither polishing nor alcohol removes the white spots, the damaged finish must be treated with abrasives. For a gentle abrasive, mix cigarette ashes to a paste with a few drops of vegetable oil, mineral oil, or boiled linseed oil. Rub the paste over the stained area along the grain of the wood, and then wipe the surface clean with a soft cloth. If necessary, repeat the procedure; stubborn spots may require several applications. Then wax and polish the entire surface.

If rubbing with ashes is not effective, go over the stained area with a mixture of rottenstone and linseed oil. Mix the rottenstone and oil to a thin paste, and rub the paste gently over the stain along the grain of the wood. Rottenstone is a fast-cutting abrasive, so rub carefully and check the surface frequently to make sure you aren't cutting too deep. As soon as the white spots disappear, stop rubbing and wipe the wood clean with a soft cloth. Then apply two coats of hard furniture wax and buff the wood to a shine.

Blushing. Blushing, which is a white haze over a large surface or an entire piece of furniture, is a common problem with old shellac and lacquer finishes. The discoloration is caused by moisture, and it can sometimes be removed the same way white spots are removed. Buff the surface with 0000 steel wool dipped in boiled linseed oil. Work

Rubbing with oil and fine abrasives often removes spots and blushing. Rub along the grain of the wood, then wipe the surface clean.

with the grain of the wood, rubbing evenly on the entire surface, until the white haze disappears. Then wipe the wood clean with a soft cloth, apply two coats of hard furniture wax, and buff the surface to a shine.

Black Spots. Black spots are caused by water that has penetrated the finish completely and entered the wood. They cannot be removed without damage to the finish. If the spots are on a clearly defined surface, you may be able to remove the finish from this surface only; otherwise, the entire piece of furniture must be refinished. When the finish has been removed, bleach the entire stained surface with a solution of oxalic acid, as directed by the manufacturer. Then refinish the piece.

Ink Stains. Ink stains that have penetrated the finish, like black water spots, cannot be removed without refinishing. Less serious ink stains can sometimes be removed. Lightly buff the stained area with a cloth moistened with mineral spirits; then rinse the wood with clean water on a soft cloth. Dry the surface thoroughly, then wax and polish it. If this does not remove the ink, lightly rub the stained area, along the grain of the wood, with 0000 steel wool moistened with mineral spirits. Wipe the surface clean, then wax and polish it. This treatment may damage the finish; if necessary, refinish the damaged spot.

Grease, Tar, Paint, Crayon, and Lipstick Spots. These spots usually affect only the surface of the finish. To remove wet paint, use the appropriate solvent on a soft cloth: mineral spirits for oil-base paint or water for latex paint. To remove dry paint or other materials, carefully lift the surface residue with the edge of a putty knife. Do not scrape the wood or you'll scratch the finish. When the surface material has been removed, buff the area very lightly along the grain of the wood with 0000 steel wool moistened with mineral spirits. After buffing, wax and polish the entire surface.

Wax and Gum Spots. Wax and gum usually come off quickly, but they must be removed carefully to prevent damage to the finish. To make the wax or gum brittle, press it with a packet of ice wrapped in a towel. Let the deposit harden, then lift it off with your thumbnail. The hardened wax or gum should pop off the surface with very little pressure. If necessary, repeat the ice application. Do not scrape the deposit off, or you'll scratch the finish. When the wax or gum is completely removed, buff the area very lightly along the grain of the wood with 0000 steel wool moistened with mineral spirits. Then wax and polish the entire surface.

SPOT REFINISHING

Any repair that involves removing the damaged finish completely, including deep scratches, gouges, burns, or any other damage, also

Spot-staining is tricky, but it is sometimes successful. Apply stain to the repair area with an artist's brush.

involves refinishing the repair area. Spot refinishing is not always easy, and it's not always successful, especially on stained surfaces. If the damage isn't too bad, it's worth trying. If you have to touch up several areas on one surface, you're probably better off refinishing the surface or the piece of furniture completely.

To stain one area on a surface, use an oil-base stain that matches the surrounding stain. You may have to mix stains to get a good match. Test the stain on an inconspicuous unfinished part of the wood before working on the finished surface.

Before applying the stain, sand the damaged area smooth with fine-grit sandpaper, and wipe the surface clean. Apply the stain to the damaged area with an artist's brush or a clean cloth, covering the entire bare area. Let the stain set for 15 minutes and then wipe it off with a clean cloth. If the color is too light, apply another coat of stain, wait 15 minutes, and wipe again. Repeat this procedure until you're satisfied with the color, then let the stain dry according to the manufacturer's instructions.

Lightly buff the stained surface with 0000 steel wool, and wipe it clean with a tack cloth. Apply a new coat of the same finish already on the surface over the newly stained area, feathering out the new finish into the surrounding old finish. Let the new finish dry for one to two days, and lightly buff the patched area with 0000 steel wool. Wax the entire surface with hard paste wax, and polish it to a shine.

SURFACE DAMAGE

Scratches, dings, dents, cracks and gouges, burns, and other maladies can also mar furniture surfaces. Here is how to treat these afflictions:

Scratches. To hide a small scratch quickly, break the meat of a walnut, pecan, or Brazil nut and rub it along the scratch. The oil in the nut meat will darken the raw scratch, making it less conspicuous.

When many shallow scratches are present, apply hard paste wax to the surface with 0000 steel wool, stroking very lightly along the grain of the wood. Then buff the surface with a soft cloth. If the scratches still show, apply one or two more coats of hard paste wax to the surface. Let each coat dry thoroughly and buff it to a shine before applying the next coat.

For one or two deeper scratches, wax furniture-patching sticks are usually effective. These retouching sticks, made in many colors, are available at hardware stores; choose a stick to match the finish. To use the wax stick, run it firmly along the scratch, applying enough pressure to fill the scratch with wax. Remove any excess wax with the edge of a credit card or other thin plastic card. Let the wax harden, then buff the surface with a soft cloth.

Badly scratched surfaces should be refinished, but to hide one or two very deep scratches, you may be able to stain the raw area to match. Apply oil-base stain with an artist's brush, drawing it

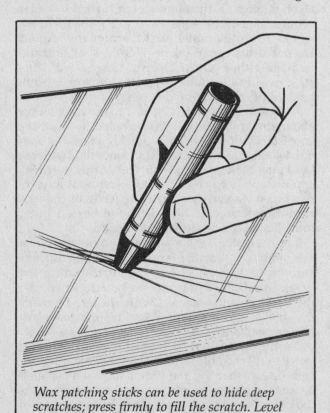

Wax patching sticks can be used to hide deep scratches; press firmly to fill the scratch. Level with the edge of a credit card.

carefully along the scratch; let it stand for 15 minutes and wipe it off. If necessary, repeat this procedure until the scratch matches the rest of the wood. Let the area dry completely, as directed by the stain manufacturer, then apply hard paste wax and buff the waxed surface to a shine.

Dings. Dings are tiny chips in the finish, usually caused by sharp blows. The wood may not be affected. To repair a ding, use a sharp craft knife to remove any loose finish in or around the ding. Scrape the damaged spot with the flat, sharp edge of the knife blade; do not scratch the spot. Then feather the edges of the ding with 0000 steel wool.

Clean the ding area with a soft cloth moistened in mineral spirits, and let it dry completely. With an artist's brush apply new finish to the spot to match the rest of the finish. The spot will be very noticeable at first. Let the finish dry; it will be glossy. Then buff the spot with 0000 steel wool, and wax and polish the entire piece of furniture. The ding should blend when the job is complete.

Dents. Small shallow dents in pine and other soft woods are usually easy to remove; large and deep dents, especially in hard wood, are harder to repair. Dents are easiest to remove from bare wood. Large shallow dents are probably best left untreated. Deep dents should be filled, using the same methods as for cracks and gouges.

On finished surfaces you'll have to remove the finish around the damaged area. Using fine-grit sandpaper, carefully remove the finish for about 1/2 inch around the spot. To raise the wood in the dent, apply a few drops of water to the dent and let the water penetrate the wood for a day or so. Do not wet the entire surface. This treatment may be enough to raise the dent, especially if the dent is shallow and the wood is soft.

If this doesn't raise the dent, soak a cloth in water and wring it out. Place the damp cloth, folded in several layers, over the dent, then press the cloth firmly with a warm iron. Be careful not to touch the iron directly to the wood. This moist heat may be enough to swell the wood and raise the dent. If it isn't, apply a commercial wood-swelling liquid to the area and give it time to work, as directed by the manufacturer.

For deep dents that can't be raised with water, heat, or wood sweller, use a fine straight pin or needle to drive a series of holes in the dent. Pound the straight pin in about 1/4 inch, and carefully pull it out with pliers; the holes should be as small as possible. Then treat the dent as previously described. The pinholes let the water penetrate the wood's surface, and if you're careful, they won't show when the wood has been raised.

After the dent has been raised, let the wood dry for about a week, then refinish the damaged area. Let the finish dry completely. Lightly buff the new finish with 0000 steel wool, then wax and polish the entire surface.

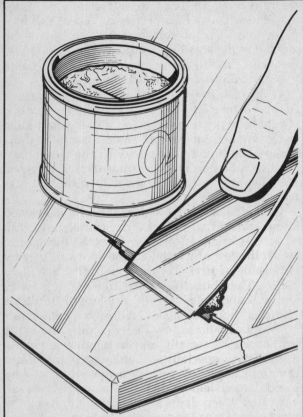

Fill deep cracks and gouges with plastic wood or water putty; leave the filler higher than the surface level to allow for shrinkage as it dries. When the patch is dry, sand it smooth.

Cracks and Gouges. Cracks and gouges should be filled so that they're level with the surface of the wood. For small holes, such as staple holes, you can use wood-tone putty sticks. If you can't match the wood, mix several colors together. To use a putty stick, wipe it across the hole and smooth the surface with your finger. If you plan to finish or refinish the wood, let the putty dry for at least a week before proceeding further.

For larger holes plastic wood and water putty are the easiest fillers. These fillers can be used on bare or finished wood; plastic wood is available in several colors, and water putty can be tinted with oil- or water-base stain. Plastic wood and water putty patches are usually noticeable and may look darker than the wood. For the best results, test the patch on an inconspicuous surface to make sure the color is right.

To use plastic wood, carefully clean the crack or gouge with the tip of a craft knife, then press the plastic firmly in with a putty knife. Plastic wood shrinks as it dries, so press it in and leave it mounded above the surface of the wood.

Plastic wood dries quickly, but let it set for at least two days. Then smooth the patch lightly with fine-grit sandpaper and buff the area with 0000 steel wool. If the surrounding finish is

involved, feather the edges so that the new patch blends in with it. If necessary, stain the patch and buff it lightly with 0000 steel wool. Apply finish to match the rest of the surface, using an artist's brush and feathering the edges. Let the finish dry, then lightly buff it with 0000 steel wool; clean the area of any residue, and wax and polish the surface.

Water putty dries flint-hard, usually harder than the wood being patched. It's best used on bare wood. Water putty can be toned with oil- and water-base stains, but you'll have to experiment to come up with a perfect match. To use water putty, mix the powder with water to the consistency of putty; then trowel it into the break with a putty knife, leaving the patch higher than the surface of the wood. Let the patch dry completely, and sand the area smooth and level with the surrounding surface. Finish the patch area, or refinish the entire piece of furniture.

For the most professional patching job, use shellac sticks to fill cracks and gouges. Shellac sticks leave the least conspicuous patch and are very effective on finished wood that is in good condition. Shellac sticks are available in many colors; use a stick that matches the finish. Practice on scrap wood before working on a piece of furniture.

Carefully clean the crack or gouge with the tip of a craft knife. Shellac sticks must be heated and melted to fill the crack. The best heat source is an alcohol lamp or a propane torch turned to a low setting. Do not use a match to soften the stick; the smoke from the match will discolor the shellac. Do not use a range burner; liquid shellac could damage either gas or electric ranges. Hold the stick over the blade of a palette knife or a putty knife to prevent it from dripping.

To use a shellac stick, hold it to the heat source above the knife, until it has softened to about the consistency of putty. Then quickly press the softened shellac into the crack and smooth it with the hot knife. Make sure the soft shellac fills the break completely; it hardens quickly, so you'll have to work fast. Leave the patch higher than the surrounding surface. Then, with the heated putty knife blade, trowel the shellac smooth.

Let the patch set for one to two hours. When the shellac is hard, plane or sand the surface smooth and level. The finish surrounding the break usually doesn't have to be retouched, but the surface can be coated with shellac. To make the shellac match a satin-gloss finish, rub the surface smooth with 0000 steel wool and linseed oil.

To fill deep holes, use plastic wood or water putty to fill the hole almost level. Let the filler dry completely, then fill the indentation with a shellac stick. If a hole or split is very large, don't overlook the possibility of filling it with a piece of wood cut and trimmed to fit perfectly. If the patching wood can be taken from the piece of fur-

Heat the shellac stick over an alcohol lamp or a propane torch; hold a palette or putty knife between the stick and the flame to keep it from dripping.

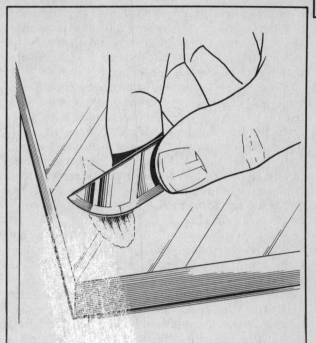

To remove a burn spot, scrape away the charred wood with a craft knife; feather the edges of the depression.

niture in a spot that won't show, the repair may be almost impossible to detect.

Fit the wood patch into the hole or split; use carpenter's glue to bond it to the surrounding wood. Leave the patch higher than the surface. When the glue is completely dry, sand the plug smoothly level with the surface of the surrounding wood. Then refinish the piece of furniture.

Burns. Burns on furniture can range from scorches to deep char, but the usual problem is a cigarette burn. Scorches from cigarettes or cigars are usually easy to remove. Buff the scorched area with 0000 steel wool moistened with mineral spirits until the scorch disappears. Then wipe it clean, and wax and polish the surface.

Deeper burns require the removal of the charred wood. Shallow burns, when repaired, will always leave a slight indentation in the wood, but this depression will be inconspicuous. Deep burn holes can be filled.

Remove the damaged wood. With the flat sharp edge of a craft knife, scrape away the charred wood. For deep burns use a curved blade. Do not scratch the burn area. Scrape away the char to the bare wood, feathering out the edges. Any burned or scorched spots will show, so all the burned wood must be removed.

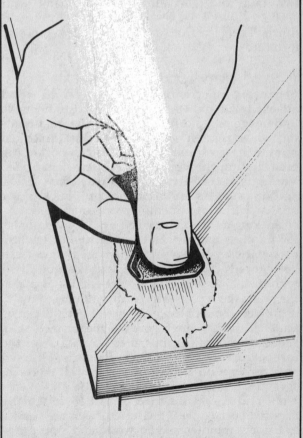

After removing the char, sand the burn area lightly to smooth and level it.

If the surface is veneer, you must be careful not to scrape through the veneer into the wood core. If the burn is deep enough to go through the veneer, the hole must be filled to the level of the core wood, before the veneer can be patched.

When the charred wood has been completely removed, lightly sand the edges of the groove or trench to level it with the surrounding surface. Press lightly into the groove with fine-grit sandpaper, removing only the char from the burned area; be careful not to damage the surrounding finish. If you're not sure all the burn has been removed, wet the sanded area. If water makes the burned area look burned again, you haven't removed all the char.

With deep burns the groove left after the char is removed probably will be quite noticeable. Level the groove as much as possible with fine-grit sandpaper, but stay close to the edges of the groove. If you sand too far out from the burn area, the damaged area will become a wide saucer-shaped indentation. If the depression isn't too deep, try swelling the wood as detailed before for dents. If you're left with a deep gouge, the burn area can be filled with wood plastic or stick shellac.

After smoothing out the burn, refinish the damaged area. Let the new finish dry for one or two days, and then lightly buff the patch with 0000 steel wool to blend the edges into the old finish. Then wax and polish the entire piece of furniture.

HOW TO REPAIR VENEER

Because veneer is only a thin layer of wood attached with glue to a solid base, it is vulnerable to damage. On old furniture, the glue that holds the veneer is often not water resistant. Prolonged humidity or exposure to water can soften the glue, letting the veneer blister, crack, or peel. Veneer is also easily damaged from the surface, and old veneers are often cracked, buckled, or broken, with chips or entire pieces missing.

As long as the veneer layer is in good shape, the thinness that makes it prone to damage also makes it easy to repair. Undamaged veneer can be reglued; chips and bare spots can be filled with matching veneer. If you're careful to match the grain, the repairs will hardly show.

Blisters. Small blisters in veneer usually can be flattened with heat. To protect the surface, set a sheet of smooth cardboard on it, and cover the cardboard with a clean cloth. Press the blistered area firmly with a medium-hot iron. If there are several blisters, move the iron slowly and evenly back and forth. Be careful not to touch the exposed surface with the iron. Check the surface every few minutes as you work, and stop pressing as soon as the blisters have flattened. Leaving the cardboard in place, weight the repair area for 24 hours. Then wax and polish the surface.

To repair a large blister in veneer, slit it and insert a little glue under the edges; then flatten it with heat.

Large blisters usually must be slit because the veneer has swelled. With a sharp craft knife or a single-edge razor blade, carefully cut the blister down the middle, along the grain of the wood. Be careful not to cut into the base wood. Then cover the surface and apply heat, checking every few seconds as the glue softens. If the glue has deteriorated and does not soften, carefully scrape it out and insert a small amount of carpenter's glue under the slit edges of the bubble with the tip of the knife. Be careful not to use too much glue. If necessary, wipe off any excess as the blister flattens. As soon as one edge of the slit bubble overlaps the other, carefully shave off the overlapping edge with a craft knife or razor blade. Heat the blister again; if the edges overlap further, shave the overlapping edge again. When the blister is completely flattened, weight the repair area for 24 hours. Then wax and polish the entire surface.

Loose Veneer. Lifted veneer occurs most often at the corners of tabletops, on cabinet and dresser edges, legs, and drawer fronts. If the loose veneer is undamaged, it can be reglued.

Remove the residue of old glue left on the back of the veneer and on the base wood. With a sharp craft knife or razor blade, scrape out as much of the old glue as possible. Don't lift the veneer any further; if you bend it up, you'll damage it. After scraping out as much old glue as you can, clean the bonding surfaces with mineral spirits or benzene to remove any residue. Glue left under the loose area will interfere with the new adhesive. If any glue remains, sand the bonding surfaces lightly with fine-grit sandpaper, and then wipe them clean with a soft cloth moistened with mineral spirits.

The veneer can be reattached with contact cement, but you may prefer to use carpenter's

Loose veneer can be reglued. Apply glue to the base wood, press the veneer into place, and clamp it firmly.

glue because it sets more slowly and allows repositioning. To reglue the veneer, apply contact cement to both bonding surfaces and let it set, as directed by the manufacturer. If necessary, set a small tack or two between the layers to keep them from touching. Or apply carpenter's glue to the base wood, spreading it on along the grain with a small brush. Starting at the solidly attached veneer and working out toward the loose edge, smooth the loose veneer carefully into place. Contact cement bonds immediately, so make sure the veneer is exactly matched; if you're using carpenter's glue, press from the center out to force out any excess glue, and wipe it off immediately. If more than one veneer layer is loose, reglue each layer.

Reglued veneer should be clamped or weighted. To protect the surface, cover it with a sheet of wax paper; make sure all excess glue is removed. Set a buffer block of scrap wood over the newly glued area, and use another block or a soft cloth to protect the opposite edge or side of the surface. Clamp the glued and protected surface firmly with C-clamps or hand screws for one to two days. Then remove the clamps and the buffers, and wax and polish the entire surface.

Cracked or Broken Veneer. If the veneer is lifted and cracked, but not broken completely through, it can be reglued; large areas may be easier to repair if you break the veneer off along the cracks. Broken veneer can be reglued, but you must be very careful not to damage the edges of the break. Do not trim ragged edges; an irregular mend line will not be as visible as a perfectly straight line.

Before applying glue to the veneer, clean the bonding surfaces carefully. Fit the broken edges

carefully together to make sure they match perfectly. Then apply contact cement to both surfaces, or spread carpenter's glue on the base wood. Set the broken veneer carefully into place, matching the edges together. Clamp the mended area. Refinishing may be necessary when the mend is complete.

Chipped or Missing Veneer. Replacing veneer is easy, but finding a new piece to replace it may not be. If the piece of furniture is not valuable, you may be able to take the patch from a part of it that won't show. The patch area must be along an edge, so that you can lift the veneer with a craft knife or a stiff-blade putty knife.

Patch veneer usually should not be taken from the same piece of furniture; you'll have to buy matching veneer to make the repair. If only a small piece is missing, you may be able to fill the hole with veneer edging tape, sold at many home centers and lumberyards. If you have access to junk furniture, you may be able to salvage a similar veneer from another piece of furniture. For larger patches, if you can't find a scrap piece of matching veneer, buy a sheet of matching veneer from a specialized wood supplier.

To fit a chip or small patch, set a sheet of bond paper over the damaged veneer. Rub a soft dull lead pencil gently over the paper; the edges of the damaged area will be marked on the paper. Use this pattern as a template to cut the veneer patch. Tape the pattern to the patching wood, matching the grain of the new veneer to the grain of the damaged area. Cut the patch firmly and carefully with a sharp craft knife; it's better to make it too big than too small.

To make a larger patch, tape the patching veneer firmly over the damaged area with masking tape, with the grain and pattern of the patch matching the grain and pattern of the damaged veneer. Make sure the patch is flat against the surface, and securely held in place. Cut the patch

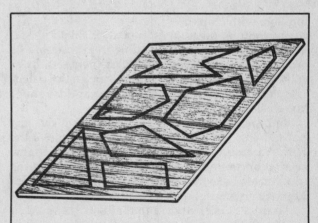

To mend veneer cut a patch in an irregular shape; any of these shapes will be less visible than a square.

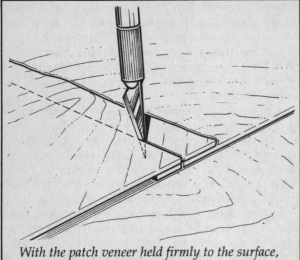

With the patch veneer held firmly to the surface, cut through the patching sheet and the veneer below it.

Before gluing the patch, test it for fit; it should fit flush with the surrounding surface with no gaps.

in an irregular shape or in a boat or shield shape; these shapes will be less visible than a square or rectangular patch would be. Cut the patch carefully with a craft knife, scoring through the patching veneer and through the damaged veneer layer below it.

Untape the patching sheet and pop out the patch. With the tip of the craft knife, remove the cutout patch of damaged veneer. If necessary, score it and remove it in pieces. Remove only the top veneer layer; do not cut into the base wood. Remove any old glue and clean the base wood.

Test the fit of the patch in the hole. It should fit exactly flush with the surrounding surface, with no gaps or overlaps. If the patch is too big or too thick, do not force it. Carefully sand the edges or the back with fine-grit sandpaper to fit it to the hole.

Glue the fitted patch into place with contact cement or carpenter's glue and clamp or weight it. Let the repair dry for one to two days; then lightly sand the patch and the surrounding veneer. Refinish the damaged area or the entire surface or piece of furniture.

HARDWARE REPAIRS

Drawer pulls, handles, hinges, locks, protective corners, decorative bands, and escutcheons on old furniture often shows signs of hard use. Sometimes hardware is missing; sometimes it's loose, broken, or bent. Loose hardware can be repaired; missing or damaged pieces should be replaced. Replacement is also the solution if you don't like the existing hardware.

Many pieces of furniture are made with common hardware; matching these basic designs is simple. If the hardware is more distinctive or unusual, it may be easier to replace all the hardware than to find a matching piece. Make sure that the new hardware's bases are at least as large as the old. If the piece of furniture is very valuable or antique, or if the hardware is very attractive, the old hardware should not be removed. Missing parts should be replaced with matching or similar hardware; a slight difference in design usually doesn't look bad.

Hardware stores, home centers, and similar stores offer a fair selection of furniture hardware; specialty hardware outlets and craft suppliers are usually better sources.

Drawer Pulls and Handles. To tighten a loosely attached drawer pull, remove the pull and replace the screw with a longer one. If the screw is part of the pull, you'll have to make the hole in the wood smaller. When the hole is slightly enlarged, you can tighten the pull by using a fiber plug with the screw. For metal pulls, fit a piece of solder into the hole and then replace the screw. When the hole is much too big, insert wooden toothpicks or thin shavings of wood, dipped in glue, into the hole; let the glue dry and carefully trim the shavings flush with the wood surface. Then dip the pull's screw into glue, replace the pull, and tighten the screw firmly. For a more substantial repair, enlarge the hole, glue a piece of dowel into it, and drill a new screw hole in the dowel.

Hinges. Hinges that don't work properly usually have bent hinge pins, and you should replace them. If the hinges are loose, try using longer screws to attach them. When the screw holes are greatly enlarged, adjust them by one of the methods detailed before. If the hinge leaves are damaged and the hinges cannot be replaced, glue the hinges into position with epoxy or a rubber- or silicone-base adhesive.

Locks. Locks on old pieces are often damaged, and keys are often missing. If the piece of furniture is antique, or the lock is unusual, have it

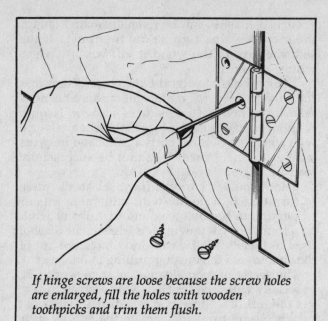

If hinge screws are loose because the screw holes are enlarged, fill the holes with wooden toothpicks and trim them flush.

repaired by a professional. Otherwise, remove the damaged lock and take it to a locksmith; order a matching or similar lock to replace it. Install a new lock the same way the old one was secured.

Loose Metal Bands and Escutcheons. Old bands and escutcheons often have an attractive design and patina; don't replace them unless they're badly damaged. To secure a loose band or escutcheon, squeeze adhesive caulking compound under the metal, and press it down to bond it to the wood. If this doesn't work, fasten the band or escutcheon with tiny metal screws of the same metal as the hardware. You must match the metals: brass to brass, copper to copper, or steel to steel. If you don't match the screws to the metal plate, the metal will corrode. Use several screws, placing them to form a pattern; drill pilot holes before inserting them.

Coverup Hardware. If old hardware holes are impossible to repair, or if you want to change the look of a piece entirely, the damage can be covered with new wood or metal escutcheon plates. Escutcheons are used particularly under drawer pulls or handles; many handles are made with escutcheon backers. Attach the escutcheons with adhesive or with screws, matched metal to metal. If you're using escutcheon handles, no other treatment is necessary. If you're using an escutcheon under other hardware, drill new mounting holes as required.

REVIVING AN OLD FINISH

Refinishing is a long, slow, and messy job. Before you strip the old finish off any piece of furniture, take a good look at it—a complete refinishing job may not be necessary. You may be able to use a simple restoration technique to revive the old finish. Restoration doesn't always work, but it's well worth trying before you resort to more drastic means. Start with the simplest techniques and work up; the easiest way is often best.

Most restoration projects require a knowledge of the finish with which you are working. If you don't know what the finish is, you could damage a perfectly good finish or you could waste your time on a technique that won't work. After identifying the finish, you're ready to restore it. Whether the problem is dirt, cracks, discoloration, or wear, it can often be solved by these restoration techniques:

CLEANING

The easiest restoration process is cleaning; what looks like a beat-up finish may be just dirt. Over a period of years, even well-cared-for furniture can acquire a dull, sticky coating of wax and dust. This coating often can be removed with an oil-based commercial wood cleaner/conditioner. These cleaners can often dig through layers of dirt and wax. They are available at furniture stores, some supermarkets, and paint stores.

Following the manufacturer's instructions, apply the cleaner generously with a soft cloth, and let it stand for an hour or two. Then wipe off the cleaner with another cloth. Repeat the process, using plenty of cleaner, until the wood is clean and lustrous. This may take as many as four or five applications. Buff the clean wood lightly to remove excess oil.

If commercial cleaner doesn't do the job, remove the built-up grime with a mild solution of warm water and liquid detergent. Work quickly, and don't soak the piece of furniture or pour the solution over it. Water can cause a white haze to appear on a shellac or lacquer finish. When the furniture is clean, rinse off the detergent with water and then carefully and thoroughly dry the wood with a soft cloth or a towel.

Let the wood dry completely. If there is a haze on the finish, you may be able to remove it with steel wool. Buff the surface along the grain of the wood with 0000 steel wool. Then apply a commercial conditioner, and buff the wood with a soft cloth.

If detergent cleaning doesn't work, use a solvent—depending on the kind of finish—to clean the wood. Solvent cleaning is the last resort to consider because it may damage the finish, but it is worth a try. Use mineral spirits or turpentine on any finish; use denatured alcohol on varnish or lacquer. Do not use alcohol on shellac or on a shellac-lacquer mixture. Working in a well-ventilated area (outdoors is best), apply the solvent with a rough cloth, such as burlap or an old towel. Then wipe the wood clean with another cloth. Apply a commercial conditioner, and buff the wood lightly.

Detergent and solvent cleaning also can be used to rejuvenate wicker and rattan furniture; use the same techniques, but be especially careful not to use too much water. Let the piece of furniture dry thoroughly; if possible, set it in the sun to dry. If the old finish is very thin or worn, apply one or two coats of spray varnish, spraying carefully to cover the wicker or rattan evenly. Let the new finish dry for several days before using the furniture.

REAMALGAMATION: THE QUICK NEW FINISH

Reamalgamation is a grand revival technique that can make alligatored, crazed, cracked, and scratched furniture look like new. Reamalgamation is the near-liquefaction of a marred finish so that it dries solid and unblemished. It works like magic, it's easy, and it can eliminate the need for a refinishing job; if it doesn't work, you haven't spent too much time and effort trying.

Alligatoring, crazing, and cracking are the same. They're caused either by sunlight or by temperature changes, and they can be eliminated by reamalgamation. Alligatored finishes have many small lines intersecting into a rough pattern; crazed finishes have erratic lines running everywhere; and cracked finishes have larger lines, or just one line, running across the surface.

An alligatored finish, usually the result of excessive sunlight or temperature changes, shows a pattern of many small intersecting cracks.

Scratched finishes can be reamalgamated only if the scratches don't go below the finish. If the scratches are in the wood itself, you'll have to refinish the area.

The kind of finish on the furniture determines the solvent used for reamalgamation: Shellac is reamalgamated with denatured alcohol, lacquer with lacquer thinner, a lacquer-shellac mixture with a mixture of three parts alcohol and one part lacquer thinner. Varnish cannot be successfully reamalgamated.

Before you work on the finish, clean the piece of furniture thoroughly with mineral spirits or turpentine to remove wax and dirt. Don't work on a humid day if the finish is shellac; the alcohol used to liquefy shellac can draw moisture out of the air and into the finish, resulting in blushing.

The secret of reamalgamation is to work fast, especially with lacquer. Start with a small area to get the feel of it; once you're satisfied with your results, go on to reamalgamate the entire finish. Apply a moderate amount of solvent with a brand-new, absolutely clean natural-bristle brush. Work in small sections, no larger than 2 square feet, so that the solvent doesn't dry while you're still reamalgamating.

To reamalgamate the finished surface, apply solvent along the grain of the wood in quick, long strokes; work quickly, and don't let the brush get dry. Don't try to brush out all the cracks or scratches at this point; many of them will disappear as the finish dries. If you work on individual marks too much, you may be removing the finish instead of liquefying it.

As the solvent dries, the finish will have a high gloss, and then, after 30 minutes or so, will become dull. If the reamalgamation was successful, the scratches and nicks will have disappeared, and the finish will look solid.

Reamalgamation is not always a one-step process. If the cracks in the finish are deep, it may take two or three applications of solvent to remove them. If repeated reamalgamation doesn't work, the problem is probably the wood; you'll have to refinish it.

After the reamalgamated surface has dulled, lightly buff the finish with 0000 steel wool, working in one direction along the grain. Don't exert much pressure; just lightly polish the finish. Then wipe the surface clean with a dust-free cloth. If the reamalgamated finish is very thin, clean the surface with a tack cloth and apply a new coat of the same finish, right over the old one. Let the finish dry, buff it lightly with 0000 steel wool, then wax the piece of furniture with a hard paste wax. Buff the waxed wood with a clean cloth.

SALVAGING A DISCOLORED FINISH

Blushing, a milky discoloration in the finish, is a common problem with shellac-finished furniture and also can be a problem with lacquered wood, but it never affects varnish finishes. Blushing is caused by prolonged high humidity, exposure to water, or just age. If the haze isn't too deep in the finish, you may be able to remove it with 0000 steel wool and oil, or by reamalgamating the finish. Deep-set blushing can be eliminated only by refinishing.

When blushing is present in an alligatored or cracked finish, try reamalgamation first; this may remove the blush and eliminate the cracks. If the finish is not cracked or if reamalgamation doesn't remove the blush, use steel wool to remove the discoloration.

Before you start, make sure the surface is clean; remove wax and dirt with mineral spirits or turpentine. Then dip 0000 steel wool in mineral oil, linseed oil, or salad oil, and rub it gently along the grain of the wood. Work slowly, and make sure the steel wool is always well oiled. The abrasive removes the top part of the finish, leaving a clean finish behind. Then dry the wood with a soft cloth and polish it with a hard paste wax. If the blushing is only in the top part of the finish, rubbing with steel wool will remove it.

OVERCOATING: COVERING A WORN FINISH

Any material wears down over time, and furniture finishes are no exception. Sometimes the entire finish is worn, sometimes only heavy-use spots. Worn spots are most common around doors and drawers. On an antique wear is part of the patina of the piece and is used to date and decide the value of the furniture; it should not be covered or restored. The same consideration applies to almost any piece of furniture: wear and tear add character. A thin old finish can be recoated, and where refinishing is the only alternative, you may be able to repair the worn spots.

Clean the surface carefully with mineral spirits or, for lacquer or varnish, denatured alcohol. If the entire finish is worn, clean the whole piece of furniture; you must remove all dirt and grease. Then apply a new coat of the finish.

If you're touching up worn spots and not recoating an entire finish, clean the worn surface, then sand the worn spots with fine-grit sandpaper. Be careful not to exert too much pressure.

Once the wood is bare, it must be refinished. If the piece of furniture isn't stained, this is easy; if it is stained, you'll have to restain the bare spots to match. This may not always be easy, but it's worth a try.

To touch up the worn spot, use an oil-base stain that matches the stain on the piece of furniture. You may have to mix stains to get a good match. Test the stain on an inconspicuous unfinished part of the wood before working on the worn spots.

Apply the stain to the damaged area with an artist's brush or a clean cloth, covering the entire bare area. Let the stain set for 15 minutes and then wipe it off with a clean cloth. If the color is too light, apply another coat of stain, wait 15 minutes, and wipe again. Repeat this procedure until you're satisfied with the color. Let the stain dry according to the manufacturer's instructions.

Buff the stained surface with 0000 steel wool, and wipe it clean with a tack cloth. Apply a new coat of the finish that is already on the surface over the newly stained areas, feathering out the new finish into the surrounding old finish. Let the new finish dry for one or two days, then buff the patched areas with 0000 steel wool. Wax the entire surface with hard paste wax, and polish it to a shine.

DECORATING AND OTHER ALTERNATIVES

Restoration including cleaning or reamalgamating, spot-patching or buffing, is the easiest way to make old furniture look better, but it isn't always successful. If the old finish is in good shape, you can salvage an old piece of furniture with decorative accents or special finishing effects. If the old finish is damaged, you can cover it completely with enamel instead of refinishing. Before you remove the old finish, consider the alternatives; you may not have to refinish to give an old piece of furniture new life.

Special-effect finishing can do a lot for a dull piece of furniture. Antiquing, flyspecking, striping, stenciling, and decaling can add interest and charm to many pieces. They are especially effective for country furniture. Where you want a bright, distinctive accent piece, an enamel finish may be the answer. Enamel can be applied over an old finish, and it hides many flaws. It also lends itself to further decoration; enamel can be dressed up with stripes, stencils, or decals, and is the most common base coat for antiquing.

Refinishing

Refinishing a piece of furniture is a lot of work. First you have to strip away every bit of the old finish. Then you have to prepare the bare wood with meticulous sanding. The grain may have to be filled, bleached, or stained. Then you must apply the new finish.

Refinishing takes time and patience, but there are plenty of rewards, from the moment you expose the treasure of a handsome wood buried under paint, discolored old varnish, or accumulated grime to the day you put the final coat of wax on your prize. This section tells how to get results that will make you proud.

STRIPPING

There are many ways to remove an old finish, some of them are more difficult than others.

PROFESSIONAL STRIPPERS

These businesses are listed in the telephone advertising pages as "Professional Furniture Strippers." They use huge tubs of methylene chloride or other wash-away chemicals. Your piece of furniture is dipped into the solution, which eats off the old finish down to the bare wood. The furniture is then dipped into a neutralizing chemical and sprayed with water to remove the remover.

The cost of commercial finish removal usually depends on the size of the item to be cleaned; for example, a chair would cost less to clean than a dresser. The cost for most items is not prohibitive. Professional strippers will remove the finish from almost any item that has a finish, including woodwork and railings; their work isn't limited to furniture.

There are some advantages and some disadvantages to professional strippers:

Pros: The item you have stripped comes out extremely clean. If there are several layers of finish on the item, a commercial stripper can definitely save you hours of labor. The cost is probably less to have the piece stripped than to buy the remover to strip it yourself.

Cons: The chemicals used by commercial strippers are thought by some furniture buffs to take the "life" or "oil" out of the wood and render it "dead wood." The chemicals sometimes soften or destroy the adhesive that holds the furniture together. You should think hard about having a professional strip a valuable antique, but for run-of-the-mill furniture, thick with layer on layer of old finish, the professional way may be easiest and best. To help you make the decision, visit a professional stripper and examine some of stripped furniture; discuss your project with the professional. He or she may recommend that you remove the old finish yourself. They might even recommend the best method and show you a couple of tricks to make the job go easier.

Shellac and lacquer finishes are the easiest to remove, requiring only alcohol or lacquer thinner and a little muscle. The tougher finishes, such as paint and varnish, usually are removed with chemical paint-and-varnish remover. Oil, wax, and penetrating sealer finishes also are removed with paint-and-varnish remover.

Unless you know exactly what the finish is and how much of it is on the furniture, you should start with the easiest techniques and work your way up. Don't do any more work than you have to. If you want to paint the piece, and the old finish is sound, it isn't necessary to remove the finish; preparation involves sanding and sealing. If you want to use a clear finish, you may be able to remove the old finish without using paint-and-varnish remover. For any clear finish, the first step is identifying the old finish.

Before you use paint-and-varnish remover on a piece of furniture, test the finish with denatured alcohol and lacquer thinner. It is hard to know what the finish is just by looking. Shellac and lacquer are clear finishes, like varnish, but they're much easier to remove.

Test the finish first with denatured alcohol. If the finish liquefies, it's shellac; if it gets soft but doesn't dissolve, it's a mixture of shellac and lacquer. Test the surface again with lacquer thinner; if it liquefies, it's lacquer. Shellac can be removed with denatured alcohol, lacquer with lacquer thinner, and a shellac-lacquer combination with a 50-50 mixture of denatured alcohol and lacquer thinner. Stripping with chemical compounds is not necessary to remove these finishes.

Apply the appropriate solvent to a section of the piece of furniture, using an old or throwaway brush. Let the alcohol or thinner work for 5 to 10 seconds and then wipe it off with a rough cloth or steel wool. If the finish comes off easily, you can remove the entire finish with the alcohol or thinner. Work quickly: Alcohol and lacquer thinner evaporate fast. Clean small sections at a time, and change cloths frequently.

When the finish is off, go over the entire piece with a scraper to remove any traces of finish. You also can use steel wool dipped in thinner. Always scrape with the wood grain, and be careful not to dig into the wood. Then sand the wood as necessary to smooth it. No neutralizing is necessary; after sanding the piece of furniture is ready to be sealed, bleached, stained, or finished.

Most home centers, hardware and paint stores, drugstores, variety stores, and even grocery stores carry a variety of paint-and-varnish removers. All soften old finishes so that they can be scraped, washed, wiped with steel wool, or sanded off. There are differences among removers in chemical content, removal techniques, and price.

Inexpensive paint-and-varnish removers soften old finishes, but they're not necessarily the bargain they appear to be. These removers may contain paraffin. This waxy substance gives the wood an oily look and feel, and prevents the new finish from adhering properly. It must be removed with turpentine or mineral spirits before the new finish can be applied. Not only is this another step in the stripping process, but the additional money spent on turpentine or mineral spirits can be considerable. You may spend as much as you would have for a more expensive paint-and-varnish remover.

ALTERNATIVE REMOVAL TECHNIQUES

Someday, some helpful person will recommend that you use an easier, faster method than chemical remover. There is only one answer to this: Don't do it. The usual alternatives are power sanding, lye, and heat. While these methods work and professionals sometimes use them, they can do considerable damage to wood and, sometimes, to you. If you don't want to spend time to remove a thick finish with paint-and-varnish remover, consider having it professionally stripped. You won't save anything by using other methods.

Power Sanders. Power sanders remove a lot of old finish fast. If a piece of furniture isn't valuable and has several thick layers of old finish, power sanding can be useful. Of the alternatives it offers the least risk.

There are several kinds of power sanders, but only two should be considered for removing the finish: orbital and straight-line sanders. Either one of these sanders can do a good job of removing the old finish from furniture, without too much danger of grooving the wood surface if you know what you're doing. An orbital sander may leave tiny swirls in the wood surface, despite the fineness of the abrasive; a straight-line sander can groove the wood.

Lye. Lye is an effective finish remover. It also can remove skin and clothing, cause blindness, discolor wood, and kill vegetation so thoroughly that nothing at all will grow in that spot for decades. If you're tempted to use lye, take your piece of furniture to a professional stripper instead.

Ammonia. Ammonia is the only thing that removes old milk paint, sometimes found on antiques. It is effective, but the fumes are strong. It should never be used without a respirator. Ammonia also darkens wood; fumed oak has been ammonia treated. If you must use ammonia, work outside, and keep children and pets away. Rub the ammonia on and the finish off with medium-grade steel wool.

Heat. Heat is strictly a last resort method of removing finish, and it can very easily remove the wood, too. Two devices are available: propane torches, with special fittings to spread the heat, and electric paint removers. The electric tool looks like a blow dryer.

Heat can be used only on flat or slightly curved surfaces, so that a scraper can be used to remove the softened finish. It doesn't work readily on clear finishes, such as lacquer, shellac, and varnish. Heat can be dangerous.

Inexpensive removers also may be flammable and highly toxic; check the label carefully. This makes good ventilation, preferably outdoors, a must. You have to keep the area free of open flame: No smoking while you work, and avoid appliances with pilot lights.

The more expensive paint-and-varnish removers probably don't contain paraffin, but they might contain a special wax that helps prolong chemical evaporation. This wax, like paraffin, must be removed after the furniture is stripped, despite the product's no-cleanup claims. A turpentine or mineral spirit rubbing, or a light sanding with 0000 steel wool or fine-grit sandpaper will remove the wax.

Some paint-and-varnish removers don't have wax. While you have to take precautions against evaporation, a cleaning step is eliminated. Expensive paint removers probably contain methylene chloride, which decreases the flammability of the other chemicals in the remover. They are probably nontoxic, although good ventilation is always desirable.

The most expensive removers usually are labeled "water rinsing," "wash-away," or "water cleanup." After application the finish is washed off with water, instead of scraped or sanded off. The claims are true if you follow the manufacturer's directions to the letter; the chemicals in these removers contain special emulsifiers that mix with the rinse water, resulting in a squeaky-clean finish.

The problem with these wash-away removers is that water is the natural enemy of wood and certain glues. The water used to remove the chemicals must be removed from the wood as soon as possible to avoid raising the wood grain or dissolving the glue. This water problem is especially pronounced with veneer finishes and inlays. To be safe never use wash-away remover on veneers or inlays.

Most removers are available in liquid or semipaste forms. The semipaste removers contain a starch or stiffener; they're designed for vertical surfaces, such as the legs of a chair. Semipaste removers are susceptible to the same problems (wax, flammability, and toxicity) as other removers. You can buy a nonflammable, nontoxic, nonwax semipaste. These thick removers can be used on flat surfaces as well as verticals.

For many jobs the most expensive wash-away remover may be worth the price in time and work saved. The nonflammability of a remover is a big consideration, and any remover that is toxic may not be worth the price you pay for it. Semipaste removers are the easiest to work with, although you may want to experiment with a liquid remover as well. No remover is necessarily better than another. The key to finding a remover you're comfortable with is experimentation: Try different kinds of removers until you find one you like.

Packaged finishing systems also are available. These systems contain paint-and-varnish remover, steel wool, stain, and top finishes. These products are excellent, and you should check them out before starting any refinishing job.

Whichever paint-and-varnish remover you choose, the techniques are the same. The basic steps are simple: After preparing the furniture, you apply the remover, let it work, and then take off both remover and old finish.

Preparing the Furniture. Before you start to apply paint-and-varnish remover, take off all the hardware, including knobs, handles, hinges, decorative locks, and escutcheons. Make a sketch of the furniture and key the hardware to it, so you'll be able to replace it correctly. If the piece of furniture has doors or drawers, remove them and work on them separately.

If the hardware is clean, set it aside. Otherwise, polish it as appropriate. If it's blemished with paint or finish, drop it into a shallow plastic pan or bucket filled with paint remover, and let it soak while you work on the furniture. A couple of hours in the solution won't hurt it.

Some pieces of furniture may have gilded edges, special finishes in fluting, insets, and so on that you can't remove. If the special finish on

If hardware has been painted, drop it into a shallow plastic pan filled with paint remover, and let it soak while you work on the wood.

your furniture will stand up to it, you can protect these areas with masking tape. Make sure the edges are pressed firmly against the wood so the remover can't seep under them.

Some finishes can be damaged by the adhesive on masking tape; the tape can pull off delicate gilding, for instance, when it's removed. If the finish is too delicate for masking tape, simply stay a couple of inches away from the area when you apply the remover. For further protection, tear a strip of cloth and apply the strip to the area with tape—like a bandage—to help protect the finish. No matter how careful you are, finishing residue always seems to find its way onto the parts you want to protect. The cloth will provide added insurance.

If the piece of furniture is upholstered, it probably needs new upholstery. Remove the old fabric before you refinish, and make any necessary webbing or support repairs; replace the upholstery after refinishing. If you want to keep the old upholstery, it's best to remove the fabric before you work on the finish. Just be sure you can put it back on again. If the piece is large, have a professional upholsterer remove and replace the fabric.

Stripping Techniques. There are two unbreakable rules for using paint-and-varnish remover: Use plenty of remover and give it plenty of time to work. Don't skimp on materials or on time; you won't save a thing.

Applying paint remover is a slow, sloppy, and smelly job, so it's important to protect your workshop. Cover your worktable and the floor around it with a thick layer of newspaper or with a plastic drop cloth. Be careful with drop cloths; the plastic is slick. Make sure you have plenty of ventilation, keep the remover away from any open flame, and cover your skin to prevent irritation.

All removers are applied in the same way. Considering the quick evaporation of chemicals, it's best to work in small sections, such as 3-by-3-foot areas. It's always easiest to work on a flat surface to keep the remover from dripping off; you may want to turn the furniture from time to time while you work.

Apply the paint remover with a wide brush, or just pour it on and distribute it with a brush. The quality or condition of the brush doesn't matter. Lay it onto the surface with the flat of the brush, and don't spread out the mixture as you would paint. Use what you think is plenty of remover, then add some more, coating the surface thickly. Use the brush only to distribute remover; brushing back and forth causes the remover to lose a lot of its removal power. The chemicals evaporate even more rapidly when you brush the solution.

After applying a thick coating of remover, cover the surface with aluminum foil to help slow evaporation. Aluminum foil is especially important for removers that don't contain wax, although it also helps slow the evaporation of

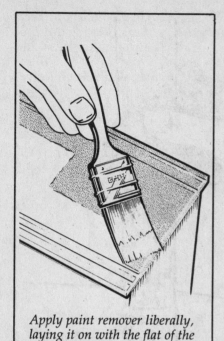

Apply paint remover liberally, laying it on with the flat of the brush to coat the surface. Do not brush the remover; this interferes with its action.

Cover the surface with aluminum foil to slow the evaporation of the chemicals, especially with removers that don't contain wax.

After 30 minutes, remove the foil and test the treated area. If you can easily rub down to bare wood, the finish is soft enough to be removed.

waxed removers. If you're applying remover to a vertical surface, use a semipaste remover.

Wait about 30 minutes before testing the results of the remover. Experimentation will show you the optimum time, but taking time at the outset will save you time later.

While you're waiting, apply the remover to another section of the furniture, following the same procedures. Don't remove any old finish from areas that won't show when the piece has been restored. Once you start working on these surfaces, you're stuck with finishing them. The obvious areas are work enough; leave table bottoms and the insides of drawers alone.

After 30 minutes remove the foil and test the results. The treated area should look bubbly and cracked. Rub your rubber-gloved finger into a small part of the bubbly area. If you can easily work your way to the bare wood, the remover and the old finish are ready to be removed. If you can't easily reach bare wood, wait another 10 minutes and try again. Paint remover stops working after 40 minutes. If you can't easily reach bare wood after this time, scrape away the old finish with a wide-blade putty knife, if you're using a non-wash-away remover. If you're using a wash-away remover, rinse off the remover and as much finish as you can with water.

Apply another thick coat of the remover and wait again. Try the finger test again. If it still doesn't work, scrape or wash off all the old gunk you can and apply more remover. Keep doing this until you've reached the bare wood, always giving the remover time to work.

Different removers require different removal techniques. Once your testing proves that the finish is ready for final removal, use the appropriate technique for wash-away, wax, or nonwax removers.

To remove wash-away compounds, use water and medium-fine steel wool. Do not use a scraper, putty knife, sandpaper, power equipment, or heat. It's easiest to hose off the furniture outside. If that is impossible, use a brush to apply the water, and steel-wool the wood clean. When the finish is off, thoroughly dry the wood with a soft towel or other absorbent cloth. Remember that water is harmful to wood; dry the wood immediately. Let the wood air-dry for several days before you continue refinishing.

Remove other kinds of removers with a scraper and steel wool; scrape carefully so you don't gouge the wood. To minimize the mess, dump the scrapings into a bucket as you work.

If the remover contains paraffin or wax, immediately scrub the surface with turpentine or mineral spirits. Work the turpentine or mineral spirits into all the dips, dings, cracks, and carvings. Change the cleaning cloth frequently so that the paraffin or wax will not be transferred from the cloth back onto the wood. The paraffin or wax should be removed now, not sanded off later.

During a stripping project, you may be tempted to change removers, especially when the remover you're using isn't doing a good job. Make the switch, but do not mix paint-and-varnish removers. Completely remove the first chemical before you apply another.

Remove scrape-away compounds with a putty knife or steel wool; minimize the mess by dumping the scrapings into a bucket. Be careful not to gouge the wood.

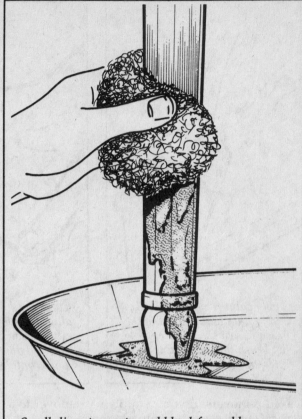

Small-diameter parts could be deformed by a scraper; wipe off the remover with a medium-fine steel wool.

Treat the stripped piece with denatured alcohol. Liberally spread the alcohol over the bare wood with a clean soft cloth. Dry the wood thoroughly. Wipe the wood with mineral spirits to prepare it for refinishing.

When you finish working, throw away newspapers, plastic drop cloths, brushes, and cloths used to apply the paint-and-varnish remover. Do not wad waste materials up and stuff them into a wastebasket or trash can; the chemicals in the remover could cause spontaneous combustion.

Special Finish Removal Tricks. It's easy to apply chemical finish remover to flat surfaces, but most furniture has vertical and curved surfaces, carvings, cracks, joints, and other areas that aren't as easy to work as their flat counterparts. Here are some tricks you can use to make the job go quicker:

•Rungs, Rounds, Arms, and Legs. These furniture components are hard to clean because paint-and-varnish removers don't stick well to their vertical or cylindrical surfaces. The trick is packaging or enveloping.

Apply a thick coating of semipaste remover to the rung, round, or slat, then fold a piece of aluminum foil over the part to enclose the remover in a package or envelope. The aluminum foil helps hold the remover against the part and prevents the remover from evaporating too quickly.

The legs of furniture are especially hard to strip because the remover will run down the legs onto your worktable. The result is a mess. To reduce the mess, drive a single 10d finishing or common nail into the bottom of each leg before applying the remover. Set the legs in aluminum-foil pie pans. The nails elevate the legs so that you can remove the finish right down to the bottom of the leg without lifting the furniture, and

the pie pans catch the remover that drips off. You may even be able to salvage some remover for reuse. Be careful when driving the nails; you don't want to split the leg. The nail trick may not work if the diameter of the legs is small.

Wipe the remover off with medium-fine steel wool after the remover has properly softened the finish. Don't use a scraper or sandpaper on small-diameter components; these tools can flatten rounds.

•Crevices, Cracks, and Joints. Use a fine twisted "rope" of steel wool, a piece of string, or a length of hemp rope to clean crevices on turnings. Insert this string into the crevice and pull back and forth to wipe away the remover. For slight tapers on turnings, a thick rope of steel wool makes the best tool to remove the stripping solution.

Crevices, cracks, and joints usually need several applications of remover to clean away the old finish. This is because finish builds up in these spots. Sometimes the crevices are so packed with finish that you don't even know they're crevices until the old finish has been removed. By removing the finish, you restore the original design of the piece.

Tools for cleaning crevices and cracks also include nutpicks, plastic playing cards, ice-cream

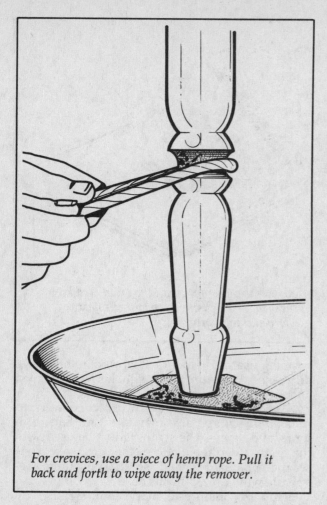

For crevices, use a piece of hemp rope. Pull it back and forth to wipe away the remover.

To strip slats apply semipaste remover thickly; then wrap the part with aluminum foil to cover it completely.

sticks, old forks, orange sticks, wooden toothpicks, or old spoons.

•Curves and Carvings. Curves and carvings, especially shallow carvings, must be treated carefully; scraping could damage or change the shape of the wood. Clean curves with medium-fine steel wool, wiping firmly along the curve. Clean carvings with steel wool, a toothbrush, and the crevice-cleaning tools listed above; be careful not to gouge the wood. On delicate carvings, use wooden or plastic tools.

•Cleanup Stripping. After you complete the chemical removal process, there may still be some spots of finish that refuse to come off. There are a few ways to handle these spots. The most gentle method is to use steel wool and paint remover on them; this technique minimizes the chance of rough spots and uneven surfaces. Sandpaper should be used when steel wool fails. Some scrapers fit into corners where sandpaper won't, but there is some possibility you'll damage the wood. Electric drill attachments also are used to get off the last bits of finish, but you run a risk of damaging the wood.

•Steel Wool. Steel wool is the best way to remove leftover spots from flat, round, and other easy-to-get-at areas. Dip medium-fine steel wool into chemical paint remover and try to scrub off

the remaining finish. If necessary, repeat the stripping process with another application of the remover. Once the finish comes loose, wash it off with water if it's a wash-away remover; rub it down with turpentine or mineral spirits if the remover contains wax; or rub it down with denatured alcohol if the remover is neither washable nor waxed.

•Sandpaper. If steel wool doesn't completely remove residual spots, try sandpaper, but be careful not to leave depressions in the surface. No matter how fine it is, sandpaper works by scratching the surfaces of the wood. The final scratches are usually so tiny that you can't see them when the wood is finished, but always remember that you are making scratches and don't sand too much.

Work with a sanding block on flat surfaces and a foam block on curves; sand rounds gently with the paper alone. Sand with the wood grain; sanding across the grain may scratch the wood permanently. Use medium-grit paper to remove the last traces of the old finish, and then lightly sand along the wood grain with fine-grit paper. This last fine-grit sanding prepares the wood for finishing.

•Scrapers. Sometimes flat-surface techniques can't remove the finish from hard-to-get-at areas.

If spots of finish are left after stripping, remove them with steel wool dipped in paint remover; scrub along the grain of the wood until the finish loosens.

Always use a scraper with the grain, and keep the blade sharp, using a smooth-cut file to sharpen it regularly.

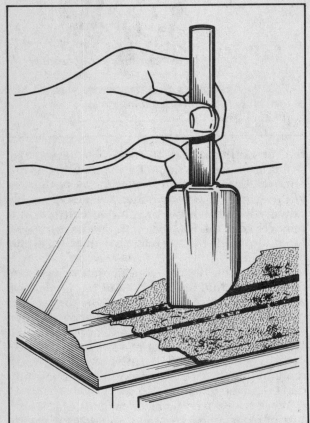

A good tool for refinishing is a rubber kitchen scraper; use it to remove the softened finish from moldings and other hard-to-get-at and easily damaged areas.

When this is the case, you can remove the stubborn spots with scrapers. Used with caution, these are very effective tools, but they can easily scratch or gouge the wood, so be careful. After scraping use sandpaper or steel wool to minimize differences in texture and height between scraped and sanded surfaces.

A sharp pull scraper fits into corners to remove finish; you also may use it on flats, contours, and tapers. The scraper must be used with the grain. Keep the blade of the scraper sharp—scraper blades dull fast, so sharpen them frequently with a smooth-cut file.

Scrapers come in all shapes and sizes: putty knives, paint scrapers, pull scrapers, cabinet scrapers, scraper blades (which are just pieces of metal with a sharpened edge), and broken glass. On some projects you may be able to use a sharp butt chisel as a scraper; for tiny jobs the edge of a coin can be effective. Don't overlook other scraping tools, including rubber spatulas, knives, bottle caps, golf tees, utility knife blades, screwdriver tips, and your thumbnail. For some jobs you may find that a car windshield scraper works best.

•Electric Drill Attachments. Useful electric drill attachments include a wire brush and a rotary sanding attachment—not a disc sanding attachment. The sanding attachment is small strips of sandpaper that spin around as the drill spins. These attachments can be used on hard-to-get-at places when the hand-powered methods fail, but they can damage the wood quickly. If you use electric drill attachments, work slowly and carefully.

PREPARING THE WOOD
Refinishing furniture isn't just a matter of stripping off one finish and slapping on another; it also involves preparation of the stripped wood: sanding, sealing, filling, bleaching, staining, and repairing. Preparing the wood takes time and elbow grease, but it's essential to the success of

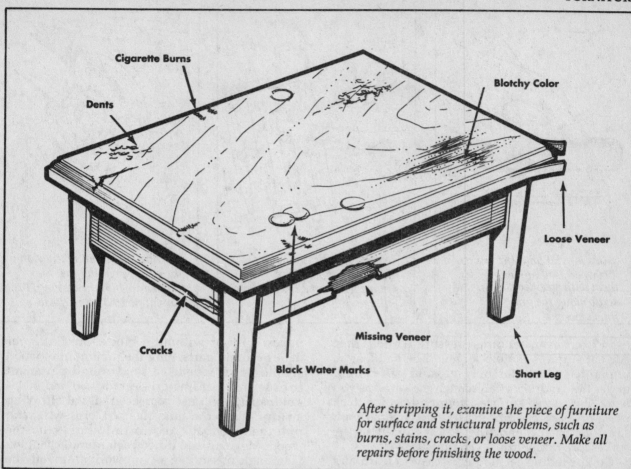

Cigarette Burns

Dents

Blotchy Color

Loose Veneer

Cracks

Black Water Marks

Missing Veneer

Short Leg

After stripping it, examine the piece of furniture for surface and structural problems, such as burns, stains, cracks, or loose veneer. Make all repairs before finishing the wood.

your refinishing job. The finish is only as good as the preparation for it. You may spend more time on this step than you did on stripping, but the results will be worth your effort.

Take a good look at the piece of furniture. How has the stripping process affected it? Are the joints loose? Do burns, stains, or other blemishes still show? Are veneers loose or bubbled? Before you prepare and finish the wood, repair the damage. Any problems you ignore now will show up later, because the finish will definitely accentuate the damage.

Look at the wood itself. What kind of wood is it? Is the grain open or closed? The kind of wood determines the preparation: Open-grained woods usually should be filled. Some wood may need special treatment. Is the piece of furniture made with more than one kind of wood? If it is, you may have to bleach or stain the less conspicuous wood so that it matches the main surface.

Look at the color and texture of the stripped wood. Is there an old stain or filler left in the wood? It usually should be bleached out. Is the color blotchy or uneven? Is one part of the furniture darker than another? Is the wood darker or lighter than you want it to be? Can you see a distinct grain pattern? With bleach or stain you can correct almost any color problem or achieve any color effect you like.

With any piece of furniture, the finish you choose will determine how the wood should be prepared. Not all finishes require the same amount of preparation. Before you prepare a piece of furniture for finishing, make sure you're familiar with the special characteristics and requirements of the finish you plan to use. Read the ingredient and application information on the container, and follow the manufacturer's instructions and recommendations. Make sure you use compatible sealers, stains, and fillers.

Sanding. Whatever the wood and whatever color problems it may have, it must be thoroughly sanded before the finish can be applied. This step takes priority over all other surface preparations. You also may want to bleach, stain, or fill the wood, but you should always sand it first.

More than any other part of refinishing, sanding is a process that can't be rushed. It must be done by hand; power tools can damage the wood. It must be done carefully and thoroughly, and always with the grain. This demanding technique only requires time and patience. The care you put into sanding will determine the quality of the final finish.

The first rule of sanding is to work with the grain of the wood, because cross-grain sanding can leave permanent and obvious scratches. The second rule is to use a sanding block, because you

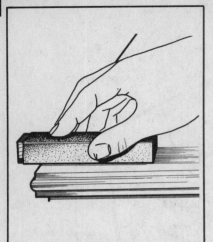

Always sand with the grain of the wood, making long light strokes with a padded sanding block.

To sand spindles and other rounds, wrap a strip of sandpaper around the part and pull the ends to sand it.

On carvings sand lightly along the grain, pressing the sandpaper into the carving. Be careful not to flatten the wood.

can't exert even sanding pressure without one. For flat surfaces the block should be padded; an unpadded block has no give, and grit caught under the sandpaper can scratch the wood as you work. For curved surfaces, your best bet is a thick piece of foam padding or sponge covered with sandpaper; the padding shapes itself to the curves, providing firm, even pressure.

Good sanding technique is easy to learn and apply. Using a sanding block, sand in long, light, and even strokes along the grain of the wood. Don't press hard; too much pressure can cause gouging at the edge of the sanding block. Change the sandpaper when it clogs or wears smooth.

To smooth the wood evenly and thoroughly, work with successively finer grades of sandpaper. The slight roughness left by the first sanding will be removed in the next sanding; the final sanding will remove the last traces of roughness. Start sanding with coarse-grit paper, using grade 20 for most woods or grade 40 for soft woods, such as pine or poplar. Work up to grades 40, 80, and finally 100 sandpaper. Although finer-grit paper produces a smoother surface, sanding with too fine paper can clog the wood and interfere with finishing.

Sand the entire piece of furniture with each grade of sandpaper before moving on to the next grade. Between sandings, brush or vacuum the sanding debris, and then wipe the wood clean with a tack cloth. Dust or grit caught under the paper can scratch the wood. If there are tight corners you can't get at with the sandpaper, use a sharp scraper to smooth the wood. Scrapers can leave gouges or scratches, so use them only when sanding isn't possible.

•Rungs, Rounds, and Spindles. Narrow rungs, spindles, legs, and other round parts need special treatment. Hard sanding with coarse-grit paper, with or without a block, can flatten or deform round parts; only the minimum of wood should be removed. To sand round parts, cut narrow strips of fine-grit—grades 80 and 100—sandpaper; don't use coarser grades at all. Wrap a strip of paper around the part, crosswise, and pull the ends back and forth to buff-sand the wood. Move up and down each round, changing your angle of sanding as you work to smooth the wood evenly. Be careful not to leave horizontal grooves in the wood at the edges of the sandpaper strips.

•Carvings. Carvings, especially shallow ones, must be treated carefully. Because coarse sanding could blur the lines of the carving, use only fine-grit sandpaper to smooth the stripped wood; work without a sanding block. Sand lightly along the grain of the wood, pressing the paper into cut-out areas with your fingertips. Sand as far down into the carving as you can, but be careful not to flatten rounded surfaces.

•Crevices and Curved Edges. Sand along crevices with a strip of sandpaper, creased to fit into the angle of the crevice. Sand only along the crevice, and use slow strokes, keeping the pressure even. Make sure the sandpaper doesn't slip; you could damage the edges of the wood at the sides of the crevice. Sand convex curves carefully along the curve, pressing lightly with your fingers and being careful not to damage any adjoining surfaces or edges. To smooth concave curves, use a piece of dowel the same diameter as the curve. Wrap sandpaper around the dowel, and push it carefully back and forth along the curve. At the ends of the curve, be careful not to slam the dowel into any adjoining surfaces.

•Veneers and Fine Patinas. If the piece of furniture you're working on is veneered, it must be treated carefully; the usual sanding techniques

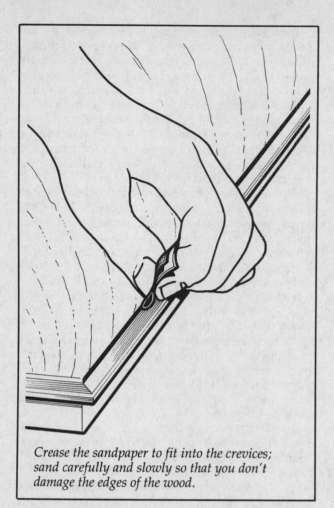

Crease the sandpaper to fit into the crevices; sand carefully and slowly so that you don't damage the edges of the wood.

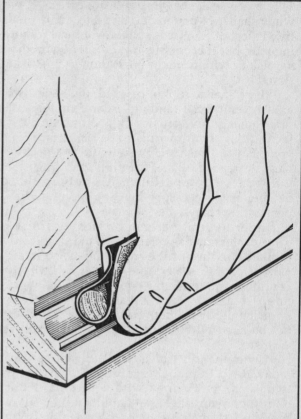

To sand a concave curve, use a piece of dowel that is the same diameter as the curve, wrapped with sandpaper.

could cause serious damage to the wood. The same thing is true for wood with a fine patina; sanding will remove the patina. For the best results, veneers and pieces with a fine patina should be smoothed gently.

Smooth sturdy whole-surface veneers with fine-grit sandpaper. Do not use coarser grades. On very thin veneers and wood with a patina, smoothing is best done with steel wool. The technique is the same as for sanding.

Start working with coarse steel wool if the surface is rough, and work up to 00 and 000 for the final smoothing. If the surface is smooth, use only the finer grades of steel wool. Between grades brush or vacuum dust and steel wool debris, then wipe the wood with a tack cloth.

Raising the Grain. When the wood is moistened, the cells that make up the grain swell, raising the grain above the surface of the wood. Any liquid causes this reaction; even when the wood is smoothly sanded, the finish itself acts to raise the grain. To prevent the appearance of a raised grain in the finished piece of furniture, the grain should be purposely raised and then sanded down before the finish is applied, after the final sanding.

The simplest grain raiser is water. Sponge the sanded piece of furniture with cold water, soak-ing the wood evenly and thoroughly; then wipe off any excess. The wood must be evenly wet with no dry spots and no puddles, or it may dry with water stains. Do not soak veneers; the glue that holds them may be water soluble.

Let the wood dry completely. When it's thoroughly dry, the raised fibers of the grain will stick up stiffly above the surface. With grade 80 or 100 sandpaper, lightly smooth these raised fibers down to the surface of the wood; use 000 steel wool on very delicate surfaces. Be careful not to roughen the surface. Then brush or vacuum the sanding debris, and wipe the wood clean.

Sealing. Like good sanding, careful sealing can make all the difference to your results in refinishing furniture. Sealer coats are used between finishing steps to ensure even penetration of stains and finishes, to prevent bleeding of stains and fillers, to form a good base for the finish, and to make the finished surface smoother. Sealing is not difficult, and it's well worth the extra time it takes. For professional results seal all surfaces before and after staining and filling, and before finishing. Some sealers have a built-in stain; the label on the container specifies that the product is a stain and sealer.

The traditional sealer for shellac, lacquer, and natural varnish finishes is thinned white shellac.

This basic sealer is simply a mixture of 1 part white shellac (4-pound cut) and 3 to 4 parts denatured alcohol. Shellac is suitable for most refinishing jobs, but it cannot be used with polyurethane varnish or with water or NGR (non-grain-raising) stains.

Where shellac cannot be used, the easiest sealer is a commercial sanding sealer. Sanding sealer dries quickly, and provides a good sanding base; it can be used with varnish, shellac, or lacquer. If you plan to finish the piece with polyurethane varnish, read the label carefully; sanding sealer may not be compatible with polyurethane. Sealing is unnecessary before finishing with a penetrating resin sealer.

Under natural varnish or lacquer finishes, some professionals prefer to seal the wood with a thinned mixture of the same finish. To make a natural varnish sealer, thin the varnish with turpentine or mineral spirits to make a 50-50 mixture. To make a lacquer sealer, mix lacquer and lacquer thinner in equal parts. These sealers cannot be used with shellac or with polyurethane varnish.

Polyurethane varnish demands special treatment. Read the label carefully. Some polyurethanes can be thinned with a specific thinner; with these varnishes the manufacturer may recommend thin varnish coats as sealers. Some polyurethanes do not require sealers. If you must seal stain or filler before polyurethane is applied, make sure the sealer is compatible with the varnish. Otherwise, use a penetrating resin sealer; this finishes the wood completely, but you can apply polyurethane over it if you want a smoother finish.

Because sealers should not interfere with other finishing steps, they must be applied in thin coats. Before applying the sealer, make sure the wood is clean; remove any dust with a tack cloth. Apply the sealer with a clean brush, flowing it on evenly and quickly along the grain of the wood. Make sure all surfaces are evenly covered, and pay particular attention to any end grain. End grain that isn't properly sealed will absorb stains and finishes more deeply than the rest of the wood in a piece.

Let the sealer dry completely. This takes about two hours for thinned white shellac or about one hour for commercial sanding sealer. Then sand the surface lightly with grade 120 sandpaper. The wood must be very smooth, but the sanding shouldn't penetrate the sealer. Remove all sanding debris by wiping thoroughly with a tack cloth.

If you're applying a finish directly over sanded wood, more than one coat of sealer may be necessary to close the wood's pores completely. Let the first coat of sealer dry completely before applying another coat. Very porous woods may require several coats of sealer.

Bleaching. Bleaching is a first-aid measure, not a routine part of refinishing. A piece of furniture should be bleached if the surface is marked by stains, black rings, or water spots, if the wood is discolored or blotchy, if the color is uneven, or if an old stain or filler is left after the finish is removed. Old filler is often a problem with oak, walnut, and mahogany. Bleaching also can be used to even the color of a piece of furniture made with two or more woods, by lightening the darker wood to match the lighter one.

Bleach also can be used cosmetically to lighten the color of a whole piece of furniture. This technique obviously isn't recommended for delicate inlays, veneers, or antiques, or for furniture made with rare wood, but it can be used to lighten a dark piece to match your other furniture.

Before you use bleach on any piece of furniture, make sure the wood is suitable for bleaching. Some woods, including cherry and satinwood, don't accept bleach well and should never be bleached. Other woods, such as bass, cedar, chestnut, elm, redwood, and rosewood, are difficult to bleach, and some woods, notably pine and poplar, are so light that bleaching makes them look lifeless. Birch, maple, and walnut can be bleached, but bleaching destroys their distinctive color. Rare woods, including mahogany and teak, seldom benefit from bleaching. Common woods that are easy to bleach and may benefit from it include ash, beech, gum, and oak.

Not all bleaching jobs call for the same kind of bleach; depending on the problem you want to correct, you may need a strong bleaching agent or a mild one. To remove ink stains or white marks, to even a mottled surface, or to remove an old stain or filler left after stripping, use liquid laundry bleach. To remove black water marks or lighten chemically darkened wood, use oxalic acid, available in paint stores and drugstores. Oxalic acid also removes old stain or filler. To change the color of the wood itself, you'll need a two-part commercial wood bleach.

Whatever bleach you use, remember that the results are permanent—you may be able to restain if you make the wood too light, but uneven bleaching is very hard to remedy. Make sure the wood is absolutely clean, and touch it as little as possible. The bleach must penetrate the wood evenly. Before applying the bleach, test it on a scrap piece of furniture. Make sure you know exactly what the bleach will do and how fast. Bleaches act quickly on soft woods, slowly on hard woods.

Bleaching isn't difficult, but it does require some precautions. Bleaches are strong chemicals, and the stronger ones can damage skin, eyes, and lungs. Wear rubber gloves and safety goggles when working with bleach, and make sure your working area is well ventilated. Follow the manufacturer's instructions exactly.

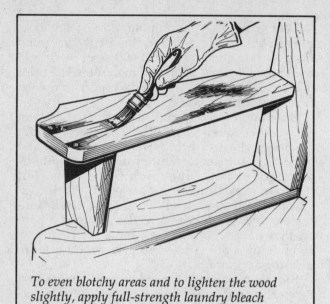

To even blotchy areas and to lighten the wood slightly, apply full-strength laundry bleach along the grain of the wood.

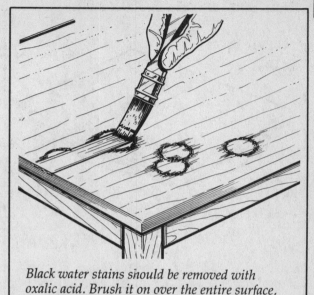

Black water stains should be removed with oxalic acid. Brush it on over the entire surface, then neutralize the acid with ammonia.

Bleaching requires careful application and removal. With any bleach, use a synthetic-bristle brush; the chemicals will damage natural bristles. Apply the bleach along the grain of the wood, wetting the surface evenly and thoroughly; there should be no dry spots and no puddles.

After bleaching, wipe the wood clean with a damp cloth. To remove any residue, neutralize the wood thoroughly; use an ammonia solution for oxalic acid or a borax solution for laundry bleach or two-part bleach. Wash the bleached wood thoroughly with the appropriate neutralizer; be careful not to soak it. Then, working quickly to prevent water damage, rinse the wood with clean water and dry it thoroughly with a soft cloth. Let the piece of furniture dry for at least two days before doing any further work on it.

•Laundry Bleach. This chlorine bleach can solve most refinishing color problems, from stain or filler not removed in stripping to ink stains and water spots. It works well for evening blotchy areas and for slight general lightening, but it won't drastically change the color of the wood. Before you use a stronger bleach on any piece of furniture, try laundry bleach; it usually does the trick.

Apply laundry bleach full-strength, brushing it evenly over the entire surface. If you're removing spots or lightening discolored areas, apply bleach full-strength to those areas. Laundry bleach works quickly; after a minute or two, you should be able to see the stain fading. If you're bleaching out an old stain, wipe the bleach off with a damp cloth when the stain has lightened. If you're spot-bleaching to remove spots or blend color areas, wait until the bleached spots are roughly the same color as the rest of the wood; then apply bleach again over the entire surface. Remove the bleach with a damp cloth when the color is even.

Then neutralize the treated wood with a solution of 1 cup of borax dissolved in 1 quart of hot water. Rinse with clean water, and dry.

•Oxalic Acid. Oxalic acid, sold in powder or crystal form, is used to remove black water marks from wood. It is also effective in restoring chemically darkened wood to its natural color. You're unlikely to encounter this problem unless you have a piece of furniture commercially stripped. Lye and ammonia, the chemicals that discolor wood, are not recommended for nonprofessional use. Oxalic acid must be used on the entire surface of the wood, because it also bleaches out old stain. You must bleach the entire piece of furniture to get an even color. Oxalic acid is more effective in lightening open-grained wood than close-grained wood.

Oxalic acid is not caustic, but it is poisonous; wear rubber gloves and safety goggles, and make sure ventilation is adequate. To prepare the acid, mix a saturated solution with warm water: 1 ounce of powder or crystals per 1 cup of warm water. Prepare enough bleach to treat the entire surface or piece of furniture.

Apply the acid solution evenly to the wood, brushing it on along the grain to cover the entire surface. On softwood you'll see results quickly; on hardwood bleaching takes longer. Let the acid work for about 20 minutes and then wipe it off with a damp cloth. If the surface isn't fully or evenly bleached, reapply the acid as necessary. On hardwood complete bleaching may take up to an hour. Wipe the wood clean with a damp cloth, wash it with clean water, then neutralize it with a solution of 1 cup of household ammonia and 2 quarts of water. Rinse it again with clean water, and dry it thoroughly.

•Two-Part Bleach. The two-part commercial wood bleach is often used to lighten or remove

Bleached   Not Bleached

To lighten or remove the color of the wood itself, use a two-part commercial wood bleach.

the natural color of wood. If you want a dark old piece to fit in with a roomful of blond furniture, this is the bleach to use. Two-part bleach is very strong, and must be used carefully; wear rubber gloves and safety goggles. This kind of bleach is also expensive.

Two-part bleach is easy to use and usually works quickly. The two components of the bleach, labeled "1" and "2" or "A" and "B," are applied separately. Read the manufacturer's instructions and follow them exactly. The first solution is usually allowed to work for about 20 minutes before the second solution is applied. One treatment usually bleaches the wood completely, but if the wood isn't light enough, treat it again. Wipe the bleached wood clean with a damp cloth, then neutralize it with a solution of 1 cup borax dissolved in 1 quart of hot water. Then rinse the wood with clean water, and dry it thoroughly.

•Post-Bleach Treatment. Treatment with any bleach raises the grain of the wood, even when the piece of furniture has already been thoroughly sanded. To prevent the raised grain from affecting the finish, it must be resanded.

After bleaching, let the piece of furniture dry for at least two days. Then sand the grain down lightly with grade 80 or 100 sandpaper; be careful not to roughen the surface. Because there may still be some chemical residue in the wood, wear a mask, and use a vacuum to remove sanding dust. Wipe the wood clean with a tack cloth.

One other complication of bleaching, especially with laundry bleach, is that the wood may be left with a whitish or grayish color. This is not serious; it shows that the bleach has dried out the fibers of the wood surface. On hardwood it disappears when the finish is applied. On softwoods

the gray color may be pronounced and the loose fibers obvious. To remove them rub the wood firmly along the grain with 000 steel wool; rub the entire bleached area, and make sure the color is even. The grayish cast will disappear completely when the finish is applied.

Staining. Wood is a beautiful material, but not all wood is equally beautiful. The choice woods are prized chiefly for the beauty of their color and grain; the common furniture woods are less desirable, not because they don't work well but because they don't look as good. Antiques, whether hardwood or softwood, are often beautiful simply because the wood has acquired a patina that new wood doesn't have. In furniture refinishing stain is used to give wood a more pleasing appearance.

Staining is done for a variety of reasons. Properly used, stain can emphasize the wood grain and give a light wood character. It can make new wood look old or common wood look rare. It can pull together a two-wood piece, restore color to bleached areas, and change or deepen the color of any wood. Staining is not always advisable, but it can solve many problems.

Before you stain any piece of furniture, take a good look at it. If it's made of cherry, maple, mahogany, rosewood, aged pine, or any rare woods, the wood probably should not be stained; these woods look best in their natural color. If the wood is light with an undistinguished grain, it may benefit from staining. Beech, birch, poplar, ash, gum, and new pine are usually stained before finishing. Some woods, such as oak, are attractive either stained or unstained. It's best not to stain if you're not sure it would improve the wood.

The kind of wood is not the only guideline for staining; your own preference should be the deciding factor. To get an idea how the piece of furniture would look unstained, test an inconspicuous spot, such as the bottom of the table, with whatever finish you plan to apply. The finish itself will darken the wood and bring out the grain. If you like the way it looks, there is no need to stain the wood; if you want a darker color or a more pronounced grain pattern, go ahead and stain it.

Several kinds of stains are available: wiping stains, water stains, varnish and sealer stains, and NGR stains. Some stains are combined with a sealer, and these are usually labeled as stain sealers. Not all are easy to use or guaranteed to give good results, so take a few minutes to read the labels.

The first consideration is the finish you plan to use. Most finishes can be applied over most kinds of stain, but polyurethane varnish cannot. If you want to use a polyurethane finish look for a stain that is compatible with polyurethane. If you can't find a compatible stain, you'll have to apply a clear penetrating resin sealer over a incompatible stain. Varnish can be applied over this sealer if you want a shiny finish.

The second consideration in choosing a stain is the job you want it to do. The most commonly used furniture stains are based on pigments mixed in oil or turpentine, or on aniline dyes mixed in turpentine, water, alcohol, or a volatile spirit. Other kinds of stains include varnish stains, sealer stains, and organic stains.

•Pigmented Oil Stains. The pigmented oil stains are nonpenetrating; they consist of pigments mixed in linseed oil, turpentine, mineral spirits, or a similar solvent, and are sometimes also available in gel form. They are inexpensive and easy to apply, but unless the grain of the wood is very open, they usually blur or mask the grain pattern. These stains usually don't work well on hardwood, but can be used for slight darkening on close-grained hardwood, such as maple. Lightening stains are pigmented oil.

Pigmented oil stains are applied by wiping and removed after the desired color is achieved. The intensity of the color is controlled by the length of time the stain is left on the wood. Drying time can be long, and the stain must be well sealed to prevent bleeding through the finish; the wood also should be sealed before application. The colors fade over time.

•Penetrating Oil Stains. The penetrating oil stains are very popular; they consist of aniline dyes mixed with turpentine or a similar solvent. They are inexpensive and easy to apply, but they tend to penetrate unevenly; they don't work well on hardwood, and are best used on pine and other softwood. They can be used for slight darkening on close-grained hardwood, such as maple.

Penetrating oil stains are applied by wiping and removed after the desired color is achieved. The intensity of the color is controlled by the length of time the stain is left on the wood. Drying takes a long time, and the stain must be well sealed to prevent bleeding through the finish. It is difficult to remove once it's dry. The colors are rich and clear, but fade over time.

•Water Stains. Water stains consist of powdered aniline dye mixed with hot water. They are inexpensive and produce a rich color, but are difficult to use. Water stains are extensively used by manufacturers but are not recommended for refinishing.

Water stains are hard to apply evenly, and they have a very long drying time. They raise the grain of the wood, so sanding is necessary after staining, and color may be lost in high spots. Water stains don't bleed through the finish, but the wood must be sealed before and after staining to ensure even staining and smooth finishing.

•NGR (Non-Grain-Raising) Stains. The NGR stains consist of aniline dye mixed with denatured alcohol or a volatile spirit, such as methanol. They are expensive, and they can be difficult to use. Alcohol-base stains fade over time and must be well sealed to prevent bleeding; they cannot be used with shellac. Spirit-base NGR stains don't fade or bleed, and produce a more uniform color.

Alcohol- and spirit-base NGR stains dry quickly. Apply them with quick even brushing; repeated thin applications are best to minimize overlaps. One color can be applied directly over another, but too dark a color must be bleached out. NGR stains are recommended for use on hardwood, especially close-grained woods, where oil stains would not be absorbed properly. They should not be used on softwoods.

•Varnish Stains. Varnish stain is a nonpenetrating stain, consisting of aniline dye in a varnish base. It is used by manufacturers to finish drawers, backs, and other hidden parts, because it is inexpensive and no further finish is required. Since it looks cheap, it is not recommended for refinishing.

•Sealer Stains. The sealer stains are nonpenetrating mixtures of dye in a varnish, shellac, or lacquer base. Two coats are usually required, and the surface must often be protected with paste wax. No further finishing is required.

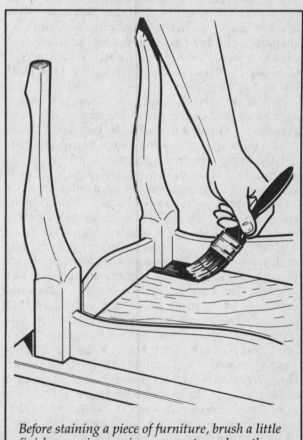

Before staining a piece of furniture, brush a little finish on an inconspicuous area to see how the wood looks without a stain.

•Organic Stains. Several organic-base stains can be made for use on pine and other woods; the most common uses tobacco as the color, but stains also can be made from bark, roots, tea, berries, and other natural sources. These stains are interesting, but they're not recommended unless you're an accomplished refinisher.

Before staining the piece of furniture, make sure the wood is absolutely smooth. Any surface irregularities will cause uneven stain absorption, and will result in a blotchy effect. To make sure the wood is smooth, rub it firmly along the grain with 000 steel wool; touch the wood as little as possible. Remove all dust and steel wool debris with a tack cloth.

To ensure even stain penetration, many woods should be sealed before staining. Close-grained wood may not need sealing. Thinned shellac can be used as a sealer under pigmented and penetrating oil stains; it should not be used under NGR or water stains. Commercial sanding sealer should be used with these stains. If you plan to finish the piece of furniture with polyurethane, make sure the sealer is compatible.

Apply the shellac or other sealer with a clean brush, stroking it lightly along the grain of the wood. Make sure any end grain is sealed completely. Otherwise, it will absorb too much stain and turn out darker than the rest of the wood. The grain should be lightly coated but not filled; the surface should dry dull. Let this sealer coat dry completely. This takes about two hours for shellac or one hour for commercial sanding sealer. Then sand the surface lightly with fine-grit sandpaper. Remove the dust with a tack cloth before applying the stain.

Whatever kind of stain you're using, the most important part of the process is getting the color you want. You may be able to buy stain in the color you want, or you may have to mix colors to get the right effect. Experiment, mixing small amounts of stain and applying test batches to scrap wood, until you get the right color.

Although a wide range of stain colors is available, you can mix almost any color with two or more of the four basic shades: light oak (tan), walnut (brown), maple (yellow-orange), and mahogany (red). Most manufacturers provide mixing proportions for various effects. To dull any color, add a drop or two of black. Mix small amounts of stain at once; then, starting full-strength and thinning the stain gradually with the proper solvent, test the stain on scrap wood until you have the right color. Keep track of the proportions so you'll be able to duplicate the mixture. When you like the color, test it again on a hidden part of the piece of furniture. If the piece is made of two or more woods, you may have to mix stain separately for each wood, but this is often not necessary.

When you're satisfied with the stain color, mix enough stain to treat an entire piece of furniture.

Do not mix brands or kinds of stain, and do not change brands or kinds of stain in the middle of the job. Better to have stain left over than to run out of stain with one table leg or chair arm to go.

Whatever stain you're using, it's best to go carefully. If you're not sure the color is right, thin the stain to lighten it, and apply several coats of stain until the color is as deep as you want it. Always test the stain in an inconspicuous spot, and stain the least conspicuous surfaces first. It may take longer this way to get the effect you want, but the only way to salvage a badly applied stain is to bleach it out and start over.

To prevent drip marks and uneven color, turn the piece of furniture so that the surface being stained is always horizontal. If you're working on a large piece and this isn't practical, start at the bottom and work up. Always work quickly, applying stain smoothly and evenly over the entire surface.

•Pigmented or Penetrating Oil Stains. Apply pigmented or penetrating oil stain with a clean brush, flowing stain evenly on along the grain of the wood; you also may use a clean cloth or sponge to apply penetrating stain. Let pigmented oil stain set for about 10 to 15 minutes, until the surface of the stain starts to turn dull, then firmly wipe off the excess stain with a clean cloth dampened with stain. Penetrating oil stains work more quickly than pigmented ones; wipe off the excess immediately for a light color, or let it set as long as 15 to 20 minutes for a darker color.

Oil stain can be modified if you don't like the effect. If the wood is too dark, soak a clean cloth in turpentine or mineral spirits, and rub the wood firmly and evenly along the grain. This will lighten the stain but not remove it. If part of the grain is too dark, wrap a cloth around your index fin-

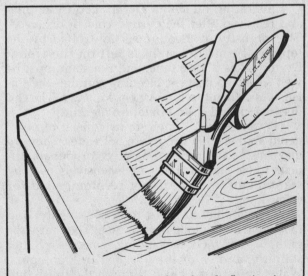

Brush on oil stain with a clean brush, flowing it evenly along the grain of the wood to cover the entire surface.

Let oil stain set to produce the desired color; the longer you leave it on, the darker it will be. Wipe off the excess.

Oil stain allows some leeway for color adjustment. If part of the grain is too light, use an artist's brush to apply more stain.

Apply water stain in long strokes, with as little overlap as possible. Overlaps will dry darker than the rest of the surface.

ger, dip it into turpentine or mineral spirits, and lightly rub the grain you want to lighten. If part of the grain is too light, use an artist's brush to apply more stain just to the grain. Let the completed stain dry for about 24 hours. If the color isn't dark enough, repeat the staining procedure.

•Water Stains. Water stains should be used only on absolutely clean bare wood or on new wood. Apply water stain with a new brush, flowing it on quickly and evenly along the grain of the wood; use long, smooth strokes. Try not to overlap your strokes; a double layer of stain will dry twice as dark as a single one. It's better to use several thinned coats of stain than one dark one to minimize brush overlap marks.

Water stain cannot be adjusted, but if you're working on small surfaces, the stain can be evened out by wiping. To apply water stain by this method, flow it liberally onto the surface, then wipe off the excess with a clean cloth, stroking along the grain. The intensity of the color is determined by the length of time the excess is left on the wood. Wipe immediately for a light color, or let the stain set for a darker shade. Let the completed stain dry for about 24 hours. If the color isn't dark enough, repeat the staining procedure.

•NGR Stains. NGR stain, either alcohol- or spirit-base, is applied like water stain, but this kind of stain dries so quickly that it can be hard to apply. Use a medium-size new brush to apply NGR stain, flowing it on quickly and evenly along the grain of the wood. Make long, smooth strokes and try not to overlap the strokes; brush overlap marks will dry twice as dark as the rest of the stain. To minimize overlap marks, it's better to use several thinned coats of stain than only one dark coat.

NGR stains cannot be adjusted, and should not be applied in very humid weather. An unsatisfactory stain must be bleached out. Let the stain dry completely for about 30 minutes before finishing the wood.

Lightening. Dark wood can be lightened with stain for an interesting light-dark effect. Lightening is not recommended for fine woods, because it covers the natural color and grain of the wood. As a last resort it can be effective. Lightening works best on open-grained wood; the effect of a lighter color is produced because the grain is filled with a light or white pigment. The lightening agent is sometimes thinned white oil-base paint, but more often it is pigmented oil stain.

Apply the oil stain as discussed previously, and let it set to achieve the desired effect. Wipe off excess stain and let the stained wood dry completely.

Any stain, even an oil-base stain, may raise the grain of the wood. If necessary, remove this slight roughness when the stain is completely dry, but smooth the wood carefully to avoid removing the stain. To smooth wood treated with oil-base stain, rub it gently with 000 or 0000 steel wool. To smooth wood treated with water or NGR stain, sand it lightly with fine-grit sandpaper. Remove sanding debris with a tack cloth. Sanding may remove water stain in spots; if the surface is uneven in color, you may have to apply another coat of stain.

Most stains should be sealed to prevent bleeding. After smoothing the stained wood, apply a sealer coat of thinned shellac, sanding sealer, or other appropriate sealer. Do not use shellac with NGR or water stains. If you plan to finish the piece with polyurethane, make sure the sealer is compatible. Let the sealed wood dry completely; then sand the surface lightly with fine-grit sandpaper. Remove the sanding debris with a tack cloth.

Filling. Softwood and close-grained hardwood, such as maple and poplar, are ready to finish after staining; open-grained hardwood may require further treatment. Even after the surface is stained or sealed, open-grained wood still has open pores, and a finish applied over open pores may look uneven. To give it a smooth and evenly finished surface, open-grained wood is usually treated with a filler after staining.

Whether you should fill the wood depends on both the wood itself and the finish you want. What is the piece of furniture made of? Bass, hemlock, maple, pine, poplar, redwood, willow, cedar, cypress, and ebony should never be filled; they can be finished immediately after staining and sealing. Ash, beech, mahogany, oak, rosewood, walnut, teak, satinwood, butternut, chestnut, elm, hickory, and lauan are open-grained; they are usually filled. Most other hardwood, including cherry, birch, and sycamore, is close-grained and should not be filled.

Filling is also a matter of personal taste. Do you want a smooth finish on a formal table, or are you aiming for a natural finish on an informal piece? Filler produces a smooth, glassy surface; if you want a natural look, you may want to leave the pores open. This also affects the finish you plan to use. Under most finishes open-grained woods should be filled, but if you don't want the piece of furniture to have a smooth surface, you can finish it with a penetrating sealer, which makes filling unnecessary.

One drawback of filling is that most finishes don't bond well to filled surfaces. Use a filler only when a varnish, shellac, or lacquer finish will be applied over an open-grained wood. If you're not sure the wood should be filled, don't fill it.

Fillers are available in two forms: liquid and paste. Liquid filler is too thin to be effective on open-grained woods. Tinted liquid filler is sometimes used like lightening stain to change the color of the wood. Filling should be done with paste filler, thinned as necessary to penetrate the pores of the wood. If you plan to finish the piece of furniture with lacquer, use a lacquer-base filler, or let the filler dry for at least 48 hours before sealing and finishing. If you plan to use a polyurethane finish, make sure that the filler is compatible.

There are two kinds of paste filler. The most commonly available filler is based on cornstarch; it's available in a neutral tone and in several colors. This kind of filler should be matched to the color of the wood; it dries lighter than its wet color. If you can't find a color to match the wood, use oil stain to mix a filler darker than the wood; check the label to make sure you can mix it. More than one application may be required with this kind of filler.

The second kind of paste filler is called sanding filler; it dries transparent and does not have to be matched to the wood. Sanding filler has a silicate base and requires only one application. Because it doesn't have to be color matched, it is easier to use than cornstarch-base filler.

Stained surfaces should be sealed after staining to prevent bleeding; they need no further treat-

Apply filler first along the grain of the wood. Then work across the grain to fill the pores completely.

ment before filling. Unstained surfaces also must be sealed; apply a coat of thinned shellac, sanding sealer, or other appropriate sealer. If you plan to finish the piece with polyurethane, make sure the sealer and the filler are compatible. Let the sealed wood dry completely, then sand the surface lightly with fine-grit sandpaper. Remove the sanding debris with a tack cloth, and apply the filler.

To use paste filler, thin the paste as directed with turpentine, working it to a smooth, creamy batter. Wood with large open pores requires a thicker consistency than wood with smaller pores. Apply the filler with a clean brush, working it firmly into the pores along the grain of the wood, then work it in across the grain. On large surfaces fill one area at a time to cover the entire surface evenly.

Let the filler set for about 15 minutes or as directed by the manufacturer, until the surface of the filler is dull. Then firmly wipe off the excess filler, across the grain of the wood, with a coarse towel or a piece of burlap. You want to remove the filler from the surface of the wood but leave it in the pores; you may have to experiment with the drying time to find the right timing. After wiping off the excess filler, wipe the wood slowly and carefully with a clean cloth in the direction of the grain. Let the filled wood dry for at least 24 hours.

The filled wood should look clean. If you can see a dull haze on the surface, the excess filler was not completely removed. This haze must be sanded off to prevent clouding in the finish. Sand the hazy areas lightly with fine-grit sandpaper, being careful not to remove either the filler in the pores or the stain. Remove sanding debris with a tack cloth.

To prevent the filler from bleeding through the finish before bonding of the finish to the filler,

When the surface of the filler dulls, wipe off the excess with a coarse cloth, first across and then along the grain.

Whatever finish you choose, it's important to know exactly what you're working with. Some finishes can be mixed, and some cannot. Each finish has its own application techniques; each finish requires different tools and materials. Before you buy and apply a finish, always read the ingredient and application information on the container. Always follow the manufacturer's instructions and recommendations.

The one requirement common to all finishes is a dust-free environment during application. Providing this environment isn't easy, but it can be done. Consider using a finish that dries with a matte, or flat, surface; this kind of finish gives you the opportunity to remove dirt and lint with rubbing abrasives. Before you start to work, clean your working area thoroughly, then let the dust settle for about 24 hours. Keep doors and windows closed. Don't work near heating or cooling registers or next to open windows, and never work outside. Wear lint-free clothes, and don't wear gloves.

Before you apply any finish, make sure you have all the materials you need. Set up your working space so that the piece of furniture will always be between you and the light; this makes it easy to see dust and lint on the newly finished surfaces. Work with clean tools and new finish materials, and make sure you have adequate light and ventilation. Clean all surfaces carefully with a tack cloth before applying the finish. If it is necessary, give the piece of furniture a final swipe with mineral spirits to remove dirt and fingerprints. Let the wood dry thoroughly before applying the finish. To keep the new finish smooth, remove specks of dust and lint from wet surfaces with an artist's brush.

How a piece of furniture stands up to wear is as important as how it looks, and durability is a primary consideration in choosing a finish. The most durable finishes, varnish and penetrating resin, are the two basic finishes for refinishing. Varnish is the more protective of the two because it is a surface coat; damage to the varnish does not always extend to the wood. Penetrating resin hardens in the wood itself. Although it doesn't protect the surface from damage as effectively as varnish, it may stand up to heavy use better because it's easy to reapply and doesn't chip or craze.

seal the filled surface before finishing, using the appropriate sealer. Apply a coat of thinned shellac, sanding sealer, or other sealer. If you plan to finish the piece with polyurethane, make sure the sealer is compatible; some polyurethane may not require sealing over some fillers. If you plan to finish the piece with penetrating resin sealer, sealing is not necessary. Let the sealed wood dry completely, then sand the surface lightly with fine-grit sandpaper. Remove sanding debris with a tack cloth, and apply the finish.

APPLYING THE NEW FINISH

Putting the finish on a piece of furniture is the final payoff for the hours you've spent removing the old finish, making repairs, sanding, staining, and smoothing. The finishing step is the fun step. It may be routine; it may be creative. Either way, it is usually easy to do.

A furniture finish can be classified as varnish, penetrating resin, shellac, lacquer, wax, or oil. All these finishes are designed to protect wood and to bring out its natural beauty. Choosing a finish comes down to two factors: How you want the wood to look and how durable you want the finished surface to be.

Of the six basic finishes, all can be beautiful, but when it comes to durability, two kinds outperform the others: varnish and penetrating resin. Varnish, the most durable of all finishes, is available in high-gloss, satin, and flat forms. Applying varnish can be difficult, but the results are worth the work. Penetrating resin sinks into the wood to give it a natural look and feel; it is easy to apply and durable. The other furniture finishes have their advantages. Oil produces a natural finish; shellac dries fast and is easy to use. For most refinishing, varnish or penetrating resin is probably the best choice.

Varnish. Varnish enhances and gives warmth to the grain of the wood, and it is resistant to impact, heat, abrasion, water, and alcohol. It can be used as a top coat over worn finishes. Varnish provides a clear finish, but it darkens the wood. It is available in high-gloss, semigloss, or satin, and matte, or flat, surface finishes. Varnish dries slowly and can be difficult to apply. Dust can be a problem.

The traditional varnish is based on natural resins and oils, and is thinned with mineral spirits or turpentine. Spar varnish is a natural varnish formulated to stay tacky; it's strictly for outdoor use and should never be used for furniture. Synthetic varnishes are based on synthetic resins and require special thinners. The best of the synthetic varnishes is polyurethane. It is clear, nonyellowing, and tough. Other synthetic varnishes are the phenolics, used for exterior and some marine work, and the alkyds, often used in colored preparations. Phenolic and alkyd varnishes yellow with age and are not recommended for refinishing. With any kind of varnish, look for quick drying to minimize dust problems. Use spray varnish only where brushing is impractical, such as on wicker or rattan.

Natural varnish can be used with any stain or filler. The sealer for natural varnish is thinned shellac or a mixture of 1 part varnish and 1 part turpentine or mineral spirits. Do not mix brands or kinds of varnish. Polyurethane varnish is not compatible with all stains and fillers. Before buying polyurethane, read the label to make sure you're using compatible materials. Some polyurethane can be thinned for use as a sealer; others do not require sealers. Some sanding sealers are compatible with polyurethane.

Apply varnish with a new, clean, natural-bristle brush. Use only new varnish. A can of varnish that has been used several times may contain lumps of hardened varnish from around its sides and rim. These lumps can cause trouble. If you plan the job properly, you probably won't have much leftover varnish to waste.

Bare wood to be finished with varnish must be properly prepared, sealed, and sanded. Finished wood to get a topcoat must be cleaned and lightly sanded. Immediately before applying the varnish, clean each surface thoroughly with a tack cloth.

It's much easier to apply varnish to horizontal surfaces than to verticals. Before you start to work, turn the piece of furniture so that its major surfaces are horizontal. If the piece has drawers, doors, shelving, and other removable parts, take them out or off, and finish them horizontally. Work on only one surface at a time, and work on large surfaces last.

Apply varnish to the prepared wood with long, smooth strokes, laying the varnish on along the grain in strips the width of the brush. Do not touch the brush to the rim of the varnish container; shake or tap off excess varnish inside the container or on a strike can. The varnish should flow onto the surface of the wood, with no drag. If the brush starts to pull, or if you see small missed or thin spots, add about 1 ounce of the proper thinner to the varnish, being careful not to raise any bubbles.

After laying on an even coat of varnish in strips along the grain of the wood, apply more varnish in even strokes across the grain to level and even the surface. The varnish should be as

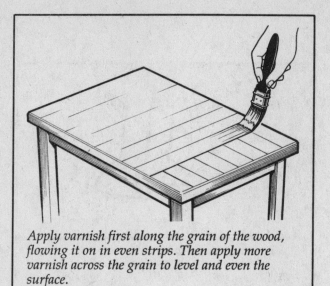

Apply varnish first along the grain of the wood, flowing it on in even strips. Then apply more varnish across the grain to level and even the surface.

even and level as possible, with no thick or thin spots, but a thin coat is better than a thick one, which takes longer to dry and may crack as the varnish ages. As you work, remove dust and lint from the wet finish with a rosin lint picker.

To finish each surface, tip off the wet varnish in the direction of the grain. Use an almost dry brush for this step. Holding the brush at a slight angle to the surface, lightly stroke the surface of the varnish to remove brush marks and even the surface. Smooth the entire varnished surface, working in strips along the grain of the wood. As you work, pick off dust and lint with a lint picker. Any remaining brush marks will disappear as the varnish dries.

Varnish must be applied carefully to prevent thick spots. At outside corners work from the flat surface toward the corner, lifting the brush as it nears the corner and before it flips down over the edge. This prevents a buildup of varnish along the edge. At inside corners work an inch or two away from the corner, then brush the varnish into the corner, tip it off, and leave it alone. This method prevents buildup on many flat-surface brushings.

Spots that tend to hold varnish should be coated just once with varnish and tipped just once with the brush. Repeated tipping will leave a bulge.

Brush lengthwise along rungs, spindles, and other turnings. On carved moldings apply the finish to the carvings first with a dry brush; then finish the flat surfaces with the tip of the brush. With a dry brush, go over the carvings and then the flats, leveling the finish and removing any fat edges, sags, or runs. On raised panel doors, finish the panels first and then move on to the flat framing. The finish will build up at the miters in the frame where they meet the panel, so remove the excess varnish with a dry, clean brush, working from the corner out.

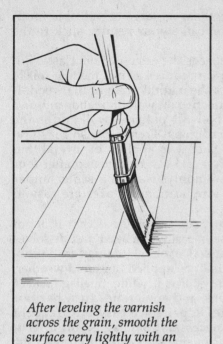

After leveling the varnish across the grain, smooth the surface very lightly with an almost dry brush.

At outside corners, apply varnish from the flat surface to the corner; lift the brush before the bristles go over the edge.

Where two surfaces meet, varnish the flat surfaces first, then finish the corner; varnish from the corner out.

Drying times for varnish average about 24 hours, but polyurethane often dries more quickly. Dampness slows drying, so it's recommended that you extend all drying times, especially if you're applying varnish in humid or wet weather. Drying times are not necessarily curing times, and new varnish is easily damaged. Always let the finish dry at least 24 hours or as long as the manufacturer recommends; if possible, let it dry a couple of days or more. Pick off lint and dust only while the surface is wet or sticky, but too much interference could damage the finish.

Many varnishes require two or even three coats for a smooth finish. Use your own judgment, and follow the manufacturer's recommendations. Between coats of varnish, let the first coat of varnish harden or dry as recommended by the manufacturer. Some two-coat varnishes should be applied 10 to 15 hours from the time the first coat was applied, but it is usually best to wait at least 24 hours and longer if possible. When the first coat is completely dry, lightly sand the varnished wood in the direction of the grain, using grade 120 sandpaper on a padded sanding block. Abrade the surface evenly, but don't cut it deeply. Clean away sanding residue with a tack cloth and apply the second coat of varnish the same way as you did the first. Repeat this procedure, sanding the varnished wood carefully, if a third coat of varnish is required.

Penetrating Resin. Penetrating resin finishes are not surface finishes; they soak into the wood to harden the fibers themselves. Wood treated with penetrating resin has a natural look and feel; the grain is strongly highlighted. Penetrating resin is durable, and withstands heavy wear; it is easy to apply and easy to repair. It dries clear, but it darkens the wood. It also is available in several stain colors. The finish may lack depth.

Because penetrating resin must soak into the wood, it is best used on open-grained woods; close-grained woods may not absorb it deeply. On stripped wood all old filler must be removed. If filler is left in the wood, the finish will not be absorbed. Penetrating resin is recommended for use on oily hardwood, such as rosewood and teak, and is especially effective on oak and walnut. It is often preferable to varnish for use on large pieces of furniture and complex carvings. It dries slowly, but because it is not a surface finish, dust is not a problem. A penetrating resin finish is hard to remove for future refinishing.

Penetrating resin finishes are formulated with two different kinds of resins: phenolic and alkyd. There is little difference in performance between these kinds, but phenolic-base compounds may penetrate the wood more deeply than alkyds.

Penetrating resin can be used over any stain except varnish- or vinyl-base stains. No filling or sealing is required. Before applying penetrating resin on bleached or stained surfaces, test it on a hidden part of the piece.

Wood to be finished with penetrating resin must be properly prepared and sanded. Because the finish does not coat the surface of the wood, any rough spots or other defects will be accentuated when the resin is applied. Immediately before applying the resin, clean the piece of furniture thoroughly with a tack cloth.

Whenever possible, penetrating resin should be applied to horizontal surfaces. If the piece of furniture has removable parts, remove them and finish them horizontally. Apply penetrating resin with a clean brush or cloth, or 0000 steel wool, or pour it directly onto the wood. Work on small areas at a time. On rungs or spindles, apply the resin with a clean cloth, one rung at a time.

Spread the resin liberally and evenly over the wood. The appearance of the surface isn't critical, but the amount of resin used on each surface should be consistent. As you work, watch the wood surface. Some open-grained wood soaks up the finish quickly; close-grained hardwood absorbs it slowly and may not absorb much at all. Apply resin until the wood stops absorbing it.

Let the resin set for about 30 to 45 minutes. During this time, keep the surface wet, adding more resin to any dry spots that appear. All surfaces should be shiny. After 30 to 45 minutes, when the wood will not absorb any more resin and the surface is still wet, firmly wipe off the excess finish with clean, absorbent cloths. The surface of the wood should be completely dry, with no wet, shiny spots.

Let the newly applied resin dry for 24 hours. If glossy patches appear on the wood during the drying period, remove them immediately; add resin to these areas to soften the dried finish, and wipe off the liquid resin so that the wood is dry.

After 24 hours smooth the wood gently with 0000 steel wool, then clean it thoroughly with a tack cloth. Apply a second coat of penetrating resin, let it penetrate and wipe off the excess as before. If necessary on open-grained wood, apply a third coat of resin; wait 24 hours and smooth the surface with steel wool before the application. No wax or other surface coat is needed.

The other traditional finishes, shellac, lacquer, wax, and oil, are not as tough nor as durable as varnish. Because each has its own distinctive advantages and characteristics, the classic finishes are still widely used today.

Shellac, the least durable of all finishes, is also the easiest to apply, and it dries quickly. Used with linseed oil, it's the basis of French polish. Shellac is easily damaged by water or alcohol. Lacquer is similar but tougher; it dries even faster than shellac but is difficult to apply evenly. Lacquer is used chiefly by furniture manufacturers. The other two traditional finishes are used less frequently. Wax is not really a permanent finish, but it's easy to apply and maintain. Sealer stain systems use wax as a protective top coat. Oil, the original wood sealer, is still used where a rich, natural finish is needed. The traditional oil is linseed oil, which is difficult to apply and maintain properly. Modern finishing oils, both natural and synthetic, are much easier to use.

Although these finishes are not recommended for most refinishing jobs, they can be effective where durability is not important or where you want to achieve a particular character. Experiment with the classics on small pieces before you use them on large or valuable furniture; if you don't like your results, stick to the basic finishes.

Shellac. Shellac is the easiest of the classic finishes to apply. It produces a fine, mellow finish, and accentuates the natural grain of the wood. It is especially attractive on walnut, mahogany, and fine veneer woods. It polishes well and is the basis for the traditional French polish finish on fine furniture. Shellac is applied in several thin coats. It dries fast and can be recoated after four hours. It is commonly used as a sealer under other finishes. Application mistakes are easy to correct.

The big drawback to shellac is that it is not durable. Shellac is easily damaged and dissolves in both water and alcohol; white rings are a problem. Shellac cannot be applied in humid weather, because humidity turns it white. Shellac finishes absorb moisture, and sometimes turn hazy or white with age. Repairs are easy but frequent retouching is necessary. Shellac is soft after it dries, so waxing is almost essential to protect the surface. It is best used on decorative pieces that don't have to stand up to hard wear.

Shellac is available in two colors: white and orange. White shellac is used for light-color wood and is thinned with denatured alcohol for use as a sealer. It can be tinted with alcohol-soluble aniline dye and is sometimes available in colors. Orange shellac gives an amber color to wood; this is often desirable on dark-color wood. It is especially attractive on walnut, mahogany, and teak.

Shellac is sold in several cuts, or concentrations; the most common kind is a 4-pound cut. Shellac usually must be thinned or cut with denatured alcohol before application, as directed by the manufacturer. For sealer thin 1 part of 3- or 4-pound-cut white shellac with 4 parts denatured alcohol; for finish coats thin 1 part 4-pound shellac with 2 parts alcohol.

Shellac can be used over any stain, except alcohol-base stain (NGR), and over any filler. Thinned shellac is recommended for sealer coats. Use denatured alcohol to thin shellac; use alcohol or ammonia for cleanup. Shellac has a short shelf life; old shellac does not dry properly. Buy just enough for the job, and throw out any leftover shellac. Some manufacturers shelf date shellac.

Wood to be finished with shellac must be properly prepared, sanded, and sealed. Immediately before applying shellac, clean each surface thoroughly with a tack cloth. Use a new good-quality brush. Work on one area at a time.

To apply shellac, flow it liberally onto the surface, working in long, smooth strokes along the grain of the wood. Keep the surface really wet with the shellac, and apply the finish from dry to wet edges. After coating the surface completely, tip off the shellac along the grain of the wood. Use an almost dry brush for this step. Holding the brush at a slight angle to the surface, lightly stroke the surface of the shellac to remove brush marks and even the surface. Smooth the entire shellacked surface, working in strips along the grain of the wood.

Shellac dries in about 30 minutes and can be recoated after four hours. Let the new shellac set for a full four hours. Make sure drying time is adequate. Because shellac is soft, it can pick up sandpaper grains or steel wool shreds if it isn't completely dry. This can result in a nightmare of smoothing to remove the debris. When the shellac is completely dry, lightly sand the surface with grade 120 open-coat sandpaper on a padded sanding block. Clean the sanded surface thoroughly with a tack cloth, then apply a second coat of shellac. Let the shellac dry for four hours, then repeat sanding and cleaning the surface, and apply a third coat. Additional coats of shellac can be added, if you want a smoother surface; let each coat dry thoroughly before applying a new one, and buff the finish with fine steel wool between coats.

Let the final coat of shellac harden for 48 hours. With 0000 steel wool, remove the gloss from the finished surface, rubbing carefully along the grain of the wood. Do not rub across the grain. When the gloss is completely removed, let the piece of furniture stand for 48 hours. Then apply a good-quality paste wax to the finished wood, and buff the surface to a shine with a soft cloth or the buffing attachment of an electric drill.

French Polish Finish. This shellac finishing technique produces a more durable surface than the standard shellac finish. French-polished surfaces have a distinctive velvety sheen, and the grain and color of the wood are emphasized. It is best used on close-grained woods and fine

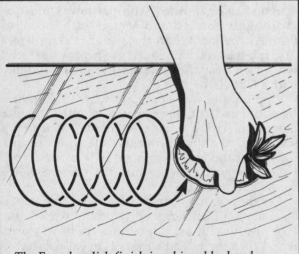

The French polish finish is achieved by hand-rubbing. Apply the shellac-and-oil mixture and rub it in with a circular or figure-eight motion; continue rubbing for 45 minutes.

veneers. Use only water stain or spirit-base NGR stain under French polish; other kinds may bleed or lift.

To apply a French polish finish, mix 2 tablespoons of boiled linseed oil into 1 pint of 1-pound-cut shellac. Make a palm-size pad of cheesecloth, and wrap it in a clean, lint-free linen or cotton cloth. The pad should just fit in your palm. Dip the pad into the shellac-oil mixture; don't soak it. Make sure the surface of the pad is not wrinkled.

Apply the shellac/oil mixture to the prepared wood, spreading it evenly along the grain to cover the entire surface. Work with a quick stroke, blending your strokes carefully. Then rub the wet surface with the pad, using a firm circular or figure-eight motion over the wood. Continue this circular rubbing for about 45 minutes, using plenty of downward pressure and adding shellac as the mixture is worked into the wood. The surface should be evenly glossy, with no dark spots or stroke marks.

Let the rubbed shellac-oil finish dry for 24 hours, then apply another coat. Rub in the second coat for 45 minutes, and let it dry for two to three days. Apply a third coat in the same way.

Let the piece dry for at least a week, but not more than 10 days, after the final coat. Clean the surface, wax the finished wood with a good-quality paste wax, and buff it to a fine sheen.

Lacquer. Lacquer dries faster and is more durable than shellac. It is thin, and must be applied in many thin coats. It is available in high-gloss, satin, and matte finishes, in clear form and in several clear stain colors. Dust-free drying is not a problem, but because lacquer dries so fast, it is difficult to work with. Brushing lacquers are not recommended for amateur use; spraying lacquers must be applied with an air-compressor-driven spray gun. Application is tricky, and lacquer fumes are both toxic and explosive. Lacquer is not usually used in amateur refinishing. For small jobs lacquer can be applied with aerosol spray cans. This is expensive, but it works well.

Lacquer can be used on most woods, but it cannot be used on mahogany and rosewood; the oils in these woods will bleed through the finish. Lacquer can be used over lacquer-base, NGR, and water stains, and over lacquer-base fillers. It cannot be used over other finishes, or over oil-base stains or many fillers. The solvents in lacquer will dissolve other finishes and incompatible stains and fillers. Thinned lacquer or shellac or a compatible lacquer-base sanding sealer should be used as a sealer under a lacquer finish.

Wood to be finished with lacquer must be properly prepared, sanded, and sealed. Immediately before applying lacquer, clean the piece of furniture thoroughly with a tack cloth. Protect your working area with drop cloths or newspaper. Make sure ventilation is adequate.

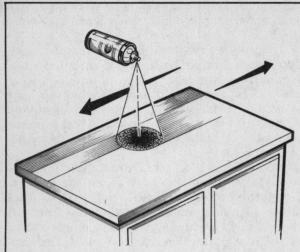

With the can about 18 inches from the surface, spray lacquer in even strips from side to side, top to bottom. Overlap the strips to equalize the thickness of the lacquer film.

Before applying lacquer, test the spray can on a piece of newspaper or cardboard. Spray cans have different patterns of spray; practicing and watching the test spray pattern will give you enough control to cover the surface.

Apply lacquer slowly and evenly, holding the spray can upright about 18 inches away from the surface of the wood. If you work farther away than this, the lacquer will tend to "orange peel," dimpling like the skin on an orange. If you work closer than 18 inches, too much lacquer may be applied to the surface, causing runs and sags in the finish. Spray the top edge of the surface first, then cover the entire surface in horizontal strips, from side to side, top to bottom. As you work, overlap the lacquer spray patterns. The edges of each sprayed area are thin; the centers are thick. Overlapping equalizes the thickness of the lacquer film, keeping the surface even. Never try to equalize the film by brushing the lacquer. Apply only a thin coat of lacquer.

Lacquer dries in no more than half an hour, but it must cure completely between coats. Let the newly sprayed wood dry for about 48 hours or as directed by the manufacturer. Then lightly smooth the surface with 000 steel wool, and clean it thoroughly with a tack cloth. Apply a second coat of lacquer. For a smoother finish, let the second coat dry for 48 hours, smooth the surface with 000 steel wool, and apply a third coat.

Runs and sags are usually caused by too much lacquer, but they don't always appear on the first couple of coats. The solvent in each coat of lacquer softens the dried lacquer under it to meld the coats together. As you apply more coats of lacquer, the bottom coats soften, and the lacquer film gets thicker; any unevenness can cause sags. For a rich, deep finish, use many thin coats of lac-

quer. Let the lacquer dry completely between coats, and rub the surface between coats with grade FFF powdered pumice and boiled linseed oil on a cheesecloth or felt pad.

After applying the final coat of lacquer, let the piece of furniture dry for 48 hours; then lightly buff the lacquered surface with 0000 steel wool. Clean the surface thoroughly with a tack cloth, and apply a good-quality paste wax. Buff the waxed surface to a fine gloss.

Waxes and Sealer Stains. Paste wax, often used to protect finishes, is sometimes used to finish bare wood. This is most successful on hard, close-grained wood, such as maple, that has been sanded absolutely smooth. Some waxes have color added, for use on dark wood, such as walnut. These waxes add color to the wood and are especially helpful if the finish on the wood is blotchy, but they do not stain the wood or restore the finish. Paste wax is easy to apply, and is non-sticky and heat resistant, but it is easily damaged and liable to wear. It must be reapplied periodically. Paste wax is more commonly used over a sealer stain to color, seal, and finish new or stripped wood.

Sealer stain finishes are available in several colors. Sealer stains produce an even color, with no lap marks or dark spots. They are tough and are easy to apply, but they are not water resistant and must often be recoated periodically.

Paste wax can be applied directly over prepared bare or stained wood; thinned shellac is recommended as a sealer coat. Sealer stains should be applied directly over prepared bare wood; no other sealer is required. Open-grained wood should be filled before a wax finish is applied; any paste filler is compatible. Wax and sealer stain finishes can be used on new or stripped wood.

Wood to be finished with paste wax must be thoroughly sanded and sealed with a coat of thinned shellac. When the sealer is completely dry, rub the wood along the grain with 0000 steel wool; then clean the piece of furniture thoroughly with a tack cloth.

Apply paste wax sparingly with a clean, lint-free cloth pad, rubbing the wax on with a circular motion to form a thin, even coating. Work on a small area at a time. Some manufacturers recommend that the wax be applied with a damp pad. If you use water, make sure the surface is dry before you polish it.

Let the wax dry completely as recommended by the manufacturer, then wipe the waxed surface firmly with a clean cloth to remove excess wax. When the waxed surface is even, polish it to a shine with a clean cloth. To complete the finish, apply one or two more coats of wax. Polish each coat completely before applying the next coat.

Wood to be finished with a sealer stain finish must be properly prepared and sanded; no other preparation is necessary. Thoroughly mix the sealer stain. Apply the stain evenly along the grain with a clean brush or cloth, let it stand for 10 to 15 minutes, then wipe off the excess with a clean cloth. Let the finish dry for 24 hours and apply a second coat of stain. To complete the finish, apply one or two coats of paste wax. Polish each coat thoroughly with a clean cloth.

Oils. Hand-rubbed oil finishes can be beautiful, but only if they're properly applied. Oil is penetrating and durable; it is water- and alcohol-resistant and gives the wood an attractive natural sheen and texture. Danish- and tung-oil finishes are far superior to the traditional linseed oil, which is sticky and difficult to apply. Any oil finish must be reapplied periodically, but Danish and tung oil require far less frequent reapplication than linseed oil.

Synthetic Danish oil and natural tung oil are penetrating finishes, but they should be reapplied periodically. Tung-oil finishes are available in semigloss and high-gloss, and in several stain colors. Danish oil usually has a satin finish.

A linseed-oil finish is rich and glossy, but many applications are required for a good finish. The classic linseed-oil finish is a mixture of equal parts of boiled linseed oil and turpentine. There are many variations on this finish. One of the best consists of equal parts of boiled linseed oil, turpentine, and natural varnish. Mix linseed-oil finishes several days before you use them. For most pieces a pint of each ingredient is plenty.

Oil finishes can be applied directly over prepared bare or stained wood. Only water or NGR stains should be used; oil-base stains interfere with the penetration of the oil. Colored tung-oil sealers stain and finish in one operation. Open-grained wood should be filled before an oil finish is applied; any paste filler is compatible.

Wood to be finished with oil must be thoroughly sanded, but no sealing is necessary. Before applying the finish, clean the piece of furniture thoroughly with a tack cloth.

Apply the oil with a clean cheesecloth pad, using a circular or figure-eight motion to work it into the wood. Apply oil evenly and liberally, until the wood has stopped absorbing it; work on one surface at a time. Rub the oil firmly into the wood with the heel of your hand, working along the grain. Continue rubbing for about 15 minutes; as you rub, the warmth you generate will help the oil penetrate into the wood. Danish oil and tung oil may not require extensive rubbing; follow the manufacturer's specific instructions. After thoroughly rubbing all the surfaces, wipe the piece of furniture with a lint-free cloth. You must remove all excess oil; there should be no oil on the surface of the wood, unless you're using a linseed finish, then only a thin film of oil.

Danish oil and tung oil dry more quickly than linseed oil. They can be reapplied after 12 to 24 hours; follow the manufacturer's specific instructions. Linseed-oil finishes must dry for about a week, and drying takes longer in humid weather. Do not recoat a linseed-oil finish until it's completely dry, with no trace of stickiness.

When the first coat of oil is completely dry, apply further coats until the finish is rich and hard. Danish oil and tung-oil sealers may require only one additional application, but linseed-oil finishes should be given 10 to 20 additional coats. Rub each additional coat of oil thoroughly into the wood, then wipe off all excess oil. Let each coat of oil dry thoroughly before applying the next, allowing at least one week between the first several coats, longer between later coats. If the oil isn't completely dry between coats, the finished surface will be sticky and hard to work with.

Special Effects. When you're aiming for a special look, or want an accent piece or a particular decorative effect, there is more to refinishing than the basic finish. With a few special-effect finishing techniques, you can decorate newly finished furniture, refurbish an old piece without stripping it, or add distinction to an inexpensive unfinished piece. Any finish can be dressed up with these techniques. Use your imagination to create any effect you like.

Whatever finish you're working on, it must be clean and smooth. If you're covering it completely, it must be properly prepared. For special effects done with paint or varnish, make sure the materials you use are compatible with the finish on the piece. This is especially important with lacquer finishes.

•Enameling. Unlike clear finishes, enamel can be used over an old finish. It is tough, attractive, and easy to care for. It covers many flaws, including poor-quality or uninteresting wood, badly stained surfaces, and pieces made with different kinds of wood. Used over bare wood or over an old finish, enamel can create a striking accent piece. Used under a glaze, it is the most common base for antiquing a piece of furniture.

Where furniture is concerned, enamel should never be confused with paint. Paint consists of pigments in an application vehicle, or medium. Enamel consists of pigments in a varnish, lacquer, or oil base. While enamel is as tough as varnish, paint produces a soft finish and is not recommended for use on furniture. Oil-based enamel is generally superior to latex.

Enamel is available in high-gloss, semigloss, and flat or matte finishes. If you're enameling a piece of furniture as an accent for a room, you may want a shiny finish, but most fine enameled furniture has a satin finish, not high-gloss. Buy enamel in stock colors, or have it mixed at the paint store.

On bare wood enamel can be used with any filler. Finished surfaces to be enameled must be sealed with thinned shellac. Before enamel is applied, all surfaces should be undercoated. Shiny enamel emphasizes flaws, so surfaces to be covered with this kind of enamel must be smooth. Enamel cannot be used over wax.

Unless a piece of furniture has intricate carvings already clogged by the old finish, stripping is not required before enamel is applied. To prepare a finished piece for enameling, sand it to remove any obvious flaws and chip marks. The surface must be smooth, but it isn't necessary to remove the old finish completely. Clean the sanded wood thoroughly with a tack cloth, and apply a sealer coat of thinned shellac. Let it dry completely, sand the piece lightly with grade 120 sandpaper, and remove the sanding debris with a tack cloth. To prepare a stripped or unfinished piece, sand and seal the wood as for any finish application, and clean it with a tack cloth.

Wood to be finished with enamel must be properly sanded, filled and sealed; finished surfaces must be sanded and sealed. Before applying enamel, clean the piece of furniture thoroughly with a tack cloth.

Undercoat the piece of furniture with commercial enamel undercoat. It is usually white; use it white or have it tinted to match the enamel. It should never be darker than the enamel. Apply the undercoat with a clean, good-quality brush; make sure it is thoroughly mixed. Brush the undercoat smoothly and evenly along the grain of the wood, flowing it on to cover the surface completely. Carefully smooth the surface to even out any thick spots. Brush marks will almost disappear as the undercoat dries.

Let the undercoat dry for at least three days or as directed by the manufacturer. Lightly sand the undercoated surfaces with grade 120 sandpaper. Remove sanding debris with a tack cloth.

When the undercoat is complete, apply the enamel. Use a clean, good-quality brush of the kind specified by the enamel manufacturer. Mix the enamel thoroughly but gently. Apply the enamel with long, smooth strokes, laying it on along the grain or length of the wood in strips the width of the brush. Use enough enamel to flow smoothly onto the surface but not so much that you leave thick spots.

After laying on an even coat of enamel in strips, apply more across the grain or width of the wood to level and even the surface. The enamel should be as even as possible, with no thick or thin spots. As with varnish, a thin coat is better than a thick one. Thick coats of enamel dry slowly and stay soft for a long time.

To finish each surface, tip off the enamel along the grain or length of the wood, using an almost dry brush. Holding the brush at a slight angle to the surface, lightly stroke the surface of the enamel to remove brush marks and even the surface. Smooth the entire enameled surface, working in strips along the grain or length of the wood. As you work, pick off dust and lint with a lint picker. Brush marks will disappear as the enamel dries.

On vertical surfaces enamel is likely to sag or run. Work with a fairly dry brush, applying enamel from dry to wet surfaces. As you finish each surface, carefully inspect it for runs and sags. With the brush in a tipped position, and moving the brush as you come onto the surface with the bristles, tip the finish. Keep the stroke in motion as you come through the sag or run and as the tip of the brush leaves the surface. By keeping the brush in motion before, during, and following the tipping, you will avoid brush marks. Watch the enamel carefully as it dries; sags and runs are especially liable to occur after the enamel has set for 10 to 15 minutes. Tip off sags and runs immediately when you spot them.

Enamel must be applied carefully to prevent thick spots. At outside corners, work from the flat surface toward the corner; lift the brush as it nears the corner and before it flips down over the edge. This prevents a buildup of enamel along the edge. At inside corners, work an inch or two away from the corner, then brush the enamel into the corner, tip it off, and leave it alone. This method prevents buildup on many flat-surface brushings. Spots that tend to hold enamel should be coated just once with enamel and tipped just once with the brush.

Brush lengthwise along rungs, spindles, and other turnings. On carved moldings, apply the finish to the carvings first with a dry brush, then finish the flat surfaces with the tip of the brush. With a dry brush, go over the carvings and then the flats, leveling the finish and removing any fat edges, sags, or runs. On raised panel doors, finish the panels first and then move onto the flat framing. The finish will build up at the miters in the frame where they meet the panel; remove the excess enamel with a dry brush, working from the corner out.

Let the enamel dry for several days or as directed by the manufacturer. Then sand the surface with grade 120 sandpaper and a padded sanding block, and clean the piece of furniture thoroughly with a tack cloth. Apply a second coat of enamel and let it dry completely.

Enamel can be finished in several ways. For a tough, shiny surface, apply a third coat of enamel. Sand the second coat lightly before applying more enamel. Or let the piece of furniture dry for at least a month, and then apply a coat of paste wax and buff it to a shine.

•Antiquing. This technique glazes a base finish to simulate age or create an interesting color effect. Enamel is the most common base for antiquing, but varnished, shellacked, and lacquered surfaces also can be glazed. Antiquing is not recommended for real antiques, but it can work wonders with a thrift-store find or an unfinished piece.

Antiquing kits, sold in paint and hardware stores, include both base enamel and a coordinated or contrasting glaze. Many colors and combinations are available. Any sound flat or gloss enamel, varnish, shellac, or lacquer finish can be treated with glaze. Look for transparent antiquing glaze in muted tones of umber and burnt sienna or in white, gold, black, or other colors. The greater the contrast between base and glaze, and the brighter the glaze color, the more obvious it will be that the furniture is antiqued. If you're working over an existing finish, be sure the glaze is compatible.

A piece of furniture to be antiqued must be clean and in good repair. Remove all hardware. If you're antiquing an unfinished piece of furniture or covering an old finish, sand and seal the wood. On finished pieces to be covered completely, clean the wood thoroughly and then treat it with sanding deglosser to dull the surface. If there are still any shiny spots, buff them with 0000 steel wool. Sand out any chips in the old finish so that the surface is smooth. On pieces to be glazed over an existing finish, clean the wood thoroughly with a detergent solution and dry it well; then wipe it with denatured alcohol. Let the prepared wood dry for 24 hours.

If you're working on an unfinished piece or covering an old finish, apply a base finish coat or flat or gloss enamel. Let the enamel dry completely. If necessary, apply a second base coat. Sand the surface lightly, clean it, and apply the enamel. Let the final coat of enamel dry completely, at least two days.

When the base coat is completely dry or the existing base finish is prepared, apply the antiquing glaze. Use a contrasting color for an obvious antiqued look, a muted umber or burnt sienna to simulate age. Apply the glaze with a clean brush.

Antiquing glaze sets quickly, and the surfaces you glaze first will retain more color than the ones you glaze later. Working on one surface at a time, apply glaze to moldings, carvings, and decorated areas, and then to flat areas. On large surfaces, the glaze can be applied in several stages, if necessary.

Let the glaze dry until it starts to dull, as directed by the manufacturer. Then carefully wipe the glaze off with a soft cloth, flat surfaces first, so that the base coat retains color only at areas to be highlighted. Work from the center of each surface out to the edges, wiping carefully along the grain of the wood. Remove the glaze completely from high spots; leave some of it in low spots, in corners, in carvings or decorations, and along edges and moldings. The surfaces wiped last will retain the most glaze; leave the parts you want to highlight until last. Let the glazed surface dry completely or as directed by the manufacturer.

For a bolder look, you can get different design effects by texturing the glaze with different materials and leaving on more glaze. Before using these texturing methods on a piece of furniture, experiment on a piece of scrap wood given an enamel base coat. Texturing the glaze can be done with almost anything, including cheesecloth, crumpled newspaper, plastic wrap, a sponge, or whatever you have on hand. Remove a little glaze or almost all of it, whichever you prefer. For a wood-grain texture, use a cheesecloth pad; wipe the glaze off in long, even strokes, and then dab it with a scrap piece of carpeting or a stiff-bristled

When the enamel base is dry, brush the glaze on over it, one surface at a time. Cover highlight areas first, then flat surfaces.

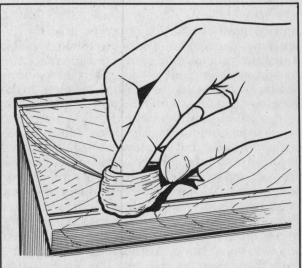

Let the glaze dry until it starts to dull; then wipe it off. Work from the center out, leaving glaze in low spots, in carvings, and along the edges.

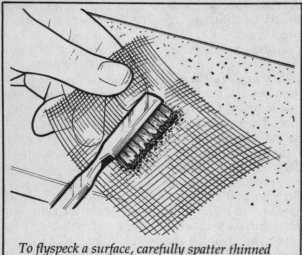

To flyspeck a surface, carefully spatter thinned paint or shellac with a toothbrush, through a piece of wire screening.

brush. Crumpled newspaper or plastic wrap produces a marble effect; a dry sponge makes a random stipple. Use a burlap bag or a towel for a scratched look. For a leather texture, let the glaze get almost dry, then pat it with a piece of fiberglass insulation.

Antiqued finishes can be left uncoated, but for a more durable surface, seal the piece of furniture with semigloss or high-gloss varnish. Make sure the varnish is compatible with the antiqued finish. Apply the varnish directly over the antiquing.

•Flyspecking. Flyspecking is the random spattering of furniture with tiny drops of paint; the effect is of aged and worn wood. Some expensive furniture is flyspecked, but this technique can be especially effective in finishing inexpensive pieces.

Any thin flat black paint can be used for flyspecking. For colored specks use thinned shellac tinted with aniline dye; orange or brown is effective on medium-brown wood. Thin the paint or shellac so that it spatters in fine droplets; make sure it's compatible with the finish.

A piece of furniture to be flyspecked must be clean; if you're finishing the piece, add flyspecking after sealing but before the finish is applied. Before working on a piece of furniture, practice the specking technique on a piece of cardboard or scrap wood. The easiest way to apply the specks is by spattering the thinned paint or shellac through a piece of wire screening. Dip a toothbrush into the paint or shellac, and flick the bristles with your thumb. Work just far enough away from the surface to produce a fine, even spatter. Experiment to find the best brushing angle. Practice until you can cover the test surface evenly, then apply the specks to the piece of furniture.

Flyspecking can be used over an entire surface or to accentuate edges and corners. Apply the

specks in any density, working evenly over the surface. Use only tiny spatters of paint or shellac; to speck an area more heavily, use repeated spatters. Let the flyspecked piece dry completely. Flyspecked surfaces should be sealed with varnish. Apply the varnish directly over the flyspecking after the specks have dried.

•Gilding. Ornate carvings or turnings and carved mirror and picture frames can be finished with gold. The traditional gilding method is to apply gold leaf, which are thin sheets of gold foil. Gold leaf is beautiful and durable, but it is also expensive and isn't used much in furniture work. Bronzing, a more recent technique, is done with powdered gold, either mixed into a vehicle or applied directly; it may fade with time. Bronze powder is made in gold, silver, bronze, copper, and colors; it is often used for stencils on furniture.

The easiest way to apply gold or other metals is wax gilding. Wax gilt is a paste made in gold, silver, bronze, copper, and colors, and sold at craft and art supply stores. It's inexpensive and looks much like gold leaf. For moldings, small-area highlighting, and striping, wax gilt is the best choice. Use it over gold-leaf paint for the best results.

A surface to be gilded must be clean; remove all wax and dirt. If you're working on a picture frame, clean the surface gently with a damp cloth, and let it dry thoroughly.

For the deepest gold effect, paint the area to be gilded with liquid gold-leaf paint, using a 1/2-inch brush. Let the paint dry completely, about 30 minutes, and then apply the wax gilt.

To apply the gilt, dip an artist's brush or a piece of soft cloth into turpentine and then into the gilt. If the gilt is in a tube, squeeze out a little. Wax gilt is thick; apply it sparingly, smoothing it on. Press gently as you work, smoothing or brushing back and forth, to bring out the sheen of the gold. When the entire surface is covered, let the gilt set for about an hour; then carefully buff the surface, in one direction only, with a soft cloth. The buffing distributes and highlights the gilt. No surface protection or further finishing is necessary.

•Stenciling. Whether you want art deco or Pennsylvania Dutch, a drawing or a child's name, stencils are a quick and almost foolproof way of getting your design onto furniture. Stencils can be applied over any finish, but they are easiest to work with when used over varnish that is still tacky. When the surface to be decorated is completely dry, the stencil must be carefully attached so that the edges of the design don't blur. Use paint for informal designs, bronze powder for a more formal effect.

Use stencil paper or architect's linen, available at art supply stores, to make the stencil. If your design has more than one color, make a separate

Spray paint onto the stencil in short, even bursts. To prevent spattering, mask the piece of furniture with paper.

stencil for each color. For large or complex designs, make several small stencils instead of one large one. Trace your design carefully onto the stencil paper or architect's linen, and cut it out with a sharp craft knife. Make sure all corners and curves are sharp and accurate.

Brushing paint over a stencil is tricky and requires a special brush. Use high-gloss or semigloss spray paint or enamel. Make sure the stencil paint is compatible with the finish.

Surfaces to be stenciled must be clean; remove all wax and dirt. If you're decorating a newly varnished piece of furniture, work while the varnish is still tacky. Carefully press the stencil into place on the tacky surface, smoothing it down flat on the wood. Make sure all cut edges adhere to the varnish, but be careful not to touch the varnish or you'll leave fingerprints. On dry surfaces attach the stencil carefully with masking tape. If the finish is new, make sure it's completely set or the tape may damage it. Mask the entire piece of furniture with newspaper.

Spray paint onto the stencil in short, even applications. Cover the stencil surface completely, but don't let the paint get thick enough to sag or drip. Let the paint dry almost completely, then remove the stencil. Repeat the process for each color of the design, making sure each color is completely dry before applying the next color.

Bronze powder must be applied over varnish. If you're working on a newly varnished piece of furniture, apply the stencil while the varnish is still tacky. If you're working on an old or completely dry finish, apply a thin coat of varnish over the surface to be stenciled, and let it dry until it's just tacky. This should take between 30 minutes and two hours. Make sure that the varnish is compatible with the existing finish. Carefully press the stencil into place on the varnished surface, smoothing it down flat. Make sure all cut edges adhere to the varnish, but be

careful not to touch the varnish. Masking the piece of furniture is unnecessary.

Apply the bronze powder with a piece of velvet or soft flannel over your index finger, or make a small pad out of the fabric. Working with only a little powder, dip the velvet into the bronze powder and smudge it into the exposed areas of the stencil. Bronze powder can be applied evenly, but you can give your design depth by shading it and rounding your strokes. Work from the edges in to bronze each area of the stencil.

Repeat the process for each color of the design. If you must overlap stencils to apply the colors, let the varnish dry completely between colors. Remove excess bronze powder with warm water and a soft brush, then blot the wood dry and let it air-dry for about an hour. Apply another thin coat of varnish to the unfinished area, let it get tacky, and repeat the stenciling process. When the design is complete, let it dry and then remove excess bronze powder.

To prevent damage to paint or bronze powder, stenciled surfaces should be sealed with varnish. Apply the varnish directly over the stenciled designs.

•Striping. On enameled or antiqued furniture, edge stripes can add distinction to flat surfaces. Use one thin border stripe or paint multiple stripes or geometric borders. Tabletops, chair seats, and similar areas are good candidates for striping, but any flat surface can be decorated with stripes. Use high-gloss or semigloss enamel, slightly thinned. Make sure it's compatible with the existing finish.

Freehand stripes take a steady hand and a good brush, but they aren't difficult on a small piece. The surface to be striped must be clean; remove all wax and dirt. Use a good-quality artist's brush, with a small diameter and a good point. Practice striping on a piece of cardboard before you work on a piece of furniture.

Stripes close to the edge of a surface can be applied without a straightedge or other guide. Hold the brush with your thumb and first two fingers, and rest your other two fingers on the edge of the surface. Keeping the brush steady on the surface, draw your hand along the edge. This method is effective for edge stripes on curved or straight surfaces. For stripes too far from an edge for this technique, use a yardstick as a guide to draw your hand along. Have an assistant hold the stick in place while you paint.

Apply enamel carefully, loading the brush enough to make a complete stripe but not enough to blob or drip. Keep your pressure steady as you draw the brush along the edge of the surface. If the brush doesn't hold its point or spreads out too far, try turning it as you draw it along. This will re-form the brush as you work.

For double stripes or designs with more than one color, let each stripe dry completely before

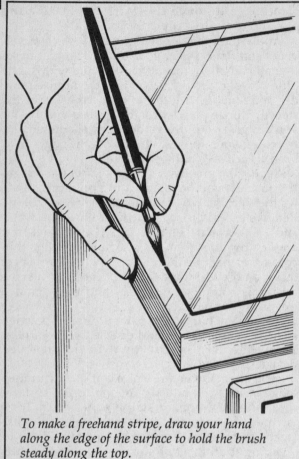

To make a freehand stripe, draw your hand along the edge of the surface to hold the brush steady along the top.

you paint the next one. Work from the inside stripe out to avoid smudging.

On long edges or for wide stripes, use masking tape to define the stripes. The surface must be clean, with all wax and dirt removed. Carefully press the tape along the surface, making sure it is straight and at a consistent distance from the edge. Seal the edges of the tape carefully to keep the paint from seeping under it by pressing each tape edge along its length with your thumbnail.

Apply the enamel with a good-quality artist's brush, roughly the same width as the masked stripe. Use enough paint to cover the surface completely, but smooth it out well; don't let the stripe get thick or uneven. Let the paint dry completely, then remove the tape, pulling it gently away from the surface. Do not leave the tape on the surface for more than 12 hours, or it may damage the finish.

For double stripes or designs with more than one color, let each stripe dry completely before you tape the next one. Apply tape carefully where stripes cross, to keep it from damaging the earlier stripe. Work from the inside of the surface toward the edges.

To prevent damage to the stripes, the surface should be sealed with varnish. Apply the varnish directly over the stripes.

•Decals. On informal furniture decals can add a down-home, cheerful touch. They shouldn't be used on expensive furniture, but they look right on some Early American reproductions. Pennsylvania Dutch decals or other country designs can be attractive on kitchen furniture or in a child's room. Home center and hardware stores often carry decals, but you'll probably find a better selection at a craft or art supply store.

A surface to be decorated with decals must be clean; remove all wax and dirt. Decals consist of a printed image on a varnished or lacquered paper base. To apply a decal, soak it in warm water until the paper loosens; then carefully smooth the decal onto the surface to be decorated and peel off the backing paper.

If you don't like the effect of a decal or if it isn't positioned correctly, peel it off while it's still wet, dip it into warm water again, and reapply it. To remove dry decals, buy special decal-removing strips. Soak the remover strip in warm water as directed by the manufacturer, and place it over the decal to be removed. Let it set for about 30 minutes or as directed, then peel off the decal.

To prevent damage to the decals, the surface should be sealed with varnish. Apply the varnish directly over the decals.

Making Structural Repairs

Structural problems in furniture are defined in three ways: the material itself, the way it's put together, and the way it functions. The material itself is the problem when a part is broken, warped, or missing. The way it's put together is involved when joints fail or parts aren't fitted properly. The way a piece of furniture functions depends on both material and construction. Functional problems always can be traced to one or both sources. Nothing can turn an all-around loser into a quality piece of furniture, but with a few basic repair techniques, you can handle most structural problems. If you plan to refinish a piece of furniture, make structural repairs after stripping off the old finish and before preparing the piece for refinishing.

With extensive structural repairs, where parts are missing or support is inadequate, you'll probably need wood to match the piece of furniture. Pine and oak are sold at most lumberyards and at home centers, but other furniture woods, including walnut, cherry, and mahogany, are harder to come by. Woodworking and millwork outlets usually stock and sell a variety of hardwood. Don't overlook auctions, used furniture outlets, and wrecking contractors; you may be able to pick up some real bargains in wood or old furniture.

Whenever possible, repairs should be made with the same wood used in the piece of furniture. If you can't find the wood you need, use a light-colored wood, such as maple, gum, birch, or even pine. It's always easier to stain a light repair area than to refinish an entire piece of furniture to match one part or patch. You also may be able to borrow a piece of wood from a hidden part of the piece, such as a drawer bottom or a back leg. Use the borrowed wood to make the repair, and use the new wood to replace the borrowed wood.

REBUILDING LOOSE JOINTS

When a joint fails, you have two problems to deal with: the immediate functional problem and the long-term effect of the failure on the rest of the frame. A loose joint that is not repaired today may not break tomorrow, but it will put stress on other joints. In time, one wobbly leg may become two. To prevent simple structural problems from turning into more serious ones, loose or separated joints should be repaired immediately.

Basic joint repair techniques can be applied to all kinds of furniture, but each kind of frame has its own individual structural problems. Chairs are prone to broken rungs and split seats, tabletops warp, drawers stick or tip, and caning and upholstery wear out.

Gluing. The simplest solution is usually the best one. When you discover a loose joint, first make sure the screws (if there are any) are tight, then try to repair the joint with an adhesive, such as plastic resin, epoxy, or resorcinol. Force the adhesive into the loose joint with a glue injector. If you can, wiggle the joint to distribute the adhesive. Clamp the joint for about a day, until the adhesive is completely cured. If possible, strengthen the glued joint with a glue block.

After gluing the loose joint, put the piece of furniture back into service. Check the joint again in a few weeks. If it has worked loose again, it can't be permanently repaired by gluing. You'll have to reinforce it, resecure it, or rebuild it completely.

Reinforcing: Glue Blocks and Steel Braces. Glue blocks are solid pieces of wood used to reinforce joints and provide additional support. Steel corner plates and angle braces perform the same functions, but they can lower the value of a piece of furniture. Valuable pieces of furniture, antiques, and good reproductions should always be repaired with glue blocks instead of steel braces.

Glue blocks for corner braces can be either square or triangular. Square blocks are used chiefly as outside support braces. Triangular glue blocks usually are preferable.

Glue blocks can be cut from any square stock, but hardwood is preferred. To make a glue block, cut a square piece of wood in half diagonally. The larger the piece of wood, the greater the gluing

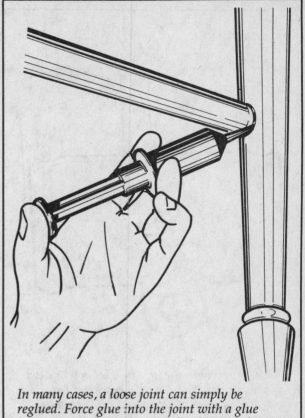

In many cases, a loose joint can simply be reglued. Force glue into the joint with a glue injector, and clamp the piece firmly until the adhesive is cured.

surface of the block. The length of the blocks will depend on the project. To strengthen chair and table legs, cut triangular braces from 1-inch nominal boards, as long as necessary. At the right-angle corner of the block, cut off a diagonal or make a notch to fit around the leg.

To install a triangular glue block, spread adhesive on the two right-angle sides. Set the block into the corner, and twist it to distribute the adhesive on the bonding surfaces. Small glue blocks can be strengthened by nails driven through the block and into the furniture frame; drill pilot holes for the nails to make sure you don't split the wood. To strengthen chair and table braces, drive three screws through the block and into the frame: one screw straight into the corner and one straight into each side at an angle to the inside block edge. Predrill the screw holes in both block and frame.

Sometimes a corner joint is held by a steel bracket instead of a glue block. If the leg wobbles, first make sure the nut that holds the bracket is securely tightened. If this doesn't solve the problem and the bracket is set into notches in the frame, it may not be seated properly. Remove the nut and reseat the bracket, then replace the nut securely.

Resecuring: Screws and Glue. If a loose joint would be difficult to take apart, you may be able

Some corner joints are held by steel brackets, set into notches in the frame. If a bracketed leg wobbles, tighten the bracket nut; if necessary, reseat the bracket.

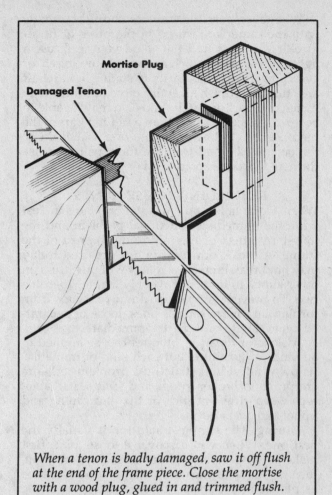

When a tenon is badly damaged, saw it off flush at the end of the frame piece. Close the mortise with a wood plug, glued in and trimmed flush.

to solve the problem with a long screw. Align the joint and drill a pilot hole for the screw. Then enlarge the top of the pilot hole so that a dowel plug can be installed over the screw head. Coat the screw with glue and drive it into the joint so that it pulls the joint tightly together. Before you tighten the screw, try to force adhesive into the loose joint; this will help strengthen the joint. Then tighten the screw firmly.

To cover the screw head, insert and glue a dowel plug into the enlarged hole. The end of the plug will protrude above the surface of the frame. Sand it smooth. You'll probably refinish the frame so the dowel matches, and you may want to install false dowel plugs at the other joints in the frame so that they match. The dowels will give the frame a hand-made pinned, or pegged, look.

A screw and plug also can be used to repair loose rungs and backs, but the pieces involved must be large enough to accept the screw and dowel. Small parts such as turnings and slats may split when a screw is driven into them.

For the strongest screw-reinforced joint, the screw should be driven into a piece of dowel instead of into the frame itself. This isn't always possible, but if you can, disassemble the joint, drill a hole at the screw point, and plug the hole with a dowel, gluing the dowel into place. Then reassemble the joint with a screw and glue. If you want to hide the head of the screw, enlarge the hole for a dowel plug, or countersink the screw and fill the depression with wood putty.

Rebuilding: Disassembly and Doweling. Rebuilding a joint is not as tough as it might sound, although it does require patience. You must work slowly to make sure all the parts are in the right places and all parts fit tightly. To disassemble the joint, pull it carefully apart. If it doesn't come apart easily, use a rubber mallet to tap the frame pieces apart, but be careful not to damage the wood. Don't overlook the possibility that the joint was assembled with nails or screws as well as adhesive. You should remove the fasteners before you break the adhesive. If you can't remove them, break the adhesive bond and pry the joint apart carefully. Don't force the joint apart; if the nails or screws are embedded too firmly, you'll split or splinter the wood. If prying would damage the wood, consider sawing the joint apart. Use a hacksaw with a thin blade that will go through metal and not leave a wide cut.

After the joint is disassembled, it must be thoroughly cleaned. If the old adhesive is brittle or crumbling, scrape it off with a knife or a narrow chisel. If it is difficult to remove, use sandpaper, hot water, or a hot vinegar solution. You must remove all dirt and old adhesive.

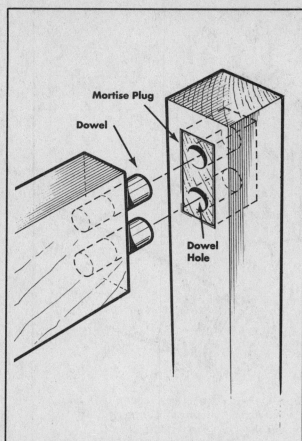

Use dowels to rebuild the joint. Drill holes in the end of the frame piece, where the tenon was, and in the mortise; then glue the dowels into place.

Whatever method you use, be careful not to damage the wood, or the joint won't fit together properly when you reassemble it. Structural problems are most common in chairs and tables, and the joints involved are usually mortise-and-tenon. The tenon usually is worn or broken. If the damage isn't too bad, you may be able to clean the joint and then reassemble it with epoxy. This is a good joint filler as well as a bonding agent. Wipe off any excess epoxy after assembling the joint, and clamp the joint until the epoxy is completely dry. Keep the piece of furniture out of service for a week to make sure the glue has cured properly.

If the tenon is badly damaged or the joint was sawed apart, you'll have to rebuild the joint with hardwood dowels in place of the tenon. Two dowels are adequate for most joints. Use dowels about the same width and about twice the length of the damaged tenon. Cut off the damaged tenon, and remove any broken wood from the mortise. Plug the mortise completely with a wood plug, glued in and trimmed flush with the surface. Then use dowels to connect the parts again.

To make the holes for the dowels in the tenon base and in the plugged mortise use a doweling jig clamped to the edge of the wood and adjusted to center the dowel holes. Dowel center points also can be used, but they aren't as accurate as a jig. Drill the holes to a total depth of about 1/4-inch deeper than the length of the dowels to allow for glue buildup under the dowels.

Score the sides of the dowels with pliers and round the ends with sandpaper or a file. This improves glue distribution, and makes insertion easier and more accurate. Apply glue to the dowels and insert them into the holes in one side of the joint; then coat the edge of the wood with glue and slip the other joint piece onto the dowels. Tap the joint together with a rubber mallet, wipe off any glue that oozes out of the joint, and clamp the joint firmly for about a day, until the glue is completely set.

REPAIRING CHAIRS
Humidity, uneven flooring, accidents, and everyday wear and tear subject chairs to stress that can loosen joints, split seats, and break arms, legs, and spindles. Here is how to repair an ailing chair:

Loose Joints. Seat frames are held by mortise-and-tenon or doweled joints supported by triangular glue blocks, notched to fit the legs. If you catch a loose joint in time, repair it with glue. If the joint is broken, you'll have to disassemble it and replace the dowels, as detailed before. Triangular glue blocks probably will be glued and screwed to the frame, and the dowel joint

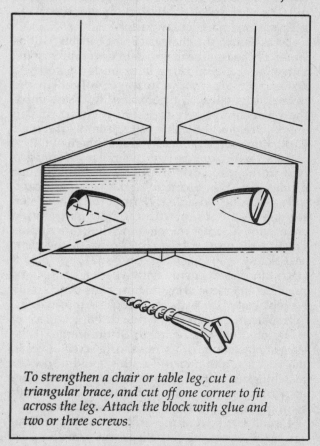

To strengthen a chair or table leg, cut a triangular brace, and cut off one corner to fit across the leg. Attach the block with glue and two or three screws.

might even be supported with hidden nail or screw fasteners. Separate the joint carefully with an old screwdriver or a stiff-blade putty knife, then replace the dowels. Make sure the joint is clean and dry before you begin to reassemble it.

Sometimes you can use a mechanical fastener, such as an angle brace or a chair-leg brace, to mend the frame. This depends on the value of the furniture; do not lower the value of an antique with a piece of metal. Metal reinforcements are useless unless the joint is tightly fitted together, but they can be used to make a firm joint stronger. Fasten the braces with brass screws, and make sure the screws are long enough.

Fasten the metal angle to one side of the chair frame; predrill the screw holes. Insert a piece of thin cardboard under the opposite part of the angle; then drill the screw holes for that side. Drive in the screws tight, remove the cardboard, and finish tightening the screws. When the screws are final-tightened, the angle will pull the joint tightly together to bridge the gap left by the cardboard.

Back Rails, Spindles, and Slats. On chairs with horizontal rails across the back, the rails are mortised into the side posts. On chairs with vertical spindles or slats, these parts are mortised into a curved or straight top rail. Rails, spindles, and slats can be replaced easily, but replacement may be expensive, so don't bother if the chair isn't worth the investment. To replace a broken or missing part, have a millwork or woodworking shop custom make a new part.

Disassemble the chair back; it probably will be joined at the legs, seat, and rail. Carefully pry the joints apart, removing any nails or screws. Disassemble only the joints involved in the repair; it usually isn't necessary to disassemble the piece completely to get at the part. If you aren't sure you'll be able to reassemble the chair back, number the parts as you take them out.

Take the broken part and a similar undamaged part to the millwork or woodworking shop for duplication. When you have the new part, carefully clean the old adhesive from the joints. Then reassemble the chair with the new part, gluing each joint. Clamp the chair with strap clamps until the adhesive dries, then refinish the chair completely.

Outdoor chairs made with wooden slats can be repaired the same way, but the slats can usually be replaced with wide moldings or thin boards. To replace a broken slat, cut and shape a piece of wide molding or a board to fit the frame. If the slats are fastened with screws, drill screw holes in the new slat and attach it with the old screws or matching new ones. If they're fastened with rivets, drill the old rivets out, and replace them with self-tapping or pan-head sheet-metal screws.

Loose Legs, Rungs, and Spindles. Loose rungs, spindles, and loose legs can sometimes be

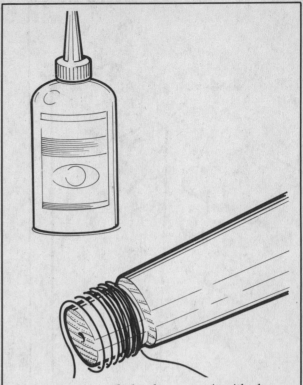

If the tenon is cracked or loose, coat it with glue and wrap it with silk thread. Let the glue dry; then glue the tenon back into its socket.

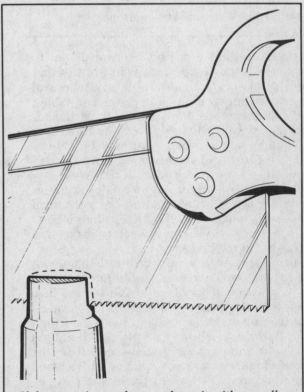

If the tenon is very loose, enlarge it with a small wedge. Saw straight into the tenon, and cut a thin wedge to fit the saw cut.

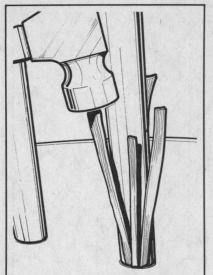

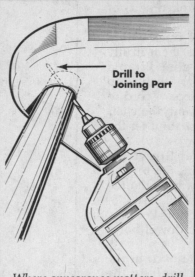

Drill to
Joining Part

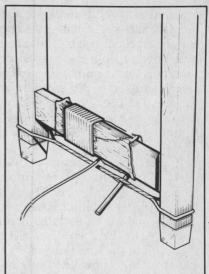

Extremely loose joints can be wedged from the outside. Dip thin wedges in glue and pound them in around the loose part.

Where appearance matters, drill through the side of the joint into the loose part. Pin the joint with a nail through the drilled hole.

Wrap a piece of waxed paper around the glued part, bind it with cord, and clamp it firmly until the glue is dry.

mended by forcing glue into the joints, but a part mended this way may work loose again. For a more permanent repair, carefully separate the part from the frame. If both ends are loose, remove the entire piece. For stubborn joints twist the part to break the glue bond. If necessary, use self-locking pliers, padding them to prevent damage to the wood.

Remove the old adhesive completely from the part and from its socket; glue does not bond well to old glue. Be careful not to remove any wood from the end of the part, or it won't fit right. After removing the old glue, test each end of the part in its socket. If the ends fit snugly, apply glue to the sockets and reinsert the loose part. Clamp the reglued part and let it dry completely.

If the part is loose in its socket, you'll have to enlarge it to make a firm joint. If the tenon end is cracked, you'll have to reinforce it. Apply a thin coat of glue to the tenon, and wrap it tightly with silk thread. If necessary, apply more glue and cover the tenon with another layer of thread. Let the threaded tenon dry for a day, then glue the reinforced end into the mortise. Insert the tenon carefully so you don't disturb the thread. Clamp the joint, and let it dry completely.

Loose legs or rungs can be wedged to fit if the tenon is sound. Clamp the part in a vise or have a helper hold it; then saw carefully into the center of the tenon's end. The cut must be square and centered, roughly the depth of the part that fits into the mortise. For small parts use a hacksaw or a coping saw to make the cut; for thicker parts, use a backsaw or a combination saw.

From a piece of pine quarter round, cut a thin wedge to fit the width and depth of the saw cut in the tenon. The object here is to spread the saw cut with the wedge, enlarging the tenon to fit the mortise. When you're satisfied that the wedge is the right size, carefully tap the wedge into the saw cut. When the tenon is enlarged, stop pounding and trim off any excess wood from the wedge with a utility knife or a pocketknife. Be careful not to pound the wedge too far; excessive wedging will split the tenon. To test the wedge, insert the end of it into the saw cut and tap it down with a screwdriver handle. If you see the wood on both sides of the cut start to spread, the wedge is too wide. Finally, apply glue and reassemble the joint.

You may not be able to disassemble the piece of furniture for this wedging procedure. There are two ways to do the job. If the joint is extremely loose, and appearance is not important, remove as much adhesive as you can. Make several thin wedges from pine lattice. Dip the ends of the wedges in adhesive and drive the wedges with a hammer around the loose part, between the part and the mortise. With a utility knife, trim the ends of the wedges flush with the surrounding wood surface. Equalize the pressure from the wedges as you drive them in; unless you place them carefully, the wedges can pull the part out of alignment and weaken the joint.

Where appearance is more important, drill a 1/16-inch hole into the side of the joint through the loose part. Then make a pin from a 10d common or finishing nail. Cut off the head of the nail with a hacksaw; apply a drop or two of glue to the drilled hole and drive in the nail. Countersink the pin with a nail set, and fill the hole with wood filler.

Broken Rungs and Spindles. Splits and breaks in nonstructural rungs and spindles can be repaired with glue. Separate the broken ends of the part and apply glue to each piece. If the part is only cracked, force glue into the crack with a glue injector. Join the pieces, press them firmly together, and remove any excess glue. Wrap a piece of waxed paper around the part, then wrap the mended break firmly with a piece of cord to keep the part aligned properly. Clamp the chair firmly with a strap clamp or a rope, and let the glue dry completely.

Broken Arms, Legs, and Other Structural Parts. Where strength is important, the broken part must be reinforced. The best way to pin the broken pieces together is with a dowel. Use 1/8-inch to 3/8-inch doweling, depending on how thick the broken part is. Drill the dowel holes with a bit of the same size.

Separate the broken ends of the part. In the center of one end and at a right angle to the break, drill a 1-inch-deep hole, the same diameter as the dowel. This hole marks the dowel location. Insert a dowel center point into the hole, point out. To mark the dowel location on the other piece of the broken part, match the pieces and press them firmly together to force the point of the dowel center point into the center of the matching piece of the broken part. Pull the pieces apart, and remove the dowel center point; then drill straight into the second piece at the marked point, about 1 inch deep.

Measure the dowel holes, and cut a piece of dowel 1/4 inch shorter than their total depth to allow for glue buildup. Score the sides of the dowel with pliers and round the ends with sandpaper or a file to improve glue distribution and make insertion easier. Apply glue to one end of the dowel and insert it into the hole in one end; then apply glue to the protruding dowel and to the face of the break, and push the other piece of the broken part onto the dowel. Match the parts perfectly, wipe off excess adhesive, and clamp the mended part.

Where doweling isn't possible or where you want to provide extra strength, use a steel mending plate to reinforce the break. Mending plates can be used on any flat surface. Glue the break, and let it dry completely. Then add a mending plate, long enough to span the break and narrow enough to be inconspicuous; use a plate with screw holes beveled to accept flathead screws.

Place the mending plate on the inside or least-obvious face of the mended part. If appearance doesn't matter, secure the plate directly over the break, using flathead brass screws. For a less conspicuous repair, mortise the plate into the wood. Carefully trace the outline of the mending plate onto the wood with a scratch awl or a sharp nail. Score the wood along the outline with a series of straight-down chisel cuts, as deep as you want the mortise, allowing space to cover the plate with wood filler. Score the wood at right angles

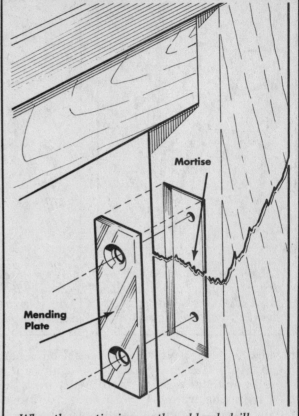

When the mortise is smooth and level, drill screw holes and glue the mending plate into place. Secure it with flathead screws, and cover it with wood filler.

to the outline; then turn the chisel over, bevel side down, and remove the excess wood in the scored outline, working with the grain of the wood and removing only a little wood at a time.

When the bottom of the mortise is smooth and level, test the plate for fit, and make the necessary adjustments. When the plate fits exactly, drill pilot holes for the screws and coat the mortise with a thin layer of glue. Dip the screws in glue, position the plate in the mortise, and drive in the screws. Let the glue dry for several days, and then cover the mending plate evenly with wood filler or a veneer patch; finish the filler to match the wood.

Split Seats. Split chair seats can be repaired with a series of 1/4-inch dowels along the break, reinforced with metal mending plates. The seat must be completely removed for doweling.

Drill holes for the dowels in each side of the broken seat, about 1 inch deep and spaced 4 to 6 inches apart. Use a doweling jig, clamped to the broken seat, to drill the dowel holes; dowel center points also can be used, but they aren't as accurate. Cut each dowel 1/4 inch less than the total length of the dowel holes.

Apply glue to one end of each dowel, and insert the dowels into the holes along one side of

FURNITURE

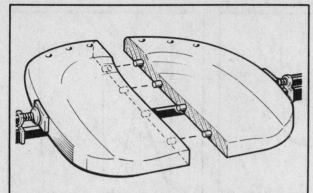

Repair a split chair seat with a series of 1/4-inch dowels, placed about 4 inches apart along the split. Clamp the seat firmly until the glue is completely cured.

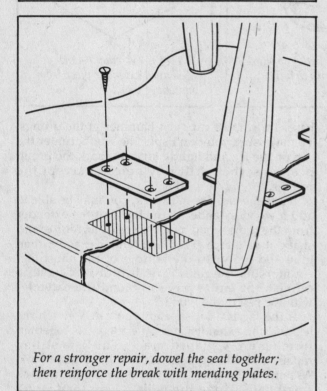

For a stronger repair, dowel the seat together; then reinforce the break with mending plates.

the broken seat; then apply glue to the protruding dowel ends and to the broken edge, and join the two parts. Tap the pieces of the seat together with a rubber mallet, and wipe off any excess glue. Clamp the glued seat, and let it dry for at least two days. For extra strength you can add metal mending plates to span the break.

Insert Chair Seats. Chair seats set in or on frames are usually boards or plywood, covered with padding and cloth. These seats seldom split, but when they do, the simplest solution is to replace the seat with a new piece of 3/8-inch plywood. If 3/8-inch plywood won't fit properly after the padding has been added, you may have to use 1/4-inch plywood. Use the old chair seat as a pattern to cut out the new one.

Padded chair seats are usually held to the frame with screws driven through glue blocks. Look carefully for these screws; the cloth covering the padding may hide them. Remove all fasteners, and replace them the same way to hold the new chair seat.

If the upholstery on insert seats is worn or damaged, it can easily be replaced. Dining room chairs are usually padded with cotton batting; some chairs have foam padding or a combination of foam and cotton. Both kinds of padding are available precut for chair seats. The padding should be about 3/4 inch to 1 inch thick.

To recover an insert chair seat remove the seat from the chair. The seat is usually a piece of plywood, held to the chair frame by screws; the screws may be counterbored into the frame or may go up through the corner glue blocks. Remove the tacks or staples that hold the old upholstery fabric to the seat, and lift off the fabric. If refinishing is necessary, refinish the chair before proceeding further.

Using the old fabric as a pattern, cut the new fabric to fit. If the old padding on the chair seat is in good shape, it can be reused; if it's damaged, replace it with new padding. You may be able to fluff and smooth old cotton padding. If it's badly flattened, add a layer of foam padding to build the seat cushion up to 3/4 to 1 inch.

Lay the new fabric flat, wrong side up, and center the padded seat on it upside down. Fold the edges of the fabric up over the seat, stretching it firmly onto the plywood; if needed, tape the fabric firmly down with masking tape. Starting at the center of one side, fold the fabric under and attach it to the seat with heavy-duty staples. If the new fabric is heavy, flathead upholstery tacks may be more secure. Set staples or tacks 1 to 1 1/2 inches apart along the side of the seat.

When the first side is completely attached, restretch the fabric; then staple or tack the opposite side. Turn the seat over and smooth the padding; be sure the fabric is straight, with no wrinkles. Then turn the seat over again and fasten the other two sides. At the corners fold the fabric in to miter it neatly; if necessary, staple or tack each layer separately. Staple a scrap piece of the new fabric to the seat in case repairs are necessary in the future.

Replace the chair seat in the frame, and secure it. Replace all the screws and tighten them firmly.

REPAIRING LEGS AND FEET

The legs and feet of furniture pieces, especially heavy cabinets, dressers, and bookcases, are subjected to great stress. Pushing a heavily loaded piece of furniture can cause problems even if it doesn't cause immediate breakage, and these problems are common in old pieces.

Loose Casters. A caster is secured by a metal rod, driven into a hole drilled in the bottom of the

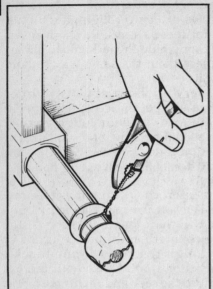

When the leg is split, remove the caster completely; glue the split together and bind the leg with wire to reinforce the break.

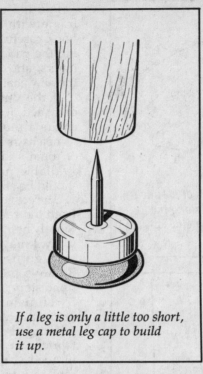

If a leg is only a little too short, use a metal leg cap to build it up.

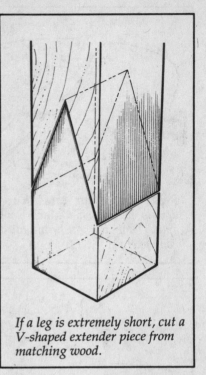

If a leg is extremely short, cut a V-shaped extender piece from matching wood.

leg. When the piece of furniture is moved, stress on the caster rod can damage the wood around it, enlarging the hole and loosening the caster. If the damage isn't too bad, the casters may be loose. If it's been ignored for too long, the casters may fall out when the piece is lifted, or the ends of the legs may be split. Both problems can be solved.

To tighten loose casters, use metal or plastic caster sleeve inserts, available in several sizes. Remove the loose caster and tap the insert into the hole in the leg; no adhesive is needed. The sleeve should fit snugly; if it doesn't, use larger inserts. Insert the caster into the sleeve; this should solve the problem.

If the leg is split, remove all the casters on the piece. Apply glue along the split, and press the glued edges firmly together; wipe off any excess. To reinforce the break, bind the split with several wraps of fine black steel wire. On many pieces of furniture there is a ridge or a crevice at the caster point; if you wrap the wire around the leg at this point, the repair will not be obvious. If the leg doesn't have any carving or decoration at this point, you can notch the wood all the way around with a triangular file, and then wrap the wire in the notch. Treat all legs the same way so that they match.

One Leg Shorter Than the Rest. When this happens, you may be tempted to cut the other legs down to match the shorter one, but don't do it. Build up the short leg to match the others. Cutting usually results in serious mismatching, besides shortening the piece and ruining its design.

If the leg is only a little too short, use a metal leg cap to build it up. These caps, made in several sizes, have from one to three prongs on a metal base. To install a cap, just hammer in the prongs. To make sure you don't split the wood, center the cap on the leg and lightly tap it to mark the prong positions; then drill tiny holes to accept the prongs.

If a metal cap doesn't work, you may be able to add a wood extender to the leg. Cut the extender from the same wood as the piece of furniture, and shape it to match. Fit the extender exactly, then glue and nail it to the bottom of the short leg; countersink the nails. You'll probably have to refinish the entire piece to blend the extender with the rest of the wood.

If the leg is a lot shorter, you can V-notch the leg and the extender and glue the parts together, forming an A-shaped brace. This is a strong repair, and will give the piece a handmade look. Assemble the joint with glue and countersink small nails; drive the nails where they won't show, and fill the holes with wood filler. Even if the holes are visible, the repair won't look bad.

REPAIRING DOORS AND OTHER FLAT PARTS

A door that is splitting, sagging, or binding is only going to get worse until you do something about the problem. Door repairs are simple.

Splits. Split doors, panels, cabinet backs, and other flat parts should be repaired with glue and dowels. Thin door panels and cabinet backs cannot be repaired and should be replaced. Where appearance is not important, as on the back of a door that is always left closed, metal mending plates can be used for reinforcement.

Sagging or Binding Doors. Sagging is usually caused by faulty hinge operation; make sure the

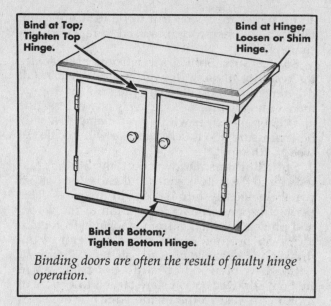

Bind at Top; Tighten Top Hinge.

Bind at Hinge; Loosen or Shim Hinge.

Bind at Bottom; Tighten Bottom Hinge.

Binding doors are often the result of faulty hinge operation.

hinges are working properly. Binding can be caused by faulty hinges or by excess humidity. Swelling from humidity is most common in spring and summer, and is most likely to affect wood that hasn't been properly sealed. In fall and winter, when the humidity is lower, the wood will shrink again.

Before you work on the wood, adjust the hinges. If the door binds at the top on the latch side, the top hinge is probably loose; tighten the screws. If the door binds at the bottom on the latch side, the bottom hinge probably needs tightening. If the door binds on the hinge side, the hinges may be too tight, or may be mortised too deeply into the wood. Remove the affected hinge or hinges, add a shim of thin cardboard under each, then replace the hinges.

If hinge adjustment doesn't work, you'll have to remove some wood at the binding points. Be careful in removing any wood; use sandpaper. To prevent future swelling, seal the raw edge with shellac when the weather and the wood are dry.

Replacing Door Panels. Many cabinets have flat door panels, either veneered or covered with cloth, cane, metal, or glass. Split panels should be replaced. If the covering of one panel is damaged, all panels should be recovered, if necessary, to match.

Door and drawer panels are usually held in place by molding strips nailed around the edges, sometimes surface-mounted and sometimes set into a rabbet joint. These molding strips may be hard to see, but by carefully prying around the panel, you'll be able to see the way in which they are attached.

To replace or recover a panel, remove the molding, using a butt chisel, a knife blade, or the tip of a screwdriver. Be careful not to damage either the molding or the wood. After removing the molding on all four sides, lift the damaged panel out of the frame. Some raised door panels

are fastened with screws from the back of the door frame; these screws must be removed before the panel can be taken out. Raised panel doors may be in one piece; the panel usually cannot be removed. To repair this kind of door, remove the door from its hinges.

On old furniture, door panels often require special repair techniques. If the panels are held by moldings, remove the moldings carefully. Try not to bend or damage the nails that hold the moldings; it's best to reuse these nails when you replace the moldings. If the panel is held in the frame in grooves (dadoes), the best way to remove it is to soften the adhesive around the panel with heat or moisture—a hot towel is a good tool. Most old furniture was put together with animal or fish glue, and this adhesive usually can be softened. If this method doesn't work, take the piece to a professional; the door must be taken completely apart.

Panels set in square or rectangular frames are seldom really square. To cut a replacement for any panel, use the old panel as a pattern. Don't try to force a replacement panel in or you may break the frame; if necessary, cut the panel down to fit the frame.

REPAIRING DRAWERS

A drawer's main job is to slide in and out smoothly. When one doesn't or a front or bottom splits, take these measures to repair it:

Loose Joints. Drawer-frame construction is similar to chair construction, with dovetail joints in old or expensive furniture or butt joints, glued and held with corrugated nails, in newer furniture. Dovetail joints seldom separate; if they do, force adhesive into the loose joint and tap the joint together with a hammer. Butt joints are another problem. To tighten a loose butt joint, try gluing the joint and tapping it together as tightly as you can; clamp it firmly until the glue is dry. If this doesn't work, you may be able to nail the joint through the face of the drawer; countersink the nail heads and fill the holes with wood filler.

Binding. Problems with drawer frames are usually the cause of sticking and binding drawers. When a drawer sticks, it's jerked to get it open and slammed closed; this causes the joints in the frame to separate. First make sure the joints are tight. Then lubricate the drawer guides and the top and bottom edges of the sides with stick lubricant, wax from a candle, paraffin, or silicone spray. Do not use a petroleum lubricant; oil will collect dirt and dust, and cause more problems than the binding.

If lubrication doesn't solve the problem, carefully sand down the binding points. Remove only as much wood as necessary, and seal the raw wood with shellac to prevent future swelling. If sanding doesn't eliminate binding, examine the drawer's runners and guides.

Worn Guides and Runners. Drawers are built with wood or metal runners, and move back and forth on guides or tracks. In old furniture, the runners are parallel pieces of wood fastened to the drawer bottom, and the guides are strips of wood across the frame. Sometimes the runners or guides are missing; sometimes they're split, warped, or badly worn. Rough guides or runners can cause the drawer to bind.

If the drawer guide is missing, install metal guides, available in several lengths and sold in hardware stores and home centers. Complete installation instructions are provided with the guides. If a wood drawer guide is rough, smooth it carefully with sandpaper. If the drawer still binds, remove the guide completely. Break a hacksaw blade in half and wrap one end of it with electrician's tape; wearing gloves, cut the guide out with short strokes of the saw blade.

After removing the old guide, you may be able to install metal guides. For a neater job, cut and fit a new wooden guide, the same size as the old one. Use hardwood to make the guide; softwood wears too quickly. Glue the new guide into position and secure it with nails; countersink the nail heads so they won't interfere with the drawer's operation.

When the runners are worn, the drawer moves unevenly because the wood is uneven. To replace a worn runner, plane and rabbet the worn edge to form an even, smoothly mortised strip along the drawer edge. Glue a thin strip of hardwood into each mortised runner edge, building it up to its original height. Secure the runners with small nails, and countersink the nails so that they won't interfere with the drawer's operation.

If the drawer frame has a wood kicker above the sides, and the kicker is worn, smooth it and add a new hardwood strip to build it up again. Follow the same procedure used to replace worn runners.

Split Fronts. Split drawer fronts are usually the result of missing drawer guides. First install drawer guides, then repair the split with glue forced into the break. Wipe away any excess glue and clamp the edges with a strap clamp. Use only light pressure; too much pressure will buckle the wood at the split.

Split Bottoms. Drawer bottoms are not fastened into the drawer sides and ends; the bottom panel fits loosely into dadoes in the sides. This permits expansion and contraction of the wood, and prevents the joints from cracking. To replace a drawer bottom, just remove one end of the drawer and slide the bottom panel out. Replace it with a new plywood or hardboard panel cut to fit. Some drawer bottoms are tacked to a piece of molding nailed to the inside edges of the sides and back, and some drawer bottoms are set on triangular glue blocks. Remove these fasteners or braces before disassembling the drawer.

STRAIGHTENING WARPED BOARDS

Table leaves and other flat parts can warp unless they're properly sealed, and years of uneven humidity can leave them severely cupped. Unwarping them isn't too difficult.

To unwarp a board, work in summer; the traditional cure is exposure to wet grass and hot sun. Water a grassy area thoroughly and set the board convex side up on the wet grass. As the concave side of the board absorbs moisture from the grass, the convex side is dried out by the sun, and the board unwarps. Unless the warp is caused by stress in the wood, the board should straighten out within a day.

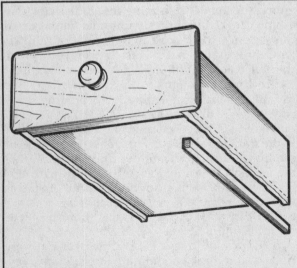

Plane and rabbet worn runners to form an even mortise along the drawer edge; glue and nail a new hardwood runner into the mortised edge.

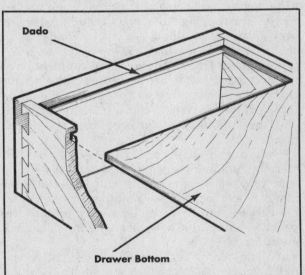

Dado

Drawer Bottom

The drawer bottom is held by a dado around the sides. To replace it, remove the drawer end; slide the old bottom out and the new one in.

When the board has straightened out, clamp it between two straight boards so that it will dry evenly. Before replacing it in the piece of furniture, seal the unfinished side with shellac to prevent it from warping again.

REPLACING WORN CANING

In antique furniture, caning is usually hand woven; it is threaded through individual holes in the frame, and woven in strand by strand. This kind of caning should be replaced by a professional. In most newer furniture, the cane is prewoven; an entire sheet of cane is attached in a groove around the open frame. Sheet cane is easy to replace.

Remove the old cane. If you can, pull the cane out of the groove, using a chisel to pry up the spline that holds it. If the spline is stubborn, you may have to soak the area with a warm damp towel. When the adhesive has softened, place a block of wood under the caning and tap the block with a hammer. This should dislodge the caning and the spline from the seat frame. After removing the cane, clean out the groove with a chisel. Make sure it's completely clean and dry before you install the new cane.

To replace the cane, buy a new spline and new prewoven sheet caning, about 1 to 1 1/2 inches larger all around than the opening. Make sure the spline is the right width for the groove. Soak the cane and the spline in warm water for 10 to 15 minutes to soften the fiber.

When the spline and the cane are pliable, blot them dry with a towel. Lay the caning over the groove, shiny side up. Starting at the center of one short side, pound the edge of the caning into the groove with a narrow wooden wedge. Cut the wedge from a 1 x 2 or a 1 x 3, and use a hammer to tap it along the caning. The bottom of the taper on the wedge should be smaller than the groove. Work along the side of the frame toward the corners, wedging the cane firmly and squarely down into the groove. If it isn't securely wedged, it will come loose.

When the first side of the cane is in place, clamp the caned edge between two pieces of 1 x 2 or 1 x 3 to prevent the caning from popping out of the groove. Then stretch the sheet of cane across the frame and wedge the opposite side, starting at the center and working out. Repeat the procedure, clamping each side as you go, to secure the remaining sides. As you work, the caning may start to dry out; wet it again to keep it pliable.

When the caning has been tapped into the groove all around the frame, trim off any excess

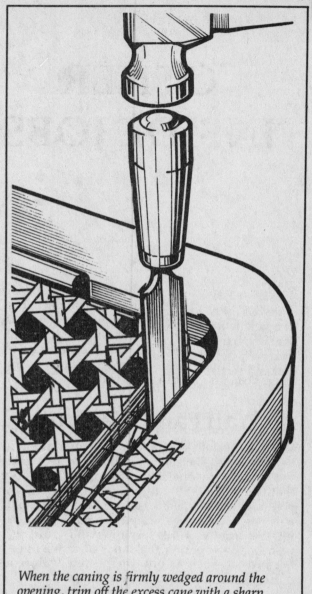

When the caning is firmly wedged around the opening, trim off the excess cane with a sharp chisel, set straight into the outside of the groove.

at the outside corner of the groove; set a sharp chisel into the groove to cut the cane. Then lay a narrow bead of white glue all around the groove on top of the caning. Blot the spline dry and force it into the groove over the caning, using a rubber mallet to drive it into the groove. Pull the spline tight as you go, and ease it around the corners. You may have to install the spline in several pieces, making sure the ends butt together tightly to form a continuous spline.

Let the glue and the cane dry completely. As it dries, the caning will become taut. Let the seat set for at least a week before you use it.

OTHER INSIDE JOBS

Painting, papering, and furniture projects are among the most popular do-it-yourself activities, but they're far from the only around-the-house tasks that anyone with a little time and the right information can accomplish. This chapter delves into more than two dozen other repairs and improvements you can add to your repertoire.

Walls and Ceilings

Walls and ceilings get a lot of attention from do-it-yourselfers. The shelves at home centers reflect this attention by offering a wide array of products that can make wall and ceiling jobs easier than you might think. Thanks to products sold in kits, paneling a wall, for example, or putting up ceiling tile often requires less time and effort than painting or papering the same surfaces. Even a big project, such as building a new wall, goes quickly once you know how.

HANGING THINGS ON WALLS

Pictures, mirrors, shelves, lamps, tools, sports equipment—the list of items you can hang on walls is almost endless. To keep them up there, you need to choose the proper fastener and install it in the proper way.

Most wall framing is covered with either plaster, backed up with wire or wood lath, or drywall that measures 1/2 or 5/8 inch thick. To hang lightweight and medium-weight objects, you need only to pierce this covering with a nail or expandable plastic screw anchor. Heavier objects, such as a large mirror, should be supported by hardware that either attaches to the wall framing or clamps securely to the wall surface from behind.

Framing members usually are on 16-inch centers, which means that the center of one stud or joist is 16 inches from the center of the next. You can locate studs with a magnetic or electronic stud finder, which detects nails holding the wall covering to the studs or the density of the studs themselves. If you don't have a stud finder, measure 16 inches from a corner of the room and begin knocking the wall with your knuckles. If the wall sounds more solid at a point exactly 16 inches from the corner, a stud is there; it's likely you'll find other studs along the length of the wall spaced in increments of 16 inches from the first. If you hear a hollow sound at a point 16 inches from the corner, go to the opposite end of the wall, measure 16 inches, and knock. You'll probably find a stud there, because carpenters always space studs from one end of the wall or the other.

Hanging Light Objects. To hang most lightweight objects, such as small pictures, use a picture hanger. Place the hanger flat against the wall, and drive the nail through the hanger. Before you drive the nail, stick a tab of cellophane tape over the spot to prevent the plaster or drywall from crumbling when the nail is driven in and later removed.

Hanging Medium-Weight Objects. To hang medium-weight objects, such as drapery rods, use plastic or nylon wall anchors. Buy anchors

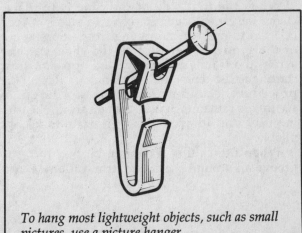

To hang most lightweight objects, such as small pictures, use a picture hanger.

made for the size screws you have, and read the package to find out what size drill bit to use for the holes. To install these anchors, follow these simple steps:

- Drill a hole in the wall for the plastic anchor.
- Tap the anchor all the way in with a hammer.
- Insert the screw through the item it is to hold, and then turn it into the anchor; the screw expands the anchor to make it grip the sides of the hole.

Hanging Medium-Weight and Heavyweight Objects. When you hang heavyweight objects, such as shelves and mirrors, the best device is the expansion anchor, or bolt. This kind of fastener comes in different sizes to fit differences in wall thickness and in the weight of the things they are to hold. Once you get the right fastener, here is how to install it:

- Check the package to see what size drill bit you must use, and then drill a hole in the wall.
- Lightly tap the fastener into its proper place with a hammer.
- Turn the slotted bolt clockwise. When you can't turn it any more, back it out. The fastener is then secure against the inside of the wall, and you are ready to hang the object.
- Put the bolt through the object or its hanger, and reinsert the bolt in the expansion anchor.

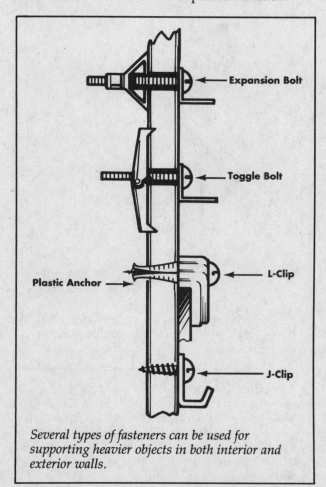

Several types of fasteners can be used for supporting heavier objects in both interior and exterior walls.

Hanging Very Heavy Objects. For really heavy objects, such as cabinets or bookshelves, use toggle bolts, which are available in several sizes. Toggle bolts also require you to drill holes in the wall. If you buy the packaged kind, you will find the size of the hole specified on the package. Here is how to install them:

- Drill the proper-size hole.
- Remove the bolt from the toggle.
- Put the bolt through the object to be hung, or through its hanger, before you insert it into the wall; you can't remove the bolt after the device is in the wall without the toggle falling down behind the wall. Reinsert the bolt in the toggle.
- Squeeze together the toggle with your thumb and forefinger and push it into the hole. You must hold the object you are hanging right next to the wall as you insert the toggle. When it goes through, pull the bolt back toward you until you feel the toggle open and hit the back of the wall.
- Turn the bolt clockwise until the hanger or the item itself is flat and secure against the wall.

REPLACING MOLDINGS

For wide seams, joints, and gaps between materials, moldings, along with wood putty, caulking compound, and other fillers, are the solution. When the molding itself gets damaged, you can't hide the problem. You must replace the molding, at least the section that is damaged.

Because baseboards are down at floor level where they can be struck by all sorts of objects, they are the most easily damaged moldings. The following procedures guide you on how to replace baseboard molding. You also can apply the same techniques to other kinds of moldings.

Removing a Molding. The first task in replacing molding is to remove the old molding. Begin by removing the shoe molding; this is the piece that fits against both the baseboard and the floor. Because the shoe molding is nailed to the subfloor, apply gentle prying pressure with a putty knife at one end to get it started. Then use a short pry bar and a wood block for leverage. Once started, the shoe molding should come up easily. Try not to break it, adding to replacement costs and work.

Pry off the damaged baseboard. Start at one end, inserting a small flat pry bar between the baseboard and the wall. Pry gently, and move farther down the molding, slipping small cedar-shingle wedges into the gaps. Work all the way along the baseboard, prying and wedging. Then work back between the wedges, tapping the wedges in deeper as the baseboard comes out further. Continue until the molding comes off.

Check to see if any nails have been pulled through either the shoe molding or the baseboard. If so, pull them out completely.

Using a Miter Box. If the old baseboard came off intact, you can use it as a pattern for cutting

To remove molding, pry it gently with a putty knife. Then use a short pry bar and a wood block.

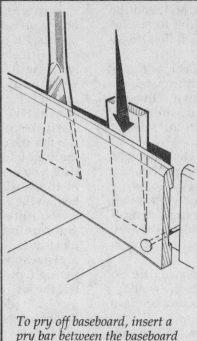

To pry off baseboard, insert a pry bar between the baseboard and the wall, slipping small wedges in the gaps.

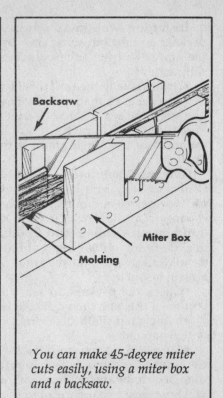

You can make 45-degree miter cuts easily, using a miter box and a backsaw.

the new one. If part of it is missing or if it is badly damaged, you must cut the new molding to fit without the aid of a pattern. You will need a miter box to cut moldings. An inexpensive wooden or plastic miter box will be adequate for this work. Slots in the box allow you to cut molding at 45-degree angles. Use either a backsaw or a fine-toothed blade in a hacksaw to do the sawing. Before sawing, place the molding you are about to cut next to the molding against which it will rest to make certain that the cut you plan to make is the correct one. To make two 45-degree cuts to join molding so it forms a right angle, place a length of molding in the miter box. Hold the molding tightly against the back of the miter box to prevent it from slipping as you saw. Repeat the procedure for the other length of molding; the two lengths should form a perfect right angle.

How to Cope Molding. If you must cut an inside right angle, you'll have to cope the joint using a coping saw. The blade of the saw is mounted so it can be turned to match the cutting angle, if necessary.

First, blunt-cut a piece of molding to fit tightly into the corner along one wall. Hold the molding in place or fasten it lightly with a nail driven in partway.

Hold a second blunt-cut piece of molding—a scrap will do—along the other wall, butted against the corner-fitted piece. With a pencil, trace the outline of the second piece of molding carefully onto the side of the fastened piece, keeping the pencil at a constant angle so the traced outline will be exact.

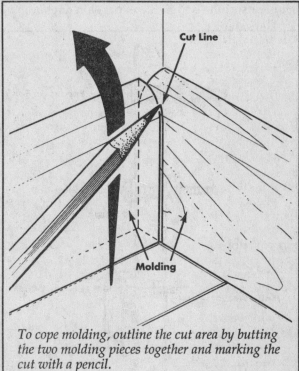

To cope molding, outline the cut area by butting the two molding pieces together and marking the cut with a pencil.

Unfasten the corner-fitted molding and cut it slowly and carefully along the traced line with a coping saw, following the pencil mark exactly. Complete the coped joint by installing a blunt-cut piece of molding along the wall you traced from, and then install the traced and trimmed piece of molding in place against it.

Installing Molding. When you finish all the mitered and coped joints, you are ready to install the new baseboard molding and reinstall the shoe molding.

Fit all the pieces together before nailing to make sure that you cut them correctly. Locate the wall studs. If you're replacing a molding, they'll be at the points where the old one was nailed. If the molding is new, locate studs with a stud finder. Nail the baseboard in place with finishing nails, and then use a nail set to drive the nail heads below the surface of the molding.

Install the shoe molding with finishing nails as well. Shoe molding must be nailed to the floor and not to the baseboard. Drive the nail heads below the surface of the shoe molding with a nail set. Paint or stain the moldings to match your walls.

INSTALLING PANELING

If you're looking for a way to cover deteriorated walls, finish off a basement room, or give any area a new look, consider a product that was designed for do-it-yourselfers: manufactured wall paneling. Large but lightweight sheets of paneling go up fast, and once they're up, the job is usually over because most paneling requires no finishing.

You can buy plywood paneling that is finished or ready to finish. Or you can buy hardboard panels that simulate finishes ranging from barn siding to marble. Some paneling has a composition core. This material breaks easily and should be used only over drywall or plaster walls.

The plastic-coated finishes on both hardboard and plywood panels are almost impervious to scratches and stains, and they are washable as long as you don't soak them. To clean the panels, go over the finish with a damp cloth and mild detergent.

The ease with which panels go up makes paneling a wall a simple do-it-yourself project. Modern adhesives eliminate nailing, and the preparation and basic installation steps are the same for both plywood panels and hardboard.

In new construction you can apply panels to the wall studs. Because the panels give a little and are far from soundproof, it is best to provide a drywall backing. Many building codes require a drywall backing, particularly in basements. If you decide to apply paneling directly to the studs, make sure that the studs are free of high or low spots. Plane away high spots and attach cedar shingle shims to compensate for any low spots.

With existing walls, remove the molding and trim and check for high or low spots by moving a long, straight board against the wall and watching for any gaps as you draw it along. Build up any low spots with drywall joint compound and sand down any high spots. If the walls are badly cracked or extremely uneven, you should install furring strips on which to attach the paneling. Masonry walls must always be furred and waterproofed.

Installing Furring Strips. Furring strips are 1 x 2s or 1 x 3s that are nailed or glued to the wall, with pieces of cedar shingle under them to even up low spots. Use 1 x 3s because they provide a better bearing surface and are easy to install.

Exactly how much furring you need depends on how uneven your walls are. If they're smooth, with a variation of only 1/2 inch or so between high and low spots, you need only to put up vertical strips, nailing or gluing them over studs and compensating for low spots by wedging shingles under the strips. Once the verticals are up, cut short horizontal pieces to fit between them at the floor and ceiling levels.

If your walls are very uneven, you may need to double fur them. With double furring, you create a grid with two layers of strips. Start by nailing up vertical strips spaced 16 inches on center from floor to ceiling. Even these with shims and

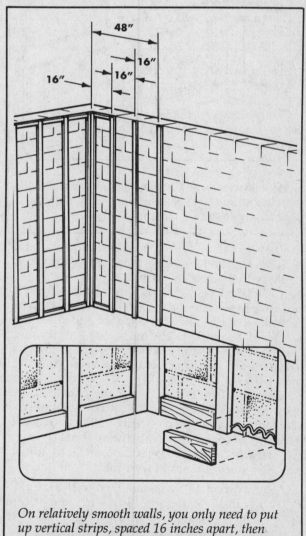

On relatively smooth walls, you only need to put up vertical strips, spaced 16 inches apart, then cut short horizontals to fit at the top and bottom.

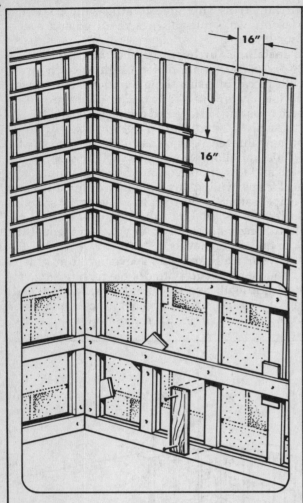

With uneven walls you may need to double-fur with a second layer of horizontal strips. Shim as necessary to smooth the grid.

note any problem spots. Next install horizontal strips, also spaced 16 inches from center to center; nail these to the vertical strips.

At electrical wall switches and outlets, you'll need to compensate for the increased thickness of the wall. Remove the cover plates and reset the electrical boxes out the necessary distance. **Caution: Turn off the electrical power to the circuits you are working on before removing the cover plates.**

Putting Up the Panels. Stack the panels in the room to be paneled, placing strips of boards between each one. Leave them there for at least 48 hours before installing them. This step is important because it allows the panels to adjust to the moisture content of the room.

After the panels have stabilized to the humidity and temperature in the room, lean them against the walls where you want them. This lets you match the wood graining in the most pleasing manner. When you have the panels arranged the way you want them, number them.

Measure the distance from floor to ceiling at several different points. If the panels have to be cut for height, you can cut all of them the same, provided the height varies by no more than a 1/4 inch. If the variance is more than 1/4 inch, you should measure the height for each panel and cut it to fit. If you are not going to use a ceiling molding, each panel must be cut to conform to the ceiling line, but you should use ceiling moldings and leave as much as a 1/4-inch gap at the top. There also should be a 1/4-inch gap at the floor, which will be concealed by baseboard molding.

Because few corners are plumb (vertically level), place the first panel in a corner next to the wall and check for plumb with a level. Get the panel plumb and close enough to the corner so that you can span the space with a scribing compass. Then run the compass down the corner, with the point in the corner and the pencil marking a line on the panel. Cut the panel along the marked line using a saber saw equipped with a fine-toothed blade or use a coping saw. Install the first panel so that it is plumb. If it isn't, the error will compound itself with each additional panel you install.

If you plan to nail the panels, use nails of a matching color. You can use 3d finishing nails to attach the panels to furring strips, but if you must

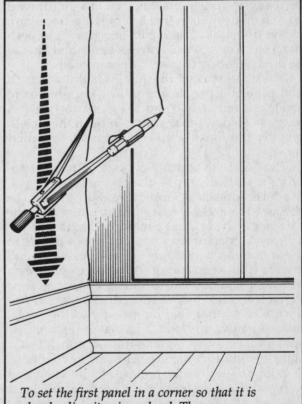

To set the first panel in a corner so that it is plumb, align it using a level. Then run a compass down the corner with the compass point in the corner and the pencil marking a line on the panel. Trim the marked edge of the panel.

go through wall material to reach the studs, be sure to use nails long enough to penetrate about one inch into the studs. Drive nails about every six inches along the edges of the panel and about every 12 inches through the center. Check frequently to make sure you are nailing into the furring strips.

If you are using panel adhesive, get it in cartridges so it can be applied with a caulking gun. Run a ribbon of adhesive across all furring strips, or if there are no strips, in about the same pattern as if there were furring strips on the wall. Place the panel against the wall or furring strips, and press it down. Then pull it away from the wall, and reset it. This helps distribute the adhesive for a better bond. Nail the panel in place at the top with a pair of nails. Then pull the bottom of the panel out from the wall, and prop it with a scrap block of wood until the adhesive gets tacky. When this happens, remove the block, and press the panel against the wall. Then secure the panel by pounding it with a padded block and hammer.

When you come to a door or window, use one of the large sheets of paper that came between the sheets of paneling to make a pattern. Tape the paper in place, press it against the door or window frame, mark it with a pencil, and cut it to fit with scissors. Use this pattern to transfer the

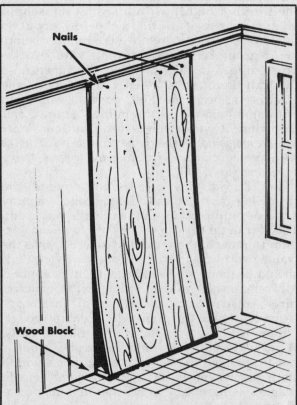

Nails

Wood Block

After applying adhesive to the wall, set the panel in position and press it down. Then pull it away and reset it; this helps distribute the adhesive for a better bond.

marks to the panel; then cut with a fine-toothed crosscut handsaw or with a power saw equipped with a fine-toothed blade. If you use a handsaw or a table saw, cut the panel with the face side up. If you use a hand-held power saw, cut with the face side down.

To make cutouts for electrical outlets or switches, trace the outline of the switch or outlet box on the panel, and drill pilot holes at opposite corners. Then use a keyhole or saber saw to connect the corners with a saw cut.

Next comes the molding. Most panel manufacturers offer prefinished moldings to match. You can get floor moldings, ceiling moldings, inside or outside corner moldings, and just about anything else you need. Use a miter box and a fine-toothed backsaw to cut moldings. Be sure to countersink the nails and fill the holes with matching wood putty.

REPAIRING CERAMIC TILE

Ceramic tile is durable, but it can show signs of wear. Tiles crack or loosen, and the grout between tiles wears down and crumbles out. These are more than simple cosmetic problems, because unless you repair the damage, water can seep behind the tiles and cause more serious trouble. To keep the problem from getting worse, make the repairs as soon as you can.

Replacing a Tile. The hardest part of this job, especially if your bathroom is old, is finding a tile to match the broken one. If you can't find a new tile that matches, try looking in a junkyard for an old tile. Remove the cracked tile. The easiest way to do this without damaging the tiles around it is to break up the old tile. Put a piece of masking tape at the center of the tile and drill a hole into the taped spot with an electric drill fitted with a carbide bit. Be sure to wear safety goggles while you do this; tile chips can damage your eyes. After drilling a hole in the tile, peel off the tape and score an X across the tile with a glass cutter. Then, still wearing safety goggles, carefully break up the tile with a cold chisel and hammer, and remove the pieces.

After removing the old tile, you'll have to clean out the gap left by it. Use a scraper or a chisel to remove old adhesive and grout from the wall where the old tile was. If chunks of plaster have been pulled out of the wall, fill the holes with spackling compound, and let the compound dry. Make sure there is no loose grout around the opening.

To attach the new tile, you'll need ceramic tile mastic, sold at hardware stores, and ceramic tile grout. Spread mastic on the back of the tile with a putty knife or a notched spreader; leave the tile's edges clean. Then carefully set the new tile into the opening on the wall. Press the tile in firmly, moving it from side to side to distribute the mastic, until it is flush with the surrounding tile sur-

To remove a damaged ceramic tile, drill a hole through its center and score an X across it with a glass cutter. Then chisel out the pieces.

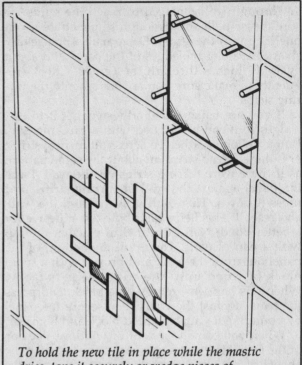

To hold the new tile in place while the mastic dries, tape it securely or wedge pieces of toothpick firmly into the open joints around it.

face. The space around the tile should be even, and the tile should be aligned. To hold it in place while the mastic dries, tape it in place with masking tape or adhesive tape; if the tile is large, wedge pieces of broken toothpick around it to keep it from slipping. Let the mastic cure as directed by the manufacturer, and keep the tile dry during this curing period.

When the mastic has cured, remove the tape or toothpicks holding the tile in place. Mix ceramic tile grout to fill the joints around the tile; follow the grout manufacturer's mixing instructions, making sure all lumps are removed. Use a damp sponge to apply the grout all around the new tile, filling the gaps completely. Grout is caustic, so wear rubber gloves. Let the grout set for 15 minutes, and then wipe the wall with a clean damp sponge or towel to remove any excess grout. Be careful not to disturb the grout around the new tile. After removing the excess, let the grout dry completely for at least 12 hours. Don't let the grout get wet during this drying period. Then rub the tile firmly with a damp towel to remove any remaining grout from the wall.

Loose ceramic tiles can be removed and then reattached with the same procedure. Scrape out the old grout around the loose tile with the corner of a putty knife, and then carefully pry out the tile. If it cracks, it must be replaced by a new one. You can locate loose tiles by tapping across the wall with the handle of the putty knife.

Regrouting Tile. Crumbling grout should be replaced as soon as possible to prevent mildew

and water damage. Before you regrout, scrub the tile thoroughly with a strong household cleaner; rinse it well. If the old grout is mildewed, you must remove the mildew before you regrout; scrub the tile joints with a toothbrush dipped in chlorine bleach, and then rinse the wall thoroughly. When you're sure all the chlorine has been rinsed off, wash the wall again with ammonia to kill the mildew spores, and then rinse it with clean water. **Caution:** *Before you use ammonia, make sure no chlorine is left on the wall; ammonia and chlorine combine to form a very dangerous gas.*

Let the wall dry, and then remove all the crumbling grout you can. Use the edge of a putty knife or a nutpick to scrape out the old grout. Then brush up any big chunks of grout, and vacuum to remove the remaining debris. Rinse the wall again to make sure it's absolutely clean; it should be damp when the new grout is applied. Mix ceramic tile grout according to the manufacturer's instructions; make sure all lumps are removed. Apply the grout with a damp sponge, wiping it firmly over the wall to fill the joints. Wear rubber gloves while you work; grout is caustic. Smooth the newly grouted joints with a clean damp sponge. Add more grout and smooth it again as necessary to fill the tile joints completely.

When the joints are smooth and evenly filled, carefully wipe the wall clean with a damp sponge. Get the wall as clean as possible, but make sure you don't gouge the grout out of the joints. Let the grout dry for at least 12 hours; don't let the wall get wet during this period. Then scrub the wall firmly with a clean dry towel to remove any grout that is left on the tiles. Finally, to protect the new grout, seal the tile joints with a silicone tile grout spray.

Recaulking Fixtures. Because tubs and sinks are subjected to widely varying loads as they're filled and emptied, grout or caulking between the fixture and the wall often cracks or pulls loose. When this happens, water seeps into the opening and damages the joint, and the surrounding wall. A cracked fixture joint may not look bad, but it should be fixed as soon as possible to prevent it from getting worse. Use silicone caulk or bathtub caulk to make the repair; these caulks are more flexible and durable than other kinds. Bathtub caulk is available in colors and white.

First, remove all the old grout or caulk from the joint. Use a putty knife to pry out pieces of grout; peel out old caulk. If old caulk can't be peeled out, cut it out with a utility or craft knife to form a clean corner. After removing the old joint material, clean the joint thoroughly with a strong household cleaner. If the joint is mildewed, scrub it out with chlorine bleach, rinse, and then scrub it again with ammonia as described above. Rinse it well. **Caution:** *Make sure all chlorine is removed before you apply ammonia; ammonia and chlorine combine to form a very dangerous gas.*

The joint must be completely dry before you recaulk it, or the caulk won't stick properly. Dry it thoroughly with a clean rag wrapped over the blade of a putty knife; if the joint is deep, dry it with a hair dryer. Then cut the nozzle of a caulk tube at an angle, making the opening a little larger than the open joint. If you're caulking several joints, start with the smallest joint and work up, recutting the nozzle of the tube as necessary for the larger joints. Bathtub caulk is simply squeezed out of the tube by hand; with a large cartridge of silicone caulk, use a caulking gun. Apply the caulk evenly all along the open joint, starting at a corner and working across the wall and around corners. Don't try to hurry the job; the bead of caulk must bond to the joint surfaces all around the fixture. As soon as you finish applying the caulk, smooth it along the joint with your finger or thumb, pressing it evenly into the open joint. Very deep joints may require more than one application of caulk, because the first bead can be pushed all the way into the opening.

When the joint is completely filled and smooth, remove the caulk from your hands with a clean cloth or paper towel; it should come right off. Wash your hands as soon as you finish. Let the new caulk dry for several hours, and don't let it get wet during the drying period. Let the caulk cure completely, according to the manufacturer's instructions, before you touch it.

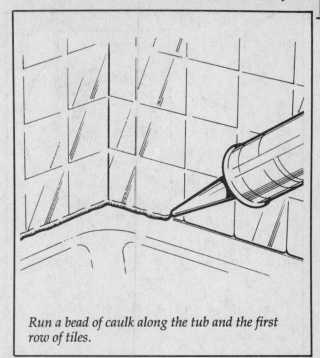

Run a bead of caulk along the tub and the first row of tiles.

INSTALLING NEW CERAMIC TILE

Installing ceramic or marble tile is not difficult if you use fast-setting mastic and grout. Many styles of ceramic tile are available pregrouted with flexible latex grout. Whatever style or size you choose to install, the principles are the same.

Before you begin, assemble the following tools and supplies: hammer, chalk line, level, saber saw with carbide blade (helpful but not necessary), rubber gloves, tile mastic, tile grout sealer, grooved trowel, tiles, rubber squeegee, and a paint-stirring stick or old toothbrush to use for forcing grout deeply into the tile joints. You can rent tile nippers and a tile cutter.

Inspect the walls; they must be smooth and free of loose plaster, dust, or peeling paint. Read the mastic instructions; on new plaster or unfinished drywall, a primer may be necessary.

Tiling around a tub presents one of the biggest challenges to a do-it-yourself tile setter, so let's look at what's involved. Start at the back wall (the wall opposite the faucet end of the tub). Using a level, draw a vertical line from the outside edge of the tub up as high as you want the tile on the wall. Check the tub for level, and if one side is higher or lower by more than 1/8 inch, you must make the adjustment on the starter row of tiles.

Temporarily place the starter row of tiles (start with an edge cap tile) along the top edge of the tub. The tile next to the corner wall must be cut to fit. Adjust the run so that not less than half a tile must be cut. Remove the tiles.

Spread as much mastic along the wall of the tub as you'll be able to cover with tiles in half an hour. As you progress, spread more mastic as needed.

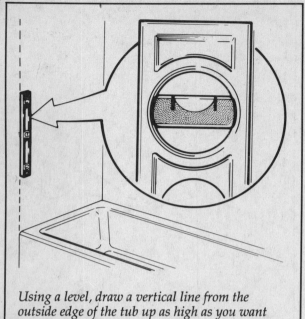

Using a level, draw a vertical line from the outside edge of the tub up as high as you want the tile on the wall.

Put the first row of tiles in place. Push each tile with a slight twisting motion to spread the mastic, but don't slide the tile around or the mastic will rise in the grout line. Leave a 1/8-inch gap between the tub and the first row of tiles. Put the edge cap and first two tiles of the next row in place. Then put the edge cap and first tile of the third row in place. You now have the beginning of a stair-step pattern. Continue placing tiles in a stair-step pattern until all the tiles on this wall except the top row of cap tiles are in place. Finish by placing the row of cap tiles along the top of the tiled area, starting with an outside corner cap.

The tiles are placed on the long wall in the same stair-step fashion. Start by placing a row temporarily along the top of the tub to find how much must be trimmed off the last tile. Spread the mastic as you did for the first wall, and install a row of tiles along the edge of the tub. Then place the tiles of the next two rows to start a stair-step pattern. Fill in the rest of the wall, and finish the top with a row of cap tiles.

The faucet wall is next. The procedure is the same as it was for the other two walls. Use a saber saw equipped with a carbide blade or use tile nippers to cut the openings for the spout, faucets, and shower arm. The openings don't have to be exact, because the chrome trim rings (escutcheons) will cover minor imperfections.

When you've finished placing the tiles, clean up any excess mastic and clean the tools. Allow the mastic at least 24 hours to dry thoroughly.

Mix the grout to a creamy consistency, and set it aside. Wet the tiles to prevent them from removing moisture from the grout. Wearing gloves, spread grout evenly over half the back wall. Then use a rubber squeegee to work the grout well between the tiles. Wipe the excess away with a wet sponge.

Use a blunt stick (the end of a toothbrush or paint stirrer is ideal) to force the grout deep into the tile joints. Remove the excess grout with a sponge, and continue in the same manner for the remaining area. Allow the grout to dry overnight, and polish off the thin film of grout that has dried on the tile. Run a bead of tub caulk around the 1/8-inch gap between the tub and the first row of tiles. If you have tiled around a window, be sure to caulk it carefully.

Apply a grout sealer according to the manufacturer's directions.

FRAMING A PARTITION

If your plans call for converting your basement, garage, or attic into living space, you probably will have to build a partition wall. Even if you have not done much carpentry, you will find that framing a wall isn't a difficult job. The basic components of a partition wall include the top plate; the sole, or floor, plate; and the wall studs. The

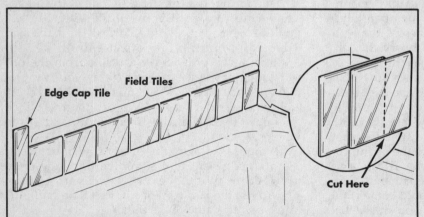

Temporarily place the starter row of tiles along the top edge of the tub. The tile next to the corner wall will have to be cut to fit. Adjust the run so that no less than half the tile will need to be cut.

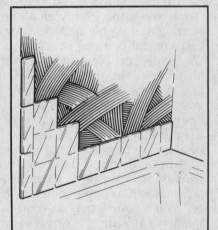

Apply mastic, and then place the tiles in a stair-step fashion.

After placing the tiles and allowing them to dry for at least one day, spread grout evenly over the wall. Use a rubber squeegee to work the grout deep into the spaces between the tiles.

Use the end of a toothbrush to force the grout into the tile joints.

studs are usually on 16-inch centers, which means that the distance from the center of one stud to the center of the next measures 16 inches. All framing lumber for the project is of the same size, usually 2 x 4s.

Note that the framing described here is for a non-load-bearing partition wall. Because it isn't designed to support the ceiling or the floor above, you need not worry about preventing the roof from caving in.

When you plan a wall, make sure that you consider all the uses the room will be put to and what furniture or equipment will go into it. Think also about the best place for a door. To get an idea of how a new wall would affect existing space, put tape or 2 x 4s on the floor to mark the spot for the proposed new wall. Shift these if necessary until you're satisfied with your plan.

When the planning is completed, cut the top plate and sole plate for the wall. Use long lengths of lumber to make the plates all one piece, if possible. Remember that the sole plate doesn't run through a doorway. After these plates have been cut, lay them side by side and mark them for stud locations. The studs should be 16 inches on center.

If the wall runs across the joists in the ceiling above, you can nail the top plate to each joist. If the wall runs parallel to the joists and cannot be positioned so that the top plate can be nailed to a joist, then you must install bridging of 2 x 4s between the joists to provide solid nailing for the top plate. Space the bridging pieces on 16-inch centers, and nail them to the joists with two nails through each end of each bridging piece.

Snap a chalk line on the floor where the sole plate is to go to guide you as you install it. Install the sole plate by nailing it; make sure it's aligned with your chalk line. If necessary, shim under the plate with cedar shingles to compensate for any unlevel sections of flooring.

With the plate in place, use a long, very straight 2 x 4 to decide where the top plate should go so that it will be directly above the sole plate. Place the straightedge against the 2 x 4, and use a level to make it vertically level, or plumb.

If a heating and cooling duct is in the way of the top plate, you must cut the top plate at the duct and continue it on the other side. Butt the top plate against the duct, leaving a gap of about 1/4 inch on each side for expansion of the wood. Then install a stud against one side of the duct, and nail the stud to the top plate and to the sole plate. Do the same on the other side of the duct. Run a length of 2 x 4 across the bottom of the duct and nail it to the studs on both sides. Finally, under the midpoint of this horizontal 2 x 4, install another stud for support, nailing it to the 2 x 4 under the duct and to the sole plate.

If the floor and ceiling are even, assemble the studs and top plate on the floor as a unit, which will be raised as an assembly. This allows you to nail through the top plate and straight into the top of each stud. If the studs must vary in length, install the top plate, cut each stud to fit, and then "toenail" each stud in place. Toenailing is driving 16d nails into the side of the stud at about a 45-degree angle so that the nails penetrate the plate. Drive two nails into each stud.

Toenail the studs in place to the sole plate. Openings for doors in the framing must be about three inches wider and 1 1/2 inches higher than the actual size of the door. Nail additional 2 x 4s, called trimmers, on both sides of the door opening; nail a header at the top. Then place a short cripple stud between the header and the top plate, and nail it in place.

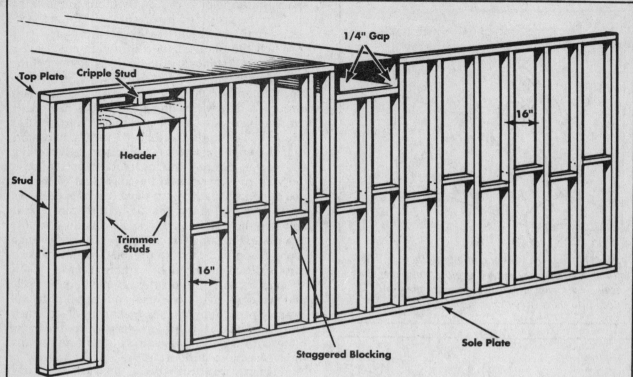

The basic components of a partition wall include the top plate; the sole, or floor, plate; and the wall studs. All framing lumber for a project is of the same size, usually 2 x 4s.

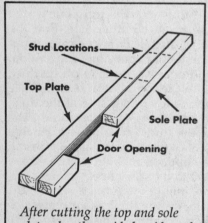

After cutting the top and sole plates, lay them side by side and mark them for stud locations.

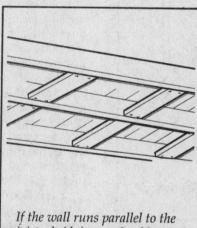

If the wall runs parallel to the joists, bridging made of 2 x 4s provides solid nailing.

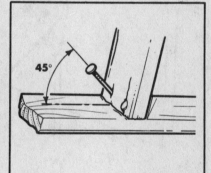

Toenailing consists of driving a nail into the side of a stud at about a 45-degree angle.

Nail 2 x 4s between studs at the midpoint of the wall. This blocking may be staggered so the pieces can be end nailed.

Complete the job by covering the stud partition with paneling or drywall.

INSTALLING DRYWALL

Drywall is also known as gypsum wallboard. A rocklike gypsum core makes drywall as fire resistant as plaster, and its heavy paper facing eliminates cracking problems. Drywall is also easier to work with than plaster.

Although they are heavy, large sheets of drywall go up fast, and you can cut them easily with a utility knife or handsaw. Once in place, drywall can be paneled, wallpapered, or painted.

Installing drywall calls for basic carpentry skills, but taping the joints between panels (a process that involves embedding a paper tape in special drywall joint compound, then covering up the seam with more applications of compound) requires practice.

Although it's easy to figure how much drywall to buy (just compute the square footage of the

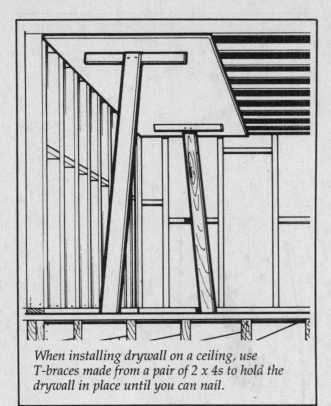

When installing drywall on a ceiling, use T-braces made from a pair of 2 x 4s to hold the drywall in place until you can nail.

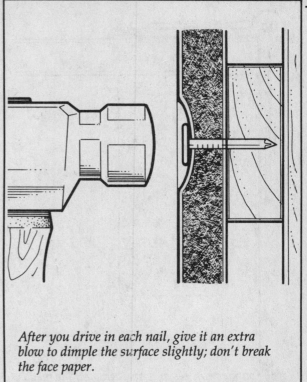

After you drive in each nail, give it an extra blow to dimple the surface slightly; don't break the face paper.

walls and ceiling), it takes planning to end up with as few joints as possible. The standard sheet measures 4 by 8 feet. You usually install them with the long side running from floor to ceiling, but you can place them horizontally if by doing so you eliminate a joint. You can buy longer sheets. All drywall sheets are 4 feet wide, but many building material outlets offer 10-foot lengths. Other sizes may be specially ordered. Most walls are made of drywall that is 1/2 or 5/8 inch thick; check your local building code to learn which thickness is required for the wall you are building.

For the number of nails and tape rolls and the amount of joint compound you will need, consult a dealer. For example, 1,000 square feet of drywall requires about 7 pounds of coated drywall nails, a five-gallon pail of joint premixed compound, and a 500-foot roll of tape. Each outside corner requires metal corner bead; drywall tape is used for inside corners.

Installing Drywall. To install drywall on the ceiling and walls of a framed room, you'll probably need an assistant, especially for the ceiling.

Cover the ceiling first. If possible, try to span the entire width with a single sheet of wallboard to reduce the number of joints. Before you can work on the ceilings, though, you need to construct a pair of T-braces from 2 x 4s that are about an inch longer than the distance from floor to ceiling. Nail 2 x 4s about 3 feet long to one end of each longer 2 x 4 to form the Ts, and then position and wedge the braces against the drywall sheet to hold it in place until you finish nailing it. Drive

nails at 6-inch intervals into all the joists covered by the sheet. Start in the center of the drywall panel and work out. After you drive each nail in, give it an extra hammer blow to dimple the surface. Take care not to break the face paper.

When you need to cut panels to complete the coverage, use a sharp utility knife along a straightedge. All you want to do with the knife is to cut the face paper. After you make the cut, place the board over the edge of a sawhorse, a length of 2 x 4 laid flat on the floor, or another kind of support, and snap the scored section down. The gypsum core will break along the line you cut. Then turn the panel over, cut the paper on the other side, and smooth the rough edges with coarse-grit sandpaper on a sanding block.

When the ceiling is finished, put up the walls. Space the nails 6 inches apart, but start nailing 4 inches from the ceiling. Butt the wall panels against the ceiling sheets. Dimple all nails. If outside corners are involved, nail the metal outside-corner beads in place.

Be sure to measure carefully for any cutouts in the drywall, including electrical outlets, switches, or light fixtures. To make cutouts, draw a pattern of the cutout on the wallboard, drill a hole, and then use a keyhole saw to follow the pattern.

Taping Drywall. Once you have nailed the drywall to the walls, you have to cover the nails and joints. This is where you use joint compound and joint tape. Here is the procedure:

Use a 5-inch-wide drywall-taping knife to spread joint compound into the slight recess created by the tapered edges of the drywall sheets.

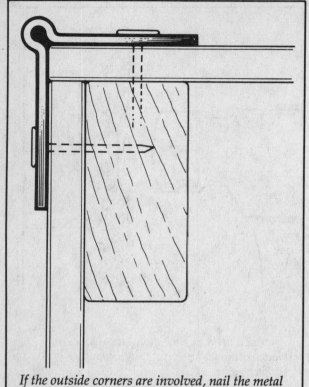

If the outside corners are involved, nail the metal outside cornerbeads in place; there's no need to dimple these nails.

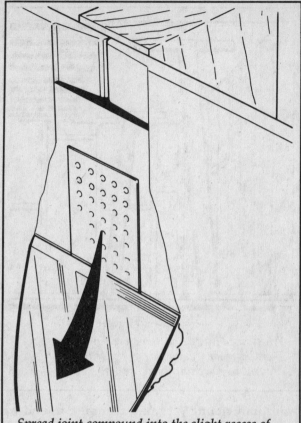

Spread joint compound into the slight recess of butting edges, center the tape over the joint, and press it firmly into the compound. After the tape is embedded, apply more compound.

Smooth the compound until it is even with the rest of the board surface. Center the drywall tape over the joint, and press it firmly into the compound. Because some compound will squeeze out, you should make sure that there is still a good bed underneath. When you get the tape embedded into the compound all along the joint, smooth it with the taping knife.

When the compound is completely dry, usually 24 hours later, apply a second, thin coat of compound that extends out a few inches from either side of the first coat. After the second coat dries completely, apply a third coat, this time with a 10-inch-wide taping knife, extending the compound to about six inches from either side. When the third coat is dry, feather all the edges with a sanding block covered with medium-grit sandpaper.

Fill all the dimples with compound. They also require three coats as well as drying time between coats. After the final coat, sand to feather and smooth the dimpled spots.

Inside corners, including spots where the walls and ceiling meet, also must be taped. Cut the tape to length and then fold it in half. After laying the bed of compound, press the folded tape into the compound and then feather the compound out at least 1 1/2 inches to each side. The corners also require three coats, and the last coat should extend about eight inches to each side. Sanding is required.

If you have any outside corners, apply three coats that taper up to the bead. The last coat should extend the compound on each wall to about eight inches wide. Sand and if there are cracks at the floor, install molding to hide them.

Let the walls dry for five days. If you are installing paneling, you can apply it directly over the gypsum wallboard. If you are going to paint or wallpaper, give the surface of the drywall a coat of sealer and a coat of primer made for paint or wallpaper. When the primer is dry, sand the drywall surface lightly with fine-grit sandpaper on a sanding block. Be sure to sand between each additional coat of paint with fine-grit sandpaper.

REPLACING DAMAGED CEILING TILES

When you look at a ceiling covered with tile, the idea of replacing a damaged tile somewhere in the middle of the ceiling may seem impossible. If a tile or a series of tiles has been damaged by water and has become stained, you may not have to replace the tiles. Instead, brush a coat of 4-pound-cut white shellac over the tiles, and allow the shellac to dry for one hour. Then paint the tiles with a color to match the undamaged tiles. The shellac seals the tile surface so the stain won't bleed through the paint.

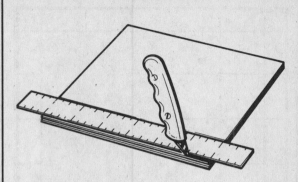

Before installing a replacement tile, cut the tongue or grooved edge with a utility knife; you can determine which by holding the tile in position over the opening.

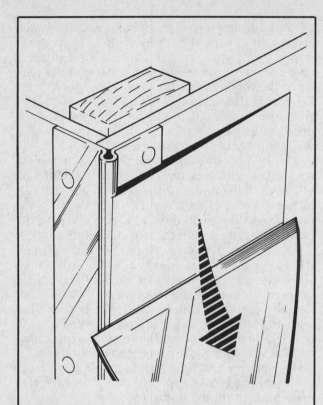

On outside corners, apply three coats of compound that taper up to the bead. The last coat should extend about eight inches on each side of the bead.

To remove and replace one or more damaged tiles, follow this procedure:

If the tile is applied to furring, cut a hole in the center of the damaged tile large enough to stick your hand through. Use a keyhole saw for cutting the hole, being careful not to damage adjoining tiles or anything behind the tile. Carefully remove the damaged tile with your fingers. If the tile is glued directly to a plaster or drywall ceiling, you'll have to make a hole with some sharp tool and carefully pry off the pieces.

Using a carpenter's square or a straightedge, cut either the tongue or grooved edges from the replacement tile with a utility knife. Which edges to remove can be determined by holding the tile in position over the opening in the ceiling. Match the cut tile to the opening. It may need special trimming to fit. Use the utility knife for sharp, clean-cut edges. Remove any old staples or adhesive from the furring strips or ceiling. Be careful not to damage the edges of adjoining tiles.

Place a walnut-sized daub of ceiling-tile adhesive at each corner of the new tile and press the new tile into the opening. Hold the tile in position for several minutes until the adhesive sets enough to support the tile. Before the adhesive dries, examine the tile. If it is not aligned with surrounding tiles, you can slip the tile into the proper position before the adhesive dries.

TILING A CEILING

The fast way to have a new ceiling is to install ceiling tiles directly to an existing plaster or drywall ceiling. If the ceiling surface isn't sound or if you're dealing with open joists, the tiles can be stapled to furring strips. If the ceiling is in really poor condition, you can lower the ceiling with a suspended ceiling system, provided that the ceiling is high enough.

To decide how much tile you need, multiply the room's length by the width to obtain the square footage. Most tile is sold in boxes containing 64 square feet, although smaller quantities are available. To find how much tile you need, divide 64 into the square footage; allow for some extra tiles in case of mistakes.

If the room doesn't have a square or rectangular shape, you can draw a sketch of the room on graph paper, using each square on the paper to represent 1 square foot. Then count the squares to find how many tiles you need.

Installing Tile With Adhesive. If you plan to apply tile directly to the existing ceiling surface with adhesive, first find the center of the ceiling. Measure and mark the midpoint of each wall. Stretch a chalk line between opposite midpoints and snap the chalk line; where the lines cross is

---

STAY CLEAN ALONG WITH THE TILE

Installing ceiling tile with adhesive can turn into a messy job. Your hands will become covered with adhesive, which picks up dirt. The dirt is then smudged onto the tile. These smudges can be very difficult to remove because they are adhesive-based. When working with ceiling tile, wear clean, inexpensive cotton gloves. You should buy three pairs. This way, you can put on a clean pair while the dirty ones are being laundered.

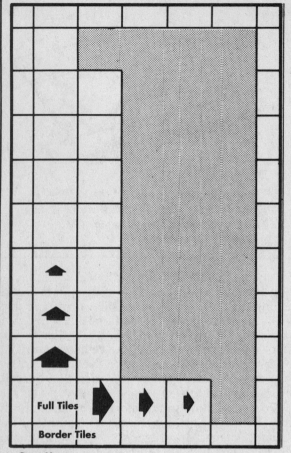

Full Tiles

Border Tiles

Start Here

Start by setting the corner tiles first. Then cut border tiles to work out along the corner walls. Fill in between the border tiles with full tiles.

the center. Check it with a carpenter's square to make sure the lines form 90-degree angles. Measure the ceiling to determine the width of the tiles that will go around the edges of the room, across both chalked centerlines.

To calculate the width of border tiles, consider only the inches measured past the last full foot in each direction—5 inches, for example, from 17 feet 5 inches. Add 12 inches—the width of one full tile—and divide by 2. The result is the width of the border tiles at each end of each row of tile laid in that direction. If the inch measurement is 5, for example, border tiles in rows across the direction measured will be 8 1/2 inches wide.

Calculate the width of border tiles along both directions. Start in one corner of the room; from this corner, measure out the width of the border tiles in each direction. Mark these points on the ceiling. Snap a chalk line on the ceiling at a right angle through each of these points, making sure each of the two new lines is parallel to one of the chalk lines across the center of the ceiling.

Set the corner tile first. Mark it to the measured size with a pencil; cut it, face up, with a sharp

utility knife and a steel straightedge. Ceiling tiles are made to lock together, with two grooved edges and two tongued edges. The tongued edges of the starter tile must face toward the center of the room, so cut the grooved edges to trim the corner tile to size. The border tiles along the two starter walls also will be trimmed along a grooved edge; the tiles bordering the two far walls will be cut along the tongued edges.

Apply adhesive to the back of the trimmed corner tile with a putty knife, putting daubs of adhesive in the center of the tile and about 1 1/2 inches in front of each corner. Place the tile into the corner, tongued edges out, and slide it into position exactly within the two chalked lines.

Cut border tiles to work out from the corner tile along the two corner walls. As you work, slide the grooved edges of each tile over the exposed tongues of the last tiles to lock the tiles firmly together. Fill in between the border tiles with full-size tiles in an expanding wedge pattern, gradually extending the rows of border tiles and fanning tiles out to cover the entire ceiling.

To work around light fixtures, hold the tile tip to the ceiling before applying adhesive; carefully mark and cut off the portion to be removed, then apply adhesive and slide the tile into place.

Continue setting tiles until you reach the far corner of the room. Before cutting border tiles for the two far walls, measure the gap left beyond the last full tile. Mark and cut border tiles along these walls one by one to make sure they fit the gap. Finish the job by installing cove molding along the edges of the ceiling.

Installing Tile on Furring Strips. To install tile over an uneven or badly damaged ceiling, nail furring strips across the ceiling. Begin by locating each ceiling joist in the room and marking it on the ceiling. Nail 1 x 2 or 1 x 3 furring strips at right angles across the joists and along the edges of the ceiling with 6d common nails 12 inches apart from center to center; use a carpenter's square to make sure the strips are even and properly angled.

Measure and calculate the border-tile width. To mark the lines from the starting corner for the corner tile and the first two border rows, carefully snap a chalk line each way on the furring strips. Trim tiles to this dimension.

To attach tiles to the furring strips, you'll need a heavy-duty stapler and staples of a length specified by the tile manufacturer. Staple through each tile's grooved edges; slide in the next tile's tongued edge to interlock the tiles.

Cut the corner tile, and set it into place, grooved side toward the center of the room and centered on the furring strips. Staple it to the furring strips, setting three staples along each exposed grooved edge. Nail the other two sides firmly into place with 4d common nails, as close to the walls as possible.

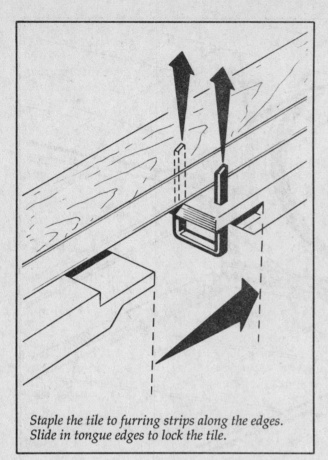

*Staple the tile to furring strips along the edges.
Slide in tongue edges to lock the tile.*

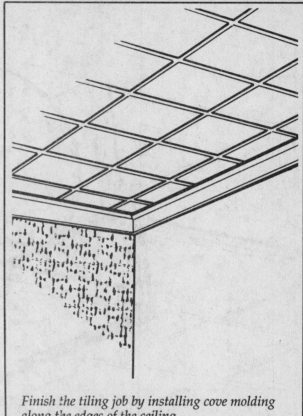

*Finish the tiling job by installing cove molding
along the edges of the ceiling.*

Continue across the room, setting border tiles
and then filling in with full tiles, sliding new tiles
in to lock over old ones as you go. Staple each
new tile with three staples along each grooved
edge.

To fasten border tiles into place at the wall,
drive three nails along each trimmed tongued
edge, as close to the wall as possible. These nails
will be covered by molding. Trim and set border
tiles for the far walls one by one as you work.
Finish the job by installing cove molding along
the edges of the ceiling.

Tiling Around Beams and Ducts. There are
two methods of installing ceiling tile around
ducts and metal support beams. Which one you
use depends on the obstruction's shape and how
far down from the ceiling it is. If it is just a matter
of a few inches, you can build a plywood box
around the duct. If the distance is a foot or more,
the tile can be applied directly to rectangular
ducts. The plywood-box method is best for metal
support beams and other irregularly shaped
obstructions.

Tiles may be installed directly on rectangular
ducts. First, install ceiling tile to the edge of the
metal duct. The fit doesn't have to be perfectly
accurate because cove molding will be used to
hide the joints. Use tile adhesive to stick the tiles
to the sides and bottom of the duct. If strap duct
hangers won't let tiles lay flat, mortise the back of
the tiles with saw kerfs made with a crosscut saw.

After tile has been installed over the duct, measure, cut, and install a strip of prefinished metal
wall angle made for suspended ceilings on the
bottom edges of the duct over the tiles. Because
the wall angle is very light in weight, you can
affix it over the tile with tile adhesive or panel
adhesive.

At the top of the duct, where the ceiling tile
meets the tile on the sides of the duct, install prefinished cove molding with panel adhesive. You
probably will have to hold the molding for several minutes to give the adhesive time to set
enough to adhere to the tiles. You can use a pair
of 1 x 3s wedged between the floor and the molding to hold the molding until the adhesive sets.

You can use 1 x 3 furring strips to go around
round ducts and I-beams, but it's a lot of work. A
faster and easier way is to use 1/2-inch plywood
sheathing.

Cut the plywood sheathing into strips for the
sides of the obstruction; they should match the
width and the height (distance from ceiling to
bottom of duct or beam) of the obstruction. Using
10d threaded nails, nail one strip of plywood to
the side of the joist nearest the duct or beam.
Then nail the other strip of plywood on the other
side to the nearest parallel joist.

Bridge the two plywood strips with a strip of
plywood for the bottom of the obstruction. Nail
through the face of the bottom strip into the
edges of the vertical strips. Use threaded nails

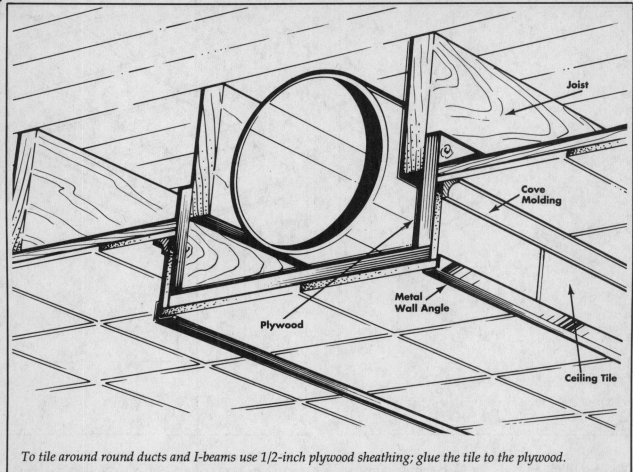

To tile around round ducts and I-beams use 1/2-inch plywood sheathing; glue the tile to the plywood.

and panel adhesive on the edges for strength. When you are finished, you have a boxed enclosure onto which you can glue or staple the ceiling tile.

INSTALLING A SUSPENDED CEILING

A suspended ceiling can cover a lot of flaws and obstructions, including pipes, wiring, and ducts. It works only where you can afford to lose some ceiling height. Suspended-ceiling panels are sold in 2-by-2-foot and 2-by-4-foot sizes; use the smaller size for smaller rooms.

To install a suspended ceiling, first measure the ceiling and plot it on graph paper, marking the exact locations of windows and doors. Mark the direction of ceiling joists. Mark the joists on the ceiling itself, using a pencil or chalk to draw the joist lines across the ceiling.

Take the diagram with you when you buy the ceiling materials. With the dealer, plan the layout for the ceiling, figuring full panels across the main ceiling and evenly trimmed partial panels at the edges. To calculate the width of the border panels in each direction, find the width of the gap left after full panels are placed all across the dimension; divide by 2. The dealer should help you calculate how many panels you'll need and tell you how many wall angles (in 10-foot lengths), main runners (in 12-foot lengths), and cross tees (in 4-foot or 2-foot lengths) and how much 12-gauge hanger wire to buy.

Begin by marking the level at which the new ceiling will hang; allow at least 4 inches clearance between the panels and the old ceiling. Snap a chalk line at this height across each wall, using a level to keep it straight. Make sure the lines meet exactly at the corners of the room. Nail wall angle brackets along the chalk line all around the room, with the bottom leg of the L-angle facing into the room and flush along the chalk line. Use 6d common nails to fasten the brackets, setting them every 1 1/2 to 2 feet. Cut the bracket to the required lengths with tin snips or a hacksaw.

Locate the points where screw eyes should be driven in by consulting your final ceiling layout diagram. The long panels of the ceiling grid are set parallel to the ceiling joists, so the T-shaped main runner must be attached at right angles to the joists, every 4 feet across the ceiling. Hanger wire threaded through screw eyes in the joists suspends the main runners of the grid system. Locate on the diagram the joints between the short sides of two long panels; if you're using 2-by-2-foot panels, count every joint at right angles to the joists. Mark these points along the angle bracket on each wall, measuring carefully accord-

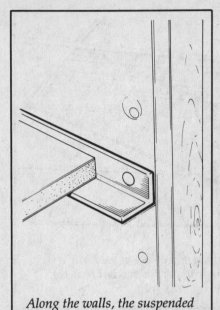

Along the walls, the suspended ceiling panels are supported by wall angle brackets fastened to the wall.

The panels are supported by a grid of main runners and cross tees attached to the ceiling with wire and screw eyes.

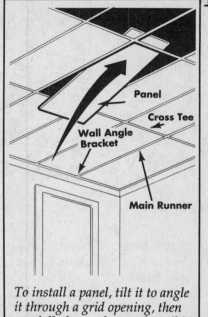

To install a panel, tilt it to angle it through a grid opening, then carefully lower the panel until it rests on the grid.

ing to the diagram. Stretch strings across the room from wall to wall at these points to show you where the main runners will hang.

Drive screw eyes into the joists directly above each string, placing one screw eye at the last joist on each side and one in every third joist across the ceiling. If you're covering a finished ceiling, drive the screw eyes at the marked joist lines; use long screw eyes to hold through the thickness of the ceiling.

For each screw eye, cut a length of hanger wire long enough to fasten securely through the screw eye, extend down to the stretched runner string, and fasten the runner. Thread a wire through each screw eye, and twist the end firmly around the dangling wire. Exactly at the point where the wire crosses the string beneath it, bend the wire sharply with pliers to a 90-degree angle.

Set the main runners into place. Cut T-shaped main runner sections to required lengths with tin snips or a hacksaw; if you must put two sections together to cover a long span, snap the pieces together with the preformed tabs. Lift each long main runner and set one end into place on the wall angle bracket at one side of the ceiling, with the single leg of the T up; swing the other end up and position the runner exactly along the marker string and under the screw eyes in the joists. Thread the bent end of each hanging wire through a hole in the runner leg, bend the end of the wire up, and secure it. Check each runner with a level and adjust the length of the hangers if necessary. Repeat until all main runners have been installed.

Working from your ceiling diagram, install the cross tee sections of the ceiling grid. These sec-

tions snap into place in slots in the main runner sections; because they're sold in 4-foot lengths, no cutting is necessary. Snap the sections into place every 2 feet along the main runners. If you're using 2-by-2-foot ceiling panels, use 2-foot cross tees to divide each 2-by-4-foot panel in half; snap the sections together.

After all main runners and cross tees are in place, install the panels. Tilt each panel to angle it through a grid opening, then carefully lower it until it rests on the bracket edges of the grid sections. Measure border panels carefully; cut them to size with a utility knife.

If you have to fit a panel around a post, carefully measure across the opening to the post in both directions; sketch the opening and mark the post. Measure the diameter of the post. Mark the panel lightly where the post will go through it; cut the panel in two exactly through the center of the post, across the shorter dimension. Carve an opening for the post on the inside cut edge of each panel, forming two semicircular or rectangular cutouts. Cut only a little at a time; hold the cut sections up to the post frequently to fit them exactly. Set the two sections into place in the suspension grid; the cut will show hardly at all.

INSTALLING RECESSED CEILING LIGHTING

Recessed lighting fixtures are readily available for a variety of ceilings. For ceilings with 12-inch-square tiles on furring strips over joists, the fixtures are the size of a single tile. For suspended ceilings with 2-by-4-foot panels, you can buy fixtures that fit above a single panel and attach to the joists, subfloor, or to the main tees of the sus-

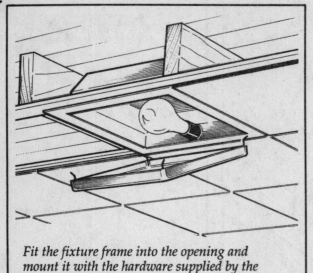

Fit the fixture frame into the opening and mount it with the hardware supplied by the manufacturer.

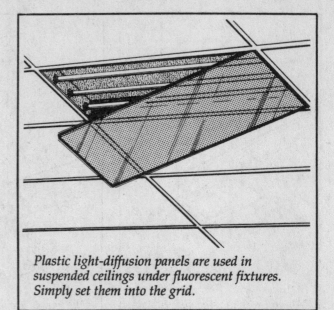

Plastic light-diffusion panels are used in suspended ceilings under fluorescent fixtures. Simply set them into the grid.

pended system. A special light panel replaces the ceiling panel below the light fixture.

To power a lighting fixture, you may be able to use an existing ceiling fixture junction box and wall switch, or you may have to route wiring from an existing circuit into a ceiling junction box for the new fixture. If a new circuit is required, call a professional. In any case, the wall switch and wiring for the fixture should be routed to the site of the ceiling fixture before the ceiling tile or panels are installed.

At the fixture site, fasten a junction box to the joists, using hangers for the box that span the joists. Some fixtures come wired with their own junction boxes. With this kind of fixture, the circuit wires can be connected directly to the fixture's junction box with wire nuts.

After the wiring has been routed to the site of the fixture, you can proceed to install the ceiling tile or suspended ceiling system.

Lighting in a Tiled Ceiling. Lighting fixtures for a ceiling with 12-inch-square tiles are usually incandescent lighting fixtures that fit between joists above furring strips; the light fixtures mount to the furring strips or joists.

To install lighting in a tiled ceiling, first tile the ceiling to the location of the fixture. Next fit the fixture frame in the opening, and mount it in place with the provided hardware.

Turn off the power to the fixture circuit by removing the proper fuse or tripping the proper circuit breaker to the "off" position. Connect the circuit wiring to the fixture, using wire nuts to join white wire to white wire, black wire to black wire, and bare or green wire to the fixture's green wire or grounding clip.

Install the reflector in the fixture according to the manufacturer's instructions; it usually snaps into position around the light socket and the fixture frame.

Screw in the light bulb and install the light diffuser panel over the frame of the fixture and reflector, according to the manufacturer's instructions. On some fixtures, the diffuser is hinged to the fixture frame and is snapped into place.

Lighting in a Suspended Ceiling. Lighting fixtures for suspended ceilings are almost always fluorescent fixtures. To install such a fixture in a suspended ceiling, first install the suspended ceiling, and then turn off the power to the fixture circuit by removing the proper fuse or tripping the proper circuit breaker to the "off" position.

Disassemble the new fluorescent fixture, if necessary, to expose its wires. Have someone hold the fixture while you connect the circuit wiring to the fixture; attach black wire to black wire, white wire to white wire, and bare or green wire to the fixture's green wire or grounding clip. Then, reassemble the fixture, if necessary, and position it against the ceiling. Mount the fixture with the hardware provided. Most fluorescent fixtures come with installation screws. Use these screws if you can drive them into ceiling joists or another solid wood. Otherwise, use expansion fasteners or toggle bolts for drywall or plaster ceilings, or masonry anchors and screws for concrete ceilings. Drill pilot holes to size for bolts and anchors; drill pilot holes of smaller diameter for wood screws. Then firmly screw or anchor the fixture to the ceiling.

Place the fluorescent tubes into the fixture's contact slots, and restore the power to the circuit. After you've determined that the installation works, install the plastic light diffusion panel into place in the ceiling.

Floors and Stairs

When you consider the punishment meted out by everyday foot traffic, it's surprising that floors

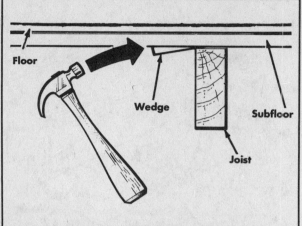

Working under the floor, look for gaps between the joists and the subfloor. Drive wedges into the gaps to keep the floor from moving and to stop the squeaks.

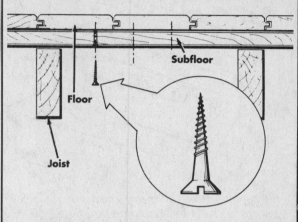

To eliminate squeaks between joists, drill pilot holes and drive wood screws up through the subfloor and the floorboards to pull the layers together.

and stairs hold up as well as they do. Eventually wear and tear take their toll. Squeaks develop, minor damage afflicts resilient tile and sheet flooring, or the entire surface begins to show its age and needs replacing or refinishing.

ELIMINATING SQUEAKS

Squeaky floors and stairs aren't serious structural problems, but they can be very annoying. If your floors are exposed hardwood, you may be able to stop the squeak by sprinkling talcum powder over the noisy boards and sweeping it back and forth to force it into the cracks. On stairs, use packaged graphite powder or talcum powder in a squeeze bottle; apply the lubricant along all the joints in the problem area. The powder will lubricate the edges of the boards, eliminating the noise. For a more permanent repair, tackle the squeak with the procedures below:

Squeaky Floors. If a basement or crawl space is under the noisy floor, work from this area to locate the problem. You'll need a helper upstairs to walk on the squeaky spot while you work. Watch the subfloor under the noisy boards while your helper steps on the floor above. If the subfloor moves visibly, or if you can pinpoint the noise, outline the affected areas with chalk. At the joists closest to your outlines, look for gaps between the joist and the subfloor. Where there is a gap, the floorboards can move. To stop squeaks here, pound thin wedges into the gaps to stop the movement; shingles or wood shims make good wedges. If there are no gaps along the joists, or if the squeaks are coming from an area between joists, there is probably a gap between the floorboards and the subfloor. To pull the two layers together, drive wood screws up through the subfloor in the squeaky areas; drill pilot holes before inserting the screws. The wood screws must be long enough to penetrate into the floor above

you, but make sure they aren't so long that they go all the way through the boards. If this happens, you'll have sharp screw points in your floor.

If you can't get at the floor from underneath, you'll have to work from the top, with spiral flooring nails. Locate the squeak, and try to find whether it's at a joist or between joists. To eliminate the squeak, drive two spiral flooring nails, angled toward each other in a V, through the floorboards and the subfloor. At a joist, use longer spiral flooring nails, and drive them through the floorboards and the subfloor and into the joist. Drill pilot holes before driving the nails; countersink the nail heads with a nail set, and cover them with wood filler.

If the floor is tiled or carpeted, and you can't get at the floorboards from above or below, you probably won't be able to eliminate the squeak without removing the floor covering. Before you do this, try to reset the loose boards by pounding. Using a hammer and a block of scrap wood as a buffer, pound the floor firmly over the squeaky boards, in an area about 2 or 3 feet square. The pressure of the pounding may force loose nails back into place.

Squeaky Stairs. Stairs are put together with three basic components: the tread, the riser, and the stringer (the side piece). In most cases squeaks are caused by the tread rubbing against the riser or the stringer. If you can, work from under the stairs to fix the squeak. You'll need a helper to walk up and down the stairs while you work. Watch the stairs from below while your helper walks on them; look for movement and for cracks in the wood, loose nails, or other problems. The simplest way to fix the squeak is to wedge the treads, risers, or stringers that are moving. Cut small wedges from wood shingles or shims. To install a wedge, apply carpenter's glue

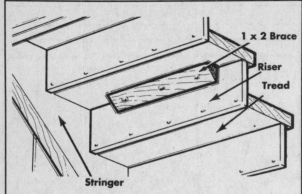

If the gaps between stair components aren't wide enough to accept wedges, brace the joints with triangular 1 x 2 blocks to stop the movement of the stairs.

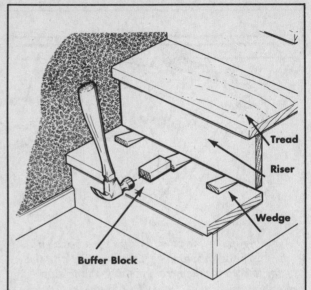

To stop squeaks at the back of a step, use a buffer block to drive thin wedges between the tread and the riser. Trim the wedges flush.

to the side that will lie against the stairs. Drive the wedge into the squeaking joint, either tread-riser or tread-stringer. When the wedge is tight, secure it with small nails, being careful not to split the wedge. The nails must be long enough to hold the wedge securely, but make sure they don't go all the way through the stair component and stick out on the other side.

If the joints aren't wide enough to take wedges, use 1 x 2s to stop the movement of the boards. Use one long or two or more short blocks for each stair joint. Apply carpenter's glue to the sides of the block that will lie against the stairs; then set the block into the squeaking joint, and nail it into place.

If you can't get at the stairs from underneath, you'll have to work from the top. For squeaks at the front of a tread, where it meets the riser below it, drive pairs of spiral flooring nails, angled toward each other in a V, across the tread and into the top of the riser. Countersink the nail heads with a nail set, and cover them with wood filler. For squeaks at the back of a tread, where it meets the riser above, drive thin wedges into the joint at the back of the tread. Coat the wedges with carpenter's glue, and use a hammer and a wood buffer block to pound them in. Then carefully trim the wide ends of the wedges flush with the riser. If the wedges are noticeable, cover the joint with quarter round or other trim molding; treat all other joints the same way so that they match.

REPAIRING RESILIENT FLOORING

Today's resilient floors can lose their attraction quickly when they're damaged. Even the worst damage is easy to repair, whether the floor is tile or sheet vinyl.

Tile Floors. Tile repairs are simple because only the affected tiles must be considered. If a tile is loose, it can be reglued with floor-tile adhesive. If it's loose at one edge or corner, there may be

enough old adhesive left on the tile to reattach it. Cover the tile with aluminum foil, then with a clean cloth. Heat the loose edges with an iron, set to medium heat, to soften the old adhesive and rebond it. When the adhesive has softened, weight the entire tile and let the adhesive cure for several hours or overnight.

If the old adhesive isn't strong enough to reattach the tile, use a floor-tile adhesive made for that kind of tile. Heat the tile, and lift the loose edges with a paint scraper or a putty knife. Scrape the old adhesive off the edges of the tile and apply a thin coat of new adhesive, using a notched spreader or trowel. Then smooth the tile firmly from center to edges, and weight the entire tile. Let the adhesive cure as directed by the manufacturer, then remove the weights.

If a tile is damaged, you can easily replace it. To remove the tile, heat it with a propane torch with a flame-spreader nozzle; be careful not to damage the surrounding tiles. Then pry it up with a paint scraper or a putty knife. Instead of heating the tile, cover it with dry ice; wear work gloves to protect your hands. Let the dry ice stand for about ten minutes and remove remaining ice. Then chisel out the tile from the center to the edges. The cold will make the tile brittle so that it shatters easily. After removing the tile, scrape all the old adhesive off the floor to make a clean base for the new tile. Fill gouges in the tile base with spackling compound or wood filler, and let the filler dry completely.

Check the fit of the new tile in the prepared opening. If the new tile doesn't fit exactly, sand the edges or slice off the excess with a sharp utility knife and a straightedge. When the tile fits perfectly, spread a thin coat of floor tile adhesive in

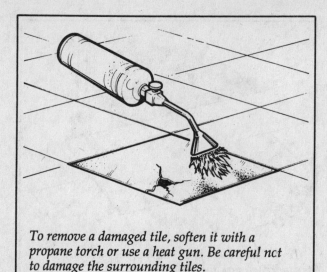

To remove a damaged tile, soften it with a propane torch or use a heat gun. Be careful not to damage the surrounding tiles.

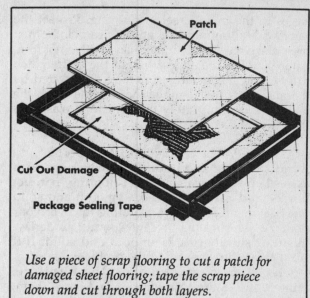

Use a piece of scrap flooring to cut a patch for damaged sheet flooring; tape the scrap piece down and cut through both layers.

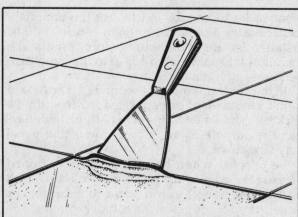

When the tile is soft, pry it up with a paint scraper or putty knife; then scrape the adhesive off the floor so the new tile will bond cleanly.

the opening, using a notched trowel or spreader. Warm the new tile with an iron to make it flexible, and then carefully set it into place, pressing it firmly onto the adhesive. Weight the entire tile, and let the adhesive cure as directed by the manufacturer. Remove the weights when the adhesive is completely cured.

Sheet Flooring. Damaged sheet flooring looks worse than damaged tile, but if you have a matching scrap of flooring, you can cut in a patch to replace the bad spot. You also can make a patching compound from scrap flooring, to fill deep scratches without patching. To make the compound, bend a piece of scrap flooring in half, right side out. Scrape the folded edge with a utility knife, making a fine powder; catch the scrapings in a small shallow pan. Rebend the flooring as you work to keep the scrapings the color of its top surface. When you have more than enough powder to fill the scratch, mix a few drops of clear nail polish with it; use only enough to make a thick paste. Cover the floor around the patch with masking tape, and then fill the scratch with

your patching paste; smooth it along the scratch with a putty knife. Let the patch dry for about an hour, remove the tape, and buff the patch lightly with 000 steel wool.

When the floor is badly worn or damaged, use scrap flooring to patch it. You'll need a piece of flooring a little bigger than the bad spot. Position the scrap over the bad spot so that it covers the damage completely, and align the pattern with the floor pattern. Tape the patch firmly in place on the floor, using package sealing tape all around the edges. With a straightedge and a sharp utility knife, cut a rectangle through the scrap piece and through the flooring below it, to make a patch bigger than the damaged area. Cut along joints or lines in the pattern, if possible, to make the patch harder to see. You'll probably have to go over each cut several times to cut completely through the two layers of flooring; stay on the original score lines. Be sure that the corners are cleanly cut.

When the flooring is cut through, untape the scrap piece and push out the rectangular patch. Soften the old flooring inside the cut lines by heating it with an iron, set to medium heat. Cover the patch area with aluminum foil and then with a cloth, and press until the adhesive holding the flooring has softened. Pry up the damaged piece with a paint scraper or putty knife. Scrape off the old adhesive to make a clean base for the patch. If there are gouges in the floor, fill them with water putty and let it dry completely.

Try the patch in the opening; it should fit perfectly. If it binds a little, you can sand the edges with medium- or fine-grit paper to adjust the fit. When the patch fits exactly, spread a thin coat of floor tile adhesive in the opening with a notched trowel or spreader. Set the patch carefully into the gap, press it in firmly, and wipe off excess adhesive around the edges. Then heat-seal the edges to the main sheet of flooring. Protect the floor with aluminum foil and a clean cloth, then press the edges firmly but quickly with a hot iron. After bonding the edges, weight the entire patch firmly, and let the adhesive cure as directed by the manufacturer. Remove the weights when the adhesive is completely cured; don't wash the floor for at least a week.

INSTALLING UNDERLAYMENT

Almost without exception, floor coverings such as resilient tile, resilient sheet flooring, parquet blocks, and carpeting need a smooth and solid underlayment. If you are planning to cover your floors, make sure the present flooring, underlayment, or subflooring is smooth and solid. If it isn't, here is how to correct the problem:

Clear the room: Move out the furniture, remove the doors to the room and store them, and remove the moldings and trim at the base of the walls. Also remove registers, electrical outlet covers, and pipe escutcheons.

Now remove the carpeting. Inspect the tile, blocks, or hardwood flooring to make sure it is solidly in place. If not, the flooring should be removed or at least fastened down with adhesive, nails, or other permanent fasteners. Drive in protruding nail heads with a nail set. Flatten the bumps and ridges you find, with a chisel or sander. Fill large holes and cracks with water putty and sand smooth. After making repairs, inspect the floor to be sure it is smooth, then sweep the floor and vacuum it.

For the underlayment you'll need sheets of 1/4-inch or thicker tempered hardboard, particle board, or lauan plywood. Try to buy 4-by-4-foot pieces, or cut 4-by-8-foot sheets in half to make

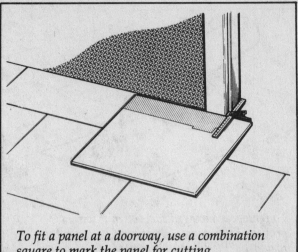

To fit a panel at a doorway, use a combination square to mark the panel for cutting.

them easier to handle and fit. Set the underlayment on edge around the room in which it will be installed for about 36 hours before installation; this allows the material to adjust to the room temperature and humidity.

If the underlayment is tempered hardboard (don't use standard or perforated hardboard), the slick side should be facing down. If the underlayment is particle board, either side of the panel may face down.

Be careful when handling particle board because the edges chip easily. Before laying each hardboard panel, you'll have to chamfer, or bevel, the top edges with a block plane. One swipe with the plane should be sufficient.

Using threaded or ring-shank underlayment nails, nail each underlayment panel every 6 inches around its perimeter. In hardboard the nails should be about 1/2 inch from the edge. In particle board the nails should be about 1 inch from the edge to prevent chipping. Place the next panels against those laid and nailed. If possible, the panels should not have common joints on all four sides; stagger the joints as much as you can. Four corners should never meet. Space the panels about 1/32 to 1/16 inch between joints to allow for expansion and contraction from humidity.

As you set each panel, check to see that it's level. If not, raise it with thin wooden strips or shims made from cedar shingles; make sure that the underlayment over these strips is solid. Set trimmed panels against the walls, next to doorways, and other places to complete the job. For smaller pieces, you should both glue and nail the underlayment to the floor with subflooring adhesive. This product is available for use in a caulking gun. Apply the adhesive to the floor, then press the underlayment down and pick it up again. Reset it and nail it. Pressing the panel down and picking it up before resetting it helps spread the adhesive over the surface for a better bond.

Place the first underlayment near the center of the floor. Place the next two panels against the first so there are no common joints.

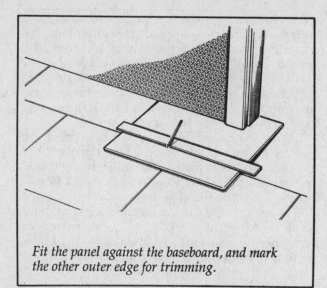

Fit the panel against the baseboard, and mark the other outer edge for trimming.

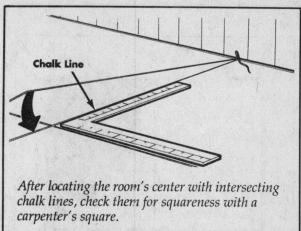

After locating the room's center with intersecting chalk lines, check them for squareness with a carpenter's square.

After all underlayment panels have been fastened down, carefully walk over the floor. If you find loose or spongy spots, nail the panels in such places with underlayment nails; the floor should be solid before the finish flooring is installed. Complete the job by vacuuming the floor.

LAYING A RESILIENT TILE FLOOR

The beauty of a resilient tile floor is its finished appearance plus the relative ease of installation. Most do-it-yourselfers should be able to tile an average 12-by-15-foot room in less than four hours.

When you shop for resilient tiles, you'll find solid vinyl and rubber tiles. With solid vinyl, the wear layer goes all the way through the tile's thickness; solid vinyl tiles are durable. Rubber tiles are highly durable but tricky to install.

Many solid vinyl tiles come with a self-stick backing, so you don't need a separate adhesive. If you do need adhesive, make sure you get the one specified for the product you'll be using. Buy a notched trowel for spreading the adhesive. Most tiles come with clear installation instructions. Here's the way a typical tile-laying job proceeds:

Remove the moldings and trim from the bases of the walls. Also remove metal thresholds in doorways, heating and cooling register covers, and other items that might interfere with the job. You'll need a hammer, screwdriver, and a stiff-blade putty knife, which is an excellent tool for prying up moldings.

Clean the floor, removing all wax, dirt, grease, and other debris from the surface. Sand down high spots, and make sure there are no nails sticking up. Because resilient tiles are flexible and tend to conform to whatever is under them, irregularities in the floor will eventually show through. Make sure the floor is clean and solid or tiles may become loose in time.

If there is an old floor covering that is bonded to the subflooring, you may not have to remove

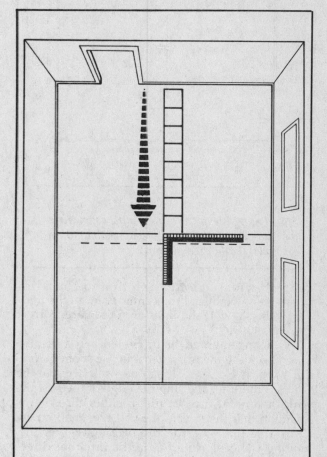

With uncemented tiles, lay a row of tiles from the centerline. If the last tile is less than half the width of a full tile, snap a new chalk line.

it. If the old floor covering is in poor condition, remove it. If old tile has to be removed, the best way is with a spade or long-handled ice scraper; remove one tile and wedge the spade or scraper under the adjoining tiles and pry up.

With a tape measure, find and mark the exact center of each wall. Stretch a chalk line across the floor between opposite center points. Where the lines intersect is the center of the room. Lay a car-

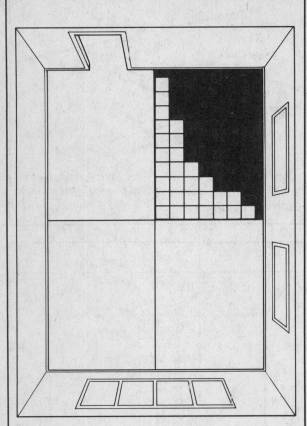

Start laying tile at the center of the room where the chalk lines cross. Set tiles alternately toward each wall, building a pyramid.

penter's square along each line to check for squareness. Do this at the center point in the middle of the floor. If the lines aren't square, correct them.

With uncemented or unpeeled self-adhesive tiles, check the measurements in the room by laying a full row of tiles along one wall. Begin at the wall's centerline, aligning the edge of the first tile with the line. If the last tile in either direction is less than half the width of a full tile, snap a new chalk line mark beside the original centerline, moving the centerline half a tile in either direction. This will give you even-sized tiles at both ends of a room and save cutting and fitting time. Repeat the procedure for the other centerline.

Pick up the tiles and thoroughly clean the floor. Vacuum the dust and dirt particles. Before you lay any tiles, store the tile in the room to be tiled for about 24 hours; this lets the material adjust to the temperature and humidity within the room. Tiles should be laid when the room temperature is 70° Fahrenheit or warmer. This temperature level also should be maintained for about ten days after the job has been completed.

Start working at the center of the room, where the chalk lines cross. The first tile is extremely critical because it is the key for all other tiles to be laid; make sure it is aligned perfectly along the centerline marks. If you are using tile adhesive, spread enough adhesive for about six to eight tiles at a time. This number may vary, depending on your arm reach. Just set as many tiles as you can comfortably reach without sticking your hand in the adhesive for support.

If you are using self-adhesive tiles, peel the backing off each tile as you go. Don't peel a lot of tiles and set them aside. The adhesive on peel-and-stick tiles is extremely sticky and bonds tightly. Once the tile is in place, you may not be able to remove the tile for refitting without damaging it. After the backing has been removed, bend the tile and butt just the edges of the tile against the adjoining tiles on two sides. Then "drop" it in position, using the straight edges on the adjoining tiles as guidelines.

If you are setting the tiles with floor adhesive, tiles should be set in place the same way as self-adhesive tiles, using adjoining tiles as guidelines. With floor adhesive, the tiles may be slid into alignment. Most floor adhesives are applied with a notched spreader, although some may be brushed on. Either way, follow the adhesive manufacturer's recommendations. Also be sure to note adhesive setting times. Some adhesives must be allowed to cure for 20 minutes or so before the tiles are applied.

After the first, or key, tile is set, lay tiles alternately toward each wall, building a pyramid. Do just one quarter of the room at a time, except the row of tiles along the walls. Note that some tile products, especially those with patterns, have directional arrows printed on the back of each tile. If the product you're using has these arrows, make sure that the tile is laid so the arrows point in the same direction.

Clean up adhesive that oozes from the tile joints as you work; it's easier to do this now before the adhesive dries. When you finish laying tiles in one quarter of the room, go over the tiles with a rolling pin to compress the tiles evenly into the adhesive. You may consider renting a tile roller for this job.

Once you've laid the tiles in one quarter of the room, set tiles in another quarter of the room until you finish laying all the uncut field tiles. Now cut and fit the border tiles along the walls. To fit a border tile, place a tile precisely on top of a tile in the row adjoining the border row to be laid. Then, butt a second tile against the wall, with its sides aligned with the first tile. Mark the first tile where the first and second tiles overlap, using the second one's edge as a guide. Cut the first tile along your mark; it should fit exactly. Some types of tile products can be cut more easily if they are heated until they are pliable. This is especially helpful when you must cut small pieces and irregular shapes.

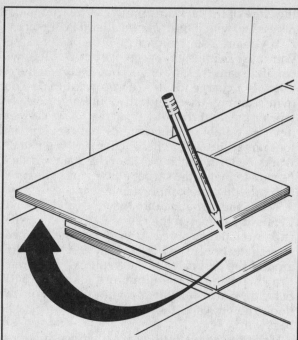

To fit a border tile, place a tile precisely on top of the tile in the row adjoining the border row. Then butt a second tile against the wall with its sides aligned with the first tile. Mark the first tile where the first and second ones overlap. Cut the first tile; it should fit exactly.

To fit tiles around objects, such as a pipe, heat register opening, toilet, or bathtub, you have a choice of two methods. One way is to use a compass with a point on one leg and a pencil on the other leg. Guide the pointed leg along the irregular surface of the object while the pencil draws this shape on a tile that is positioned exactly on top of the tile in the adjoining row.

Another way is to use thin cardboard that is the exact size of the tile, and cut a template to fit around the irregularity. Make a pattern of the obstacle from the cardboard. Trace your cardboard template onto the tile, and then cut the tile along your marks.

With effort, you can make each tile fit perfectly against the wall surfaces, but it is easier to cover imperfections along the walls with molding or trim. When the entire floor has been laid, add the molding along the walls and across the thresholds. Reinstall heat register covers and anything else you removed. Caulk joints that butt against bathtubs or pipes.

Don't scrub the new tile floor for about ten days. You should clean up excess adhesive as soon as the floor is down.

REPAIRING BURNS IN CARPETING

Professional reweaving is expensive, but what else can you do when your carpeting is damaged by cigarette burns? With a little patience, you usually can repair the damage yourself.

When only the tips of the carpet fibers are burned, cut off the charred fiber with a pair of small sharp scissors. Then sponge the area lightly with a mild detergent solution, and again with clean water. The low spot won't be noticeable when the carpet dries.

If the burn goes down to the backing, you can remove the charred fibers and insert new ones. Cut out the burned fibers, then pull the stubs out of the backing with tweezers. Clean out the entire burned area, so that you have a hole in the carpet with the woven backing exposed. To fill the hole, ravel fibers from the edge of a scrap piece of carpet; you'll need enough tufts of yarn to place one tuft in each opening in the backing. If you don't have a scrap piece, use tufts from an inconspicuous area of the carpet, such as the back corner of a closet.

When you have enough fibers, apply a little latex adhesive to the exposed backing. Use a carpet tuft-setting tool, which is a small punch with a forked tip, to insert the new fibers, one fiber in each opening. Fold each fiber in half to form a V, and place the folded tuft into the tuft setter. Set the tip of the tuft setter into the opening in the backing and strike the handle lightly with a hammer. When you lift the tuft setter, the fiber will stay in the carpet backing. Set fibers across the entire burn area, one at a time. The repair area should match the rest of the carpet in density and depth; if a tuft doesn't match in height, you can adjust by pulling it up a little with tweezers or tapping it down again with the tuft setter. When the hole is completely filled, cut protruding fibers flush with the rest of the pile.

Retufting works well for small burns, but if the backing is burned through or if a large area of carpet is damaged, you'll have to replace the burned area with a patch cut from a piece of scrap carpet. Cut out a rectangle or square of carpet, a little larger than the burned area. The patch must match any pattern in the carpet, and the pile must run in the same direction as the damaged pile, or the patch will be obvious. Press the patch firmly over the damaged area; holding it carefully in place, use a utility knife to cut around its edges and through the carpet under it. Cut completely through the backing, but don't cut into the carpet padding. When the entire damaged area is cut out, lift the burned piece out of the hole. Check the patch for fit, and trim the edges, if necessary, so that it fits the opening exactly.

To install the patch, use double-faced carpet tape or latex carpet adhesive. On each side of the hole, stick a piece of tape to the padding or apply adhesive. Position the patch and press the edges of the patch firmly onto the padding. The pattern and pile of the patch should blend with the surrounding carpet. Weight the patch with a heavy book. Let the adhesive dry for several hours before walking on the patch.

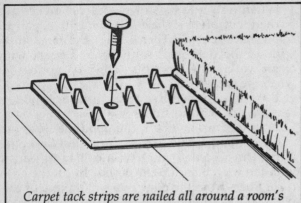

Carpet tack strips are nailed all around a room's perimeter leaving a 1/4-inch space between the strips and the wall.

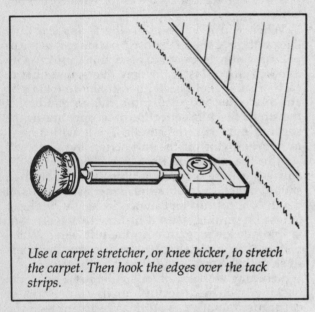

Use a carpet stretcher, or knee kicker, to stretch the carpet. Then hook the edges over the tack strips.

INSTALLING WALL-TO-WALL CARPET

Wall-to-wall carpeting must be stretched so that it's under tension. If it isn't, the carpeting is likely to ripple and wad. To stretch the carpet, you'll need to rent a carpet stretcher, commonly called a knee kicker. Installing carpet isn't too difficult, but there are some tricks to doing the job correctly. Here is what's involved:

Move all furniture out of the room to be carpeted. Also remove the doors to the room and metal thresholds. If the room is presently carpeted, pull up the old carpet and remove all tacks. Also eliminate squeaks in the floor, and drive in protruding nails with a nail set and hammer. If there are large cracks in the floor, fill them with wood putty. Vacuum and scrub the floor.

Now nail the carpet tack strips to the floor all around the perimeter of the room, leaving a 1/4-inch space between the strips and the walls. The teeth of the strips must face the walls.

Install the carpet padding by stapling it to the floor. Space staples at 12-inch intervals just so the padding won't slide. The padding should go to the edge of the tack strips and can be trimmed, if necessary, with a utility knife after it is in place.

If you are using two or more pieces of carpet, you must seam them. Many carpet retailers will cut and seam the carpet you buy before delivery. There is a charge for this. If you want to do your own seaming, use standard double-faced carpet tape or the kind that is activated by a special heat device available from some carpet retailers and tool rental firms. The heat-activated tape usually works better for seaming than the standard tape. Be sure to match the carpet pattern and pile direction carefully to obtain invisible seams.

Move the carpeting into the room and unroll it. Center the carpet in the room. Use the knee kicker to stretch the carpet. After the carpet has been stretched, hook the edges over the tack strips around the perimeter of the room. As you stretch the carpeting, have someone stand directly behind you to weight the material so you can hook the edges without having the carpet slip backward.

Trim the edges of the carpet with heavy-duty scissors or a utility knife, leaving about 1/8 inch of carpet beyond the tack strips. Use a wide putty knife to poke excess carpet down between the wall and the strip. If the carpet pops out, try holding it in place with double-faced carpet tape.

Install strips designed to hold down carpet at doorway thresholds. These strips, which are similar to tack strips, have points to grip the carpet, but they also have a decorative metal lip that may be bent flat against the edge of the carpet. If the carpet and pad are thicker than the previous floor covering, you may have to plane the bottom of the door so it clears the carpeting.

When the carpeting job is complete, carefully vacuum the carpet. If you find spots that aren't laying properly, you may have to restretch the carpet in this area. You may be able to pull it tight against the wall and tack it with nails; the carpet pile should conceal nail heads.

REFINISHING A HARDWOOD FLOOR

If you are tired of floor coverings and want to restore the natural warmth and beauty of hardwood, the job is difficult, but it can be done. You must remove old finishes and adhesives, and strip the floor down to the bare wood before you can apply the new finish.

At a tool rental store, rent a drum sander with a dust bag and a disk sander or edger. The store also furnishes sandpaper. Buy open coat sandpaper in 20, 40, and 100 grits.

Move everything out of the room, including curtains, draperies, and pictures. Floor refinishing is messy, especially the sanding operation.

Seal heating and cooling outlets with masking tape, and around all doorways except the one you will use (seal that one too, when you are ready to start). Some sanding dust will get into

A floor sander with a dust bag attachment.

the rest of the house, but sealing doorways and duct outlets helps reduce the mess.

Carefully remove shoe molding, baseboard and other molding at the floor. Check the entire floor for nails, and countersink any that protrude. Open the windows.

For the first sanding, use 20-grit paper in the drum sander. Go back and forth over the entire floor, with the grain, overlapping each pass about 3 inches. At the end of each pass, you must lift the sander and move it over but be careful in doing this to avoid digging into the floor. Go slowly. Use the disk sander in areas near the walls where the drum sander cannot reach.

Repeat the procedure with 40-grit paper, and then again with 100 grit. When you are satisfied that you have removed the old finishes, you can return the rental equipment.

Vacuum the room thoroughly, including the walls and around windows, to remove all the dust. Be sure to remove all the dust, or you will obtain an inferior finish.

If your floor is pine, use a special primer to seal the wood. Give the primer an hour to dry before applying your finish. If your floor is oak, rub some turpentine on a small section to see what the wood would look like with a natural finish. If you like the way the floor looks, you need not stain it. If you decide to stain the wood, apply the stain evenly and let it dry thoroughly according to the directions.

An easy, clear finish to apply is plastic resin, such as polyurethane varnish. The first coat will

be tack dry in about 15 minutes, and will be ready for the second coat in about an hour. When the second coat dries, wax and buff. For a high gloss, wait overnight and apply a third coat using a mixture of one part reducer to four parts finish. Let this coat dry overnight before use. After the third coat, the floor will not require waxing and can be shined with a dry mop.

Natural varnish is a traditional finish coat that requires more care to apply. It is slower drying, and there is more chance for dust to foul the finish. It is also subject to checking as it grows older, although when varnish is applied properly it dries clear for a beautiful finish. Follow it with a coat of wax and buff.

Windows

The openings in your home's walls are often trouble spots. Along with doors, windows are the major heat loss areas in most homes. They may stick shut when they're painted or swell shut from humidity. Shades and venetian blinds may not work right. Glass gets broken and screens get damaged or torn.

UNSTICKING A WINDOW

Double-hung windows, especially in older homes, often stick. They may be hard to open and close, or they may refuse to open at all. The most common cause of this problem is that the window has been painted shut, and the paint has sealed it closed. The solution is usually simple: Break the seal, clear away paint chips, and lubricate the sash tracks. The procedure takes strength, but it isn't difficult.

Before you start to work, make sure the window is unlocked. Then look for evidence of a paint seal between the sash and the window frame. The seal usually extends all around the window. To break the seal, push the blade of a stiff putty knife or paint scraper into the joint, cutting straight through the paint. If necessary, tap the knife lightly with a hammer to force in the blade. Work all around the window to break the seal; if the window was also painted on the outside, repeat the procedure to break the seal on the outside. This should release the window.

If the window still doesn't open, look at the tracks in the window frame above the sash; they're probably blocked with built-up paint. Using a chisel, clean the excess paint out of the tracks. Cut out the thickened paint, but be careful not to gouge the wood of the tracks. Smooth the cleaned-out tracks with medium-grit sandpaper on a narrow sanding block, and then spray them with silicone lubricant. The window should slide freely in the cleared tracks.

If the window still sticks, paint in the lower part of the tracks is probably holding it. Set a

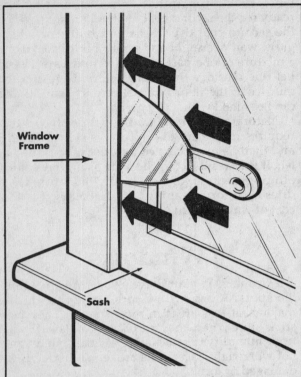

Window Frame

Sash

To free a window that has been painted shut, use a scraper or putty knife to cut the paint seal between the sash and the window frame. If necessary, tap the tool with a hammer.

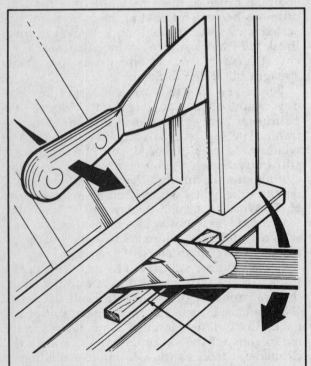

Working from the outside, insert the blade of a pry bar under the sash and pry gently from the corners in; lever the bar over a block of scrap wood.

block of scrap wood against the sash at the window frame. Tap the block of wood with a hammer gently to force the sash back from the frame. Don't exert too much force; all you want to produce is a slight movement. Move the block of wood all around the window sash, tapping the sash back from the frame; then try the window again. If it opens, clean and sand the tracks, and lubricate them with silicone spray. If it doesn't open, use a small pry bar, preferably from the outside. Insert the flat end of the pry bar under the sash, and set a block of scrap wood under it for better leverage. Pry gently at the corners of the sash and then from the corners in toward the center. Use the pry bar carefully; too much pressure could damage both the sash and the frame. If the window opens, clean and lubricate the tracks as above. If it doesn't, the sticking may be caused by extreme humidity, poor construction, or uneven settling. Don't try to force the window open; call a carpenter to fix it.

REPLACING BROKEN GLASS

Broken glass is easy to fix. You can buy replacement glass, cut to measure, at paint-and-glass stores and some home centers.

The first step is to remove the broken glass from the window frame. Wearing heavy gloves, work the pieces of glass back and forth until they're loose enough to pull out. Knock out stubborn pieces with a hammer. Then remove the old putty from the frame, using a chisel or scraper to pry it out. Look for the fasteners that held the glass in place: metal tabs called glazier's points in wood-frame windows and spring clips in metal frames. Set the points or clips aside; you'll need them to install the new glass. If the putty doesn't come out easily, soften it with a propane torch or heat gun. Scrape out the softened putty, being careful not to gouge out the window frame.

Measure the window frame from inside edge to inside edge up and down and sideways. Have the new pane cut 1/8 inch smaller each way.

Glazier's points hold the glass in place. Set one point every 6 inches around the pane; push the points in with the blade of a putty knife.

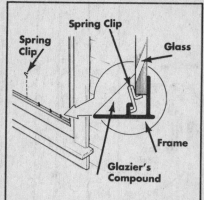

In a metal-frame window, the glass is held by spring clips instead of glazier's points. Install the clips by snapping them into the holes in the frame.

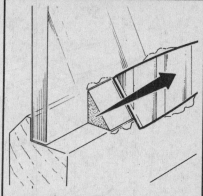

Seal the pane with glazier's compound, using a putty knife to smooth the compound at an angle and cut it off cleanly along the glass.

When you've removed the old putty, paint the raw wood around the pane with linseed oil to prevent the new putty from drying out too fast. If the frame is metal, paint it to prevent rusting. Let the oil soak in or the paint dry, then measure the frame for the new glass. The glass must be just enough smaller than the opening to allow for expansion and contraction, and for imperfections in the frame or the glass. Measure both ways across the opening, inside edge to inside edge, and subtract 1/8 inch each way. If the lip of the frame is wide, subtract as much as 1/4 inch each way. Have the replacement glass cut to these precise dimensions. You'll need glazier's points or clips every 6 inches or so around the pane. If there aren't enough old ones, buy new ones when you get the glass.

Use glazier's compound to install the new glass. Roll a large chunk of compound between your palms to make a long string about the diameter of a pencil. Starting at a corner, press this cord into the outside corner of the window frame, where the glass will rest. Cover the entire diameter of the frame. With the compound in place, carefully set the new pane of glass into the frame, pressing it firmly against the cord of compound. Press hard enough to flatten the compound, squeezing out air bubbles and forcing out some compound around the frame. To hold the glass in place, install glazier's points or spring clips every 6 inches or so around the pane. Push the points partway into the wood with the blade of a putty knife, held flat against the glass. If the frame is metal, snap the spring clips into the holes in the frame.

When the glass is firmly held in place, seal the new pane with glazier's compound all around the outside edge. Roll another thicker cord of glazier's compound, and press it firmly into the glass-frame joint around the pane. Then use a putty knife to smooth the compound along the joint around the pane, to match the putty around the other windows nearby. Hold the putty knife at an angle to the lip of the frame, so that the knife cuts the compound off cleanly and evenly along the glass. If the putty knife sticks or pulls at the glazier's compound, dip the blade into linseed oil and shake off the excess. Use long, smooth strokes to keep the joint even.

While the glazier's compound is still fresh, carefully remove the excess from both sides of the new glass and the frame, with a razor blade or a glass scraper. Then let the compound dry completely, for about three days. To finish the job, paint the new compound and the frame to match the rest of the window frame. Lap the paint over the edge of the compound and onto the glass, to seal the pane completely. Make sure the paint is dry before you clean the glass.

REPLACING A BROKEN SASH CORD

Double-hung windows, the kind found in most older homes, are still popular today in new home construction. Their most common problem is a broken sash cord. Double-hung windows operate on a rope-and-pulley system. Each window unit, or sash, is held on each side by a sash cord or chain, extending from the sash up to a pulley in the window frame and over the pulley into the inside the wall. A heavy weight at the end of each sash cord or chain balances the weight of the window and holds the sash in place when you open the window. When the sash cord breaks, the weight falls to the bottom of the frame, and there is nothing to hold the sash in place. You can replace the broken cord with a new cord, but to eliminate rope failure entirely, use sash chain.

You'll have to remove the sash from the window frame. On both sides of the window, remove the inside stop molding along the side of the sash frame. If the molding has been painted over, cut the paint seal between the frame and the mold-

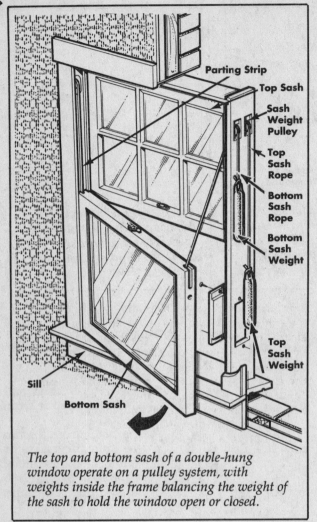

Parting Strip

Top Sash

Sash Weight Pulley

Top Sash Rope

Bottom Sash Rope

Bottom Sash Weight

Top Sash Weight

Sill

Bottom Sash

The top and bottom sash of a double-hung window operate on a pulley system, with weights inside the frame balancing the weight of the sash to hold the window open or closed.

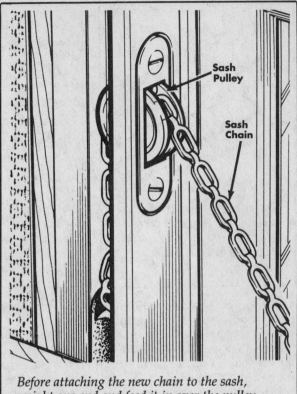

Sash Pulley

Sash Chain

Before attaching the new chain to the sash, weight one end and feed it in over the pulley.

ings; use a utility knife or a sharp single-edge razor blade. Then pry off the molding strip with a stiff scraper or a flat pry bar.

After removing the stop molding, ease the sash out of the window frame on the side with the broken cord until you can get at the slot at the top of the sash where the cord is attached. Cut or untie the knot in the end of the cord, and pull it out of the sash frame. Then ease the other side of the sash toward you out of the frame; you may need help to balance the sash on the sill while you work. Untie the knot that holds the cord on this side, and pull it out of the sash frame; don't let go of the end, or it will be pulled into the window frame. Knot the loose end of the cord to keep it from being pulled in, and then lift the sash down out of the window frame. Set it aside while you work on the cord. If the broken cord operates the top sash, you'll have to remove the bottom sash and pry out the parting strip between the two sashes, then remove the top sash.

Many double-hung windows have access plates set into the sides of the frame, so that you can get into the window frame to replace the cord. Some old windows do not have access

plates, and the entire window frame must be disassembled to replace the cord. Look closely at the lower part of the window frame to find the access plate on the side with the broken cord; it may have been painted over. If the outline of the plate isn't clear, tap the track lightly with a hammer to show the edge, then cut around the plate with a utility knife or a sharp razor blade. Remove the screws that hold the plate and lift the plate out of the window frame. Then reach into the opening in the frame and lift out the sash weight. Remove the old cord from the weight. Use the two pieces of the broken cord to measure a piece of sash chain to the correct length; leave several inches extra for fastening.

Before you attach the new sash chain to the window, feed it over the pulley at the top of the frame. Attach a small weight to one end of the chain, and push it in over the pulley. Slide a large nail through the end of the chain so that it cannot go over the pulley. Let the chain down until you can see the end in the access plate opening. Remove the small weight from the inside end. Attach the sash weight to the inside end of the chain, looping the chain through the opening in the weight and binding the loop securely with sturdy wire. Pull the wire tight with pliers, and make sure the weight is firmly fastened. It must be able to support the entire weight of the sash. Set the weight back into the access hole and pull the top end of the chain to eliminate slack, but don't replace the access plate yet.

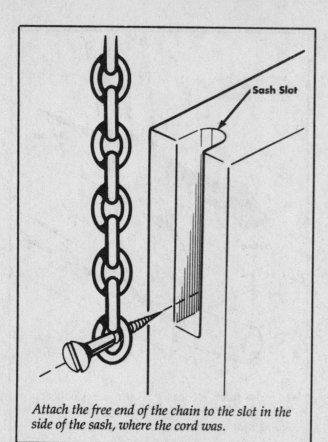

Attach the free end of the chain to the slot in the side of the sash, where the cord was.

With the weight secured to the chain, you're ready to install the sash. Since the frame is already accessible, replace the sash cord on the other side, too. Follow the same steps to remove the old cord, measure the chain, and attach the weight to the chain.

When both chains are secured to the weights, you can replace the sash in the window frame. You'll probably need help to balance the sash while you work. Before you lift the sash back, attach one chain to the slot in the sash. Use two 3/4-inch wood screws to secure the chain through two links. Then lift the sash back into the window frame. With the sash in place, attach the chain on the other side to the slot on that side of the sash. To check the operation of the chains, raise the sash as far as it will go in the track, keeping it braced against the parting stop as it moves. Have your helper look at the weights in the access holes at the sides of the window frame; the bottom of the weight on each side should be about 3 inches above the window sill. If a weight isn't the right distance from the sill, you'll have to adjust the chain at the slot in the sash to lengthen or shorten it as required.

When the weights are properly adjusted and the sash hangs evenly, let the sash down. While your helper holds the sash in place, replace the access plates and then the stop molding. If the sash is the top one, you'll have to replace the parting strip first, then the bottom sash and the stop molding.

REPAIRING OR REPLACING SCREENS

Screens are essential in summer to let in air and keep out bugs. When your screens develop holes, from abuse or just old age, take action. It isn't hard to repair the holes or, when the screen is badly damaged, to install new screening.

Patching Holes. Pinholes in screening are simple to fix. If the screening is metal, use an ice pick or a similar sharp tool to push the strands of wire toward the hole. You may be able to close the hole completely. If there is still a hole, paint a little clear nail polish or household cement over it. Let the sealer dry and apply another coat. Repeat, applying sealer sparingly, until the opening is filled. If the screening is fiberglass, you may be able to move the threads back into place. If you can't do this, fill tiny holes with clear nail polish or household cement. Be careful not to let the sealer run down the screen; blot excess immediately.

Clean cuts and tears in screening can usually be stitched together, use a long needle and strong nylon thread or on metal screening fine wire. Sew the edges of the tear with a close zigzag stitch across the cut, and be careful not to pull the thread or wire so tight that the patch puckers. After stitching the tear closed, apply clear nail polish over the thread or wire to keep it from pulling loose.

To close a large hole, cut a patch from a scrap piece of screening, the same kind (fiberglass or metal) as the damaged screening. Don't use metal screening made of a different metal; placing two metals together, such as steel to copper, can cause corrosion.

A fiberglass patch is easy to install, if you can lay the screen flat. Cut a patch about 1/2 inch bigger than the hole, and set it over the hole. Place a sheet of aluminum foil over the patch area, shiny side down, and press the patch firmly with a hot iron. Be careful not to touch the screen directly with the iron. The heat will fuse the patch onto the screening. If you can't lay the screen flat, sew the patch into place with a needle and nylon thread; use a firm running stitch, but don't pull the thread too tight. Apply clear nail polish over the edges of the patch to keep it from fraying.

To patch metal screening, cut a square or rectangular patch about 1 inch bigger than the hole all around. Pull out the wires on all four sides to make a wire fringe about 1/2 inch deep all around the patch. Then bend the fringe wires down sharply at a right angle. Use a block of scrap wood to make a clean bend on each side of the patch. When the fringe wires are evenly bent, set the patch over the hole in the screen, and press it to insert the bent fringe wires through the screening around the hole. The patch should be flat against the screen, covering the hole completely. When it's properly positioned, fold the fringe wires down flat toward the center of the

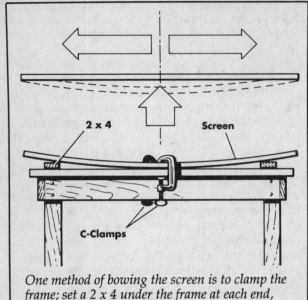

One method of bowing the screen is to clamp the frame; set a 2 x 4 under the frame at each end, and clamp the center firmly with C-clamps.

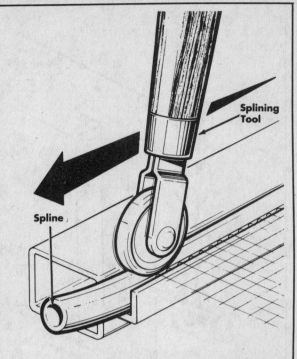

In metal-frame screens, a plastic spline holds the screening. To install the screening, roll the spline into the groove with a splining tool.

patch on the other side of the screen. Then stitch the patch down all around with a needle and nylon thread or fine wire.

Replacing Damaged Screening. When a screen has so many holes or such big ones that it isn't worth patching or when metal screening becomes bulged and rusted, replace the screening entirely. If the frame is in good shape, this isn't difficult. You can use either fiberglass or aluminum screening. You may be able to buy screening cut to size. If you buy it on a roll, use scissors to cut it about 1 1/2 inches larger all around than the opening. If you're working on an aluminum-frame screen, you'll also need plastic splining, a few inches longer than the perimeter of the screen, to replace the old spline.

To replace a screen in a wood frame, use a stiff putty knife to pry up the molding around the edges. Be careful not to crack the molding. When the molding is off, pry out the tacks or staples that held the screening in place, and remove the screening. Pull out staples or tacks left in the frame.

To stretch the screening into place in the frame, you must bow or arch the frame. There are two ways to do this, by weighting or clamping. To use the weight method, set the frame the long way across two sawhorses, and hang a weight from a rope around the center of the frame. To clamp the frame into a bow, set it on a workbench or a wide board across two sawhorses. Place a C-clamp at the center of each long side, holding the frame to the work surface, and set a long piece of scrap wood, such as a 2 x 4, between the frame and the work surface at each end. As you tighten the C-clamps, the frame will bow.

When the frame is securely clamped, set the screening across it, aligned along one unclamped end. Use a staple gun loaded with heavy-duty staples to attach the screening to the frame. Place the staples at right angles to the frame, 2 to 3 inches apart. If you're using fiberglass screening, turn the cut edge under about 1 inch before stapling it down. When the first end is securely stapled, pull the loose screening over the clamped frame, and stretch it firmly and evenly across to the opposite end. Holding it firmly as you work, staple the second end into place, setting the staples 2 to 3 inches apart at right angles to the frame. Then unclamp or unweight the frame; the screening should be pulled tight as it straightens out. Staple the two sides into place, and trim off excess screening. To finish, replace the molding to cover the stapled edges of the screening.

To replace a screen in an aluminum frame, you don't have to bow the frame, but you'll need a special splining tool to install the plastic spline. Pry up the spline that holds the old screening in place, using a screwdriver or a putty knife, and remove the old screening. Lay the frame flat, and position the new screening over it. Trim the edges so that the screening extends just to the outside edges of the frame. To keep the screening level with the frame, set scrap boards under it, the same thickness as the frame.

When the screening is trimmed correctly, position it so that one end and one side are lined up on the outside edge of the splining groove in the frame. Hold the screening in place. With the convex roller of the splining tool, force the edge of the screening into the splining groove; be careful not to let the screening slip out of place. Secure the other two sides the same way, stretching the screening taut as you work. When all four sides of the screening are in place, cut off excess screening with tin snips or scissors. Using the concave end of the splining tool, drive the plastic spline into the groove to hold the screening in place. Start installing the spline at a corner and work around the frame. Where the ends meet, cut off the excess splining. With the spline in place, your screen will be as good as new.

REPAIRING WINDOW SHADES

Everyone who has ever used window shades is familiar with the many problems that beset them. There is the shade that is so tightly wound it snaps all the way up, the one that is so loose it won't go up at all, and the one that binds at the edges or falls out of its brackets. A simple adjustment usually is all that is needed to get your shades working properly.

A shade that binds is probably being pinched by brackets set too close together. If the brackets are mounted on the wall or on the outside of the window frame, this is easy to remedy; simply tap the brackets outward with a hammer. This technique also may work on brackets mounted inside the window frame. If the shade still sticks, take it down; you'll have to remove some wood from the roller. Remove the round pin and the metal cap on the round-pin end of the roller, and sand the end of the roller with medium-grit sandpaper. Badly binding shades may require further adjustment. If the brackets are outside-mounted, you can move out one bracket. If the brackets are inside-mounted, the shade must be cut down; have it professionally cut to fit the frame.

The opposite problem occurs when the mounting brackets are set too far apart. The shade may even fall when you try to use it. If the brackets are mounted outside the frame, tap them gently with a hammer or move one bracket in closer to the other. If the brackets are mounted inside the frame, you'll have to adjust the space with cardboard shims. Take the shade down and cut a piece of thin cardboard a little smaller than one bracket. Unscrew the bracket, set the shim behind it, and screw the bracket on over the shim. If necessary, add one or more shims to each bracket.

When the shade won't go up or down properly, the roller mechanism itself usually is at fault. Shades are operated by a strong coil spring inside one end of the roller. The pin that holds the shade up at this end of the roller is flat; this flat pin tightens or loosens the spring when you roll the shade up or down. At the flat-pin end of the roller, the spring is controlled by a pawl and ratchet, which stop the movement of the spring when the shade is released. If the shade is too tight or too loose, or if it doesn't stay in place

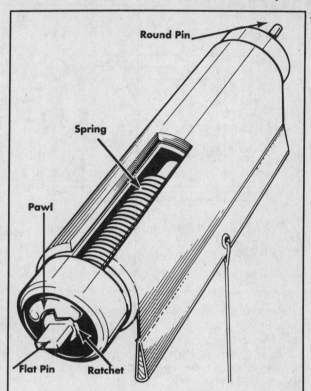

The shade is operated by a spring inside the roller. At the roller's flat-pin end, a pawl-and-ratchet mechanism stops the movement of the spring when the shade is released.

when you release it, there is usually a problem with the spring or with the pawl-and-ratchet mechanism. Unless the spring is broken, this is easy to fix.

If the shade won't stay up, the spring is too loose. Pull the shade down enough to turn the roller a few times; if it's extremely loose, pull it down about halfway. Lift the flat-pin end of the roller out of its bracket; then roll the shade up by hand, keeping it tightly rolled. Set the roller back on the bracket and try the shade again. If it still doesn't stay up, repeat the procedure.

If the shade snaps up and is hard to pull down, the spring is too tight. With the shade rolled up, lift the flat-pin end of the roller out of its bracket, and unroll it two or three turns by hand. Replace the roller on the bracket and test its operation; adjust it further if necessary. If the shade won't stay down, the pawl-and-ratchet mechanism may need cleaning. Take the shade down and remove the cap at the flat-pin end of the roller. Vacuum out dust, and clean the mechanism with a soft cloth; then spray a little silicone lubricant into the mechanism. Replace the metal cap and rehang the shade; the mechanism should now catch properly.

A shade that works unevenly also can be repaired. If the roller rocks when the shade is raised or lowered, one of its pins may be bent.

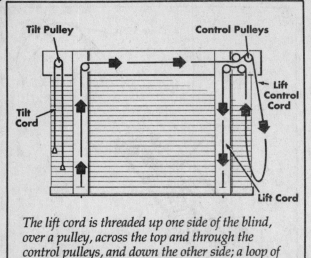

The lift cord is threaded up one side of the blind, over a pulley, across the top and through the control pulleys, and down the other side; a loop of cord from the control pulleys forms the lift control.

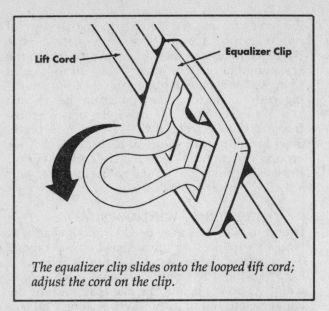

The equalizer clip slides onto the looped lift cord; adjust the cord on the clip.

Take the shade down and examine the pins. If one is bent, straighten it with pliers. If the shade is crooked on the roller, it must be reattached. Take it down and unroll it completely onto a flat surface; pry out the staples that hold the shade to the roller.

Reposition the roller so that it's at a right angle to the shade fabric, and if there is a big difference, cut off excess at the roller end of the fabric. With a staple gun and heavy-duty staples, reattach the fabric to the roller, setting the staples close together and parallel with the roller. Then carefully reroll the shade and rehang it.

REPAIRING VENETIAN BLINDS

Venetian blinds are a practical and long-lasting window treatment, but they can develop problems. When the cords break or the tapes look frayed and shabby, you can give your blinds new life by installing replacement cords and tapes, which often are sold in kits. Always replace both cords, the lift cord and the tilt cord, at the same time. If you're also replacing the tapes, make sure you buy tapes for the same width slats, and with the same number of ladders, as the old ones.

If the blind is clean and otherwise in good condition, and the old cord is not broken, you can install a new lift cord without removing the unit from the window. With the blinds down, tilt the slats to horizontal. The ends of the cord are secured to the bottom of the bottom rail. If the bottom rail is wood, the knotted ends of the cord are simply stapled under the ends of the tapes; if it's metal, remove the end caps and the clamps from the rail to expose the knotted cords. Untie the knot on the side opposite the lift cord, and butt the end of the new cord to this end. Tape the two ends firmly with masking tape.

Pull gently on the old cord to draw the new cord up through the slats on this side, across the top, and through the control pulleys; leave a loop of excess cord for the new lift cord, and then continue to draw the cord down through the slats on the lift cord side. When the taped end of the new cord reaches the bottom rail, untape the old cord and discard it; cut off excess cord at the starting end. Knot both ends of the new cord, and secure them the same way the old cord was secured. Replace the end caps on the bottom rail, and slide the equalizer clip off the old lift cord and onto the new one. Adjust the cord with the equalizer until the blind works smoothly.

This procedure takes care of the lift cord, but not the tilt cord. To replace the tilt cord, untie the knots at the ends of the cord, and remove the pulls. The tilt cord is simply threaded over a pulley and out again; it doesn't connect with the lift cord. Remove the old cord by pulling it out; thread one end of the new cord over the pulley and feed it in until it comes out over the other side of the pulley. Slip the cord pulls over the ends of the cord and knot the ends to hold the pulls on.

If the lift cord is broken, the slats need cleaning or painting, or the ladder tapes are going to be replaced, you'll have to take the blind down. Lay the blind out flat, all the way open, and untie both ends of the lift cord. Remove the staples if the bottom rail is wood; remove the clamps if it's metal. Pull the cord out of the blind, and set the equalizer clip aside. Remove the blind's slats one by one, stacking them in order. If they're dirty, this is a good time to clean them. Soak them in a bathtub, in a mild solution of liquid detergent, and then rinse and dry them thoroughly. The slats also can be repainted. Use a fast-drying spray lacquer.

When the slats are ready, pull out the hooks that hold the tapes in place at the top of the blind; one hook holds the tapes on each side. Position the new tapes in the top box and slide the hook into each pair of tapes, front and back, at the

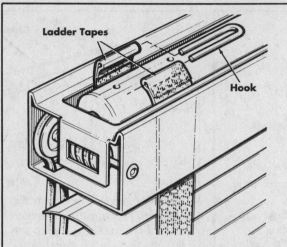

At the top of the blind, slide the hooks into the sleeves in the front and back ladder tapes at the sides of the box. One hook holds the tapes at each side.

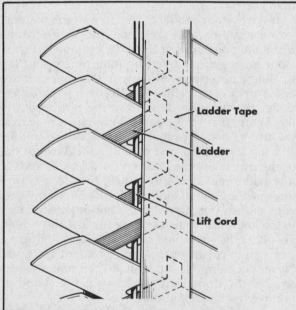

Insert the lift cord at the center of the tapes, passing the ladders first on one side and then on the other.

sides of the box. Slide the slats into place between the tapes; make sure they're all right side up and facing the right way. Fold the ends of the tapes under and fasten them to the bottom rail under the last slat.

With the slats in place, thread a new lift cord into the blind, starting at the tilt cord side and working up that side, across the top, through the control pulley, and down the other side. The tapes have woven strips connecting the front and back pieces, on alternating sides. Insert the new cord right at the center of the tapes, so that these ladders are placed on alternate sides of the cord.

At the control pulley, leave a long loop of cord for the new lift cord, and then keep threading the cord down through the slats on that side. When you reach the bottom rail, cut off excess cord, knot both ends of the cord, and secure the ends to the bottom rail. To finish, slide the equalizer clip onto the lift cord and install a new tilt cord.

Before you rehang the blind, check the control pulley mechanism to make sure it is working properly. If you can see dirt or lint in the pulleys, vacuum it out and wipe the mechanism clean with a soft cloth. Then spray silicone lubricant into the pulleys to keep them working smoothly.

Doors

Are you dissatisfied with a door or doors in your home? Perhaps one is sticking or won't entirely close, or perhaps you'd like to replace a door with a different style. Repairing or replacing a door calls for patience and a few carpentry skills, but neither job will take more than a few hours of your time.

UNSTICKING A DOOR

Doors stick for many reasons, from poor construction to extreme humidity. It usually is easy to unstick the stubborn door. To diagnose the problem, close the door, watching it carefully to locate the binding point. If there is a gap between the door and the frame opposite the binding edge, the hinges probably need adjustment. If you can't see a gap anywhere between the door and the frame and you had to slam the door to close it, the wood has probably swollen from extreme humidity. If the hinges and the wood are both all right, the door frame itself may be out of alignment; check the frame with a carpenter's square to see if this is the case.

If the binding is caused by poorly adjusted hinges, first examine the hinges for loose screws, on both the door and on the frame. Tighten loose screws securely. If a screw doesn't tighten, the screw hole has become enlarged. When the hole is enlarged, you may be able to correct the problem by replacing the screw with a longer one; make sure the head is the same size. Or use a hollow fiber plug with the old screw; spread carpenter's glue on the outside of the plug, and insert it into the screw hole. Then drive the screw into the hole. When the screw hole is badly enlarged, use wooden toothpicks to fill it. Dip the toothpicks in carpenter's glue and insert them around the screw hole; let the glue dry and then trim the toothpicks flush with the surface. Drive the screw into the filled-in hole; it should hold securely.

If the screws are not loose, the hinges may have to be readjusted on the door frame. Close the door, watching to see where it sticks and where it gaps. If the door is tilted in the frame, it

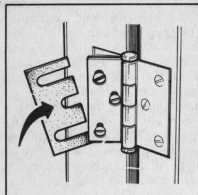

To shim a hinge, loosen the screws on the door frame side. Cut a shim from thin cardboard, and slide it behind the hinge.

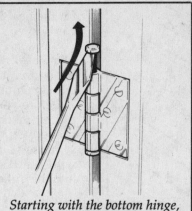

Starting with the bottom hinge, tap the hinge pin up and out with a screwdriver. Carefully pull the door from the frame.

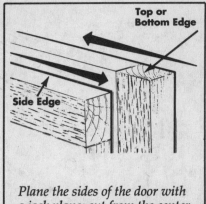

Plane the sides of the door with a jack plane; cut from the center toward the ends. On the top and bottom, use a block plane; cut from the ends toward the center.

will stick at the top on one side and at the bottom on the other; there will be a gap between the door and the frame opposite each binding point. To remedy this situation, you'll have to shim the hinge diagonally across from the binding point on the latch side. If the top-latch edge sticks, shim the bottom hinge; if the bottom-latch edge sticks, shim the top hinge. If the door has three hinges, shim the middle hinge as well as the top or bottom one.

Shimming the hinges is simple, but you must hold the door in place while you're working. Open the door as far as it will go, and push a wedge under it to hold it firmly. At the hinge to be adjusted, loosen the screws from the hinge leaf on the door frame; don't touch the screws in the door itself. Cut a piece of thin cardboard to the same size as the hinge leaf, and mark the location of the hinge screws on it. Cut horizontal slots in the shim to fit over the screws; then slide the shim over the screws behind the loosened hinge leaf. Keeping the shim in place, tighten the screws to resecure the hinge. Remove the wedge holding the door and close the door. If the door still sticks, but not as much as it did before, add another shim under the hinge. This should eliminate the gap between the door and the frame, and also should eliminate the binding.

If the door sticks even after shimming, or if there is no gap anywhere around the frame, you'll have to remove some wood at the binding points. Use a block plane on the top or bottom of the door, a jack plane to work on the side. If the door sticks at the sides, try to plane only on the hinge side; the latch side is beveled slightly, and planing could damage the bevel. Remove only a little wood at a time; keep your cuts even across the entire binding edge.

The top of the door can be planed without taking the door down. Wedge the door as far open as it will go, and work from a stepladder. With a block plane, cut carefully from the ends of the door toward the center. Don't cut from the center out; this could split the wood. Test the door after planing only a little bit; don't cut off more wood than you have to.

If the bottom or side of the door needs planing, you'll have to take the door out of the frame. Close the door most of the way, but don't latch it. Door hinges are secured by long hinge pins; tap the hinge pins out, starting with the bottom hinge and working up. Hold the tip of a screwdriver under the pin's head, and tap the pin up out of the hinge. If it sticks, tap a long nail up against the pin to dislodge it. Then tap out the middle and top hinge pins, and carefully lift the door out of the frame. Set the door on its side. Clamp it to a workbench or heavy crate, or use a clamp designed to hold a door steady. Plane the binding edge of the door. To plane the bottom, use a block plane, and cut from the ends toward the center. To plane the sides, remove the hinges and use a jack plane; cut from the center toward the ends. Never cut from the ends toward the center on the side of the door; this could split the wood or remove too much material.

After planing evenly all along the binding edge, set the door back into the frame, and open and close it. If it still sticks, plane off a little more wood. Before you replace the door permanently, you must seal the planed edges. If you fail to do this, the raw wood will absorb moisture and the door will stick again. Coat the raw edges with thinned shellac, and let the shellac dry for at least an hour. Then rehang the door.

If the door sticks because the frame is out of alignment, there is not much you can do to fix it. At the binding point, set a piece of 2 x 4 flat against the frame, and give it several firm hammer blows. This may move the frame just enough to solve the problem. If this doesn't work, you'll have to adjust the hinges or plane the edges to allow for the unevenness of the frame. The door may be crooked, but it won't stick.

HANGING AN INTERIOR DOOR

Hanging a door is an exacting job that must be done correctly for the door to open and close properly. If you are replacing a door and take your time, the job isn't difficult. If you are installing a new door, consider purchasing a prehung door so you don't have to build the door frame yourself. A prehung door comes with a frame.

Swinging Doors. Before buying a door, measure the inside of the door opening exactly, top to bottom and jamb to jamb. Be sure to measure between the side jambs of the frame, not between the stops. Allow 1/2-inch clearance at the top of the door and 1/4-inch clearance at the bottom. If the door will open or close over carpeting, allow 7/8-inch clearance at the bottom. Subtract this clearance from the measured top-to-bottom height of the opening. Allow 1/8-inch clearance at each side; subtract 1/4 inch from the measured side-to-side width of the doorway opening.

Place the door across the sawhorses and cut off the stile extensions, if any, at the top. Cut off enough at the bottom of the door to provide the necessary clearance in the door opening. With a pencil, draw a line parallel to the latch edge of the door to show how much must be trimmed off the width of the door to fit the opening.

After you have planed the door to the correct size, slightly bevel or chamfer the latch edge of the door.

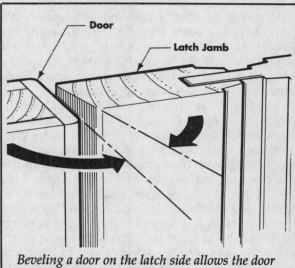

Beveling a door on the latch side allows the door to clear the jamb as the door swings open and shut.

Place the door on the floor, hinge-edge down, and clamp the door to a workbench or use a specially designed door vise. The door must be perfectly vertical. With a jack or jointer plane, remove wood from the latch edge of the door down almost to the pencil line. Before you plane down to the line, set the door in the opening to make sure the planed edge is parallel to the jamb. If the edge of the door isn't parallel to the jamb, mark the edge of the door and finish planing.

After you have planed the door to the correct size, bevel, or chamfer, the latch edge of the door to allow it to clear the jamb as the door swings open and shut. Round off the door's corner edges slightly to prevent them from splintering, and sand all surfaces smooth; use fine-grit sandpaper on a sanding block.

Set the door in the opening and force it tight against the hinge jamb by driving a wooden wedge into the gap on the latch side.

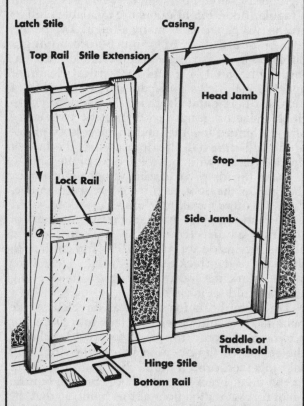

Before buying a door, measure the inside of the door opening exactly, top to bottom and jamb to jamb.

Lay a 6d nail across the top of the door and drive a wooden wedge under the door until the nail is snug against the head jamb; this procedure provides the proper amount of space between the top of the door and the head jamb.

Mark the positions for the top and bottom hinges on both the door and the hinge jamb. The hinges should be 3 1/2-inch butts with loose pins. The pin's cap must be at the top of the hinge. If the door frame already has mortises for hinges match these to the new door.

With a sharp pencil, draw the outlines of the hinges on the edge of the door and on the jamb. The hinges should be set 1 1/8 inches in from the face of the door and from the front edge of the jamb. To simplify this operation and the next one, you can buy a butt marker for a 3 1/2-inch hinge. This device marks the position and outline of a hinge. When you hit it with a hammer, it cuts the outline into the wood to the proper depth.

If you don't have a butt marker, use a wide butt chisel or knife to cut the outlines of the hinges in the door edge. Chisel out the wood within the outlines to make the mortises for the hinge leaves. Make a series of closely spaced cuts across the wood and rake out the chips.

Smooth the bottom of the mortise and set the hinge leaf into it. The top of the leaf should be flush with the surrounding wood; continue chiseling out wood and testing the depth until the leaf is flush with the surface. After you complete the mortises in the jamb and in the edge of the door, take the hinges apart and screw the leaves firmly into the door edge. Screw the other leaves into the jamb, but drive in only one screw per leaf; don't make holes for the other screws yet.

Set the door into the opening and fit the hinge leaves together. If they fail to fit, loosen the jamb leaves and try again. If you still cannot make them fit, adjust the jamb leaves up or down in the jamb as necessary. When you get the right fit, slip the hinge pins into the hinges. Then finish driving the remaining screws into the jamb.

If the door strikes the latch jamb when you push it closed or if there is too much of a gap between the door and the latch jamb, loosen the screws in the hinge and insert narrow cardboard shims under the leaves. A shim placed under the inner edge of a hinge forces the door away from the latch jamb; placed under the outer edge (pin edge), the shim forces the door toward the latch jamb. The thicker the shims, the greater the movement of the door.

Step into the room and pull the door shut. Draw pencil lines on the jambs around the sides and top of the door. Cut stops to fit around the door, position them along the pencil lines, and tack them to the jambs temporarily. Close the door against the stop moldings. If the door fits snugly against them, nail the stops, and countersink the nail heads with a nail set. If the stops don't fit snugly against the door, remove the tack nails and reposition the moldings. The door must be plumb (vertically level) in the opening to swing properly; make sure it's plumb before you nail the stops.

Fill nail holes with wood putty, and finish the moldings and door, including the edges, with sealer, stain, paint, varnish, shellac, or whatever finish you wish.

Prehung Doors. Prehung doors are easy to install. These doors come already set in a frame, and one side of the frame has been trimmed with molding. The hardware often has been installed, making installation even easier. To buy a prehung door, you need to know the size of the rough door opening. There are approximately 3 inches at the side jambs and 1 1/2 inches at the head jamb for fitting purposes. To install a prehung door, set the door into the rough opening, and plumb the jamb sides, filling gaps at the top and sides with shims.

Nail the head and side jambs to the rough framing, using 16d finishing nails. Countersink the nail heads into the face of the jambs. Fill the holes with wood putty. Nail the finished casing or molding to the doorway with 10d finishing nails; countersink the nail heads.

Folding Doors. If you need a door where there isn't room for it to open, you might install a folding door. A bifold door uses only half the space of a regular door. Bifold doors are available with as few as two panels or as many as eight; two panels fit a standard door opening. Before buying a bifold door, measure the inside of the door opening. Subtract 1 1/4 inches for vertical clearance and 1/2 inch (for a four-panel door subtract 3/4 inch) for horizontal clearance. Buy a door cut to fit this size opening; make sure the panels are already hinged together and the necessary pivots are included. Install the door so that the face of the door aligns with the front edges of the jamb.

Insert the top pivot bracket into the metal track that guides the door, as directed by the manufacturer. If you're installing a four-panel door, insert the second top pivot bracket into the other end of the track as directed. Set the track in position across the inside top of the door opening, with the edge of the track flush with the edges of the jambs. Mark the location for screw holes along the track and set it aside.

Drill pilot holes for screws as directed by the manufacturer and fasten the track into place. For a two-panel door, from the top pivot bracket at the corner of the opening where the door will fold together, drop a plumb bob from the center of the pivot bracket to the floor. Set the bottom pivot bracket on the floor at this point, so that the holes in the two brackets line up exactly. Mark the screw holes for the bottom pivot bracket. Drill pilot holes for the screws and screw the bracket into position on both the floor and door frame.

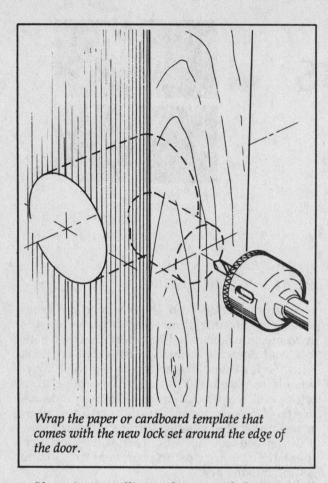

Wrap the paper or cardboard template that comes with the new lock set around the edge of the door.

If you're installing a four-panel door, install the second bottom pivot bracket in the same way, aligning it exactly under the top pivot bracket at the other side of the door frame.

If you're installing the door in a carpeted area, allow adequate clearance over the carpeting. Decide the position of the bottom pivot bracket or brackets as before, but don't attach them. Trace the outline of each bracket exactly on a block of scrap wood that is the same thickness as the carpeting. With a handsaw, cut the block of wood to the same size as the bracket. Cut out a similar size section of carpet, set the block in place, and screw the bottom pivot bracket into the block and the door frame.

Fold the door panels together. The pivot panel has pivot pins at top and bottom to fit into the pivot brackets; the guide panel has a wheel that moves along the track. Set the bottom pivot pin into place in the bottom pivot bracket and tilt the folded-together door into the door frame. Slide the top pivot bracket over to the top of the tilted door and insert the top pivot pin into the bracket. Tilt the door slowly into position, sliding the top bracket back toward the pivot corner; insert the guide wheel in the track when the angle of the door allows. Open the door to bring it firmly upright.

If you're installing a four-panel door, repeat this procedure to install the second pair of panels on the other side of the door frame. Test the door for proper operation. If it sticks or doesn't hang evenly, adjust it according to the manufacturer's instructions.

Complete the installation by attaching doorknobs on both sides of the hinge joint. Mark and drill pilot screw holes, then screw in the knobs with the screws provided. If you're installing a four-panel door, attach doorknobs to each set of panels; close the door and attach the aligning plates provided to hold the panels together.

INSTALLING A LOCK SET

Once you've hung a new door, you need to fit it with a lock set. Some doors come predrilled for standard-sized lock sets. With other new doors, you need to drill the holes yourself, using a template provided by the lock manufacturer. With a door, you also need to cut mortises in the door edge for the lock set and in the frame for the strike plate that engages the lock's bolt.

Wrap the paper or cardboard template that comes with the new lock set around the edge of the door, according to the manufacturer's directions. Use it to locate two holes. One hole is for the lock cylinder; the other hole goes into the edge of the door for the bolt. Mark the centers for these two holes on the door.

Use a brace and an expansion bit or a power drill with a hole saw attachment to drill a hole of the size specified for the lock cylinder. Be careful not to damage the veneer on the opposite side of the door. When you see the point of the drill coming through, stop and finish boring from the other side.

Drill a hole of the appropriate size for the bolt into the edge of the door. Be sure to hold the drill at a right angle to the door, and keep drilling until you reach the cylinder hole. You can use a combination square against the edge of the door and the drill bit to keep the bit at a right angle to the door.

Smooth the edges of the holes with sandpaper. Insert the bolt into its hole, and place the bolt plate in position over it. Then, trace the bolt plate's outline on the edge of the door. Remove the bolt, and mortise the edge for the bolt plate so it will be flush with the surface. Use a butt chisel to cut the mortise. Insert the bolt and plate in the mortise, and drill pilot holes for the mounting screws. Install the screws to secure the bolt in place. Insert the outside lock cylinder so that the stems or the connecting bar fits into the bolt assembly. Attach the interior lock cylinder and secure with screws, then locate the proper spot for the strike plate on the jamb, and drill a proper-sized hold in the jamb. Using the strike plate as a pattern, mark the jamb for mortising, and cut the mortise. Install the strike plate with screws so that it fits flush with the jamb. Test the operation of the lock.

OUTSIDE JOBS

The outside of your home and its landscaping are the first things visitors see. This chapter tells how you can keep your yard and house looking their best, season after season. Outside jobs are more than just keeping up appearances. A lawn that is neglected soon goes to seed and begins to erode. A small crack in concrete collects water that can freeze and widen the crack. Ignore a roof leak, and it will soon wreak havoc inside.

Most outside jobs are neither expensive nor especially time consuming. All they require is a few tools and materials, some know-how, and a few Saturday mornings distributed throughout the spring, summer, and fall.

Yard Work

Although you'll probably have to mow and water throughout the summer, spring and fall are the best times to catch up on yard work. Your first task may be to get your landscaping into an easily maintained condition. After that, you only need to do yard work from time to time.

MINIMIZING YARD MAINTENANCE
No matter what you do, your yard will take some maintenance to keep it presentable. By planning ahead, you can keep your yard work to a minimum and still have a good-looking lawn.

Here are some suggestions to make caring for your yard easier:

Mowing and Edging. Mowing is not a problem unless there are slopes or other tough-to-mow areas. If there are steep slopes, you could plant a ground cover, terrace with rocks or stones, or change the slope. These are not easy solutions, but after they are in place, the mowing problem is licked. You may be able to eliminate mowing by using a ground cover instead of grass. There are living ground covers, such as ivy, ajuga, and sedum, and inert ground covers such as pebbles, bark, or gravel.

You must edge your lawn where the grass ends. You can install mowing strips where the lawn meets a flower bed or where the lawn runs to a wall. Mowing strips are strips that are flush with the lawn and wide enough for the mower wheels to ride on. You can make these from bricks, concrete blocks, railroad ties, or landscaping ties. Be sure to put a good bed of sand or gravel under the mowing strip so it doesn't sink. If flower beds are not a big part of the yard, corrugated edging strips help prevent grass from getting into the beds.

Watering. The best answer to watering problems is to install an underground sprinkler system and automate it. Short of that, select the right sprinkler. Moving sprinklers are better than a

An effective way to control weeds is to feed your lawn with an organic fertilizer distributed with a spreader.

steady spray. Let the shape and size of your yard guide you in selecting a sprinkler. Buy one that will adjust to odd shapes without too much waste, but also get one that will cover as much territory as possible without your having to move it. You may need to have more than one sprinkler. Water only when there is a need. Overwatering or everyday shallow watering isn't as good as deep-watering when needed, because it causes shallow root systems.

Weeds. In flower beds cover empty spaces with mulch or inert ground cover. Mulch helps beds retain moisture. For the lawn you can use herbicides to kill weeds, but digging them out is better for the environment. Herbicides also will kill other plants, including the grass, unless you use the right kind for your lawn. One of the most effective ways to control weeds is to feed your lawn with an organic fertilizer distributed with a spreader, give it plenty of water, and mow regularly. A healthy lawn will choke out weeds, and keeping them cut won't allow them to seed. Add some hand-pulling to that, and you should get rid of them altogether.

Insects. The biggest problem is identifying the insect, choosing a proper insecticide, and using it at the time that will be the most effective. Picture charts of insects for identification purposes, with insecticides to kill them, are available at stores that sell garden and lawn supplies.

Leaves. There isn't much you can do about leaves if you have trees that shed each fall. If you are going to plant new trees, find out which trees are native but don't create much of a leaf problem. Some trees, such as mimosas, not only drop leaves but also shed beans, flowers, and sap at different times of the year. If you have a big leaf problem, get a lawn vacuum and start a compost pile.

Other Ways to Reduce Maintenance Time. Besides the five biggest problems already discussed, here are some more things to consider:

• Don't chop up the lawn area into separate sections.

• Don't try to grow grass where it won't grow, such as in areas that receive little sunlight.

• Learn the kind of grass that grows best in your area.

• Plant trees native to the area. You can get other species to grow, but they might require more time and effort.

• Plant for the future. Remember that trees will spread. Don't plant them too closely.

PLANTING A LAWN

Owning a healthy, green lawn not only makes your home look attractive but the grass helps fight air pollution, provides some oxygen, prevents soil erosion, and reduces noise pollution. A super lawn takes super care; just an occasional mowing doesn't produce a well-manicured look.

The kind of grass that grows best in your area is determined by the climate, moisture, and soil. You can and should talk to experts, but the best ways to select a suitable grass is to pick out several healthy-looking lawns in the neighborhood and ask the owners what they did to achieve such beautiful results. Find out which species of grass is most successful and how much trouble it is to maintain. The owners will be flattered, and you should learn a great deal.

Planting a New Lawn. After you select the kind of grass you want, learn what time of year is the best for planting. If the grading hasn't been done yet, you should have it done or do it yourself. The ground should slope gradually away from the house in all directions. After grading, check for low places by turning on a sprinkler and looking for spots where water collects.

Check the soil: It should have the proper pH. The only way to find out about the soil's pH is to test it. Most county agents and many seed stores will test your soil at little or no cost to you. Lime is added to soil that is too acid, and gypsum is added to soil that is too alkaline. The soil also should be crumbly. Squeeze a handful in your fist and release it. If the blob falls apart, the soil is too sandy. If it looks like a mud ball, it contains too much clay. Make whatever soil additions are indicated by the tests, then till the soil. You can rent a tiller if you don't want to buy one. When tilling, avoid making the soil too fine. Marble-size lumps are better than fine dirt. Wet the soil to pack it down, then wait 24 hours.

Spread the grass seed at the rate recommended for the specific variety of seed you are planting. Don't spread the seed too thick. If you do, the

When tilling the soil, avoid making the soil too fine. Marble-size lumps are better than fine dirt.

young seedlings will compete for nutrients and most will die. Rake the ground lightly to cover the seeds partially with soil, then go over the ground once with a roller to press the seeds into the soil. Don't try to bury them.

Feed the lawn when you finish the seeding if this is recommended by the company that packaged the seed. Use the fertilizer recommended for your variety of grass and carefully follow directions on the bag.

Water when you finish fertilizing. During the next two weeks, water two or three times a day, keeping the top layer of soil damp. When the seedlings are up, revert to regular morning watering.

Wait until the sprigs are 2 inches tall before mowing. Mowing will help to spread the root system and make the lawn thicker. Mow weekly until you note the proper thickness; then mow as needed. Never use a weed killer on a new lawn. Pull the bigger weeds and mow the rest. As your lawn thickens, many weeds will be choked out.

Redoing an Established Lawn. The maintenance of a lawn depends on the species of grass planted, the soil condition, and the climate. A lawn specialist or county agent can tell you what kind of fertilizer you should have, how often you should apply it, and how much water you should be using. All fertilizer is numbered, with such groups of numbers as 5-10-5, 24-3-3, 10-10-10, or 1-1-1. The numbers stand for chemical contents of the products. The first number is the amount of nitrogen. The second number is the amount of phosphoric acid. The third is the amount of potash. Because the numbers and names are difficult to remember, try this system: "Up," "Down," "All Around." The first number makes the grass grow up and green. The second number makes the roots grow down and healthy. The third number increases the root growth all around. If you want your grass to be extremely green, choose a fertilizer with a high first number. If you are just starting a new lawn or reshuffling the old one, you want a high second number to encourage root growth. If you want a root growth that is healthy and even across the lawn, you want a fertilizer with a high third number.

If your existing lawn is in poor condition, try to renovate it. If there is at least 50 percent of the area still covered with grass, plant new grass in the bad spots.

Get rid of weeds, then mow the grass close to the ground. Rake the yard to remove grass clippings and leaves, and to loosen the surface of the soil. Test the soil. Correct its chemistry as needed. Then seed the bare spots.

PLANTING A SHRUB

What do you want a shrub to do? Screen a bad view? Help stop erosion? Accent the design of

Plant the shrub in a hole about 8 inches wider and 6 inches deeper than the balled roots of the plant.

your home or hide it? Buy the kind of shrub that will do the job best. A nursery will help you make this decision; there are hundreds of shrub and bush varieties from which to choose.

Most nurseries and garden centers certify that their shrubs and bushes are free from insects, disease, and other growth problems. Get this in writing so the plant will be replaced if it dies through no fault of yours. If you spot cankers, leaf rot, spots, insects, or other problems, don't buy the shrub.

After you've selected a shrub, dig a hole about 8 inches wider and 6 inches deeper than the balled roots of the plant. Carefully place the root ball into the hole. If the ball is wrapped in burlap, cut the string that holds the burlap to the plant. If the ball is in a plastic or metal container, remove it by lightly tapping down on it while you hold onto the base of the plant. The container should drop right off.

Spread out the plant's root system in the hole, and cover the roots with top soil or a rich soil mixture, then lightly pack the soil down and against the base of the plant.

Prune any stalks that are broken or dead. In fall, when the plant is dormant, prune the stalks back about a third of their length; it will promote better growth. Deeply water the roots. The soil must be kept damp until you see growth on the plant. The dealer where you purchased the plant will tell you the best watering schedule.

If you are planting a hedge, you can plant it in a trench instead of individual holes. The trench should be deep and wide enough to accept the root system without crowding it. If you want the hedge to grow about six feet high, the hedge plants should be spaced about 20 inches apart. If you want the hedge to grow higher, space the plants about three feet apart.

PRUNING TREES

Although it is sometimes difficult for people to trim away perfectly healthy foliage, trees should be pruned for several reasons. Pruning gives trees a more desirable shape, strengthens them by improving their structure, removes dead limbs and diseased portions, and increases the production of foliage, flowers, and fruit. Think of pruning as the equivalent of getting a haircut.

Begin by sharpening all pruning tools; dull tools lead to ragged cuts, and ragged cuts can lead to problems. Select the right size and kind of tool for the tree you are pruning. Too large or too small a tool can make ragged cuts.

Make all cuts as close as possible to the base of the piece being removed without damaging the larger limb to which it is attached. Try to do as much pruning work as possible while standing on the ground. When you must work from a ladder, never try to reach very far; move the ladder frequently and make certain that it is always on solid ground. Position yourself and your ladder so that the limbs you prune fall free and nowhere near you. If you are cutting away large limbs, make certain that there is no chance of them falling against electric power lines. Finally, seal all cuts with wound compound.

Late fall is the best time for pruning trees because that is when most trees are dormant. Trees that exude sap during the winter should not be pruned until the following spring. Because their root systems usually have been greatly reduced, newly transplanted trees should be pruned no matter what the season of the year.

When removing of as much as a third of the tree, don't do all the pruning during a single season. Prune it in stages over a two- or three-year period.

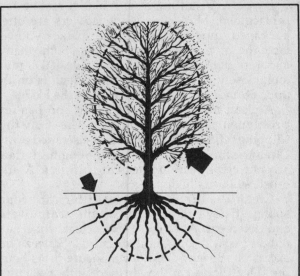

The root systems of newly transplanted trees usually have been greatly reduced, so prune back the branches too.

MAINTAINING A MOWER

Gasoline-powered lawn mowers and electric mowers are hard-working machines that will last for years if they are properly maintained and you clean away lawn debris after each mowing session. If you do nothing more than annually change the spark plug, clean the air filter, change the oil, and hose off the metal housing, your lawn mower should run trouble free.

The following procedures are for maintaining a gasoline-powered lawn mower. Electric lawn mowers have a motor that is best serviced by a professional if problems arise. The housing of the electric unit is maintained in much the same way as a gas-powered engine.

Always disconnect the spark plug cable before inspecting or servicing the mower. **Caution:** *Disconnect the spark plug wire to prevent accidental starting of the engine. With an electric machine, always unplug the mower before working on it.* Tilt the mower over so that you can inspect the blade. If it is not sharp, remove the blade and sharpen it, or replace the blade. To remove the blade, block the blade so it will not turn with wrench pressure. A block of wood and a C-clamp should work. You usually must apply some penetrating oil on the nut to loosen it. Follow the manufacturer's directions in the mower's instruction manual.

Dress the cutting edges of the blade with a file, giving each cutting edge the same number of strokes with the same amount of pressure on the file. Don't worry about nicks in the blade. Before the blade is replaced, it must be balanced. This can be done by filing a notch along the blade on the heavy side. However, don't notch the cutting edge. Rest the blade on a pencil to check its balance.

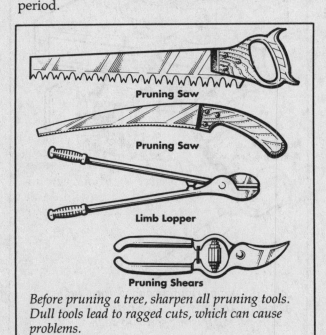

Pruning Saw

Pruning Saw

Limb Lopper

Pruning Shears

Before pruning a tree, sharpen all pruning tools. Dull tools lead to ragged cuts, which can cause problems.

If you're installing a new blade, realize that replacement blades for lawn mowers are often packaged "upside down." The surface you see faces the lawn mower, not the grass. Some manufacturers stamp the metal "grass side." You must look closely to see this imprint, which is on the opposite side of the label stickers on the blade.

A clean mower runs efficiently and has few problems. Clean underneath the housing. Clippings that are caked on can be scraped away. Clean the fins that stick out on the engine. If these are not clean, the mower can run hot. A stiff brush will usually do the job.

Clean the air filter. Most filters are foam sponge. They can be cleaned with warm water and detergent. After the filter is clean, squeeze it out and coat it with lightweight oil. Squeeze out excess oil. Be sure the filter is secure in its housing. Dry filters can be cleaned with a vacuum cleaner and by brushing. When filters refuse to come clean, replace them. Some mowers have an oil-bath filter. They are cleaned with a solvent. Be sure it is a safe solvent such as kerosene. **Caution:** *Never use gasoline as a solvent; it is too dangerous.* Air-dry the parts of the filter and the filter assembly, and put in new oil.

Check the spark plug. To remove it you need a spark-plug wrench. If you have a socket set, you can buy a special socket for spark plugs. If not, you can get an inexpensive wrench made just for spark plugs. Because lawn mower spark plugs are not expensive, it is best to replace the plug annually or even twice a year if the mower is used to cut a large lawn.

To set the gap on the plug, use a wire gapping gauge made for this purpose. If a gauge isn't available, try using a matchbook cover. Your owner's manual is the best guide. If you don't know the correct gap, 0.025 inch should work.

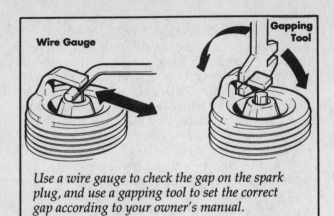

Use a wire gauge to check the gap on the spark plug, and use a gapping tool to set the correct gap according to your owner's manual.

When you put the plug back in, be sure its threads are clean. Oil them. Hand tighten the plug, then give it about a third of a turn with the wrench. Don't overtighten.

Inspect the spark-plug cable. If it is frayed, replace it. Some are not easily replaced because doing so requires the removal of the flywheel. To do this you will need a special puller made for your mower's engine and engine size. These tools are available at lawn-mower repair centers. **Caution:** *Don't try to pry up the flywheel with a wrench handle or screwdriver; the force will break the flywheel.* Be sure that the cable connection is tight. If the cable terminal fits loosely on the plug, squeeze it gently with pliers.

Check the oil level. If the oil is dirty, change it. It will drain completely when hot. Oil should be changed at the end of each mowing season, no matter how clean it may appear.

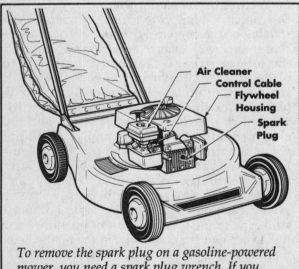

To remove the spark plug on a gasoline-powered mower, you need a spark plug wrench. If you have a socket set, you can buy a special socket for spark plugs.

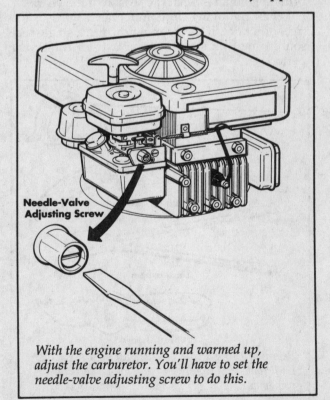

With the engine running and warmed up, adjust the carburetor. You'll have to set the needle-valve adjusting screw to do this.

Lubricate all moving parts on top of the mower. Also use a spray lubricant on the throttle and cable.

Check to see if the choke is properly adjusted. To do this remove the air-filter unit, and look into the carburetor. There will be a round plate. With the control set to "choke," this plate should move down to close the opening. If it does not, loosen the screw and the clamp that hold the choke cable in place. Move the cable forward until the plate closes. Tighten the cable and check again. Replace the air filter, reconnect the spark plug cable, and start the mower.

With the engine running and warmed up, adjust the carburetor. Turn the needle-valve adjusting screw clockwise one-eighth turn. Wait a few seconds, then make another one-eighth turn. Do this until the engine slows. Now turn it counterclockwise in one-eighth turns, counting the eighths. When the engine falters, stop. Divide the number of one-eighth turns by two and turn back (clockwise) that number of eighths. This sets the needle valve to its best setting. To set the proper idle, turn the throttle to its top speed, then back to its slowest speed. Turn the idle-speed adjustment screw until the engine sounds as if it is running at half the maximum speed.

If the lawn mower won't start, and you know the spark plug is okay, chances are that the mower needs new points and a condenser. A clue to this is the way the mower stopped running—quit suddenly without sputtering—or how it won't start—absolutely no kick over. The condenser and points are under the flywheel. You will need a flywheel puller to get at these parts. Once the flywheel is off, a round metal container should be visible. Remove the lid on it and the points and condenser will be exposed. You can buy points and condenser kits for mower tune-ups at most stores that sell lawn-and-garden supplies.

Masonry Repairs

More than any other structural part of your home, the masonry, including concrete, blacktop, or concrete block, is supposed to be permanent. Wood rots, glass breaks, shingles tear, and other components wear out or break, but masonry endures. What happens when the driveway cracks, the steps crumble, or a brick falls out of the chimney? You may be hesitant to tackle masonry problems, even if you've worked on all the other components of your home. Like every other structural component, masonry is easy to repair when you know the right techniques.

PATCHING CONCRETE SLABS
Cracks and holes in concrete should never be ignored, because temperature changes and water

penetration, especially in cold weather, can quickly break up the sound concrete around them. To keep the damage to a minimum, patch cracks and holes when weather permits. Buy a liquid concrete bonding agent and ready-mix sand concrete mix to repair the slab. For large or deep cracks or holes, use a gravel concrete mix.

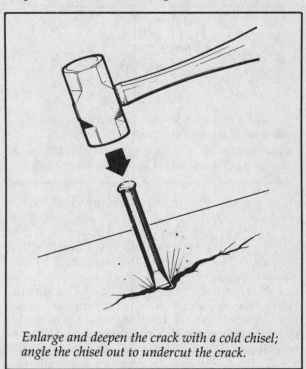

Enlarge and deepen the crack with a cold chisel; angle the chisel out to undercut the crack.

Cracks. Before a crack can be filled, it must be deepened and undercut so that the patch will bond properly. Use a cold chisel and hammer to enlarge the crack and deepen it to between 1 and 2 inches. Wear safety goggles. Angle the chisel into the crack to make the bottom of the opening wider than the top; this will lock the patch concrete into the gap. Then remove all chunks of concrete, and brush the remaining debris out of the crack with a stiff brush or whisk broom. Flush the cleaned crack thoroughly with water, then sponge out any standing water. If the crack goes all the way through the slab, and the ground underneath is eroded, pour sand into the crack just to the bottom edge of the slab. Dampen the sand thoroughly with water.

While the crack is still wet, mix the concrete as directed. A sturdy wheelbarrow is the most convenient container; use a shovel to mix the concrete. When the concrete is mixed, pour liquid concrete bonding agent into the crack to coat the inside surface entirely. Spread the bonding agent with a stiff paintbrush, and clean the paintbrush when you finish. Then quickly fill the crack with the wet concrete. Pack the concrete with a trowel, and make sure there are no air spaces along the bottom of the crack. Smooth the concrete along the surface of the crack with the trowel. If the

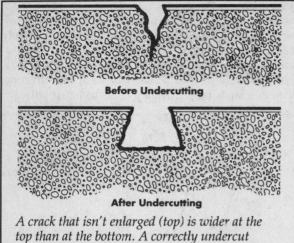

Before Undercutting

After Undercutting

A crack that isn't enlarged (top) is wider at the top than at the bottom. A correctly undercut crack (bottom) is wider at the bottom than at the top. The patch concrete is locked into the opening.

crack is wide, the surface of the patch should be leveled with the surrounding surface. Set a piece of 2 x 4 on edge across one end of the crack, and pull the 2 x 4 in zigzags along the entire length of the crack. This will level the patch and remove excess concrete.

Let the concrete set for about 45 minutes. When the sheen of water has disappeared from the surface, smooth the concrete again with a steel finishing trowel or a clean piece of 2 x 4. A trowel will give the concrete a dense, polished finish. Then let the concrete cure for about a week. During this time, spray the patch two or three times a day with water to keep the concrete from drying out too quickly. If the patch is wide, cover it with a sheet of plastic during the curing period. Lift the plastic two or three times a day to spray the patch.

Holes. Before you can fill a hole, you must undercut it. If it's shallow, it must be deepened to at least 1 inch. Remove all loose concrete. Wearing safety goggles, deepen the hole with a cold chisel and hammer. Cut down to sound concrete, and angle the chisel out at the edges so that the bottom of the hole is wider than the top. Remove the broken concrete and sweep out the debris with a stiff brush. Then flush the hole thoroughly with water. Sponge out any standing water left in the hole. If the hole extends all the way through the slab, and the ground underneath is eroded, pour sand into the hole to the bottom edge of the slab, and moisten the sand thoroughly.

While the hole is still wet, mix the concrete in a wheelbarrow. Then quickly cover the inside surface of the hole with the concrete bonding agent. Spread the bonding agent with a stiff paintbrush, paying particular attention to the undercut edges. Clean the paintbrush immediately. As soon as you've spread the bonding agent, shovel new concrete into the hole; pack it into the undercut

edges with a trowel. Mound the concrete above the surface of the slab, then pound it down with the back of the shovel. Cut through the concrete with the blade of the shovel to make sure there are no air spaces, then pound the patch down again. Leave the new concrete higher than the surrounding surface.

Use a piece of 2 x 4 to level the patch. You can do this by yourself if the patch is small; you'll need a helper to level a large patch. Set the 2 x 4 across the filled hole, and pull it in zigzags over the new concrete; the 2 x 4 will remove the excess and bring the concrete level with the surrounding surface. The new concrete will have a sheen of water on the surface. Let it set for about 45 minutes to an hour. When the surface water has disappeared, smooth the concrete with a wooden float until the surface is filmed with water again. Use long, smooth strokes and press lightly so you don't mark the new concrete; stop smoothing when the water sheen reappears.

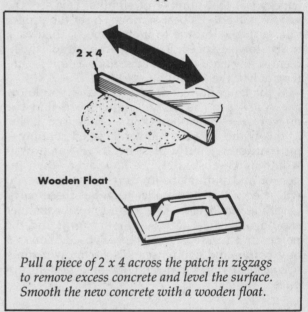

2 x 4

Wooden Float

Pull a piece of 2 x 4 across the patch in zigzags to remove excess concrete and level the surface. Smooth the new concrete with a wooden float.

Let the concrete set again until the water sheen has disappeared. If you want to match a dense, highly polished concrete surface, smooth the patch again with a steel finishing trowel, using long, even strokes and working until the film of water appears again. If you want a rougher, nonskid texture, finish the surface of the patch with a push broom. Set the broom on the old concrete to one side of the patch, then push it slowly and evenly across the patch and onto the old concrete on the other side. Don't push the broom hard enough to dig into the concrete. You want an even, brushed look. After this final texturing, let the concrete cure for at least a week. To keep it from drying out too quickly, cover the patch with a sheet of plastic. Two or three times a day during the curing period, remove the plastic and spray the patch lightly with water.

MENDING CONCRETE STEPS

When concrete steps start to crumble along the edges, they usually go fast. More concrete is broken off as people use the steps, and the crumbling edges can be hazardous as they deteriorate further. Repairing the steps isn't as hard as you might think; you can recast the edges with sand concrete mix, using the same techniques described before. Use liquid bonding agent to bond the new concrete properly.

As with any concrete repair, the first step is to chisel out and undercut the damaged area with a cold chisel and hammer. Wearing safety goggles, cut into the crumbled edge at least 1 inch, or go down to solid concrete. Cut a deep open V all along each damaged edge, with one arm of the V straight into the riser and the other arm angled into the tread of the damaged step. Even if only one end of the step is crumbling, chisel out the entire edge. Clean out the debris with a stiff whisk broom, and flush the open V thoroughly with water.

For each damaged step, build a form to recast the open edge. For the front of the form, use a board as long as the step and as wide as the step is high, so that the top edge of the board is flush with the top of the step. Set the board against the riser under the broken edge, and hold it in place with several bricks. Complete the form by closing in the ends of the step with a board set against each side. Use boards tall enough so that the top edges are flush with the surface of the step. To brace these side boards, nail a piece of 2 x 4 across the top of each, and wedge each board into place against the step with another piece of 2 x 4 placed under the crosspiece. Drive a stake at the bottom of the wedge 2 x 4 to keep it from slipping.

When the forms are in place, wet the steps again with water. Mix the concrete as directed. With a stiff paintbrush, spread liquid concrete bonding agent over each chiseled-out edge, making sure the corner of the V is completely coated. Clean the brush immediately. While the bonding agent is still wet, fill the open V on each prepared step with concrete. Pack the concrete in with a trowel, forcing it well into the undercut edge. Make sure there are no air spaces in the concrete; cut through it with the point of the trowel to fill any gaps. Then smooth the surface of the concrete roughly level with the surface of the step. The front and side of the new edge are shaped by the forms.

To finish the step, smooth the top surface of the edge with a wooden float to level it. Let the concrete set for 45 minutes to an hour, until the water sheen disappears from the surface. Then smooth it again with the wooden float, so that it matches the texture of the old concrete. If you want to match a dense, polished texture, let the concrete set for another 45 minutes until the water sheen disappears again, then final-smooth it with a steel finishing trowel. Stop smoothing when the water comes to the surface again.

Let the concrete cure for at least a week, and leave the forms in place during this time. To keep the concrete from drying out too quickly, cover the steps with a sheet of plastic. Two or three times a day during the curing period, lift the plastic and spray the concrete lightly with water so it dries out evenly.

PATCHING BROKEN BLACKTOP

Asphalt deteriorates much more quickly than concrete, and once it starts to crumble, the process accelerates. But blacktop is as easy to patch as it is quick to break down. Blacktop patching mixture, sold in bags, requires no mixing or heating, and you can prolong the life of the whole driveway with liquid blacktop sealer. Make all your blacktop repairs in warm weather; blacktop is brittle and slow to bond when it's cold.

Unlike concrete, blacktop must be dry when it's repaired. With a shovel or a trowel, chop out all the loose blacktop from the damaged area. Cut down and out on the sides to solid blacktop. Remove the crumbled blacktop and clean out the hole with a stiff broom or whisk broom. If the hole is very deep, fill it with gravel to within 3 or 4 inches of the surface. Pound the gravel in with the back of the shovel.

To fill the hole, pour blacktop patching mixture into it, right from the bag. Spread the patch mixture evenly to just below the surface, then tamp it in firmly with the end of a piece of 4 x 4. When this layer is firm, pour in more blacktop patch, mounding it to about 1/2 inch above the surrounding surface. Tamp the patch again to level it with the surface. For a firmer patch, drive your car over the filled hole several times to compact the new asphalt. Add more patching mix, and tamp it down to level the hole again. To keep the fresh blacktop from being tracked on shoes, sprinkle the patch with sand.

Small cracks in blacktop can be filled with sand and liquid blacktop sealer. Pour sand along the crack to fill it partway, then pour the blacktop sealer into the crack over the sand. The sand will absorb the sealer quickly. If necessary, add more sealer to fill the crack completely. To fill large cracks, mix sand and blacktop sealer to a thin paste, and pack this paste with a trowel. Force the patching paste into the full depth of each crack, and smooth the surface level. Sprinkle sand along newly patched cracks to keep the sealer from being tracked around while it dries.

To prevent further damage to the driveway, you may want to coat the entire surface with liquid blacktop sealer. Applied every two or three years, the sealer can prolong the life of an asphalt drive. If you plan to seal the driveway after patching it, do not sprinkle sand on the newly patched areas.

Chop out loose blacktop and clean out the debris; keep the hole dry. Then pour blacktop patching mixture directly into the hole.

Tamp down the loose patching mixture with the end of a 4 x 4; add more blacktop and tamp again until the patch is firm and level.

To prevent further damage, coat the entire driveway with liquid blacktop sealer, spread with a push broom.

Spread the blacktop sealer with a push broom, coating one section of the driveway at a time. Throw the broom head away when you finish the job. Block off the driveway until the sealer is completely dry, as directed by the manufacturer.

TUCK-POINTING LOOSE MORTAR JOINTS

Brick and concrete block don't deteriorate as quickly as wood, but they do need regular maintenance. Over the years and especially in very cold and wet climates, the mortar between bricks can loosen or crumble. This can result in further damage, both inside and out. As water seeps through the open joints, interior walls may be damaged, and the mortar outside will crumble even more. Professionals charge a lot to repair loose mortar joints. The repair work, called tuck-pointing, requires little skill but a lot of strength and patience. You can save yourself the expense

of tuck-pointing by repairing loose mortar joints yourself, as soon as possible. Buy mortar mix and, if the old mortar is colored, mortar coloring. If the mortar joints are rounded, you'll also need a tool called a jointer, or a piece of pipe or rod the same diameter as the joints, to smooth the mortar.

The first step is to clean out the damaged mortar. Wear safety goggles while you work. With a cold chisel and hammer, cut out the crumbling mortar to a depth of at least 1/2 inch or down to sound mortar. Work on the vertical joints first, then on the horizontal ones. Brush the debris out of the joints, and flush them with water. Keep your safety goggles on until the joints are completely cleaned out.

After cleaning the joints, mix a small amount of mortar, as the package directs. Use a scrap of corrugated cardboard to test the color. Spread a little mortar on the cardboard; it will dry very quickly. If the dried mortar doesn't match the color of the old mortar, add mortar coloring as necessary. Test the colored mortar on the cardboard with each mixture. When the test mortar is the right color, mix and color as much mortar as you'll need to repair the wall.

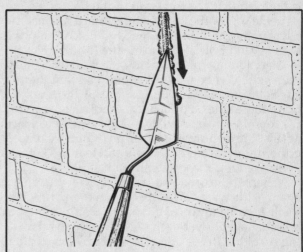

Cut out crumbling mortar to a depth of at least 1/2 inch, first in vertical joints and then in horizontals. Press mortar firmly into the cleaned joints to fill them completely, with no gaps in the mortar.

Mortar should be applied to a wet surface, so it won't dry out too quickly. Spray the wall so that it's wet but not streaming. With a small sharp trowel, press the mortar firmly into the cleaned-out joints. Fill the vertical joints first, then the horizontal ones. Force the mortar into the full depth of the open joints, making sure there aren't any gaps. As you finish each joint, go back over it to remove excess mortar and make the joints look like the old ones. For V-shaped joints, use the point of the trowel to shape the mortar. For a smooth, concave U-shaped joint, use a mortar jointer or finish the joints with a piece of metal rod or pipe the same (or a little smaller) diameter as the joints. Holding the trowel or jointer at a steady angle to the mortar, draw it smoothly and firmly along the newly filled joint. At the end of the joint, remove the excess mortar. Then go on to the next joint.

Scrape excess mortar off the wall as you work. After all the joints are filled, the mortar must be kept damp for several days while it cures. Spray the wall lightly two or three times a day during this curing period. If there is still excess mortar on the wall, you can remove it with a stiff brush when the mortar has cured.

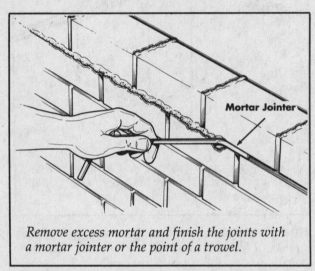

Remove excess mortar and finish the joints with a mortar jointer or the point of a trowel.

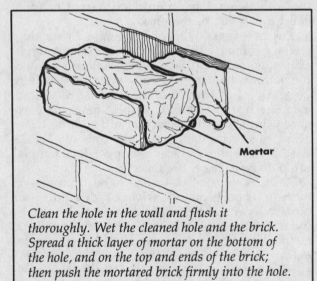

Clean the hole in the wall and flush it thoroughly. Wet the cleaned hole and the brick. Spread a thick layer of mortar on the bottom of the hole, and on the top and ends of the brick; then push the mortared brick firmly into the hole.

REPLACING A BRICK

On old buildings, where tuck-pointing has been neglected and especially on chimneys, there may be loose or broken bricks. This situation is obviously more serious than damage to the mortar. Besides causing further damage, it also can be hazardous. Particularly when a chimney is involved, you should replace loose or damaged bricks as soon as you can. Use mortar mix, coloring as needed, and to replace broken bricks, new bricks of the same texture and color.

First remove the brick. If it's very loose, you may be able to pull it right out. If you cannot, cut out the old mortar around the brick with a cold chisel and hammer; wear safety goggles. Be careful not to damage the surrounding bricks or, if it's not broken, the loose brick. If the loose brick is damaged or if you can't get it out by removing the mortar, break it up with the hammer and chisel, and remove the pieces. Then chisel out all the mortar left in the hole, and wire-brush the hole to remove all traces of the old mortar. If the old brick is not damaged, also chisel off any old mortar adhering to it. Flush out the hole with water, and put the old brick or the replacement brick in a bucket of water.

After cleaning the hole, mix a small amount of mortar, according to the package directions, and spread a little on a scrap of corrugated cardboard to test it for color. When you have a good color match, mix enough mortar to replace the brick. Spray the hole with water so that it's wet but not streaming. Spread a thick layer of mortar on the bottom of the hole but not on the back, sides, or top. Then remove the brick from the bucket of water, shake it to remove excess water, and spread a thick layer of mortar on the top and the ends of the brick. Don't spread mortar on the back of the brick; as the brick is pushed into the hole, the mortar on the bottom will be forced behind the brick.

Set the mortared brick into the hole, pushing it firmly in so that its face is flush with the surrounding bricks. With a small sharp trowel, press in the mortar that has squeezed out around the brick. If the brick is crooked, add more mortar as necessary to even it out. Then scrape off any excess mortar and finish the mortar joints.

The newly replaced brick should be kept moist for several days while the mortar cures. Spray the brick lightly two or three times a day during the curing period. If there is still excess mortar on or around the brick, remove it with a dry stiff scrub brush when the mortar is fully cured.

Fences and Walls

Sun, wind, snow, rot, and below-ground frost subject fences and walls to a terrific beating. Here is how to keep your fences mended, how to build new ones the right way, how to build a mortarless stone wall, and how to hold back a shifting slope with a railroad-tie retaining wall. As you work with fences and walls, always keep nature in mind. Stone and concrete have natural immunities to many elements, but even they can deteriorate over time. Wood is more vulnerable to nature's punishments, especially rotting. This

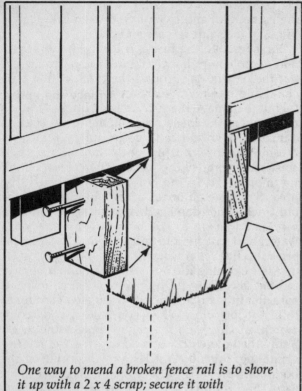

One way to mend a broken fence rail is to shore it up with a 2 x 4 scrap; secure it with galvanized nails.

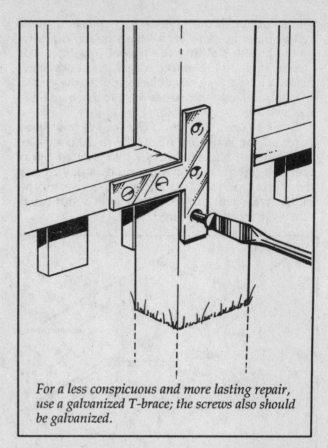

For a less conspicuous and more lasting repair, use a galvanized T-brace; the screws also should be galvanized.

means you should always repair or construct fencing with the most rot-resistant lumber you can afford. Here are your major choices:

•Pressure-treated lumber has been saturated with preservatives and lasts almost indefinitely, even when wood is buried in the ground. Pressure-treated wood is costly.

•Cedar and redwood also stand up well underground and are also costly.

•Creosote and asphalt roofing compound can be painted on just about any wood for an underground coating that stands up almost as well as pressure-treated pine, cedar, or redwood. Creosote has a medicinal smell and can't be painted over. With roofing compound, apply three coats, leaving a lot of time for drying between coats. These are inexpensive, but they take time to apply.

•Pentachlorophenol also works below ground and can be painted. Though inexpensive, it can harm plants until it's completely dry. Apply at least two coats.

•Copper napthenate is odorless and non-toxic, but it imparts a greenish cast to wood. It's moderate in price. Apply at least two coats.

•Exterior paints and stains work all right above ground, but are almost useless below or on parts of fences in frequent contact with water.

REPAIRING FENCES

The components of a fence fall into three main categories: vertical posts, rails that run horizon-tally from post to post, and screening material, such as pickets, attached to the rails. Examine your fence, and you probably can identify each of these elements. Each requires different maintenance and repair techniques.

Rot is a fence's biggest enemy. Posts that weren't properly treated or set in concrete typically rot away at ground level. Bottom rails and the bottoms of screening can suffer, especially if vegetation has been rubbing against them and trapping water. Carefully inspect fences at least once a year, paying particular attention to these areas. When you find a problem, correct it before the damage spreads. One weak post, for example, can pull down the entire fence.

Rails. A rail that has come loose from one or more of its posts may be salvaged, depending on how badly rotted the joint is. You may be able to mend the break with a scrap 2 x 4 or a couple of metal T-braces, or you may have to replace the entire rail.

Before you make a repair, saturate the damaged areas with copper-napthenate wood preservative. This keeps the rot from spreading. If you choose to use a 2 x 4, soak it with preservative. With the 2 x 4 make a cleat that supports the rail. Level the rail, fit the 2 x 4 snugly underneath, then nail the 2 x 4 to the post with galvanized nails. You also may need to drive a couple of nails down through the rail into the cleat. Caulk the top and sides of the repair to keep out moisture.

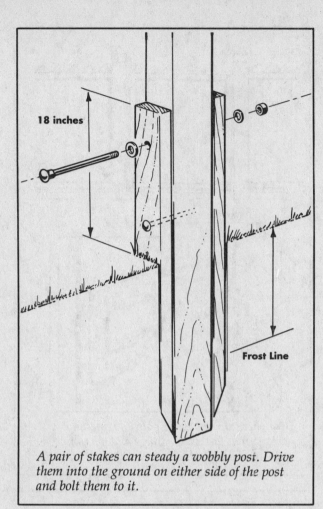

18 inches

Frost Line

A pair of stakes can steady a wobbly post. Drive them into the ground on either side of the post and bolt them to it.

Galvanized steel T-braces, available at most hardware and home stores, are less conspicuous and make a more lasting repair. Level the rail, drill pilot holes into the post and rail, and secure with galvanized screws. Caulk the joint, then paint the braces to match the fences.

If the entire rail needs to be replaced, you'll probably have to dismantle that section of fence and rebuild it.

Screening. Replacing broken or rotted screening takes only basic carpentry skills. If rot is the problem, treat boards or pickets with coppernapthenate wood preservative. Measure an unbroken piece to get the correct length and width for the new piece or pieces you'll need. Use lumber the same width as the old screening, or rip boards to the proper width.

If you're replacing pickets or other curved-top screening, set the board against an unbroken picket and trace the top onto the new board. Make these cuts with a saber, coping, or keyhole saw. If yours is a painted fence, give the new screening a coat of top-quality exterior primer. If the fence is natural wood, stain the new boards to match.

Remove the broken pieces by hammering and prying them away from the rails. Pull out any nails left in the rails, set the board or picket

against the rails, align it, and nail it firmly into place with galvanized 8d nails. Paint the new pieces to match the rest of the fence.

Posts. When a post begins to wobble, your first task is to decide why. If the post is rotted or broken you may be able to repair it with a pair of splints, or you may have to replace the entire post. If the post seems intact but has come loose in its hole, it's most likely suffering from frost heaving. A pair of stakes or a new concrete base can steady the post.

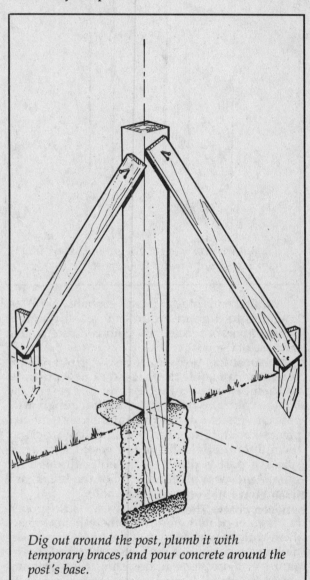

Dig out around the post, plumb it with temporary braces, and pour concrete around the post's base.

To stake a post, you'll need a pair of 2 x 4s long enough to reach below the frost line and extend at least 18 inches above the ground. Use only pressure-treated lumber, cedar, or clear all-heart redwood. Bevel-cut one end of each stake, and drive two stakes into the ground along opposite sides of the post. After you've driven the stakes, bore two holes through the stakes and the post, and bolt the three with galvanized carriage bolts.

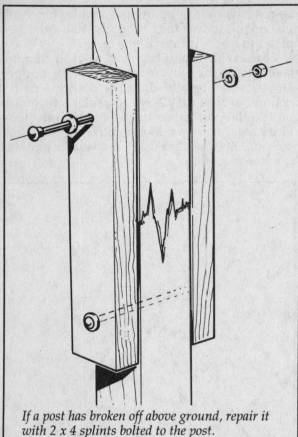

If a post has broken off above ground, repair it with 2 x 4 splints bolted to the post.

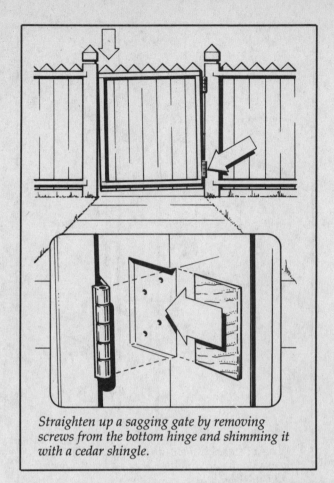

Straighten up a sagging gate by removing screws from the bottom hinge and shimming it with a cedar shingle.

An alternate method that probably will last longer is to dig out around the post, plumb it with temporary braces, and pour concrete around the base of the post.

If a post has broken off below ground level, you must dismantle the fence, set a new post, and reassemble everything. For an above-ground break, you may be able to make a repair with pressure-treated or rot-resistant 2 x 4s. Cut two pieces about 18 inches long, and nail or clamp them to opposite sides of the post. Check to be sure the post is plumb, bore holes through the splints and post on either side of the break, and secure them with steel carriage bolts.

Gates. When a gate sags or won't close properly, first check its hinges. If they're bent, replace them with heavier hinges. If the hinge screws are pulling loose, remove them and plug the holes by gluing in short pieces of doweling, then drill new holes and install longer screws or carriage bolts. All hardware should be galvanized steel.

With a gate that is sagging only slightly, you may be able to straighten it by shimming under the bottom hinge. Prop up the gate in its open position, remove screws from the post side of the hinge and cut a thin piece of cedar shake to fit into the hinge mortise. Reattach the screw by driving longer screws through the shim.

Sometimes a gate sags because its own weight has pulled it out of square. One quick way to

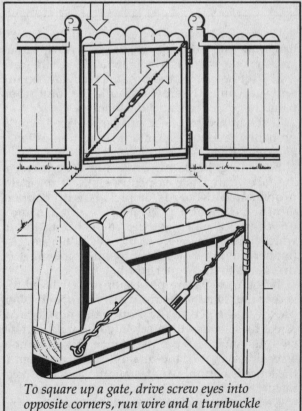

To square up a gate, drive screw eyes into opposite corners, run wire and a turnbuckle between them, and tighten the turnbuckle.

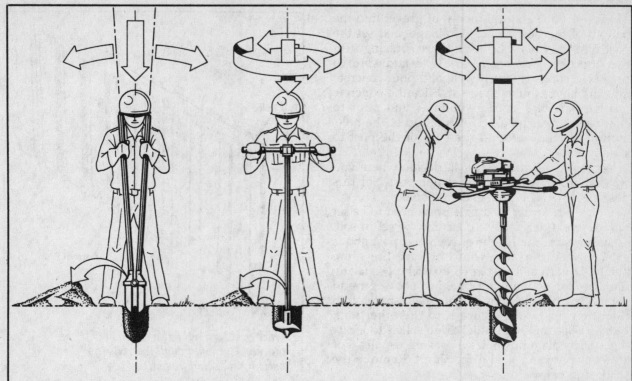

Dig postholes with a hand-operated digger or a power-driven auger. These tools are available at rental outlets.

square up a gate is to drive a screw eye into the upper corner of the gate on the hinge side and another into the lower corner on the gate side. Run wire and a heavy-duty turnbuckle from one screw eye to the other and tighten the turnbuckle until the gate frame is square.

Another possible cause of a malfunctioning gate is that a post on one side of the opening is wobbling or out of plumb. If this is the case, shore it up.

BUILDING A NEW FENCE

The most arduous part of constructing a fence comes at the beginning, when you have to dig holes for the posts. You will need a posthole digger, available at tool rental outlets. Hand-operated clamshell and auger diggers work well in sandy, rock-free soil. If your soil is rocky or you have many holes to dig, rent a power-driven auger.

For a weather-resistant fence, use pressure-treated lumber, cedar, or redwood. No finishing is necessary, and the fence can be left to weather naturally. Use untreated wood only for screening and top rails, and for bottom rails that are at least 4 inches above the ground. You'll need 4 x 4s for fence posts, 2 x 4s for rails, and 1 x 4s or 1 x 6s for screening.

Lay out an approximate fence line, making sure you're not on your neighbor's property, then establish the exact location of the first end or corner post. Dig a hole that is 18 to 24 inches deep. For a fence that is five or six feet high, go down

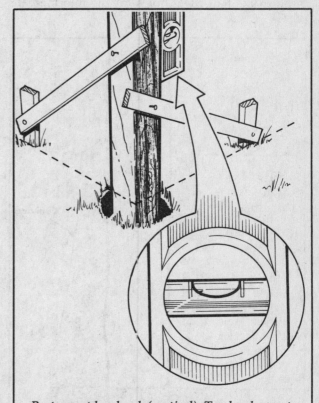

Posts must be plumb (vertical). To plumb a post, set it in its hole, hold a level to one side, and adjust the post until the level's bubble is centered; do the same on an adjacent side of the post, then brace it with outriggers.

24 inches. Pour about 3 inches of gravel into the bottom of the hole to help drainage, and set the post into the hole. Plumb the post, bracing it in two directions with outriggers. Now add water to premixed concrete, stir it well, and pour concrete into the hole around the post. Slice the concrete mix periodically with a spade as you pour to eliminate any air pockets. At the top of the hole, mound concrete around the base of the post to shed water.

After you set the first post, decide where you want the opposite end or corner post. Set this post the same way you set the first one.

Only end, corner, and gate posts need to be set in concrete. Intermediate posts can be set in soil. First, measure the height of each end post above grade level to assure that both are the same height. Drive a nail partway into each post, facing the direction of the fence line, just above ground level. Tie a piece of twine to one nail, stretch it to the other post, and secure it to the other nail. Using the string as a guide, drive stakes to locate the intermediate postholes. Posts are usually 8 or 10 feet apart and 4 to 6 feet high. Remove the string and nails.

Now drive nails into the top centers of each end post and stretch twine between them, securing it to the nails. Dig holes for the intermediate posts.

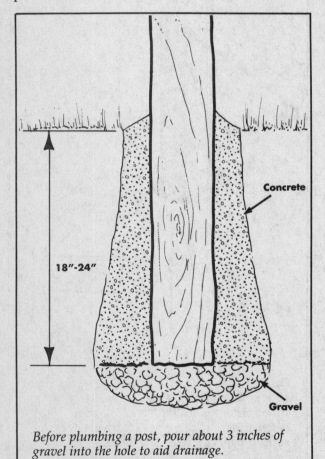

Before plumbing a post, pour about 3 inches of gravel into the hole to aid drainage.

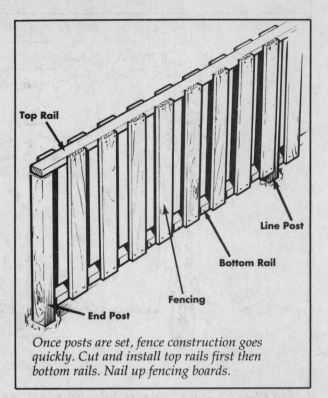

Once posts are set, fence construction goes quickly. Cut and install top rails first then bottom rails. Nail up fencing boards.

Pour about 3 inches of gravel into each hole. Set a post into the hole and use the twine as a guide for checking the post's height. If necessary, make height adjustments by varying the depth of gravel in each hole or shimming up posts with stones. Set and plumb each post, then fill around its base with about 6 inches of gravel. Fill the rest of the hole with soil, shoveling in about 4 inches at a time and compacting each layer with a scrap of 2 x 4.

Cut 2 x 4 rails to fit flat along the tops of the posts. The rails can extend from post to post, or a rail can span two sections. Measure and cut each rail individually, to allow for slight variations in fence-post spacing. Butt the ends of the rails together. Beginning at one end of the fence line, nail the rails into place, using two 10d galvanized common nails at the ends of each rail.

Measure and cut a 2 x 4 bottom rail to fit snugly between each pair of posts. Position the rails flat between the posts, anywhere from just above grade level to 12 inches high. Toenail the bottom rails into place with a 10d galvanized nail driven through the fence post and into the end of the rail on each side. Use a level to keep the rails even.

When the rails are in place, measure and cut the fence boards. The boards should be of uniform length, as long as the distance from the bottom of the bottom rail to the top of the top rail, as measured at one post. Starting at one end, nail the boards to one side of the rails, with a space equal to a single board width between each; use a board as a spacer as you work. Secure each board to the rails with two 8d galvanized nails at the top and two at the bottom. Nail the tops first, flush with the top, then nail the bottoms, pulling or pushing the bottom rail into alignment as you proceed.

If your fence will have boards on both sides nail up all the boards on one side first, then nail alternate boards to the other side of the rails, positioning the boards to cover the spaces left by the boards on the opposite side of the fence.

BUILDING NEW WALLS

Constructing a wall with mortar and bricks, blocks, or stones is heavy work that calls for specialized masonry skills. Laying up a stone wall without mortar or building a retaining wall with railroad ties is equally hard work, but all you need is muscle and an understanding of a few simple principles.

Building a Mortarless Stone Wall. If you have a handy source of fieldstone, you can build an attractive and economical mortarless stone wall. It is demanding work, but you can do the job a little at a time.

Before you start building, prepare a foundation for the wall. If the ground is level, lay out the line of the wall and dig a trench about 1 1/2 feet wide and 1 foot deep. Make the bottom level. On uneven terrain change elevations in the trench bottom stair-step fashion not in slopes.

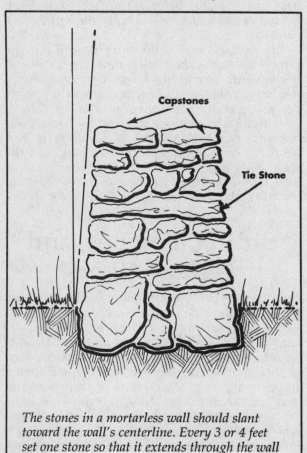

The stones in a mortarless wall should slant toward the wall's centerline. Every 3 or 4 feet set one stone so that it extends through the wall and ties it together.

Pile your fieldstones near the wall site so you'll be able to choose stones as you work. Use a crowbar to lift the edges and a wheelbarrow for heavy hauling. Wear heavy leather gloves and heavy work boots.

Set the first course of stones on the bottom of the trench in a double row. Use the worst stones here, including those with awkward shapes or poor faces. Bed each stone firmly into the earth, fitting the stones carefully together side by side with the flattest faces upward. Don't use stones with very smooth or rounded faces in the wall; they don't provide enough surface friction for good bonding. Pack earth in around the stones and tamp firmly. Spray them lightly with water to pack the earth, but don't turn it into mud.

If you need another course of stones to reach approximate grade level, lay them down. Fit these stones together, twisting and turning and nesting them as tightly as possible so they cling to one another. This is a trial-and-error process, and it will take some time for you to get the feel of it and recognize what stones will fit where. Pack soil into all the cracks and crannies between the stones, but don't depend on the soil to support the rocks. Spray the packed stones lightly with water.

Pick out some of your better stones, and start laying the above-grade courses. At least every three or four feet, set one stone in each course extending through the wall from front to back, solidly nestled. This helps tie the wall together. Whenever possible, make the stones slant inward toward the centerline of the wall, so they push against one another; stones tilted toward the outside faces of the wall have a tendency to slide out. You can shim and fill small gaps by chinking them with small stones, but do this as little as possible. Try to do filling-in work on the inside face of the wall.

If you have to break large stones or trim away knobs and protrusions, use a heavy sledgehammer or a hand sledge and brick chisel to fit the stones. Wear safety goggles and heavy leather gloves for stone-breaking.

Continue laying courses of stone until the wall reaches a height of about four feet. Build the sides of the wall in a vertical line on each face; they can slant inward on either or both faces, but they should never slant outward. Set aside the best and flattest stones, as you work, to use as capstones for the top course of the wall. Fit this last course together carefully to make the top of the wall as flat as you can.

Building a Railroad-Tie Retaining Wall. If your landscaping includes two or more grade levels, a retaining wall can keep earth from shifting and add interest to your yard. There are easier ways to make a railroad-tie retaining wall, but this setback method is the most effective. It takes extra effort, but you won't have to do it again.

A setback retaining wall is built stair-step fashion, with each successive course of ties set back from the leading edge of the course below by 2 inches, or a third of the width of the tie.

The first step in building the wall is to prepare the site where the wall will be built. Shovel out the soil as required on the low side of the grade, and rough level the soil for the first row of ties. If you want to sink the first row of ties into the ground, cut a channel 2 or 3 inches deep for the base ties. Lay out the first row of ties along the ground, butted together end to end; do this by eye or stretch a string between nails driven into the ties.

In the middle and at each end of each tie, drill a 1/2-inch hole, centered on the tie width, completely through the tie; use a power drill with a 1/2-inch wood-boring speed bit and a bit extension. Drive a length of 1/2-inch concrete-reinforcing bar, commonly called rebar, through each hole and into the ground. Use rebar that is 2 or 3 feet long, depending on the thickness of the ties. Drive the rebar with a heavy sledgehammer; keep pounding until the top of the rebar is flush with the tie surface. This holds the base row in place. Shovel dirt and rocks in against the back of the line of ties on the high side of the grade, tamping it firmly up to the level of the ties. Dampen the soil with a garden hose to aid in compaction, but don't let it get too muddy.

Line up the next row of ties on top of the first ones, set back about 2 inches from the outside face of the first row, so the joints of the rows of ties are staggered like brick joints. If all your ties are the same length, cut a tie in half with a chain saw and use the halves as end ties to stagger the joints. Stagger each successive row of ties so that no two rows have corresponding joints.

At the end of every third or fourth tie, depending on their lengths, insert a tie beam, a railroad tie lying at right angles to the wall, with its outward end flush with the face of the row of ties. Calculate the tie beam's length and cut it so that at least a foot at the far end of the beam extends into the bank and rests against undisturbed soil.

Secure the second row of ties to the base row with spikes long enough to go completely through one tie and two-thirds of the way through the tie beneath it. With the second row of ties in place, drill a hole at each end of each tie, completely through the tie and into the tie below it. You'll be driving long spikes through these holes, so use a drill bit the same diameter as the spikes. Drive the spikes with a sledgehammer, securing the second course of ties to the first.

Fasten the exposed end of the tie beam with two spikes set diagonally into the end. Don't place the spikes side by side; you could split the end grain. At the banking end of each beam, drill a 1/2-inch hole through the beam and drive a length of rebar through the beam and into the

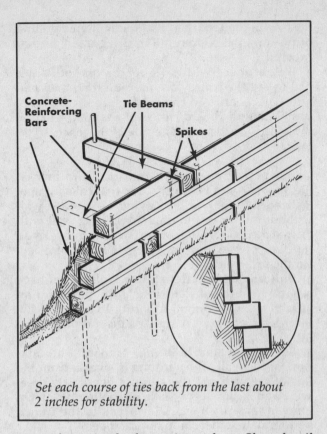

Set each course of ties back from the last about 2 inches for stability.

ground to pin the beam into place. Shovel soil behind the second row and tamp the earth down hard.

Lay out and fasten the third row of ties the same way, but without tie beams. Use tie beams in the fourth course and in every other course as you work. Stagger the tie beams so that no tie beam lies above a tie beam in a lower course. Continue setting course ties and tie beams, setting each row back about 2 inches from the row below it, until you reach the full height of the wall. Pack earth in firmly behind the retaining wall as you go. The last course of the wall should reach just above the grade level behind the wall.

Siding, Porches, and Garage Doors

Your home is built to withstand wear and weather, and if you don't look at the outside too closely, it's easy to assume that everything is in good shape until one day it's too late, and all the little problems have become big ones. To prevent this kind of structural deterioration, make a periodic tour of inspection around the outside of your home, so that you can repair the damage before it becomes serious. One of the most important of the routine jobs is caulking. When siding or porch flooring is damaged or a garage door doesn't operate properly, you can forestall more serious problems by taking care of the repairs immediately.

CAULKING

No matter how well your home is built, it also must be well caulked if it is to function properly. Caulking serves three important purposes: It finishes the joints where outside surfaces meet; it prevents drafts and heat loss; and it prevents water, dirt, and insects from entering and damaging your home. Caulking is important everywhere two outside surfaces meet. To make sure your home is sealed against the elements, you should inspect it yearly for missing or damaged caulking, and recaulk as necessary to repair the damage.

There are several kinds of caulking compound. Oil-base caulks are the least expensive, but also the least durable. For most applications, acrylic latex or silicone caulk is better. Acrylic latex, an all-purpose caulk, can be painted. Silicone caulk is more durable and is easy to work with, but it's expensive and usually can't be painted. For masonry-metal joints, where pipes go through the foundation wall use butyl rubber caulk. Polyvinyl acetate (PVA) caulk is also available, but it's less durable and less widely used than other kinds. For caulking wall-to-roof or chimney-to-roof joints, use roofing compound. Caulking is sold in bulk tubes to be used with a caulking gun. Caulking is generally available in white, gray, black, brown and clear forms. When you buy caulking compound, read the label to estimate how much you'll need, and buy one or two extra tubes.

Plan routine caulking for dry, warm weather; caulking should not be done when it's very cold or very hot. If you must work in cold weather, warm the caulk to room temperature before you start. If you must work in hot weather, chill the caulk briefly in the refrigerator to keep it from getting runny. All surfaces should be dry when you apply caulking compound.

Caulking is not a difficult procedure; all it really requires is patience and attention to detail. When you're ready to work, inspect your home

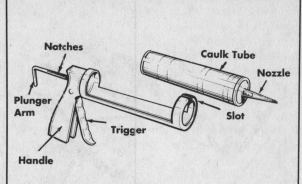

To use a caulking gun, pull out the plunger arm to disengage the notches, and insert a tube of caulk, base first, so that the nozzle sticks out through the slot at the end of the gun. Turn the plunger arm and push it in to engage it. To apply the caulk, squeeze the trigger.

carefully to find the places that need caulking. There should be caulking around windows and doors, at the point where the house walls meet the foundation, where porches or steps are attached, and around air conditioners, pipes, and vents. Every corner seam should be caulked, and every seam between sheets of siding. On the roof there should be caulking where the chimney meets the roof and along every flashing edge, at the chimney surface, and at the roof surface. If caulking is missing or damaged at any of these points, you should recaulk the entire joint.

Before you can apply new caulk to a joint, you must remove the old caulking. Sometimes you can peel out the old caulk in long strips. If you can't and if it's hard to dislodge the caulk with a putty knife, use a sharp utility knife to cut the old caulk out, forming a clean, square joint. Be careful not to damage the joint surfaces. After removing the old caulk, go over the joint with a dry paintbrush to remove dust and other debris.

Once you get the feel of it, caulking is very simple. With a sharp utility knife, cut off the tip of the caulk tube's nozzle, cutting at an angle. Most tubes have cutting guidelines marked on the nozzle. The open tip of the nozzle should be roughly the same diameter as the width of the narrowest cracks to be caulked; the bead of caulk must be wide enough to overlap both sides of the joint. For larger cracks or joints, you'll have to recut the nozzle to make a wider bead of caulk. With the nozzle cut to the correct width, pull out the plunger of the caulking gun and set the tube of caulk into the gun, base first, so that the nozzle of the tube sticks out through the slot on the end of the gun. Then turn the plunger of the gun to point up, and push it in just until it engages. Break the seal between the tube and the nozzle; push a piece of stiff wire or a long nail into the nozzle to puncture the foil or plastic seal.

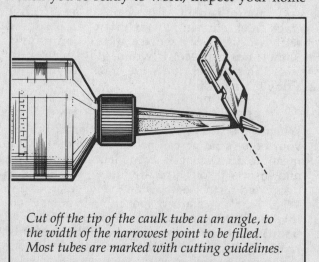

Cut off the tip of the caulk tube at an angle, to the width of the narrowest point to be filled. Most tubes are marked with cutting guidelines.

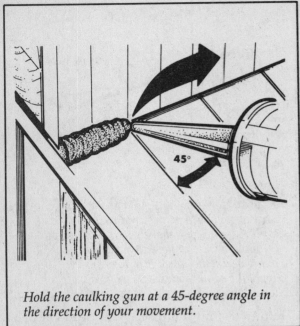

Hold the caulking gun at a 45-degree angle in the direction of your movement.

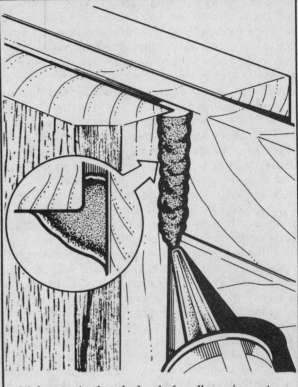

Make certain that the bead of caulk coming out of the tip of the cartridge is the proper size for the job. The bead must overlap both surfaces on either side of the crack.

To use the caulking gun, hold the nozzle at a 45-degree angle to the joint you want to fill. With the plunger of the gun engaged and the seal of the tube broken, squeeze the handle firmly. In a few moments, caulk will begin to flow out of the nozzle. The caulk is forced out of the tube by the pressure of the plunger. As you squeeze the handle of the gun, the plunger moves in, notch by notch, and the caulk flows out. Draw the nozzle of the tube slowly along the open joint, with the tip slanted in the direction you're caulking. The caulk should flow out behind the nozzle as you go; don't try to push it ahead of the nozzle. As you work with the caulking gun let the caulk flow at its own rate; don't try to hurry it. The gun releases caulking compound at a steady rate, one click at a time. You can't speed it up by squeezing the handle harder; all you can do is adjust your rate of movement to use it well.

Fill each joint with one steady movement from end to end, adjusting your speed as necessary to the flow of caulk. The caulk should fill the joint completely, overlapping both side surfaces, with no gaps or bubbles. At the end of the joint, twist the nozzle out and turn the gun nozzle up to minimize the flow of caulk. Don't expect the caulk to stop flowing instantly; the caulk released by the last click will keep coming. If caulk builds up on the nozzle between joints, wipe the excess off the nozzle with paper toweling. When you're finished caulking, stop the flow of caulk by turning the plunger to point down and pulling it out to disengage it from the tube of caulk.

Let the caulk cure as directed before you touch it. To clean hands and tools, remove as much excess caulk as you can with paper toweling, and finish the job with the appropriate solvent. Fresh acrylic latex caulk can be removed with soap and water; dried silicone caulk will peel off like rubber cement. Use leftover caulk as soon as possible; it will eventually harden in the tube.

What About Big Cracks? Gaps that measure 1 inch or more in width cannot be bridged by caulking compounds. Any crack more than 1/2 inch wide or 1/2 inch deep requires something besides caulking compound.

Oakum, which is a treated hemp rope that is available in plumbing supply stores, is often used to seal big cracks. Fiberglass insulation and sponge rubber strips can act as effective crack fillers, leaving a crack that can be closed with a double bead of caulking compound. Sometimes a piece of wood molding can be added in a corner of a wide crack, leaving only a tiny seam to caulk.

REPLACING DAMAGED SIDING
When clapboards or shakes are rotten or broken, your home's siding can no longer do the job it is meant to do. Damaged siding lets air, water, dirt, and insects through to the inside, and leads to decay and further damage in the wood around it. When you notice a bad spot in your home's siding, repair it as soon as you can. The damaged board or shake is the only part that must be replaced. Replace the old board with a new one the same size and shape.

Be sure to caulk wherever plumbing pipes go through holes in the walls to enter the house. Always caulk along seams where two different materials come together.

Oakum is a treated hemp rope, which is available in plumbing supply stores, that is often used to fill big cracks. Cracks more than 1/2 inch wide or 1/2 inch deep should not be filled with caulk.

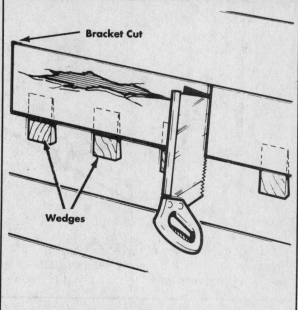

To remove a damaged clapboard, drive wedges to pull it away from the house, and pry out the nails. Then cut out the damaged section with a backsaw.

Clapboards. To remove the damaged board, you'll have to wedge it away from the house. Drive wedges under the damaged board to pull it out from the sheathing below it. Look for the nails in this section of clapboard, and pull them out. If you can't remove them with a claw hammer or pliers, cut them flush with the sheathing, using a hacksaw. To release the top of the board, drive wedges under the clapboard that overlaps the damaged board, and remove the nails from the top of the board you are replacing.

Once the siding has been released, you can cut the damaged section out. Leave the wedges in place under the clapboard. Cut through the board on both sides of the damaged area, using a backsaw. If you don't have much room, use a hacksaw blade with one end wrapped with electrical tape or a keyhole saw. Cut all the way through the board, moving the wedges to make room for the saw. When the board is cut through on both sides of the damage, the damaged section should pull down and out easily. If it won't come out, break it up with a hammer and chisel, and remove it in pieces. Be careful not to damage the surrounding boards.

Cut the new clapboard to fit the opening, and test it for fit; it should slide easily into place, with its top edge under the board above and its bottom edge over the board below. Plane the edges for an exact fit. When the new board fits, paint it with a primer coat; make sure both sides and all edges are covered. Also paint the raw edges of the opening, where the old siding was cut out. Let the paint dry completely. Then set the new

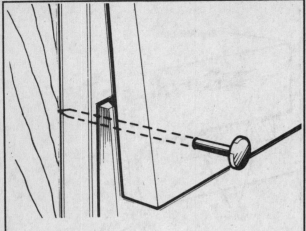

Slide the new clapboard into the gap, with its top edge under the board above and its bottom edge over the board below.

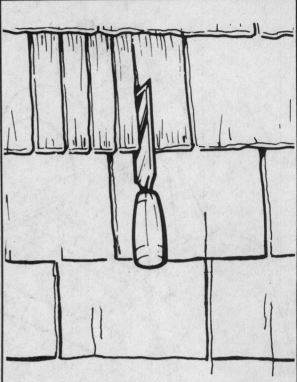

If a damaged shake doesn't come out easily, split it into several pieces with a hammer and chisel; remove the pieces and pull out the nails.

board into the opening, and adjust it so that it fits perfectly. Nail the board into place with 16d nails, driven through the bottom and through the board above into the top edge. Caulk the edges of the patch with acrylic latex caulk. When the caulk is dry, paint the new siding to match the rest of the house.

Shakes or Shingles. Damaged shakes or shingles are replaced the same way clapboards are. If they're natural unstained cedar, take replacement shakes from an inconspicuous area of the house, and use the new shingles on that spot. This trick eliminates an unweathered patch in the repair area.

Wedge out each damaged shake or shingle, driving wedges under the damaged shake and under the shakes that overlap it. Pull out or cut off all nails, then remove the damaged shake. If it doesn't come out easily, split it into several pieces with a hammer and chisel, and remove the pieces. Insert the new shake and nail it into place with 16d aluminum nails; do not use steel nails. If the shake doesn't have predrilled nail holes, drill pilot holes for the nails to keep the wood from splitting.

REPLACING DAMAGED PORCH FLOORING
Wooden porches are a pleasure to live with, but they are also subject to heavy wear and damage. When porch flooring breaks or wears out, more than the looks of the porch are involved. A weak spot in the floor is dangerous, and it can lead to further damage. Unless the whole floor is weakened, you can easily replace the damaged boards.

Porch flooring is nailed directly to the joists of the framing. To repair the damaged area, you'll have to replace the boards in a square or rectangle from joist to joist. Look at the boards to see where the joists are; you'll see a line of nails along each joist. Using a carpenter's square, draw an outline around the damaged area, from board edge to board edge, from inside a joist to inside another joist. If the boards are damaged where they cross a joist, draw the outline out to the joists on either side of it. The boards in this outlined area will be replaced.

Bore a hole inside two diagonally opposite corners of the outline, using a brace and a 3/4-inch bit. Position each hole so that it touches the marked outline on both sides, but does not touch the sound boards outside the repair area. With a saber saw or a keyhole saw, cut across the damaged boards, working from the hole at one outside board across the damaged boards to the other side of the marked outline. You should have to cut only across the boards; the long edges are joined by tongue-and-groove edges, and should pull apart. Carefully pry out the damaged boards with a pry bar. At the outside board edges, don't damage the tongue or the groove of the sound board outside the outline. You may have to use a chisel to remove the last pieces.

Cut new tongue-and-groove flooring strips, the same width and thickness as the old ones, to replace the old ones. Test them for fit in the opening; they should fit exactly in the gap left by the old boards. On the last board, you'll have to cut off the bottom part of the groove to make the board fit flat. Cut the groove piece off with a sharp chisel; be careful not to damage the rest of the board. Then sand the raw surface.

To brace the boards at each end, install 2 x 4 cleats along the inside faces of the joists at the sides of the hole. Cut a piece of 2 x 4 as long as the hole for each joist. Before you install the cleats, paint the floorboards and 2 x 4 cleats with two coats of wood preservative, on all sides. Make sure all surfaces are covered. Let the preservative dry as directed, then nail the 2 x 4 cleats flat to the side joists, with their top edges flush. The top edges of the cleats must be exactly level with the top edges of the joists.

With the cleats in place, set the new floorboards into the opening with their ends resting on the cleats along the joists. Set the first board in tongue first, and insert each board to lock its tongue into the groove of the previous board. Nail each end of each board to the cleat with two or three 16d finishing nails. At the last board, lock the tongue in and set the groove side flat over the tongue of the adjoining board. It won't lock to the joining board, but with the bottom of the groove removed, it will fit into place. When all the nails are in place, countersink them with a nail set, and cover the nail heads with water putty. Do not use wood plastic; it isn't strong enough. Water putty dries rock hard.

To finish the job, let the water putty dry, then sand the patch. Paint the patched area with a primer coat of porch and floor enamel, and let the paint dry. Then repaint the whole porch.

If the old boards were rotten, you should take steps to prevent further decay. Cover the ground under the porch with heavy plastic, lapping the plastic about 6 inches up at the sides. Set a few stones or bricks on the plastic to hold it in place. For the most effective rot preventive, paint the

framing, joists, and floorboards with a coat of wood preservative. These preventive measures will keep your porch strong and healthy for years to come.

REPAIRING A GARAGE DOOR

Overhead garage doors operate on spring tension; the door moves in metal tracks on the garage walls, and a heavy spring or springs provide the power. When the door doesn't work easily, repairs usually are simple.

The first thing to check is the metal tracks inside the garage. Look at the mounting brackets that hold the tracks to the walls; if they're loose, tighten the bolts or screws at the brackets. With the garage door closed, and working inside the garage, examine the tracks for dents, crimps, or flat spots. If there are any damaged spots, pound them out with a rubber mallet or with a hammer and a block of scrap wood. If the tracks are badly damaged, they should be replaced; this is a job for a carpenter.

Now check the tracks with a level to make sure they're properly aligned. Horizontal tracks should slant down toward the back of the garage. Vertical tracks should be plumb. Both tracks must be at the same height on the garage walls. If the tracks are not properly aligned, loosen but do not remove the screws or bolts that hold the mounting brackets, and tap the tracks carefully into position. Recheck the tracks with the level to

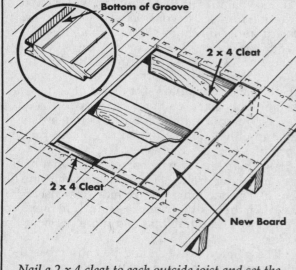

Nail a 2 x 4 cleat to each outside joist and set the new boards into the opening; cut off the bottom of the groove on the last board.

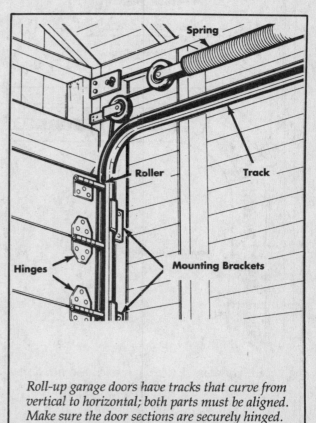

Roll-up garage doors have tracks that curve from vertical to horizontal; both parts must be aligned. Make sure the door sections are securely hinged.

make sure they're in the right position, then tighten the screws or bolts at the mounting brackets.

When you're sure the tracks are straight, clean them out with concentrated household cleaner to remove dirt and hardened grease. Clean the rollers thoroughly, and wipe both tracks and rollers dry. Then lubricate both the tracks and the rollers, using garage-door lubricant or powdered graphite in the tracks and household oil or silicone spray on the rollers. If there are any pulleys, lubricate them with the same lubricant you used on the rollers.

Binding or difficult operation also can be caused by loose hardware. Check the hinges that hold the sections of the door together; tighten loose screws, and replace any damaged hinges. Sagging to one side of the door can often be corrected by servicing the hinges. If a screw hole is enlarged, replace the screw with a longer one of the same diameter, and use a hollow fiber plug, dipped in carpenter's glue, with the new screw. If the wood is cracked at a hinge, remove the hinge and fill the cracks and the screw holes with wood filler; let the filler dry, then replace the hinge. If you can, move the hinge onto solid wood.

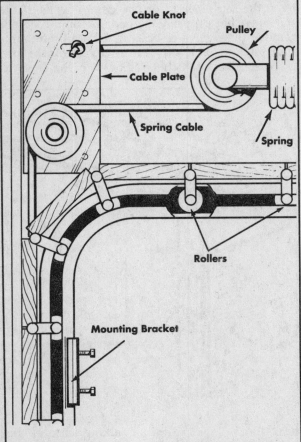

On roll-up doors the spring tension is controlled by a cable on a pulley. To adjust the tension, pull the cable and reknot the end to shorten or lengthen the cable.

If the tracks and the hardware are in good condition but the door still doesn't work right, the problem may be in the springs. **Caution:** *If a roll-up door has only one torsion spring, at the center of the door, do not try to repair it; the tension is so great that the spring could injure you.* For doors with this kind of spring, call a professional repair service.

On roll-up doors, the spring on each side is controlled by a spring cable on a pulley. To adjust the tension of this kind of spring, pull the cable farther through the plate above the door, and reknot the end to maintain the tension.

Sometimes garage doors are hard to open because the wood has swollen; an unpainted door can bind at the edges. To remedy this situation, let the door dry out thoroughly, over several dry days; then paint it on both sides. Paint all the edges of the door; on sectional roll-up doors, make sure the paint penetrates to the edges between the sections. This will prevent the wood from swelling again.

Exterior Painting

You'll never realize just how big your house is until you start to paint it. House painting is a job that consumes time, energy, patience, and no small sum of money. Exterior painting is no more difficult than interior painting, and many tools and techniques are the same. The most persuasive argument for doing exterior painting yourself is that hiring the work can easily cost you two, three, or four times as much.

SELECTING THE RIGHT EXTERIOR PAINT

One of the major differences between indoor and outdoor painting is that there is a wider range of exterior surfaces to consider. They include clapboard and aluminum siding, wooden shingles, cedar shakes, brick, concrete block, stucco, and who-knows-what-kind of old paint. On many homes there is a combination of surfaces, but there is also a paint for every kind of surface and some paints that are suitable for more than one.

Like interior paints, exterior paints are available in either water-thinned or solvent-thinned formulas and three finishes: flat, semigloss, and gloss. There are several characteristics that distinguish exterior coatings from those used inside the house. For one thing they're more expensive. For another they contain more resin (for moisture resistance and durability) and more pigment (for color).

The paint you use should be chosen based on the paint that was used before. Latex works best over latex, and alkyd works best over alkyd. If you can't tell or are unsure about what kind of paint is on the house, use an alkyd-base paint.

Latex paints are easier to apply, they dry quickly, and can minimize moisture problems because they "breathe." Cleaning up only requires soap and water. Latex does not adhere well to alkyd-base paints or to poorly prepared surfaces. Alkyds are durable, but they're trickier to apply, and they dry slowly. Solvents must be used to clean brushes, rollers, paint trays, and drips.

A special alkyd exterior paint has a regulated, self-cleaning property. It's called "chalking," because that is what it does. Over a period of years, the paint surface slowly oxidizes. Each rainfall washes off a minute quantity of the paint along with dirt. Because of this shedding, the paint surface is constantly renewing itself. The price of this convenience used to be chalky residue on foundations and shrubs, but the newest formulas control the shedding so it doesn't stain adjacent surfaces.

Chalking paint is not recommended for every house. In areas with little rainfall, the powder remains on the surface, dulling the paint. In wet regions chalking paint may not be worth the expense because frequent rainfall will keep the outside of the house clean no matter what kind of paint is used.

Once you've selected the proper coating, wait for a weather report that forecasts a string of clear, mild days. Paint adheres best when the temperature is between 50 and 90 degrees Fahrenheit. In most parts of the country, late spring or early fall are the best times to tackle the job, although both seasons can be rainy, which may cause scheduling problems. Wait at least 24 hours after a rain to start or resume painting, and inspect the exterior of your house carefully to be sure that all the moisture has evaporated.

IDENTIFYING PAINT PROBLEMS

Exterior paint will cover many exterior problems, but it won't repair them or even cover them for long if the conditions that created the problem aren't corrected before the paint is applied.

Most paint failures can be attributed to incompatible paints, improper surface preparation, careless painting, or moisture. Rain, snow, fog, and humidity are always at work on the outside of your house, but moisture from inside usually is responsible for deteriorating paint. The more energy-efficient your house is, the more likely it is to suffer from moisture-related paint problems. Well-insulated and tightly sealed houses hold moisture as well as heat. Without adequate ventilation in baths, kitchens, laundries, and attics, moisture vapor penetrates the walls and undermines exterior paints.

Inspect your house thoroughly before you paint and correct the causes of paint failure. Here are some common paint problems and their usual causes:

Peeling. When paint curls away from the surface, it is usually because there is moisture in the wood. You must find the source of the moisture and stop it. Install siding vents to help dispel moisture vapor in problem areas.

Peeling also may result from painting over wet wood. It can be caused by moisture within the house pushing its way out. If you cannot control the moisture with exhaust fans, try latex primer and latex paint. Latex allows some moisture to pass through the paint.

Another cause of peeling is that the paint was applied over a dirty or a glossy surface. To undo the damage, all loose paint flakes must be scraped off with a wire brush and the surface sanded to feather sharp edges. Bare spots must be primed before painting.

Alligatoring. This problem looks just like the hide of an alligator. Paint shrinks into individual islands, exposing the previous surface, usually because the top coat is not adhering to the paint below. Perhaps the paints are not compatible, or perhaps the second coat was applied before the first coat had dried. Scrape, sand, prime, and repaint.

Blistering. This is paint that rises from the surface and forms blisters. It is due to moisture or improper painting. Scrape off a blister. If you can see dry wood behind, the problem is moisture. If you find paint, then it's a solvent blister and is probably attributable to painting with an oil- or alkyd-base coating in hot weather. The heat forms a skin on the paint and traps solvent in a bubble.

Wrinkling. New paint can run and sag into a series of droops. This can occur when the paint you are using is too thick and forms a surface film over the still-liquid paint below. It also can happen if you paint in cold weather. A cold surface slows drying underneath. To recoat, make sure the new paint is the proper consistency and be sure to brush it out as you apply. Before you paint, you must sand the wrinkled area smooth or remove the old paint.

Chalking. This is paint that has a dusty surface. Some oil- and alkyd-base paints are designed to chalk so that when it rains, a powdery layer is removed, automatically cleaning the surface. This usually is desirable, but if it stains foundations, sidewalks, and shrubs, then the process is going on at an accelerated rate. Too much chalking may be caused by a chemical imbalance in an inferior paint, but it usually is due to painting over a porous surface that has absorbed too much of the paint's binding agents. The best solution is to wash down the chalking surfaces thoroughly, then paint over them with a nonchalking paint.

Mildew. This moldy growth appears where there is dampness and shade. If you paint over it, it's likely to come right through the new paint.

Use a fungicide, such as chlorine bleach or a commercial solution, to kill patches of mildew before repainting.

Running Sags. A wavy, irregular surface results from improper brushing. To correct it after the paint is dry, sand and repaint, smoothing out the new coat to a consistent thickness.

Paint Won't Dry. This is the best reason to buy high-quality paint. Prolonged tackiness is an indication of inferior paint. If you apply the paint too thickly or during high humidity, it will stay tacky for a long time. Good paint dries quickly. If you think you may be dealing with an inferior paint, experiment on an inconspicuous portion of the house first.

REMOVING OLD PAINT

If you're lucky, all your house may need before repainting is a bath. Wash it down with water and go over stubborn dirt with a scrub brush and warm soapy water.

If you're not so lucky, then you have a time-consuming, dirty job to do before you can apply a new coat of paint. Do the job right and your paint job will not only look better, it will last for five to eight years.

Start by examining the outside of the house thoroughly, not just the walls but under the eaves, around windows and doors, and along the foundation. Look for split shingles and siding, popped nails, peeling or blistering paint, and mildew and rust stains. Once you've identified the areas that need attention, make the repairs.

Brushing and Scraping. Remove small areas of defective paint with a wire brush or a wide-blade putty knife. Scrub under the laps of clapboard siding and on downspouts and gutters. For speedier work on metal, a wire brush attachment on an electric drill will remove rust and paint with less effort on your part.

For more extensive paint removal, use a sharp pull scraper. This tool has a replaceable blade that can strip old paint down to bare wood with a single scrape. Hold the scraper so that the blade is perpendicular to the wood, apply moderate to firm pressure, and drag it along the surface. Keep the blade flat against the wood so that it doesn't gouge the surface.

Sanding. For feathering the edges of scraped spots, you can wrap a piece of sandpaper around a wood block. For larger areas it is less tiring and more effective to use an electric orbital sander. Move it up and down or back and forth across the surface to remove old paint and feather rough edges at the same time. An electric disc sander or a belt sander can leave swirls or dips in the wood that will show through a new coat of paint.

Melting and Burning. For particularly heavy deposits of paint, heat rather than muscle may be more effective. One way to apply heat is with an electric heat gun that cooks the paint. Use a putty

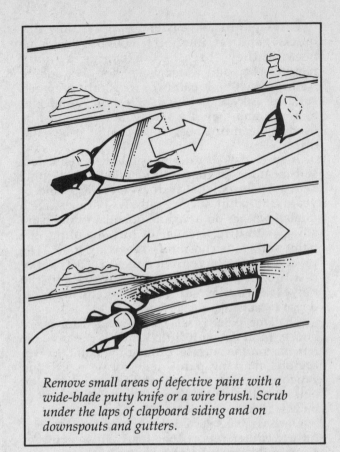

Remove small areas of defective paint with a wide-blade putty knife or a wire brush. Scrub under the laps of clapboard siding and on downspouts and gutters.

Move an electric orbital sander up and down, or back and forth to remove old paint and feather rough edges.

knife in your other hand. Hold the heat gun above the surface until the paint sizzles. Scrape it off with the putty knife.

You also can burn off old paint with a propane torch fitted with a spreader tip that produces a thin, fan-shaped flame that burns off wide bands of paint. Hold the torch in one hand, a wide-blade scraper in the other. The heat from the flame will blister and loosen the paint so you can remove it with the scraper. Keep a fire extinguisher nearby, and take every precaution against setting the house on fire.

Priming. Once the loose paint has been removed, apply an appropriate primer to distressed areas, particularly if your paint-removal system has exposed raw wood or bare metal. The kind of primer you use depends on the kind of paint you'll be using later. For latex paint use latex primers; for solvent-thinned paints use solvent-base primers and for metals metal primers. These coatings not only provide extra protection against the elements, but they form a firm foundation for finishing paints. Priming is always required when you're working on new wood.

OTHER PREP WORK

Even if you're fortunate enough to be able to skip scraping, sanding, and priming, there are still some prepainting chores you must do. Airborne dirt that has affixed itself to the outside of your home should be washed off so that the new coating bonds well to the old. Rust stains on siding, overhangs, and foundations need to be removed. Leaks in gutters and downspouts have to be repaired. Loose caulking should be replaced, along with split shingles. Cracks in siding must be filled, sanded, and primed; mildew has to be scrubbed off and steps must be taken to eliminate its return. To make painting easier, storm windows, screens, shutters, light fixtures, the mailbox, and the house numbers should be taken down, cleaned, and painted separately.

You usually can complete these preparations in a single day or over a weekend. If you're painting with latex you can start the following day. If you're using a solvent-base paint, remember that it does not adhere well to moist surfaces. Wait several days until all the washed surfaces are absolutely dry before applying a new coat of paint.

Washing Down the House. Not only will this process get the outside of your house clean and provide a dirt-free foundation for the new coating, it also will help you find surface flaws that need your attention.

Depending on just how dirty the outside of the house is and on its size, there are two ways to approach this job. If you live in an average size house, use a garden hose with a car-wash brush attachment to bathe the big areas. For caked-on dirt, use a scrub brush or a sponge and a pail of warm water with a strong household detergent in it. Work from the top down, and rinse the areas you scrubbed with clean water.

For bigger houses or faster work on smaller ones, rent a high-pressure spray cleaner. This electrically driven device, attached to your home's water supply system, puts out a jet of water at a pressure of about 600 pounds per square inch. It is equipped with a hand-held wand tipped with a trigger-activated nozzle. The pressure is high enough to dislodge not only stubborn dirt, mildew, stains, and dried-on sea-spray salt, it's enough to remove peeling paint. If you hold the jet nozzle too close to the surface, it can peel off perfectly sound paint, split open shingles, and drill a hole in siding. Follow the manufacturer's directions and wear goggles and protective clothing.

To remove caked-on dirt, use a scrub brush or a sponge and pail of warm water with a strong household detergent in it. Work from the top down and rinse the areas you scrubbed with clean water.

You can use the spray while working from a ladder, although scaffolding is better, but practice at ground level first. The force of the spray against the house could knock you off a ladder if you're not careful. Some of these machines come with separate containers you can fill with cleaning or anti-mildew solutions. Sprayers are so powerful that ordinarily you probably won't need to use a cleaning solution. If you do, remember to rinse the surface with clean water afterward.

Setting Popped Nails. The house bath may reveal the location of nails that have popped out of the siding or rusting nail heads that have left streaks of rust on the exterior walls. Use a nail set and a hammer to reset them. Use sandpaper or steel wool to clean the nail head. On clapboard siding, use the nail set to recess the nail head about 1/4 inch below the surface of the wood. Dab on a coat of rust-inhibiting primer (unless the nail is aluminum or non-rusting galvanized steel) and let it dry. Then fill the nail hole with spackle or putty. When the filler is dry, give it a coat of primer. For flathead nails, which cannot be recessed, sand the heads until they're shiny and coat with a primer.

For rusting nail heads and rust stains, go over both siding and nail heads with sandpaper. If the rust is just on the surface, this should remove it. If it does, then follow up with a coat of primer. If the rust stain doesn't come off with a light sanding, it has soaked into the wood too deeply to remove without damaging the wood itself. Your only option is to sand the nail head, apply a primer to it and the rust stain, then paint over it.

Removing Fixtures, Masking Shrubs. Painting the outside of your house will go faster if you remove all the obstacles in your path: wall-mounted light fixtures, ornaments, shutters, house numbers, mailbox, and awnings. You may even want to remove downspouts because it's sometimes difficult to get a paint brush behind them. Be sure to turn off the power supply before dismantling light fixtures.

Trees, bushes, and shrubs also can get in your way. Prune any branches that overhang the house or brush up against walls. For evergreen trees and tall bushes growing close to the house, wrap them with canvas drop cloths. Then tie one end of a rope around the trunk at least half way up. Pull the top of the tree out and away from the house and tie the other end of the rope to a stake in the yard. Cover smaller shrubs, flower beds, sidewalks, and driveways with drop cloths to protect them from paint drips and spills.

PAINTING SIDING

With the surface preparations out of the way, you're almost ready to brush, roll, or spray on a new coat of paint. Mix all the paint in one or two large containers, especially if you're using a custom-mixed color. Paint colors vary even though they have been mixed by the manufacturer or the paint dealer. The last thing you want is a color change in the middle of a wall. Leftover paint should go back in the original paint cans and be resealed.

Plan to paint from top to bottom so you don't have to worry about dripping paint on freshly painted areas. Do the walls first, then the trim.

Plan your painting day so that you follow the sun, working in the shade after the sun has dried off the early-morning moisture. Try not to let the setting sun catch you in the middle of a wall at the end of the day. If you have to stop, try to finish painting an entire course of siding all the way across the house.

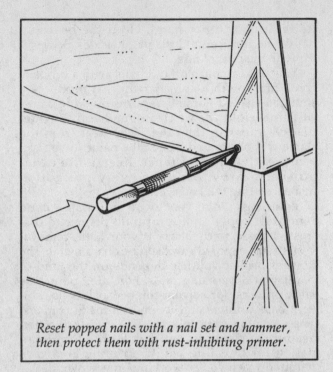

Reset popped nails with a nail set and hammer, then protect them with rust-inhibiting primer.

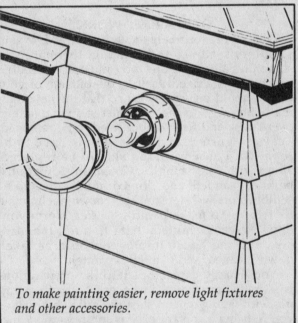

To make painting easier, remove light fixtures and other accessories.

Plan to paint high places in horizontal sections across the top of the wall. Never lean away from an extension ladder or reach more than an arm's length to either side. Paint one high section, move the ladder, and paint another, creating a painted band as you go. Repeat all the way across the wall. Then lower the ladder to work on a lower section. When you get to a point where you can use a stepladder, lean it (closed) against the wall.

An extension ladder can be perilous. Make sure it's on firm footing, about one-quarter of its length out from the foundation of the house, and does not tilt to the left or right. Always make sure both extension hooks are firmly locked on the

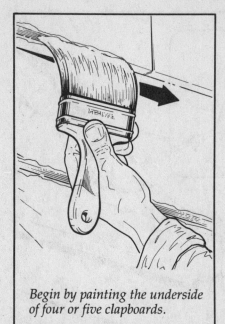

Begin by painting the underside of four or five clapboards.

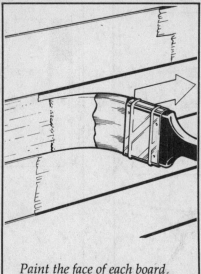

Paint the face of each board, using short strokes to cover the surface.

Level the paint with smooth, broad horizontal strokes.

supporting rungs. The two sections of the ladder should be lapped no less than three rungs. When moving the ladder, watch for power lines. So you can hang on to the ladder with one hand while painting with the other, hang your paint bucket on a rung with an S-shaped bucket hook.

If your house has dormers, you may have to paint them from the roof, instead of a ladder. If so, the ladder should reach at least 3 feet above the edge of the roof so you can step onto the roof without standing on the top rungs of the ladder.

To paint clapboard siding, use a 4-inch brush. To begin, just dip the tips of the bristles in the paint and coat the underside edges of four or five clapboards to a length of 3 feet. With a fully loaded brush paint the face of each board, using short strokes to cover the surface. To finish, level the paint with smooth, broad horizontal strokes.

The same sequence can be used for painting shingles and shakes, except that you'll be applying the paint with vertical strokes. Painting pad applicators, specially designed for shingle painting, are easier to use than a brush. They have a carpet of short nylon bristles embedded in a foam rubber pad attached to the applicator. For edge painting on shingles, just dip the edge of the pad in a paint tray. For the face of the shingles, load the face of the pad, place it against the face of the shingle, apply some pressure and pull it downward. These pads also can be used horizontally on clapboard siding.

A corner roller is another time-saving tool. Use it to apply paint to the underside of either shingles or clapboards. Pay attention around door and window casings. At the top of each casing you'll find a drip cap (metal flashing that tucks up under the siding). Paint a tight seal between metal and wood. At the sides of the casings, jab your brush into joints, then smooth out the paint

to seal them. At casings and for the underside of siding laps, you may prefer to use a corner roller.

Before dismounting and moving the ladder, check your work for drips, runs, sags, thin areas, and missed spots.

PAINTING TRIM

Painting trim is a slow process, but diligence and patience in dealing with details pays off. Done

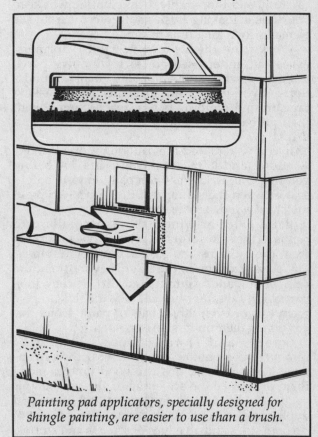

Painting pad applicators, specially designed for shingle painting, are easier to use than a brush.

A corner roller makes short work of the underside of shingles or clapboards.

Paint a tight seal between the drip cap and siding atop windows and doors.

carefully and thoroughly, trim painting will keep your house looking fresh and protect it from the elements for a long time to come.

Work from the top down: gables, dormers, eaves and gutters, second-story windows, porch railings, porches and stairs, and finally, foundations. If you don't want to bother with masking tape around window panes, use a paint shield, then go back later and scrape off spatters and drips.

If you've replaced the caulking around doors, windows and joints, make sure it's dry before painting over it. Use enough paint to form a tight seal between the siding and the trim to keep out moisture, wind, and insects.

Paint exterior windows, sashes, sills, and jambs in the same order as interior ones, working from the muntins and sashes out to the frames. Pay close attention to the sills. They must endure rain, snow, and accumulated dirt. If they look particularly weather-beaten, take the time to give them two or even three coats of paint. Don't forget to coat their underside edges.

Screens and storm windows should be removed and painted separately. If the screens have holes in them, this is a good time to mend them or replace the screening. If the screening is sound, but needs painting, coat it first (use a pad applicator), then paint the frame. Don't forget to do both sides and all edges of screens and storms.

At the sides of window and door casings, jab your brush into joints, then smooth out the paint.

Paint double-hung windows in the sequence shown, moving the top and bottom sashes for access to all surfaces.

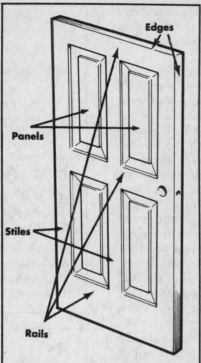

When painting a door, paint the panels first. Then paint the rails, the stiles, and finally the edges, working from top to bottom.

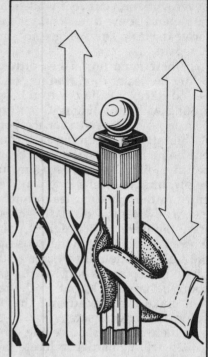

For railing and ornamental iron work, you might prefer to use a mitten applicator instead of a trim brush.

Doors are easier to paint if you remove the knobs, latch plates, and the door knocker. If you can, remove the entire door, lay it flat and paint one side at a time, working on recessed panels first, then raised areas. It's not a bad idea to sand the bottom and top edges and apply a thin coat of paint to keep out moisture and prevent rot. While the door is open or off its hinges, paint the jambs and the frame and give the wooden threshold a coat of urethane varnish. Do not paint the hinges.

Gutters and downspouts made of galvanized metal should be scraped with a wire brush to remove loose paint, then primed and painted. On downspouts paint in the direction of the flutes, usually up and down, to prevent runs, drips, and sags. Because some downspouts are flat on all four sides and attached closely to the house, you may even want to take them down to paint them. As long as you're up there, it won't hurt to coat the inside of gutters with an asphalt-base paint, which waterproofs them and seals tiny holes and joints.

On ornamental metal work and porch railings, you may want to use a lamb's wool applicator instead of a trim brush. The mitten applicator, which can be used on either hand and is cleanable and reusable, allows you to grasp a railing support as you would a broom handle, smearing on the paint as you move your hand from top to bottom. A plastic liner inside the mitten keeps your hand clean.

Paint all the risers on stairs at the same time, then the treads. If the stairs must be used while the paint is still wet, paint alternate treads. When they're dry, paint the other ones.

Roofs and Gutters

Structural damage is always disturbing, but as anyone who's gone through it knows, few things can make you feel as helpless as watching water drip through your ceilings as the rain pours outside. The leak could be anywhere: in the roof itself, in the chimney flashing, in the seal around a vent pipe. If the gutters aren't running freely, water could be backing up at the downspouts and forcing its way in. No situation is hopeless. While it's raining, you should try to locate the problem. Once the rain stops, you usually can repair the damage.

FIXING A LEAKY ROOF

The average lifetime of a shingle roof is 15 to 20 years. If your roof is old, leaks may be the result of general deterioration, and there isn't much you can do to remedy this except to buy a new roof. Leaks usually are caused by localized damage somewhere on the roof, such as cracked or missing shingles or shakes, or on a flat roof, a blistered or cracked area. The hardest part of repairing this kind of damage is locating it. You should never work on your roof while it's wet or windy, but spend some time while it's still raining to locate the leak. This will greatly simplify the actual repairs.

If there is an unfinished attic or crawl space below the leaky roof, finding the leak shouldn't be too difficult. Climb into this space, and look around with a flashlight. Don't turn on a fixture or trouble light; it's easier to spot a leak with a flashlight. Water coming in through the roof at one point often runs down the beams or along the ceiling joists before dripping into the space below. It may travel a long way from the point of entry to the apparent leak point. Watch for the gleam of water in your flashlight beam, and try to trace the water to its highest point on the roof, where it's coming into the house. When you find the leak, outline the wet area with chalk. If you can, push a piece of stiff wire up through the bad spot, so that it sticks out on the roof above. This will make it easier to find the bad spot when you're working outside.

If there is a finished ceiling directly under the leak, it will be harder to locate the problem, but you can make an educated guess. Draw a rough plan of the roof in that area, and mark chimneys, vent pipes, ridges, and wall intersections on it. Every place where two surfaces meet, or the roof changes pitch, is a potential trouble spot. Any one of these spots anywhere near the leak is a good place to start looking.

Caution: *Never work on the roof while it's still wet; it must dry out completely before you can fix the leak. When you work on a roof, wear rubber-soled shoes and old clothes. On gentle pitches, tie a rope to the chimney for use as a safety rope. On*

Adequate safety measures must be taken for any roof repairs. Always use safety ropes; on steep roofs, use a ladder framework to provide secure anchoring.

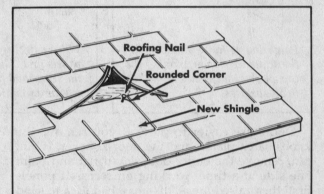

Round the corners of the new shingle and slide it up into the gap. Lift the corners of the overlapping shingles and drive a roofing nail at each corner.

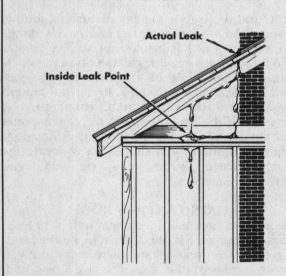

Water leaking in at one point may travel long distances before dripping into a room below. While it's still raining, use a flashlight to trace the leak.

a steep roof, you'll need an anchor hook or framework for the ladder; don't try to make repairs unless the ladder is secured to the ridge of the roof. Use an extension ladder to get up to the roof; brace the ladder firmly against the house, with the top of the ladder extending above the roof. Don't rest the ladder on a gutter. Always work away from power lines.

Shingle Roofs. Shingle roofs are usually easy to fix. At the marked leak point or where you think the leak might be, look for damaged, curled, or missing shingles. At every place where two surfaces meet and around every chimney or vent, look for breaks in the flashing or caulking, or gaps in lines of roof cement. If you can't see any damage to the shingles or flashing in the leak area, you'll have to call a professional roofer; the problem may be inadequate flashing or simply deterioration of the shingles.

If you do find evidence of shingle problems, the repairs are simple. Curled-back shingles can be reattached with roof cement or compound. Use the troweling-consistency cement or buy roof cement in tubes for use with a caulking gun. In warm weather, you can easily straighten out the curled shingle. In cold weather, shingles become brittle and must be softened before they can be flattened out. To soften a brittle shingle, use a propane torch with a flame-spreader nozzle or a heat gun. Apply the flame carefully to the curled edges of the shingle; it should get just warm enough to soften but not hot enough to catch fire. Then flatten the edges of the shingle. To reattach the shingle, apply roof cement generously to the bottom; a good dollop of cement at each corner is usually enough. Then press the shingle firmly into place.

If shingles are torn, rotten, or missing, they should be replaced with new ones. Any shingle that lifts off the roof with no effort is rotten and should be replaced. If you find a large area of rotten shingles, you may need a new roof, and should call a professional. If the area is small, replace the damaged shingles with shingles left from the installation of the roof. If you can't get matching shingles, you can make do with non-matching ones. In an emergency cut shingle-sized patches from sheet aluminum or copper. To make it easier to slide the new shingle up into place, round its back corners with a sharp utility knife. For sheet-metal patches, use tin snips.

Remove the damaged shingle. Lift the edges of the surrounding shingles and carefully remove the nails with a pry bar. Slide the old shingle out; if there is loose or brittle roof cement left under it, scrape the opening clean. When shingles are blown off by a storm, remove any protruding nails left in the roof. Nails that don't stick up can be left in place. With the old shingle removed, slide the new shingle into the gap, with its front edge aligned with the shingles on each side and its back edge under the shingles in the row above it. If you're using a piece of sheet aluminum or copper, coat the back of the patch with roof cement before you slide it into place. Lift the corners of the overlapping shingles and fasten the top of the new shingle with a 6d galvanized roofing nail driven through each corner. Cover the nail heads with roof cement, then smooth down the overlapping shingle edges to make a watertight fit.

If you're replacing rows of shingles, it isn't necessary to round the back corners, except where the top row meets the row above. Ridge shingles, the tent-shaped shingles along the peak of the roof, can be replaced the same way; overlap them along the ridge and over the shingles on both sides. Do not try to use flat shingles; you must use new ridge shingles. Cover the back of each new ridge shingle with roof cement before

setting it into place; secure each corner of the shingle with a roofing nail, and cover the nail heads with roof cement.

After replacing the damaged shingles or if the shingles are undamaged, inspect the chimney flashing, the flashing around vents or vent pipes, and any line of roof cement where two surfaces meet. If the metal flashing around a chimney or dormer is not thoroughly caulked, fill the joints with roof cement in a caulking gun. Along joints sealed with a line of roof cement, apply roof cement with a putty knife to areas that look worn or cracked. Apply the cement liberally; cover the questionable areas completely. If there are any exposed nail heads in the flashing, cover them with roof cement.

Flat Roofs. Flat roofs are built up of layers of roofing felt and tar; leaks usually occur at low spots, or where the roofing felt has been damaged. The leak usually is directly below the damaged spot, and the damage to the roofing felt is easy to see. If there is still water pooled in the leak area, mop it up or soak it up with rags, and let the surface dry. Brush off any gravel. Look for cracks in the felt or for large blisters where the top layer has separated.

To mend a blister, use a sharp utility knife to slice it open down the middle. The cut should penetrate to the full depth of the blistered layer, but should not reach the sound roofing felt beneath it. Lift the cut edges of the blister. If there is water inside the blister, press from the edges in toward the center to squeeze the water out from between the layers of roofing. If there is water under a large area of the roof, the problem is more than a simple blister; water may be running in from an adjoining pitched roof surface, and you should call a professional roofer.

Before you can repair the blister, the inside layers of roofing felt must be dry. If there was water inside the blister, soak up all you can; then prop up the edges to let the layers dry. In cold weather or if the layers are thoroughly saturated, you'll have to use a propane torch, heat gun, or hair dryer to dry out the felts. With a flame-spreader nozzle on the torch, play the flame carefully over the inside layers of the blister. Roofing felt and tar are very flammable; don't let the layers get hot enough to burn or bubble. Use a heat gun or blow dryer in the same way. When the layers of roofing are dry, spread a thick coating of roof cement on the bottom edges of the loose felt, and press down the sides of the blister. Close the blister permanently with a row of 6d galvanized roofing nails along each side of the slit, then spread roof cement over the entire blister; make sure the nail heads are well covered.

When a flat roof has a hole in it, you must patch each damaged layer of roofing felt. With a sharp utility knife, cut out a square or rectangle of roofing around the hole; keep the edges as

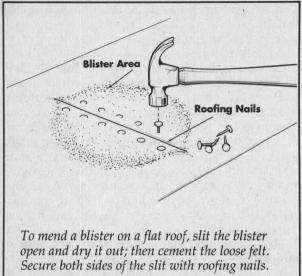

To mend a blister on a flat roof, slit the blister open and dry it out; then cement the loose felt. Secure both sides of the slit with roofing nails.

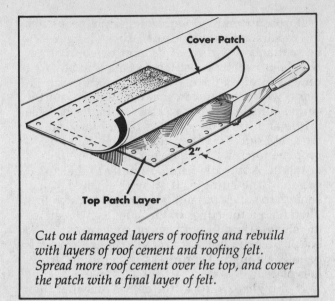

Cut out damaged layers of roofing and rebuild with layers of roof cement and roofing felt. Spread more roof cement over the top, and cover the patch with a final layer of felt.

even as you can. Cut through each damaged layer of roofing felt, one by one, to the depth of the hole, but don't cut any more than you have to. When all the damaged layers have been removed, you should have an evenly cut-out square or rectangle. If there is water between the layers, soak up what you can. Then dry out the roofing felt with a propane torch or heat gun.

When the surrounding roofing is dry, fill in the hole with pieces of 15-pound roofing felt cut to the same size as the hole, rebuilding the damaged area to the same level as the rest of the roof. Cut the patches with a utility knife, one patch for every layer of roofing you removed. Spread roof cement thickly on the bottom of the hole, set a patch into the hole, and press it into place; then spread more roof cement over the patch. Fill the entire hole this way, building up layers of felt and roof cement, until the top patch is flush with the surrounding surface. Finish the job by cutting a larger patch, 2 inches bigger all around than the filled-in hole. Spread roof cement over the top patch, extending it at least 2 inches out onto the roof all around, then set the large patch over this coating. Nail this cover patch down with 6d galvanized roofing nails, set about 1 inch apart, and coat the nail heads with roof cement.

After patching the damaged area, look at the entire roof, and especially at flashing and joints finished with roof cement. Caulk flashing joints with roof cement in a caulking gun. Spread roof cement on any joint that looks worn or damaged. If you can see thin spots or cracks all over the roof, it should be recoated with liquid asphalt not roof cement. This won't solve the problem permanently, but it will extend the lifetime of an old roof. Paint the liquid on with an old broom, and wear clothes you don't mind getting rid of, because this is a messy job. Clean your hands and your tools with mineral spirits, and be sure to dispose of waste materials properly.

Wood Shake or Shingle Roofs. Repairing a shake roof is similar to repairing a shingle one, although it may be more difficult. Use the same kind of shakes or shingles to replace the damaged ones. If a ridge shingle is damaged, use a new specially cut ridge shingle instead of trying to make do with regular shingles.

Damaged wood shakes or shingles usually must be split before they can be removed. Use a hammer and a sharp chisel to split the damaged shake; slant the chisel into the shake at the same angle as the pitch of the roof. Be careful not to gouge the surrounding shakes. Pull the pieces of the shingle out, and cut off the nails that held it in place. Since shakes aren't flexible, you cannot pry out the nails. Use a hacksaw blade, wrapped with electrical tape at one end, to cut off the nail heads, as far down the nail shaft as you can. If you can't reach the nails without damaging the other shakes, you'll have to work around them.

Measure the gap left by the old shake, and cut a new one about 3/8 inch less than this measurement using a saw with a fine-toothed blade. You must allow this 3/8-inch clearance, because the first time it rains the shake will swell. If you were able to cut off the nails that held the old shake, you can just slide the new one up into place, with its top edge under the overlapping shingles, and nail the shake down with two galvanized roofing nails, one at each side of the exposed top edge. If you weren't able to cut off the nails, you'll have to notch the new shake to fit around them. Push the shake up into the gap, hard enough so that the edge is marked by the two old nails. Then carefully cut slots at the marked points with a coping saw or saber saw. Clamp the shake to your workbench so that it doesn't split. Slide the notched shake into place, and nail it with two roofing nails. To finish the job, set the heads of the nails with a nail set, and seal them with caulking compound.

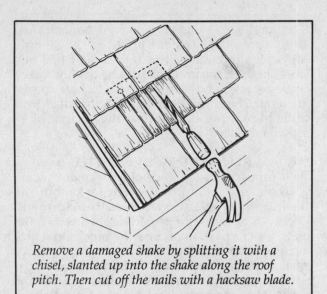

Remove a damaged shake by splitting it with a chisel, slanted up into the shake along the roof pitch. Then cut off the nails with a hacksaw blade.

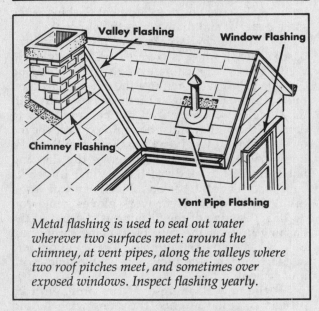

Valley Flashing

Window Flashing

Chimney Flashing

Vent Pipe Flashing

Metal flashing is used to seal out water wherever two surfaces meet: around the chimney, at vent pipes, along the valleys where two roof pitches meet, and sometimes over exposed windows. Inspect flashing yearly.

REPAIRING FLASHINGS

The metal seals around chimneys and dormers, called flashings, can eventually pull loose, collecting water. Chimney flashing that is pulled out of place can channel water down into your home, with disastrous results. Flashing is also used where two roof pitches meet; this is called valley flashing. When flashing is badly damaged or when a leak is severe, you need a professional repair job. But you often can repair the damage yourself. Use ladders and safety ropes to get to the roof. Make sure the roof is dry.

To prevent leaks at the flashing, inspect it every spring. If you can see thin spots or gaps along a flashing joint, at a chimney, or along a valley, spread roof cement over the entire joint, applying it generously, with a trowel. The flashing edge should be covered completely. At the chimney examine the flashing carefully. Chimney flashing is installed in two parts: the base, which covers the bottom of the chimney and extends

onto the roof, and the cap, which is mortared into the chimney bricks. If the mortar holding the cap flashing is crumbling or the flashing has pulled loose, you must resecure the flashing.

Pull the lip of the cap flashing out of the mortar joint as far as it comes easily. Do not yank the entire flashing out, or pull it completely away from the chimney. The less you have to separate it, the easier it will be to fix. With the flashing out of the mortar joint, clean out the old mortar with a hammer and chisel. Wear safety goggles to protect your eyes. Then clean debris from the joint with a wire brush. Use cement mortar mix to fill the open joint; mix the mortar as directed. Wet the joint with a paintbrush dipped in water. With

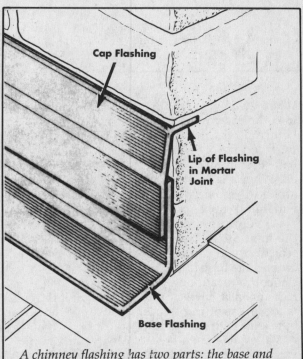

Cap Flashing

Lip of Flashing in Mortar Joint

Base Flashing

A chimney flashing has two parts: the base and the cap. The lip of the cap is embedded in mortar between the chimney bricks.

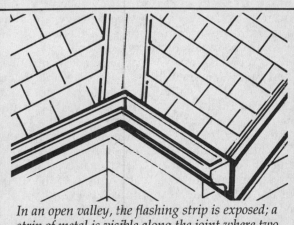

In an open valley, the flashing strip is exposed; a strip of metal is visible along the joint where two roof pitches meet. Repair this yourself.

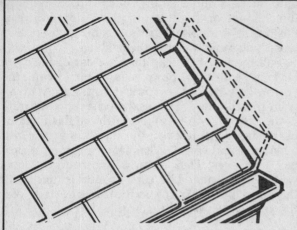

In a closed valley, the flashing is covered by shingles; no exposed metal is visible. Problems here should be repaired professionally.

a small trowel, fill the joint firmly with mortar. When the joint is full, press the lip of the flashing into the mortar, in the same position it was in before. Press the flashing in firmly, but don't push too far or it may pop back out, and you'll have to start all over. Let the mortar dry as directed. When the joint is completely cured, caulk all around the joint, over the lip of the cap flashing, with butyl rubber caulk.

At vent pipes or metal chimneys, make sure the joint at the base of the pipe or chimney is sealed. If you can see gaps at the roof line, caulk around the base of the pipe or chimney with roof cement in a caulking gun. Vent pipes on pitched roofs usually have a protective collar; if the collar is loose, tap it into place, then caulk the collar-base joint with roof caulk.

Valley flashings are not always repairable. If you see a strip of metal along the joint where two roof pitches meet, the valley is open. If the joint is shingled over, it's closed. Open valleys are easy to get at; you can see the damage and you can repair it. Because closed valleys aren't visible from the roof, the only sign of damage is usually a leak directly under the valley. This kind of valley must be repaired by a professional roofer.

To repair an open valley, inspect it for holes. You can patch small holes with sheet metal, the same metal the valley is made of. Do not use a different metal to patch the valley; this would cause corrosion. Clean the surface of the valley with a wire brush. Cut a sheet-metal patch about 2 inches bigger than the hole. Spread a thick coating of roof cement on the damaged area and press the patch into place, bending it to the shape of the valley. Spread more roof cement over the edges of the patch to seal out water.

If you can't see any holes along an open valley, but it has leaked, look for loose shingles along the edges of the valley. Working from the bottom up,

reset any loose shingles with roof cement; then apply more roof cement to cover the shingle edges all along the valley. If you can't find any loose shingles, the problem may be that the valley is too narrow, and simply isn't adequate to seal the joint. This situation should be handled by a professional roofer, because the entire valley must be replaced.

REFLASHING A VENT PIPE

Vent pipes and appliance chimneys are sealed with metal flashing to prevent leaks, but the flashing may eventually need replacement. Pitched-roof vents are usually flashed with a flat metal sheet, cut to fit around the pipe, and a protective collar that fits around its base. Flat-roof flashing usually covers the entire vent, with a flat base and a pipe casing that slides on over the chimney. Replacing either kind of flashing is easy if you make sure your replacement flashing is the same material and diameter as the old one.

Vents on Pitched Roofs. On a pitched roof, the base of the flashing is covered with shingles on the side above the chimney, and left exposed on the side below it. To remove the old flashing, you must remove the shingles on the up-roof side. Lift the shingles with a pry bar, but be careful not to damage them; they must be replaced to cover the new flashing. If you break a shingle, you'll need a new one to replace it. To remove the flashing itself, insert the blade of the pry bar under its edge, and lever the bar on a block of scrap wood to lift the flashing. Wear work gloves while you do this; the edge of the flashing is sharp. Lift the flashing up over the vent pipe, being careful not to knock the pipe out of place. Then pull out any nails left around the pipe, and fill the holes with roof cement.

Set the new flashing over the pipe, with its protective collar aligned the same way the old one was. Nail down the flashing with 6d galvanized roofing nails, and cover the nail heads with roof cement. Apply more roof cement to seal the base of the protective collar. If the top of the collar is loose around the pipe, tap in the lead caulking against the pipe with a screwdriver. With the flashing secure, replace the shingles over the top of the flashing. Starting with the bottom row and working up, nail each shingle into place at the top; use two 6d galvanized roofing nails for small shingles, four nails for large ones. As you work, cover the nail heads with roof cement. Slide the top edges of the top row of shingles under the overlapping bottom edges of the row above.

Vents on Flat Roofs. On a flat roof, the base of the flashing is embedded in the roofing material; to replace it you must cut a hole in the roof, then rebuild it. If there is gravel on the roof, sweep it away from the vent pipe to clear a 4-foot-square area. Locate the edge of the flashing base and, with a sharp utility knife, cut a slit through the

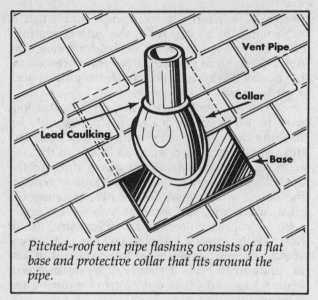

Pitched-roof vent pipe flashing consists of a flat base and protective collar that fits around the pipe.

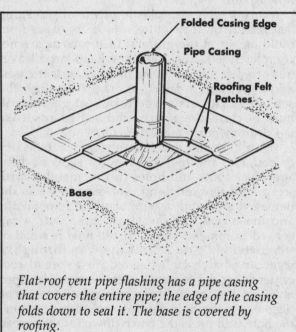

Flat-roof vent pipe flashing has a pipe casing that covers the entire pipe; the edge of the casing folds down to seal it. The base is covered by roofing.

roofing felt along one side of it. Wearing work gloves, insert the blade of a pry bar into the slit and under the edge of the flashing. Lever the bar over a block of scrap wood, working along the slit in the roofing, to release the flashing. Cut around the remaining three sides to free the flashing completely. Lift the old flashing out and over the pipe. You should now have an evenly cut-out square in the roof.

The new flashing is not built into the same hole, but set on top of the roof; your first step in installing it is to fill the hole. For each layer of roofing that you can see in the hole, cut a patch of 15-pound roofing felt. Use the base of the old flashing as a pattern to cut the felt. On each piece of roofing felt, mark the location of the vent pipe, and cut a hole at that point so that the patch will

fit over the pipe. When all your patch pieces are ready, spread roof cement thickly on the bottom of the hole. Set the first patch over the pipe and press it firmly into the hole, then spread more roof cement on top of it. Fill the entire hole, building up layers of roofing felt and roof cement, until the top patch is level with the surface of the roof. Spread a thick layer of roof cement over the top patch, and fill any gaps around the vent pipe with more cement.

Set the new flashing carefully into place over the vent pipe. Wear work gloves while you do this; the edges of the flashing are sharp. Press the new flashing down firmly, so that the vent pipe is encased in the flashing pipe and the base is aligned the same way the old one was. Nail down the flashing with 6d galvanized roofing nails, and cover the nail heads with roof cement. Using pliers, fold the top edge of the casing pipe down over the top edge of the vent pipe to seal the new flashing.

To finish the job, cover the base of the flashing with two more layers of roofing felt. The first one should be 3 inches larger and the second 6 inches larger all around than the flashing. Cut a hole in the center of each piece so that it will fit over the vent pipe. Spread roof cement thickly over the base of the flashing, extending it 3 inches onto the roof all around. Set the smaller piece of roofing felt over the pipe and press it into place. Cover this piece of felt with another layer of roof cement, again extending it 3 inches onto the roof all around, and set the larger patch into place. Press this final patch down and nail it into place with 6d galvanized roofing nails, about 1 inch apart; cover the nail heads with roof cement. If you removed gravel from the patch area, you can now spread it back over the bare spot, but this isn't necessary.

MAINTAINING AND REPAIRING GUTTER SYSTEMS

Good drainage is very important to your home's structural integrity. Gutters and downspouts, the primary components of your drainage system, must be kept clear to prevent storm water from overflowing or backing up. Blocked gutters can cause erosion around the house, damage to the exterior walls, basement leaks, and uneven settling of the foundation. To prevent these drainage problems, you should give your gutters and downspouts regular periodic maintenance, and repair them at the first sign of trouble. When you work on your gutters, follow roof safety procedures.

You should clean your gutters at least twice a year, in late spring and late fall. If you live in a wooded area, more frequent cleaning is advisable. A plastic scoop is an ideal gutter-cleaning tool. To clean the gutters, shovel out leaves and other debris with the scoop; wear work gloves to

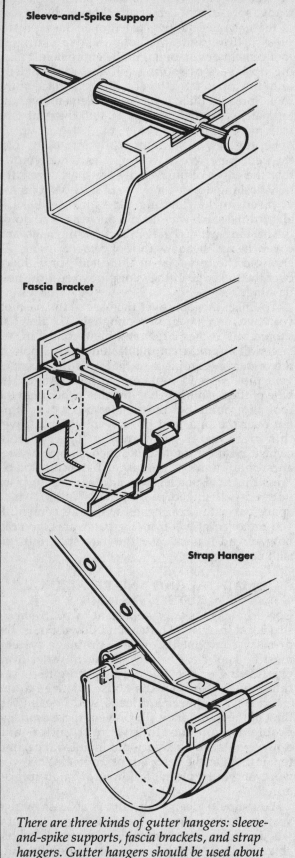

Sleeve-and-Spike Support

Fascia Bracket

Strap Hanger

There are three kinds of gutter hangers: sleeve-and-spike supports, fascia brackets, and strap hangers. Gutter hangers should be used about every 2 1/2 feet.

protect your hands. Work from a ladder that is tall enough to let you reach the gutters comfortably. As you work, move the ladder frequently; don't bend out to reach to either side. After cleaning out all the loose debris, flush the gutters with a garden hose.

Even when the gutters look clear, a downspout may be blocked. Check your downspouts by flushing them with water from garden hose. If a downspout is clogged, you can break up the clog with a plumber's snake, fed down through the opening in the gutter; then clear out any remaining debris with water. To keep the downspouts clear, use a wire leaf strainer over each: copper wire for copper gutters and stainless steel for all other kinds. Insert a leaf strainer into each downspout opening along the gutters; push it in just far enough to hold it steady. The strainer will keep sticks and other debris from entering the downspout.

Many people use plastic or metal screening leaf guards on their gutters, to keep leaves from building up in the gutters. Leaf guards are not completely effective, but they keep large leaves out of your gutters. Leaf fragments, leaf cases, and other small debris go right through the screening. Gutters covered by leaf guards still must be cleaned regularly, and leaf guards make the cleaning much more difficult.

After cleaning out the gutters, let them dry thoroughly, and inspect them for signs of damage. Rust spots and holes can be mended with scrap wire screening and roof cement. Clean the damaged area with a wire brush to remove dirt and loose rust, then wash the area with a rag soaked in mineral spirits. If the hole is small or the metal isn't rusted all the way through, a screening patch isn't needed; just spread roof cement over the damaged area. To repair an open hole, cut a piece of wire screening, 1/2 to 1 inch bigger than the hole. Spread roof cement around the hole, and press the patch down into it; spread a thin layer of cement over the screening. Let the patch dry. If the holes of the screening are still open, spread another layer of cement over the patch to close it completely.

If the gutter is damaged extensively or has a large hole in it, patch it with sheet metal instead of wire screening. If the gutters are copper, be sure to use copper for this repair; use sheet aluminum for other kinds of gutters. Cut a piece of sheet metal big enough to cover the inside of the gutter completely and wrap around the outside edges. The patch must extend at least 1 inch beyond the damage each way along the gutter. Bend the patch to the exact shape of the inside of the gutter. Coat the entire inside of the gutter, where the patch will go, with roof cement, and press the patch down into the cemented gutter to cover the hole. Bend the edges back over the gutter lips with pliers, then coat the entire patch

Foundation Work

Large holes can be patched with sheet metal, bent to the shape of the gutter. Spread roof cement on the damaged gutter before installing the patch.

Sheet Metal Patch

Roof Cement

The problems you see in your home's main living areas, such as cracked walls, sticking doors, and even leaks in the roof or walls, are caused by problems farther down, in the foundation of the building. Foundation problems may make themselves known in several ways. One obvious sign of trouble is a sagging floor, which shows that the joists supporting the floor have given way. The classic trouble spot is the basement, which may be damp all the time or may flood during heavy rains. If you don't have a basement, your first indication of trouble may be a crack in the foundation wall, sudden cracks in inside walls, or gaps at door and window frames. Most problems can be traced to poor drainage of storm water away from the house. Whatever the problem, there is a good chance that you can fix it. You can't make major structural repairs yourself, but if you act promptly, you can take care of most foundation maintenance and repair work.

inside the gutter with roof cement. Make sure the edges of the patch are well covered.

Besides patching obvious damage, inspect the gutters for sags, loose sections, and loose hangers. Gutters are held by three kinds of hangers: sleeve-and-spike supports; fascia brackets, which are nailed to the face of the wall; and strap hangers, which are nailed to the roof. Loose sleeve-and-spike supports can be adjusted or renailed. Loose fascia brackets and strap hangers also can be renailed; use 6d galvanized roofing nails to reset them. Cover the nail heads with roof cement to prevent leaks. If you can't get at a fascia bracket to renail it, or if the gutter sags although all its supports are solid, you must add supports. There should be a support about every 2 1/2 feet along the gutter. Make sure you cover all nail heads on the roof with roof cement.

If a section of downspout or an elbow is loose, it should be reattached. You can do this temporarily with duct tape, but duct tape should not be left in place indefinitely. For a sturdier repair, reattach the loose section with pop rivets; you'll need a pop-rivet tool for this job. Pop rivets can be installed from the outside, so it isn't necessary to take the sections of downspout apart. Hold the loose section in the proper position. With an electric drill and a bit of the correct size for the pop rivets you're using, drill through the overlapping sections. Make one hole on each exposed side of the downspout. Then set a pop rivet through each drilled hole: set a rivet in the pop rivet tool, insert the tip of the tool into the hole, and squeeze the handles of the tool until the rivet pops off. Pop rivets will hold the section of downspout in place permanently.

LEVELING SAGGING FLOORS

Sagging floors can be caused by uneven settling, but severe localized sags on the ground floor are usually the result of problems in the floor joists. If you can get at the beams under the sagging floor, the problem is easy to fix. Before you start, check your local building code to make sure your repair conforms with code. You'll need a jackscrew to make this repair; jackscrews are available from rental outlets.

Before you start working, you should know where the sag is; look for the low spot in the floor. In the crawl space or basement under the sag, examine the exposed floor joists to locate the low point and find the extent of the sag. At the lowest point of the sag, set a 4 x 8 timber flat on the floor under the sagging beam. This timber will serve as a footing or support base for the jackscrew. Measure across the entire sag area, from the sagging beam out past several sound beams in each direction. Cut a 4 x 6 timber to this measurement, and nail the 4 x 6 flat across the center of the sag with long spikes. The 4 x 6 should cross the sagging joist, extending past it across several sound beams on each side. Drive nails through the 4 x 6 into every joist it crosses.

Set the jackscrew, adjusted to its lowest position, on the 4 x 8 timber under the 4 x 6. It should be centered under the low point of the sagging joist. Measure the distance from the top of the jackscrew to the bottom of the 4 x 6, and cut a 4 x 4 timber to this length; make sure the ends are square. Then set the 4 x 4 on end on the jackscrew, forming a post between the jackscrew and the 4 x 6 beam. The 4 x 4 must be solidly set and exactly plumb; check it with a level to make sure it's accurately placed.

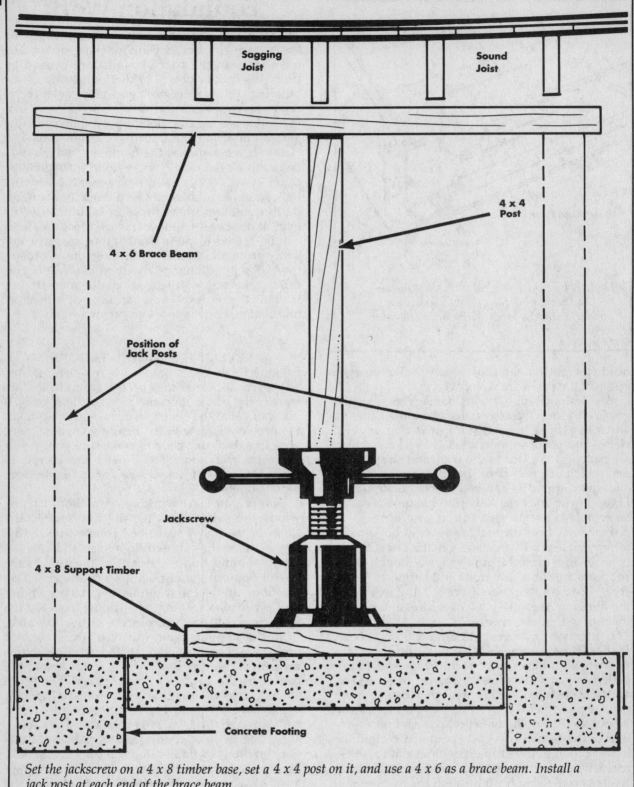

Sagging Joist

Sound Joist

4 x 4 Post

4 x 6 Brace Beam

Position of Jack Posts

Jackscrew

4 x 8 Support Timber

Concrete Footing

Set the jackscrew on a 4 x 8 timber base, set a 4 x 4 post on it, and use a 4 x 6 as a brace beam. Install a jack post at each end of the brace beam.

With the post in place, turn the handle of the jackscrew just until you feel resistance, then stop. **Caution:** *Do not turn the handle of the jackscrew after you feel resistance, or you could cause serious structural damage to your home.* Wait a full 24 hours, then turn the handle one-quarter turn tighter. Wait another 24 hours and again turn the handle one-quarter turn; repeat this procedure as necessary until the sagging beams straighten out. Before you make each adjustment, check the beams with a level to see how far they've changed position. **Caution:** *You must wait at least 24 hours between adjustments; don't worry if you miss a day. Do not turn the jackscrew handle any more than one quarter turn a day; if you try to hurry the process, you could cause serious structural damage.*

As you continue to jack them up, the sagging beams will eventually level out. When all the beams in the sag area are even, stop jacking up the brace beam. To hold it in place, you'll have to install a post at each end of the beam; leave the jackscrew in place for the time being. Steel Lally columns or adjustable jack posts are the best supports; the jack posts are easier to install. Jack posts are available at building supply outlets. They must be left in place permanently, so you'll have to buy them instead of renting. The posts work the same way the jackscrew does.

Whether you use jack posts or Lally columns, you must provide a concrete footing for each; the concrete of the basement floor is not strong enough to support them. Set the posts in place at the ends of the brace beam and mark the position of each on the floor; then set the posts aside while you prepare the footings. Leave the jackscrew in place while you work.

Break up a 2-foot-square section of the floor, centered on the marked post area, for each footing. Wear safety goggles, and use a brick chisel and a heavy sledgehammer to break up the old concrete. Break through the floor to a depth of at least 1 foot; the opening doesn't have to be perfectly level, but it must be at least 1 foot deep at its shallowest part. Then remove the debris, clean out the hole, and flush it thoroughly with water.

While the opening is still wet, blend ready-mix sand concrete according to the package directions. A wheelbarrow is the best mixing container, because you also can use it to pour the concrete; use a shovel as a stirring tool. When the concrete is ready, spray the hole lightly with water; it should be wet but not streaming. Then paint all exposed surfaces of the opening with liquid concrete bonding agent. Without this step, the footing will not bond properly to the old floor. Use a stiff throwaway paintbrush to apply the bonding agent. While the bonding agent is still wet, pour the prepared concrete into the hole. Spread the concrete with the shovel, making sure there are no gaps.

To finish the job, strike off the footing with a long piece of 2 x 4. Set the 2 x 4 on the edge across the new concrete, and pull it back and forth over the footing in a firm zigzag stroke. This smoothes and levels the surface of the footing. After striking off, use a wooden float (a concrete tool that looks like a large trowel) to smooth the surface. As you smooth the footing, a sheen of water will appear on the surface of the concrete. Wait until this film of water disappears, about 45 minutes to an hour; then smooth the footing again with a flat steel trowel. This second smoothing will make the surface harder. A sheen of water will again come to the surface during this step; wait until the water disappears, then cover the footing with a sheet of heavy plastic to keep it from drying out too fast. Weight the edges to hold the plastic in place. Let the concrete cure for a week. During this period, remove the plastic and spray the concrete lightly with water, two or three times a day.

When the new footings are completely cured, you can set the jack posts in place permanently. Set each jack post into place, centered on its footing under the brace beam. With a level, adjust each post to exact plumb. Then set the posts so that they meet the brace beam exactly. Stop turning when you feel resistance. Finally, with the jack posts in place, remove the jackscrew. The sagging floor is now permanently leveled.

HOW TO KEEP YOUR FOUNDATION HEALTHY

Foundation damage can be caused by poor construction, but the problem is far more likely to be poor drainage, which leads to shifting and uneven settling of the soil under and around the house. There isn't much you can do once settling has occurred. If the damage is slight, you can live with it; if it's extensive, you must call a professional engineer. There is something you can do, no matter how old your house is, to prevent uneven settling from becoming a structural problem: Keep water away from the house.

Fix downspout leaks immediately. Walk around the house and look at the ground near the foundation; the soil should always slope away from the house. If the ground is level or slopes in toward the house around the foundation, you'll have to regrade the soil to slope it properly. Water should never be allowed to collect around the foundation. Go outside during a heavy rain and watch the course of the runoff around the house. There should be shallow runoff channels in the ground to carry water away from the foundation. If these natural drainage routes have been filled, open them so that rainwater can flow away from the house. If you have to dig channels or regrade, reseed or sod to prevent erosion.

See that vegetation around the house is properly maintained. Check flower beds near the house to make sure they slope away from the foundation; if they're curbed or edged, make sure the edging doesn't trap water. When you plant trees or shrubs, keep them away from the foundation. Any large plant draws water out of the soil, and can cause areas of unequal moisture, which may cause shifting of the soil. When you water grass and flowers, water all around the house, even where there are no plants to keep the soil evenly moist around the foundation.

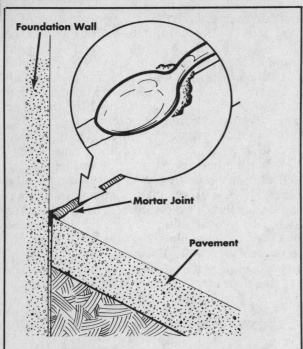

To keep water from collecting where a paved area meets the foundation, undercut the joint, and fill it with mortar. Shape the mortar into a smooth curve.

Look at walks, drives, or patios that butt directly against the house. Paved areas should slope away from the house, and paving should meet the foundation wall in a smooth, rounded joint. If this joint is cracked or if it holds water, you should cut it out and remortar it. Use packaged mortar mix, available at hardware and building supply stores. Cut out the joint with a hammer and chisel, undercutting it so that it's wider at the bottom than at the top. Wear safety goggles as you work. Clean the joint with a wire brush to remove the debris, and flush it thoroughly with water. Mix the mortar as the package directs. While the joint is still wet, fill it with mortar. Use the back of an old spoon to shape the mortar into a smooth curve, so that the joint curves up from the pavement to the foundation wall. Let the mortar cure for two to three days, or as directed. During this time spray it lightly with water two or three times a day to keep it from drying out too quickly.

Your gutter and downspout system is another important factor in foundation moisture control. Clean the gutters and downspouts regularly to make sure they're open and flowing freely. Runoff from downspouts must be kept away from the foundation; if the downspouts empty directly at the foundation, install long drainage sleeves or concrete splash blocks to break its force. If your gutters are not adequate to handle rainwater drainage, you should extend the system or have new gutters installed.

When uneven settling does occur, deal with the problem immediately. If cracks in the foundation wall are serious or if they're getting noticeably worse, call a professional to do the work.

DRYING OUT A WET BASEMENT

For many people, keeping a basement livable is a constant struggle.

Seepage. Where seepage through the entire foundation wall is occurring because the original waterproofing was inadequate, you may be able to eliminate moisture in the basement by painting the walls with waterproofing paint. Several basement paints and waterproofing compounds are available. Some must be mixed, as the manufacturer directs; others must be applied to a wet surface. Before applying the compound, scrub the walls with a wire brush to remove dirt and chips. Wear safety goggles. After cleaning the walls, mix the compound and wet the walls, as directed by the manufacturer. Apply the compound to the walls with a stiff masonry brush; work it in to fill rough and uneven surfaces. Let the compound dry as directed. A second coat usually is required; apply it the same way.

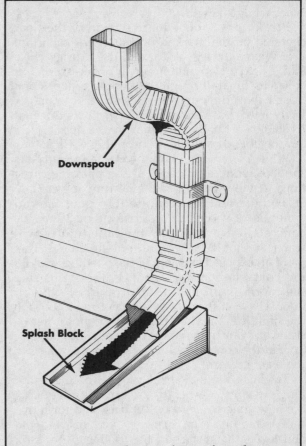

Storm water must be routed away from the foundation. Clean downspouts regularly, and install concrete splash blocks to break the force of runoff water.

If the problem is seepage through the wall-floor joint, you can seal the joint with epoxy mortar, sold as a two-part mix. This can be done only when the floor is dry. Cut open the joint with a hammer and chisel, deepening it to a depth of 1 to 2 inches and undercutting it so·that it's wider at the bottom than at the top. Wear safety goggles. Use a wire brush to remove debris from the joint, then vacuum it thoroughly. Mix the epoxy compound as directed on the package, and pack it into the open joint with a small trowel. With the back of an old spoon, shape the epoxy into a smooth curve all along the joint. The epoxy must cure for at least 24 hours.

Cracks. Leaks through cracks in the foundation wall also are easy to repair. If the damage is serious or if the cracks are widening visibly, you should call a professional. But you can repair less serious damage yourself. If the foundation wall has large cracks that extend below the surface of the ground, it should be professionally repaired and waterproofed. When the outside of the wall has been repaired, you can work on the inside to stop leaks in the basement.

To repair cracks inside, deepen and undercut them with a hammer and chisel. Wear safety goggles. Remove debris with a wire brush, and flush thoroughly with water. Mix mortar as directed. While the cracks are still wet, fill them with mortar, smoothing it level with a small trowel. Let the mortar cure for two or three days, or as directed. During the curing period, spray the patched area lightly with water two or three times a day to keep the mortar from drying out too quickly.

Wet Cracks and Constant Leaks. When water comes in constantly through a crack or hole in the wall, you can repair the damage with hydraulic cement. Hydraulic cement, unlike mortar, hardens even in flowing water. It's sold as a mix, in hardware and building supply stores.

Hydraulic cement is not applied with a trowel; it's formed into a long plug and inserted into the hole. If there is a long open crack, it should be filled gradually, top to bottom, with plugs of hydraulic cement. This reduces the flowing crack to one open hole, which is then filled with a final plug.

Deepen and undercut the crack or hole with a hammer and chisel. Wear safety goggles. Remove debris with a wire brush. Mix the hydraulic cement as directed. Wearing heavy-duty rubber gloves, shape a long, carrot-shaped plug of cement, the same diameter as the hole or the same width as the crack. Let the plug set briefly, as directed. When it starts to harden, push the plug into the hole. Hold the plug in place until you can feel that it's set, then trowel the surface smooth.

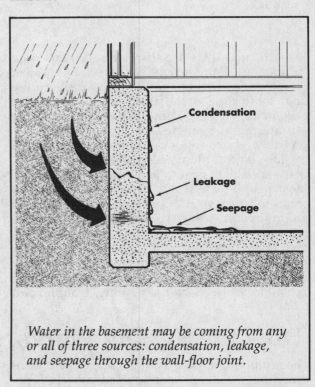

Water in the basement may be coming from any or all of three sources: condensation, leakage, and seepage through the wall-floor joint.

PLUMBING

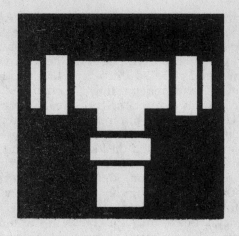

Many homeowners are scared of even the word "plumbing." Cartoonists have played on this fear for years, picturing the victim of a plumbing calamity floating on the rising waters of a flooded basement. There is some truth in this. Severe plumbing emergencies do arise, and there is probably no one so lucky as never to be plagued by some kind of plumbing problem.

It's usually not the calamities that bother you. Most people worry about plumbing because it seems to be a mysterious system, but plumbing is no mystery. It works according to the basic laws of nature: gravity, pressure, and water seeking its own level. You can easily understand the way your plumbing system works. Once you know the basics, you can take care of many plumbing problems yourself and save time, trouble, and money.

How the System Works

The plumbing in your home is one system composed of two complementary but entirely separate subsystems. One subsystem brings in freshwater, and the other subsystem takes out wastewater. If you and your family are to stay healthy, you must avoid cross-connections between the supply and disposal lines.

THE SUPPLY SYSTEM

The water that comes into your home is under pressure. It makes no difference whether your water supply is public or private; water that comes from either a storage tank or a well enters your home under enough pressure to allow it to travel upstairs, around corners, or wherever else it's needed.

In urban and suburban areas, the community water department pumps water into a tank or tower that is higher than the surrounding homes; the force of gravity supplies the water pressure. If you have your own well, you probably have a pump to bring water into your home under pressure.

From the supply tank or tower, water travels through a water main to the supply line for your home. Before you use the water for drinking, bathing, and washing clothes and dishes, it may pass through a meter that registers the number of gallons or cubic feet you use. The water meter may be somewhere on your property outside the house, or it may be inside, at the point where the supply pipe enters. An outside meter has a metal cover; you can lift the cover for access to the meter.

Even if you never look at the water meter itself, you should be familiar with one device that is generally located close to the meter. This is the main shutoff, or stop valve. In a plumbing emergency, close the main shutoff valve as fast as you possibly can. When a pipe bursts, it can flood your house in no time, but you can minimize damage by closing the main shutoff valve to shut off all the water coming into the house. The shutoff may be a stop-and-waste valve, which drains the water from the pipes as well as shutting off the supply. If the emergency is confined to a sink, tub, or toilet, you may not want to turn off your entire water supply. Most fixtures have individual stop valves.

Once the water has passed from the public facility's tower or tank through the main supply line to your individual supply line, and through your home water meter and main shutoff valve, it travels to the different fixtures in the house for your use. Water must be heated for your hot-water supply, but the water from the main supply is immediately ready for your cold-water needs.

The hot-water supply requires another step. One pipe carries water from the cold-water system to your water heater. From the heater a hot-water line carries the heated water to all the fixtures, outlets, and appliances that require hot

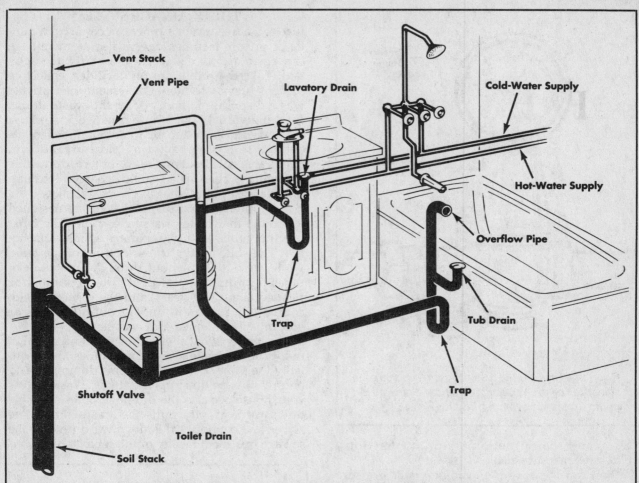

Vent Stack

Vent Pipe

Lavatory Drain

Cold-Water Supply

Hot-Water Supply

Overflow Pipe

Tub Drain

Trap

Trap

Shutoff Valve

Toilet Drain

Soil Stack

Your home's water supply and drainage systems must always be two distinct subsystems with no overlapping. At the fixtures (bridges between the two systems), the air admitted by the vent stack and vent pipes keeps the traps sealed and prevents sewer gases from backing up through the drains.

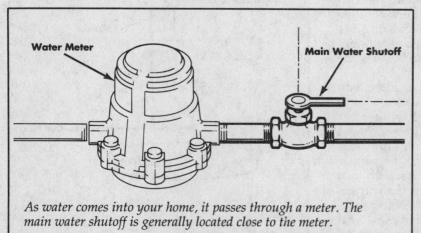

Water Meter

Main Water Shutoff

As water comes into your home, it passes through a meter. The main water shutoff is generally located close to the meter.

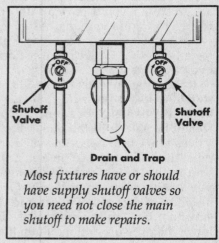

Shutoff Valve

Shutoff Valve

Drain and Trap

Most fixtures have or should have supply shutoff valves so you need not close the main shutoff to make repairs.

water. You can adjust the water temperature by raising or lowering the temperature setting on the water heater. A thermostat on the heater maintains the temperature you select by turning the device's heating elements on and off as required. The normal temperature setting for a home water heater is between 140 and 160 degrees Fahrenheit, but 120 degrees Fahrenheit usually is adequate and more economical.

The water pressure in your home is like any other good thing; too much of it can be bad. Residential water pressure that reaches or exceeds 70 to 80 psi (pounds per square inch) can cause your pipes to bang and faucets to leak. It

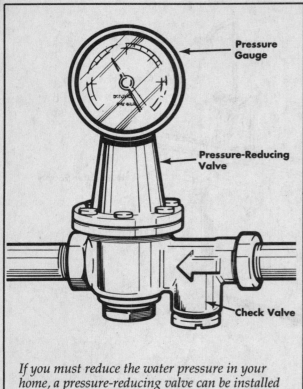

If you must reduce the water pressure in your home, a pressure-reducing valve can be installed in the supply pipe coming into the house.

also can break pipe joints and connections. Excessive pressure also wastes water.

You can measure the average water pressure in your home by attaching a pressure gauge to the cold-water faucet nearest the main shutoff valve. Be sure to test the pressure at several different times during the day to find an average. Water pressure fluctuates, but it shouldn't fluctuate greatly or you'll have an uncomfortable time trying to take a shower. When measuring the water pressure, make sure no water is running from any other outlet in your home besides the one the gauge is attached to.

If the gauge registers 70 to 80 psi or more, you should install a pressure-reducing valve. This is an inexpensive device, and a do-it-yourselfer should be able to install one easily. Most of these valves work best when installed on a horizontal pipe; the valve can be connected into the supply line with union fittings (fittings used to join pipes) without much difficulty. Once the valve is installed, you can simply set it to the water pressure that best suits your needs. The valve will lower the pressure and maintain it at that setting.

Decreasing excessive water pressure is easy; increasing inadequate water pressure is more difficult. It could involve such major projects as building your own water tower, installing a pump, or even ripping out all the pipes in your home and installing new ones. Too little water pressure is something many people learn to live with.

THE DRAINAGE SYSTEM

Just as the freshwater supply can come from public or private facilities, the wastewater drainage can go to a public sewer line or private septic tank. Like the public supply facilities, collective sewer systems are more convenient than private waste disposal methods. After the waste drains from individual houses into a network of pipes, it's carried to a sewage treatment plant, where it's aerated to hasten bacteriological breakdown. Solids are settled out and used for fertilizer, while the liquid is chlorinated and discharged into natural water supplies, such as rivers and lakes.

A septic tank and disposal field are designed to handle the waste of a single home. The tank, like the public facility, separates solids from liquid. The solids settle to the bottom of the tank, while the liquid runs out through a network of pipes into the disposal field. The tank must be cleaned every few years, and the disposal field, composed of pipes in underground trenches or pits, must be enlarged as it becomes clogged.

No matter what method of waste disposal is used, the drainage systems in homes are essentially the same. Drainage systems do not depend on pressure, as do supply systems. Waste leaves your house because the drainage pipes all angle downward; gravity pulls the waste along. The sewer line continues this downward flow to the sewage treatment facility or the septic tank.

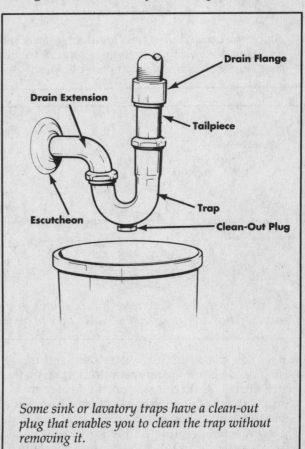

Some sink or lavatory traps have a clean-out plug that enables you to clean the trap without removing it.

While the system sounds simple, there is more to waste drainage than pipes tilted downward. There are also vents, traps, and clean outs. You can see the vents sticking up from the roof of your house; they allow air to enter the drainpipes. If there was no air supply coming from the vents, wastewater would not flow out properly, and the water in the traps could be siphoned away.

Traps are vital components of the drainage system. You can see a trap under every sink or lavatory; it is the curved or S-shaped section of pipe under the drain. Water flows from the basin with enough force to go through the trap and on out through the drainpipe, but enough water stays in the trap to form a seal that prevents sewer gas from backing up into your home. If there was no seal at the drain, bad odors and dangerous gases would back up through the pipes.

Every fixture must have a trap. Toilets are self-trapped; they do not require an additional trap at the drain. Bathtubs frequently have drum traps; these not only form a seal against sewer gas but also collect hair and dirt to prevent clogged drains. Some kitchen sinks have grease traps, which collect grease that goes down the sink drain that might otherwise cause clogging. Because grease and hair generally are the causes of drain clogs, traps often have clean-out plugs that give you easier access to remove or break up any clogs.

Since the drainage system involves all these components, it usually is called the DWV (the drain/waste/vent system). If water is to flow out freely and waste is to exit properly, all components of the DWV must be present and in good working order. Examine the pipes in your basement or crawl space. The larger and heavier pipes are for drainage. It's always a good idea to tag as many pipes as possible and to know exactly what each does. Locate the clean-out plugs on the traps and in the drainage lines, and make sure you know where all the vents are.

PUTTING IT TOGETHER

The supply and drainage subsystems are two distinct operations with no overlapping. There are bridges between the two, and the bridges are what make the plumbing system worth having. A bridge between the supply and drainage systems is a fixture.

Toilets, sinks, and tubs are fixtures. An outside hydrant is a fixture and so is an automatic washing machine. All devices that draw freshwater and discharge wastewater are fixtures, and all are designed to keep the supply and drainage systems strictly segregated.

Repairing Sinks, Tubs, and Drains

Many people who rush to call a plumber when a pipe springs a leak or a toilet clogs draw the line at calling in professional help when it comes to sinks and tubs. They feel that it takes no great expertise to fix a dripping faucet or to clear a slow drain. Don't hesitate to tackle faucet prob-

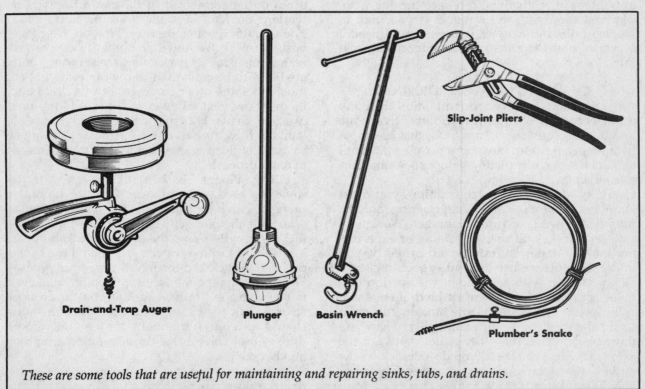

Drain-and-Trap Auger   Plunger   Basin Wrench   Slip-Joint Pliers   Plumber's Snake

These are some tools that are useful for maintaining and repairing sinks, tubs, and drains.

lems and toilet troubles, and you should be able to take care of most sink and tub problems.

SPECIAL TOOLS

You already probably own many tools necessary for working on sinks and tubs. They are tools that can be used for many other do-it-yourself projects besides plumbing chores, or they are tools that are so well known that no detailed explanation of them is needed. Essential for every household is the plumber's friend, also called a plunger or a force pump. The best models have long handles, and their suction cups are large enough to cover different drain openings.

Plumber's snakes, or drain-and-trap augers, come in various lengths; you should have a short and a long one. When you buy an auger, look for one that comes encased in a metal housing; it's less messy to use.

You'll need wrenches for most faucet repairs and for various other connections. A medium-size adjustable wrench can be used on nuts of many different sizes; with one adjustable wrench you can handle the same tasks that would otherwise require a complete set of open-end wrenches. The advantage of open-end wrenches over an adjustable wrench is that they provide a secure grip on the nut. You frequently can substitute a pair of long-handle slip-joint pliers for either kind of wrench.

A basin wrench is a specialized tool that allows you to reach tight spots under sinks and basins. The jaws of a basin wrench not only adjust to fit nuts of different sizes but also flip over to the opposite side, so that you can keep turning without first removing the wrench. If you plan to work on tub and shower fixtures, you'll need a socket wrench set to help remove recessed packing nuts.

CLEARING CLOGGED DRAINS

Clogged drains receive more attention than any other common plumbing problem. Everyone knows the inconvenience and mess that accompany a sluggish drain, but many people wait until the drain stops completely before they take corrective action.

When you take corrective action, you must know how to use the best drain-clearing tool: the plumber's friend, or rubber plunger. Working a plunger requires no special training or expertise, but if the plunger is to do its job properly, you must know a few facts. If you expect to clear a clogged drain with a plunger, the suction cup must be large enough to cover the drain opening completely. The water in the sink or tub must cover the plunger's cup completely. Then you must block off all the other outlets between the drain and the blockage. If you don't block off the outlets, all the pressure you create will be dissipated long before it can get to the clog.

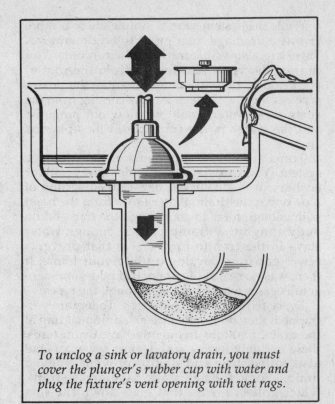

To unclog a sink or lavatory drain, you must cover the plunger's rubber cup with water and plug the fixture's vent opening with wet rags.

For clogged lavatory, sink, and tub drains, use this procedure with the plunger: Cover the overflow opening in the basin or tub with a wet cloth. Most kitchen sinks don't have an overflow vent, but if you're working on one of two side-by-side basins, you'll have to plug the other basin's drain opening with wet cloths. There may be another drain outlet connected to the drain line you're working on, and this outlet must be blocked too. You'll find it if water starts backing up in a previously unsuspected outlet. In homes that have two bathrooms back to back in adjacent rooms, both are likely to be connected to the same drain. You must block the other basin at both its drain and its overflow vent. Shower facilities seldom have overflow vents, but bathtubs do have vents, and laundry tubs may have two or three. You must cover all of them with wet cloths for your plunger to work properly.

Fill the clogged basin with enough water to cover the head of the plunger. Coat the lip of the plunger with petroleum jelly; this assures a better seal. Slide the plunger's cup over the drain opening and rapidly pump the plunger up and down. You should feel the water move in and out of the drain. This back-and-forth water pressure eventually builds up enough force to dislodge whatever is blocking the drain. After about a dozen firm strokes, jerk the plunger up quickly. The water should rush out. If it doesn't, try the same procedure two or three more times before attempting another method.

If the plunger doesn't remove the clog in the drain, many people turn to a chemical drain opener, in either dry or liquid form. In a drain that is completely blocked, it's best not to use chemicals. Most chemical drain openers contain caustic agents that can harm fixtures. If you must later remove a trap or clean out to free the blockage, you will be exposed to the harmful solution.

Your safest course is to use a drain-and-trap auger. To use it remove the pop-up stopper or strainer from the clogged drain, and insert the auger wire into the opening. As you feed the flexible wire in, crank the handle of the device clockwise, loosening and then tightening the thumbscrew on the handle as you advance the wire. If the wire encounters something, move it back and forth while you turn the auger handle. Then continue to turn the handle while withdrawing the auger slowly.

If the auger has cleared the drain of most of the debris inside, you can pour hot, soapy water into the drain to remove any remaining debris. If the auger didn't work, move on to the trap to unclog the drain.

If the trap under the basin is equipped with a clean out, remove the clean-out plug, catching the water in the trap in a bucket. You can use a wire coat hanger with a hook shaped in one end to try to reach the clog. If this fails, insert the wire of the drain-and-trap auger through the clean out, then work toward the basin and toward the drainpipe to remove the blockage.

If the trap does not have a clean out, remove the trap. With the trap removed, clean it out with a wire coat hanger and then with a stiff brush and hot soapy water; then replace the trap. If the clog wasn't in the trap, insert the drain-and-trap auger into the drain extension that goes into the wall, and continue working the auger down into the drainpipe itself. You should be able to reach the blockage, unless it's in the main drain.

If a bathtub drain is clogged and a plunger doesn't clear the drain, use the drain-and-trap auger first through the tub drain opening. If this doesn't work, remove the overflow plate and insert the auger directly into the overflow pipe and down into the drainpipe.

Some older bathtubs have a drum trap, usually located near the tub at floor level. Unscrew the lid of the drum trap counterclockwise with an adjustable wrench, and clean out the trap. If the debris is elsewhere, try to reach it through the drum trap with the drain-and-trap auger.

For floor drains, such as those in basements and showers, a garden hose can be effective in unclogging drains, especially if the clog is not close to the opening. Attach the hose to a faucet, feed the hose into the drain as far as it will go, and jam rags around the hose at the opening. Then turn the water on full force for a few moments.

If you suspect a clog is in the main drainpipe, locate the main clean out; this is a Y-shaped fit-

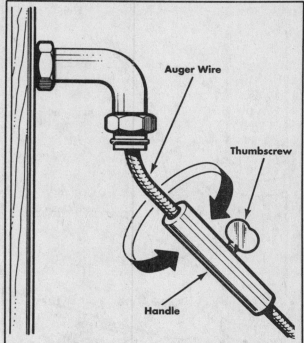

If the clog is not in the fixture's trap, insert a drain-and-trap auger into the drain extension that goes into the wall, and work the auger into the drainpipe.

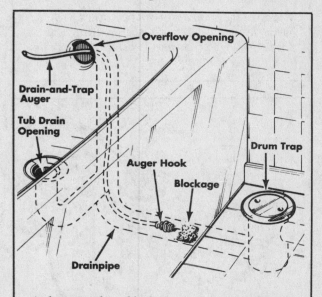

A clog near the tub's drain can be attacked from several places: the overflow opening (as shown), the tub drain opening, or the drum trap. Start working at the tub drain; if you can't remove the obstruction there, move on to the overflow and then the drum trap.

ting near the bottom of your home's soil stack or where the drain leaves the building. Set a large pail or container under the clean out and spread papers and rags around the site to soak up the backed-up water. Using a pipe wrench, slowly

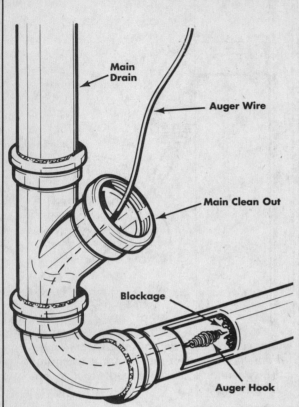

A clog in the main drain can be reached from the main clean out. This is a Y-shaped fitting near the bottom of your home's soil stack or where the drain leaves the building.

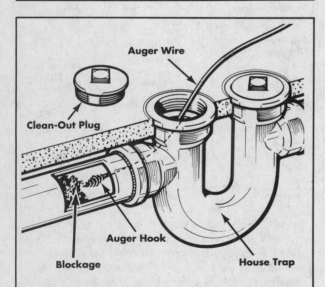

The house trap is a U-shaped fitting installed underground. You can locate it by finding two adjacent clean-out plugs in the basement floor. A blockage between the trap and the main clean out can be reached by removing the plug closest to the main clean out.

unscrew the clean-out plug counterclockwise, trying to control the flow of water that will seep from the clean out. Once the flow has stopped and you've cleaned up the flooded site, insert the auger to remove the debris.

If you still haven't located the blockage, another place you can try is the house trap; this is a U-shaped fitting installed underground. You can locate it by finding two adjacent clean-out plugs in the floor, if the main drain runs under the floor. Place papers and rags around the site before opening the clean out nearest to the sewer outside. If the clog is in the house trap or between the trap and the main clean out, you should be able to remove it. If the water starts to flow out of the trap as you unscrew it, check quickly beyond the house trap with an auger. If you can remove the clog rapidly, do so. Otherwise, replace the trap plug and call in a professional to do the job.

If the clog is between the house trap and the main clean out, insert the wire from the auger into the trap in the direction of the main clean out. If the blockage is not in the trap but is in the drain itself, remove the adjacent clean-out plug and try to reach the blockage from there with the auger.

A clog can collect in the soil stack (the vertical drainpipe that leads from the main drain and ends at the roof vent). If you have an auger long enough to reach the bottom of this pipe from the opening in the roof vent, you can try to remove the blockage from the roof. This can be risky work on a steeply pitched roof, and it may be better to call in a professional to do this chore.

There is one drain clog that will not respond satisfactorily to plunger or auger. This is when the main drain outside the building or a floor drain in the basement gets stopped up from tree roots that have grown in at the joints. The most effective solution is an electric rooter, which is inserted into the pipe and cuts away roots from the pipe walls as it moves along.

You can rent one of these power augers at a tool rental firm. Feed the auger cable into the clean-out opening closest to the blockage. When the device's cutting head encounters roots, you should be able to feel the cable strain. Keep feeding the cable slowly until you feel a breakthrough; then go over the area again. Remove the cable slowly and run water from a garden hose through the pipe to wash away the root cuttings. Before you return the power auger to the rental firm, replace the clean-out plug and flush a toilet several times. When you're sure the drain is clear of tree roots, clean the cable and return the machine.

STOPPING FAUCET DRIPS

Although a dripping faucet is the most common plumbing problem and one of the easiest to repair, many people try to ignore it and leave the

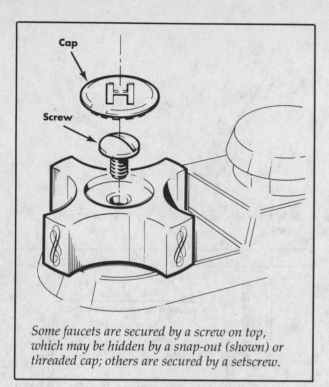

Some faucets are secured by a screw on top, which may be hidden by a snap-out (shown) or threaded cap; others are secured by a setscrew.

dripping faucet unrepaired. You may not think that a tiny drip is worth the effort to fix, but you'd be amazed how much that tiny drip costs. A steady drip can add up to so many gallons over a year's time that it can cost $50 or more in wasted water. Multiply that figure by the number of faucet drips in your home, and you can calculate how much of your money is literally going down the drain. If that isn't enough to convince you, just think about the drip that comes from a hot-water faucet; you're also paying to heat the water before you waste it.

A drip is caused by seepage from the water supply. The water supply enters your house or apartment under pressure. There must be a watertight seal holding back the incoming water when the faucet handle is in the "off" position. That seal is usually created by a washer pressed tightly against the faucet seat. When the washer or the seat is not functioning properly, a little water can seep through and drip out of the faucet spout. To stop the drip, all you usually have to do is replace the washer or repair the seat.

The first thing to do when you fix a faucet drip is to turn off the water supply. You should be able to turn off the supply at a nearby shutoff; but if your house is not equipped with shutoffs for individual fixtures, you'll have to go to the main shutoff and turn off the entire water supply throughout your home.

Compression Faucets. With the water flow stopped, you can start to disassemble the faucet. No matter what the faucet looks like, whether it has separate handles for hot and cold water or one handle that operates both hot and cold, it works according to certain principles. The first

thing to do is to remove the faucet handle, which is held to the main body of the faucet by a tiny screw, either on the top or at the back of the handle. You may not be able to see a top-mounted screw at first because some of them are hidden by a metal or plastic button or disc. These buttons usually snap out, although some are threaded. Once you get the button out, you'll see the top-mounted handle screw. If a handle's screw is difficult to turn, use penetrating oil to help loosen it. A standard blade or Phillips screwdriver can be used to remove the screw, unless the handle is secured by a set screw; an Allen wrench (hexagonal wrench) is required to loosen it.

Take the handle off and look at the faucet assembly. You'll see a packing nut (sometimes called the bonnet); remove the nut with either a large pair of slip-joint pliers or an adjustable wrench, but take special care not to scar the metal. It's a good idea to wrap plastic tape around the packing nut to protect it from the teeth of your pliers or wrench. Once you get the packing nut off, twist out the stem (sometimes called the spindle) by turning it in the same direction you would to turn on the faucet.

You can see the washer at the base of the stem, but to remove it you must first take out the brass screw that holds it. That can be difficult, but penetrating oil should make a stubborn brass screw easier to remove. After you remove the screw, examine it to see whether it should be replaced along with the washer. If you can't get the brass screw out, you can buy a new stem.

You must put on a replacement washer that is exactly the right size; washers that almost fit will almost stop the drip. Also note whether the old washer is beveled or flat; the shape is important too. If you can't determine the precise size, take the stem with you to the hardware store. You also can buy an assortment pack of washers that contains just about every size and shape you might need.

Some washers don't work well on a hot-water faucet. A washer designed only for cold water expands when it gets hot, closing the opening and slowing the flow of hot water. Perhaps you've experienced a hot-water faucet that works fine until the water gets quite hot and then slows to a trickle; its problem is the washer. Be sure to tell your hardware dealer whether the replacement washer you need is for the hot side or the cold side. Some washers will work for either. You also can buy a swivel-head washer with a fitting that snaps into the threaded screw hole in the base of the stem.

Fasten the new washer to the stem, and reinstall the assembly in the faucet. Turn the stem the same way you'd turn the faucet handle to stop the water flow (clockwise). With the stem in place, put the packing nut back on, but be careful not to scar the metal with the wrench. Once you

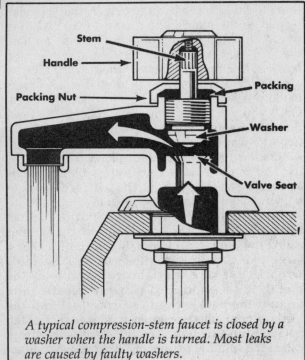

Stem
Handle
Packing Nut
Packing
Washer
Valve Seat

A typical compression-stem faucet is closed by a washer when the handle is turned. Most leaks are caused by faulty washers.

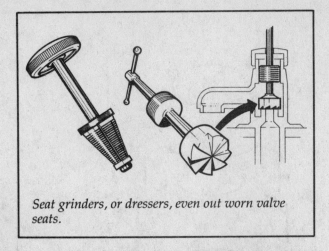

Seat grinders, or dressers, even out worn valve seats.

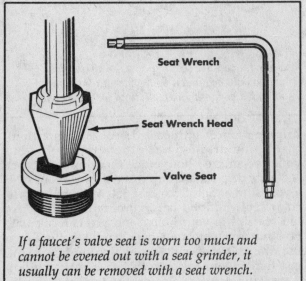

Seat Wrench
Seat Wrench Head
Valve Seat

If a faucet's valve seat is worn too much and cannot be evened out with a seat grinder, it usually can be removed with a seat wrench.

screw on the handle and replace the button or disc, your faucet is completely reassembled. Turn the water supply back on, and you should find that your days of wasting water are over.

Other Faucets. Instead of washers, some faucets use rubber diaphragms to control the flow of water. If you have this kind of faucet, you may have to remove the faucet stem from the faucet body with a pair of pliers. Be sure to wrap the top of the stem with tape to protect it from the teeth of the pliers. The rubber diaphragm covers the bottom of the stem, and you may have to pry it off with a screwdriver. Make sure the replacement diaphragm fits snugly over the base of the stem before you reassemble the faucet.

Another faucet uses a rubber seat ring that acts like a washer. To remove it from the stem, hold the end of the faucet stem with pliers while you unscrew the threaded center piece that holds the seat ring in place. Remove the sleeve to insert the new seat ring, but be sure the seat ring's lettering faces the threaded part of the stem.

Cartridge-stem faucets may have a spring and a rubber washer. To replace these, lift the cartridge out of the faucet body and remove the washer and spring from the faucet body. Insert the new spring and washer, and carefully align the cartridge so it fits correctly into the slots in the faucet body when reassembling it.

There also are faucets with washers that have the faucet seat built into the stem itself. This assembly lifts off the base in a removable sleeve, which contains the valve seat. Unscrew the stem nut from the base of the stem and remove the metal washer and the washer retainer, which con-

tains a rubber washer. Insert the new washer, bevel side up, into the washer retainer.

One faucet doesn't have washers at all; it works by means of two metal discs. Turning the faucet on aligns holes in the discs and allows water to flow through the faucet. If something goes wrong with this faucet, the valve assembly usually must be replaced.

Repairing a Faucet Valve Seat. Sometimes a faucet may still drip after you've replaced a washer. This shows that there may be something wrong with the faucet valve seat. Perhaps a defective washer at some point in the past allowed the metal stem to grind against the seat and leave it uneven, or else chemicals in the water have built up a residue that now prevents the washer from fitting tightly against the valve seat.

What do you do to repair a bad faucet seat? You can use a valve seat grinder, or dresser, an inexpensive tool that will even out a worn seat. You must be careful not to use the tool too long or with too much force, because the seat is made of soft metal and you easily can grind away too much of it. To use this tool, remove the faucet stem and insert the seat grinder down to the valve seat in the faucet body. Using moderate pressure, turn the tool clockwise a few times. Then clean the valve seat with a cloth to remove any metal shavings.

The other thing you can do is to replace the seat. This is a necessity if you grind it down too far with the tool. Removal of the old valve seat is easy if you have the right tool, called a seat wrench. Just insert the seat wrench into the seat and turn it counterclockwise. Once you get the old seat out, be sure the replacement seat you buy is an exact duplicate. If you cannot remove the valve seat, you can insert a seat sleeve, which slides into place in the old seat and provides a tight seal.

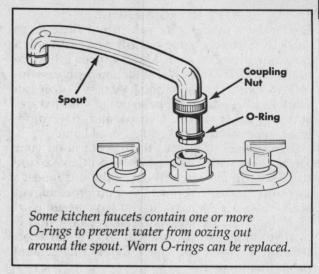

Some kitchen faucets contain one or more O-rings to prevent water from oozing out around the spout. Worn O-rings can be replaced.

STOPPING FAUCET LEAKS

A drip occurs when the faucet is turned off; a faucet leak occurs when the water is running. If you see water coming out around the handle, you have a faucet leak.

First make sure the faucet's packing nut is tight, but be careful not to scratch the nut with pliers or a wrench. If you find a loose nut is not causing the leak, you should replace the packing. Faucet packing can be a solid piece of packing, or it can consist of one or more rubber O-rings. It also can resemble string or soft wire wrapped around the stem under the packing nut.

To replace the packing, shut off the water supply and remove the faucet handle. Loosen the packing nut and slip both the nut and the old packing off the stem. Put the new packing on. If you use the stringlike packing material, wrap a few turns around the stem; packing that resembles soft wire is wrapped around the stem only once. Before you finish reassembling the faucet, smear a light coat of petroleum jelly on the threads of the stem and on the threads of the packing nut.

Kitchen faucets in which the spout swings from side to side present a different situation. These faucets have one or more O-rings to prevent water from oozing out around the spout. If the ring wears out, you'll see water at the base of the spout every time you turn on the water. To replace an O-ring, shut off the water supply and remove the threaded coupling nut that holds the spout in place by turning it counterclockwise. Be sure to wrap the nut with tape to prevent scratching it with pliers or a wrench. With the coupling nut removed, work the spout up and out of its socket, where you will find the ring(s). Replace the defective ring(s); be sure to use the same size. Then reassemble the faucet.

Single-lever faucets are easy to fix, but there are so many different kinds that you must buy a specific repair kit for the faucet you have. Most faucet companies make repair kits for their products and include detailed instructions and diagrams with the replacement parts. The hardest part of repairing a single-lever faucet may be tracking down the hardware dealer or plumbing supply store that carries the appropriate kit. Once you have the kit, you should have little difficulty in eliminating the leak. Just make sure the water supply is shut off before disassembling the faucet, and carefully follow the kit's instructions.

SILENCING NOISY FAUCETS

Faucets can scream, whistle, or chatter when you turn them on or off. There are several possible causes for these ear-shattering noises. If your house is newly built, you may have pipes that are too small to allow the water to pass through them properly. Pipes in older homes can become restricted by the formation of scale, which also will result in a noisy faucet. You must replace the pipes to get rid of the noise.

Your noisy faucet probably is caused by a washer, either the wrong size or not held securely to the stem. Turn off the water supply before starting this or any other faucet repair job. Replace the washer or tighten it, and you should eliminate the noise. If the faucet still makes noise, check the washer seat; the seat can become partially closed with residue, and the restricted water flow can cause whistling or chattering. If this is the case, clean the seat.

A terrible squealing noise when you turn the faucet handle means that the metal threads of the stem are binding against the faucet's threads. Remove the stem and coat both sets of threads with petroleum jelly. The lubrication should stop the noise and make the handle easier to turn. If the stem threads or faucet body threads have become worn, the resulting play between them causes vibration and noise in the faucet. You'll need more than just lubrication to quiet the faucet. Install a new stem and see if the noise stops. If not, the faucet body threads are worn, and the only solution is a completely new faucet.

REPLACING A FAUCET

Replacing a faucet gets you into a little more work than just changing a washer or putting in a new faucet valve seat. Many faucet units are made for do-it-yourself installation with easy-to-follow instructions included. A new faucet can work wonders for the appearance of your fixtures and will eliminate leaks, drips, and other problems you may have had with your old one.

If you want to replace the old faucet on your kitchen sink with a single-handle unit, make sure the unit you choose will cover the old faucet's mounting holes. This usually is no problem, but some sinks are unusual. If you have an unusual sink, look for an adjustable faucet unit that is made to fit many different sinks. Once you select the faucet model you want, follow this general procedure to install it properly.

Turn off both hot- and cold-water supplies to the sink faucets. Disconnect the old faucets from their water supply lines under the sink. The connections probably will be threaded compression fittings that are held by locknuts. Loosen the nuts with an adjustable wrench or basin wrench, and disconnect the water supply pipes from the faucets.

The old faucets are probably held in place by nuts under the sink. Loosen and remove these nuts. The nuts often are impossible to remove without a basin wrench.

If the old assembly has a spray head and hose, remove the spray-head mounting nut under the sink; also disconnect the hose from its spout connection. Now you should be able to remove the old faucet assembly from the sink. Clean the sink around the faucet mounting area.

Before you install the new faucet, apply plumber's putty around its base; if gaskets are supplied with the faucet for this purpose, putty is not necessary. Then insert the new faucet assembly into the mounting holes in the sink.

If the new faucet has a spray hose, attach the hose first, if possible. Run the spray hose down through its opening in the faucet assembly, through its opening in the sink, and up through the sink's center opening. Then attach the hose to the supply stub on the faucet.

With the new faucet assembly in position, place the washers and nuts on the assembly's mounting studs under the sink and hand tighten them, making sure the assembly is in proper position and any gaskets are correctly aligned. Then tighten the nuts with a basin wrench.

Align the original water supply lines with the flexible supply tubes coming from the new faucet, and connect them with compression couplings. Make sure the hot- and cold-water lines are connected to the proper supply tubes on the faucet assembly. When you attach the lines, be sure to use two wrenches: one to hold the fitting, the other to turn the nut on the water supply line.

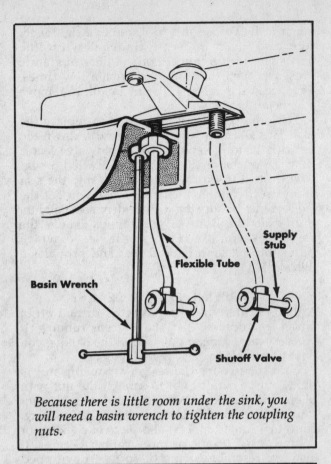

Because there is little room under the sink, you will need a basin wrench to tighten the coupling nuts.

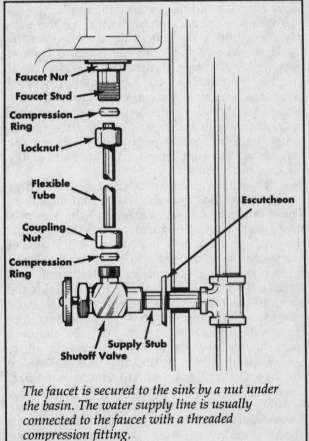

The faucet is secured to the sink by a nut under the basin. The water supply line is usually connected to the faucet with a threaded compression fitting.

If the combined length of the old and new supply lines is inconveniently long, you can cut off a portion of the original lines before attaching the coupling. Conversely, if the new supply tubes reach all the way to the shutoff valves under the sink, the tubes can be connected directly to the valves with a compression fitting. On some installations you may need adapters or transition fittings to join different size supply lines and tubes or to connect one kind of pipe to another.

Turn on the hot- and cold-water supplies to the fixture, and run both hot and cold water full force to clear the supply lines and to check the fixture for leaks. If there is any evidence of leakage, go back over the procedure to check for loose or improper connections.

A bathroom lavatory faucet can be replaced using the same procedures. One difference may be the presence of a pop-up drain that is connected by a linkage to a knob or plunger on the old faucet assembly. There should be one or two places in the linkage where it can be easily disconnected from the faucet before removing the original unit from the basin; the instructions provided with the new faucet will tell you how to connect the new drain assembly. Be sure to reconnect the drain linkage when installing the new faucet.

Shower and tub faucets can be a bit more complicated because the connections are made not under a sink but behind a wall. Whoever built your home should have provided an access panel so that you can get at the pipes without ripping the wall apart. If you find that you must cut into the wall, be sure to add an access panel for future pipe and faucet repairs.

Once you get to the tub faucet connections behind the wall, the job is no harder than working on your kitchen sink. Shut off the water supply, remove the faucet handle on the tub side, and then disconnect the old faucet unit from the back. If there is an old shower-head pipe, unscrew it from its pipe inside the wall; do the same thing with the tub spout. Now you're ready to install all the new parts.

REPAIRING A SPRAY HOSE

Many sink faucets are fitted with spray-hose units, and these units occasionally leak or malfunction. The assembly consists of a special diverter valve located within the spout body, a flexible hose connected to the spout under the sink, and a spray head with an activating lever and an aerator assembly. The spray-head body and lever are generally a sealed unit, and if it malfunctions or fails, the unit must be replaced with another identical unit. Other parts of the spray system can be repaired.

The aerator portion of the spray head is similar to a regular faucet aerator, although the parts are usually held with a small retaining screw. If aeration is inadequate or water squirts off at various angles, the aerator screen has become clogged with sediment or mineral deposits, and must be cleaned. Remove the aerator and disassemble it, usually by unscrewing. Flush the screens and the perforated disc with a strong stream of water; be careful not to let the parts get washed down the drain. Dry the parts, and brush them gently with a fine-bristled stiff brush. Mineral deposits sometimes can be removed by soaking the parts in vinegar, or you may be able to scrape the deposits away with a penknife. Reassemble the aerator, making sure that you get all of the parts positioned in the proper order and direction.

Water dripping off the flexible hose beneath the sink indicates a leak at the hose-to-spout connection, the hose-to-spray-head connection, or somewhere in the hose itself. Dry the hose thoroughly and check the head connection; this may or may not be repairable. If the leak is at this point, tighten the connection, disassemble and make repairs, or replace the head and hose assembly. Check the spout connection under the sink. Tightening may stop a leak here; if not, disconnect the hose, apply plumber's joint compound or wrap plumber's joint tape around the threads, and reconnect it. The easiest way to spot a leak in the hose is to inspect it inch by inch under a strong light while water is running through it. Look for tiny cracks, chafes, or indications of some mechanical damage. Temporary repairs can be made by wrapping a damaged section of hose with vinyl electrical tape, but replacing the hose eventually will be necessary.

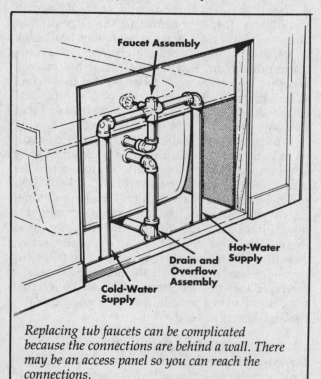

Replacing tub faucets can be complicated because the connections are behind a wall. There may be an access panel so you can reach the connections.

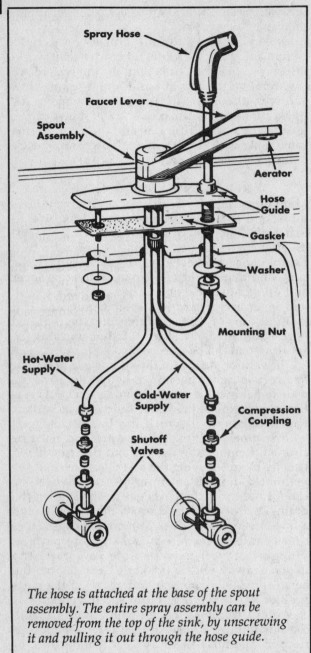

The hose is attached at the base of the spout assembly. The entire spray assembly can be removed from the top of the sink, by unscrewing it and pulling it out through the hose guide.

Uneven water flow, low pressure when the pressure at other faucets seems all right, or troublesome switching back and forth from spray head to sink spout can be caused by a malfunctioning diverter valve or by a restricted hose. To check the hose, remove the spray head at the coupling and disconnect the coupling from the hose by prying off the snap-ring retainer. Turn on the water and let a strong stream of water flow into the hose. If a strong stream of water flows out of the open end of the hose, then you know the diverter valve is the source of the trouble. A weak stream flowing from the open end of the hose may indicate a blockage in the hose itself. Running the water full force for a brief time may clear the hose. If this doesn't work, remove the

hose from the spout attachment, stretch it out straight, and sight through it toward a strong light source. If the hose is clear, the problem lies in the diverter valve. If the hose is blocked, you may be able to clear it with a wire coat hanger or a length of wire. Failing that, replace the hose; if you can't get an exact replacement, adapters are available for connecting other kinds and sizes.

To service the diverter valve, you first must remove the sink spout: Loosen the screw on top, unscrew the threaded spout ring or nut, and lift the spout out of its socket. This exposes the valve. Some valves are just set in place, and can be lifted straight out by gripping them with a pair of pliers; others are secured by a screw. If there is a screw, turn it enough to free the valve. If possible, disassemble the valve. Flush all the parts with water and clean all the surfaces and apertures with a toothpick. Never use metal instruments; they could damage the unit. Reassemble and reinstall the valve, and test the unit. If it still operates poorly, you probably will have to replace the valve.

FIXING SHOWER HEADS

Shower heads are subject to several problems. Leaks can occur where the head connects to the shower arm (the curved, chrome-plated pipe that protrudes from the wall) or at the connection between the shower-head body and the swivel ball. If the arm connection leaks, unscrew the entire shower head from the pipe, using a pair of strap wrenches if necessary. If you use another kind of wrench, tape the pipe to avoid scratching it. Clean the arm threads and coat them with plumber's joint compound or a wrap of plumber's joint tape. Screw the shower head back and hand tighten it only. Remove any excess compound or tape. If the leak is at the swivel, unscrew the shower-head body from the swivel ball ring; you'll find an O-ring or a similar seal inside. Replace it and screw the shower head back into place.

Problems also can be caused by grit or sediment lodged in the head or by a buildup of scale or mineral deposits. The solution is to remove the shower-head body at the swivel ball, take it completely apart, and start cleaning. Soaking in vinegar may be necessary for some parts, scraping for others, but be careful not to scratch or gouge anything. If the shower head has an adjustable spray, examine all of the moving parts carefully for signs of excessive wear. If the adjustment handle binds or does not work smoothly, or the internal cam is fouled up, usually the only solution is to replace the entire head.

REPLACING A TRAP

Directly beneath the drain outlet of your kitchen sink and every bathroom lavatory is the trap. This element is vital not only to the proper functioning of the drainage system, but to your health and safety as well. Each trap contains and maintains a plug of water within its curved section that acts as a seal against the entrance of harmful sewer gases. If the trap leaks, this water barrier may disappear and create a hazardous situation. All traps must be kept in proper working order and good condition. Restrictions and clogging are immediately noticeable, because the drainage flow is slowed or stopped; clearing the blockage takes care of the problem. Leakage or seepage can often go undetected for a time, so check your traps from time to time and make quick repairs if anything seems wrong.

Trap assemblies are comprised of several parts. The short piece of pipe that extends downward from the drain outlet flange in the sink or lavatory is the tailpiece. The curved section of pipe connected to the tailpiece is the trap itself; it may be one piece or two coupled sections. The piece of pipe extending from the end of the trap to the drainpipe outlet in the wall or floor is the drain extension; it may be straight or curved. All these pieces may be made of thin metal, such as chrome-plated brass, and they are subject to eventual corrosion, failure of seals, and in exposed traps, mechanical damage. A plumber's auger also can damage a trap. Whatever the reasons for failure, a malfunctioning trap should be repaired immediately.

Sometimes the problem is simply that the slip nuts that hold the trap assembly together and secure it to the drain and the drainpipe have loosened; tightening them may solve the problem. If the metal has corroded through, the slip-nut threads are damaged, or other damage has occurred, the only solution is replacement. Trap assemblies and parts to fit every possible installation requirement are readily available at most hardware and all plumbing supply stores. Chrome-plated thin-wall brass traps are popular, especially where appearance is important. Polypropylene (PP) plastic traps, notable for their ruggedness and longevity, will outperform other kinds. ABS plastic traps also are in use, but they deform and eventually fail when handling frequent passage of boiling water and caustic household chemicals. They may not be allowed by your local plumbing code. Whatever the material, you're likely to encounter two trap diameters: 1 1/2-inch traps for kitchen sinks and 1 1/4-inch traps for lavatories. Take the old trap with you when you buy the new one; if possible, also take the old tailpiece and drain extension.

Trap replacement is simple. If the trap is equipped with a clean-out plug on the bottom of the curved section, remove the plug with a wrench and let the water in the trap drain into a bucket. If there is no plug, unscrew the slip nuts and slide them out of the way. If the trap is a swivel, the curved trap section(s) will come free.

Keep the trap upright as you remove it, and pour the water out after the part is free. If the trap is fixed and does not swivel, remove the tailpiece slip nut at the drain flange and the slip nut at the top of the trap, and shove the tailpiece down into the trap itself. Then twist the trap clockwise until you can drain the water in the trap, pull the tailpiece free, and unscrew the trap from the drain extension or drainpipe.

Installation of a new trap is merely a reverse procedure of the disassembly. Buy a trap of the proper diameter or a universal trap, which works on either size drain, as well as a new tailpiece, a drain extension, or other fittings as necessary. A swivel trap is the easiest to work with, because it can be easily adjusted for angled or misaligned drainpipe/fixture installations. A clean-out plug on a trap is handy but not essential, because the trap can be taken apart for cleaning if necessary. Replace the new parts in appropriate order, making sure you have the slip nuts and compression seals or large washers lined up on the proper pipe sections. Couple the parts together loosely with the slip nuts, make the final adjustments for correct pipe alignment, and tighten the nuts down snug, but not too tight. Plumber's joint compound or tape is not usually necessary, but you can use either if you prefer. Run water into the new trap immediately, both to check for leaks and to fill the trap with water to provide that important barrier against sewer gases.

Repairing Toilets

The toilet is one of the most important fixtures in your home. Although toilets are sturdy and reliable components of the plumbing system, it's a rare person who never has any problems with a toilet. Clogging is perhaps the most serious toilet trouble, but it is far from the only one. The tank can make strange noises, or water can run continuously, but most toilet troubles can be fixed by any do-it-yourself plumber.

SPECIALIZED TOOLS
Few special tools are required for toilet repairs. For changing a toilet seat, you'll need a wrench, a deep socket wrench, or a hacksaw. The most frequently used toilet tool is the plumber's friend, also known as a plunger or a force cup. Get one with a long handle, and be sure the suction cup is large enough to cover the toilet's drain opening.

A closet auger is a version of the plumber's snake, but it's designed specifically for clearing clogs in toilets. The closet auger is shorter than a regular snake, and it comes encased in a metal housing with a crank.

If you plan to remove a toilet for replacement or repairs, you may well need a spud wrench. Older toilets frequently have a large pipe that

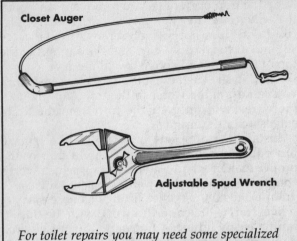

Closet Auger

Adjustable Spud Wrench

For toilet repairs you may need some specialized tools, including a closet auger and an adjustable spud wrench.

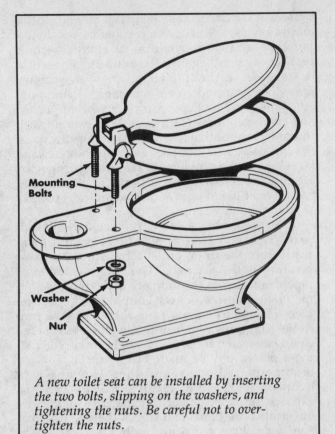

Mounting Bolts

Washer

Nut

A new toilet seat can be installed by inserting the two bolts, slipping on the washers, and tightening the nuts. Be careful not to over- tighten the nuts.

connects the tank to the bowl; this pipe is called a spud, and it is held to the bowl and tank by extra-large hexagonal slip nuts. A spud wrench is designed to remove these slip nuts. An adjustable spud wrench is much more versatile than the nonadjustable one, which has a fixed opening at each end.

REPLACING A TOILET SEAT

The easiest toilet repair is replacing the lid and seat. There are so many styles of replacement seats available that you should have no trouble finding one to match any bathroom color scheme or motif. Most toilets are manufactured in two standard sizes, and replacement seats are made to fit them. If your toilet is extra wide or very old, you may not be able to use a standard replacement seat and may have to special order the seat with a company that deals in plumbing fixtures.

Once you have the right size seat, remove the old one. All you have to do is remove two nuts and lift your old toilet seat up and out. If you can get to the fasteners easily, apply penetrating oil to help loosen them. Give the oil plenty of time to soak in. Use a wrench or, if you can't reach the nuts with a regular wrench, a deep socket wrench. Be sure you don't use too much force; if the wrench slipped off a stubborn nut, it could strike and crack the tank or the bowl or anything else it happened to hit.

If you can't remove the nuts, you'll have to cut off the bolts with a hacksaw. To protect the bowl's finish, apply tape to the bowl at the spots the hacksaw blade is likely to rub against. Then insert the blade under the hinge, and saw through the bolts. A careless slip with a hacksaw can crack the fixture just as easily as a blow with a wrench can.

With the nuts removed or the bolts cut, you can remove the old seat without further difficulty. Clean the area before installing the new seat.

The new one can be fastened simply by inserting the bolts and tightening the nuts, but be careful not to overtighten the nuts since someday you may want to replace this seat.

If the toilet lid and seat are still in good condition, but the small rubber bumpers on the bottom are in bad shape, you can buy replacement bumpers at the hardware store. Some bumpers screw in; others must be nailed into place. Whichever kind you have, try to install the new ones in holes that are close enough to conceal the original holes.

CLEARING A CLOGGED TOILET

You can generally clear a clogged toilet with the plumber's friend, or plunger. Just make sure that there is enough water in the toilet bowl to cover the rubber suction cup, and then work the handle of the plunger up and down. There are two kinds of plungers, and the one with a bulb head is especially effective. Some have a foldout head that is designed for toilet use. If there isn't enough water in the bowl, do not flush the toilet; flushing a clogged toilet will just cause the bowl to overflow. Bring a pot or bucket of water from another source to supply the water you need to cover the plunger cup.

Whatever is blocking the toilet drain usually is not far away. If the plunger's action doesn't dislodge the clog, you can try to hook the blockage and pull it free. A wire coat hanger can some-

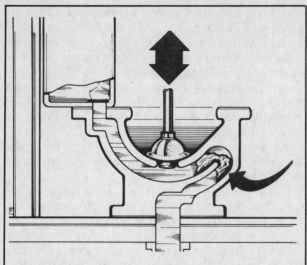

Before using the plunger, make sure there is enough water in the toilet bowl to cover the suction cup. Pump the plunger to dislodge the clog.

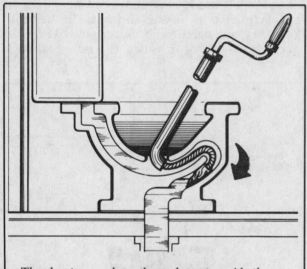

The closet auger has a long sleeve to guide the snake and auger hook into the trap. A crank enables you to turn the hook and dislodge the blockage.

times do the job. The coat hanger is a substitute for the closet, or toilet, auger. This tool has a long sleeve or tube to guide the snake and auger hook into the trap. A crank on the end enables you to turn the hook in the drain or trap.

Insert the auger into the toilet and turn the crank until it feels tight. This means that the snake has twisted its way to and into the blockage. Pull in the auger and you should be able to remove whatever is clogging the toilet. If you aren't successful, try the closet auger several more times.

When all else fails, the toilet may have to be removed from the floor and turned upside down

so you can get at the blockage. This is not an easy job, so you should try the simpler methods before you remove the toilet. But removing the toilet is not beyond the capabilities of the average do-it-yourselfer.

TOILET TANK PROBLEMS

Compared with a clogged toilet, tank troubles can seem insignificant. Strange noises or water running continuously is more than annoying; they cost you money in wasted water. You can eliminate most tank troubles quickly and easily.

Before you can solve tank problems, you must know how this fixture works. When you trip the handle on the tank to flush the toilet, a trip lever is raised inside the tank. This lever lifts wires that raise the tank ball (or rubber flap) at the bottom of the tank.

When the flush-valve opening is clear, the water in the tank rushes out past the raised tank ball and into the toilet bowl. This raises the level of water in the bowl above the level of water in the toilet trap. While the water is rushing out of the tank, the float ball, which floats on top of the water in the tank, drops down. This pulls down on the float arm, raising the valve plunger in the ball-cock assembly and allowing fresh water to flow into the tank. Since water seeks its own level, the water from the tank pushes the bowl water out into the drain, causing a siphoning action that cleans everything out of the bowl. When all the water is gone from the toilet bowl and air is drawn into the trap, the siphoning stops. The tank ball falls back into place, closing the flush-valve opening.

As the water level rises in the tank, the float ball rises until the float arm is high enough to lower the valve plunger in the ball-cock assembly and shut off the incoming water. If, for some reason, the water should fail to shut off, there is an overflow tube that carries excess water down into the bowl to prevent the tank from overflowing.

Lift the lid off your toilet tank, and you should be able to follow this procedure quite easily. Once you know how the toilet works, you can start to look for the sources of toilet tank problems.

If your toilet never stops running and water flows continuously out of the tank to the bowl and down the drain, try lifting the float arm. If the water stops, you know the problem is that the float ball doesn't rise far enough to lower the valve plunger in the ball-cock assembly. One reason could be that the float ball is rubbing against the side of the tank. If this is the case, bend the float arm to move the ball away from the tank side.

The problem also could be in the float ball itself. If the ball doesn't touch the tank, continue to hold the float arm, and remove the ball from the end of the arm by turning it counterclockwise. Then shake the ball to see if there is water inside it; the weight of the water inside could be preventing the ball from rising normally. If there is water in the ball, shake it out and put the ball back on the float arm. If the ball is corroded, replace it with a new one. If there is no water in the ball, put the ball back on and bend the float rod down to lower the level the float ball must reach to shut off the flow of fresh water into the tank.

When you lift the float arm and the water doesn't stop running, the problem is not in the float arm. The next logical place to check for trouble is the tank ball at the flush valve seat. Chemical residue from the water can prevent this ball from seating properly, or the ball itself may have decayed. This causes water to seep through the flush valve opening into the toilet bowl.

Turn off the water at the toilet shutoff valve, and flush the toilet to empty the tank. You can now examine the tank ball for signs of wear, and install a new ball if necessary. If the problem is chemical residue on the lip of the flush valve opening, use wet-dry emery cloth, steel wool, or even a knife and clean away the debris. You can retard any further formation of residue by putting a few slivers of soap into the tank.

There are still other possible causes for a toilet running continuously. The guide or the lift wire that raises and lowers the tank ball may be out of line or bent. Make sure the guide is in place so that the wire is directly above the flush valve opening. Rotate the guide until the tank ball falls straight down into the opening. If a lift wire is bent, try to bend it back to the correct position, or install a new one. Make sure the trip lever rod is not rubbing against anything, and the lift wire is not installed in the wrong hole of the rod; either situation could cause the tank ball to fall at an angle and not block the opening as it should. If neither the float ball nor the tank ball is at fault, then the problem must be caused by the ball-cock assembly.

WORKING WITH THE BALL-COCK ASSEMBLY

The ball-cock assembly looks far more complicated than it is. Just make sure the water shutoff valve for the toilet is turned off.

With many ball-cock assemblies, you'll find a pair of thumbscrews that hold the valve plunger. If the unit in your toilet tank has a different linkage arrangement, you should still be able to determine how to remove the valve plunger. Remove the valve plunger, and you'll see one or two washers, or an O-ring. If any of these parts is faulty, water will flow out past the plunger continuously and the toilet will run constantly. Examine all of the washers, and replace any defective ones.

Some ball-cock assemblies are completely sealed, and there is no way you can get inside this kind of unit without breaking it. If this is what you find when you lift the lid off the toilet tank, you'll have to buy a replacement ball-cock assembly. If you discover either a sealed ball-cock assembly or a damaged one, remove all the water from the tank so that you can take out the old unit and install a new one. Shut off the toilet water supply at the shutoff valve, and flush the tank. Unscrew the float arm from the old ball-cock unit, and remove the refill tube from the overflow tube; the refill tube may be clipped on or bent into position.

Look under the tank. You'll see a coupling, or slip, nut where the water inlet pipe enters the base of the tank. Loosen the coupling nut to free the water inlet pipe. Then use an adjustable wrench to grip the retaining nut or locknut immediately above the slip nut under the tank. Use another wrench to grip the base of the ball-cock assembly shaft inside the tank. Unscrew the locknut under the tank to remove the ball-cock assembly. If the nut is stubborn, use penetrating oil to loosen it. Lift the old assembly out of the tank, but be sure to save all the washers from all connections, both inside and outside the tank. You may not need them, but always keep old parts until you've installed the new ball-cock assembly.

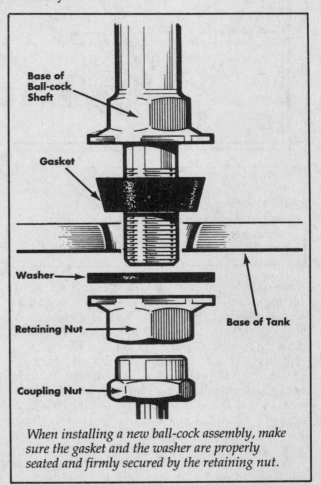

When installing a new ball-cock assembly, make sure the gasket and the washer are properly seated and firmly secured by the retaining nut.

Insert the new ball-cock assembly into the hole in the tank, with the inside washer in place. Tighten the locknut on the outside sufficiently to make the inside washer fit watertight against the hole, but don't overtighten it. Replace the coupling nut and water inlet pipe, reinstall the float arm, set the refill tube into the overflow tube, and the job is done. Turn the water back on at the toilet shutoff valve, and check for leaks at all points. Also check that the float ball does not rub against the back of the tank.

When you go to a hardware or plumbing supply store to buy a new ball-cock assembly, you'll find that both plastic and metal units are available. Plastic costs less and will not corrode, but plastic assemblies are not as sturdy as metal ones. Plastic units usually cannot be repaired because many of them are sealed. You can purchase a different kind of unit than the one you're replacing if the new assembly has a threaded shank the same size as the old one. If possible, bring the old assembly with you when you go to buy the replacement.

New ball-cock assemblies eliminate the float arm and the float ball. One kind features a plastic cup that floats up to cut off the water as the tank fills. You can set the water level in the tank by adjusting the position of the plastic cup on a pull rod. One advantage to this ball-cock assembly is that it lets the water run full force until the tank is filled; it then shuts the water off immediately, eliminating the groaning noises some toilets make as a float arm gradually closes the valve.

Another model also eliminates the float ball and float arm. This is a small unit that rests almost on the bottom of the tank; its diaphragm-powered valve senses the level of the water. Since installation of the unit requires no tools, this assembly is easy to install.

The first step in installing this unit is to turn off the tank's water supply shutoff valve. Then flush the toilet to drain the tank. Sponge up any water remaining in the tank. Remove the old ball-cock assembly. Slip the parts over the water inlet pipe under the tank in this order: coupling nut, friction washer, cone washer, and retaining or mounting nut.

Now install the new unit inside the tank, fitting the threaded shank down through the hole over the water supply pipe and making sure the gasket fits into the hole. Start the retaining or mounting nut under the tank onto the threaded shank; hand tighten it only. Push the washers into place, and hand tighten the coupling nut under the tank; don't overtighten it.

Inside the tank, attach one end of the refill tube to the tank's overflow pipe, and place the other end on the stem of the replacement unit. Open the water supply valve to fill the tank. The water level in the tank can be adjusted by a knob on the new valve unit.

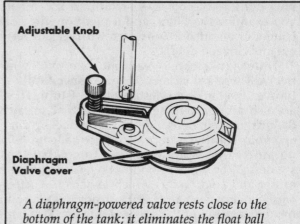

A diaphragm-powered valve rests close to the bottom of the tank; it eliminates the float ball and float arm.

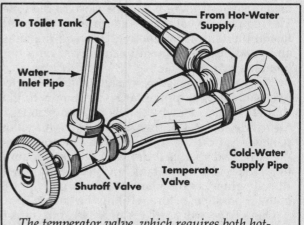

The temperator valve, which requires both hot- and cold-water supply connections, can reduce toilet tank sweating.

INADEQUATE FLUSHING, SWEATING, AND OTHER PROBLEMS

If too little water comes from the tank to flush the toilet bowl, the first thing you should check is the water level in the tank; it's probably too low. If the water level doesn't reach within 1 1/2 inches of the top of the overflow tube, try bending the float arm up to let more water enter the tank.

The water level may be correct, but there is still not enough water coming from the tank to clean the bowl properly. The culprit in this situation is the tank ball at the flush valve seat at the bottom of the tank. The ball is probably dropping too soon because the guide is set too low. Try raising the guide, but make sure it stays in line with the lift wire. If the guide and the wire are out of alignment, the tank ball will not drop straight into the valve seat opening, and the toilet will run continuously.

There is one other possible cause for inadequate flushing. The small ports around the underside of the toilet bowl's rim can get clogged with residue from chemicals in the water and prevent a sufficient amount of tank water from running out into the bowl. A small mirror can help you examine the holes, and a piece of wire coat hanger or an offset Phillips screwdriver can ream out any clogged debris.

Toilet tanks can sweat and drip onto your floors. There are jackets designed specifically to fit over the tank and absorb the moisture. There are also drip pans that fit under the tank to catch the dripping condensation so that it doesn't damage your bathroom floor. A device called a temperator valve is another way to combat tank sweating. The valve provides a regulated mixture of hot and cold water, which lessens the difference between the temperature inside the tank and the temperature of the surrounding air. This temperature difference causes condensation.

A temperator valve requires you to hook up a hot-water line to the valve, which may be quite inconvenient if there is no line close to the toilet. The temperator valve does not prevent the water inside the tank from cooling between flushings, and condensation can still occur even on a temperator-equipped toilet.

The simplest, least expensive, and most effective method of stopping tank sweating is to glue thin (1/4- to 1/2-inch) panels of foam rubber to the inside surfaces of the tank walls. To install the panels, shut off the fixture's water supply, flush the tank, and sponge it dry. Cut pieces of foam to fit all four sides of the tank, and secure them with silicone glue. Let the glue cure thoroughly, for 24 hours if possible, before refilling the tank.

One of the worst effects of a sweating tank is that it can hide a genuine leak in the tank. You may see water on the floor, but fail to attribute it to a leak, believing that it's just condensation from the tank. There is an easy way to check for leaks. Pour enough bluing into the tank to give the water a noticeably blue color; some toilet-bowl cleaners also turn the water blue and can be used. If the tank does have a leak, the moisture on the floor will show traces of blue.

The leak may be due to loose connections or defective washers on the spud pipe, if your toilet has an exposed pipe from the tank to the bowl, or where the water inlet pipe and ball-cock assembly are attached to the tank. Replace any worn gaskets or washers and tighten all of the nuts; then test with bluing in the water again. It is also possible that water is seeping out from under the toilet bowl; the wax ring seal that joins the bowl to the drain outlet may be defective. If this is the case, the bowl and the tank, if it's supported by the bowl, must be removed, and a new gasket installed. If the leak is due to a crack in the tank or bowl, the whole toilet must be replaced.

REMOVING AND REPLACING A TOILET

Removing and replacing a toilet is not a task to be undertaken without good reason, but it is not beyond your skill. When you can't unclog the toi-

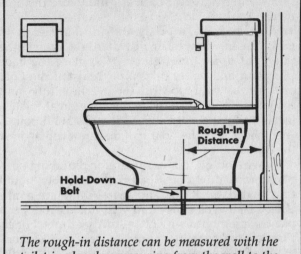

The rough-in distance can be measured with the toilet in place by measuring from the wall to the center of the hold-down bolt or to the center of the rear bolt if the fixture is held by two pairs of bolts.

let by less drastic means, removing it is the answer. Maybe you want a new toilet; maybe the bowl or the tank is cracked; maybe the fixture leaks around its base. All these situations call for removing the old toilet and reinstalling it or installing a new fixture.

Many communities prohibit anyone but a licensed plumber from removing and replacing a toilet. Check the code for your community. If it doesn't prohibit do-it-yourself toilet replacement and if you feel confident of your plumbing skill and knowledge, go ahead.

If you're installing a new toilet, the first step is to measure the rough-in distance, the distance from the wall behind the bowl to the center of the toilet floor drain. You can do this with the old bowl in place by measuring from the wall to the center of either of the two hold-down bolts, one on each side of the toilet, that hold the fixture to the floor. If there are two bolts on each side, measure to the center of the rear bolt. Use this measurement when you buy the new toilet so that it will fit properly in your bathroom. You can replace your old toilet with a new fixture, but you must make sure that the new unit will fit into the space between the drainpipe and the wall. You can install a smaller unit, leaving a space between it and the wall, but you cannot put a larger toilet into the same space that was occupied by a smaller fixture.

Once you have the new toilet, shut off the water supply to the toilet tank, and then remove all the water from both the tank and the bowl. Trip the flush handle to eliminate most of the water from the tank, and then soak up whatever water is left with a sponge. Bail out the water in the bowl with a small container, and then sponge it dry.

If you're unclogging the toilet or fixing a leak at the base, you'll have to remove only the bowl, leaving the tank in place. See if there is a spud pipe between the bowl and the tank. This is a large pipe, found most frequently on older units, that is connected at both ends by a slip nut similar to the nuts that hold a sink trap. The nuts that hold the spud are much larger than those on a sink. Use a spud wrench to remove the slip nuts. Once you loosen the slip nuts, slide them onto the spud itself. You should have just enough room now to remove the connecting pipe and then the bowl while the tank is still fastened to the wall.

If there is no spud pipe or if you want to remove the tank as well as the bowl, disconnect the water supply inlet pipe at the base of the tank. Older tanks are probably connected to the wall; newer tanks are most likely supported by the bowl. If the tank is connected to the wall, remove the hanger bolts inside the tank that secure the tank to the wall. Then remove the pair of bolts at the bottom of the tank that connect the tank to the bowl. Remove the tank and set it out of the way. Be sure to keep the rubber gaskets you find under all the bolts; you'll need them if you reinstall the old tank. With the tank removed from the wall mounting or the bowl support, you're ready to work on the bowl itself.

Remove the toilet seat, so it won't get in your way as you work on the bowl. If there are caps over the hold-down bolts at the base of the bowl, take them off. Most caps are made of ceramic to match the bowl. Some are held on by plumber's joint compound and can be pried off with a putty knife; others are threaded and can be unscrewed. If you don't know what kind of caps are on your toilet, wrap the caps with masking tape to protect their finish, and try to unscrew them. If they don't come off this way, you'll have to pry them off. After removing the caps, brush away the dried compound before proceeding.

With the caps off, remove the hold-down nuts or bolts. These may be extremely stubborn, but penetrating oil should make removing them easier. Be sure to save the washers and bolts if you will be reinstalling the bowl. Once the hold-down nuts or bolts are out, there is nothing else holding the bowl to the floor. Because the bowl and the tank can crack from just one sharp blow to the porcelain, put the fixtures on a piece of carpeting. You also should have a bucket and sponge handy to soak up the water you couldn't bail out earlier. With your work surface prepared, rock the bowl gently back and forth to loosen it, and then lift it straight up; it weighs about 60 or 70 pounds. Set the bowl on the carpeting.

With the toilet bowl out of the way, you'll find yourself looking down into an uncovered soil pipe. If you're dealing with a clog, the obstruction is probably somewhere in this pipe; you can now clear the drain. Once the pipe is clear, you can replace the toilet. **Caution:** *To prevent sewer gas from backing up the soil pipe, you should plug the opening while you work. Tie a cord around an old towel so it won't fall through into the opening, and jam this plug into the soil pipe.*

Once you have removed the toilet from its moorings, you might as well take the opportunity to consider any other work that might make your toilet function better than it does. If the ball-cock assembly has been malfunctioning, this is a good time to install a new one, especially since you've already done most of the work in disconnecting the tank for removal.

Putting in a new toilet and reinstalling the old one are done in the same way. With a putty knife, scrape away all the old putty (or other sealing material) from both the bottom of the bowl and the metal or plastic floor flange. Inspect the floor where the toilet was. If the floor has rotted, it must be rebuilt before the toilet can be installed. Depending on how bad the damage is, the rebuilding may involve the floor, the subfloor, and even the joists. Have a carpenter rebuild the damaged area before you install the toilet. Also inspect the flange and the bolts that come up from the flange. If the flange is damaged or the bolts are stripped, replace the faulty part or parts before you go any further. These parts are inexpensive, and it's far better to replace them than to try to get by with parts of doubtful quality.

The next step is to put a new sealer ring on the water outlet opening on the bottom of the new bowl. The best and easiest to install is the wax toilet-bowl gasket. With the fixture upside down, set the wax ring into place on the bottom of the bowl. If the floor flange is recessed, you'll need a gasket with a plastic sleeve in the wax; this sleeve faces toward you as you position it, since it will go into the soil pipe. Now apply a uniform 1/8-inch-thick layer of toilet-bowl setting compound around the edge of the bowl at the base. You can buy the compound at most hardware stores and at all plumbing supply stores. With the gasket and the compound in place, remove the plug from the soil pipe. Turn the bowl right-side up and place it down over the flange, guiding the bolts into place. Press down firmly, and give the bowl a slight twist to make sure the wax ring seats properly against the flange. It is important that the bowl is level; check this by placing a level across the bowl. Either press down on any higher portion or insert thin wedges (you can hide them with toilet-bowl compound) under any lower portion of the bowl to even it. Make sure you don't disturb or break the seal of the wax ring; if this seal is broken, the toilet will leak.

Once you get the bowl positioned properly, you can install the nuts to hold the bowl to the floor. Do not overtighten the nuts; if you do, you can crack the fixture. Hand tightening is all that is required. Coat the hold-down nuts and bolts with

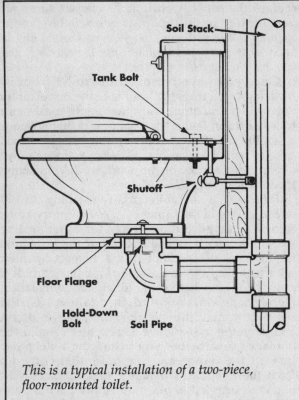

This is a typical installation of a two-piece, floor-mounted toilet.

toilet-bowl setting compound and reinstall the caps.

This completes the installation of the bowl; now you're ready to attach the tank. Rebolt a wall-mounted tank, or reinstall the bolts and washers that connect a bowl-supported tank. Before you put them back, make sure all washers, gaskets, and bolts are in sound condition, and replace any damaged parts. If the tank and bowl are connected with a spud pipe, apply pipe joint compound to the threads of the spud slip nuts and tighten them in place. Reconnect the water supply inlet pipe to the tank, make sure the ball-cock assembly is properly attached, and turn the water back on.

Solving Pipe Problems

Most plumbing problems occur at or near sinks, tubs, and toilets. Less often the pipes themselves can leak, sweat, freeze, or bang. Here is how to deal with these difficulties:

STOPPING LEAKS IN PIPES AND JOINTS

There are many kinds of leaks; some can flood your home, while others do little damage. Your approach to stopping a particular leak depends on the kind of leak it is.

If the leak is at a pipe joint, tighten or remake the joint. If the leak is in a pipe, remove the section that has the leak, and replace it with a new section. This is easier said than done. When you

turn a threaded galvanized steel pipe to unscrew it from its fitting at one end, you tighten the pipe into its fitting at the other end. With copper pipe, the new section must be sweat soldered in place. Most pipe replacement jobs are best left to a plumber, but consider using a pipe patch.

You'll find patch kits for plumbing leaks at hardware stores, or you can make your own with a piece of heavy rubber from an old inner tube and a C-clamp. Another possibility is to use a hose clamp with the rubber patch. The factory-made kits contain a rubber pad that goes over the hole in the pipe and metal plates that bolt tightly together to compress the rubber pad over the hole. A homemade rubber patch and a C-clamp do the same thing, but to spread the clamping pressure, place a block of wood against the pad or cut a tin can along its seam and wrap the can around the rubber patch. A quick and easy way to stop a leak, the patch kit can even be used permanently if the pipe is otherwise sound.

Other easy but temporary measures for stopping pipe leaks include wrapping waterproof tape over the bad spot and rubbing the hole with a stick of special compound. Applying epoxy paste to the leak or inserting a self-tapping plug into the hole are other alternatives. When using waterproof tape, be sure to dry the pipe thoroughly before you start wrapping. Start the tape 2 to 3 inches from the hole, and extend it the same distance beyond. For tiny leaks in pipes, there is

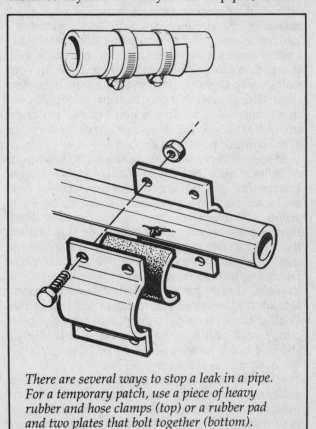

There are several ways to stop a leak in a pipe. For a temporary patch, use a piece of heavy rubber and hose clamps (top) or a rubber pad and two plates that bolt together (bottom).

probably no easier cure than the compound sticks that are available at most hardware stores. Rub the stick over the hole to stop the leak; it can stop small leaks while the water is still running in the pipe. Epoxy paste can be applied only to dry pipes, and the water must be turned off. Self-tapping plugs are best used for leaks in large pipes or tanks; they impede the flow of water in smaller pipes. When it is tightened, the screw of a self-tapping plug applies enough pressure to stop the leak.

The problem with these solutions is that a pipe that is bad enough to spring one leak often starts leaking in other places. You may fix one spot only to see the pipe burst somewhere else. Especially in cases where the leak results from substantial corrosion, the entire section of pipe most likely needs replacing. This is a job for a professional plumber.

SWEATING PIPES

Sometimes there is so much water dripping from a pipe that you're sure there must be a leak somewhere. On closer examination you may discover that there is no leak, although your floors and furnishings have suffered as much damage as if there were. What you are witnessing is a natural event called condensation, or sweating.

Sweating occurs when the water inside a pipe is much colder than surrounding humid air, a situation that exists nearly year-round in many homes. During the summer the surrounding air is naturally hot; during the winter the air is heated by the furnace. When warm humid air reaches cold pipes, drops of moisture form and drip as if there were a tiny hole in the pipe.

It is worth your time, effort, and expense to eliminate condensation problems. The moisture that drips from sweating pipes can harm your floors, encourage mildew, and cause other kinds of damage.

One good way to control the moisture problem of a sweating pipe is to insulate the pipes. There are several kinds of thick "drip" tape in rolls of self-sticking material made to adhere easily to problem pipes. Before applying the tape, wipe the pipes as dry as you can. Wind the tape so that it completely covers the pipe and the fittings; you should see no further signs of sweating.

Insulating tape also stops sweating. For straight runs of pipe, fiberglass pipe jackets are excellent. There are also no-drip compounds that you can brush on pipe to form a coating of insulation.

THAWING FROZEN PIPES

You may think that your entire plumbing system is in perfect working order, and that there is no danger of a pipe bursting and flooding your house. But there is one situation that you may not have considered. Water that freezes during the winter in an unprotected pipe expands, and that expansion can rupture an otherwise sound pipe. A frozen pipe is always an inconvenience, but it can result in a more serious situation than just a temporary loss of water. If there is one example of how a little prevention is superior to a lot of cure, fighting frozen pipes is it. By taking the proper preventive steps, you may never need to worry about thawing frozen pipes or repairing a pipe that bursts when the water in it freezes solid.

If you're building a new house or adding pipes underground, follow these freeze-fighting tips: Bury the pipes below the frost line. Since this depth varies in different regions, check with the local office of the National Weather Service to learn about the frost line in your area. Make sure the new pipes are well insulated, and run as many pipes as you can along your home's inner walls instead of along its outside walls. If you have pipes on outside walls leading to outside faucets, when it begins to get cold, shut off the water to the outside faucets and open the faucet to drain the exposed pipe. If you know you have a stretch of pipe that is likely to freeze, wrap the pipe with heat tape or pipe insulation. You can buy heat tape that has an automatic thermostat to start the heat when the temperature drops to about 38 degrees Fahrenheit.

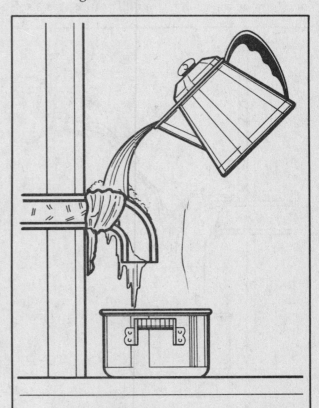

The safest and most popular method of thawing a frozen pipe is pouring boiling water over a towel wrapped around the frozen section. Catch the runoff in a pan.

Before doing anything about a frozen pipe, open the faucet so that the steam produced by your thawing activities will be able to escape. Start thawing the pipe at the faucet and work back toward the other end of the frozen section. As you melt the ice, water and steam will come out the open faucet. If you started in the middle, the steam produced by the melting ice could get trapped and build up enough pressure to burst the pipe.

You can use any of several pipe-thawing heat sources. The safest is hot water. Wrap and secure a heavy towel or a burlap bag around the pipe to concentrate and hold the heat against the pipe. Pour boiling water over the towel, but be careful because most of the water will run off the towel onto the floor. Position a bucket to catch the runoff.

A less messy but more dangerous heat source for thawing frozen pipes is a propane torch equipped with a flame-spreader nozzle. With this heat source, you must be extremely careful to keep the torch flame from damaging or igniting the wall behind the pipe. A scrap of fireproof material between the pipe and the wall is a good precautionary measure, but the way you use the torch is the main factor in safe pipe thawing. Move the flame back and forth; never leave it in one spot. Be especially careful if you're near a sol-

dered pipe joint; pass over it quickly or it may melt and cause leaks. Never use a torch or other direct high heat on plastic pipe.

If you want to avoid the messiness of thawing with hot water and the danger of melting soldered joints with a propane torch, you can use a heat gun, a hair dryer, or an electric iron as the heat source. They may work a little slower, but they are safer.

The special technique for thawing a frozen drainpipe involves melting the blockage with hot water. If the ice is some distance from the drain opening, the hot water you pour in could cool considerably before it reaches the trouble spot. For more effective thawing, remove the trap and insert a length of garden hose into the drainpipe. When the hose reaches the ice and can't push it in any farther, raise your end of the hose and feed hot water in through a funnel. This way, the hot water is sure to get to the problem area. You must be careful when using this technique. Until the ice melts and drains down the pipe, the hot water you pour in will back up toward you.

QUIETING NOISY PIPES

Some people call the sound of banging pipes "water hammer," but water hammer is only one of several different noises that can come from your plumbing system. If you hear the sound whenever you turn on the water, then the problem is not water hammer; it probably results from the pipes striking against something.

Banging pipes are easy to cure if you can see them. Turn on the water and look for movement. Once you find the trouble, you should have no problem stopping the pipe or pipes from hitting against whatever is nearby. Even if the moving pipe is between the walls, you may be able to silence it without tearing your house apart. Place rubber stops or other padding at each end where the pipe emerges from behind the wall.

You'll often find that the moving pipe is loose within its strap or U-clamp and is banging against the wall to which it's supposed to be secured. To eliminate the noise completely, slit a piece of garden hose or cut a patch of rubber, and insert it behind the strap or clamp to fill the gap. Pipes that strike against a masonry wall can be silenced by wedging a block of wood between the pipe and the wall. Nail the block to the wall with masonry nails or with a screw installed in a masonry wall anchor, and attach the pipe to the block with a pipe strap.

In a basement or crawl space, you may find galvanized steel pipes suspended from the joists by perforated pipe straps. Although this is a proper installation, a long run of suspended pipe can move within the straps, strike against something, and create a racket. A block of wood strategically wedged along the run can eliminate the pipe's movement and the noise.

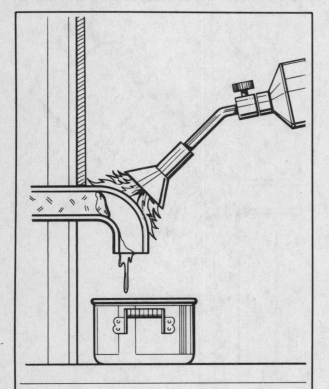

A propane torch also can be used to thaw a frozen pipe. This method is fast, but it could melt soldered pipe joints or cause a fire. Never use a torch on plastic pipe.

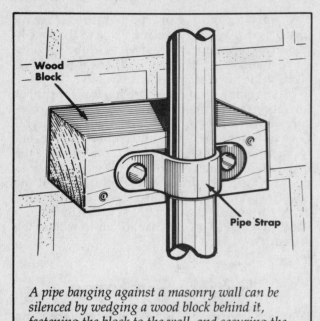

A pipe banging against a masonry wall can be silenced by wedging a wood block behind it, fastening the block to the wall, and securing the pipe to the wood.

Whenever you secure a pipe, be careful not to anchor it so tightly that it can't expand and contract with changes in temperature. If you place a bracket on a pipe, be sure to include a rubber buffer between the pipe and the bracket. You can make buffers from garden hose, radiator hose, foam rubber, rubber cut from inner tubes, or even kitchen sponges.

You may find that supply pipes and drainpipes that run right next to each other are striking one another and creating a clatter. One solution to this problem is to solder the two pipes together; another is to wedge a piece of rubber between them. Because vibration and noises are often caused by water pressure that is too high, try reducing the water pressure.

If the knocking sound occurs only when you turn on the hot water, your water heater is set too high; the noise is steam rumbling through the hot-water system. Turn down the heat setting to silence the pipes.

A pipe that is too small or that has become clogged with scale or mineral deposits can be a big noise problem. It's almost impossible to clean clogged supply pipes (a water filter can sometimes prevent such clogging), and you must replace pipe that is too small if you want to stop the noise. You can diminish the sound level of clogged pipes by wrapping them with sound-damping insulation.

Drainpipes rarely clatter, but they can make a sucking noise as the water leaves the sink or basin. This kind of sound means that a vent is restricted or that there is no vent attached to the drain. You have a potentially serious plumbing problem not because of the noise but because a nonfunctioning or nonexistent vent could result in the water seal being siphoned from the fixture's trap, allowing sewer gas to back up into your home. Run a plumber's snake through the vent from the fixture, if possible, or from the roof vent to eliminate any clogging. If there is no vent on the drain, install an antisiphon trap (available at the hardware store) to quiet the noise and to prevent any problem with sewer gas.

Water hammer occurs when you shut off the water suddenly, and the fast-moving water rushing through the pipe is brought to a quick halt, creating a shock wave and a hammering noise. Plumbing that is properly installed has air chambers or "cushions" that compress when the shock wave hits, softening the blow and preventing this hammering. The chambers can fail because water under pressure gradually absorbs the air. If you formerly experienced no hammering and then it suddenly started, most likely your plumbing system's air chambers have become waterlogged.

You can cure water hammer by turning off the water behind the waterlogged chambers (perhaps

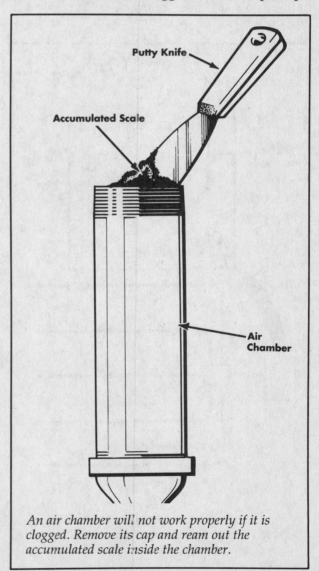

An air chamber will not work properly if it is clogged. Remove its cap and ream out the accumulated scale inside the chamber.

even at the main shutoff), opening the offending faucet, and permitting the faucet to drain thoroughly. Once all the water drains from the chamber, air will fill it again and restore the cushion. If the air chamber is located below the outlet, you may have to drain the main supply lines to allow the chamber to fill with water again.

The air chamber will not drain properly if it's clogged with scale or residue from chemicals or minerals in the water. The chamber should be a bit larger than the supply pipe to preclude such clogging. Since the chamber is simply a capped length of pipe, all you have to do to clear it is to remove the cap and ream out the scale.

If there are no air chambers built into your plumbing system, you must do something because water hammer pressures are often sufficient to cause failure of fittings or burst pipes. The problem is most often caused by water pressure that is too high, so reduce the water pressure, if possible. Sometimes this isn't feasible, because a reduction in pressure may result in only a dribble of water at an upper-floor faucet if one on the first floor is turned on. Where it is

appropriate, you can reduce pressure by installing a pressure-reducing valve in the supply line that comes into the house. A globe valve (a valve that halts water flow with a washer) at the head of the affected pipeline may solve the problem, but it may create pressure too low for proper operation when other faucets are open. If pressure reduction is infeasible or ineffective, you must install the necessary air chambers to prevent water hammer. If you have no room to make the installation without tearing into a wall, go to a plumbing supply dealer and find out about the substitute devices that are designed for such problem areas. Many of these devices have a valve that makes it very easy for air to reenter the system.

Septic Systems

People who live in an area where there is no municipal sewage-disposal system must have private sewage systems, which usually are septic tanks. New methods of waste disposal are now appearing, such as the composting toilets used together with separate gray-water disposal systems and full-cycle waste treatment plants designed for individual residential application.

HOW THEY WORK

Septic systems differ in minor construction and operational details, but they are similar in design and function. Waste travels down the house's main drain to a sewer line and into a large underground tank. Heavier solids settle to the bottom of the tank, forming a layer of sludge. Lighter substances rise to the top, forming a layer of scum. Anaerobic bacteria, enzymes, and fungi go to work on the waste, liquefying most of the solids and reducing the materials to different chemical constituencies. Gases that are formed in the process percolate up through the liquid and the scum layer, and escape through the venting system.

As new waste enters the tank, a like amount of effluent pours from the tank's outlet pipe into a distribution box from where it is channeled into a network of perforated or loosely jointed drainpipes; it then seeps into the ground and evaporates into the air. During this process, aerobic bacteria further reduce the waste until eventually it is rendered harmless. The bacterial action is a natural phenomenon, but the addition of certain chemicals into the system can speed up the liquefying process. What chemicals are used depends on soil conditions and the kind of sewage. Bacterial action also is speeded up by introducing yeast into the septic system. Put 1/2 pound of brewer's yeast in a bucket of warm water, empty the contents of the bucket into a toilet bowl, and flush it into the septic tank system.

As waste enters the septic tank through the inlet pipe, a like amount exits through the outlet pipe into a distribution box. From there it flows into a network of perforated or loosely jointed drainpipes and seeps into the ground.

TESTING AND CLEANING THE TANK

A septic tank should be checked about once a year, but it may require cleaning only after several years (some tanks go as long as 10 years between cleanings). Never allow the layers of solids, both top and bottom, to get so close to the opening in the tank's outlet pipe that the solids can be carried out into the drainage field. The same firm that cleans out and removes the solid waste matter can check the tank annually, but the homeowner also can make the inspection.

Most tanks have an inspection extension that comes from the top of the tank. Usually a pipe with a screw-on plug, this extension and its plug may be buried only a few inches below ground level. **Caution:** *When you uncover and uncap the opening, allow the gas in the tank to disperse before you try to make the inspection. Do not breathe the gas; it can asphyxiate you. Also make sure that there are no flames or sparks; the gas is explosive.*

You must make a wooden device to test the scum level. Hinge a foot-long flap piece of 1 x 2 to a long 1 x 2. The hinge allows the flap to fold upward. The exact length of the long piece of 1 x 2 depends on how deep your tank is buried. Position the flap at the end of the long stick, and tie a stout cord to it so that you can fold the hinged flap, and hold it next to the stick with the cord. Fold the flap up and insert the stick into the inspection extension vent, forcing it through the layer of scum. After it passes through the layer and beyond the top of the folded up flap, release the cord. The flap will unfold down. Move the flap until it is against the bottom of the outlet pipe, and make a mark on the stick at the top of the extension pipe. Now, move the flap away from the outlet pipe and bring it up against the bottom of the scum layer; you will feel resistance from encountering the layer of scum. Mark the stick again. The distance between the two marks tells you how close the scum layer is to the bottom of the outlet pipe. If this distance is 3 inches or less, your septic tank needs cleaning.

The sludge test stick is a long piece of 1 x 2 with cloth wrapped and secured around the bottom portion. The length of wrapped stick should equal the distance from the bottom of the outlet pipe opening to the floor of the tank. Place the test stick in the inspection extension pipe, and move it through the scum and down to the bottom of the tank. As the stick goes into the sludge, gently turn it so that the end goes down to the bottom of the tank. The turning also causes the sludge to mark its level on the cloth. Remove the stick slowly. Measure the distance between the top of the sludge layer and the top of the cloth wrap to see if the sludge level is high enough to warrant cleaning. The cleaning firm will leave a small layer of the sludge in the tank to assure that the bacterial action will continue uninterrupted.

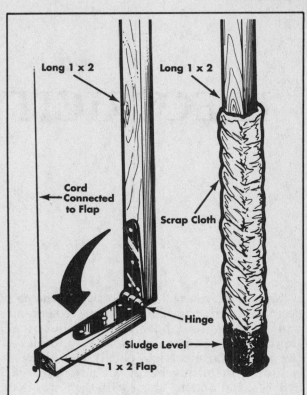

To inspect your septic tank, you should make two simple testing tools: the scum test stick (left) and the sludge test stick (right).

DISPOSAL FIELDS AND SEEPAGE PITS

The septic tank itself cannot purify the sewage. All it does is liquify some solid waste matter. The still-contaminated liquid leaves the tank and goes into either a disposal field or seepage pit. The disposal field usually is preferable. The liquid goes through the outlet pipe to a distribution box, which is nothing more than a small closed tank with several openings to which pipes are attached to allow the liquid to follow several different routes. From the distribution box, the liquid flows into the disposal or absorption field via pipes that are either perforated or loosely jointed. Released either through the perforations or the loose joints, the liquid waste seeps down into a bed of crushed stone or gravel, and a natural purification process begins.

Where there is not enough room for an adequate drainage field, seepage pits are dug. Seepage pits are large dry wells, which also can be used where the terrain is too steep for easy disposal field construction. The walls of the pits, which are made of concrete blocks, bricks, or stone, usually are not held together by mortar, so the liquid from the septic tank flows into the pits and seeps through the openings between the blocks, bricks, or stones. The bottom of the tank is filled with crushed rock, and sometimes, if the walls weaken, the entire pit fills with loose stones.

ELECTRICITY

In this chapter you will learn about your home's electrical system, how to make simple repairs and replacements, and how to make electrical improvements that are safe and easy to make. The work that electricians call "roughing," including installing boxes for new fixtures, switches, and outlets, along with the wires that bring power to them, is best left to licensed professionals.

This chapter is limited to electrical repair and improvement projects that require no license or special expertise.

How the System Works

Your home's plumbing and electrical systems may seem as different as any two things could be, but there are parallels. Water enters your home through a pipe under pressure (hydraulic pressure, measured in pounds per square inch), and when you turn on a tap, the water flows at a certain rate (gallons per minute). Electricity enters your home through copper or aluminum wires, also under pressure (electrical pressure, called electromotive force or voltage, measured in volts). When you turn on an electrical device, the electricity flows at a certain rate; this is current, measured in amperes, or amps. Unlike water that is used as it comes from the tap, electricity is meant to do work; it is converted from energy to power, measured in watts. Since household electrical consumption is high, the unit of measure most often used is the kilowatt, 1,000 watts. The total amount of electrical energy that you use in any period is measured in terms of kilowatt-hours (kwh).

The electric meter records how much electricity you use and determines the amount of your electric bill. There are two kinds of electric meters.

One displays a row of small dials with individual indicators on its face. Each dial registers a certain number of kilowatt-hours of electrical energy. If you leave a 100-watt bulb burning for 10 hours, for example, the meter will register 1 kilowatt-hour (10 x 100 = 1,000 watt-hours or 1 kwh). The meter dial at the far right is the one that counts individual kilowatt-hours from 1 to 10; the next one to the left counts the electricity from 10 to 100 kilowatt-hours; the third dial counts up to 1,000; the fourth counts up to 10,000; and the dial at the extreme left counts kilowatt-hours up to 100,000. If the arrow on the dial is between two numbers, always read the lower number.

The other electric meter performs the same function, but instead of individual dials, it has numerals in slots on the meter face, much like the odometer in your car. This meter is read from left to right, and the numbers show total electrical consumption. Some meters also use a multiplying factor; the number that appears must be multiplied by 10, for example, for a true figure in kilowatt-hours. Once you know how to read your meter, you can verify the charges on your electric bill, and become a better watchdog of electrical energy consumption in your home.

The electrical service drop, or supply line, and the meter are as far as the local utility company is involved in your home's electrical system. From that point on, the system is the homeowner's responsibility. Electricity passes from the meter to the service equipment through three lines (older houses may have two) that supply 110-120/220-240 volts AC (alternating current). The three-wire system gives you 110-120-volt power for lighting, outlets, and small appliances, as well as 220-240-volt power for air conditioning, an electric range, an electric clothes dryer, a water heater, and electric heating.

THE SERVICE ENTRANCE
Electricity enters your home through the power company's service equipment, which is a discon-

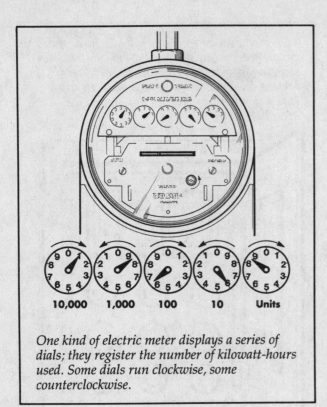

One kind of electric meter displays a series of dials; they register the number of kilowatt-hours used. Some dials run clockwise, some counterclockwise.

10,000   1,000   100   10   Units

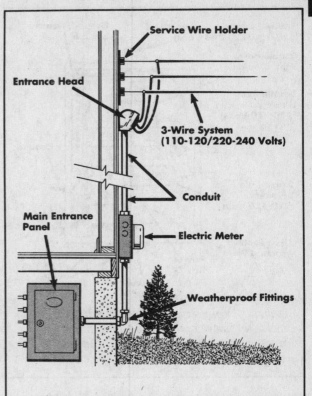

The electrical service drop, or supply line, and the meter are as far as the local utility company is involved in your home's electrical system. The rest of the system is your responsibility.

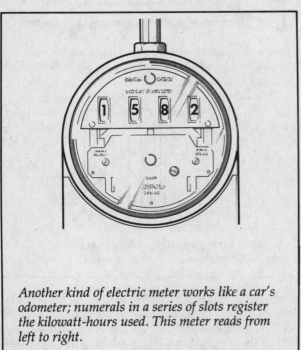

Another kind of electric meter works like a car's odometer; numerals in a series of slots register the kilowatt-hours used. This meter reads from left to right.

nect device mounted in a suitable approved enclosure. Its purpose is to disconnect the service from the interior wiring system. This disconnect might be a set of pullout fuses, a circuit breaker, or a large switch. The disconnect device usually is called a main fuse, main breaker, main disconnect, or simply "the main." It can be in a separate enclosure, and although it's usually installed inside the building, it can be mounted outdoors in a weatherproof box.

Main disconnects usually are inside the house, in a large enclosure that also contains the fuses or circuit breakers, which handle the distribution of power throughout the house. This is called a main entrance panel, main box, or entrance box. The three wires from the meter enter this box. The heavily insulated black and red lines are secured in lugs to the tops of a parallel pair of exposed heavy copper bars, called buses, that are positioned vertically toward the center of the box. These two lines are the "live" or "hot" wires. The third wire, which usually is bare, is the neutral. It is attached to a separate grounding bar, or bus, a silver-colored strip usually found at the bottom or to one side of the main box. In most homes this ground bus is connected to the ground (the earth) by a heavy solid copper wire, clamped to a cold-water pipe or to an underground bar or plate.

OVERLOAD PROTECTION
Power in your house is distributed through various electrical circuits that originate in the main entrance panel. The 110-120-volt circuits have two conductors: one neutral (white) wire and one hot (black) wire. Three conductors may be used inside one jacket to serve as two circuits, with one red (hot) wire, one black (hot) wire, and a common neutral or white wire. The 220-240-volt circuits may consist of two hot wires alone, or a

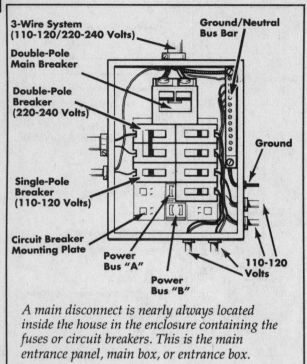

3-Wire System (110-120/220-240 Volts)

Double-Pole Main Breaker

Double-Pole Breaker (220-240 Volts)

Single-Pole Breaker (110-120 Volts)

Circuit Breaker Mounting Plate

Ground/Neutral Bus Bar

Ground

Power Bus "A"

Power Bus "B"

110-120 Volts

A main disconnect is nearly always located inside the house in the enclosure containing the fuses or circuit breakers. This is the main entrance panel, main box, or entrance box.

third, neutral wire may be added. The hot lines are attached directly to the hot main buses. The neutral wire is always connected to the ground bus, and never passes through a fuse or circuit breaker.

Fuses and circuit breakers are safety devices built into your electrical system. Since few people know about wire current-carrying capacity, the fuses or circuit breakers prevent overloading of the circuits. If there were no fuses or circuit breakers and if you operated too many appliances on a single circuit, the cable carrying the power for that circuit would get extremely hot, short-circuit, and possibly, start a fire.

To prevent electrical overloads, fuses and circuit breakers are designed to blow or trip, stopping the flow of current to the overloaded cable. For example, a 15-ampere fuse should blow when the current through it exceeds 15 amperes; a 20-ampere circuit breaker should trip when the current through it exceeds 20 amperes. A fuse that blows or a circuit breaker that trips is not faulty; it is doing its job properly, indicating that there is trouble somewhere in the circuit. When a fuse blows or a circuit breaker trips, too many appliances are plugged in to the circuit, or a malfunctioning device, such as an appliance with an internal short, is connected to the circuit.

A blown fuse or a tripped circuit breaker is the signal that you should look for trouble. It makes no sense to replace a blown fuse or reset a tripped circuit breaker until you've located and eliminated the cause of the trouble. **Caution:** *Never try to defeat this built-in safety system by replacing a fuse*

To protect against serious overloads, fuses and circuit breakers are designed to blow or trip, stopping the flow of current to the overloaded cable. A 15-ampere fuse, for example, should blow when the current passing through it exceeds 15 amperes.

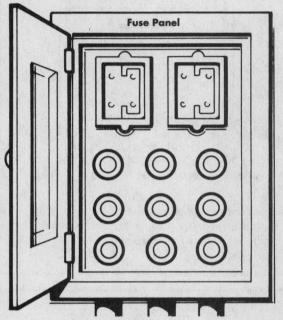

Fuse Panel

Along with screw-in fuses, a typical main fuse panel has a main disconnect and other pull-out blocks with cartridge fuses.

To reach cartridge fuses, simply pull the fuse blocks out of the main entrance panel.

with one of a larger current-carrying capacity. The fuse or circuit breaker capacity should equal or be less than the current-carrying capacity (or ampacity) of the conductors. Edison-base plug fuses can be interchanged in certain sizes, as can some cartridge fuses. If you replaced a 15-ampere fuse with a 25-ampere fuse, you could be placing yourself in danger. Placing a copper penny behind a blown fuse is also sure to lead to disaster. Certain circuit breakers also can be interchanged, but like fuses, they never should be.

BRANCH AND FEEDER CIRCUITS

From the fuses or circuit breakers, circuits go to all the devices in your home that require electrical

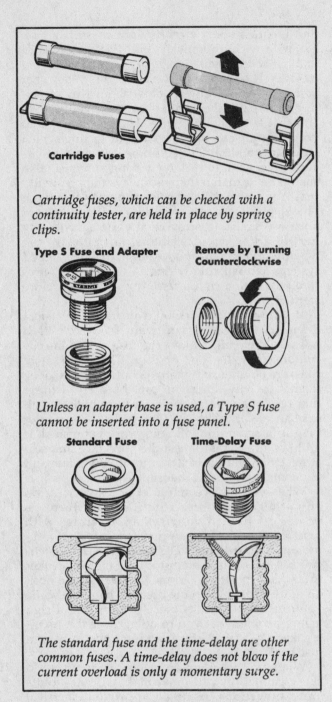

Cartridge Fuses

Cartridge fuses, which can be checked with a continuity tester, are held in place by spring clips.

Type S Fuse and Adapter

Remove by Turning Counterclockwise

Unless an adapter base is used, a Type S fuse cannot be inserted into a fuse panel.

Standard Fuse

Time-Delay Fuse

The standard fuse and the time-delay are other common fuses. A time-delay does not blow if the current overload is only a momentary surge.

Circuit Breaker Panel

Main Circuit Breaker

Single Circuit Breaker

Double Circuit Breaker

Push Tripped Circuit Breaker to "On" to Restore Power

Circuit breakers do not blow like fuses; they are switches that automatically trip open to interrupt the flow of electrical current when it overloads the circuit.

power. There are two kinds of circuits: feeder and branch. Feeder circuits, which are not found in every house, are heavy cables that travel from the main entrance panel to other smaller distribution panels, called subpanels or load centers. These auxiliary panels are located in remote parts of the house or in outbuildings, and are used for redistribution of "bulk" power, such as in a garage.

All of the circuits that run from either the main entrance panel or other, smaller panels to the various points of use are branch circuits. For 110-120-volt needs, a circuit branches out through a circuit breaker from one of the main buses and from the ground bus. For 220-240 volts, many circuits use only the two main buses. But all three wires are needed for devices that operate on both 110-120 and 220-240 volts, such as an electric range, and for 220-240-volt appliances that require the third wire for a neutral.

The 110-120-volt branch circuits go through fuses or circuit breakers, which are labeled either 15 amperes or 20 amperes. The 15-amp branches go to ceiling lamps and wall outlets in rooms where less-energy-demanding devices, such as floor and table lamps, are found. The larger 20-amp branch circuits go to outlets in the kitchen, dining and laundry areas, and anywhere else heavy-duty appliances are used.

A 15-amp circuit can handle a total of 1,800 watts, and a 20-amp circuit a total of 2,400 watts, but these figures represent circuits that are fully loaded. Limit the load on a 15-amp circuit to no more than 1,440 watts, and the load on a 20-amp line to no more than 1,920 watts. Add up the individual wattage for all lamps and appliances plugged into each circuit to make sure there is no overload anywhere in your home.

When computing the load on each branch circuit, be sure to allow for the fact that many motor-driven appliances draw more current when the motor is starting up than when it's running. A refrigerator might draw up to 15 amps initially but quickly settle down to around 4 amps. Suppose the refrigerator is plugged into a 20-amp branch circuit, and a 1,000-watt electric toaster, which draws a little more than 8 amps, is also plugged into that circuit. If the refrigerator motor starts while the toaster is toasting, the total current load exceeds the current-carrying capacity of the circuit, and the fuse blows or the circuit breaker trips.

ELECTRICAL SAFETY

The insulation around a conductor protects you from danger. An electric shock is always distressing, always hazardous, and occasionally fatal. Electrical safety is avoiding physical contact with any live, or hot, part of the circuit. All electrical devices and electrical wires are designed to provide the greatest measure of safety, but you can defeat built-in safeguards through carelessness. To work safely with electricity, you must understand both the hazards and the precautions those hazards require you to practice.

Never do anything that would break the conductor's insulation. Do not staple an extension cord to a baseboard or to a wall (an illegal practice). The staple can cut through the insulation

For safety, examine wiring regularly. Replace cords that have brittle or damaged insulation.

and create a short circuit that can start a fire. Examine wiring regularly and discard any cord that has brittle insulation.

There is one wire in the electrical system that you can theoretically touch without fear of getting shocked (if the circuit is correctly connected), and that is the neutral wire. The problem is that you can't always be sure without testing which wire is the neutral. The equipment-grounding circuit, present only in later wiring systems, also should be dead, but there is always the possibility that it might not have been properly installed. The identifying marks or colors on the wires are not always reliable, so avoid any contact with any part of a live circuit. This is particularly true when working with poorly done or jury-rigged systems and with old wiring. Always check wires carefully with a circuit tester or voltmeter before starting work.

If you plan to work on a portable electrical device, unplug it. If you want to work with a household circuit, remove the fuse or trip the circuit breaker to its "off" position. These two safety rules are obvious, but many people forget to obey them. The only thing you can do safely without first unplugging is changing a light bulb. Do all appliance work with the unit "cold," and do not plug it in again until all your work is finished. If it blows a fuse, disconnect the appliance immediately. Don't plug it in again until you locate and eliminate the cause of the trouble.

When you replace an outlet or a switch, or do any other work on a circuit, always turn the power off first. If your system operates with fuses, remove the fuse for the circuit you're working on. If your home's electrical system uses circuit breakers, trip the appropriate circuit breaker to its "off" position. To make sure no one accidentally flips the circuit breaker back on while you're working, put a piece of tape and a sign telling people what you're doing over the circuit breaker's handle. A sign also is a good idea for a fuse box.

When you work on an electrical circuit, for a safe installation you must make all wire joints and connections inside an approved electrical box. There are several ways to join wires, but the best way is to use solderless connectors of either the crimp-on or the screw-on kind. Never connect wires together in a behind-the-wall or in-the-ceiling location that is not accessible by simply opening an electrical box. In addition, when joining insulated wires to one another or when fastening them under terminal screws, make sure no uninsulated (bare) wire extends beyond the connection. The insulation should go right up to the solderless connector or the terminal screw.

ELECTRICAL GROUNDING

Proper grounding of your electrical system is essential to your safety. Electricity always follows

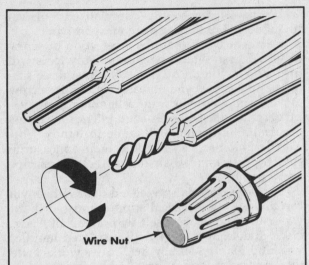

One of the most popular ways to join wires is to use solderless connectors, called wire nuts. The conductor ends are twisted together and the wire nut is screwed onto the twisted ends; make sure no bare conductor is exposed.

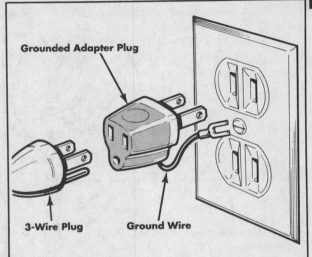

If your home's circuitry is not of the three-wire grounding type, you can ground appliances by equipping all three-wire plugs with a grounded adapter plug. The adapter's grounding wire is secured to the outlet plate's mounting screw.

the path of least resistance, and the path could be you whenever an appliance or another electrical component is not grounded.

The idea behind grounding is simply to direct electrical energy into the earth by providing a conductor that is less resistant than you are. This often is accomplished by attaching one end of the wire to the frame of an appliance and fastening the other end to a cold-water pipe.

Most nonmetal-sheathed cable contains a bare wire, which carries the grounded connection to every electrical box, outlet, and appliance in your home. You usually can tell whether your electrical system is grounded by checking the outlets. If you have outlets that accept plugs with two blades and one prong, your system should have three wires, one of which is a grounding wire. The prong carries the safety ground to the metal frame of any appliance that has a three-wire plug and cord.

The metal frame poses a safety hazard. If some insulation on the power cord of a major appliance (refrigerator, dishwasher, washing machine, or dryer) wears away at the point where the cord enters the frame, the contact between the metal current conductor and the metal frame could make the whole appliance alive with electricity. If you touched a charged metal frame while simultaneously touching a water faucet or a radiator, the current would surge through you and could kill you.

There are other places throughout the electrical system where conductor-metal contact is a distinct possibility: wherever wires enter a metal pipe (conduit), where the cord enters a lamp or lamp socket, and where in-wall cable enters an electrical box. Surfaces at these points must be

free of burrs that could chafe the wire and damage its insulation. Washers, grommets, and special fittings have been devised to protect wire at these various points of entry, but the best thing you can do is to make sure that the whole system is grounded and that the ground circuit is electrically continuous (without breaks).

If your circuitry is not of the three-wire grounding type, you should ground all of your appliances. You can do this without going to the expense of installing completely new wiring. An inexpensive and easy way to ground appliances is to equip all three-prong appliance plugs with a grounded adapter plug. Some adapter plugs have a metal tab near the prongs; some have a short grounding wire, or pigtail, with a metal tab at the end. The plug fits into any two-blade outlet; with the pigtail type, the small grounding wire connects under the screw of the outlet plate. **Caution:** *Never remove the prong from a three-wire plug to make it fit a two-slot receptacle. Always use an adapter.*

Even if appliances are properly grounded, dampness can cause a potential shock hazard. If you touched a charged metal frame in a damp location or while touching a water faucet or radiator, the current would surge through you. There are three things you can do to eliminate this hazard: Make sure your appliances are properly grounded, and follow all electrical safety rules. Make sure appliance cords are in good repair and are not chafing against burrs or rough spots where they enter the appliance frame. Add a ground-fault circuit interrupter (GFI or GFCI) to the circuit. Ground-fault circuit interrupters are monitoring devices that instantly shut off a circuit when a current leak occurs; they are required by

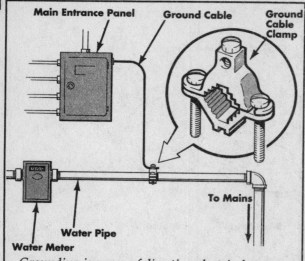

Main Entrance Panel — **Ground Cable** — **Ground Cable Clamp**

To Mains

Water Pipe

Water Meter

Grounding is a way of directing electrical energy into the earth so that you never become the path of least resistance. All major appliances, all electrical boxes, receptacles, and many other appliances should be grounded. The system usually has a ground cable running to a cold-water pipe that goes into the earth.

the National Electrical Code on all new 15- and 20-amp outdoor outlets and for wiring in bathrooms where dampness is a common problem. GFIs are available to plug into existing outlets, to replace outlets, and to replace circuit breakers in the electrical entrance panel. A professional electrician should install the circuit-breaker type; you can install the other types yourself. Ground-fault circuit interrupters are available at electrical-supply and home-center stores.

Repairing and Replacing Electrical Components

Lamps stop lighting, doorbells stop ringing, and outlets stop holding plugs. When you're faced with a malfunctioning electrical component, you could call an electrician, but there are many simple repairs you can do yourself. These electrical tasks probably require tools you're likely to have around the house, and they demand no more technical expertise than reading and following directions. Make safety your priority, and you'll be amazed at what you can do to maintain and upgrade the electrical devices in your home.

TOOLS FOR ELECTRICAL JOBS

To make simple electrical repairs, you'll need a few hand tools. The more extensive and complex your repair work and the more rewiring you eventually do, the more tools you'll need. Most are inexpensive or can be found in your home

workshop. There are a few specialized tools you might need, but they also are inexpensive.

Electrical work requires a selection of screwdrivers. These should be good-quality tools with insulated handles. You'll need at least three sizes for slotted screws and at least one Phillips screwdriver. You also will want a hammer, long-nose pliers, and adjustable slip-joint pliers. One or two adjustable wrenches will come in handy. Your electrical toolbox also should contain a measuring rule, a putty knife, a small level, electrical tape, and wire nuts.

You'll need some specialized tools, which you can buy at any electrical supply house or hardware store. Equip yourself with a pair of electrician's diagonal cutters with insulated handles. The kind that has stubby, wide jaws works better than one with long, narrow jaws. For stripping the insulation off conductors, you should use a wire stripper. You'll also need a voltage tester, used to determine whether a circuit is live or dead. You can buy a more sophisticated tester that will measure voltages and currents in the circuit.

If you'll be working with circuits that have three-slot outlets and an equipment-grounding loop, a polarity-checking device is useful. You also may want to buy a continuity tester for determining whether a dead circuit is open or closed and checking ground loops.

RESTORING A CIRCUIT

The overload devices, fuses or circuit breakers, in your electrical system are there to blow or trip if the circuit is overloaded. When that happens, as it does from time to time in almost every home, what do you do?

The first step should be taken before a circuit trips. If you haven't already done so, list all the branch circuits in your home, by number and by what area each controls. Then you can figure out which outlets and fixtures are on each branch circuit. If you aren't sure the list is accurate and complete, you can verify it through this simple procedure: Remove a fuse or trip a circuit breaker to its "off" position, and check to see what equipment or devices are de-energized. It's easy to see when a ceiling light goes out; you can check an outlet by plugging in a lamp. Once you know what outlets, fixtures, and appliances are connected to each branch circuit, write the information on a card and attach the card inside the main entrance panel's door.

When a circuit goes off, there may be a visual or audible indication of the trouble spot, such as a bright flare from a lamp or a sputtering, sparking sound from an appliance. Immediately disconnect the faulty equipment. If you don't know what is wrong, go to the main entrance panel. Check to see what fuse is blown or what breaker has tripped, and determine from your informa-

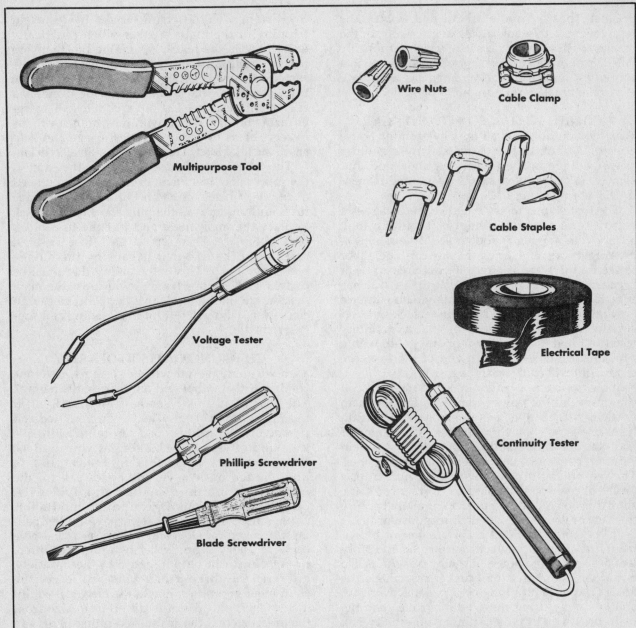

Some specialized tools are needed for electrical work: a multipurpose tool, screwdrivers, and testers. Keep electrical tape, wire nuts, cable clamps, and cable staples on hand.

tion card what outlets, appliances, and lighting fixtures are on the circuit. Then disconnect everything on that circuit that you can, and inspect those fixtures that you can't easily disconnect for signs or smells of malfunction.

Replace the fuse or reset the breaker. If the circuit holds, perhaps something you disconnected is faulty; check for short circuits or other problems. If there is no evidence of electrical fault in the fixtures, the problem may be an overload (too much current draw for the circuit to handle). Remove some of the load from the circuit.

If the new fuse blows or the circuit breaker refuses to reset, the problem is in equipment that is still connected or, less likely, in the circuit cable

itself. Examine each device for faults until you find the offending equipment. If the circuit still goes out when there are no loads connected to it, the wiring itself is faulty, probably because of a short in a junction or outlet box, or possibly in the cable itself. With the circuit dead, start at the far end of the line and inspect all of the connections. If there is no visible evidence of a problem, call an electrician, who will check each segment of the circuit with a continuity tester.

A circuit breaker is a remarkably trouble-free device, but occasionally a breaker does fail. The result is that the circuit will not energize, even when it's fault free. When a circuit goes out, if the circuit breaker itself has a distinctive, burnt-plastic smell, the trip handle is loose and wobbly, the reset mechanism seems all afloat internally, or the breaker rattles when you shake it, it has probably failed. You can make certain by checking it with a continuity tester. The only remedy is to replace the circuit breaker; they are not repairable.

COPING WITH A POWER OUTAGE

What do you do when all the power in the house goes off? Usually this is caused by a general power outage in the entire neighborhood, but sometimes the problem lies in the individual residential wiring system.

The first step is to see whether the outage is a general one or yours alone. If it's night, look around the neighborhood to see if your neighbors' lights are off. During the day call a neighbor to see if others are affected. If you have a circuit breaker main disconnect, check to see if it has tripped to the "off" position. If the main entrance is wired with fuses, pull the fuse block out and slip the fuses free. Check them with a continuity tester to see if they're blown or still good; with a probe lead touched to each end of the fuse, the tester light will come on if the fuse is good.

If the trouble is a general power outage, all you can do is call the power company. If your main breaker is still in the "on" position or both main fuses are good, but your neighbors have power and you don't, the fault lies between your main entrance panel and the power transmission lines. The reason could be a downed service drop, a faulty or overloaded pole transformer, or some similar problem; call the power company because this part of your system is their responsibility.

If you find a tripped main breaker or blown main fuses in your main entrance panel, the problem lies within the house and may be serious. Do not attempt to reset the breaker or replace the fuses. The difficulty may be a general overload; you're simply using more total current than the main breaker can pass. Another possibility is a dead short somewhere in the house.

The first step is to go through the house and turn off everything you can. If you have a circuit breaker panel, flip all the breakers to the "off" position and reset the main breaker to the "on" position. One by one, trip the branch circuit breakers back on. If one of them fails to reset, or the main breaker trips off again as you trip the branch breaker on, the source of the trouble lies in that circuit, which must be cleared of the fault.

If all the breakers go back on and the main breaker stays on, you're faced with two possibilities. One is that something you disconnected earlier is faulty. Go back along the line, inspect each item for possible fault, and plug each back in. You'll eventually discover which one is causing the problem, either visually or by the fact that a breaker trips out when you reconnect it. The other and more likely possibility is system-wide overloading. This is characterized by recurrent tripping of the main breaker when practically everything in the house is running but there are no electrical faults to be found. There are two remedies for this problem. One is to lessen the total electrical load; this should be done as a short-term measure. The other is to install a larger main entrance panel, with new branch circuits to serve areas of heavy electrical usage and help share the total load. This is a job for an electrician.

The troubleshooting approach is the same if the main panel has fuses, except that you'll need a supply of fuses on hand. Pull all the cartridge fuses and unscrew all the plug fuses in the panel. Replace the main fuses and put the fuse block back into place. Then replace each fuse or set of fuses until the one that is causing the outage blows out again. This is the circuit that must be cleared. General overloading will cause the main fuses to go out again. If this happens, call in an electrician, who will test for overloading and suggest remedies.

CHECKING OUTLET POLARITY

Two-wire residential wiring systems have one conductor that is hot and another that is neutral. The neutral also may serve as a ground, but it usually does not. The system is ungrounded and potentially hazardous. You can tell if you have this kind of circuit by looking at your outlets; there are only two slots for each plug in ungrounded outlets. Wiring codes call for the installation of a third conductor, a bare wire, called the equipment grounding conductor. Outlets used with this system have three openings: two vertical slots and a third, rounded hole centered above them. Either two-prong or three-prong plugs can be plugged into these outlets, but only the three-prong kind will carry the equipment grounding line to the electrical equipment. One vertical slot is different in size from the other, so that the many two-prong plugs can be inserted in only one direction. This ensures that equipment will be polarized, hot side to hot side and neutral to neutral.

For proper operation and safety, all outlets on each circuit should have individual conductors going to the correct terminals, so that there are no polarity reversals along the line that would negate the effectiveness of the system. Outlets are not always connected this way, even in new wiring systems. You can check your outlets with a small, inexpensive tester, called a polarity checker, designed for this purpose. It looks like a three-prong plug and contains three neon bulb indicators. Simply plug the checker into an outlet; the lights will tell you if the polarity is correct and if it isn't which lines are reversed. If there is a reversal, turn off the circuit, pull the outlet out of the electrical box, and switch the wires to the proper terminals. If the

To make sure outlets are installed properly, with the individual conductors going to the correct terminals, you can use a plug-in analyzer to check polarity.

Receptacle Polarity Checker

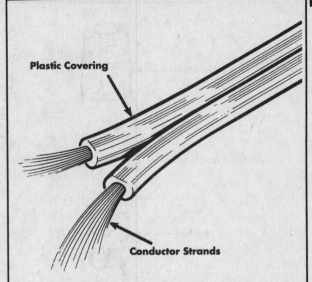

Plastic Covering

Conductor Strands

The most common lamp and small appliance cord is Type SPT, which is often called zip cord. The conductor sheath is plastic; it splits easily along a molded groove.

equipment-grounding circuit is open (discontinuous), trace the circuit until you find the disconnection or missing link, and reconnect it to restore the circuit.

REWIRING A LAMP

There is no reason to live with lamps that don't work properly. The plug, cord, and socket, which are the parts that probably are causing the lamp to malfunction, are easy and inexpensive to replace. You can get them at any well-stocked hardware store and at any store that specializes in electrical parts. Why put up with a plug that is misshapen or broken, or that doesn't make a good electrical connection in the outlet? With a quick-clamp plug, which eliminates the need for fastening wires under terminal screw, you can have a new one on in seconds.

You can install a new socket almost as easily. Replacement sockets come in brass or nickel metal and black or brown plastic, so you should be able to find a socket that approximates the color of the existing socket. If you plan to replace a socket, why not put in a three-way socket for greater lighting versatility. Wiring a three-way socket is as simple as wiring the standard "on-off" version.

Lamp cord is known as Type SPT, but if you ask for zip cord at a hardware or electrical supply store, you'll get what you need. The number 18 size is satisfactory for most lamp applications.

Zip cord is available in many colors, the most common are black, brown, white, and transparent. Match the cord color to the lamp, and order a sufficient length for your needs. The customary length is 6 feet, but you can use as much cord as you need to reach from the lamp to the outlet; add the length of the cord hidden in the lamp, plus 1 foot for attachments to socket and plug and for some slack. In terms of safety and appearance, it's better to have an adequate length of cord than to compensate for a short one with an extension cord.

To rewire a lamp, first pull the plug out; never do any work while the lamp is connected. Remove the shade, unscrew the bulb, and squeeze the socket shell at the switch to separate the shell and the cardboard insulator from the socket cap. Do not use a screwdriver to pry the socket apart if you plan to reuse the socket. Pull the socket out of the shell as far as the attached wire permits. If this doesn't give you enough wire to work with, push some cord up from the bottom of the lamp for additional slack.

Loosen the socket's terminal screws, and remove the cord wires from under them. If the lamp is a small one and the cord goes through in a straight path, you should be able to slide the old wire out and easily feed the new wire through from one end or the other. If the lamp is large and the cord twists inside it, replacing the wire can be more difficult. If the old cord offers any resistance, don't tug on it; check to see if you can disassemble the lamp to make removal easier. Also check to see if the cord is tied in a knot to keep it from being pulled out at its base. To remove a tight cord, cut the wire about 12 inches from the

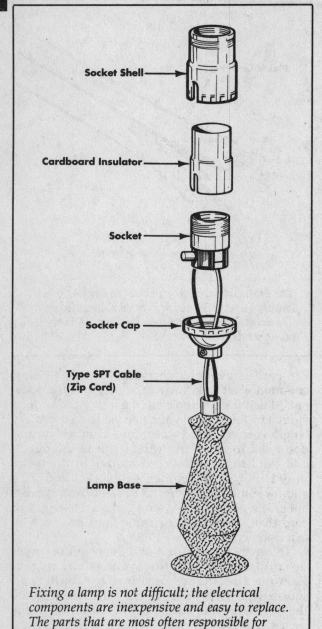

Socket Shell

Cardboard Insulator

Socket

Socket Cap

Type SPT Cable
(Zip Cord)

Lamp Base

Fixing a lamp is not difficult; the electrical components are inexpensive and easy to replace. The parts that are most often responsible for lamp failure are the socket, the cord, and the plug.

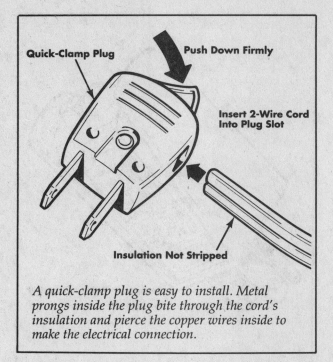

Quick-Clamp Plug

Push Down Firmly

Insert 2-Wire Cord Into Plug Slot

Insulation Not Stripped

A quick-clamp plug is easy to install. Metal prongs inside the plug bite through the cord's insulation and pierce the copper wires inside to make the electrical connection.

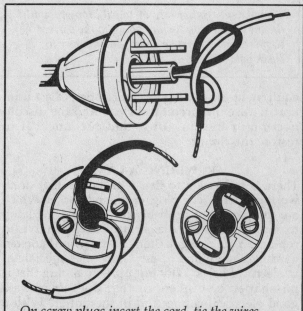

On screw plugs insert the cord, tie the wires into a knot, and pull the knot down into the plug. Then loop each wire around a prong before tightening the bare end under the screw head. This helps keep the wires from touching each other accidentally and provides some resistance to stress.

lamp's base, slit the cord's two conductors apart, and strip about 1 inch of insulation off the ends; do the same to one end of the new length of cord. Twist the bare new and old conductor ends together and fold the twists flat along the cord; wrap plastic electrician's tape around the splice in as small a lump as you can, with the wrapping smooth and tapered so that it won't catch on anything. Pull on the old cord from the top of the fixture and work the new cord through; push on the new cord from the bottom to aid the process. When you have a sufficient length of new cord through the top, clip off the old cord. Once you pass the new cord through the lamp, split the end so that you have about 3 inches of separated con-

ductors. Strip about 3/4 inch of insulation from the end of each conductor and twist the strands of each together. Use a wire stripper with the correct size of cutting slots; this tool is designed to remove insulation without damaging the wire.

Bend the twisted end of each wire into a clockwise loop, and place each loop under a terminal screw on the socket with the loop curled clockwise around the screw. Then tighten the screws. As each screw is tightened, the clockwise loop will pull the wire tighter under the screw head; a counterclockwise loop would tend to loosen the wire. When both screw heads are tightened over the bare conductor ends, clip off any excess bare wire with your diagonal cutters. It is important that all the uninsulated wire is under the screw heads, with no loose strands or exposed bare wire. If the bare wire is visible beyond the screw heads, unscrew the terminals, remove the wires, and make the connection again.

Now slide the socket shell over the cardboard insulator, and slip shell and insulator over the socket. Then snap the shell and socket into the cap. A new cord also requires a new plug. A quick-clamp plug is the easiest kind to connect. Stick the end of the cord into a slot on the side of the plug, and push down on the lever at the top. Metal prongs inside the plug will bite through the cord's insulation, piercing the copper wires to make the electrical connection.

If you use a screw plug, you must prepare the wire ends just as you did when making the socket screw connections, then knot them together. Loop each wire around a prong of the plug before tightening the bare end under the screw head. The knots and loops keep the wires apart and make it more difficult to loosen the connections by pulling on the cord. You should never disconnect a lamp or any other electrical device by yanking the cord out of the wall socket, but the knot will give some strain support if the cord is jerked. Tighten the wires under the screw heads, and clip off any excess uninsulated conductor before you plug in the lamp.

REPLACING INCANDESCENT LIGHTING FIXTURES

As far as the electrical work is concerned, replacing a lighting fixture is simple. You can even put in fluorescent lighting where you now have incandescent fixtures without encountering any great problems. **Caution:** *Before you replace or repair any lighting fixture, you must de-energize the appropriate electrical circuit. Even in a house that is properly wired (with switching done in the hot wire), turning off the wall switch may not de-energize the fixture. So always de-energize the entire circuit by pulling the appropriate fuse or tripping the proper circuit breaker.*

With the circuit de-energized and an alternate light source in position, take off the globe, unscrew the bulb(s), and disassemble the mounting hardware. Screws usually hold the fixture against the wall or ceiling, but you may discover no visible mounting hardware at all. If you don't see any screws or bolts, look for a decorative feature that could double as a fastener. Take off the mounting hardware and withdraw the fixture from the electrical box.

Disconnect the lamp fixture wires from the circuit wires. You may find that the wire joint is fused with old insulating tape that defies easy removal, and it is simpler to cut the wires close to the tape. **Caution:** *If the wire insulation or the conductors coming into the electrical box are brittle or frayed, that part of the circuit or switch loop should be professionally rewired.*

Once you remove the old fixture, examine the electrical box and the new fixture to decide which of the following installation procedures you should use.

Standard Electrical Box. Make sure you have about 3/4 inch of bare copper conductor on the end of each line wire before you start to connect the wires of your new lighting fixture. If necessary, remove enough insulation from the line wires so that you can twist each line wire's end with the end of each light fixture wire, white wire to white and black to black. Screw a wire nut over each pair of twisted ends. Hold onto the fixture to support its weight until you attach the mounting screws; otherwise, you might break a connection or damage the fixture wires.

If the fixture has more than one socket, connect the black wire from each socket to the black line wire, and the white wire from each socket to the white line wire. Three or four socket wires joined to a line wire require a large wire nut.

Now mount the fixture. Mounting screws of the proper length will be included with your new

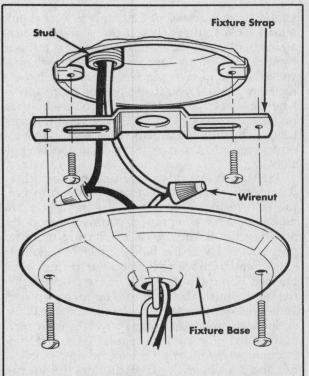

The simplest fixture installation uses a fixture strap secured to the electrical box; connect white wire to white and black to black.

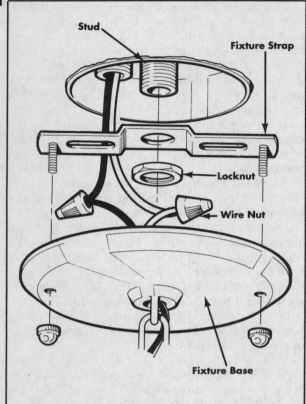

When the electrical box has no threaded ears, the fixture strap can be secured to the stud with a threaded locknut.

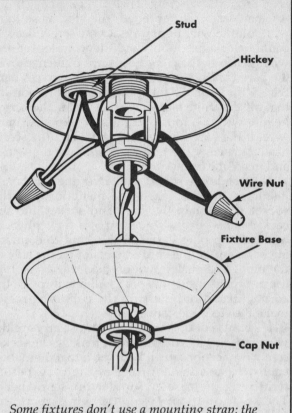

Some fixtures don't use a mounting strap; the fixture is secured to the stud with a hickey, or reducing nut.

lamp fixture; screws 2 or 2 1/2 inches long should attach most fixtures. Insert the screws into the attachment screw holes in the electrical box and tighten each screw four or five turns, which is enough to hold it in place. Examine the base of the new fixture; you'll see two or more sets of keyhole-shaped slots. Mount the fixture by passing the fixture's keyhole slots over the screw heads. Then rotate the fixture enough so that the screws go into the narrow parts of the keyhole slots.

Tighten the screws, but don't overtighten them; they should be just snug enough to hold the fixture firmly in place. If you tighten the mounting screws too much, you may distort and misalign the fixture. With the fixture mounted properly, screw in the bulbs, attach the globe or cover, and replace the fuse or trip the circuit breaker. Flip the wall switch. If the fixture lights, the job is finished. If nothing happens, go back and figure out which connection needs remaking.

Some fixtures are mounted with a short piece of threaded pipe, called a nipple. To mount these fixtures, screw the nipple into the center hole of the strap and set the fixture onto the nipple. Screw a cap nut onto the nipple to hold the fixture in place.

Electrical Box With No Threaded Ears. The electrical connections in a box with no threaded

ears are similar to those in the standard electrical box. The only difference is in mounting the new fixture. After you remove the old fixture, fasten a fixture strap to the threaded stud inside the electrical box using a locknut that fits the stud threads. Manufacturers often package a strap with the fixture, but if you have to buy one, make sure the screw holes are spaced so that they match the new fixture's mounting holes. Insert the screws into the threaded holes at the outer ends of the fixture strap, and tighten them two or three turns.

Connect the circuit line wires to the fixture wires, mount the fixture in place, and tighten the mounting screws. Before you tighten the screws completely, make sure all the wires and solderless connectors are tucked inside the fixture and the electrical box. They should never be squeezed between the fixture strap and the fixture. Screw in the bulb(s), attach the globe or cover, and replace the fuse or trip the circuit breaker.

Box With No Mounting Strap. Some light fixtures are not strap mounted. A nipple is connected to the box stud with a reducing nut, which is a nut threaded at one end to fit the stud and at the other end to fit the nipple, or an adapter called a hickey. To mount a fixture that uses a reducing nut, screw the nut onto the stud and the nipple onto the nut, set the fixture onto the nipple, set

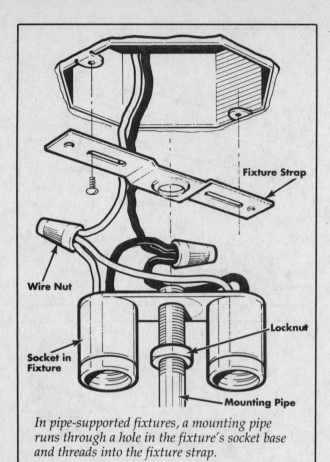

In pipe-supported fixtures, a mounting pipe runs through a hole in the fixture's socket base and threads into the fixture strap.

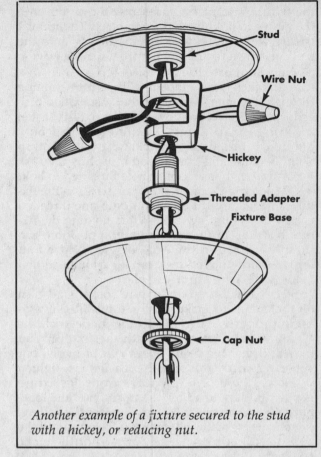

Another example of a fixture secured to the stud with a hickey, or reducing nut.

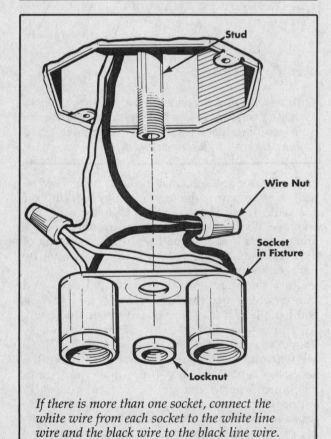

If there is more than one socket, connect the white wire from each socket to the white line wire and the black wire to the black line wire.

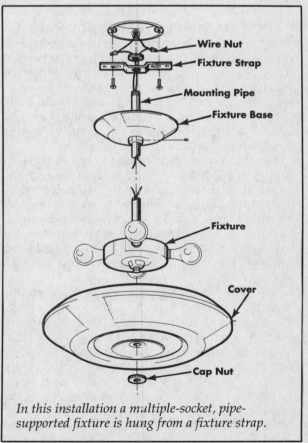

In this installation a multiple-socket, pipe-supported fixture is hung from a fixture strap.

217

the fixture into place, and screw a cap nut onto the nipple to hold the fixture in place. To mount a fixture with a hickey, screw the hickey onto the stud, and then mount the fixture the same way.

Pipe-Supported Fixtures. A replacement fixture that includes a globe held by a pipe running through its center demands other installation procedures. After you remove the old fixture, fasten a fixture strap firmly to the electrical box. Manufacturers usually package a fixture strap with the new lamp, but if you must buy one, ask for a strap that has a center hole threaded to hold a 1/2-inch pipe. Connect the line wires to the fixture wires, and turn a locknut onto one threaded end of the mounting pipe. While holding the fixture body up in its final mounting position, run the pipe through the hole in the fixture and thread it into the fixture strap far enough so that it holds the fixture firmly in place.

Screw a bulb into the fixture socket, and turn on the circuit to make sure you installed everything properly. Then attach the globe with the threaded cap that comes with the fixture. You may find that the globe doesn't fit properly, but you can remedy this situation easily; just tighten or loosen the pipe a few turns from the fixture hanger. Be sure to adjust the position of the locknut to keep the fixture secure against the ceiling. Keep working with the pipe and locknut until the right length of pipe hangs down to fit the globe and its mounting knob.

INSTALLING FLUORESCENT LAMPS

Consider replacing some of your old incandescent fixtures with fluorescent lamps. Fluorescent lamps provide even and shadow-free illumination. They also produce more light, watt for watt, than incandescent bulbs. In an incandescent bulb, much of the electric power is discharged as heat instead of light; the fluorescent bulb remains cooler, which saves electricity.

In a fluorescent circuit, beginning at the left-hand prong of the plug, current goes through the ballast, then through one of the lamp filaments, through the closed switch in the starter, through the other filament in the lamp, and out the right-hand prong of the plug. The current heats the two small elements in the ends of the fluorescent tube; the starter then opens and current flows through the lamp.

The ballast is a magnetic coil that adjusts the current through the tube. It makes a surge of current arc through the tube when the starter opens, and then keeps the current flowing at the right rate once the tube is glowing. In most fluorescent fixtures, the starter is an automatic switch. Once it senses that the lamp is glowing, it stays open. The starter closes whenever you de-energize the fixture.

Many fluorescent fixtures have more than one tube to provide more light. These lamps must

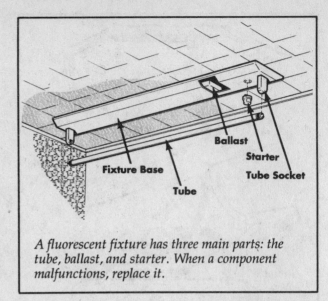

A fluorescent fixture has three main parts: the tube, ballast, and starter. When a component malfunctions, replace it.

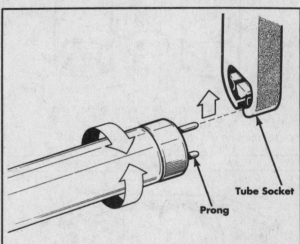

To install a new fluorescent tube, insert the tube's prongs into the holder and twist the tube to lock it into place. Change the tube when it dims, flickers, or flashes on and off.

have a starter and a ballast for each tube. The fixture may appear to have two tubes working off one ballast, but there are two ballasts built into one case. Fixtures with four tubes, similarly, have four starters and four ballasts. In some kinds of fixtures, the starters are built in and cannot be replaced individually.

Since there are only three principal parts in a fluorescent lamp, the tube, starter, and ballast, you usually can take care of any repairs yourself. All fluorescent lamps grow dimmer with age. They also may flicker or flash on and off. These are warning signals, and you should make the necessary repairs when you notice any change in the lamp's performance. A dim tube usually requires replacement, and failure to replace it can strain other parts of the fixture. Repeated flickering or flashing will wear out the starter, causing the insulation at the starter to deteriorate.

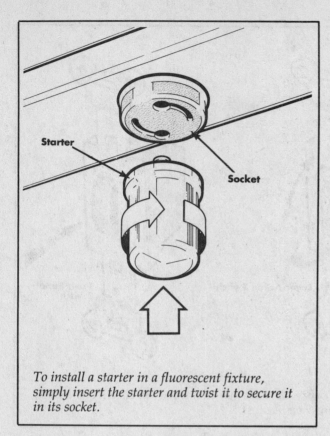

To install a starter in a fluorescent fixture, simply insert the starter and twist it to secure it in its socket.

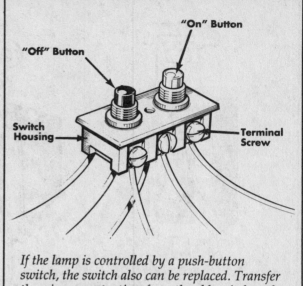

If the lamp is controlled by a push-button switch, the switch also can be replaced. Transfer the wires one at a time from the old switch to the new one.

Fluorescent fixtures can be serviced by the replacement method. If you suspect that a part may be defective, install a new part. Start with the fluorescent tube or bulb. You can either install a new one or, if you're not sure the tube is burned out, test the old tube in another fluorescent fixture. Doing both gives you double verification. Remove the old tube by twisting it out of its sockets in the fixture. Install the new tube the same way; insert the tube's prongs into the socket and twist the tube to lock it into place.

Caution: *Discard old fluorescent tubes properly. Call you local garbage-collection agency to find out the correct method of disposal.*

If the problem is not in the tube, change the starter, if possible. Fluorescent lamp starters are rated according to wattage, and you must use the right starter for the tube in your fixture. Remove the old starter by twisting it out of its socket in the fixture. Install the new one by inserting it into the socket and twisting it to lock it into place.

The ballast is also rated according to wattage, and a replacement ballast must match the wattage of the tube and the fixture. The ballast is the least likely part to fail, and it is the most difficult to replace, so leave the ballast for last when you start replacing parts. If neither the tube nor the starter is defective, the problem must be the ballast. To replace a faulty ballast, you must de-energize the circuit, disassemble the fixture, transfer wires from the old ballast to the new ballast, one at a time to avoid an incorrect connection, and then reassemble the fixture.

If the tube, the starter, and the ballast are all working properly, and the lamp still doesn't light, the only other possibility (if the lamp is receiving power) is a defective switch. If the lamp is controlled by a wall switch, replace the switch. If the lamp has a push-button switch, the old switch can be replaced by a new one of the same kind. You must de-energize the circuit before working on the switch; remove the circuit's fuse or trip the circuit breaker.

The switch usually screws into a threaded mounting nut on the inside of the lamp. Two wires from the switch are connected to four wires from the fluorescent tube. Disassemble the fixture as far as necessary to get to the back of the switch and unscrew the old switch. Then screw in the new switch and transfer wires from the old switch to the new switch, one at a time to avoid an incorrect connection. Then reassemble the fixture and re-energize the circuit.

If you're installing a new ballast or switch, think about putting in a new fixture. An old fluorescent fixture suffers the same aging effects that an outmoded incandescent fixture does. You also can replace an old incandescent lamp with a new fluorescent model. Either replacement is well within the capabilities of a do-it-yourselfer.

Caution: *Before you install a fixture, be sure to de-energize the old fixture. Simply turning off the wall switch may not de-energize the fixture. So be sure to remove the circuit's fuse or trip the circuit breaker.*

Remove the old hardware that holds the existing lamp fixture in place, and disconnect the lamp wires from the circuit line wires. Then disassemble the new fluorescent lamp to get to the fixture wires, and connect the fixture wires to the line wires with wire nuts or crimping solderless

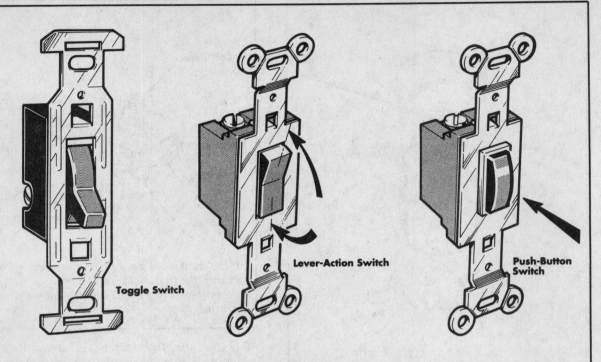

Toggle Switch

Lever-Action Switch

Push-Button Switch

There are different kinds of switches available, but all work on the same general principles. Usually, you can base your selection of a replacement switch on the features you like best.

connectors. Match the wires by color: white wire to white, black to black. Position the fixture against the ceiling, and fasten it with the screws that are packaged with the new lamp. You may have to reassemble the fixture, either before or after mounting it; this depends on its design. Once you get the lamp back together, restore the power and turn on your new fluorescent lighting fixture.

REPLACING A WALL SWITCH

Sometimes a lamp that is in perfect operating condition doesn't work because the wall switch is faulty. There are four primary symptoms of switch failure:

•When the switch loses its snap, when the handle hangs loosely in any position, or when there is no clear distinction between the "off" and "on" positions.

•When flipping the switch no longer turns the light on or off.

•When flipping the switch makes the light flicker, but doesn't make it stay on or off.

•When the switch may work occasionally, but you have to jiggle the handle back and forth several times to keep the light on.

If you spot any of these symptoms of switch failure, install a replacement wall switch as soon as you can. **Caution:** *First de-energize the electrical circuit that powers the switch.*

After de-energizing the circuit, remove the switch cover plate. If the cover plate doesn't come off easily, it is probably being held in place by several layers of paint. Use a razor blade or a craft or utility knife to cut the paint closely around the edge of the plate to free it. Then inspect the old switch to learn the replacement model you must buy; you must use the same kind, but you usually can install a better grade of switch than the one you had before. All switches work on the same principles, and you can usually choose a switch to get the features you like best.

The traditional single-pole toggle switch is the most popular. When the toggle switch is mounted properly, the words "on" and "off" are upright on the toggle lever, and the light goes on when you flip up the switch. You also can buy a silent toggle switch. A variation of the traditional toggle switch is the lever-action switch. The lever-action switch is designed to lie almost flush with the wall. It turns the fixture on when someone pushes in the top of the switch. The push-button switch has a single button that turns the light on when pressed, and off when it's pressed again. Some switches have a built-in neon lamp that glows when the switch is off, making it easy to locate the switch in the dark.

Dimmer switches, which have a dial to control the brightness of the light, turn the light off when the dial is turned all the way down or pushed in. Some dimmer switches look like toggle switches. Sliding the toggle upward increases the light's intensity; sliding it all the way down turns off the light.

Some kinds of wall switches have no terminal screws for conductor attachments. These switches

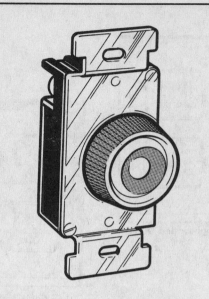

Dimmer switches have a dial that controls the brightness of the light, from bright to off. A dimmer can be used to replace almost any existing switch.

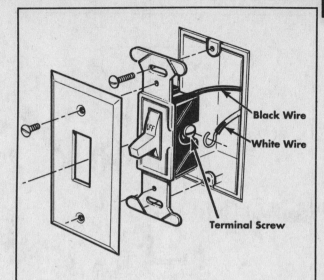

If a switch has only two terminal screws with wires attached, it's a single-pole switch. This switch is easy to install; connect the line wires to the screws, secure the switch, and replace the cover plate.

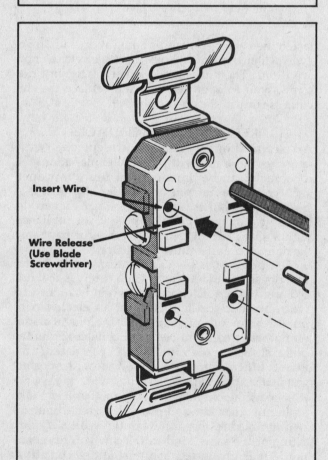

Some switches and receptacles do not have terminal screws; they have holes into which the stripped wire ends are inserted. Others like this one have both holes and terminal screws.

have small holes that are larger than the bare copper conductors. After removing about 1/2 inch of insulation from the ends of the wires, you push the bare ends into the holes. Locking tabs make the electrical connection and grip the wires so that they can't pull out. To release the wires from the switch, you have to insert a narrow-blade screwdriver in the slots next to the wire-grip holes.

After you buy the replacement switch you want to install and turn off the electric current to the old switch, remove the mounting screws on the switch cover plate and take off the plate. With the plate removed, you'll see two screws holding the switch in the switch box. Remove the screws and carefully pull the switch out of the box as far as the attached wires allow. If there are two screws with wires attached, the switch is a single-pole type. If there are three screws with wires attached, you're working with a more complicated three-way switch. The new switch must be the same kind as the old one.

Three-way switches allow you to turn a light on and off from two different locations, such as at the top and the bottom of a stairway. Look carefully at the three terminal screws; you'll see that two are one color, while the third is a different color. Do not disconnect any wires until you compare the old switch with the replacement switch to make sure you know which wire goes to which terminal screw.

Loosen one of the old terminal screws, remove the wire, and attach the wire to the corresponding terminal screw on the new switch. Then do the same with the remaining wires. Take care to con-

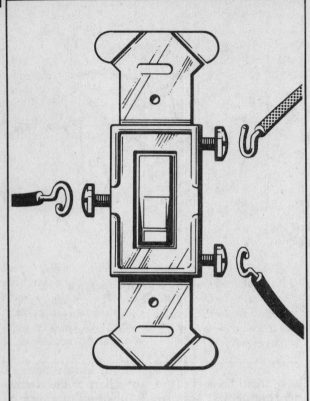

Three-way switches allow you to turn a light on and off from two different locations, such as at the top or at the bottom of a stairway.

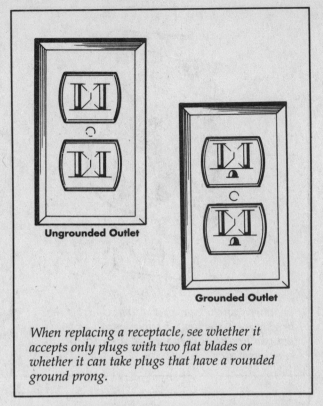

Ungrounded Outlet

Grounded Outlet

When replacing a receptacle, see whether it accepts only plugs with two flat blades or whether it can take plugs that have a rounded ground prong.

nect the wires so that all the bare wire is safely under the screw heads, and clip off any excess uninsulated wire. The procedure is the same whether you're working with a single-pole or three-way switch, but you must be more careful with the three-way switch. Verify your wiring by comparing it with the diagram on the package of the new switch.

If you're installing a wire-grip wall switch, cut off the end of each wire to leave only 1/2 inch of bare wire. Push one bare end of wire into each wire-grip hole, and check that the wires have caught properly by tugging gently on them. **Caution:** *If the wire insulation or the conductors coming into the switch box are brittle or frayed, that part of the circuit or switch loop should be professionally rewired.*

Now replace the switch in the electrical box and install the cover plate. Push the switch into the box carefully, and make sure the wires fit neatly into the box behind the switch. There are small tabs extending from the switch's mounting bracket; these tabs are supposed to lie flat against the wall outside the electrical box. They hold the switch flush with the wall no matter how much the electrical box is angled inside.

Put the switch back into place, using the two mounting screws provided with the new switch. Oval holes in the mounting bracket allow you to

fasten the switch so that it's straight up and down even when the screw holes in the electrical box are tilted. Then attach the cover plate with the screws you took out earlier, and replace the circuit fuse or trip the circuit breaker.

REPLACING A RECEPTACLE

An electrical outlet is called a receptacle. When one fails there are two possible explanations: A receptacle can be damaged through improper use. Sticking a hairpin or a paper clip in it is a sure way to shorten an outlet's life. You can do the same damage when you plug in an appliance with a short circuit. No matter how it happens, the damaged outlet must be replaced.

The other possible explanation for an outlet that doesn't work efficiently and safely is that it is old and worn out. There are two indications of a worn-out outlet: the weight of an electric cord pulls a plug out of the outlet or the plug's blades do not make constant electrical contact within the outlet slots. The old outlet must be replaced. This is not difficult, but you must follow the correct installation procedures.

Inspect the old outlet to see whether it can take a plug that has a round prong for grounding and two flat blades. Buy a new outlet with a 20-amp rating of the same kind as the one you're replacing, either grounded or ungrounded. **Caution:** *Before working on the outlet, de-energize the circuit that powers it.*

After de-energizing the circuit, take off the plate that covers the outlet. This should be an easy task; the cover plate should fall off when

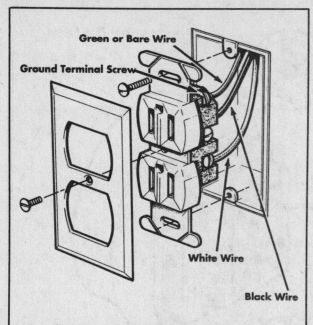

Green or Bare Wire

Ground Terminal Screw

White Wire

Black Wire

A replacement receptacle must match the one you are removing. If you have the grounded type, you must buy a receptacle that has a ground terminal screw and slots for three-prong grounded plugs.

you remove the center screw. If it doesn't, it's probably being held in place by several coats of paint. Cut the paint closely around the edge of the cover plate with a razor blade or a craft or utility knife.

Remove the two screws holding the outlet in the electrical box and carefully pull the outlet out of the box as far as the attached line wires allow. Loosen the terminal screws on the outlet and remove the line wires. **Caution:** *If you find that the wiring is old and that the insulation is brittle, that part of the circuit should be professionally rewired.*

Connect the wires to the new outlet, with the white wire under the silver-colored screw and the black wire under the dark-colored screw. If there is a green or bare wire in the box, fasten it under the screw with the dab of green color on it, and then fasten it to the box with a grounding screw or clip. Be sure to loop the line wires in a clockwise direction under the heads of the terminal screws so that the screw heads will pull the wire loops tighter. Take care to connect the wires so that all the wire without insulation is safely under the screw heads. Clip off any excess uninsulated wire.

Carefully fold the wires into the space in the electrical box behind the outlet, and then push the outlet into the box. Although there is no right-side up for a two-blade outlet, there is a correct position for outlets designed to handle three-prong grounding plugs. Grounding plugs often attach to their cords at a right angle; you should

position the outlet so that the cord will hang down without a loop.

You'll also notice that the slots in an outlet are not identical; one is wider than the other. The wider one connects to the white or neutral wire, while the narrower slot connects to the black or hot wire. Some plugs are designed with one wide and one narrow blade, and these plugs will fit into the outlet in only one way. These polarized plugs continue the hot and neutral wire identity from the circuit to the appliance.

Tighten the two screws that hold the receptacle in the outlet box, replace the cover plate, and your work is done. Restore the fuse or trip the circuit breaker.

REPAIRING A DOORBELL

Many people believe that only professional electricians can repair broken doorbells, and they put up a sign to tell friends and neighbors that the doorbell doesn't work, then settle down to wait until the electrician has to be called in for another pressing task, when the doorbell finally gets fixed. There is no reason you should not repair a broken doorbell.

When your doorbell or door chime doesn't ring, the fault could be in any part of the circuitry, from the push button to the bell or chime to the transformer. The transformer is the electrical component that steps down the 110-120-volt current to the approximate 10 to 18 volts at which doorbells and chimes operate. You can work safely on all parts of the doorbell circuit, except the transformer, without disconnecting the power.

If you don't know what part of the circuit is faulty, start by removing the screws that attach the doorbell push button to your house. Pull the button as far out as the circuit wires allow, and then detach the wires by loosening the terminal screws on the button. Now bring the two bare wire ends together. If the bell rings, you know the fault is in the button. Install a new one by connecting the two wires to the terminal screws of the new button and reattaching the button to your house. The doorbell button is a single-pole switch (two wires attached), and you can place either wire under either screw.

If the bell doesn't ring when you bring the two bare wire ends together, the problem is in the bell or chime assembly, the wiring, or the transformer. Go to the bell or chime and remove the snap-on cover. Removal may be harder than you expect; there are several different kinds of covers, and you may have to try several procedures. Try lifting the cover upward and then pulling it out. If this doesn't work, pull it straight out without first lifting it up. If the snap-on cover is held to the bell or chime assembly with prongs, depress the prongs and then pull the cover to release it. Never pull so hard that you risk damaging the decorative cover.

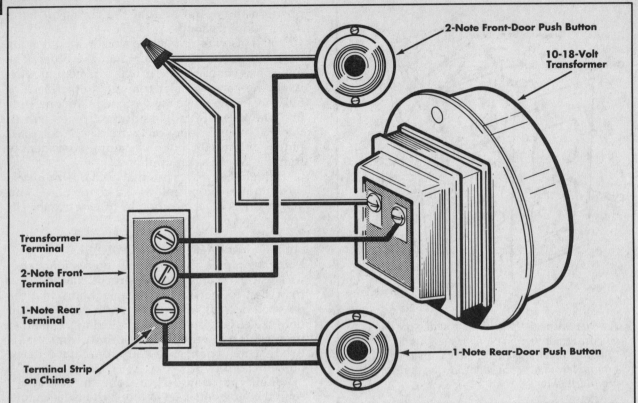

2-Note Front-Door Push Button

10-18-Volt Transformer

Transformer Terminal

2-Note Front Terminal

1-Note Rear Terminal

Terminal Strip on Chimes

1-Note Rear-Door Push Button

If your doorbell or chime doesn't work, the fault could be in any part of the circuitry, from a push button to the bell or chimes, or to the transformer. Before removing any wires at the terminal strip, it's a good idea to tag them so that they can be replaced correctly.

When you remove the cover, you will see two, three, or more terminals and wires, depending on how many tones ring in your doorbell system. A standard bell or buzzer has two wires. Detach the wires by loosening the terminal screws, and connect them to a 12-volt circuit tester or attach them to the terminal screws on a substitute bell or chime. An inexpensive bell or buzzer or a 12-volt car lamp bulb in a socket with two wires can be used for testing purposes. If the test bell or buzzer sounds or the bulb lights when you push the doorbell button, you must install a new bell or chime.

If you have a chime assembly with three or more wires, tag them with masking tape: "T" for transformer, "2" for the front-door chime, and "1" for the back-door chime. Loosen the terminal screws, remove all the wires, and connect the wires labeled "T" and "2" to the screw terminals on the test bell or bulb. If the test bell rings or the bulb lights when you push the front-door button, your old chime set is faulty. To check this conclusion, connect the wires labeled "T" and "1" to the screw terminals on the test bell. If the bell rings when you push the back-door button, then you're doubly certain that the chimes must be replaced.

If the bell doesn't ring or the bulb doesn't light at the button or at the bell or chime box, the problem must be in the transformer or the wiring.

You'll usually find the transformer mounted on an electrical junction box, a subpanel, or the main entrance panel. The transformer connections to the power lines usually are hidden from view within the box. The bell wires are attached to exposed terminal screws on the transformer. Connect the test bell directly to the exposed low-voltage transformer terminals; don't touch any other screws. If the bell doesn't ring, you can be sure that the transformer is defective or not getting power.

Caution: *Unlike the other parts of the circuit, the transformer is connected directly to the power supply and carries current that can hurt you. Before working on the transformer, you must de-energize the branch circuit that supplies power to the transformer. Remove the appropriate fuse or trip the correct circuit breaker. If you don't know what circuit controls the doorbell, throw the main switch to shut off all the electricity in your home.*

Before replacing the transformer, make sure that it's getting power from the 110-120-volt circuit. With the circuit de-energized, disconnect the transformer from the line wires. One easy way to make a line circuit test is to attach a spare screw terminal lamp socket, fitted with a 110-120-volt bulb, to the line wires. If the terminals are exposed, wrap a piece of electrical tape around

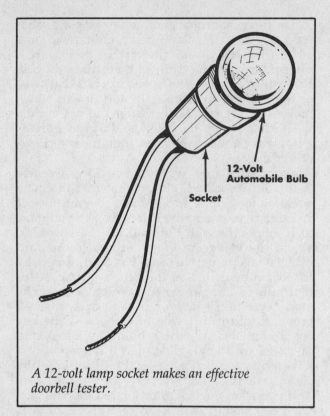

A 12-volt lamp socket makes an effective doorbell tester.

the socket to cover them. You also can use an old lamp; remove the plug and connect the lamp wires to the line wires with wire nuts. Then turn the circuit back on again. If the lamp lights, the circuit is fine; the transformer is faulty and must be replaced.

An easier method of testing is to separate the two line wires so that they cannot touch each other or any part of the electrical box. Turn the circuit back on, and gently touch the probes of a 110-120-volt circuit tester to the bare wire ends. If you get a positive indication from the tester (tester light glows or indicator reads 110-120 volts), the circuit is all right. **Caution:** *Always keep in mind that you're working with hot wires; don't touch them.*

If the transformer is defective, de-energize the circuit and remove the transformer. Buy a replacement transformer of the same voltage and wattage (or VA, volts-amps). You can find the electrical information stamped on the transformer, and you should find installation instructions on the package. Follow the instructions carefully. Use crimp-on connectors or wire nuts to attach the new transformer to the circuit line wires of your electrical system. Then connect the bell wires to the low-voltage screw terminals on the transformer, turn the power back on, and press the doorbell button. If you've installed the transformer properly, you should hear the bell or chime.

If the transformer and its power circuit prove to be all right, the only possibility left is a break or a loose connection somewhere in the bell wiring. Since a loose connection is more likely, trace the entire bell circuit from transformer to bell or chime to push buttons, and search for a loose terminal screw or wire joint. If this proves unsuccessful, you'll have to check each segment of the circuit with a continuity tester.

Disconnect the bell wires at the transformer to de-energize the bell circuit. Then disconnect the transformer wires at the bell or chime, and twist them together just enough so that they make good contact with one another. Go back to the transformer, and touch the probe leads of the continuity tester to the bare ends of the bell wires. If the tester lights up, or you get a reading on the meter dial, the circuit has continuity and there are no breaks or loose connections in the line; that part of the circuit is all right. If the tester does not register, there is a break somewhere.

If there is a break, you must try to locate it and make repairs. Where much of the bell circuit wiring is hidden within walls or is otherwise inaccessible, the easiest course is to run a new segment of bell wire.

If that particular segment of the bell circuit proves to be free of faults, go on to the next segment and check it the same way. Make sure both ends of the segment are disconnected; twist the two wires together at one end of the line and touch the tester leads to the two separated wire ends at the other end of the line. Continue this process with each segment or leg of the circuit, and eventually you'll locate the break. Once repairs are made or new wire is run, the bell or chime system will be operational.

Special Installations

You can enjoy the protection of an intrusion and fire alarm system by purchasing a kit and following these instructions. The same is true for other special wiring situations, including home intercoms and garage door openers. You can even wire your entire home to carry the sound of your stereo system to rooms far from the system itself.

INSTALLING A HOME SECURITY SYSTEM
Although there are many kinds of home security systems on the market, homeowners prefer a system that turns on a loud bell whenever an intruder breaks open a door or a window. Similar to burglar alarms used in stores and offices, this system is sold in kit form, and can be purchased at many hardware stores. You should find the system easy to install, and there can be little doubt that you will be pleased with the protection it affords.

Installation involves mounting the bell in a location where it can be easily heard, attaching a circuit of magnet-operated switches to the bell, and connecting a battery to the system. Since the bell operates from the battery, it remains an effective alarm system even if there is a power failure.

This alarm system is called a closed-circuit system. When the doors and windows are shut, the attached switches are closed. Because all the switches are in a wiring loop, opening any one of them breaks the loop and triggers the bell-ringing circuit. Reclosing the door or window does not restore the switch loop circuit continuity and does not stop the ring until either the battery becomes exhausted or someone switches off the circuit from battery to bell.

Built into the bell is an electronic switch that is turned on by breaking the magnetic-switch loop. A key-operated switch in the battery-and-bell circuit allows you to turn the alarm system completely off when it is not needed, and once the alarm goes on, operating the key switch is the only way to silence the bell. Only someone who has a key to the switch can reset the system.

The magnet-operated switch device consists of two parts that look much alike: one small plastic box contains a strong magnet; the other contains the actual switch. When magnet and switch are not near each other, the switch contacts are separated and the switch is open. When the magnet and switch are near each other, the switch contacts move together and the switch closes. The magnet part of the device is screwed to a door or window, and the switch part is screwed to the door or window frame. Opening a door or window separates magnet from switch, causing the switch to open and trigger the alarm.

The three electronic parts comprising the solid-state switch of the alarm bell are mounted on a circuit board. Under the circuit board are a solenoid coil and the plunger that strikes the bell. Below the coil is a set of breaker points that causes the plunger to vibrate up and down, which makes the bell ring. If the system did not include the breaker points, the bell would merely provide a single gong when operated from the direct current of battery.

Begin installation with the bell. Decide where you want it located, either to attract the most attention for help or to scare away an intruder. If you decide to mount the bell outdoors, you must drill a hole through the wall for the wires. To shield the bell from the weather, you should install it in a protective metal box made especially for alarm bells. Inside the box is a bracket for mounting a tamper switch, which sets off the alarm system if someone tries to open the bell box. Located in the side of the box is the key switch (an electric switch built like a lock and operated by a key), which lets a person with a key activate, service, reset, or deactivate the alarm system.

If you want the bell to be located indoors, you need not install it in a protective metal box. Mount the bell on the wall in a place where it can be heard easily. Locating an indoor bell in a closet or other confined space is not recommended.

In the kit you should find a mounting back plate attached to the bell by a mounting screw. Remove the nut, and separate the back plate from

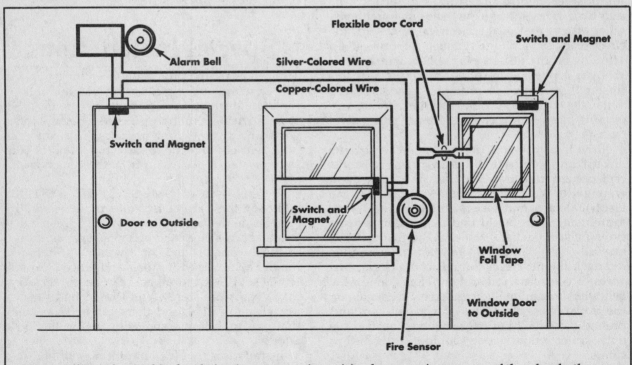

Because all switches in this closed-circuit system are in a wiring loop, opening any one of them breaks the loop and triggers the bell-ringing circuit.

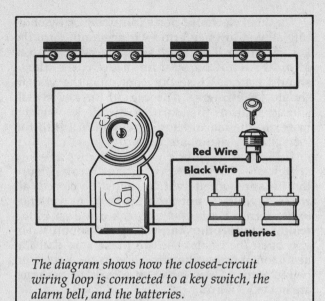

The diagram shows how the closed-circuit wiring loop is connected to a key switch, the alarm bell, and the batteries.

the bell. You will see a pattern of holes in the back plate. Using wood screws, toggle bolts, or other suitable fasteners, attach the plate to the wall at the place you have chosen to position the bell. Mount the back plate with enough fasteners to hold the bell solidly in place. Be sure that the plate is mounted right-side up and that the correct side is forward. There usually is a tongue on the back plate that should be at the top when it is mounted properly. Do not connect the bell to the back plate until later.

You will find that the protective box for an outdoor installation already contains a built-in back plate. Mount the box in the desired location.

Install the door and window switches. The magnet part goes on the door or window, while the switch part goes on the window frame or door jamb. Use the mounting screws in the kit to attach the parts. Try to position the two parts of the switch so that they are almost touching when the window or door is closed, and widely separated when the door or window just starts to open.

You can include fire sensor switches in the loop of entry-detection switches. Use the kind of fire sensor switch that breaks the loop when the air temperature in its vicinity reaches 135 degrees Fahrenheit. Since that is more than the air temperature is ever likely to reach except in attics, furnace rooms, or over wood, coal, or cooking stoves, you will never experience false alarms during hot weather. Install 190-degree-Fahrenheit sensors in normally hot locations. You should mount the fire sensor switches in the spots where you feel they will be most effective.

Consider using current-conducting window foil tape for additional security. Silver foil with a self-adhesive backing is probably available where you purchase your alarm system, and it is designed to trigger the alarm if an intruder

breaks the glass in a door or a window. Make sure there are no breaks in the foil that you stick on the glass; the tape must be continuous. Self-adhesive foil terminals or connectors at the ends of the foil tapes allow you to connect the loop circuit wiring, and a flexible door cord allows you to open a foil-taped door or window without setting off the alarm system.

After you have mounted the bell back plate and installed all the switches, fire sensors, and window foil, wire the system together. The wire for the entry-detection switch loop is a thin (nearly transparent) two-wire cord that is inconspicuous when you run up the corner of a wall, down a door frame, or alongside the baseboard. Route the wiring so it attracts the least attention.

Start at the point farthest away from the bell. Using a knife or wire stripper, bare about 3/4-inch of the wire ends. Loop each wire under a separate terminal screw on the switch or door cord. Without cutting the two-wire cord, route it to the next device, such as a magnet switch. Use small staples to keep the wire runs neat, but be careful not to damage the wire when you hammer in the staples. At the second device, use a knife to split apart the side-by-side conductors for a distance of a few inches. Cut apart just the copper-colored wire, not both. Bare about 3/4 inch of the copper wire ends and connect them to the switch's terminal screws.

Continue in this manner to the next switch, cutting apart only the copper-colored wire in the cord and attaching the bared ends of the cut wire under the terminal screws on the switch. One after the other, run the wire to all the entry-detection switches and fire sensors, finally running the two-wire cord to the bell back-plate location.

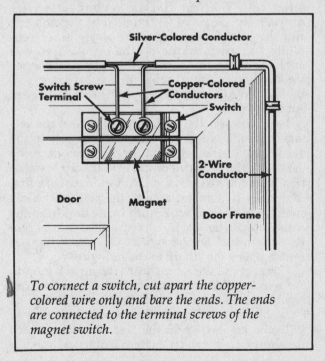

To connect a switch, cut apart the copper-colored wire only and bare the ends. The ends are connected to the terminal screws of the magnet switch.

If you need more than the spool of wire (usually 100 feet) that is included in security system kits, obtain another spool, and start the new length at the last switch reached by the first length of wire. Cut off what remains of the first length of wire at the switch, and bare the two conductors in both wires. Attach the copper-colored wires to the switch terminal screws. Twist together the two silver-colored wires, and affix a small solderless connector to them. Continue the run back to the bell with the new spool of wire, but do not connect the wire to the bell yet.

You have just finished wiring the intruder-entry sensor switch loop. If you did it properly, the circuit of the copper-colored wire will go to and through all the switches, and the silver-colored wire will return from the farthest end with no breaks or interruptions.

Now install the battery circuit. Obtain two 6-volt lantern batteries or a suitable rechargeable battery pack. Decide where you are going to locate the batteries; they can be hidden in a closet, a cabinet, or placed on a shelf you install for that purpose. The kit should contain lengths of single-conductor wire. One should be covered with red insulation and the other black. Use this wire for connecting the batteries to the bell.

In the battery-to-bell circuit, you must connect the positive (+) and negative (-) terminals of the battery to the bell to make the solid-state switches operate properly. Notice that the bell wire ends are also black and red. Such color coding helps you to wire the battery to the bell correctly. Run both a black and a red wire from the bell location to the battery location. Connect the red wire to the positive (+) terminal of one cell, and connect the black wire to the negative (-) terminal of the other cell. The last step is to connect a wire between the negative (-) terminal of the first cell and the positive (+) terminal of the other cell. While you are working on the installation, you might accidentally touch the black and red wires together. Since that discharges the batteries, you should leave the between-the-cells section of wire out until last.

Now connect the bell. Use solderless connectors to join the black wire from the battery to the black wire of the bell, and the red wire from the battery to the red wire of the bell. If your installation includes a key switch, run the red wire first to the key switch and then to the bell. At the key switch, cut the red wire, strip insulation from the ends, and fasten each cut end under a separate screw terminal on the switch. Operating the key switch opens the circuit in the red wire.

Connect the wire ends from the switch loop to the two smaller wires (wires that are neither red nor black) on the bell. Now fasten the bell to its back plate and tighten the attachment screw. With the key switch in the "off" position, attach the short wire between the two battery cells.

Close all the entry-detection switches by shutting all windows and doors in the loop. Turn the key switch on. The circuit should now be in operation. Prove it by opening a door; the alarm should sound. Close the door, and the system should keep ringing. Turning off the key switch should shut off the alarm. Turn the key switch back on; the alarm should remain off until the loop circuit is again interrupted.

If the alarm sounds when you turn the key switch on, check the loop circuit to make sure that it is intact: all switches must be closed; all wires have to be attached properly to switches under terminal screws; no break can exist in the window foil. If the alarm does not sound when you open the door, check to make sure that the key is on and that the wiring from the battery to bell is correct. Also make sure that the batteries are not exhausted.

Once you get the system into operation, set it off deliberately about once a month to make certain that the circuit is still in good condition and that the batteries still contain enough power to operate the system properly. Test the system only briefly; then turn it off and reset it.

You can leave the security system turned on in the sentry mode for a long time. Since the entry-detection switch circuit draws a standby current of only about one thousandth of an ampere, the batteries should last for months when used only to supply the entry-detection switch loop. Ringing the bell puts a heavy drain on the batteries. After a few hours of ringing the bell, the batteries become exhausted and the bell stops ringing. Know how much use your batteries can stand, and replace or recharge them before their energy is depleted.

When you combine this intruder alarm system with a timer that switches on lights and a radio, you have a home security system that compares favorably with more elaborate and expensive systems. You also have a security system that you can keep in good operating condition.

INSTALLING A HOME INTERCOM SYSTEM
A home intercommunication system can be more than an easy way to call members of the family to dinner or to summon someone for a phone call. An intercom that includes a radio provides music throughout the house. You also can enhance home security with a front-door speaker that allows you to talk with a visitor before opening the door. Installing the system requires carpentry and wiring.

An intercom system has one master station. It contains the electronic circuitry for the voice communications and, if it is a music system, the master station contains the radio, tape player, or CD player.

Intercom stations, at which you can only listen and reply, are called slave, remote, or substations.

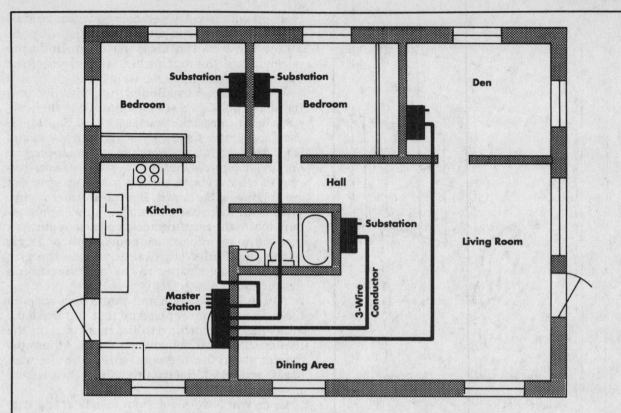

Begin the installation of the home intercom system by selecting the locations for the master station and substations. The master station often is located in the home's kitchen.

The typical substation contains a speaker, which doubles as a microphone during reply, and a switch to transfer from "listen" to "talk" modes of operation. A typical installation consists of a master station installed at a convenient location, several indoor substations, and an outdoor substation. The outdoor substation usually is at the front door and includes the button for the doorbell or chimes.

In some intercom sets, all operations are controlled by the master station: power "on/off," radio "on/off," and call station selection. You can only call one substation at a time or all at once from the master station, and only the single station you call can reply. Operating the push-to-talk button or lever, moreover, cuts off the sound of the radio for the duration of your conversation. More elaborate systems allow communication with or monitoring of any substation, call initiation from substation to substation or from substation to master station, or privacy at any substation without being monitored, plus music transmission to any or all substations.

All parts of the built-in system, even the master station, are sufficiently thin so that you can install them flush on a wall in holes cut into the wall space. The master station will usually fit in the space between wall studs. All wiring can be hidden; route it through the wall and alongside the under-floor joists. Suppose that you want to

install a one-master, four-substation system. Although such a system would be adequate only for a small home, the same principles can be applied easily in a larger building.

Begin the installation by selecting the location for the master station, and then inspect the master station box or enclosure to decide how large an opening you must cut for it. Usually the manufacturer provides a bracket or flange with mounting screw holes for installing the master station within the wall. After you measure the size and shape of the hole for the master station, locate the studs inside the wall. The hole you cut should be located between the studs. Select a convenient height above the floor; 5 feet is a good compromise for both short and tall persons. Pencil the shape of the master station hole on the wall. Drill 3/8-inch holes into the wall at the four corners of your penciled outline, then use a keyhole or saber saw to cut out the hole for the master station. Set the master station box in place to make sure that it fits the hole, and trim the edges of the hole if necessary. Then set the box aside until you finish installing the wiring.

Cut similar holes in the walls at each substation location. Try the holes for size, trim as necessary, and then set the substations aside until after you install their wiring, too.

Check your wiring diagram. In the usual master station-substation installation, only the master

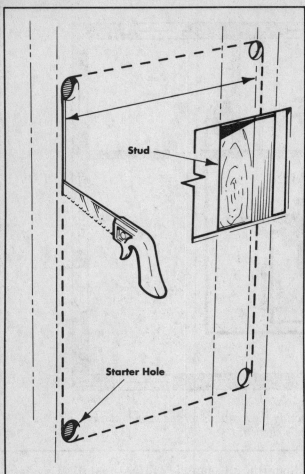

After drilling holes at each of the four corners of your penciled outline, use a keyhole or saber saw to cut out the opening for your master station.

Stud

Starter Hole

that you will find stamped alongside the terminal screws. Fasten the substation unit to the wall, and attach the trim molding that surrounds the perimeter of the unit to hide the edges of the opening that you cut in the wall.

With all the substation wiring installed and the substations themselves mounted in the wall, run line power to the master station. **Caution:** *If you have a master station that connects directly to your home's electrical system, be sure to de-energize the circuit involved and to take precautions to prevent someone else from turning it back on while you are working on the circuit.* If a transformer is supplied with the master station to power the system, locate the transformer on or near a junction box or the main entrance panel, and connect it to the electrical system (after you de-energize the circuit) according to the manufacturer's instructions.

Attach all substation and power-line wires to the master station, but be sure that you make the attachments according to the markings on the master station's terminal connections. Mount the master station in the wall, affix it to the wall studs, and attach the trim molding. Then restore power to the circuit.

Once you have the system installed, test it to see how well it performs. If any one of the substations fails to work, check the connections to its terminals and the connections to the master station. If you suspect a defective substation unit, interchange it with another. That should isolate the problem either to wiring defects or to a defective unit.

WIRING YOUR HOME FOR SOUND

If you would like to have music follow you throughout the house wherever you go, there is one speaker arrangement that is so simple that no special engineering is required. Here is the only problem: Many home sound systems have two speakers, one for each stereo channel. When you simply hook on additional speakers, you create an impedance mismatch, which not only degrades the tone quality but may damage the electronic parts of your sound system. It is the impedance mismatch that has fostered the blanket rule not to add more speakers to your system.

Look at the rear of your amplifier, and you probably will see two connections for the left channel and two for the right channel. One speaker is wired to the terminals for the left-channel output, and the other speaker is wired to the right-channel output. Each speaker is a combination of two or more speaker units: a large-diameter woofer for low sounds and a small-diameter tweeter for high sounds. The two units work together as a single wide-range speaker combination. Even in such units, all speaker leads connect back to the two-conductor cable between the speaker and the amplifier.

station connects to the household's electrical system. Multiwire cable links the substations to the master station. If such cable is not supplied with the kit you buy or if you need additional cable, you can purchase it separately from a radio-electronics parts supplier. Ask for intercom cable with the required number of conductors, preferably with a jacket covering the conductors.

Run a separate cable from each substation back to the master station. For a neat installation, run the wire from the substation inside the wall and through a small hole into the basement area. Then pass the wire through holes in the joists and alongside joists to a hole that leads up into the in-wall space below the master station. Since the cables from all the substations run to the master station, you need a large entry hole through the floor space in the wall below the master station. Maneuver each cable up to the master station opening, and label it according to its substation location.

At each substation location, connect the three wires to the terminals on the substation unit, following the wire color or other identification code

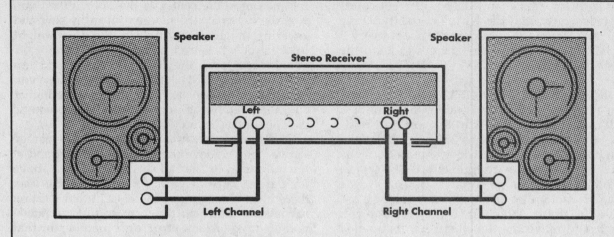

The typical home stereo system has two speakers, one for each stereo channel. Simply adding a speaker or two will result in impedance mismatch and degraded sound quality.

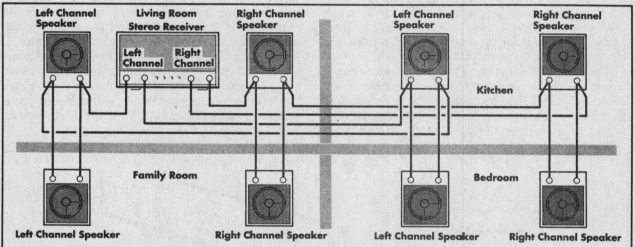

It is possible to obtain acceptable stereo sound throughout your home by adding three pairs of speakers to your present system, using series-parallel circuitry. The wiring arrangement is depicted here.

The watts and the ohms are imprinted on either the speaker or an attached label. The wattage rating tells you how much sound power (loudness) the speaker can handle without damage. If your amplifier can deliver 60 watts, your speakers must be able to handle that much power. Too much power to a speaker is called overdriving and results in distortion. Severe overdriving of a speaker can damage it. Even more important is the speaker ohms specification. Most systems are engineered for 8-ohm speakers. Connecting a second speaker to either channel results in unbalanced ohms or impedance mismatch, and the sound performance is degraded.

To connect four speakers to one channel in an unusual wiring arrangement, four 8-ohm speakers act like one 8-ohm speaker. There is some loss of sound quality, but your system will not be harmed. The arrangement is known as a series-parallel circuit, and with it you can install a pair of speakers in four different locations, or total of

eight speakers. Any combination of four locations will work, but it must be four and only four speakers on each channel, wired together for each channel and expanded to two channels.

Lamp cord, Type SPT, in number 16 gauge, is suitable for wiring the tuner-amplifier in your stereo to the extension speakers. Use lighter-gauge speaker cable only for runs of less than 25 feet. To keep the installation neat, route the extension wiring inside the walls or through the under-floor space. Unlike wiring for lights and receptacles, the speaker wire can run through small holes (5/16-inch diameter). Drill the floor hole near a corner where it will be inconspicuous, and run the wire to the hole along the baseboard. Dark-colored cord is recommended because you can run it along a dark-painted baseboard so that it is almost unnoticeable. If your baseboards are white, use white cord. If all your wiring will be hidden inside the walls or in the under-floor space though, then consider using a different color cord for each channel. The different colors will help you install the wiring correctly. Drive small staples into the baseboards about every 3 feet of the run and at the corners to keep the installation neat.

INSTALLING A GARAGE DOOR OPENER

Most garages have the kind of door that runs on a track that guides the door to an overhead position. Since a counterbalance or spring bears the main burden of raising the door, it usually can be raised and lowered with little effort. The typical garage door opener consists mainly of a reversible motor that drives a carriage along a rail above the door. Attached to the carriage is a drawbar to move the door between its opened and closed positions, with travel-limiting devices to stop the door's movement precisely at the fully opened and fully closed positions. A relay or reversing switch reverses the direction of drive from opening to closing and back again. Garage door openers have a radio receiver that allows you to open the door by sending a signal from an electronic module in your car.

The first step in installing the garage door opener is to decide the location for the mechanism. Use a folding rule or tape to measure the width of the garage door. Half this distance is the center of the door. Inside the door, toward the top, draw a verti-cal line down the center of the door. When you affix the drawbar (the mechanism for raising and lowering the door) at this line, the door weight will be evenly balanced at the lifting point.

Raise and lower the door, and observe the top point of its travel. Mark this location because you must mount the opener so that the rail is higher than the peak of the door's travel. Otherwise, as the door opens, it could strike the rail.

The door opener must be affixed to the garage at two points: above the motor drive unit and at the outer end of the rail. Inspect the area above the garage door at your vertical dividing line; there must be a support member in that location suitable for attaching the front end of the rail. If your garage lacks a structural member in that location, your first step in installing the door opener is to obtain a front mounting board. Center and fasten a length of 2 x 6 plank, with lag screws, across two wall studs over your mark of highest door travel. Transfer your high-point mark to this plank, and extend the vertical door center line that you drew earlier onto the plank.

The next phase of the installation must be done with the door down, and much of the work must be done from a stepladder. Although the job can be done by one person, you really should have someone help you throughout the installation. The helper also will require a stepladder.

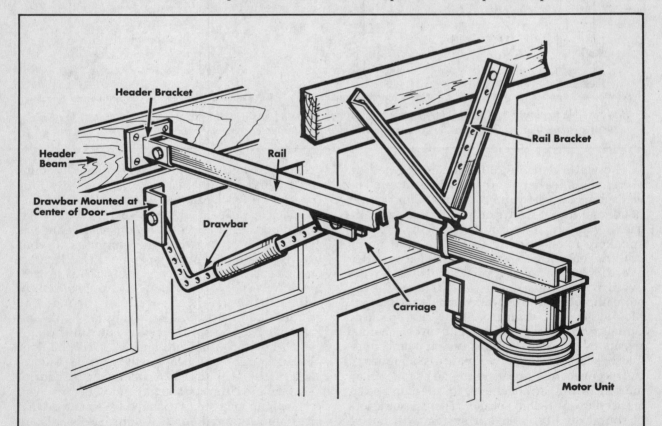

The typical garage door opener consists mainly of a reversible motor that drives a carriage along a rail above the door. Attached to the carriage is a drawbar to move the door between its opened and closed positions.

Assemble the rail to the motor unit on the garage floor, following the procedure outlined in the kit instructions. With the garage door down, lift and fasten the outermost end of the rail to the front mounting plank at a location about 2 inches above the intersecting marks you made for your door's high point and center line. The rail bracket provided for this purpose usually fastens to the front mounting plank by lag screws. If bolts and nuts are provided, you must drill suitable holes through the front mounting plank. Be sure to use washers under the heads of the bolts to keep them from pressing into the wood.

Raise the motor assembly to the point where the rail is horizontal, or parallel with the door track. With the motor assembly held or supported in this position, raise and lower the garage door by hand to make sure that the rail location does not interfere with the door's movement. Once you establish the correct position and height for the motor assembly, fasten it to the garage joists with the metal brackets in the kit. If the position of the motor assembly is between two joists, or if the garage joists run the same direction as the rail, you must fasten a length of 2 x 4 across the joists, and then mount the brackets to the 2 x 4. If your garage ceiling is finished, you can mount a 3/4-inch plywood panel overhead, fastening it to the joists with lag screws, and attach the mounting hardware to the plywood panel with heavy-duty toggle bolts.

Attach the drawbar to the rail carriage, and move the carriage to its closed-door position. Mark the drawbar mounting-screw holes on the garage door, and drill the holes in the door. With the drawbar mounted and the holes drilled, insert and tighten the attaching hardware that fastens the drawbar to the door.

Now adjust the drive chain or lead screw, observing particularly the location of the travel-limit cams. You must understand how these cams cause the device to turn off automatically at the "door open" and "door closed" positions, and how they make the motor reverse its direction and rotation. Install the radio receiver and manual push button. You can use ordinary bell wire for the push button, but be sure to locate it in a place where you can see the garage door opener in operation when you push the button.

Plug the drive assembly cord into an extension cord, and plug the extension cord into a convenient receptacle. Set the garage door in motion, using the manual push button. During the door's first test rising, pull the plug from the extension cord several times so you can check to make sure that there is no binding anywhere and that the lifting action is satisfactory. Make any necessary corrections using the adjustment provisions built into the garage door opener system, and verify the operation of the radio remote module.

Once you feel confident that the garage door opener is operating properly, disconnect the extension cord, and plug the drive assembly line cord into its permanent outlet. If possible, connect the cord to the garage overhead light socket. A pull-chain adapter then allows you to de-energize the garage door opener whenever you will not be using it for an extended period or when the unit needs servicing.

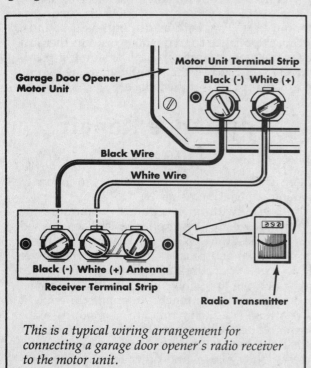

This is a typical wiring arrangement for connecting a garage door opener's radio receiver to the motor unit.

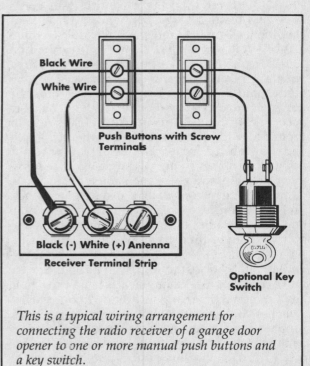

This is a typical wiring arrangement for connecting the radio receiver of a garage door opener to one or more manual push buttons and a key switch.

ELECTRIC APPLIANCE REPAIR

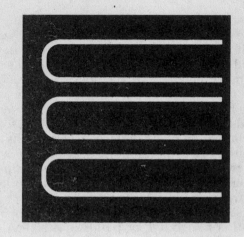

Appliances are built to perform. They work hard, year after year, and usually don't have too many problems. They're easy to take for granted. The result is that when an appliance breaks down, you may be completely at a loss. You don't know how it works or why it stopped working, much less how to fix it. Appliances are not anything you should be afraid of. All appliances work on the same fundamental principles, and all appliance repairs are based on these principles.

How Appliances Work

Most appliances operate on your home's electrical system; they use AC current from the circuit wiring in your home. Small appliances work on 110-120-volt circuits; the plugs on their cords have two blades. Large appliances, such as air conditioners, dryers, and ranges, usually require 220-240-volt wiring and cannot be operated on 110-120-volt circuits. Large appliances are wired with a grounding wire; their plugs have two blades and a prong. These appliances must be plugged into a grounded outlet, with openings to accept both blades and grounding prong, or grounded with a special adapter plug. All appliances are labeled, either on a metal plate or on the appliance casing, to show their power requirements in watts and volts, and sometimes in amps.

Small appliances usually are simple machines. They may consist of a simple heating element, a fan, a set of blades, or rotating beaters attached to a drive shaft; or they may have two or three simple mechanical linkages. Repairs to these appliances usually are simple. Large appliances are more complex. For example, a washing machine has a motor, a timer, a pump, and various valves, switches, and solenoids. In this type of appliance, problems can occur in either the control devices or the mechanical or power components. Failure of a control device may affect one operation or the entire appliance; failure of a mechanical or

power device usually affects only the functions that depend on that device. When a large appliance breaks down, knowing how to diagnose the problem is as important as knowing how to fix it.

Because large appliances are complex, it usually isn't obvious where a malfunction is. The first step is to decide whether the problem is in a control device or a mechanical device. In a dryer, for example, the control devices govern the heat; the mechanical components turn the drum. Which system is affected? If the drum turns but the dryer doesn't heat, the problem is in the control system; if the dryer heats but the drum doesn't turn, the problem is mechanical. This kind of analysis can be used to pinpoint the kind of failure in all large appliances.

To find the problem, you must check each part of the affected system to discover the malfunctioning part. This isn't as difficult as it sounds, because appliance components work together in a logical sequence; starting with the simplest possibilities, you can test the components one by one to isolate the cause of the failure.

Appliance Repair Basics

There are three very important rules to follow in making appliance repairs:

•*Always*—with no exceptions—make sure the electric power to the appliance is disconnected *before* you test the appliance to diagnose the problem or make any repairs. If you turn the power on to check your work after making a repair, do not touch the appliance; just turn the power on and observe. Never touch the appliance while it is running. If adjustments are needed, turn the power off before you make them.

•If the parts of an appliance are held with screws, bolts, plugs, and other take-apart fasteners, you probably can make any necessary repairs. If the parts are held with rivets or welds, don't try to repair the appliance yourself; call a professional service person.

•Broken or malfunctioning appliance parts often can be replaced more quickly and inexpensively than they can be repaired, by you or by a professional. Replace broken or malfunctioning parts with new parts made especially for the appliance. Appliance parts are available from appliance service centers, appliance repair dealers, and appliance parts stores. You don't *always* have to go to a specific brand-name appliance parts service center to obtain the parts and service you need for brand-name appliances. If you can't locate a parts service center in your area, order the part you need directly from the manufacturer. Give the manufacturer all the model and parts data possible. The name and address of the appliance manufacturer is usually printed on the appliance.

These three basic rules are essential for safe and successful appliance repairs. Don't try to save time or money by ignoring them. You won't save anything at all, and you could end up hurting yourself or ruining the appliance.

Before you make any appliance repair, make sure the appliance is receiving power; lack of power is the most common cause of appliance failure. Before you start the testing and diagnosis process, take these preliminary steps:

•Check to make sure that the appliance is properly and firmly plugged in, and that the cord, the plug, and the outlet are working properly. To find whether an outlet is working, test it with a voltage tester.

•Check to make sure the fuses or circuit breaker that controls the circuit have not blown or tripped. There may be more than one electrical entrance panel for your home, especially for 220-240-volt appliances, such as ranges and air conditioners. Check for blown fuses or tripped circuit breakers at both the main panel and the separate panel.

•Check to make sure fuses or breakers in the appliance are not blown or tripped. Push the reset buttons to restore power on such appliances as washers, dryers, and ranges.

•Check your owner's manual; many manufacturers include helpful troubleshooting charts. If you don't have a manual for an appliance, you probably can get one, even for an old or obsolete appliance, from the manufacturer's customer service department.

DISASSEMBLING APPLIANCES
Before you can repair an appliance, you usually must disassemble it. All appliances are different, but the disassembly procedure is always the same: You must remove the parts in reverse order of the way the manufacturer put them together. Remember that you'll have to put the

appliance back together again. Lay the parts out in order as you remove them, with fasteners kept in a safe place. If you aren't sure you'll be able to put the appliance back together, take notes and make drawings or photographs as you work. Label all terminals and wires if you must disconnect more than one wire at a time. Check your owner's manual for assembly diagrams and instructions.

To disassemble an appliance, start with the obvious knobs and fasteners. Many knobs and dials are push-fit; simply pull them off their control shafts. Knobs also may be held in place by setscrews, springs or spring clips, or pins, or they may be screwed on. These knobs are all easy to release. Housing panels are usually held by screws or bolts; they also may be held in place with tabs. Sometimes parts are force-fitted and may be hard to remove. Never force parts apart; look for hidden fasteners. For instance, there may be no obvious fasteners holding the top of a washer in place. You can locate the clips that hold the top down by sticking the blade of a putty knife into the seam where the top panel meets the side panel; run the knife along the seam until you hit an obstruction. This is a spring clip. To release the clip, push the blade of the knife directly into the clip, at a right angle to the seam, while pushing up on the top panel. Repeat this procedure to locate and remove any other spring clips holding the top panel; then lift the panel off.

Fasteners may be hidden under a nameplate or company logo, behind a scarcely visible plastic plug, under a cork pad on the bottom of the appliance, or under an attachment plate. Carefully pry up the part that is hiding the fasten-

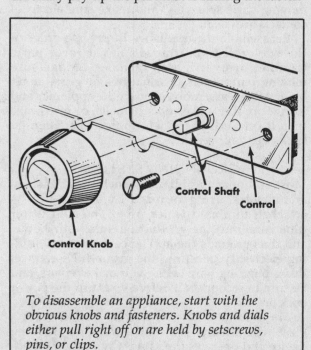

Control Shaft

Control

Control Knob

To disassemble an appliance, start with the obvious knobs and fasteners. Knobs and dials either pull right off or are held by setscrews, pins, or clips.

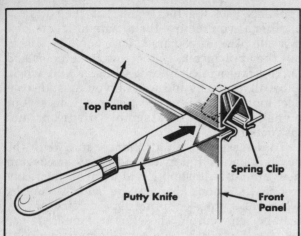

Spring clips are often hidden. To remove a panel held by spring clips, use a putty knife to find each clip; then push in against it to release the panel.

er. When you reassemble the appliance, snap the concealing part back over the fastener, or if necessary, glue it into place. If you can't find hidden fasteners on force-fitted parts, warm the parts gently with a heating pad; the heat may make disassembly easier. Inside the appliance, watch for clips holding parts to the housing panel.

After making the repair, and before reassembling the appliance, vacuum inside the appliance to remove dust and lint. Check for other problems and make any necessary repairs or adjustments. If the appliance has a motor, lubricate the motor; check carbon brushes in universal motors for wear and replace them if necessary. Lubricate moving parts sparingly, and make sure electrical contacts are clean.

Reassemble the appliance in reverse order of the way you took it apart; never force parts together or overtighten fasteners. Make sure moving parts, such as armatures or gears, don't bind. After reassembly, connect the appliance and turn it on. If it makes noise, smells, or overheats, turn it off and disconnect the power. Then go back over your repair.

GROUNDING SYSTEMS

Most stationary appliances, including washers and dryers, are grounded by a wire that is attached to a cold-water pipe. The cold-water pipe runs into the ground outside your home, and thus grounds the appliance so that any leaking electricity goes into the ground. Disconnect this grounding wire before you make repairs, and be sure to reconnect it before you turn the power back on.

Many homes have electrical outlets with a three-wire system. The third wire is a grounding device and operates the same way as the grounding wire on stationary appliances. Large appli-

ances, with plugs that have two blades and a prong, should be plugged into a grounded outlet or grounded with a special adapter plug. **Caution:** *Never remove the prong from a three-wire plug to make it fit an ungrounded outlet; always use a properly installed adapter plug.*

Proper grounding is vital for metal-framed appliances. If the insulation on the power cord of a metal-framed appliance, such as a washer or dryer, is broken or worn away just at the point where the cord enters the frame, contact between the current conductor and the metal frame could charge the whole appliance with electricity. When this happens, even if the appliance is properly grounded, dampness can cause a shock hazard. If you touched a charged metal frame in a damp location, or while touching a water faucet or radiator, the current would surge through you and could kill you.

There are three things you can do to eliminate this hazard:

• Make sure your appliances are properly grounded.

• Make sure that appliance cords are in good repair and that they are not chafing against burrs or rough spots where they enter the appliance frame.

• Add a ground-fault circuit interrupter (GFI or GFCI) to the circuit. Ground-fault circuit interrupters are monitoring devices that instantly shut off a circuit when a current leak occurs; they are required by the National Electrical Code on all new 15- and 20-amp outdoor outlets and for wiring in bathrooms, where dampness is a common problem.

GFIs are available to plug into existing outlets as adapters, to replace outlets, and to replace circuit breakers in the electrical entrance panel. A professional electrician should install the circuit-breaker type; you can install the others yourself. Ground-fault circuit interrupters are available at electrical supply and home center stores.

DOUBLE-INSULATED APPLIANCES

In double-insulated appliances and power tools, the electrical components are isolated from any parts of the appliance that could carry electrical current. These appliances are not completely shock safe; you should use caution with any electrical device. For example, never operate an electric drill while standing on a wet surface and never drill into a wall where power lines may be present. Double-insulated appliances and tools usually should be repaired by a professional, because the double-insulation depends on a plastic housing and a plastic buffer between parts that carry electricity. If these plastic parts are not properly positioned, the appliance or tool could produce a harmful electrical shock. Appliances and tools that are double insulated usually are labeled.

Tools for Appliance Repairs

For most appliance repair jobs, you'll need a few simple mechanical and electrical tools. You already may have most of them in your workshop. Some sophisticated equipment is needed for complex repair work, and this equipment is expensive, but it may be less expensive than using a professional repair service.

Buy appliance repair tools as you need them. The necessities are simple. You'll need a selection of good-quality screwdrivers: at least three sizes for standard slotted screws and at least one Phillips screwdriver. For small appliances you may need small screwdrivers. You'll also need a hammer, an adjustable wrench and a socket wrench set, a pump oil can, a utility knife, and a trouble light. Basic electrical equipment includes a fuse puller, a multi-purpose tool for stripping the insulation off conductors and crimping solderless connectors, a test wire or jumper wire with an alligator clip on each end, and a 20,000-ohm 2-watt wire-wound resistor, for work on capacitor motors. Resistors are not expensive; they're available at most appliance and television parts stores. All your electrical tools should have insulated handles.

TOOLS FOR ELECTRICAL TESTING

Many appliance repairs require electrical testing for accurate diagnosis of the problem. The tools needed for testing include a voltage tester, a continuity tester, and a volt-ohm-milliammeter (VOM). With this equipment you'll be able to tell whether the electrical current is reaching and flowing through the part of the appliance you suspect.

Voltage Tester. The voltage tester is the simplest of these three tools. It consists of a small neon bulb with two insulated wires attached to the bottom of the bulb housing; each wire ends in a metal test probe. The voltage tester is used with the current turned on, to find whether there is current flowing through a wire and to test for proper grounding. It also is used to determine whether adequate voltage is present in a wire. Look for a tester rated for up to 500 volts.

To use a voltage tester, touch one probe to one wire or connection and the other probe to the opposite wire or connection. If the component is receiving electricity, the light in the housing will glow. If the light doesn't glow, the trouble is at this point. For example, if you suspect that an electrical outlet is faulty, insert one probe of the tester into one slot in the outlet, and the other probe into the other slot. The light in the tester should light; if it doesn't, the outlet may be bad. To further test the outlet, pull it out of the wall.

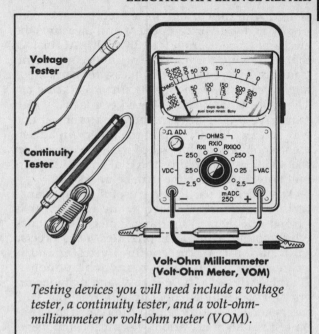

Testing devices you will need include a voltage tester, a continuity tester, and a volt-ohm-milliammeter or volt-ohm meter (VOM).

Place one probe of the tester on one terminal screw connection and the other probe on the other terminal screw. If the tester bulb lights, you know the outlet is malfunctioning, because there is current flowing to the outlet that isn't flowing through the outlet. If the test bulb doesn't light, there is no current coming into the outlet. The problem may be a blown fuse or tripped circuit breaker, or the wire may be disconnected or broken behind the outlet.

Continuity Tester. The continuity tester, the primary diagnosis tool for many appliance repairs, consists of a battery in a housing, with a test probe connected to one end of the battery housing and a test wire with an alligator clip connected to the other end. The continuity tester is used with the current turned off, to find whether a particular electrical component is carrying electricity and to pinpoint the cause of a malfunction.

To use a continuity tester, unplug the appliance and disassemble it to get at the component to be tested. **Caution:** *Do not use a continuity tester unless the appliance is unplugged or the power to the circuit is turned off.* Fasten the clip of the tester to one wire or connection of the component and touch the probe to the other wire or connection. If the component is receiving electricity and transmitting it, the tester will light or buzz; the circuit is continuous. If the tester doesn't light or buzz, or if it reacts only slightly, the component is faulty.

Volt-Ohm Meter (VOM). The voltage tester and the continuity tester are adequate for many diagnostic jobs, and they're fairly inexpensive. For serious appliance troubleshooting and repairs, you should invest in a volt-ohm-milliammeter or volt-ohm meter (VOM), also known as a multitester. A VOM is battery-powered and is used with the current turned off. It checks continuity in a wire or component and measures the electrical current, from 0 to 250 volts, AC or DC, that is flowing through the wire or component. **Caution:** *Do not use a VOM unless the appliance is unplugged or the power to the circuit is turned off.* The VOM is used with plug-in test leads, which may have probes at both ends or a probe at one end and an alligator clip at the other. An adjustment knob or switch is set to measure current on the scale, usually ohms; the dial shows the current flowing through the item being tested.

The VOM is particularly useful for appliance testing because it is used while the power is turned off; there is no danger of electric shock while you're using it. It provides more precise information than the continuity tester and is preferable for testing many components. Learning to read a VOM is easy, and manufacturers provide complete operating instructions with the meters. You also can buy information sheets on test readings of various electrical components used in appliances and in other applications, such as lights, switches, and outlets. Where a standard reading is available, this information has been included in the appliance repairs covered here. All readings are given in ohms; make sure you read the VOM dial on the ohms scale.

Repairing and Replacing Basic Components

No matter how complex they are, appliances are made with the same basic electrical components: electrical conductors, a cord and a plug, and various switches, sensors, and elements. All these components can malfunction, and what looks like a total breakdown in an appliance is often traceable to the failure of a simple component. It's important to know how these basic electrical components work, why they fail, and how to repair or replace them. With this information, you can take care of many appliance problems, with a minimum of effort and inconvenience.

POWER CORDS AND PLUGS

Many appliance "breakdowns" are caused by worn, frayed power cords or plugs that no longer make good electrical contact. To ensure safe operation, you should periodically check appliance cords for problems and replace frayed or broken cords immediately. When you suspect a cord is faulty, remove it from the appliance and test it with a continuity tester. Clip the tester to one blade of the plug, and touch the probe to one of the two wires. If it is a plug-in cord, insert the probe into one of the two holes at the appliance

end of the cord. If the tester lights or buzzes, move it to the other wire or hole and test again. Repeat this procedure to test the other blade of the plug. If the tester lights or buzzes at every test point, the cord is not faulty. If it fails to light or buzz at any point, the cord or the plug is faulty. You can pinpoint the defect by cutting off the plug and testing the cut end of the cord. If the tester lights or buzzes at all test points, the plug is the defective part. The damaged component should be replaced.

Replacing a Cord. Replacing the cords on appliances, power tools, and other equipment is simple. Some special cords can, and should, be bought as complete sets, with a plug attached to one end and special connection terminals attached to the other end. General-purpose cords can be fashioned from a separate plug, a length of an appropriate cord, and perhaps connection terminals. Electric ranges and clothes irons, for example, use complete-set cords; table saws and mixers use general-purpose cords. Always make sure you replace the old cord with a new one of the same kind.

The hardest part of the job is trying to figure out how the appliance comes apart so that you can remove the old cord and attach a new one. Sometimes all you have to do is remove the cover from a connection box, as on a water pump. In other cases, as with a small hair dryer, the unit itself must be partially disassembled before you can reach the terminals. In nearly all cases, the cord is held in place by a clamp or by a fitted strain-relief device. To remove the cord, unscrew the terminal screws or pull the pressure connectors apart, loosen the clamp or remove the strain-relief device, and pull the cord out. Installation of the new cord is simply a reverse procedure. Be sure to save the strain-relief device and replace it on the new cord. If you have to destroy the strain-relief device to remove it, replace it with a new one.

In some equipment, the conductor ends are looped around terminal screws, and making new connections is easy. Carefully strip off the outer insulation, not the insulation on the inner wires, for about 3 inches at the end of the cord. With a wire stripper, remove about 1/2 inch of insulation from the end of each conductor wire. Twist the exposed filaments of each wire, clockwise, into a solid prong. Loosen the terminal screws and loop each bare wire end clockwise around a screw; then tighten the screws firmly. Connect the wires at the appliance end of the new cord the same way the old ones were connected.

In some appliances solderless connection terminals may be clamped to the old cord, and you'll have to fit replacement terminals to the new cord. This requires terminals of a matching kind and a tool called a staker or crimper. You can find this tool at automotive or electrical sup-

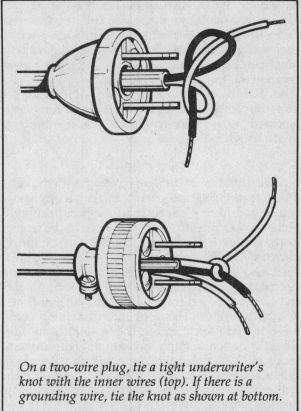

On a two-wire plug, tie a tight underwriter's knot with the inner wires (top). If there is a grounding wire, tie the knot as shown at bottom.

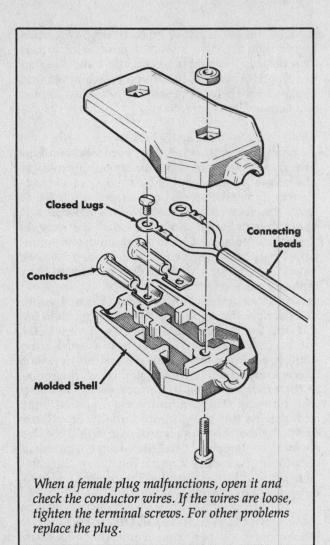

Closed Lugs

Connecting Leads

Contacts

Molded Shell

When a female plug malfunctions, open it and check the conductor wires. If the wires are loose, tighten the terminal screws. For other problems replace the plug.

ply stores. In a few cases, the terminals may be soldered to the conductor ends. You can replace them with solderless connectors.

Replacing a Plug. If only the plug of an appliance is faulty, you can attach a new plug to the old cord. Male plugs, with two blades or with two blades and a grounding prong, plug into an outlet. Female plugs, often used at the appliance end of the cord, have terminal holes instead of blades. Male plugs usually can be taken apart so you can get at the terminal screws. Female plugs may be held together by rivets or by screws; screw-held plugs can be taken apart, but rivet-held plugs cannot be repaired. When a plug malfunctions, open the plug, if possible, and check to make sure the conductor wires are properly attached to the plug's screw terminals. If the wires are loose, tighten the screw terminals. This may solve the problem; if it does not, the plug should be replaced.

To attach a new male plug, insert the cord end through the plug opening, and pull it through for 5 or 6 inches. Carefully strip off the outer insulation, not the insulation on the inner wires, for about 3 inches. With a wire stripper, remove

about 1/2 inch of insulation from the end of each conductor wire. Twist the exposed filaments of each wire, clockwise, into a solid prong. After twisting the conductor ends, tie a tight underwriter's knot with the inner wires of the cord. Then pull the plug down over the knot, leaving the exposed ends of the conductor wires sticking out. Loosen the terminal screws in the plug.

On a two-wire plug, loop each wire around one prong and toward a screw terminal. Loop the bare wire end clockwise around the screw terminal, and tighten the screw. If the screws are different colors, connect the white wire to the white screw and the black wire to the yellow screw. On a three-wire plug, use the same technique to connect each of the three wires to a terminal screw. Connect the green grounding wire to the green screw terminal. When the conductor wires are firmly secured to the terminal screws, slide the cardboard insulator over the blades of the plug. If the plug has a clamping sleeve, clamp it firmly around the cord.

WIRING
Many appliance repair tasks involve wiring, which means connecting individual wires or groups of wires to install a new electrical component. The electrical wires in appliances may be connected in one of several ways: screw terminal connection, push-in terminal, and sleeve lug terminal. Wires also may be joined with solderless connectors called wire nuts. Components that

have many wires, such as washer timers that control several operating cycles, are often connected in a wiring harness, which is a group of wires enclosed in a plastic sleeve. Each wire connection must be properly made when you install a new component, for each wire and each wire of a harness. Before you disconnect any wiring in an appliance, make sure you know how it's attached. When you install the new component, attach its wires the same way.

SWITCHES

Switches operate by making contact with the conductor of an electrical circuit. When an appliance is plugged in, it's connected to a circuit in your home; power runs through the wires of the circuit to the appliance. When the appliance's "on-off" switch is turned on, the conductors of the appliance cord are moved into contact with the circuit conductors, and electricity flows through the switch to operate the appliance. The current flows in a loop through the appliance, making a complete circuit back through the switch to the line wires. Other basic appliance components are various switches or variations of switches, including rheostats, thermostats, solenoids, and timers. These components operate inside appliances to turn on motors, open and close valves, control heating elements, and turn on different parts of the appliance during different cycles, such as the rinse and spin cycles of a washer. There are several common types of switches: push buttons, toggles, rockers, slides, and throw switches.

All switches are made up of electrical contacts in a mechanical housing, and switch failure can be caused by problems with either the contacts or the housing. When a switch malfunctions, turn it to the "on" position and watch to see if the contacts are moved into position so that they touch. If the contacts are not operating properly, the switch housing is faulty, and the switch should be replaced. If the switch's mechanical operation is all right, its contacts may be dirty or misaligned; if it has terminal screws, they may be loose. If the contacts are dirty or corroded, rub them gently with fine emery cloth and then buff with a soft cloth; if they're misaligned bend them gently back into place. Tighten any loose terminal screws. If the contacts or screws are badly corroded, the switch should be replaced.

To determine whether a switch is working properly, disassemble the appliance to get at the switch, and test it with a continuity tester or a VOM, set to the R x 1 scale. With the appliance unplugged, hook the clip of the continuity tester to one lead of the switch and touch the probe to the other; or touch one probe of the VOM to each terminal. Turn on the switch. If the switch is functioning, the continuity tester will light or buzz, and will stop glowing or buzzing when the switch is turned off; or the VOM will read zero. If

the tester doesn't light or buzz, or the VOM reads higher than zero, the switch is faulty and should be replaced. Some switches should have a higher reading than zero, as detailed for each appliance. Use a new switch of the same type as the old one, and connect it the same way.

THERMOSTATS

A thermostat is a switch that controls temperature in a heating element or a cooling device. Thermostats used in appliances may use a bimetal strip, bimetal thermodiscs, or a gas-filled bellows chamber to control the electrical contact. Faulty bimetal-strip and thermodisc thermostats should be replaced. Gas-filled thermostats sometimes can be professionally repaired; where repair is feasible, it is much less expensive than replacement.

To find whether a thermostat is functioning, disassemble the appliance to get at the thermostat, and test it with a continuity tester, or a VOM set to the R x 1 scale. With the appliance unplugged, hook the clip of the continuity tester to one lead of the thermostat and touch the probe to the other; or touch one probe of the VOM to each terminal. The continuity tester should light or buzz; or the VOM should read zero. Turn down the temperature control dial; you'll see the contact points open at the thermostat. The tester should stop glowing or buzzing when the contacts open. If it does not, the thermostat needs to be replaced or repaired.

SWITCH CONTROL DEVICES

Many appliances perform several functions, such as the various cycles of a washing machine or dishwasher. These appliances operate automatically; once the "on-off" switch is turned on, switch components inside the appliance take over to control heat, water or fuel flow, motor speed, and other variables. The most important of these devices, used to operate switches, levers, and valves automatically, are solenoids, relays, and sensor-responder pairs.

HEATING ELEMENTS

Heating elements work simply. Unlike conductors, they are made of metal with high electrical resistance, usually a nickel-chrome alloy called nichrome. When current flows through the element, this high resistance prevents it from flowing easily; it must do work to get through the element, and this work is converted into heat. When the current is turned off, the element cools. There are three kinds of heating elements: wire, ribbon, and rigid.

To determine whether a heating element is functioning, disassemble the appliance to get at the element, and test it with a continuity tester or a VOM, set to the R x 1 scale. With the appliance unplugged, hook the clip of the continuity tester to one terminal of the heating element and touch the probe to the other terminal, or touch one probe of the VOM to each terminal. If the element is functioning, the tester will light or buzz; or the VOM will read from 15 to 30 ohms. If the tester doesn't light or buzz, or the VOM reads higher than 30 ohms, the element is faulty and should be replaced. If you use a continuity tester look closely at the tester, especially if it's the kind that lights up: Some heating elements have an extremely high resistance factor, and the tester's light may produce only a dim glow or a faint buzz. This reaction does not mean that the element is faulty but that it converts current to heat efficiently.

TIMERS

The operation of an appliance that has several cycles, such as a washing machine, a dishwasher, a dryer, a frost-free refrigerator, or a range, is controlled by a timer. In some appliances the timer is electronic, but in others it is a complex rotary switch powered by a small synchronous motor. The timer consists of a shaft, gears, and a series of notched cams, one for each circuit or cycle. The timer itself is powered by a timer motor; the appliance is powered by a much larger appliance motor. When the switch is turned on, electrical contact is made with the timer motor, and a spring on a trip arm is coiled. The arm trips when the spring is tight, releasing the spring and moving the cam of the switch to the next circuit. At the last cycle, contact with the motor is broken, and the timer turns the appliance off.

When a timer malfunctions, it usually should be replaced; professional rebuilding is sometimes possible, but this is likely to be more expensive than replacement. To replace a timer, disconnect its wires one at a time, connecting the corresponding wires of the new timer as you go to avoid the chance of a misconnection.

To find whether a timer is functioning, test it with a continuity tester or a VOM, set to the R x 1 scale. Make a sketch of the timer wires, and with the appliance unplugged, disconnect all timer wires from their terminals. Touch or clip one probe of the tester or the VOM to the common terminal, and touch the other probe to each cycle terminal in turn; rotate the timer control knob as you work. The continuity tester should light or buzz at each circuit; the VOM should read zero. If one or more circuits do not give these results, the timer is faulty and should be replaced.

Maintaining and Repairing Motors

Depending on how much work it has to do, an appliance may be powered by one of several kinds of motors. Small appliances are usually powered by a universal motor or, where less power is needed, by a shaded-pole or a synchronous motor. Larger appliances are usually powered by a split-phase or a capacitor motor. Direct-current motors are used for small appliances that use batteries as their power source. Universal and direct-current motors have two blocks of carbon called brushes, which function as electrical contacts. The other motors do not have brushes; they are induction motors, in which a solid rotor spins inside a stationary piece called a stator. Both brush motors and induction motors are powered by the electromagnetic force created when electrical current passes through them.

Whatever their size and horsepower, appliance motors are usually dependable and long-wearing. You can prolong their life and increase their efficiency by keeping them clean and well lubricated. Use motor-driven appliances sensibly: Don't overload them, don't abuse them, and don't ignore problems until they become serious.

There are several basic rules for operating motor-driven appliances:

• Always connect an appliance to an adequate power source; a 220-240-volt appliance must be connected to a 220-240-volt outlet. If the outlet for a major appliance is not grounded, use a grounded adapter plug to ground the appliance.

• Never use a small appliance that is wet or operate any appliance while your hands are wet. If a large appliance, such as a washer or dryer, gets wet, do not operate it or try to unplug it. Have the motor examined by a professional before you use the appliance again.

• Never overload an appliance. Overloading causes inefficient operation and motor overheating, and can cause excessive wear. If a motor turns off because it's overloaded, reduce the load before restarting the appliance.

Regular maintenance can forestall many motor problems. To prevent overheating and jamming, vacuum the motor housing periodically to remove dirt and lint. Make sure ventilation to the motor is adequate. At least once a year, oil the motor if it has oil ports with Number 30 nondetergent motor oil (not all-purpose oil).

If the motor has belts, examine them periodically for wear and damage; damaged belts should be replaced. To quiet a squeaky belt, spray it with fan-belt dressing, available at automotive and hardware stores and some home centers. Also check the tension of all belts, about halfway between the motor shaft and the nearest pulley. The belt should give about 1/2 inch when you press on it. If it's too loose, increase the tension by tightening the adjustment bolt; if it's too tight, decrease the tension by loosening the bolt. If pulleys are misaligned, carefully bend them back into alignment, or you may want to call a professional service person.

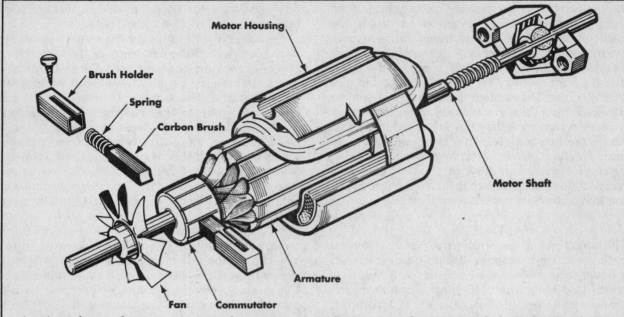

A universal motor has an armature and a rotating commutator, mounted on a motor shaft. Carbon brushes make the electrical contact; worn brushes are the most common problem.

Universal Motors. These motors consist of a rotor called an armature, with coils of wire wound around it, and a rotating cylinder called a commutator, with alternating strips of conducting and nonconducting material. The armature and the commutator are both mounted on the motor shaft. On each side of the commutator, a carbon brush carries current from the circuit. When the carbon brushes press against the commutator, the armature is magnetized and rotates. Most universal motors also have a cooling fan at the end of the shaft. Universal motors are used in many small and medium-size appliances; they provide strong power at both low and high speeds. Universal motors can operate on either AC or DC current. Their speed is controlled by a rheostat, a tapped-field control, a rectifier, or a governor, or by physical movement of the carbon brushes away from the armature.

Most universal motors are permanently lubricated and sealed by the manufacturer, and require no further attention. But some universal motors have covered lubrication ports, usually marked "oil," at the ends of the motor shaft. This kind of motor should be oiled every six months, or according to the manufacturer's instructions. Lift each port's lid and apply a drop or two of Number 30 nondetergent motor oil (not all-purpose oil); do not overlubricate.

Many universal motor malfunctions are caused by wearing down of the carbon brushes. When these brushes become worn, the motor will spark, and electrical contact may be incomplete. You can solve both problems by replacing the brushes.

Brushes can be checked visually or tested with a continuity tester. To sight-check them, remove the screws that hold the brushes and brush springs into the brush holders at the sides of the commutator. The screws will pop out of the screw holes; turn the motor over to tap out the brushes. The ends of the brushes should be curved to fit the commutator; if they're worn down, new brushes are needed. To check carbon brushes with a continuity tester, remove the motor lead wires from the circuit. Tag the wires as you disconnect them so that you'll be able to reconnect them properly. Hook the tester clip to one motor lead and touch the probe to the other lead; the tester should light or buzz. Slowly revolve the motor shaft, keeping the tester in position. If the tester doesn't light or buzz, or if it flickers or stutters when you turn the motor shaft, the brushes should be replaced. If the springs behind the brushes are damaged, they should be replaced too.

Replace worn carbon brushes and damaged springs with new ones made specifically for the motor; the model information (number and make) is stamped on a metal plate fastened to the motor or embossed on the metal housing of the motor. If you can't find the model information, take the worn brushes and springs with you to an appliance parts store to make sure you get the right kind. Insert the new springs and brushes in the brush holders, replace the brush assemblies, and secure the new brushes with the mounting screws that held the old brushes.

No other repairs should be attempted to a universal motor; if a serious malfunction occurs, buy a new motor or take the faulty motor to a professional for repairs. Most large universal motors are fastened to plate mountings. To remove the motor, disconnect the wires and take out the holding bolts and any belts that are present. If the faulty motor is in a small appliance, take the entire appliance to the repair shop. It may be less expensive to buy a new appliance than to have the old one repaired.

Split-Phase Motors. These motors consist of a rotor turning inside a stator that has two wire coils: a starting winding and a running winding. Current flows through both windings when the motor is starting up, but when the rotor has reached about 75 to 80 percent of its top speed, the starting winding is turned off, and only the running winding receives current. Split-phase motors operate on AC current; they are powerful and are used in washing machines, dryers, and dishwashers.

These motors require no maintenance except cleaning and lubrication. Split-phase motors have a special auxiliary winding, the starting winding; don't try to make any repairs yourself. When a motor malfunctions, buy a new motor or take the faulty motor to a professional service person, whichever is less expensive. You can save the expense of a service call by removing the old motor from its mounting and installing the repaired or new motor yourself.

Capacitor-Start Motors. This is a shaded-pole motor with a capacitor (an energy-storing device) wired into the starting winding. The capacitor stores current and releases it in bursts to provide extra starting power. When the motor reaches about 75 percent of its top speed, the starting winding is turned off. Capacitor-start motors operate on AC current. They are very powerful and are used in appliances that require a high starting torque or turning power, such as air conditioners and furnaces. **Caution:** *Capacitors store electricity, even after the power to the appliance is turned off. When working with a capacitor-start motor, you must discharge the capacitor with a 20,000-ohm, 2-watt wire-wound resistor.*

These motors require regular cleaning to keep them free of lint and oil. Ventilation to the motor must be adequate. If the motor has oil ports, lift each port's lid and apply a drop or two of Number 30 nondetergent motor oil (not all-purpose oil); do not overlubricate.

Capacitor-start motors are usually hard to get at, and have a capacitor and special auxiliary windings; don't try to make any repairs yourself. When a motor malfunctions, call a professional service person.

Refrigerators and Freezers

Refrigerators and freezers, like air conditioners, have two basic components: a condenser coil and an evaporator coil. A liquid coolant is circulated through these coils by a compressor and a motor. The refrigerant liquid is cooled in the condenser; it then flows to the evaporator. At the evaporator, the air in the unit is cooled by contact with the liquid-filled coil. The condenser of a refrigerator or freezer is the coil on the outside of the unit; the evaporator is the coil on the inside. The coolant is circulated through the system by a compressor.

Some refrigerators and freezers have a manual defrosting system. In this kind of unit, the temperature control is turned to the defrost setting to raise the temperature, and frost inside the unit melts slowly. After the unit has been defrosted, the control is turned back to the cooling cycle. Some refrigerators and freezers have an automatic defrost system. With this system, a heater in the refrigerator melts frost in the unit. A control switch must be turned to set the thermostat that controls this defrost heater; when the heater reaches the set point and the unit has defrosted, the switch automatically shuts off the heater and turns the unit back to the cooling cycle.

Most refrigerators and some freezers are frost free. In these units a heater is automatically turned on by a timer to melt the frost inside the unit. Frost is melted by the heater at several different spots in the unit, in a series, starting at the coldest and most frosted areas. When the frost is completely melted, the thermostat automatically switches to a cooling cycle. Because this process is automatic, frost does not build up inside the box.

The unit's compressor system, which forces the coolant through the coil system, is driven by a capacitor motor. Other basic parts of the cooling-defrosting system include switches, thermostats, heaters, condensers, and fans. You can test and replace many of these refrigerator components. **Caution:** *Before doing any work on a refrigerator or freezer, make sure it's unplugged. After unplugging the unit, check to see if the motor-compressor has a capacitor; this component is located in a housing on the top of the motor. Capacitors store electricity, even when the power to the unit is turned off. Before you do any work on a capacitor refrigerator or freezer, you must discharge the capacitor, or you could receive a severe shock.*

Unplug the refrigerator or freezer. To enter the capacitor, remove the service panel over the back rear portion of the unit or the service panel on the front of the unit below the door. The capacitor is located in a housing on the top of the motor-compressor unit; it looks like a large dry cell battery. To discharge the capacitor, use a 20,000-ohm 2-watt resistor, an inexpensive wire unit available at most electrical supply stores. Fasten the probes of the resistor to the terminals of the capacitor; this discharges the capacitor. If the capacitor has three terminal posts, connect the resistor to one outer terminal and the center terminal, then to the other outside terminal and the center terminal.

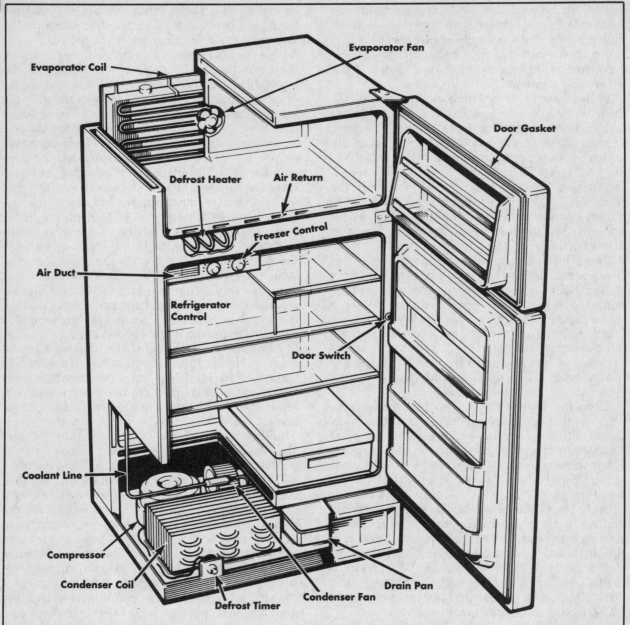

In a refrigerator coolant is cooled in a condenser; from there it flows to the evaporator, where air is cooled by contact with the coil.

After discharging the capacitor, you can make the repairs.

Disassembly. The control components of a refrigerator are usually located in the top or upper section of the unit. The motor, compressor, condenser coil, and condenser fan are located in the bottom section. To get at the components in the upper section, remove the retaining screws or pry out the clips that hold plastic or metal panels over the parts. These fasteners may be hidden by trim or molding; pry off the trim or molding with the tip of a screwdriver or a stiff-blade putty knife. Protruding controls also may serve as retainers for the various panel sections. The shelves can be removed to allow access to some panels.

To gain access to the lower section of the refrigerator, remove a service panel held by retaining screws at the back of the unit below the condenser coils. The unit also may have a front access panel below the door. This panel may be held by retaining screws or may slip up and off two side brackets. On some models, you can tip the refrigerator over and test and service parts from the bottom. Then the refrigerator must be defrosted, unplugged, and emptied before any servicing can be done.

The condenser and evaporator coils and the compressor are sealed units on most refrigerators. If a malfunction occurs within these parts, call a professional service person. Other parts usually

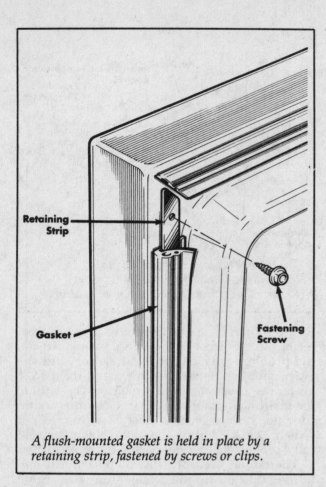

A flush-mounted gasket is held in place by a retaining strip, fastened by screws or clips.

can be unscrewed or pried loose from mounting brackets.

Cleaning and Positioning. The condenser and evaporator coils of a refrigerator collect dust and dirt over time. This decreases their efficiency. One important maintenance procedure is to clean these coils with a vacuum cleaner, a soft cloth, or a whisk broom, at least once a year.

Positioning also affects the efficiency of the unit. Refrigerators or freezers with exposed condenser coils on the back panel should be at least 2 inches from the wall, and the back of the refrigerator or freezer should not be placed against a heat register or a window or door where heat or sun could affect the temperature of the coil. To keep your refrigerator or freezer working properly, make sure it always is clean and well positioned.

Power Cord. If the cord of the unit looks frayed or you see burn marks on the prongs of the plug or at the terminal screws, on the terminal block, or under the rear access panel of the unit, the cord may be faulty. Test the cord with a VOM set to the R x 1 scale.

Door Gaskets. When a refrigerator gasket becomes hard or cracked, its seal is broken, and the unit's efficiency drops sharply. Test the door gasket for leaks by placing a dollar bill between the gasket and the door jamb, and closing the door. Pull the bill out. If it offers some resistance, chances are the gasket fits properly. If the bill

comes right out, or falls out, the gasket is faulty and should be replaced. Test the gasket at several locations around the door.

To replace a gasket, buy a gasket made specifically for the model refrigerator you own. "Fit-all" gaskets may fit after a fashion, but tailoring them to the door's configuration can be a tough job. If you aren't sure about the model number of your refrigerator, cut out a small section of the gasket and take the sample to an appliance dealer for matching. If the gasket has to be ordered, you can glue the section back into the gap with rubber cement for a make-do repair until the new gasket comes in.

Let the new gasket sit for about 24 hours in the room with the refrigerator to bring it to the correct temperature and humidity, or soak the gasket in warm water to make it pliable.

Door gaskets are held by screws, clips, or adhesive, and the gasket may have a retaining strip, which helps shape it and provides a fastening tab or guide. On some units the gasket may be held in place by the edge of the door panel; the panel is fastened with spring-steel pressure clips, bolts, or screws. The gasket also may be held by adhesive. To remove the gasket, remove the fasteners that hold it, and remove any retaining strips; or remove the fasteners that hold the door panel.

Remove the fasteners on one side of the door at a time; do not remove the entire door panel. If the gasket is held by spring clips, be careful not to pry too hard on the clips; they're under tension and could spring out of their mountings. If the gasket is held by adhesive, pry it off with a putty knife. When the old gasket is off, clean the mounting area thoroughly with mild household detergent and water. Remove stubborn adhesive with mineral spirits and fine steel wool, followed by detergent and water.

Start the replacement at one side of the top of the door, and work down the sides to replace the entire gasket. Smooth the gasket evenly into place, easing it around corners; use gasket cement to secure it if the manufacturer specifies this step. Make sure the gasket lies flat, with no lumps or curled edges. Then replace the fasteners, retaining strips, or panel that held the old gasket.

It may take some time for the new gasket to conform to the door. After the gasket is in place, tighten or loosen the mounting bolts necessary to adjust the gasket to the door jamb. If the gasket is glued in place, there isn't much you can do but wait for the gasket to conform to the door jamb.

Test the gasket on a freezer door with the same dollar-bill procedure; if the gasket is faulty, replace it with a new gasket made especially for the freezer.

Door Hinges. A worn or broken door gasket may not be the cause of door leaks. Misaligned and loose door hinges can cause the door to rock or sag slightly, making even a well-fitted gasket ineffective.

If the door won't shut tightly, try tipping the refrigerator slightly backward by propping up the front of the unit or unscrewing the front leveling legs two complete turns. Experiment with this adjustment until the door stays closed, but don't tip the unit very far out of front-to-back level.

If leveling doesn't work, tighten the hinge screws. You may have to open the door (especially freezer doors) to turn these screws. On some units, you may have to remove a hinge cap or trim to reach the screws; pry off the cap or trim with a screwdriver. Sagging and looseness can be corrected by shimming the door hinges. Loosen the hinge and place a cardboard shim, cut to the shape of the hinge, between the hinge and the door; then tighten the hinge again. Sagging also may be caused by a wrongly placed shim; you can correct the problem by removing the shim. Experiment with the shims; you may be able to eliminate the sagging.

If the door is warped, tighten the screws that hold the inner door shell to the outer door shell. You may have to change or adjust the door gasket after making this adjustment.

On some older refrigerators, the door is held shut by a latch. This latch can become misaligned or worn so that it fails to engage and the door does not close tightly. Remove the screws that hold the latch plate to the door jamb, and shim out the latch plate with thin cardboard so that the latch engages properly.

Newer units have a magnetic catch on the door. If the door doesn't latch properly, remove the magnetic strike and shim it slightly with a piece of thin cardboard. You may have to adjust the gasket to conform with the new shim.

Door Switch. On the refrigerator door jamb, locate a small push-button switch. This component operates the light inside the refrigerator. If the switch is malfunctioning, the light in the unit may stay on, and the heat from the light bulb can cause cooling trouble in the box.

If you suspect the door switch is faulty, first make sure the bulb is not burned out; then depress the push button. If the light stays on, remove the switch from the jamb. Remove retaining screws hidden by a plastic trim piece, pry the switch out of the jamb with a screwdriver, or pry off the jamb trim to expose the switch. Then test the switch with a VOM, set to the R x 1 scale. Clip one probe of the VOM to each terminal of the switch, and press the push button. The meter should read zero; if the needle on the scale moves above zero, replace the switch with a new one of the same type. Connect the new switch the same way the old one was connected.

Limit Switch. The limit switch is found only on frost-free refrigerators and freezers; its function is to keep the defrost heating element from

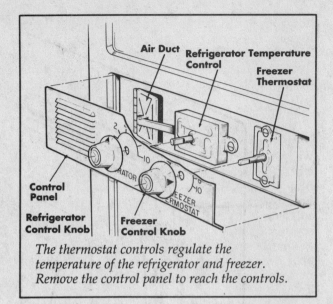

The thermostat controls regulate the temperature of the refrigerator and freezer. Remove the control panel to reach the controls.

exceeding certain set temperatures. If a refrigerator has lots of frost in the freezer compartment, the problem may be the limit switch. But the evaporator fan, the defrost timer, and the defrost heater can cause the same problem. Check these for malfunctions. If these parts are in working condition, the problem is most likely in the limit switch. Don't try to fix the limit switch yourself; call a professional service person for replacement.

Thermostat Control. This component is usually mounted inside the refrigerator; the visible control knob is turned to regulate the refrigerator-freezer temperature. The workability of this control can be tested in various ways, depending on the problem.

If the compressor runs all the time, turn the control knob to the "off" position. If the compressor still runs, unplug the unit; then pull off the control knob and remove the screws holding the thermostat in place. Pull out the thermostat, and remove either the red or the blue wire from its terminal. Plug in the unit. If the compressor doesn't run, the thermostat is faulty; replace it with a new thermostat.

If the compressor runs after the wire is removed from its terminal, there probably is a short circuit somewhere in the unit's wiring. Don't try to fix the problem yourself; call a professional service person.

If the refrigerator or freezer runs but the box doesn't cool, unplug the unit. With a screwdriver, remove the thermostat. Disconnect both wires from the thermostat, and tape the ends of the wires with electrical tape. Plug in the appliance. If the refrigerator starts and runs normally, the thermostat is faulty; replace it with a new one of the same type. If the freezer compartment is normal but the refrigerator box doesn't cool, set the dials that control both compartments to mid range. Remove the knobs; they usually are friction fitted. Then unscrew the temperature control housing; you'll see an air duct near the control. Replace the knob on the freezer thermostat, and turn the control to "off." Open the refrigerator door and look closely at the air duct. If this duct doesn't open wider in about 10 minutes, the control is faulty; replace it with a new one of the same type.

Evaporator Fan. A faulty thermostat may not be the cause of a warm refrigerator or freezer. A warm box also may be caused by a defective fan, a blocked fan, or broken or bent fan blades. If the blades are jammed, try to free them; if they're bent, straighten them with pliers. If this doesn't solve the problem, call a professional service person to make the necessary repairs.

On some refrigerators, the door switch operates the evaporator fan; if the fan seems to be malfunctioning, the door switch could be faulty. Test the switch, and replace it if necessary.

Defrost Timer. If the compressor doesn't run, chances are the defrost timer is malfunctioning. This part is located near the compressor. To test the defrost timer, unplug the refrigerator. Disconnect the wires from the timer and timer motor; remove the timer from its brackets by backing out two retaining screws. Test the defrost timer with a VOM, set to the R x 1 scale. Clip one probe of the VOM to each defrost timer wire, and turn the timer control screw shaft until it clicks. If the defrost timer is functioning, the meter will read zero. If the needle jumps, the defrost timer is faulty; replace it with a new one of the same type.

To check the defrost timer motor, clip one probe of the VOM to each motor wire, and set the scale to R x 100. If the meter reads between about 500 and 3,000 ohms, the motor is functioning properly. If the meter reads higher than 3,000 ohms, the timer motor is faulty; replace it with a new one of the same type.

Defrost Heater. This component is a heating element located on the evaporator coil; when the refrigerator or freezer switches to the defrost cycle, the defrost heater is turned on to melt the frost in the compartment. Failure of the defrost heater causes failure to defrost. Test the element with a VOM, set to the R x 1 scale. To get to the heating element, remove the compartment's wall panels. Clip one probe of the VOM to each element terminal. The meter should read between 5 and 20 ohms; if it doesn't, the heating element is faulty, and should be replaced. Replace the heater with a new one of the same type and electrical rating.

Condenser Fan. This component is located under the unit. If the fan is malfunctioning, the refrigerator or freezer won't cool properly or will run continuously or not at all. Test the fan with a VOM. Disconnect the electrical wires to the fan motor, and clip one probe of the VOM to each fan motor terminal. If the meter reads from 50 to 200

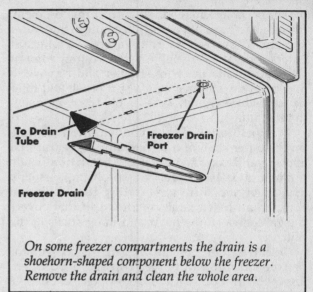

On some freezer compartments the drain is a shoehorn-shaped component below the freezer. Remove the drain and clean the whole area.

ohms, the motor is functioning properly. If the meter reads higher than 200 ohms, the fan motor is faulty; replace it with a new one of the same type.

While you're working on the fan motor, make sure the fan blades are clean and unobstructed. If the blades are bent, straighten them with pliers.

Drain Ports. The drain ports are located along the bottom of both the freezer and the refrigerator sections of the unit. These holes can become clogged with debris or ice, causing a drainage problem when the unit is defrosting. To clear the ports, use a short section of wire that will fit the holes. Do not use a toothpick; the wood may break off in the port. On some refrigerators, the drain ports are located near the defrost heater at the evaporator coils. A lot of disassembly is required to clean this type of unit; if the refrigerator or freezer is this type, you may be better off calling a professional service person to clear the ports.

On some freezer compartments, the drain is located under the freezer compartment and shaped like a shoehorn. This kind of drain usually can be unscrewed so that the drain area can be cleaned.

Drain Pan. This component is located under the bottom of the refrigerator. During the defrosting cycle, water runs through a small hose into the drain pan and then evaporates. On some refrigerators, the drain hose is rubber instead of metal. This kind of hose can become cracked, causing leaks. Examine the hose; if it's damaged, replace it with a new one of the same type. If you spot water on the floor, the drain pan may be tipped on its brackets, or the pan may be cracked or rusted. To eliminate the leak, realign or replace the pan.

Ice-Makers. Freezers with automatic ice-makers sometimes malfunction because the water inlet valve strainer that feeds the water to the ice-maker becomes clogged. To correct this problem, unplug the appliance and disconnect the water supply. Then remove the water line where it enters the valve—usually at the bottom edge of the unit. Locate the wire strainer and remove it, and clean the strainer with a stiff brush and mild household detergent. Reassemble the component in reverse fashion.

Wet Insulation. When condensation appears on the outer shell of a refrigerator or freezer in a specific and confined area, the insulation inside the unit is probably wet. This problem is usually caused by moisture penetrating the insulation through a broken jamb or trim strip that covers the gap between the outer and inner shells of the unit.

To correct the problem, unplug the refrigerator or freezer and empty it. Prop the door open. Leave the unit off, with its door open, for 36 to 48 hours; this should be ample time for the insulation to dry. During this period, examine the trim strips. If you find any cracks in them, pry out the strips with the tip of a screwdriver or the blade of a putty knife, and replace them with new ones. If this doesn't work, the insulation may be thin in spots; call a professional service person to replace or repack the insulation.

Wet insulation also may be due to broken shelf supports. Broken brackets also cause shelf leveling problems. The metal or plastic supports are easy to replace; don't try to repair them. Lift the broken support up and off its mounting bracket, and replace it with a new one of the same type.

Refrigerant Leak. Coolant leaks are identifiable by their acrid smell. There is nothing you can do to repair a coolant leak; call a professional service person to deal with the problem.

Motor-Compressor. The compressor and motor of a refrigerator or freezer are contained in a sealed unit. If you trace problems to either of these components, do not try to fix the unit yourself; call a professional service person.

Dishwashers

The control panels on dishwashers have many dials, push buttons, lights, clocks, and other features, making the machines look too complex to repair. But this is not so. You can repair most dishwasher malfunctions.

As in many appliances, dishwasher parts can be replaced as a unit, and this is often easier and less expensive than having a professional service person make repairs. If you aren't sure a part is still usable, remove it from the dishwasher and take it to a professional service person for testing, then decide whether to buy a new part or have the old one repaired.

Dishwashers usually run on 115-volt or 120-volt power; the water they use comes directly from the water heater, and wastewater is drained into the sink's drainpipe. The dishwasher is not connected to the cold-water supply. For best dishwashing results, set the temperature control of the water heater to no less than 140 degrees Fahrenheit; water cooler than this usually doesn't get the dishes clean, unless your model preheats incoming water. The water shutoff for the dishwasher is usually located below the floor underneath the unit; to turn off the water supply, you'll have to go to the shutoff in the basement or crawl space under the kitchen.

Caution: *Because the dishwasher is connected to both the plumbing system and the electrical system, you must consider both systems when working on this appliance. Before doing any work on the dishwasher, make sure the unit is unplugged or the power to the unit is turned off; remove the fuse or trip the circuit breaker that controls the circuit, at the main entrance panel or at a separate panel. Shut off the water supply to the dishwasher at the shutoff in the basement or crawl space under the kitchen.*

Basic Operating Checks. If the dishwasher does not run, first check to make sure it's receiving power. If the unit plugs into a wall outlet, check the cord, the plug, and the outlet to make sure they're functioning properly. Also check the switch that controls the outlet to make sure it's turned on. Most built-in dishwashers are wired directly into a circuit; check the main entrance panel for a blown fuse or tripped circuit breaker, and restore the circuit. If your dishwasher is wired to a separate entrance panel; look for a blown fuse or breaker at this panel, and restore the circuit. If the circuit is receiving power, and the wall outlet is controlled by a switch, the switch may be faulty. Test the switch with a voltage tester. Take off the switch cover plate; place one probe of the tester on one terminal and the other probe on the other terminal. If the tester bulb lights, the switch is functioning; if it doesn't light, the switch is faulty. Replace the switch with a new one of the same type.

Next make sure the door is tightly closed and latched; the dishwasher will not operate until the latch is properly engaged. To check the latch, close and latch the door, and hold the latch tightly in place. While you are still pressing the latch closed, turn the control knob to "on." If the dishwasher works, the latch is faulty, and should be replaced.

Also make sure the water is turned on, and the water temperature is high enough. A breakdown in the water heater could stop the flow of water to the dishwasher. Try the hot water in the kitchen sink or lavatory. If you can draw hot water, the water heater may not be at fault.

Finally make sure the controls on the control panel are properly set. Push-button controls can be very sensitive; make sure the buttons are firmly pressed into position.

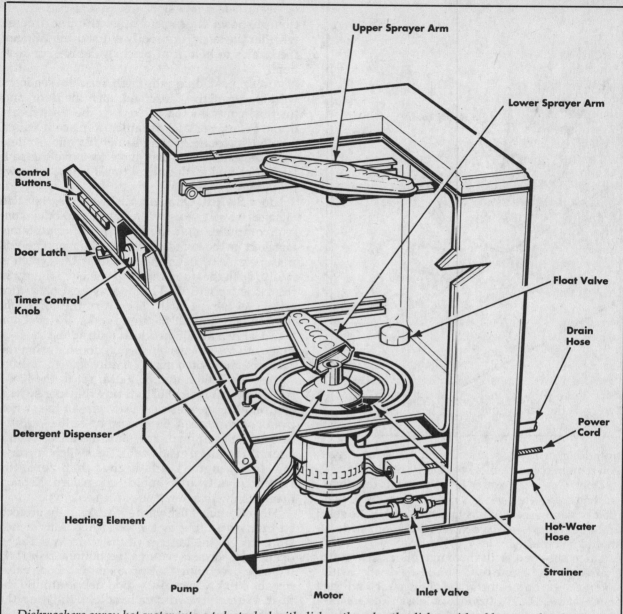

Upper Sprayer Arm

Lower Sprayer Arm

Control Buttons

Door Latch

Timer Control Knob

Float Valve

Drain Hose

Power Cord

Detergent Dispenser

Heating Element

Hot-Water Hose

Strainer

Pump

Motor

Inlet Valve

Dishwashers spray hot water into a tub stacked with dishes, then dry the dishes with a blower or heating element. Problems often involve the water-supply and drainage systems.

Disassembly. Access to the working parts of most dishwashers is through the front door of the unit. Many repairs can be made to the machine by simply opening the door and reaching into the various component parts, such as the sprayers, strainers, float switch, racks, and door latch.

To get to the control panel on the door, remove a series of retaining screws around the panel. These screws may be under molding trim strips, which usually snap onto the metal housing; pry off the strips with a stiff-blade putty knife or a screwdriver, or remove a setscrew that holds the molding. The control knobs are friction fitted on shafts, or they are held by small setscrews in the base of the knobs. In some dishwashers, the entire front door panel must be removed to gain access to the control components. This panel is held to the door by a series of retaining screws, usually found around the edge on the inside back of the door.

On many models, once the control panel is removed the door panel can be removed; unscrew a series of fasteners holding the door panel in place. Sometimes these retaining screws are covered by trim moldings, which must be pried or slipped off. For access to the motor, pump, hoses, inlet valves, and other parts, remove the lower access panel; this can usually be removed without removing the door. The panel may be held by retaining screws.

If the dishwasher is portable, tip the machine over on its back or side before removing the con-

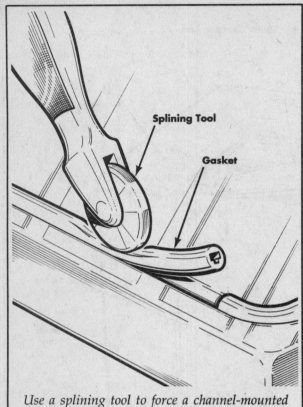

Use a splining tool to force a channel-mounted gasket into the retaining groove.

trol, door, or lower access panels. This may give you a more comfortable working position.

Door Gasket. If water leaks through the dishwasher door, the gasket is probably faulty. Open the door and examine the gasket. It should be soft and resilient; if it's worn, cracked, or hard, it should be replaced.

Once the gasket is in place, check it for fit against the door frame. It should fit tightly, with no cracks or bulges between the gasket and the frame. If necessary, tighten or loosen the retaining screws, or refit the gasket in the clips or the door channel. Then run the machine through a washing sequence, and check for leaks. If you spot a leak and the gasket seems to be properly in place, try adjusting the door latch. The trick is to seat the gasket against the frame of the door without flattening the gasket or squeezing it too flat when the door is latched properly. Adjust the latch or the gasket until it fits just right.

Door Latch. The latch on a dishwasher door is opened and closed repeatedly, and this hard use can lead to mechanical problems. The latch may be loose, or it may have slipped out of position, throwing the alignment off and preventing the door from closing properly. When this happens the latch does not engage properly, and the dishwasher will not start. You may be able to solve the problem by adjusting the position of the latch. Move the latch slightly by loosening the screws that hold it, and slide the latch with your fingers

or pliers. The screw slots are made especially for this purpose. Close and open the door to see whether the latch is properly aligned, and tighten the screws to hold it in place in the correct position.

After repositioning the latch, check to see if it's working properly. Close and latch the door, and turn the control knob to "on." If the dishwasher doesn't start, the latch is faulty. Replace it with a new latch; connect it the same way the old one was connected. You may have to move the new latch back and forth several times before it works properly.

Door Switch. On many dishwashers, the latch engages a switch to start the timer and other control components; if the latch is not completely engaged or the switch is faulty, the machine will not operate. To determine whether the switch is faulty, latch the door and hold the latch tightly in the closed position. This works best on a unit with a lever-type latch. Then turn the control to the "on" position. If the unit works, the problem is probably a misaligned lock unit; adjust the lock unit with a screwdriver. If this doesn't solve the problem, the switch may be faulty.

Test the switch with a VOM, set to the R x 1 scale. Take off the panel covering the door switch, and remove one electrical lead wire of the switch from its terminals. Clip one probe of the VOM to each switch terminal, and shut the dishwasher's door. If the meter reads zero, the switch is working. If the meter reads higher than zero, the switch is faulty and should be replaced. Replace the switch with a new one of the same type.

Float Switch. Dishwashers are usually protected from overfilling by a float switch. This switch is located in the bottom of the unit; to get at it, open the door and remove the bottom dish rack. If water overfilling is a problem, the float valve may be stuck. Clean away food debris around the float. With a screwdriver handle, lightly tap the top of the float; this may free it.

If tapping doesn't work, remove the lower access panel and locate the bottom portion of the float and float switch. Test the float switch with a VOM, set to the R x 1 scale. Unscrew one electrical lead wire to the switch terminal, and clip one probe of the VOM to each terminal. If the meter reads zero, the switch is not faulty; the trouble is probably in the timer. If the meter reads higher than zero, the switch is faulty; replace it with a new one made to fit the dishwasher. The switch is held to a mounting bracket with screws; remove the screws to get the old switch out.

Pressure Switch. Although the water level in most dishwashers is controlled by the timer, some machines are equipped with a pressure switch that does this job. You can quickly tell if your unit has one by removing the lower access panel. The pressure switch is mounted under the tub housing and has a small hose running into it.

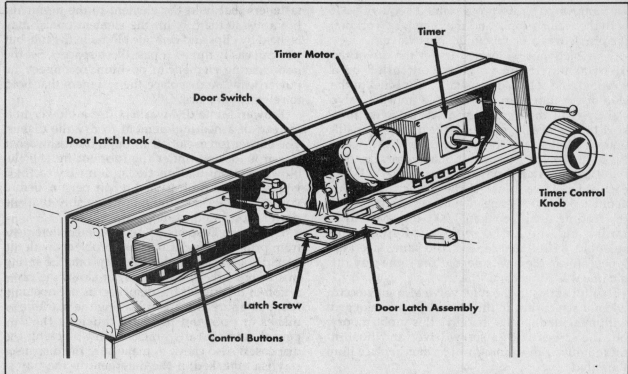

For repairs to the timer, door latch, or switches, remove the control panel. To take it off, remove a series of retaining screws and the control knobs, and lift off the panel.

The hose usually is held to the switch by a spring clip.

If the dishwasher won't fill with water, lightly tap the switch housing with a screwdriver handle; this may jar the switch loose. Also make sure that the hose and the spring clip are properly attached, and that the hose is not defective. Tighten the connections and replace the hose, if necessary. If this doesn't solve the problem, test the switch with a VOM, set to the R x 1 scale. Disconnect the electrical leads from the switch terminals, and clip one probe of the VOM to each terminal. If the meter reads zero, the switch is functioning; if it reads higher than zero, the switch is faulty and should be replaced. Replace the switch with a new one made for the dishwasher. The switch is held to the tub with retaining screws; remove the screws to take out the old switch.

Timer and Control Switches. The timer controls many operations, and a faulty timer can cause many problems. Because the timer is a complex component, don't try to fix it; if it's faulty, replace it with a new timer made for the dishwasher. Test the timer with a VOM, set to the R x 1 scale. To gain access to the timer, remove the front control panel. The timer is directly behind the main timer control knob. Disconnect one of the timer's terminal wires, and clip one probe of the VOM to each terminal. If the meter reads zero, the timer is working; if the meter reads higher than zero, the timer is faulty and

should be replaced. If possible, use the same procedure to test the selector and cycle switches. The wiring hookup may be too complicated to figure out on either of these switches. If you aren't sure you can deal with these switches, call a professional service person. Replace a faulty timer or a faulty control switch with a new one made for the dishwasher.

The timer is connected to several wires, which supply power to operate the various functions of the dishwasher. To replace the timer, have a helper hold the new timer next to the old one, and connect the wires of the new timer one by one, removing the old wire and connecting the new, to make sure you connect the wires correctly. The wires may be friction-fit on the terminals; if they are, use long-nosed pliers to remove the wires. Don't pull up on the wires or you may break the connection between the wires and the clips. After connecting the wires, set the new timer in position, secure it the way the old one was secured, and replace the control panel and knobs.

Water Inlet Valve. The water inlet valve controls the amount of water flowing into the dishwasher; it may be activated by the timer or by a solenoid. If the dishwasher doesn't fill with water, first make sure that the water supply to the unit is turned on, and that there is no problem at the water heater. A shutdown of the water heater would cause a shutdown of water to the dishwasher. Check the timer to make sure it's working through its programmed sequences. If both the water supply and the timer are working, the problem is probably in the inlet valve.

The inlet valve is located under the tub of the dishwasher. If the valve is controlled by a solenoid, the solenoid is usually connected to the side of the unit. Tap the solenoid and the valve lightly with the handle of a screwdriver; then start the dishwasher again. If the dishwasher still doesn't fill, test the solenoid with a VOM, set to the R x 100 scale. Disconnect one electrical lead to the solenoid, and clip one probe of the VOM to each solenoid terminal. If the meter reads from about 100 to 1,000, the solenoid is functioning. If the reading is higher than 1,000, the solenoid is faulty and should be replaced. Replace the solenoid with a new one of the same size and type; connect the new solenoid the same way the old one was connected.

Malfunctions of the inlet valve also may occur when a screen inside the valve becomes clogged with mineral deposits. To solve this problem, pry out the screen with a screwdriver and flush it thoroughly with running water; then replace it in the valve.

Badly worn or misshapen inlet valves cannot be repaired; if the valve is damaged, replace it with a new one made for the dishwasher. The valve is usually held to a mounting bracket with screws. Take apart the connection linking the valve to the water supply; then take out screws and remove the valve. Install the new valve by making the connections in reverse order.

Drain Valves. Some dishwashers have drain valves; these valves are used only in dishwashers with nonreversible motors. If you can't tell from the manufacturer's operating instructions whether your dishwasher has a drain valve or a nonreversible motor, remove the bottom panel of the unit and locate the motor. If the motor has two or three wires running into it, the motor is nonreversible. When the drain valve malfunctions, call a professional service person.

Heating Element. This component is used to help dry the dishes. In most dishwashers the heating element fits around the screen in the bottom of the tub housing; it looks like a round electric oven element. The heating element doesn't malfunction often, but it can burn out. If you suspect a faulty element, test it with a VOM, set to the R x 1 scale. Remove the dishwasher's bottom access panel and disconnect one of the power leads to the element. Clip one probe of the VOM to each element terminal. If the meter reads between 15 and 30 ohms, the element is working; if the reading is higher than 30 ohms, the element is faulty and should be replaced. Replace it with a new one made for the dishwasher.

Removing and replacing an element is easy. Disconnect the electrical leads to the element's terminal screws, and remove the nuts or other fasteners that hold the element to the terminals. From inside the tub, lift the element out. It may be held by clips and ceramic blocks in the tub, but you can easily thread it past these spacers. Set the new heating element in position, reconnect the power leads, and replace the fasteners that hold the element in place.

Blower. Some dishwashers use a blower unit instead of a heating element to dry the dishes. The blower forces hot air through the dishwasher tub; it is located under the tub, not in it. If the blower system malfunctions, don't try to fix it yourself; call a professional repair person. Before you call for service, though, make sure that the power is on and the timer is working.

Detergent Dispenser. Accumulated detergent from prior washings can cause problems with the soap dispenser when the soap gets into the spring that triggers the flip-out tray, or slows the pivot action of the tray. If the dispenser is not opening, first make sure you aren't loading the machine so dishes or pots and pans are touching the dispenser, and that dish racks aren't blocking the dispenser. Also check to make sure the dispenser tray isn't cracked; if the detergent in the tray is almost liquid, rather than just damp, the tray may be damaged.

If you can't solve the problem easily, replace the entire dispenser unit; this is usually better than trying to disassemble it and replace separate parts. Use a new dispenser made for the dishwasher. The screws holding the dispenser may be on the front of the unit, or you may have to remove the front door panel to get to the screws and make the replacement. Remove the old dispenser and secure the new one.

Dish Racks. Problems with the dish racks usually occur because the racks have been jammed back into the tub housing after they're fully loaded. Careless handling can exert enough force to crack or break the roller wheels, or to throw the racks off the tracks. The solution is easy: stop jamming the racks. The repair is easy, too. Remove the racks by pulling out the metal pins that hold them in the tracks; or simply lift up on the racks and pull them out of the tracks. Then replace the racks on the tracks so that they roll smoothly. If the rollers are cracked or broken, replace them with new ones of the same type. The rollers may be friction fitted to their hubs; simply pull them off for replacement. If they are held by tiny spring clips, pull the clips out with pliers, or pry them out with the tip of a screwdriver. If you can't pull the rollers off for replacement, remove and replace the entire rack.

Sprayer Arms. The sprayer arms seldom cause any trouble, but sometimes the spray holes in the arms become encrusted with detergent. When this happens, the holes must be cleaned out so that the arms will work efficiently. Remove the lower arm by twisting off the cap that holds it to

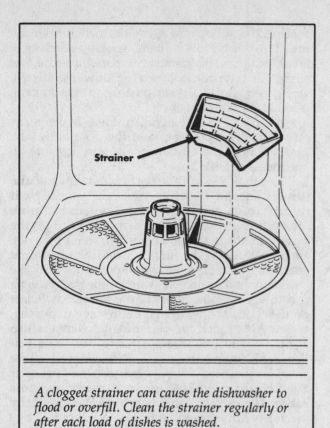

A clogged strainer can cause the dishwasher to flood or overfill. Clean the strainer regularly or after each load of dishes is washed.

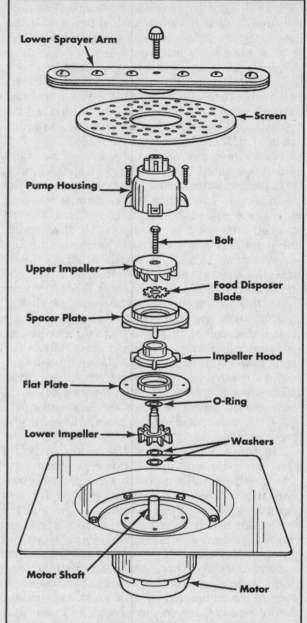

To reach the water pump, remove the sprayer arm and screen and then the pump housing. Remove a bolt, and the pump components can be disassembled.

the motor shaft; wash it thoroughly with water and mild household detergent. Sharpen a lead pencil and break off the lead point; use the tapered end of the pencil to ream out the holes. An orange stick also can be used. Do not use toothpicks, matches, or metal objects for this job; lightweight wooden sticks could break off in the ports, causing blockage, and metal could scrape and enlarge the ports. After cleaning, place the sprayer arm back on the motor shaft, and twist the cap back on to hold it in place. Follow the same procedure to clean the upper sprayer arm.

Strainer. The strainer is located directly under the lower sprayer arm. When the strainer becomes clogged with food and detergent debris, the dishwasher may flood or overfill. On some dishwashers, the strainer is a plastic or metal component consisting of two semicircular halves; to remove this type of strainer, pry it up. On other dishwashers, the strainer is a one-piece component; to remove this type, remove the cap that holds the sprayer arm on its shaft, and then remove the sprayer arm and the strainer.

Wash the strainer in the kitchen sink, with water and a mild household detergent. Use a stiff brush to get the debris out of the holes and slots in the strainer. Rinse the strainer well and replace it. If part of the strainer lifts out for regular cleaning, check it and clean it, if necessary, after each load of dishes is washed.

Leaks. If the dishwasher leaks and you know the problem is not related to tub overfilling, the

pump, or inlet valve problems, the plumbing connections may be faulty. Most dishwashers are connected to the water supply with metal pipe fittings; the leak could be at these fittings. If the fittings are threaded tighten them with an adjustable wrench. If this doesn't work, chances are the threads are stripped, or the fitting is cracked or otherwise damaged. Then replace the fitting.

Most dishwashers discharge used water through a pipe or a hose connected to the drain or garbage disposer under the kitchen sink. If the drain line is flexible hosing, it may have cracked from prolonged exposure to hot water. Examine the hose, and if it's damaged, replace it. If the hose is leaking at its connections with the disposer or dishwasher, tighten the fittings or clamps at the connections, or replace the clamps. Also check for water leaks around inlet valves, drain valves, and wherever you see flexible hoses and hose connections. Leaks at clamps can be stopped by tightening or replacing the clamps; leaks in hoses can be eliminated by replacing the hoses.

Water Pump. In most dishwashers, the water pump is located under the lower sprayer arm. This component pumps the water through the dishwasher. The pump has two impellers and these, as well as other components, can become clogged with food or detergent. To disassemble the pump, remove the cap that holds on the sprayer arm. In sequence take off the sprayer arm, the screen, the pump housing, a bolt, the upper impeller, the food disposer blade, a spacer plate, the impeller hood, a flat plate, an O-ring, and the lower impeller. Lay the parts out in order as you disassemble them so that you'll be able to put the assembly together properly. Clean the parts thoroughly with a mild detergent solution, and if any parts are worn, replace them with new ones made for the dishwasher. Replace any seals, such as the O-ring or other washers, with new ones. Then reassemble the pump, keeping the parts in order.

On some dishwashers, the lower impeller serves as a drain pump. This type of system usually has a reversible motor; machines with nonreversible motors have drain valves. If your machine has this impeller pump system and the water will not drain from the dishwasher, clean the lower pump impeller; this may solve the problem. If not, call a professional service person.

Motor. If the dishwasher motor malfunctions, don't try to fix it yourself; call a professional service person to make repairs or replace the motor. Before you call for service, check to make sure that the timer is working and that the dishwasher is receiving power.

Washing Machines

Because of the special timing cycles that operate valves and motors that turn water on, spin the tub, drain water, and control the water temperature, washing machines may be harder to diagnose than to repair. But diagnosis can be done; all it takes is common sense and patience. **Caution:** *Before you do any work on a washer, make sure it's unplugged. Disconnect the grounding wire and the water hoses.*

Basic Operating Checks. Before starting a serious appraisal, follow these procedures. Make sure the washer is receiving power. Check the cord, the plug, and the outlet; if a wall switch controls the outlet, make sure the switch is working. Look for blown fuses or tripped circuit breakers at the main entrance panel; restore the circuit. If the unit is receiving power and still won't run, press a reset button on the control panel, if the washer has one.

Next make sure the control knob is properly set to the "on" position, and the door is tightly closed. Check the latch to make sure it's free of lint and soap buildup.

Then make sure that both water faucets are turned on and that the drain and soap-saver return hoses are properly extended, without kinks. If the washer has a water-saver button, make sure the button is depressed; water may not circulate through the filter nozzle if the basket is not full and the button is not depressed.

Finally make sure the water is the proper temperature. Check the temperature selector switches on the control panel to make sure they're properly set. Also check the water heater temperature control; it should be set no lower than 120 degrees Fahrenheit.

Disassembly. The washer cabinet usually must be disassembled for repairs and maintenance. The control panel is held to the top of the machine with retaining screws spaced around the panel, usually under a piece of molding or trim that can be pried off. On some machines, you'll have to remove the back of the control panel, also held by retaining screws, to get at the working parts of the controls. Knobs on the control panel are usually friction fitted. Some knobs are held by small setscrews at the base of the knob. Loosen the setscrews and pull the knobs straight off the shafts.

Most washers have a removable service panel at the back of the machine. This panel is held by retaining screws. Tip the washer over on its front or side to gain access through the bottom of the machine; spread a blanket on the floor to protect the washer's finish. The bottom of the machine doesn't have a service panel, because the bottom of the washer is open. The top of the cabinet is usually held by spring clips. Insert a stiff-blade putty knife into the joint between the top and side panels, and give the knife a rap with your fist. This should release the spring clips so that the top can be removed.

The washer is connected both to the electric power and to the water supply. **Caution:** *Make sure the power cord and water hoses are disconnected before you disassemble the cabinet or tip the machine over for service.*

Lid Switch. The lid switch often serves as a safety switch; if the switch is not working, or the switch opening in the lid is clogged with detergent, the machine will not run. If you suspect a detergent block, try cleaning out the port with an orange stick after the power is turned off. Clean off any detergent buildup around the rim of the

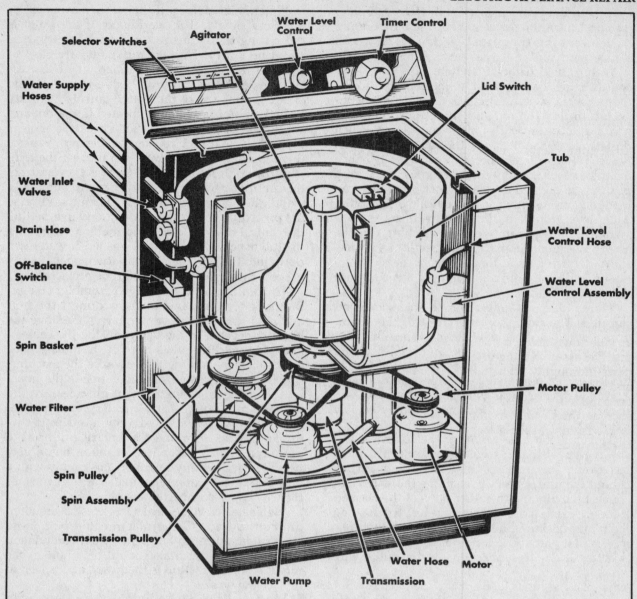

A washing machine has a tub and an agitator; various cycles control the water temperature. Problems can occur in either the electrical or plumbing system.

lid; sometimes there is enough detergent encrusted on the metal to prevent the lid from closing tightly and keep the washer from operating. If cleaning doesn't help, remove the top of the cabinet to get at the switch. With the switch exposed, check the screws for looseness; loose screws can cause the switch to move when the lid is closed or as the machine goes through its cycles. Check the terminals of the switch to make sure they're tight, and tighten the mounting screws after the switch is in alignment.

To determine whether it's functioning, test the switch with a VOM, set to the R x 1 scale. Disconnect the power leads to the switch terminals and clip one probe of the VOM to each terminal. Close the lid. If the meter reads zero, the switch is working; if not, the switch is faulty, and

should be replaced. Replace it with a new one of the same type.

If the switch still doesn't work, it is probably misaligned. Realign the switch by repositioning the screws holding it in place, testing the switch as you go until it works properly.

Temperature Selector Switch. This control panel switch regulates the temperature of the water in the tub; it also plays a role in controlling the fill cycle. If you suspect this switch is faulty, remove it by backing out the screws that hold it in place, and take it to a professional service person for testing; the test takes special equipment. You also can hook a test wire across the switch terminals; if water flows, the switch is faulty. If the switch is faulty, replace it with a new one of the same type.

If there is a problem with both water temperature and tub filling cycles, both the temperature switch and the timer may be faulty; test both components, and replace them as necessary.

Water Level Control Switch. This is another control panel switch, usually located next to the temperature switch. There is a small hose connected to this switch, and sometimes this hose becomes loose and falls off the connection. When this happens, the water in the tub usually overflows. To solve this problem, cut about 1/2 inch off the end of the hose and reconnect it, with a push fit, to the switch. The switch itself also can malfunction, resulting in tub overflow and other water-level trouble in the tub. If you suspect this switch is faulty, remove it by backing out the screws holding it in place, and take it to a professional service person for testing. If the switch is faulty, replace it with a new one of the same size and type.

Timer. Most washing machine timers are complicated. The timer controls most of the operations of the washer: water level, tub filling and emptying, length of cycles, and cycle setting sequences. Any repairs to the timer should be made by a professional service person. But there are a couple of checks you can make when you suspect the timer is faulty; and you may be able to install a new timer.

To get at the timer, remove the control knobs and the panel that covers the controls. This may be a front panel, or access may be through a panel behind the unit. Carefully examine the wires that connect the timer to the other parts of the washer. If the wires are loose or disconnected, try pushing them into position; they usually fit into their terminals like plugs. Use long-nosed pliers to avoid breaking the wire connections; never pull a wire by hand.

To test the timer, use a VOM, set to the R x 1 scale. Disconnect the power leads to the timer and clip one probe of the VOM to each lead. The VOM should read zero if the timer is working. Since the timer is a multiple switch, turn it through its cycle and test each pair of terminals. The meter should read zero at all of these points. If one or more readings are above zero, the timer is faulty and should be replaced.

Most timers are single components. To replace the timer, unscrew and disconnect the old one, and install a new timer made specifically for the washing machine. If there are many wires on the timer, have a helper hold the new timer next to the old one as you work, and disconnect the old wires one at a time, connecting each corresponding new wire as you work, to make sure the connections are properly made. You also could draw a diagram showing the connections before removing the old timer. After all the wires are connected, check the connections, and then screw the timer assembly into place.

Water Inlet Valves. If the washer won't fill or fills very slowly, if it overfills, or if the water is the wrong temperature, the water inlet valves could be faulty. These components are easy to locate and very easy to replace, at little cost. When you suspect an inlet valve is faulty, first check to make sure the water faucets are fully turned on and properly connected to the hot and cold inlets of the valves. Then check the screens in the valves; if they're clogged, clean or replace them. If water doesn't enter the tub, set the temperature control to "hot." If there is no water, set the control to "warm." If all that comes out is cold water, the hot-water inlet valve is faulty. Reverse the procedure to test the cold-water valve, setting the control first on "cold" and then on "warm." If the tub overfills, unplug the washer. If water still flows into the tub, the valve is stuck open. In any of these cases, the valves should be replaced.

To gain access to the valve assembly, take off the back service panel and disconnect the hot- and cold-water hoses to the valves. Remove the hoses connected to the valves inside the cabinet, and disconnect the wires from the terminals. Back out the screws holding the valves to the machine. The inlet valves have solenoids inside the housing. These can be tested, but chances are the valves are simply worn out. Try tapping the solenoids with a screwdriver handle; if this doesn't work, replace the entire inlet valve assembly. Repairs usually cost more than a new part. Replace a faulty inlet valve assembly with a new one of the same type; install it in reverse of the way you disconnected the old one.

Water Leaks. Water leaks in a washer are often difficult to trace. The problem could be a loose connection, a broken hose, a cracked component, or a defective seal; it also could be a hole in the tub. If a hole in the tub is the problem, it's best to replace the washer.

Most leaks can be eliminated by tightening water connections and replacing deteriorated components. To stop a leak, check these components:

- Lid seal. If faulty, replace with new gasket.
- Hoses at faucet connections. Tighten connections or replace hoses.
- Hoses at water valve connections. Tighten connections or replace hoses.
- Drain hoses. Tighten connections or replace hoses.
- Inlet nozzles. Tighten connections or replace nozzles.
- Splash guard. Tighten connections or replace.
- Any plastic valve. Tighten connections or replace.
- Outlet hose to drain. Tighten connections or replace hose.

Water Pump. Of all washing machine parts, the water pump probably takes the most punishment, because it is constantly in use. When the

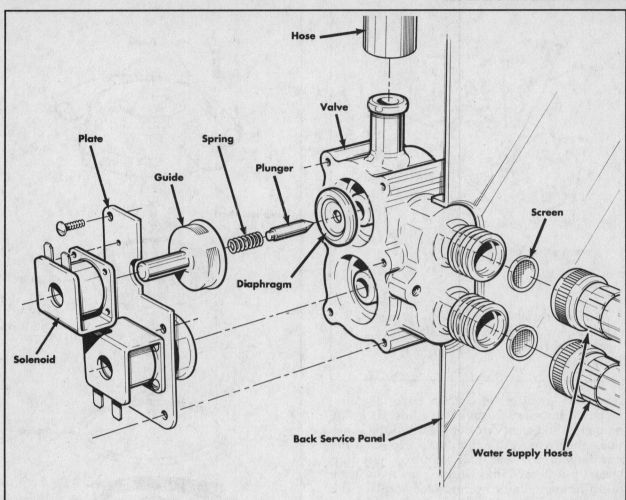

If an inlet valve is faulty, check the water connection and the valve screens. Try gently tapping the solenoids; if this doesn't work, replace the inlet valve assembly.

pump fails, you can hear or see the trouble: a loud rumbling inside the machine or a failure of the water to drain out of the tub. These symptoms also can be caused by kinked or crimped drain hoses or by blocked inlet screens, so before you start work on the water pump, make sure the drain hoses are draining properly. Remove the water supply hoses from the back of the washer. With long-nosed pliers, extract the filter screens from the valve ports in the washer, or from the hoses themselves. Wash the screens thoroughly, and then replace them and reattach the hoses. If the machine still rumbles or doesn't drain, examine the pump.

To get to the pump, bail and sponge out any water in the machine's tub, then tip the washer over on its front, using a blanket to protect the washer's finish. Remove the back service panel. The pump is usually along the bottom of the machine, but with the unit tipped on its front, it's easier to remove the pump through the back than through the bottom of the washer. Locate the pump; it has two large hoses attached to it with

spring or strap clips. If the clips are the spring type, pinch the ends of the clips with pliers to release them, and slide the clips down the hoses. If the clips are the strap type, unscrew the metal collar to loosen the clamp, and disconnect the hoses by pulling them off the connections. If the hoses are kinked or crimped at these connections, straighten and reconnect them, and try the machine again to see if this kinking was causing the problem. If the machine still doesn't drain, you'll have to remove the water pump.

To remove the pump, loosen the bolt that holds the drive belt taut and move the washer motor on the bracket to loosen the belt. Move the motor out of the way and unbolt the pump; it's usually held by two or three hex-head bolts located on the bottom of the pump housing. As you loosen the last mounting bolt, support the pump with your hand. Then lift the pump out of the washing machine.

On some washers the housing that covers the pump parts can be removed. If you can take the pump apart, do so because the trouble could be

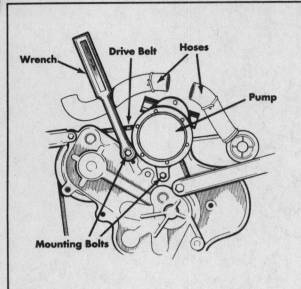

To remove the pump, unbolt the pump from the underside of the washer; it's usually held by several hex bolts on the bottom of the pump housing.

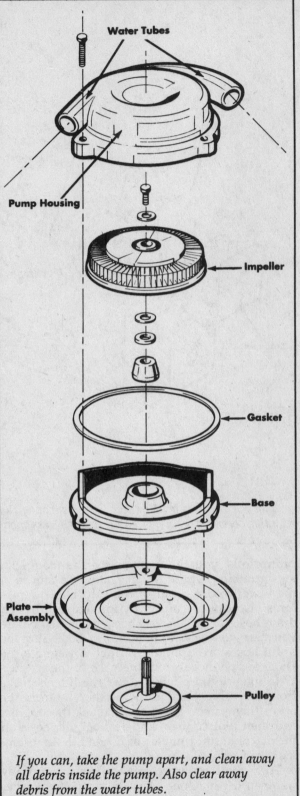

If you can, take the pump apart, and clean away all debris inside the pump. Also clear away debris from the water tubes.

lint or dirt, or pieces of cloth or paper clogging the pump impeller. Clean away all debris inside the pump, and clear any debris out of the water tubes; then reassemble the pump. Hook up the pump again and test it. If cleaning the pump doesn't put it back into working order or if the pump housing can't be removed, replace the pump with a new one.

To install the new pump, set it into position and connect the mounting bolts to the pump housing. Move the motor back into position. Tighten the drive belt on the motor by prying it taut with a hammer handle or pry bar; it should give about 1/2 inch when you press on it at the center point between the two pulleys. Then reconnect the hoses leading to the pump.

Drive Belts and Pulleys. The drive belt (or belts) of a washing machine may become worn or damaged, causing noisy operation or stopping the washer entirely. A damaged drive belt is easy to replace. Remove the back panel of the washer to get to the belt.

To remove the belt, loosen the bolt on the motor bracket, and move the motor to put slack in the belt. Remove the old belt and stretch a new one into place on the pulleys. To tension the new belt, use a hammer handle or a short pry bar to push the motor into position while you tighten the bolt in the adjustable bracket. The belt should have about 1/2 inch deflection when you press on it at the center point, midway between the pulleys. If the belt is too loose, it will slip on the pulleys, causing the machine to malfunction. If the belt is too tight, it will wear quickly and probably will become so hot that it will smoke.

Loose pulleys also can cause problems. Most pulleys are fastened to shafts with setscrews around the hub of the pulley. These screws must be tight, or the pulley or belt will slip. This malfunction may look as though it was caused by a faulty motor, but it can be corrected by tightening the pulleys and adjusting the belt. Always check the belts and pulleys before working on the motor.

Dryers

A dryer is simply a large drum into which wet laundry is loaded. A motor with pulleys, connected by a series of belts, turns the drum, and air heated by a gas heater or electric heating element is blown through the drum. The temperature and speed of the drum are controlled by a series of thermostats operated from a timer device on the control panel of the dryer. As a safety device, a dryer usually has a door switch that starts the working parts. Unless the door is properly closed, the dryer won't work, despite the settings on the control panel. Many dryers are equipped with a reset button on the control panel. If the motor won't run, let the dryer cool for about 10 minutes; then push the reset button. If there are no problems with the motor, switches, or electrical system, this should restart the dryer.

Caution: *Before doing any work on the dryer, make sure it's unplugged. Disconnect the grounding wire. If the dryer is gas-fueled, close the gas supply valve to shut off the unit's gas supply.*

Disassembly. The components that make up the dryer, except the power cord and the exhaust

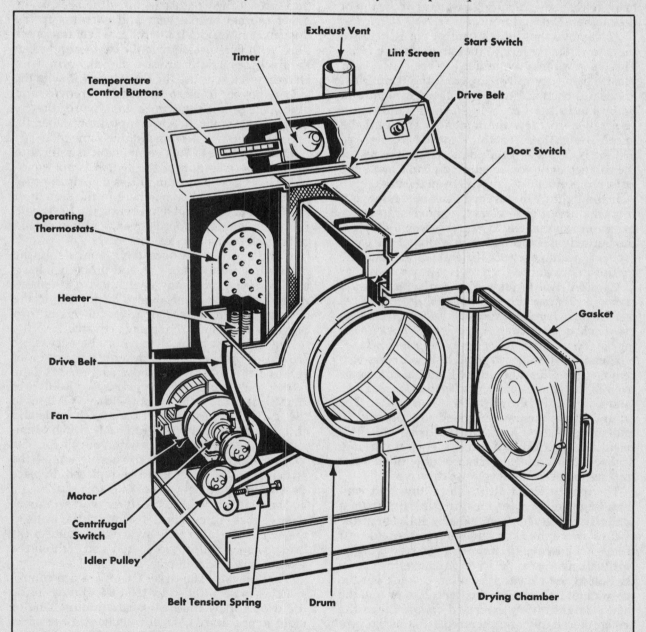

A dryer consists of a large drum into which wet laundry is loaded. A motor with pulleys turns the drum, and heated air is blown through the drum.

vent, are contained in a sheet metal box. Each component acts independently of the others, but all are interrelated. There are several different ways to disassemble the cabinet for tests and repairs, depending on the manufacturer and model of the machine. Basic disassembly procedures are simple. To remove the back panel, remove a series of screws or bolts that hold the panel to the top and sides of the cabinet. To remove the lower front panel, pull it away from the bottom of the cabinet. Remove the springs under each side of the lower panel after lifting the lower panel up and away. To remove the top panel, wedge a stiff-blade putty knife under the rim of the top and pry the top off. The putty knife helps release several spring fasteners at the top of the cabinet sides and front.

To remove the dryer's control panel, remove the screws that hold it to the cabinet top or front. These screws may be under a piece of metal or plastic trim; pry off or unscrew the trim. Most knobs are friction fitted; pull them straight out. Some knobs may be held to their shafts with setscrews; unscrew the fasteners and pull the knobs straight out. To get at most parts remove just the back panel: Don't disassemble the rest of the cabinet until you're sure you can't make the tests, replacements, or repairs from the back.

If the light in the dryer burns out, remove it from the dryer; if necessary, remove any retaining screws and panels to gain access to it. Replace the burned-out bulb with a new one of the same type and wattage; check the ends of the old bulb for this information. Then replace any panels.

Caution: *When testing or repairing the electrical parts of a gas dryer, remember that the dryer is hooked to a gas pipe. Turn off the shutoff valve on the supply pipe before disconnecting the gas supply line or moving the dryer, and before doing any electrical work.*

Cleaning. Besides drying clothes, dryers also remove lint. This fine, fuzzy material can cause trouble, because it blocks dryer lint traps, clogs vents, and fills blowers. Lint also can gather around and in the tracks of the drum rollers or in and under the pulleys and the drive belt. The result is poor clothes drying or even no drying. To avoid lint problems, clean out the dryer's lint trap system every time you use the dryer.

The exhaust vent also collects lint, and vent maintenance involves cleaning the lint from a screen in the dryer's vent exhaust collar or at the end of the exhaust vent where it sticks out through a basement window or through an exterior wall. To clean the screen, remove the clamp that holds the vent to the collar, or back out the screws that hold the vent to the collar, or pull the vent straight off an extended collar. Clean the screen thoroughly and then replace it in the vent assembly.

To clean the vent itself, bend the end of a wire hanger into a tight hook. Insert the wire into the vent and pull out any lint deposits. Also check the vent run to make sure that the vent piping or tubing isn't loose at the joints, or that flexible plastic venting isn't sagging between hanging brackets. Breaks or sags cause undue strain on the dryer's blower system, and can cause drying problems. If the vent pipe or tubing has become clogged with lint, remove the lint by pushing a garden hose or a drain-and-trap auger through the vent to a convenient joint, and disassemble the joint to remove the debris. With this procedure, it isn't necessary to disassemble the entire vent to find the blockage.

Lint also can get into pulley grooves and roller wheel tracks inside the dryer. Although the lint traps are cleaned regularly, open the back of the dryer cabinet once a year and vacuum up the dust and lint inside. If the roller wheel tracks are filled with lint, disassemble the cabinet and clean the tracks, especially around the idler arm, with an orange stick; or use the tip of a pencil, with the lead removed, to clean the tracks, grooves, and other recesses. If the wheels look worn (they're usually nylon, plastic, or composition material), replace them with new ones of the same type.

Door Switches. This component is critical to the dryer's operation; if the switch is not working, the dryer will not run unless there is a special grounding problem somewhere in the system. If such a grounding problem occurs, the dryer will run even when the door is open, and you should call a professional service person.

If the dryer has a door latch, make sure the latch is free from dirt or lint, and properly adjusted before you make any switch tests or replacements. Sometimes a misaligned latch prevents the door from being closed tightly, and this in turn prevents the switch from being activated.

The switch on the dryer may be accessible from the outside door, or you may have to remove the top of the dryer to get at it. The switch is a simple assembly, with two lead wires running to it. Test the switch with a VOM, set to the R x 1 scale. Disconnect the switch leads and clip one probe of the VOM to each switch terminal. Press the switch closed with your finger. The VOM should read zero; if the needle jumps, the switch is faulty, and should be replaced. Replace the switch with a new one of the same type.

The switch is held to the dryer with setscrews; remove these screws and disconnect the leads to the switch. Install a new switch and connect the leads; then position the switch and tighten the setscrews to hold it in place.

Thermostats. The dryer's temperature control switches are controlled by the temperature inside the dryer or by the heat of the motor. One or more temperature control switches on the panel can be adjusted to control the temperature in the dryer. Operating thermostats sometimes stick, causing control problems. These thermostats are usually positioned near the exhaust duct bulkhead or the fan housing of the dryer. Remove the back panel of the dryer to get at them. Before you make any checks, try tapping the housing of the thermostats lightly with the handle of a screwdriver. This may jar the contacts loose. Temperature control switches are located behind the dryer's control panel, and the panel must be removed for switch testing or replacement.

To check the control panel thermostat, test it with a VOM, set to the R x 1 scale. Clip one probe of the VOM to each thermostat terminal. If the meter reads zero, the thermostat is working; if the needle jumps to a high reading, the thermostat is faulty and should be replaced. Replace the thermostat with a new one of the same type. Connect the new thermostat the same way the old one was connected.

Before checking an operating thermostat, make absolutely certain that the power to the dryer has been turned off and the dryer is cool. Then disconnect the leads to one side of the thermostat. Test an operating thermostat with the VOM, set to the R x 1 scale; clip one probe to each terminal of the thermostat. Disconnect the leads to one side of the thermostat so that the meter won't give a false reading. If the meter reads zero, the thermostat is working; if the needle jumps to a high reading, the thermostat is faulty and should be replaced. Do not repair the thermostat or have the thermostat repaired; replace it with a new one of the same type.

Operating thermostats open and close circuits, turning the heating element on and off. The components of this type of switch are a thermal bulb and capillary tube, a bimetallic disc, a switch, and a control screw. To remove this type of unit, pry out the thermal bulb, which is located in the back part of the dryer, mounted on the exhaust housing. Install the new thermostat so that its bulb fits tightly on the inside of the housing; otherwise, the bulb could collect lint. Connect the new thermostat in the same position and the same way as the old one.

Timer. The dryer timer, located behind the control panel, controls several things: the drying time of the clothes in the drum, the flow of electricity to the heating element, and the flow of power to the timer motor and the drum motor in the dryer cabinet. Timers are driven by synchronous motors. Although the contact part of the timer can be cleaned and adjusted on some dryers, this is a job for a professional repair person; timer motor repairs also should be handled by a professional, but you can replace a faulty timer yourself.

To get at the timer, remove the front of the control panel. On some dryers the timer can be removed without removing the panel. In either case, pull the timer knob off the shaft, and slip off the pointer. The pointer is usually keyed to the shaft by two flat surfaces to keep the pointer from slipping when it's turned.

Test the timer with a VOM set to the R x 1 scale. Turn the timer to the "normal dry" setting, and disconnect one of the timer power leads. Some timers may have several wires connected to them; the power leads are usually larger than the other wires, and this size difference can be spotted under close examination. Clip one probe of the meter to each timer terminal. If the meter reads zero, the timer is working; if the needle jumps to a high reading, the timer is faulty, and should be replaced. Replace the timer with a new one of the same size and type.

To replace the timer, have a helper hold the new timer close to the old one, especially if there are several wires to be changed. Disconnect the old wires one at a time, connecting each corresponding new wire as you work, to make sure the connections are properly made. You also could draw a diagram detailing the proper connections. After all the wires are connected, check the connections again for correctness. The timer is held to the dryer with hex-type screw bolts; unbolt the old timer and secure the new one.

Fan. The most common dryer fan problem is lint clogging the air passages through the heater and through the dryer drum. To clear a clogged air passage, remove the back service panel of the dryer and back out the screws holding the air duct in place. Then reach into the duct and remove all the lint and dirt possible. Reassemble the parts.

Also inspect the fan for a loose screw connection where the motor shaft is set on the dryer's drum. Remove the back service panel, tighten the screw, and replace the panel.

HEATING AND COOLING

Most people take heating and cooling for granted. We expect our heating systems to keep us warm during the winter, and we depend on air conditioning to keep us cool during the summer. When a problem arises, most people call for service, but there is an alternative. You can cut your service costs drastically, while keeping your heating and cooling systems working efficiently, by doing regular maintenance chores and simple repairs yourself. Heating and cooling systems can be intimidating, but they are based on simple, easily understood principles. Adjustments and improvements often can be made without much difficulty, and if you take care of your furnace and air conditioner properly, they'll reward you with dependable service.

There is more to heating and cooling than just the machines that heat or cool a home and the network of ducts or pipes that distribute heating and cooling energy. Almost as important are the components that conserve this energy, most notably weather stripping and insulation.

How Heating and Cooling Systems Work

Climate control devices or systems have three basic components: a source of warmed or cooled air, a means of distributing the air to the rooms being heated or cooled, and a control used to regulate the system (the thermostat). The sources of warm air (the furnace) and cool air (the air conditioner) in a house often use the same distribution and control systems; if your house has central air conditioning, cool air probably flows through the same ducts that heat does and is regulated by the same thermostat. When a heating or cooling system malfunctions, any one of these three basic components (heat-cold source, distribution system, or thermostat) may be causing the problem.

FURNACES, HEATERS, AND AIR CONDITIONERS

Both heating and air conditioning work on the principle that heat always moves from a warm area to a cooler one. Furnaces and heaters put heat into the air to make your home warmer; air conditioners remove heat to make your home cooler.

All heating and cooling units burn fuel. Air conditioners use electricity. Some of the most popular home heating systems use natural gas or fuel oil; other systems use electricity. The heat pump, an electrically powered climate control unit, both heats and cools air. In summer it extracts heat from the air inside your home; in winter it extracts heat from the air outside, and uses this heat to warm the air inside.

When the furnace is turned on, it consumes the fuel (gas, oil, or electricity) that powers it. As fuel is consumed, heat is produced and channeled to the rooms and living areas of your home through ducts, pipes, or wires, and out registers, radiators, or heating panels. Some systems use the heat they produce to warm water, which in turn heats the air in your home. These systems use a boiler to store and heat the water supply. When an air conditioner is turned on, electrical power is used to cool a gas in a coil to its liquid state. Warm air in your home is cooled by contact with the cooling coil and is channeled to the rooms of your home through ducts and out registers. Room air conditioners distribute cooled air directly.

DISTRIBUTION SYSTEMS

Once air is warmed or cooled at the heat-cold source, it must be distributed to the various rooms of your home. This can be accomplished with any of three basic systems: forced-air, gravity, or radiant heat.

Forced-Air Systems. A forced-air system distributes the heat produced by the furnace or the coolness produced by a central air conditioner with an electrically powered fan, called a blower,

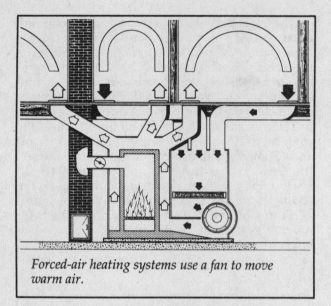

Forced-air heating systems use a fan to move warm air.

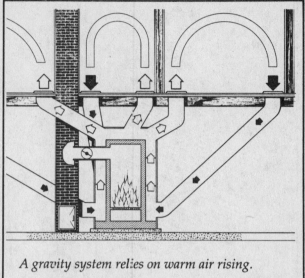

A gravity system relies on warm air rising.

which forces the air through a system of metal ducts to the rooms in your home. As the warm air from the furnace flows into the rooms, colder air in the rooms flows down through another set of ducts, the cold-air return system, to the furnace to be warmed. This system is adjustable; you can increase or decrease the amount of air flowing through your home. Central air conditioning systems use the same forced-air system, including the blower, to distribute cool air to the rooms, and to bring back warmer air to be cooled. Problems with this system usually involve blower malfunctions. The blower also may be noisy, and it adds the cost of electrical power to the cost of furnace fuel. Because it employs a blower, a forced-air system is probably the most effective way to channel airborne heat throughout a house.

Gravity Systems. Gravity systems are based on the principle that hot air rises and cold air sinks; they cannot be used to distribute cool air from an air conditioner. In a gravity system, the furnace is located near or below the floor, usually in the basement of a house. The warmed air rises and flows through ducts to registers in the floor throughout the house. If the furnace is located on the main floor of the house, the heat registers are usually positioned high on the walls, because the registers must always be higher than the furnace. Once in a room, the warmed air rises toward the ceiling; as it cools, it sinks, enters the return air ducts, and flows back to the furnace to be heated again.

The big advantage to gravity heating is that it uses no mechanical distribution device; the furnace needs no blower to circulate the heat. Gravity systems use no electric current, and the movement of the heated air is silent. There are disadvantages: Gravity-moved air doesn't move with much force, and usually cannot be filtered. The gravity system doesn't work well if the heated air must travel long distances, and the slow

movement of the heated air allows for greater heat loss before the air reaches the rooms of your home. Gravity heating systems are not adjustable and cannot warm a home as evenly as most forced-air systems.

Some wall heaters are of the gravity type, with a return air vent at the bottom and a vent for the hot air to go out at the top. These units are used in warmer climates, where heating demands are not extreme.

Radiant Heating. Radiant systems function by warming the walls, floors, or ceilings, or more commonly, by warming radiators or convectors in rooms. These objects then warm the air in the room. The heat source usually is hot water, heated by the furnace and circulated, as steam or as water, through pipes embedded in the wall, floor, or ceiling, or connected to radiators. Some systems use electric heating panels to generate heat, which is radiated into rooms; like gravity wall heaters, these panels are usually installed in warm climates. Radiant systems cannot be used to distribute cool air from an air conditioner.

Radiators and convectors, the most common means of radiant heat distribution in older homes, are used with steam and hot-water heating systems. Steam systems depend on gravity; steam rises into the radiators and as it condenses returns to the boiler. Hot-water systems may depend on gravity or on a circulator pump to move heated water from the boiler to the radiators or convectors. A system that uses a pump, or circulator, is called a hydronic system.

Radiant heating systems often are built into houses constructed on a concrete slab foundation. A network of hot-water pipes is laid within but near the surface of the concrete slab. When the concrete is warmed by the pipes, it warms the air that contacts the floor surface. The slab does not need to get very hot; it eventually will contact all the air throughout the house.

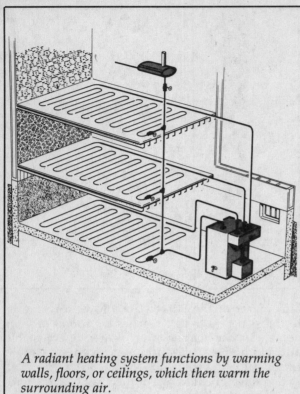

A radiant heating system functions by warming walls, floors, or ceilings, which then warm the surrounding air.

Radiant systems, especially gravity systems, are prone to several problems. The pipes used to distribute the heated water can become clogged with mineral deposits or slanted to the wrong angle. The boiler, in which water is heated at the heat source, also may malfunction.

THE THERMOSTAT

The thermostat, a heat-sensitive switch, is the basic control that regulates the temperature of your home. It responds to changes in the temperature of the air, where it is located, and turns the furnace or air conditioner on or off as needed to maintain the temperature at a set level. The key component of the thermostat is a bimetallic element that expands or contracts as the temperature goes up or down. Thermostats have three sections: a cover, a temperature control section, and a base with switches and connections.

There are two basic kinds of thermostats. Older thermostats have two exposed contacts; newer ones have contacts sealed in glass to protect them from dirt. On the older version, as the temperature drops, a bimetallic strip bends, making first one electrical contact and then another. The system is fully activated when the second contact closes, turning on the heating system and the anticipator on the thermostat. The anticipator heats the bimetallic element, causing it to bend and break the second electrical contact. The first contact is not yet broken, and the heater keeps running until the temperature rises above the setting on the thermostat dial.

Thermostats with coiled bimetallic strip elements sealed behind glass work like this: As the temperature drops, the bimetallic element starts to uncoil. The force exerted by the uncoiling of the elements separates a stationary steel bar from a magnet at the end of the coil. The magnet comes down close to the glass-enclosed contact, pulls up on the contact arm inside the tube, and causes the contacts to close, completing the electrical circuit and turning on the heater and the anticipator. As the air in the room heats up, the coil starts to rewind and breaks the hold of the magnet on the contact arm; the arm drops, breaks the circuit, and turns off the system. At this point, the magnet moves back up to the stationary bar, which holds it in place and keeps the contacts open and the heater turned off until the room cools down again.

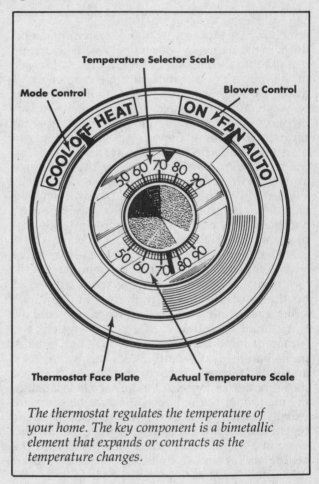

The thermostat regulates the temperature of your home. The key component is a bimetallic element that expands or contracts as the temperature changes.

Basic Maintenance Procedures

The basic components of heating and cooling systems are trouble free and easy to maintain. Efficient operation depends on regular maintenance. You'll need only a few tools and materials: screwdrivers, a flashlight, pliers, wrenches, a hammer, a level, newspaper, rags, brushes, and a vacuum cleaner. A few materials are required, including motor oil, fan belt dressing, refractory cement, and duct tape. These are available at automotive and hardware stores and at some home centers.

When a heating or cooling system malfunctions, any one of its three basic components (heat-cold source, distribution system, or thermostat) may be causing the problem. If the furnace or air conditioner doesn't run, the malfunction is probably at the source: the furnace or air conditioner may have lost power; fuel may not be reaching the unit, or if it's gas or oil, may not be igniting. If the furnace or air conditioner turns on but the warm or cool air isn't reaching the rooms of your home, the problem is likely to involve the blower or the distribution system. A faulty control, or thermostat, could keep the system from turning on or could cause it to turn on and off repeatedly. Whatever the problem, you should start with the simplest procedure.

Before you start work on a heating or cooling system, there are several steps to take:

• Check to make sure the unit is receiving power; look for blown fuses or tripped circuit breakers at the main entrance panel. Some furnaces have a separate power entrance, usually at a different panel near the main entrance panel. Other furnaces have fuses mounted in or on the unit.

• If the unit has a reset button, wait 30 minutes to let the motor cool, and then press the button. If the unit still doesn't start, wait 30 minutes and press the reset button again.

• If the unit has a separate power switch, make sure the switch is turned on.

• Check to make sure the thermostat is properly set. If necessary, raise (or for an air conditioner, lower) the setting 5 degrees.

• If the unit uses gas, check to make sure the gas supply is turned on; if necessary, turn it on. If the unit uses oil, check to make sure there is an adequate supply of oil. If necessary, have the tank refilled.

• If the unit uses gas, make sure the pilot light is lit. If necessary, relight the pilot.

There also are several important safety factors to remember:

• Before doing any work on any heating or cooling system, make sure all power to the system is turned off. At the main electrical entrance panel, remove the fuse or trip the circuit breaker that controls the power to the unit. If you're not sure which circuit that is, remove the main fuse or trip the main circuit breaker to cut off all power to the house. Some furnaces have a separate power entrance, usually at a different panel near the main entrance panel. If a separate panel is present, remove the fuse or trip the breaker there.

• If the fuse blows or the circuit trips repeatedly when the furnace or air conditioner turns on, there is a problem in the electrical system. Do not try to fix the furnace; call a professional.

• If the unit uses gas, and there is a smell of gas in your home, do not try to shut off the gas or turn any lights on or off. Get out of the house, leaving the door open, and go to a telephone; call the gas company or the fire department immediately to report a leak. Do not reenter your home.

To keep your heating and cooling systems in top shape, have them professionally serviced once a year. The best time to have a furnace serviced is at the end of the heating season; because this is the off season, you often can get a discount, and service is likely to be prompt. Also have your air conditioner checked then.

Dirt is the biggest enemy of your home's heating and cooling system; it can waste fuel and drastically lower efficiency. It affects all three basic components of the system: heat-cold source, distribution, and control. Cleaning is the most important part of regular maintenance for all three components; lubrication and belt adjustment at the furnace also are important. To keep your system working properly, follow these general procedures.

MAINTAINING THE SOURCE OF HEAT OR COLD

The heat-cold source is the most complicated part of the heating and cooling system, and the part most likely to suffer from neglect. Problems in the heat-cold source also may lead to distribution problems. Whatever heat-cold source your system uses, give it regular attention to prevent problems.

Cleaning a Furnace. Three parts of the furnace should be cleaned: the filter system, the blower, and the motor. The furnace filter should be replaced or, if it's permanent, cleaned, at the beginning of the heating season and about once a month during periods of continuous use. Check the filter by taking it out and holding it up to the light; if it looks clogged, replace it despite the length of time it's been in service. Use a new filter of exactly the same kind, material, and size as the old filter.

A disposable furnace filter consists of a fiber mesh in a cardboard frame; the size of the filter is printed on the edge of the frame. An arrow on the edge of the frame shows the correct direction of air flow through the filter. Air flows from the return-air duct toward the blower, so the arrow on the filter should point away from the return-air duct and toward the blower. A permanent filter is usually sprayed with a special filter-coating chemical, available at hardware stores and home centers. Clean this filter according to the manufacturer's instructions, which are usually attached to the furnace housing.

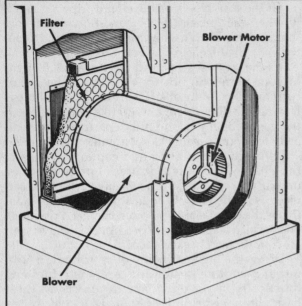

Three parts of the air-moving system should be kept clean: the filter, the blower, and the blower motor. You'll probably have to remove an access plate to get to them.

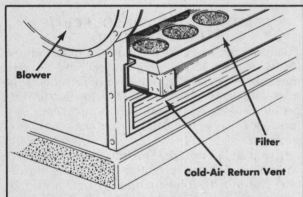

Replace a clogged furnace filter with a new one of the same kind. The arrow on the filter, indicating air flow, should point away from the return-air duct and toward the blower.

To gain access to the filter, look for a metal panel on the front of the furnace below the return-air duct, between the duct and the blower system. The panel may be marked "filter," or may form the lid or the front of a boxlike projection on the furnace housing. To remove either kind of panel, slip the panel off its holding hooks or unscrew the panel from the box or furnace housing. On some heating units, the filters are exposed; just slip the filter up and out of the U-shaped tracks that hold it in place.

After replacing or cleaning the filter, clean the blower assembly, the belts and pulleys to the blower, and the motor housing. **Caution:** *Before cleaning these areas, make sure the power to the fur-*

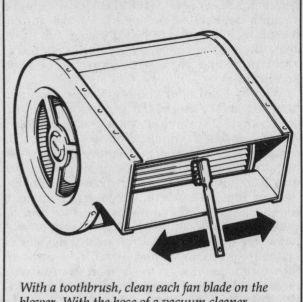

With a toothbrush, clean each fan blade on the blower. With the hose of a vacuum cleaner, remove all the dirt loosened by the brushing.

nace is turned off. Cleaning the blower is critical if the furnace has a squirrel-cage fan because the openings in this kind of blower often become clogged with dirt.

To clean the blower, turn off the power to the furnace. Remove the panel that covers the filter to get to the blower or remove a panel on the front of the furnace. This panel may be slipped on hooks or may be held by a series of retaining screws. Access to the inside of the blower is usually gained by sliding out the fan unit, which is held on a track by screws. If the power cord to the fan assembly is not long enough to allow the fan unit to slide all the way out, disconnect the cord. Mark the wire connections first, so you'll be able to reassemble the unit correctly. With a toothbrush, clean each fan blade and the spaces between the blades. With a vacuum cleaner, remove the dirt and debris loosened by the brushing. Also vacuum the belts and pulleys. Wipe off the motor housing to prevent heat buildup in the motor.

Cleaning a Central Air Conditioner. A furnace used with a central air conditioning system should be cleaned regularly, and the evaporator, which is located above the furnace, and the condenser, usually located outside the house, should be cleaned annually.

Lubrication. To keep the motor running cool, make sure it's clean. Most motors are permanently lubricated and sealed by the manufacturer; they require no further attention. Some motors have covered oil ports above the bearings near the motor shaft. If the motor has oil ports, it should be lubricated annually. Apply two or three drops of Number 10 nondetergent motor oil (not all-purpose oil) to each port; do not overlubricate. If the blower shaft has oil ports, it should be lubricated annually. You'll probably have to remove an access plate to get at the ports. If the blower has grease cups instead of oil ports, remove the screw caps that cover the cups and fill the cups with bearing lubricant, available at automotive and hardware stores.

Belt Adjustment and Replacement. On furnaces that have a blower, inspect the belts on the blower and motor when you clean and lubricate the furnace. If the belts are worn or frayed, replace them with new ones of the same kind and size. To release a worn belt, loosen the mounting bolts on the motor and slide the motor forward toward the blower unit. Remove the old belt and stretch a new one into place on the pulleys; slide the motor back and tighten the motor mounting bolts to increase the tension. Adjust the bolts so that there is about 1/2-inch deflection when you press on the belt at its center point between the two pulleys.

If the belts are not damaged, adjust the tension as necessary to achieve 1/2-inch deflection. If a belt squeaks when the blower is running, spray it with fan belt dressing, available at automotive and hardware stores and at some home centers.

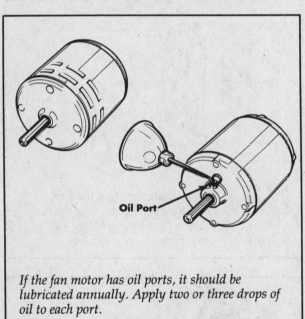

If the fan motor has oil ports, it should be lubricated annually. Apply two or three drops of oil to each port.

MAINTAINING THE DISTRIBUTION SYSTEM

Whatever the heat-cold source, warm or cool air must travel to the various rooms of your home. When the distribution system is dirty or the supply and return registers are blocked, the heat or cool generated by the furnace or air conditioner cannot reach your living spaces. A dirty system wastes energy and is inefficient. To keep your system operating at top efficiency, clean it regularly, and make sure supply and return registers are not blocked by draperies, furniture, or rugs.

Forced-Air and Gravity Systems. These two systems use the same kind of ducting to distribute heated or cooled air. To maintain the ducting, vacuum supply and return registers thoroughly at least once a month during the heating season. If your home has floor registers, lift the register grilles and clean the ducting below them, as far as you can reach, with a brush and vacuum. Cold-air returns are especially prone to dirt buildup, because air is sucked into them from the rooms back to the furnace. In forced-air systems, the blower and motor also should be cleaned and lubricated regularly.

Radiant Systems. The efficiency of radiator or convector systems, either steam or hot water, depends on free circulation in the radiators or convectors. In both systems the supply pipes and the radiators or convectors must slope toward the boiler. Check the slope of radiators and pipes with a level, and correct the tilt as necessary to restore proper operation. Lack of heat in a radiator or convector can be caused by air trapped in it. To remove air from a hot-water radiator or convector, open the air vent until the hissing stops and a few drops of water squirt out, and then close the vent. Steam radiators typically have a bullet-shaped valve that releases air with each heating cycle; if a radiator isn't heating properly, try clearing the orifice at the top of this valve with a straight pin or a paper clip. In steam systems the boiler should be flushed once a month; in hot-water systems, once a season.

In radiant systems with distribution pipes embedded in floors, walls, or ceilings, maintenance is usually not possible.

MAINTAINING AND REPAIRING THE THERMOSTAT

A thermostat is a highly sensitive instrument, responding to the slightest changes in temperature. While it has fewer parts to go wrong than the other components of your heating and cooling system, it can be a source of problems. A thermostat cover that is improperly installed or inadvertently bumped can jam the bimetallic element, causing the heater or air conditioner to fail to start. The thermostat's base may slip out of level, causing it to operate incorrectly. A more common problem is dirt on the bimetallic element, which can affect the thermostat's calibration and interfere with its operation. If a thermostat set for 70 degrees Fahrenheit, is maintaining the temperature at 73 degrees Fahrenheit, the additional energy used can add as much as seven percent to your fuel bill. Check your thermostat every year before the heating season begins.

Other problems with a thermostat often can be traced to switches on the base and wires near the bimetallic element that loosen and become corroded. Tighten loose connections with a screwdriver; use a cotton swab to clean away corrosion.

Cleaning and Checking Calibration. To check a thermostat's accuracy, tape a glass tube thermometer to the wall a few inches away from the thermostat. Pad the thermometer to prevent it from touching the wall, and make sure that neither the thermometer nor the thermostat is affected by any outside temperature influences. Often the hole in the wall behind the thermostat through which the wires come is too large, allowing cold air to reach the thermostat and affect its reading.

After taping the thermometer in place, wait about 15 minutes for the mercury to stabilize; then compare the reading on the thermometer with the reading of the thermostat needle. If the variation is more than a degree, check to see if the thermostat is dirty because dirt can cause inaccuracy. To examine the thermostat, remove the face plate, usually held by a snap or a friction catch. Blow away any dust inside it with your own breath or with a plastic squeeze bottle used as a bellows. Do not use a vacuum cleaner; its suction is too great. If the thermostat has open contact points, which are not sealed within a glass enclosure, rub a new dollar bill between them to clean these spots. Do not use sandpaper or emery cloth. If the element is coiled, use a soft brush for cleaning. If the thermostat has a mercury vial inside, make sure the unit is level. Use a level to make sure the unit is straight. If it isn't, loosen the mounting screws and adjust the thermostat until it is level; then retighten the screws.

After cleaning the thermostat, check it again with a glass thermometer, as detailed above. If the thermostat is still not calibrated properly, it should be replaced.

Replacing a Thermostat. Replace a faulty thermostat with a new one of the same voltage as the old one. The thermostat must be compatible with the heating system. **Caution:** *Before replacing the thermostat, remove the fuse or trip the circuit breaker to turn off the power to the circuit that controls it. If you aren't sure which circuit controls the thermostat, remove the main fuse or trip the main circuit breaker to turn off all the power to the house.*

To remove the old thermostat, take the face plate off the unit and look for the mounting screws. Remove the screws to release the thermostat from the wall. Remove the wires from the back of the old thermostat by turning the connection screws counterclockwise. Be careful not to let the loose wires fall down between the walls. Clean the exposed wires by scraping them with a knife until the wire ends shine; attach the wires to the new thermostat.

The new thermostat must have the same electrical rating as the old one. To complete the job, push the wires back into the wall and tape up the opening to prevent cold air inside the walls from affecting the thermostat. Install the mounting

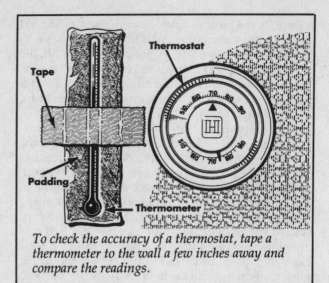

To check the accuracy of a thermostat, tape a thermometer to the wall a few inches away and compare the readings.

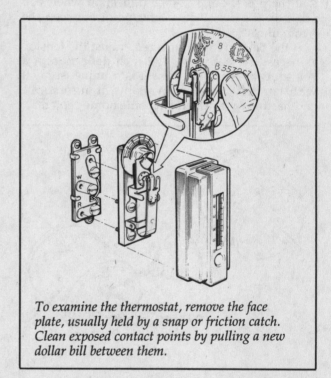

To examine the thermostat, remove the face plate, usually held by a snap or friction catch. Clean exposed contact points by pulling a new dollar bill between them.

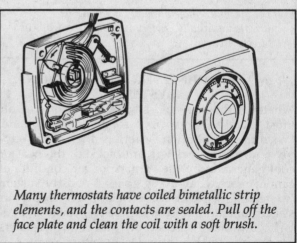

Many thermostats have coiled bimetallic strip elements, and the contacts are sealed. Pull off the face plate and clean the coil with a soft brush.

screws to secure the new thermostat to the wall. If the thermostat has a mercury tube, set the unit against a level during the installation; mercury tube thermostats must be exactly level. Snap the face plate back into place and make sure the new thermostat turns the heating-cooling system on and off when the temperature setting is adjusted.

IMPROVING HEATING AND COOLING EFFICIENCY

Although regular maintenance and repair of a central heating and air conditioning system can save you plenty, the system will operate even more efficiently if your home is sealed against the weather. Make sure the structure is properly insulated, weather-stripped, and caulked; install storm windows and doors to prevent heat loss in the winter and heat gain during the summer.

For maximum energy efficiency, follow these simple procedures:

•Protect the thermostat from anything that would cause it to give a false reading. If the thermostat is in a draft, misplaced on a cold outside wall, or too near a heat-producing appliance or register, its accuracy will be compromised.

•If you won't be home for a few days, turn the thermostat to its lowest setting. If there is no danger of pipes freezing, turn the heating system off completely.

•Install a thermostat timer to save fuel and money. The timer can be set to raise and lower the temperature automatically during peak and off hours. Installation instructions are usually included with the timer.

•Close the draperies over large windows and glass doors to form a barrier against heat loss during the winter and heat gain during the summer. Insulated draperies or shades are even more effective.

•If your home has rooms that are seldom or never used, close the vents in these rooms and shut the doors. There is no sense in heating and cooling space you don't use.

•Avoid constant thermostat adjustments; they waste fuel. When coming into the house after the thermostat has been turned down, don't set it higher than the desired temperature. Setting the thermostat high generally will not cause the temperature to reach the desired level any faster.

•One adjustment you should make is a reduction in the thermostat setting before you go to bed every night. Cutting back for several hours can make a big difference in fuel consumption.

•Reduce the thermostat setting while you're baking; heat generated by the oven will compensate.

•Reduce the thermostat setting when you have a large group of people in your home. People generate heat, and a party can quickly raise the temperature.

•Keep the damper in a fireplace or a separate wood- or coal-burning stove closed unless you have a fire going. Updrafts will suck heated air out through the chimney.

•Maintain proper humidity. A house that is too dry can feel uncomfortably cold even when the temperature setting is correct.

Additional tips for efficient air conditioning include:

•Aim the vents of room air conditioners upward for better air circulation; cold air naturally settles downward. On central air conditioning systems, adjust the registers so that the air is blowing up.

•Lighting fixtures can throw off heat; don't leave lights on unless it's absolutely necessary.

•Make sure the outside portion of the air conditioning system, whether a room unit or a central system, is not in direct sunlight or blocked from free air flow.

•If you have room units, close all heating system vents so that the cool air isn't wasted.

Troubleshooting Heating Plants

There are several kinds of heating plants in common use: oil, gas, and electric furnaces; gas or electric wall or baseboard heaters; heat pumps; and steam or hot-water boilers. Each has its own problems, depending on how it is put together and how it works. The method of distributing the heat is as important as the means of generating it.

GAS FURNACES AND HEATERS

Natural gas generally is the preferred source for heat. Natural gas burns cleaner than fuel oil, and most natural-gas furnaces present fewer operational difficulties than oil burners do. The problems that affect natural-gas furnaces usually have little to do with the fuel source. They typically involve the furnace's thermocouple, the pilot light, or some component of the electrical system. Gas space heaters have all the elements of a central gas heating system built into one compact unit.

Caution: *Gas furnaces and heaters have control shutoffs to prevent gas leaks, but they are not fail-safe. If there is a smell of gas in your house, do not turn any lights on or off, or try to shut off the gas leading to the furnace. Get out of the house, leaving the door open, and go to a telephone; call the gas company or the fire department immediately to report a leak. Do not reenter your home.*

Disassembly. On some units a plug door covers the pilot light assembly; to get to the pilot burner, pull the door out of the furnace housing. On other units remove the panel that covers the pilot and gas burners.

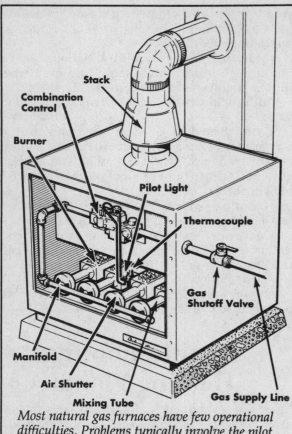

Most natural gas furnaces have few operational difficulties. Problems typically involve the pilot light, the thermocouple, or some part of the electrical system.

The pilot light control, reset button, gas valve, and thermocouple usually are contained in an assembly at the front of the furnace. The furnace limit switch is located on the plenum on the upper housing of the furnace.

Caution: *Before doing any work on the furnace, make sure the power to the furnace is turned off.*

Pilot Light. The pilot light can go out because of drafts. Instructions for relighting the pilot usually are fastened to the furnace; follow the manufacturer's instructions. If instructions for relighting the pilot are not provided, follow the general procedure below.

The pilot light assembly has a gas valve, with "on," "off," and "pilot" settings. Turn the valve to "off" and wait three minutes. Then switch the valve to the "pilot" setting. Hold a lighted match to the pilot opening while you push the reset button on the pilot control panel. Keep this button depressed until the pilot flame is burning brightly; then set the valve to the "on" position. If the pilot flame won't stay lit, the opening may be clogged; clean it with a piece of fine wire. If it won't stay lit after several attempts to light it, the problem may be a faulty thermocouple. If the thermocouple is faulty, replace it, or call a professional service person.

Some furnaces have an electrical system to ignite the gas; in these systems there is no pilot light. An electric element heats up and ignites the burners. If this electric ignition system malfunctions, call a professional.

Thermocouple. This gas furnace component, located near the pilot light burner, is a safety device; it shuts off the gas if the pilot light goes out or the electric igniter fails. If the pilot light won't stay lit, the thermocouple may be faulty and should be adjusted or replaced.

To adjust the thermocouple, tighten the thermocouple nut with a wrench. Tighten the nut but do not apply a lot of pressure. Then try lighting the pilot. If the pilot won't stay lit, replace the thermocouple with a new one of the same kind.

To replace a thermocouple, unscrew the copper lead and the connection nut inside the threaded connection to the gas line. Under the mounting bracket at the thermocouple tube, unscrew the bracket nut that holds the tube in place. Insert a new thermocouple into the hole in the bracket, steel tube up and copper lead down.

Under the bracket screw the bracket nut over the tube. Push the connection nut to the threaded connection where the copper lead joins the gas line; make sure the attachment is clean and dry. Screw the nut tightly into place, but do not overtighten it. Both the bracket nut and the connection nut should only be a little tighter than hand tightened.

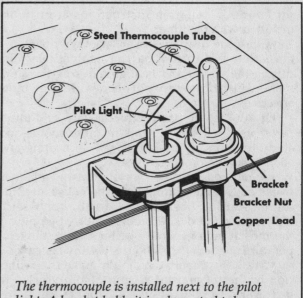

The thermocouple is installed next to the pilot light. A bracket holds it in place, steel tube up and copper lead down.

Limit Switch. The limit switch is a safety control switch, located on the furnace just below the plenum. If the plenum gets too hot, the limit switch shuts off the burner; it also shuts off the blower when the temperature drops to a certain level after the burner has shut off. If the blower runs continuously, either the blower control on the thermostat has been set to "on" or the limit control switch needs adjustment. Check the thermostat first. If the blower control has been set to "on," change it to "auto"; if the blower control is already on "auto," the limit switch needs to be adjusted.

Remove the control's cover; under it is a toothed dial. One side is marked "limit"; don't touch this side. The other side of the control is marked "fan." There are two pointers on the fan side; the blower goes on at the upper pointer setting and turns off at the lower pointer setting. The pointers should be set about 25 degrees apart. Set the upper pointer at 115 degrees Fahrenheit and the lower one at 90 degrees.

Burner Adjustment. The flames on the gas burner should be full and steady, with no sputtering and no trace of yellow. To adjust the flame height on the main burners, call a professional service person. To adjust the height of the pilot flame, turn the flame adjustment screw until the flame is from 1 1/2 to 2 inches high. The adjustment screw is near the gas valve on the pilot assembly if the control has this adjustment feature.

Gas Leaks. If you suspect leaks around the furnace unit, stir up a mixture of liquid detergent and water. Paint this mixture on the gas supply line along its connections and valves; the soapy water will bubble at any point where there is a leak. If you find a leak, try tightening the leaking connection with a pipe wrench, but be careful not to overtighten the connection. If the pipe connections or valves still leak, don't try to fix them; call a professional.

OIL FURNACES

Oil-fired burners are used in many parts of the country as the basic heat source for warm-air, hot-water, and steam heating systems. Most home oil systems in use today are called pressure burners. In this kind of system, oil is sprayed into a combustion chamber at high pressure, propelled by a blower, and ignited by an electric spark. The oil continues to burn as the mist is sprayed. There are few repairs that you can do yourself with this kind of system, so an oil furnace should be inspected by a professional service person once a year.

While there aren't many repairs you can do, good regular maintenance can help eliminate many problems. Regular maintenance should include:

•During the heating season, check the smoke from the chimney. If the smoke is black, the furnace is not burning the oil completely and fuel is being wasted. Call a professional service person for adjustments.

•Clean the blower at the beginning of the heating season and about midway through it.

•Clean the soot from the stack control about midway through the heating season.

•If the blower motor has grease or oil fittings, lubricate the fittings midway through the heating season with cup grease or Number 10 nondetergent motor oil (not all-purpose oil), available at automotive and hardware stores.

•Always clean the thermostat before each heating season.

Disassembly. An oil furnace is a complex assembly. Your maintenance and repair work is limited to simple parts, such as the filters, the blower, the motor belts, the switches, and the thermostat. The other components of the furnace, including electrodes, oil nozzle, air tubes, transformer, and pump, are best left to a professional for service, because they require special tools and testing equipment.

Remove the access panel covering the burner blower by backing out a series of retaining screws around the rim of the housing. Access to the air blower and filter is through a metal panel on one side of the furnace. The panel is held by either hooks or retaining bolts; slip the panel up and off the hooks, or remove the bolts and lift the panel off. Most furnaces have switches and reset buttons located on the motor or in a switch box outside the furnace housing. These usually are identified with stampings or labels, such as "disconnect switch" or "reset." The stack control sensor, a safety device that monitors burner operation, is positioned in the stack and held with a series of retaining bolts.

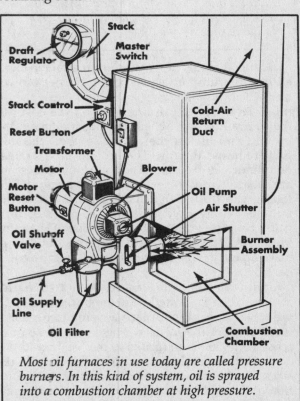

Most oil furnaces in use today are called pressure burners. In this kind of system, oil is sprayed into a combustion chamber at high pressure.

Oil Filters. The oil filter should be changed or cleaned at the start of the heating season and about midway through the season. To remove the filter, close the oil shutoff valve between the fuel tank and the filter; then unscrew the bottom or cup of the filter housing. If the filter is disposable, remove it and insert a new one of the same size and design. If the furnace has a permanent filter, wash the filter every 45 to 60 days in kerosene and replace it in the housing. **Caution:** *Kerosene is flammable; be very careful when cleaning a permanent oil filter.* After installing the filter, replace the old filter gaskets with new gaskets. Then screw in the bottom of the housing and open the oil shutoff valve.

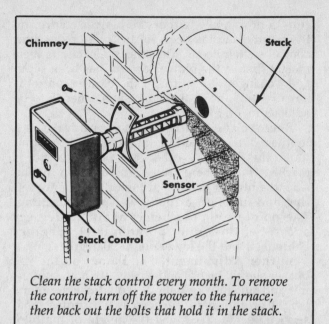

Clean the stack control every month. To remove the control, turn off the power to the furnace; then back out the bolts that hold it in the stack.

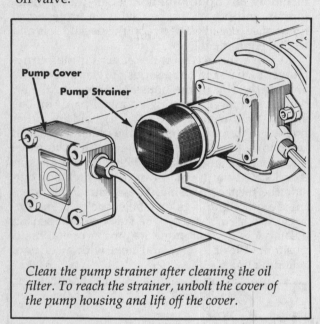

Clean the pump strainer after cleaning the oil filter. To reach the strainer, unbolt the cover of the pump housing and lift off the cover.

Some oil furnaces have a pump strainer located on the pump attached to the burner-blower unit. Clean this strainer when you clean the oil filter. To get to the strainer, unbolt the cover of the pump housing, where the oil line enters the burner, and lift off the cover. Take off the thin gasket around the rim. Then remove the strainer (a cylindrical or cup-shaped wire mesh screen) and soak it in kerosene for several minutes to loosen the sludge that has built up. Clean the strainer with an old toothbrush; if it's torn or badly bent, replace it with a new one of the same kind. Set the strainer into place on the pump, place a new gasket on the rim, and bolt the cover back on.

Switches. Some oil furnaces have two master switches; one is located near the burner unit and the other is near the furnace housing or even at a distance from the furnace. Make sure these master switches are both turned to the "on" position.

Stack Control. The stack control, located in the stack, is a safety device that monitors the operation of the oil burner. If the burner fails to ignite, the stack control shuts off the motor. A furnace

shutdown often is caused by a malfunctioning stack control rather than by the burner. If the burner fails to ignite, first check the fuel tank; if necessary, refill the tank. If the tank doesn't need to be refilled, press the reset button once on the stack control. If the burner doesn't ignite after you've pressed the button once, clean the control, as detailed below, and then press the reset button again. If the burner still doesn't operate, call a professional service person.

The stack control gradually becomes coated with soot during the heating season. To keep it working properly, clean the control every month or when it becomes soot covered. To remove the control, turn off the power to the furnace; then back out the bolts that hold the control in the stack. Pull out the sensor and its housing. With a brush dipped in soapy water, remove all soot from the control. Wipe the control dry with a soft cloth.

Before replacing the control, take the opportunity to clean the stack. Spread newspaper to protect the floor and disassemble the stack. Remove soot and debris from each section by tapping it firmly on the newspaper-covered floor. After cleaning the sections, reassemble them in reverse order. Make sure that the stack sections are properly aligned and firmly connected. Finally, reposition the stack control in the stack and reseal the connection to the chimney with refractory cement.

Some oil furnaces have an electric-eye safety switch instead of a stack control. This switch serves the same function as the stack control. If the burner has an electric-eye safety, remove the access cover over the photocell; it is held by hooks or retaining screws. Wipe the cover clean to remove accumulated soot. Reassemble the switch, replace the cover, and turn the power back on. If the burner still doesn't ignite, call a professional.

If the stack control or electric-eye safety switch is especially dirty, the furnace may not be set to burn the fuel completely. Call a professional service person to make the adjustment. **Caution:** *Do not attempt to replace either of these controls yourself.*

Draft Regulator. The draft regulator, located on the stack, is closed when the burner is off, but it opens automatically when the burner is running to let air into the chimney. Accumulated soot and rattling are signs that the draft regulator needs to be adjusted. Too much air wastes heat; too little air wastes fuel by failing to burn it completely. To increase the air flow, screw the counterweight inward; to decrease it, turn the counterweight outward. The draft regulator should be adjusted by a professional service person as part of regular annual maintenance.

Limit Switch. The limit switch is a safety control switch, located on the furnace just below the plenum. If the plenum gets too hot, the limit switch shuts off the burner; it also shuts off the blower when the temperature drops to a certain level after the burner has shut off. If the blower runs continuously, either the blower control on the thermostat has been set to "on" or the limit control switch needs adjustment. Check the thermostat first. If the blower control has been set to "on," change it to "auto"; if the blower control is already on "auto," the limit switch needs to be adjusted.

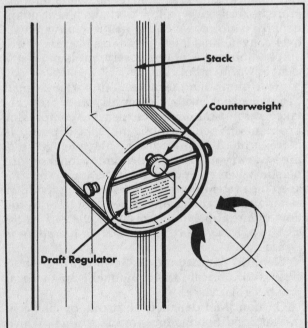

The draft regulator on the stack opens automatically when the burner is running. To increase the air flow, screw the counterweight inward.

Remove the control's cover; under it is a toothed dial. One side is marked "limit"; don't touch this side. The other side of the control is marked "fan." There are two pointers on the fan side; the blower goes on at the upper pointer setting and turns off at the lower pointer setting. The pointers should be set about 25 degrees apart. Set the upper pointer at 115 degrees Fahrenheit and the lower one at 90 degrees.

Burner Adjustments. Caution: *Do not try to adjust the burner of an oil furnace; call a professional service person.*

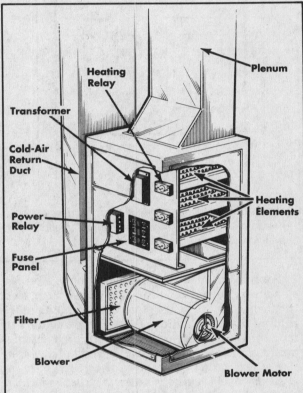

Electric furnaces use heating elements, controlled by relays, to warm the air. The elements are fused on a separate panel.

ELECTRIC FURNACES
Electric heat is expensive, whether the unit is a central furnace, a boiler system, or baseboard or wall units to heat individual rooms. Although an electric heating system has some advantages, its operating cost generally makes it less desirable than any of the other furnace systems. The high cost means that minimizing heat loss caused by improperly installed ducts or inadequate insulation is even more important than with other systems. The big advantage of electric heating is that no combustion takes place, so electric heat is cleaner. Since no flue is required to carry off undesirable combustion materials, no heat is lost through such venting, as it is in gas and oil systems. The only moving parts in an electric heating system are in the blower assembly.

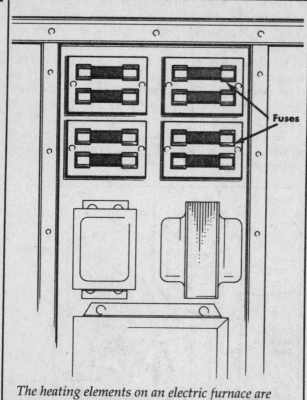

Fuses

The heating elements on an electric furnace are fused on a separate panel located on or inside the furnace housing.

For maximum energy efficiency, have a professional service person clean and adjust your electric furnace every year before the beginning of the heating season. **Caution:** *Before doing any work on the furnace, make sure the power to the furnace is turned off. Do not attempt any repairs to the heating elements, electrical connections, relays, transformers, or similar components of an electric furnace; repairs to these components must be made by a professional service person.*

Disassembly. The controls of an electric furnace, including the fuse panels, switches, and relays, may be mounted on the surface of the housing or installed behind an access panel on the front of the furnace. The access panel may be slipped on hooks or fastened to the furnace housing with a series of sheet-metal screws. To remove the access panel to the blower, filter, and blower motor, slip the panel off hooks or remove a series of sheet-metal screws.

Fuses. Electric furnaces are fused at the main electrical service entrance to the building. Many electric furnaces are on separate circuits, sometimes located in a separate fuse box away from the main panel. The heating elements of the furnace also are fused, and these fuses are located on a panel on or inside the furnace housing. If changing the fuses or resetting the breakers does not restore power to the furnace, call a professional service person.

HEAT PUMPS

A heat pump heats your home during the winter and cools it during the summer. It does not burn fuel to produce heat, nor does the electricity it consumes go through an element. The heat pump functions on the same principle as refrigerators and air conditioners: A liquid absorbs heat as it turns into a gas and releases heat as it returns to a liquid state.

During the summer the heat pump operates as a standard central air conditioner, removing heat from the house and venting it to the outside. A liquid refrigerant is pumped through an evaporator coil of tubing. The liquid expands as it moves through the coil, changing to its gaseous state as it absorbs heat from the air surrounding the coil. A blower then pushes air around the cooled coil through ducts and into the house. The gas, which now carries considerable heat, moves through a compressor, which begins the liquefying process. It then moves to a condenser coil outside the house, where the compressed gas releases its heat and returns to a liquid state.

During the winter, the heat pump reverses this process, extracting heat from the cold air outside and releasing it inside the house. The heat pump is efficient when the outside temperature is around 45 to 50 degrees Fahrenheit, but it becomes less efficient as the temperature drops. When the outside temperature is very low, an auxiliary electric heater must be used to supplement the heat pump's output. Like standard electric heating systems, this auxiliary unit is expensive to operate. In areas where the winter temperature is consistently below freezing, a heat pump usually is not practical. It has few advantages over conventional heating systems in areas where air conditioning is not necessary but is most efficient in warm or hot climates.

Heat pump maintenance is important. Small problems that are not promptly and properly taken care of can lead to expensive compressor problems. Since maintaining a heat pump is more technical than caring for the average heating system, you should call a professional service person when the pump malfunctions. You can keep the system free of dirt, by keeping the filter clean and removing any other obstacles to the flow of air. **Caution:** *Before doing any work on the heat pump, make sure the power to the pump is turned off.*

General Maintenance. Replace filters and clean and lubricate the components of the heat pump regularly.

Outdoor Maintenance. Heat pumps, like central air conditioners, have outdoor units, which contain a compressor, a coil, a fan, and other components. To function properly, this unit should be kept free of debris, such as leaves and dirt. The unit should be level on its concrete support pad.

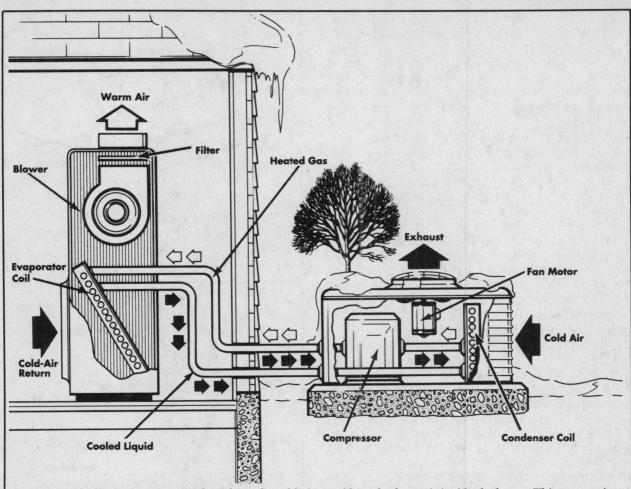

In winter the heat pump extracts heat from the cold air outside and releases it inside the house. This process is reversed for cooling during the summer.

Clean pine needles, leaves, and dirt out of updraft fans by removing the grille, which is held by a series of retaining screws. Make sure the power to the unit is off before this cleaning is done. A vacuum cleaner hose sometimes can be inserted between the fan blades to remove debris from the sides and bottom of the unit. At the beginning of each heating season, set a carpenter's level across the top of the metal cabinet and check the level from side to side and from front to back. If the unit has settled on its pad, lift the pad back to level by prying it up with a pry bar or a piece of 2 X 4; build up the ground under it with stones or crushed rock. Also check the piping insulation for deterioration. If this insulation is faulty, replace it with new insulation, available at heating supply stores. Installation instructions are usually provided by the manufacturer.

Power Interruptions. If a heat pump has been off for more than an hour because of a blown fuse, a tripped circuit breaker, or a utility power failure, the unit should not be put back into operation for six to eight hours, especially if the temperature is 50 degrees Fahrenheit or lower. The reason is that the lubricant in the pump's oil reservoir may be too cool to circulate properly. This can cause damage to the valves of the unit. Set the heat pump on "emergency heat." This turns the pump off and keeps it from running. Leave the pump in this mode for six to eight hours; then switch the pump to its normal heating setting. If little or no heat is generated at this point, call a professional service person.

Troubleshooting Distribution Systems

The way heat is distributed, through ducts, by gravity or forced air, or through pipes, is as important as how it is generated. Whatever system you have, regular maintenance is essential to make the best use of the heat your furnace provides.

FORCED-AIR SYSTEMS

Fueled by gas, electricity, or oil, a forced-air distribution system forces air from the furnace through ducts to registers in various rooms. Besides warming the air, the blower system that distributes the warmed air also returns the cold air to the furnace so it can be rewarmed and distributed to the rooms again. A forced-air system also is efficient for distributing cool air from a central air conditioner, with the same ducts, registers, and blower. There is little that can go wrong with a forced-air system. The big problems include noise and blockage of air flow, usually caused by dirt or by furniture or draperies blocking the registers. Here are specific troubleshooting procedures:

Disassembly. Floor registers are slipped into ducts or are held by retaining screws on the frame of the register. Wall and ceiling registers are held by retaining screws on the frame of the register. Duct joints usually are slip fit and held with sheet-metal screws or duct tape. The ducts are supported by wire or metal strap hangers nailed or screwed to wooden framing members, such as studs and rafters. All parts are easy to disassemble; lay them out in order so you'll be able to reassemble them properly.

Balancing the System. Forced-air systems often go out of balance, causing some rooms to be too hot or too cold. The furnace usually is not to blame; the cause of the problem is that ducts and registers are not set properly. Balance the system while the furnace is turned on.

To balance a forced-air system, open all the ducts and registers in the system. There may be dampers in various ducts; these are turned to open the ducts. The damper is open when it's turned parallel with the top and bottom of the ducting. Assemble six or seven thermometers and get them all to have about the same temperature reading. You can do this by laying the thermometers out together for about 30 minutes, and then noting any discrepancies. Tape the thermometers on the walls of various rooms, one thermometer to each room. Position the thermometers about 36 inches from the floor, away from the hot-air register or cold-air return. Then wait one hour.

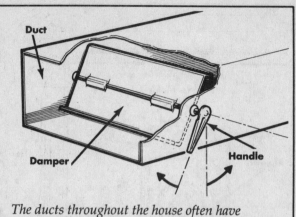
The ducts throughout the house often have dampers. The damper is open when it's turned parallel with the top and bottom of the duct.

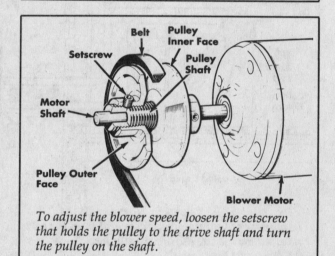
To adjust the blower speed, loosen the setscrew that holds the pulley to the drive shaft and turn the pulley on the shaft.

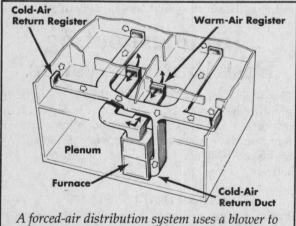
A forced-air distribution system uses a blower to distribute warmed air and return cold air to the furnace so it can be warmed.

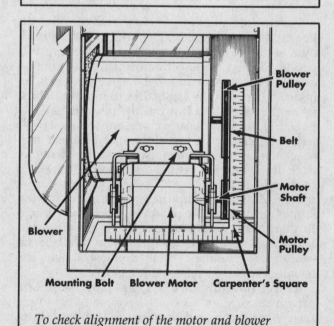
To check alignment of the motor and blower pulleys, place a carpenter's square against them. The pulleys should be in a straight line at right angles to the motor shaft.

Take a thermometer reading in each room. If one room shows a higher temperature than an adjoining room, close the damper or register in the hotter room. Follow this procedure for each room, opening and closing dampers and registers, until the same temperature is maintained in each room, or the temperature balance you want is reached. During the balancing process, the thermostat to the furnace should be kept at the same reading. For the best results, you should balance the entire system.

Adjusting Blower Speed. An increase in blower speed can sometimes improve the flow of warm air through your home; a decrease can make the system quieter. You can increase or decrease the blower speed by slightly adjusting the pulley on the blower drive motor. To increase the speed, loosen the setscrew that holds the pulley to the drive shaft. Move or turn the pulley clockwise on the shaft one turn; then tighten the setscrew. If more speed is wanted, turn the pulley clockwise two turns. To decrease blower speed, loosen the setscrew that holds the pulley to the drive shaft and move or turn the pulley counterclockwise on the shaft one turn; then tighten the setscrew. If less speed is needed, turn the pulley counterclockwise two turns.

The motor and blower pulley also may get out of alignment, causing the blower to be noisy and cutting down on the efficiency of your distribution system. To check alignment, place a carpenter's square against the outside of the motor and blower pulleys. The pulleys should be in a straight line and at right angles to the motor shaft. If the pulleys are not lined up at right angles to the motor housing, loosen the setscrew holding the motor pulley, and move the pulley backward or forward as needed to align it properly. If the setscrew is jammed or rusted and won't loosen, or if the pulleys are more than 1/2 inch out of alignment, loosen the mounting bolts on the motor and slide the motor backward or forward until the pulleys are properly aligned. Then retighten the bolts.

Noise Problems. Air forced through the ducts of the forced-air system can cause vibration and noise if the ducts are not firmly connected. The best way to stop this noise is to add duct hangers to the ducting system. The hangers are usually wrapped around or across the ducts and nailed or screwed to the stud or rafter framing. At the elbows of the ducts, where air moving through the ducts changes direction, sections can become loose or separated. Push loose sections back together and tape the joints firmly with duct tape, available at most hardware stores and home centers.

Noise also can be caused by inadequate lubrication, worn or damaged belts, or too high a blower speed. Correct these problems as detailed above.

Heat Loss from Ducts. If ducts run through cold basements or exterior crawl spaces, they should be wrapped with fiberglass insulation, spiraled around the ducting and held with duct tape, wire, or heavy cord. You also can wrap the ducts with aluminum-faced insulating tape, sold in wide rolls and available at heating supply stores.

STEAM SYSTEMS

Steam heat is no longer installed in new homes, but it is such a durable heating system that many homes and apartment buildings are still heated by steam. A steam-heat system works by gravity. A boiler in the basement of the building, usually powered by an oil or gas burner, heats water until it turns to steam. The steam rises, going up to radiators and warming the air in the rooms throughout your home. As the steam cools it condenses, and the water flows back to the boiler.

Slope. The steam system is a simple one, but for it to work properly, all pipes and radiators must slope back toward the boiler. If the water can't run back to the boiler, it collects and blocks the path of the steam. When this happens, there are hammering noises in the system, and one or more individual radiators may not function.

Correcting malfunctions caused by inadequate slope is easy. Place blocks of wood under the legs of the affected radiators to correct the angle of slope. If you suspect that the return pipes are at fault, check their angle of slope with a level; these pipes may become incorrectly tilted when the house settles. If you can get at the pipes, you can solve the problem by supporting the pipe with pipe straps to reestablish the proper slope.

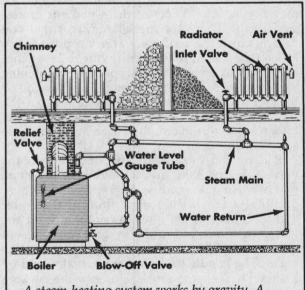

A steam-heating system works by gravity. A boiler in the basement heats water until it turns to steam; the steam rises to the radiators and warms the air in the rooms of your house.

Water Level. If the heat throughout the system is inadequate, either the boiler isn't heating or the water level is too low. If the boiler isn't heating, the furnace may be malfunctioning, and you'll have to find and correct the problem there.

A low water level in the system's boiler is easier to handle. The level of water in the boiler should be maintained at half full, and there should be an air space, called a chest, between the surface of the water and the top of the tank. Without the chest, the boiler can't work up a full head of steam; the water overfills the return lines and may trip the relief valve. To correct this problem, add water to the boiler. If the water level in the boiler is consistently low, check the pipes for leaks. If you spot a leak at a pipe connection, try tightening the connection carefully with a pipe wrench. If the connection still leaks, call a professional service person.

Radiators. If an individual radiator is cold and both it and the pipes leading to it are tilted properly, check the radiator's inlet valve; this valve must be opened all the way for the radiator to function properly. If some radiators get warmer than others, air vents may be at fault. Some air vents are adjustable. Turning a screw to a lower setting reduces the flow of heat into the radiator; raising the setting lets out more air, bringing in more heat.

If your radiators' air vents aren't adjustable, consider replacing them with units that are. Some hardware stores stock standard, bullet-shaped air vents in a range of sizes. If a radiator gets too hot, replace its vent with a smaller one; for cold radiators, go up a size or two.

Leaks. Leaks around inlet valves, radiators, and pipes are plumbing problems; you may or may not be able to correct them without professional help. There are special additives that you can put into the boiler's water supply to stop leaks. Pipe leaks are frequently due to loose connections and often can be stopped by tightening the connections with a wrench. Leaks around inlet valves are caused by deterioration of the stem packing or the washer in the valve. In order to correct this problem, the valve must be disassembled.

Radiator inlet valves are similar to faucets; the valve has a packing nut, a valve body or stem, and a washer assembly. To replace the valve packing or the washer, first shut off the boiler and let it cool. It isn't necessary to shut off the water; as the steam in the system cools, it will condense and flow back out of the radiator to the boiler. The handle to the valve is usually held by a screw; remove the screw. Unscrew the packing nut, remove the handle, and back out the valve stem or body. At the bottom of the stem is a washer, held by a screw. Remove the screw and the washer and replace the washer with a new one of the same size. The packing nut may have a

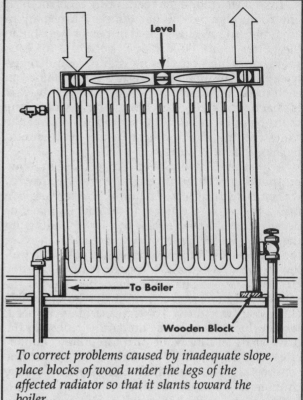

To correct problems caused by inadequate slope, place blocks of wood under the legs of the affected radiator so that it slants toward the boiler.

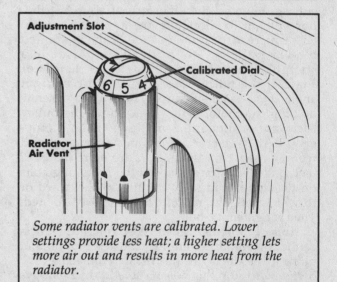

Some radiator vents are calibrated. Lower settings provide less heat; a higher setting lets more air out and results in more heat from the radiator.

washer or may be filled with packing string; replace the washer or install new packing as you reassemble the valve. When all connections are tight, turn the system back on.

Flushing the System. Once a month, the entire heating system should be flushed to keep the pipes clear and the steam flowing freely. To flush the system, open the blow-off valve and let the water run off into a bucket until it runs clear. If the water remains rusty, or if the entire system is operating at less than optimum efficiency, the

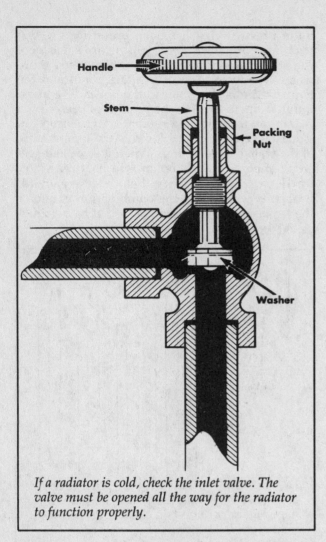

If a radiator is cold, check the inlet valve. The valve must be opened all the way for the radiator to function properly.

through return pipes. Most gravity systems heat the water to no more than about 180 degrees Fahrenheit, and the cooled water that goes back to the boiler rarely falls below 120 degrees. Open gravity systems have an overflow outlet to let water escape, preventing a buildup of excess pressure in the system. Closed systems have a sealed expansion tank; when water pressure builds up in the system, the excess water flows into the expansion tank to prevent damage to the pipes or the boiler. Hydronic hot-water systems are much like closed gravity systems, except that a hydronic system uses a motor-driven circulating pump, called a circulator, to move the water. As a result, the water in a hydronic system moves far more rapidly and arrives at the room radiator with less heat loss than the water in a gravity system.

Slope. Hot-water systems, especially gravity systems, depend on proper slope; all pipes and radiators must slope back toward the boiler. Hammering noises and failure to heat are indications of incorrect slope. To correct these malfunctions, check the slope of radiators and pipes, and prop radiators or fasten pipes so that all components are properly tilted.

Correcting malfunctions caused by inadequate slope is easy. Place blocks of wood under the legs

pipes are probably clogged with rust and scale. If you see any rust in the water level gauge tube, shut off the boiler and let it cool; then flush the system by draining and refilling it several times. Then add a commercial radiator preparation formulated to curb the buildup of rust and scale. These products are available at heating supply stores.

HOT-WATER SYSTEMS
Because water retains heat, it is used effectively to store and distribute heat in home systems. There are two kinds of hot-water systems: the gravity system and the hydronic, or forced hot-water system. Like steam systems, hot-water heating systems can be powered by gas, oil, or electricity.

Gravity systems depend on the upward flow of hot water to circulate heated water from the boiler through a system of pipes to radiators in the rooms of your home. The most-efficient radiators for hot-water systems are called convectors. These units employ a series of fins.

The heat from the water in the radiators or convectors is transferred first to the metal radiators and then to the air. As the water loses its heat, it sinks, and flows back to the boiler

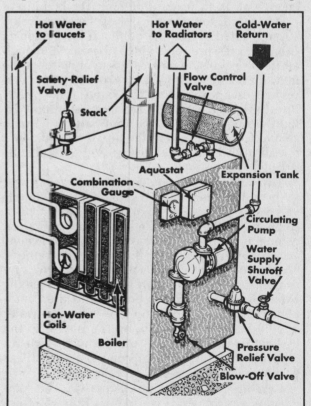

Hydronic hot-water systems use a motor-driven circulating pump to move the hot water; the water moves rapidly and arrives at the radiator with little heat loss.

of the affected radiators to correct the angle of slope. If you suspect that the return pipes are at fault, check their angle of slope with a level; these may become incorrectly tilted when the house settles. If you can get at the pipes, you can solve the problem by supporting the pipe with pipe straps to reestablish the proper slope.

Water Level. The water level in the hot-water system's boiler should be maintained, as with steam systems, at half full; there should be an air space between the surface of the water and the top of the tank. A water level that is too low can cause inadequate heating. In most systems an automatic filling unit keeps the boiler filled with the proper amount of water. If the water level of the system is consistently low, check the pipes for leaks. Close the water supply valve and note the water level for two or three days. If the level drops drastically, call a professional service person for help.

Expansion Tank. For efficient heating, the water in a hot-water system is heated well above boiling, but it doesn't turn to steam because the expansion tank and a pressure-reducing valve keep the water under pressure. Usually the expansion tank is hung from the basement ceiling, not far from the boiler; in older systems, look for the expansion tank in the attic. If there is not enough air in the expansion tank, the buildup of pressure will force water out of the safety relief valve located above the boiler. If water spurts from the pressure relief valve, there isn't enough air in the expansion tank. Without enough air the tank fills with water, which expands as it heats up and escapes through the safety relief valve. You can check for air in the expansion tank by lightly touching it. The bottom half of the tank should feel warmer than the top; if the tank feels hot all over, it has filled with water and must be drained.

To drain an expansion tank, turn off the power to the boiler; then close the water supply shutoff valve and let the tank cool. On some systems a combination drain valve lets water out and air in when it is opened. If there is a combination valve, attach a garden hose to the valve and remove about two or three gallons of water. If there is no combination valve, shut off the valve between the expansion tank and the boiler, and then completely drain the expansion tank. Turn the water supply back on, and turn on the power to the boiler to get the system running again. It isn't necessary to refill the expansion tank; it will fill as part of the normal operation of the system.

Combination Gauge and Aquastat. The combination gauge, which is different from the combination valve, is an automatic control mounted on the side or top of the boiler. It generally has three indicators. On the upper part of the gauge, a moving pointer shows the actual pressure in the system and a stationary pointer shows the mini-

mum pressure that has been preset for the system. If the moving pointer falls below the level of the stationary pointer, the system needs more water. The lower part of the gauge indicates the temperature of the water in the boiler. The maximum temperature for the system is preset by a pointer on the scale of a separate device called an Aquastat. The Aquastat controls the temperature of the water in the system. When it is set at a specific temperature, the boiler will heat the water until this temperature has been reached. Problems with either the combination gauge or the Aquastat should be taken care of by a professional service person.

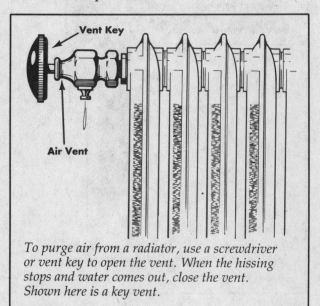

To purge air from a radiator, use a screwdriver or vent key to open the vent. When the hissing stops and water comes out, close the vent. Shown here is a key vent.

Radiators and Convectors. If an individual radiator or convector is cold and both it and the pipes leading to it are tilted properly, check the radiator's inlet valve; this valve must be opened all the way for the radiator to function properly. If some radiators or convectors get warmer than others, the vents are probably not adjusted properly. Adjust the vents so that the ones farthest from the boiler are opened more than the ones closest to it.

Air trapped in a radiator or convector can prevent water from entering it and keep it from heating. To solve the problem, turn the air vent valve on the unit until the hissing stops and water comes out; then close the vent. Use a screwdriver or the key furnished by the radiator manufacturer to open the vent; if you don't have the key, you may be able to buy one at a heating supply store. Some convectors and radiators have automatic valves; they don't have to be opened or closed.

Circulator. The circulator is a pump that forces the hot water to the radiators or convectors throughout the house. Problems with the circulator usually occur when the coupler that separates the motor from the pump breaks; this usually

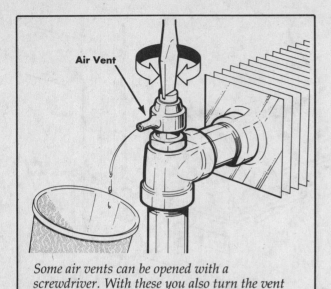

Some air vents can be opened with a screwdriver. With these you also turn the vent until the hissing stops and water comes out; then close the vent.

makes a lot of noise. Another source of trouble with the circulator is the pump seal; if water leaks from the pump, chances are the seal is damaged. If the circulator develops either of these problems, call a professional service person.

Leaks. Like steam systems, hot-water systems are prone to plumbing leaks in the pipes and at inlet valves. You may or may not be able to fix leaks without professional help. There are special additives you can put into the boiler's water supply to stop leaks. Pipe leaks are frequently due to loose connections and can be stopped by tightening the connections with a wrench. Leaks around inlet valves are due to deterioration of the stem packing or the washer in the valve.

Radiator inlet valves are similar to faucets, with a packing nut, a valve body or stem, and a washer assembly. To replace the valve packing or the washer, first shut off the boiler and let it cool. It isn't necessary to shut off the water; as the system cools, the water will flow back out of the radiator or convector to the boiler. The handle to the valve is usually held by a screw; remove the screw. Unscrew the packing nut, remove the handle, and back out the valve stem or body. At the bottom of the stem is a washer, held by a screw. Remove the screw and the washer and replace the washer with a new one of the same size and design. The packing nut may have a washer or may be filled with packing string; replace the washer or install new packing as you reassemble the valve. When all connections are tight, turn the system back on.

Flushing and Draining the System. Once a year, the entire heating system should be flushed to keep the pipes clear and the water flowing freely. To flush the system, open the blow-off valve and let the water run off into a bucket until it runs clear. If the water still looks rusty after the system has been flushed, call a professional service person.

Hot-water systems should be drained to prevent the pipes from freezing during a prolonged cold-weather power failure; it also may be necessary to drain the system to make repairs. To drain the pipes, turn off the power to the boiler at the main electrical entrance panel by removing the fuse or tripping the circuit breaker that controls the circuit. Let the water cool until it's just warm. When the water has cooled, turn off the water supply valve and attach a length of garden hose to the boiler drain. The hose should be lower than the boiler; position it in a laundry sink or at a floor drain. Open the drain valve and the air vents on all the convectors or radiators. The water from the system will flow out through the hose; give it plenty of time to drain.

To refill the system, close the air vents on all the convectors or radiators and shut the drain valve. Turn on the water supply to the boiler. If the boiler has an automatic shutoff, refilling is automatic. If the boiler isn't automatic, fill it until the combination valve gauge reads 20 pounds of pressure per square inch. Then release air from all the convectors in the system so that they'll heat properly. The gauge on the boiler should read 12 pounds per square inch. If the pressure on the gauge shows less than 12 pounds per square inch of pressure, add more water; if the pressure is above 12 pounds per square inch, drain off some water.

Troubleshooting Cooling Systems

There are two home cooling systems: central air conditioning and individual room air conditioners. Both systems have the same basic components: a condenser, which uses electricity to cool a refrigerant liquid in a coil, and an evaporator, which cools the air in your home. The condenser unit of a central air conditioner is usually located outside; the evaporator is hooked to the distribution system of your home's heat source. Room air conditioners are much smaller; both condenser and evaporator are contained in one housing, and cooled air is vented directly into the room. Heat pumps, when operated in their cooling cycle, function as central air conditioners.

CENTRAL AIR CONDITIONING
Central air conditioners are made up of two separate components: the condenser unit, usually located outside the house on a concrete slab, and the evaporator coil, mounted in the plenum (the main duct junction) above the furnace. Two coolant lines run from the condenser unit to the evaporator. When the air conditioner is turned on, the liquid refrigerant in the condenser coil is

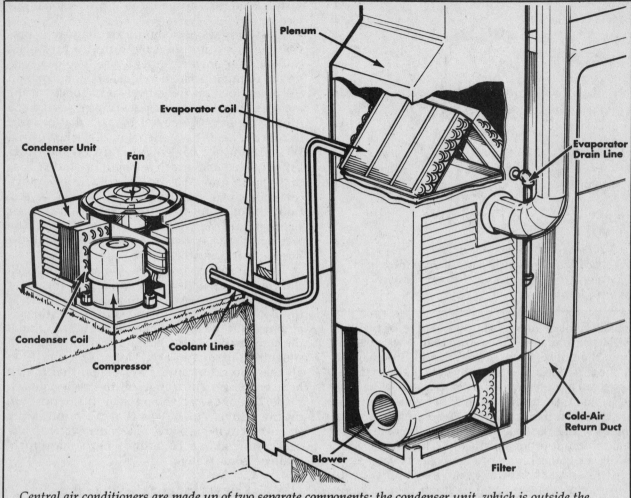

Central air conditioners are made up of two separate components: the condenser unit, which is outside the house on a concrete slab, and the evaporator coil, which is above the furnace.

cooled. The cooled liquid flows to the evaporator coil through the first line. At the evaporator warm air in your home is cooled by contact with the liquid-filled coil. As the warm air around it becomes cooler, the liquid in the coil becomes warmer and is transformed to its gaseous state. The gas flows through the second connection line back to the condenser unit, where it is pressurized and cooled again to its liquid state. As it cools, the gas gives off heat, which is vented out of the unit by a fan at the top or back of the condenser.

Most central air conditioners are hooked to a home's forced-air distribution system. The same motor, blower, and ducts used for heating are used to distribute cool air from the air conditioning system. When a central air conditioner is operating, hot air inside the house flows to the furnace through the return-air duct. The hot air is moved by the blower across the cooled evaporator coil in the plenum and then is delivered through ducts to cool the house. When the air conditioner works but the house doesn't cool, the problem is probably in the distribution system.

Refer to the section on troubleshooting forced-air systems.

Both the evaporator and the condenser are sealed, and a professional service person should be called for almost any maintenance other than routine cleaning. Central air conditioners should be professionally inspected and adjusted before the beginning of every cooling season. Don't let your maintenance go with this annual checkup. While there aren't many repairs you can make, there are specific maintenance procedures you can follow to keep your system operating at peak efficiency.

Caution: *Before doing any work on an air conditioning system, make sure the power to the system, both the condenser and the evaporator assembly, is turned off.*

Evaporator. The evaporator is located directly above the furnace in the plenum. The evaporator may not be accessible, but if it is, you should clean it once a year. If the plenum has foil-wrapped insulation at its front, you can clean the evaporator; if the plenum is a sealed sheet-metal box, do not attempt to open it.

To clean an accessible evaporator, turn off the power to the air conditioner. Remove the foil-wrapped insulation at the front of the plenum; it's probably taped in place. Remove the tape carefully because you'll have to replace it later. Behind the insulation is the access plate, which is held in place by several screws. Remove the screws and lift off the plate.

With a stiff brush, clean the entire underside of the evaporator unit; a large hand mirror will help you see what you're doing. If you can't reach all the way back to clean the entire area, slide the evaporator out a little. The evaporator can be slid out even if it has rigid pipes connected to it, but be careful not to bend the pipes. Clean the tray below the evaporator unit; this tray carries condensation away from the evaporator. Pour a tablespoon of household bleach into the weep hole in the tray to prevent fungus growth. In extremely humid weather, check the condensate drain and pan every other day; if there is much moisture in the pan, the weep hole from the pan to the drain line may be clogged. Open the weep hole with a piece of wire.

When you've finished cleaning the evaporator, put the unit back into place, reinstall the plate, and tape the insulation back over it. Turn on the air conditioner and check for air leaks; seal them with duct tape.

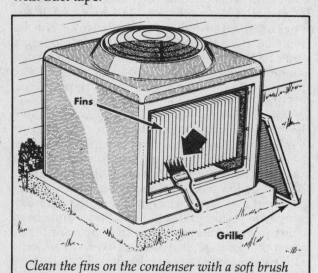

Clean the fins on the condenser with a soft brush to remove accumulated dirt; you may have to remove a protective grille to reach the fins.

Condenser. In most systems the condenser unit is located outside the house, and is prone to accumulate dirt and debris from trees, lawn mowing, and airborne dust. The condenser has a fan that moves air across the condenser coil. You must clean the coil on the intake side, so before you turn off the power to the air conditioner, check to see which direction the air moves across the coils. Then turn off the power to the air conditioner.

With the power off, cut down any grass, weeds, or vines that have grown up around the condenser unit; they could be obstructing the flow of air. Clean the condenser with a commercial coil cleaner, available at refrigerator supply stores; instructions for use are included. Flush the coil clean with a spray bottle and let it dry.

Clean the fins with a soft brush to remove accumulated dirt; you may have to remove a protective grille to reach them. Do not clean the fins with water, which could turn the dirt into mud and compact it between the fins. Clean the fins carefully; they're made of light-gauge aluminum and are easily damaged. If the fins are bent, straighten them with a fin comb, sold at most appliance parts stores. Fin combs are designed to slide into spaces between the fins.

Check the concrete pad under the condenser to make sure it's level; set a carpenter's level front to back and side to side on top of the unit. If the pad has settled, lift the pad with a pry bar or a piece of 2 X 4, and force gravel or rocks under the concrete to level it.

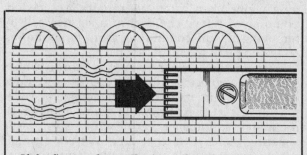

If the fins on the condenser coil are bent, straighten them with a fin comb. Use the comb carefully; the fins are made of light-gauge aluminum and are easily damaged.

During the fall and winter, outside condenser units should be protected from the elements to prevent leaf blockage and ice damage. Cover the condenser unit with a commercial condenser cover, made to fit the shape of the unit, or with heavy plastic sheeting, secured with sturdy cord.

Refrigerant. The coolant used in air conditioning systems is a refrigerant called Freon. If the system does not contain the proper amount of Freon, little or no cooling will take place. If you suspect a Freon problem, call a professional service person to recharge the system. **Caution:** *Do not try to charge your system's Freon lines; Freon is volatile and can be dangerous.*

You can make one repair to the system's coolant lines. Examine the lines running from the condenser outside the evaporator to inside the house. If the insulation is damaged or worn, it will cut down on the cooling efficiency of the unit and should be replaced. Replace damaged or worn coolant-line insulation with new insulation of the same kind as soon as possible.

ROOM AIR CONDITIONERS

Room air conditioners work the same way central air conditioners do. They are smaller than central systems, and they can be more expensive to operate if they are used to cool an entire house. Depending on its size, a room unit may cool only the room in which it is located, or it may be able to cool adjoining rooms.

Both the condenser and the evaporator are contained in one housing. The condenser coil faces outside; the evaporator faces the inside. Sandwiched between the coils are a compressor, two fans, a motor, and thermostat controls. Dirt is probably the biggest enemy of window air conditioners, because it can lower the efficiency of the evaporator coil, block the operation of the fan that blows out the cool air, clog filters, and block drain ports.

The coils, the compressor, and the motor of a room air conditioner are sealed components; so any repairs to them should be left to a professional service person. You can make minor repairs, and regular maintenance will keep your unit running well. When extensive repairs are needed, you also can save the cost of a service call by removing the air conditioner from its mounting and taking it to the repair shop.

During the winter room air conditioners should be protected from the elements; remove the unit from its mounting and store it, or cover the outside portion of the unit with a commercial room air conditioner cover or with heavy plastic sheeting, held with duct tape. Air conditioner covers are available at hardware stores, home centers, and appliance outlets.

Caution: *Before doing any work on an air conditioner, make sure it's unplugged. Room air conditioners have one or two capacitors, located behind the control panel and near the fan. Capacitors store electricity, even when the power to the unit is turned off. Before you do any work on an air conditioner, you must unplug it and discharge the capacitor, or you could receive a severe shock.*

Unplug the air conditioner or turn off the power to the circuit. To get to the capacitor—there may be one or two—remove the unit's control panel. The capacitor is located behind the control panel and near the fan; it looks like a large dry-cell battery. To discharge the capacitor, use a 20,000-ohm 2-watt resistor, an inexpensive wire unit available at most electrical supply stores. Fasten the clips of the resistor to the terminals of the capacitor; this discharges the capacitor. If the capacitor has three terminal posts, connect the resistor to one outer terminal and the central terminal, then to the other outside terminal and the center terminal. After discharging the capacitor, you can make the necessary repairs.

Disassembly. Access to the filter, controls, thermostat, and evaporator coil of a room air con-

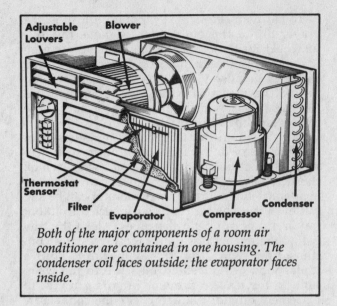

Both of the major components of a room air conditioner are contained in one housing. The condenser coil faces outside; the evaporator faces inside.

ditioner is through the front grille, which is held to the housing of the unit by retaining screws or spring clips. Disassemble the control panel by removing the control knobs and lifting off the panel. The knobs may be friction fitted on shafts; pull them straight out and off the shafts. The knobs may have tiny setscrews at the base of the knob; loosen these screws and pull off the knobs. The escutcheon plate of each knob is screwed to the frame of the appliance. On some models the working parts of the air conditioner can be removed from the housing shell by removing a series of screws. On others the cabinet can be disassembled, sides and top. For most repairs, only the grille and the control panel must be removed.

Filter. At the beginning of every cooling season, and once a month during the season, remove the front grille and clean or replace the filter. If you live in a dusty area, clean or replace the filter more often. Most room air conditioners have a washable filter, which looks like sponge rubber. Clean the filter with a solution of mild household detergent and water; rinse well. Let the filter dry completely before reinstalling it. Some units have a throwaway filter, similar to a furnace filter. When this kind of filter becomes dirty, replace it with a new one of the same kind.

Power Cord. The power cord that connects the air conditioner to the wall outlet may become worn and fail to supply electricity to the unit. To check the cord, remove the control panel. Unscrew the cord terminals and then attach a test wire across the bare lead wires. Hook the clips of a volt-ohm-milliammeter (VOM), set to the R x 1 scale, to the prongs of the cord's plug. If the meter reads zero, the cord is functioning; if the meter reads higher than zero, replace the cord.

Evaporator and Condenser Coils. Clean the evaporator and condenser coils at the beginning of the cooling season and every month during the season; if you live in a dusty area, clean the coils more often. Use a vacuum cleaner on these components. If the fins on the coils are bent, straighten them with a fin comb, sold at most appliance parts outlets. Fin combs are designed to slide into the spaces between the fins. Use the fin comb carefully; the fins are made of light-gauge aluminum and are easily damaged.

Switch. The selector switch, directly behind the control panel, turns the unit on. If the air conditioner does not run at any setting and it is receiving power, the switch may be faulty. To correct the problem, remove the control panel and locate the switch. Check the switch terminals for burnt insulation or burn marks on the terminals; if you see any indication of burning, replace the switch with a new one of the same kind. The switch is held to the control panel or frame with screws; unscrew it and connect the new one the same way. If you decide that the problem may not be the switch, call a professional.

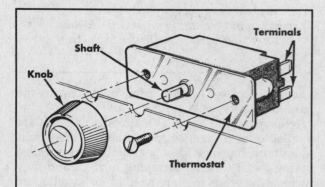

If the thermostat on a room air conditioner is faulty, remove the screws or clips that hold it in place, and replace it with a new one of the same type.

Thermostat. The thermostat is located behind the control panel; to test or replace this component, remove the grille and the control panel from the unit. The thermostat has a special sensing bulb attached to it; this part extends from the thermostat into the evaporator coil area. Its role is to sense the temperature, which is controlled by the thermostat. Remove the thermostat carefully; the sensing bulb must be returned to the identical spot. To make replacement easier, tag the location of the bulb before you remove the thermostat.

Check the thermostat with a volt-ohm milliammeter (VOM), set to the R x 1 scale. Clip the probes of the tester to the terminals of the thermostat and turn the temperature control dial to its coldest setting. If the meter reads zero, the thermostat is functioning properly; if the reading is higher than zero, replace the thermostat with a new one of the same kind. The thermostat is held to the control panel or frame with screws, clips, or metal tabs; connect the new thermostat the same way the old one was connected.

If the thermostat has more than two lead wires connected to it, not counting the sensing bulb wire, do not try to test or replace it; call a professional service person.

Drain Ports. As the air conditioner operates, condensed moisture and water vapor from the evaporator coil are funneled through drain ports or an opening between the partition or barrier between the evaporator coil and the condenser coil. At this point the fan blows the moisture against the condenser coil, where the water is dissipated. These drain ports can become clogged with dirt. The result is water leaking from the appliance, usually through the bottom of the grille. To prevent clogging, clean the ports with a short piece of clothes hanger wire or the blade of a pocket knife at the beginning of every cooling season and every month during the season. Also check the condenser side of the air conditioner. Some models have a drain port along the bottom edge of the cabinet frame. If your air conditioner has this drain port, clean it out when you clean the other ports.

Fan. When a fan malfunctions, the problem is usually loose or dirty blades. If the fan doesn't work, or if it's noisy, cleaning and tightening will usually fix it.

Open the cabinet and locate the fan. With a vacuum or a soft cloth, clean away any debris. Then check the fan blade on the motor shaft for looseness. The blade is fastened to the shaft with a setscrew at the hub of the blade; tighten the setscrew with a screwdriver or an Allen wrench. If the air conditioner has a round vent fan, tighten the fan on the motor shaft by inserting a long-blade screwdriver through a port in the fan. The fan is installed in its housing with bolts, and vibration can loosen these fasteners. Tighten them with a wrench.

Most air conditioner fan motors are permanently lubricated and sealed at the factory, but some have oil ports for lubrication. If the fan has oil ports, apply several drops of Number 20 nondetergent motor oil (not all-purpose oil) to each port at the beginning of the cooling season.

If you suspect the fan motor is faulty, test it with a VOM. Disconnect the terminal wires from the terminals and clip the probes of the VOM, set to the R x 1 scale, to the wires. If the meter reads between about 3 and 30 ohms, the motor is functioning properly; if the meter reads either zero or an extremely high number, replace the motor. To remove the motor, remove the fan, the power wires, and several mounting bolts; install the new motor with the reverse procedure. If the condenser coil must be moved to get the fan out, do not try to remove the motor; call a professional service person.

Motor and Compressor. If problems occur in the motor or compressor of the air conditioner, call a professional service person.

Conserving Energy

A cold, drafty house is a misery that grows increasingly expensive as energy costs rise. Zipping up your home with tight-fitting weather stripping and wrapping it with snug insulation can make you feel warmer all winter long and lower your utility bills.

WEATHER STRIPPING

If you had a 6-inch-square hole in the middle of your front door, you would do something to plug it up. There are thousands of homes in which a 1/8-inch-wide crack exists all the way around the door, and in terms of air flow, the gap is equivalent to a 6-inch-square hole.

Gaps around doors and windows allow heat to escape during winter and cooled air to vanish during summer. Letting these cracks exist is just like throwing dollars out the door or window. The simple procedure of installing weather stripping can keep these dollars in your hands. Weather-stripping doors and windows in your home can reduce your heating and cooling bills by as much as 30 percent.

There are simple ways to find out if your home needs weather stripping. If you can feel cold air coming in around doors and windows on a windy day, you know the answer. If you are unsure, you can create your own concentrated windstorm at the precise spot where you suspect air might be leaking. Go outside with a hand-held hair dryer and have a helper inside move his or her hands around the door or window frame as you move the blower. When testing windows, your helper can see where the blower is; but the two of you must establish voice signals when working on solid doors.

When you finish testing, you may discover that all your doors and windows are airtight, or you may find that a door or window that is airtight around three edges needs help along the fourth edge. You are likely to discover that your home has several drafty areas and that you must install weather stripping in them.

Weather Stripping. There are several kinds of weather stripping, with different situations calling for different kinds of material. The following are available to the homeowner, and unless otherwise stated, each kind of weather stripping can be used for either doors or windows.

•Pressure-sensitive, adhesive-backed foam is the easiest weather stripping to apply and the least expensive. Available in both rubber and plastic, adhesive-backed foam comes in rolls of varying lengths and thickness. When compressed by a door or window, the foam seals out the air. As an added advantage, these strips also provide a cushioning effect that silences slamming. Although not permanent, this kind of weather stripping can last from one to three years. Avoid

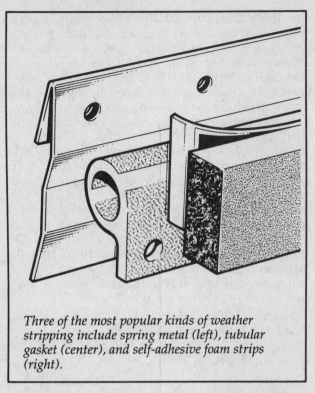

Three of the most popular kinds of weather stripping include spring metal (left), tubular gasket (center), and self-adhesive foam strips (right).

getting paint on the material; paint causes the foam to lose its resiliency.

•Spring-metal strips (V-shaped or single) are available in bronze, copper, stainless steel, and aluminum finishes. Most manufacturers package spring-metal weather stripping in rolls, and they include the brads that are needed for installation. Although this kind of weather stripping seems like a simple installation, it requires patience.

•Self-sticking spring metal has a peel-and-stick backing. This material is like standard spring-metal strips, but it is easier to install.

•Felt is an old standby and economical to install. It comes in a variety of widths, thicknesses, qualities, and colors (brown, gray, and black). Felt strips are usually nailed in place, but they are also available with an adhesive backing.

•Serrated metal is felt- or vinyl-backed weather stripping that combines the sturdiness of metal with the application ease of felt. Most manufacturers package their serrated-metal weather stripping in rolls that include brads for installation.

•Tubular gasket weather stripping is made of extremely flexible vinyl. Tubular gasket weather stripping is usually applied outside where it easily conforms to uneven places. Available in white and gray, it cannot be painted because paint causes the tube to stiffen and lose its flexibility.

•Foam-filled tubular gasket includes a foam core in the tubular part of the gasket just described. The foam provides extra insulating qualities and extra strength. The foam-filled tubular gasket will hold its shape better than the hollow tube. Like the hollow tube, it should not be painted.

•Interlocking metal weather stripping requires two separate pieces along each edge. One part fits inside the other to form the seal. One piece goes on the door, while the other is attached to the jamb. Since installation generally requires rabbeting, interlocking metal weather stripping is beyond the carpentry skills of the average homeowner. Should the pieces get bent, they no longer seal and could damage surrounding surfaces. No step-by-step installation instructions are provided for this material. If you already have interlocking metal weather stripping installed, keep it working right by straightening any bent pieces with a screwdriver, pliers, or putty knife.

•Casement window gaskets are specially made vinyl channels that slip over the lip of the casement frame. No adhesives or tools, except scissors for cutting the gasket to the proper length, are needed. This weather stripping is generally available only in shades of gray.

•Jalousie gaskets are clear vinyl tracks that can be cut to fit over the edges of jalousie louvers. They snap in place for a friction fit.

•Door sweeps fill any gap at the threshold under a door. Door sweeps come in wood and felt, wood and foam, metal and vinyl, and in a spring-operated version that is mounted on the outside of a door that opens inward.

Weather-Stripping Windows. Double-hung wood windows usually require weather stripping, although if the top sash is never opened, you can solve an air leak problem by caulking to seal any cracks. Plan to use more than one kind of weather stripping to complete the job. Be sure to follow the correct installation procedures for each.

•Spring-metal weather stripping fits into the tracks around the windows. Each strip should be about 2 inches longer than each sash so that the end of the strip is exposed when the windows are closed. Position the vertical strips so that the flared flange faces toward the outside. The center strip should be mounted to the upper sash with the flare aimed down, while the other horizontal strips are mounted to the top of the upper sash and the bottom of the lower sash with the flared flange facing out. Cut the spring-metal weather stripping to allow for the window pulley mechanisms.

After you measure and cut the spring-metal strips to size, using tin snips, follow these instructions to attach the strips to the window frame:

Position the strip properly and note any hinges, locks, or other hardware that might interfere; trim away the metal where needed. Trim the ends of the strip at an angle (miter) where vertical and horizontal strips meet. Tap in one nail at the top and one nail at the bottom of the strip. Do not put in any more, and do not drive the top and bottom nails all the way in. Since some V strips

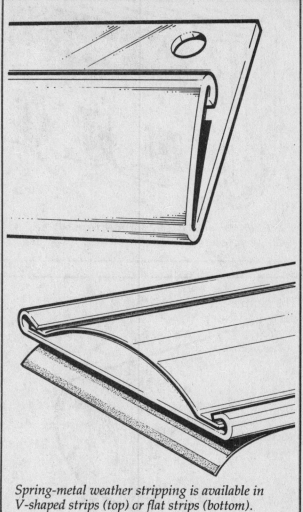

Spring-metal weather stripping is available in V-shaped strips (top) or flat strips (bottom).

Felt strips are economical to use but aren't as long-lasting as other kinds of weather stripping.

do not come with nail holes, you may have to make pilot holes with an ice pick or awl.

Check to make sure that the strips are straight and properly positioned, then drive a nail in the center of the strip, but again only part way. Add nails in between. To avoid damaging the strip,

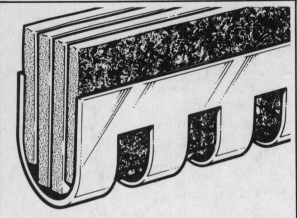

Serrated-metal strips are sturdier than felt but can be difficult to install.

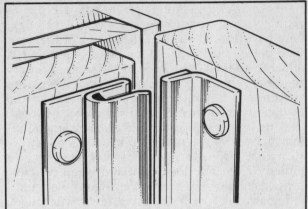

Interlocking metal weather stripping can provide a secure seal as long as the separate pieces fit together as they should. Installation is tricky, and maintenance requires careful examination for bent pieces.

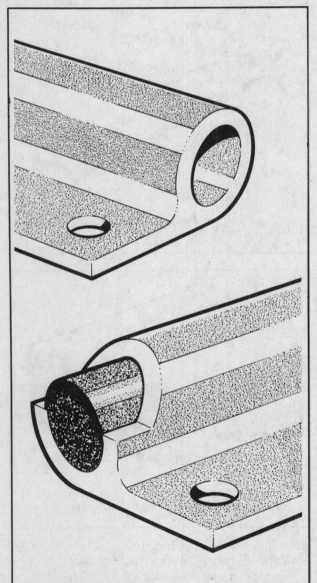

Tubular gasket weather stripping is available with a hollow tube or foam-filled tube.

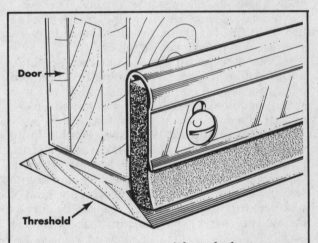

A door sweep can create a tight seal when a gap exists between the bottom of the door and the threshold. Door sweeps can be made of wood and felt, wood and foam, or metal and vinyl. All are effective in sealing out drafts.

Double-hung windows require weather stripping that surrounds both sashes.

Position the flange on spring metal so that the flared edge faces outside.

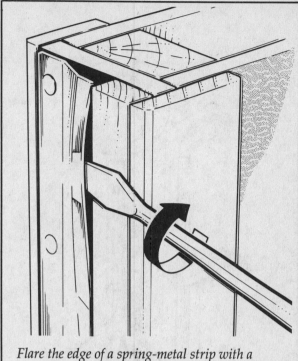

Flare the edge of a spring-metal strip with a screwdriver for a snug fit.

never drive any of the nails all the way in with the hammer. Instead, drive the nails flush with a nail set. Then flare the edge of the strip with a screwdriver to render a snug fit.

•Pressure-sensitive weather stripping can be used only on the friction-free parts of a wooden window: the lower sash or the top of the upper sash. If the strips were installed snugly against the gap between upper and lower sashes, the movement of the window would pull it loose.

To install pressure-sensitive foam weather stripping, select a warm day to do the work, and follow package instructions. The adhesive forms a better bond when applied on a day when the temperature is at least 60 degrees Fahrenheit.

Clean the surface to which the weather stripping is to be attached. Use a detergent solution and make certain that no dirt or grease remains. If pressure-sensitive weather stripping had been installed previously, use a solvent to remove old adhesive. Dry the surface. Use scissors to cut the strip to fit, but do not remove the backing paper yet. Start at one end and slowly peel the paper backing as you push the sticky foam strips into place. If the backing proves stubborn at the beginning, stretch the foam until the seal between the backing and the foam breaks.

•Self-sticking spring-metal weather stripping is applied to wooden windows this way: Measure and cut the strips to fit, then clean the surface where the strips are to go. Put the strips in place without removing the backing paper and mark the spots for trimming, such as hardware and places where vertical and horizontal strips meet. Peel off the backing at one end and press the strip in place, peeling and pressing as you work toward the other end.

•Felt strips are unsightly for sealing gaps on wooden windows. There are places where felt can be used to good advantage. Attach felt strips to the bottom of the lower sash, the top of the upper

sash, and to the interior side of the upper sash. The strips will function as horizontal gaskets.

To weather strip with felt strips, measure the felt and cut the strip from the roll with scissors. Felt strips can go around corners. Push the material snugly against the gap. Nail the ends of each strip first, but do not drive the nails flush; leave room to pry them out. Start at one end and drive a tack every 2 to 3 inches, pulling the felt tight as you go. If you find slack when you reach the other end, remove the nail, pull to tighten, and trim off any excess.

•To install pressure-sensitive felt, follow the same steps as you would to attach pressure-sensitive foam.

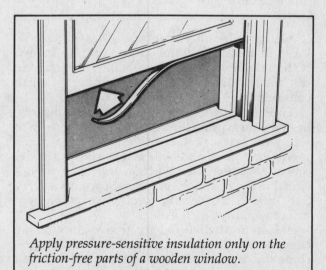

Apply pressure-sensitive insulation only on the friction-free parts of a wooden window.

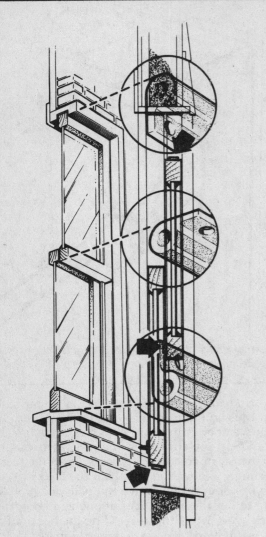

Although unsightly on wooden windows, felt strips can be placed on the bottom of the lower sash, the top of the upper sash, and the interior sides of the upper sash. Tubular gaskets also are unsightly and should be installed only on window exteriors.

•Tubular weather stripping also is unsightly. It can be installed on the outside of the window. If the window is easily accessible from outside the house, tubular weather stripping is worth considering.

To install tubular and foam-filled gaskets, begin by measuring the strips and cutting them to size with scissors. Cutting all the strips for a given window at once will save you trips up and down the ladder later. Position each strip carefully and drive a nail into one end. Space nails every 2 to 3 inches, pulling the weather stripping tight before you drive each nail.

•Most metal windows are grooved around the edges so that the metal flanges interlock and preclude the need for weather stripping. If there are gaps, you must apply weather stripping.

The only kind of weather stripping that can be applied to metal windows is pressure sensitive. Nails would go through the metal and impede movement of the window.

Apply the weather stripping to the top of the upper sash (if it is movable) and to the bottom of the lower sash; these are usually the only spots where metal windows allow for air movement. If you find other gaps, attach a vinyl tubular gasket to the area with a special adhesive formulated to hold vinyl to metal.

•Sliding windows, in which the sash moves laterally, come in both wood and metal frames. Weather-strip the wooden frames much as you would a double-hung window turned sideways. If only one sash moves, weather-strip it and caulk the stationary sash. For metal frames, follow the instructions for weather-stripping standard metal windows.

•Special gaskets are designed especially for sealing gaps in jalousie and casement windows. To weather-strip jalousies, measure the edge of the glass louver, cut the gasket to size with scissors, and snap the gasket in place. To weather-strip casement windows, measure the edges of the frame, cut strips of gasket to size, miter the ends of the gasket strips where they will intersect, and slip the strips in place over the lip of the frame.

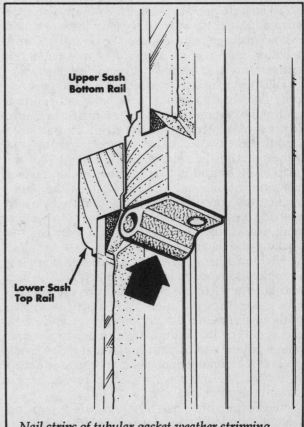

Nail strips of tubular gasket weather stripping to the outside of the window.

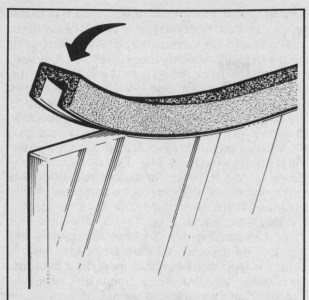

To weather-strip jalousie windows, just cut the special gasket made for this purpose to size and snap it into place along the edge of the glass.

Weather-Stripping Doors. All four edges around doors can allow air to leak in and out of your house. Many doors have more gaps than a loose-fitting window. Before you start weather-stripping, inspect your door to be sure it fits properly in the frame opening. Close the door and look at it from the inside. See that the distance between the door and the frame is uniform along both sides and at the top. The distance does not have to be the same all the way around, but if the door rests crooked in the frame, weather stripping may make it impossible to open or close. If there is great variance in the opening between the door and frame, it will be difficult to fit weather stripping snugly at all points and gaps may result.

The cause of most door problems usually can be found in the hinges. Open the door and tighten all the hinge screws. Even slightly loose screws can cause the door to sag. If the screw holes have been reamed out and are now too big to hold the screws, you can use larger screws as long as they fit in the hinge's countersunk holes. If larger screws won't work, pack the holes with toothpicks dipped in glue, and use a knife to cut the toothpicks even with the surface. Now the screws have new wood in which to bite.

Sometimes the door must be planed off to prevent binding. If so, you can usually plane the top with the door still in place. Always move the plane toward the center of the door to avoid splintering off the edges. If you must plane wood off the sides, take the door off its hinges, plane the hinge side, and always move toward the edges.

•Spring metal is a popular door weather stripping. It works effectively when installed proper-

ly, and it is invisible with the door closed. Most manufacturers include the triangular piece that fits next to the striker plate on the jamb in the packages designated as door kits. If none is provided (or if you choose to buy spring metal in bulk), you can purchase the triangular piece separately.

After you measure and cut the spring-metal strips to size, position the side strips so that the flared flange almost touches the stop. Trim away the metal where needed to fit any hinges, locks, or other hardware.

Tap in one nail at the top and one nail at the bottom of each side strip. Do not put in any more nails, and don't drive the top and bottom nails all the way in. If the strips do not have prepunched holes, make pilot holes with an ice pick or awl. Check that the side strips are straight and properly positioned. Drive a nail in the center of a side strip part way in, then add the nails in between. To avoid damaging the strip, never drive any of the nails all the way in with the hammer. Drive the nails flush with a nail set. Repeat the procedure for the other side strip. Put the top strip in last and miter it to fit. Flare the edge of each strip with a screwdriver for a snug fit.

•Self-sticking spring metal can quickly insulate a door. To install self-sticking spring-metal weather stripping around doors, first measure and cut the strips to fit and clean the surface where strips are to be placed.

Put the strips in place without removing the backing paper, and mark the spots for trimming (where there is hardware and where vertical and horizontal strips meet). Peel off the backing at one end and press the strip in place, peeling and pressing as you work toward the other end.

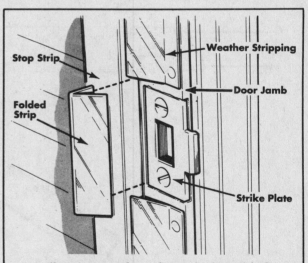

Install spring-metal weather stripping with the flared side facing out. On the latch side attach the folded strip to the edge next to the strike plate; then fasten strips above and below the strike plate.

•Pressure-sensitive foam weather stripping easily can be installed around most doors. Foams are effective, but they have a shorter lifespan than other weather-stripping materials.

To install pressure-sensitive foam weather stripping, select a warm day to do the work and follow instructions. The adhesive forms a better bond when applied on a day in which the temperature is at least 60 degrees Fahrenheit.

Clean the entire surface to which the weather stripping is to be attached. Use a detergent solution, and make certain that no dirt or grease remains. If pressure-sensitive weather stripping had been previously installed, use a solvent to remove old adhesive. Dry the surface. Use scissors to cut the strip to fit, but don't remove the backing paper.

Start at one end and slowly peel the paper backing as you push the sticky foam strips into place. If the backing proves stubborn at the beginning, stretch the foam until the seal between the backing and foam breaks. Attach the strips on the hinge side to the door jamb. Attach the other two strips to the door stop. If the corner of the door catches the weather stripping as you close it, trim the top piece of foam at the hinge side.

•Serrated-metal weather stripping, usually with a felt strip insert running the length of the serrated groove, also can be used to seal gaps around doors. To install this kind of weather-stripping material, measure the length of strips required, and then use tin snips or heavy-duty scissors to cut the serrated-metal material to the proper lengths. Nail each strip at both ends, then add a nail to the center of each strip. Drive the remaining nails, spacing them every 2 to 3 inches.

You must treat the gap at the bottom of the door differently than you do those on the sides and along the top. The hump on the floor along the bottom of the door is called the threshold. A threshold can be made of either wood or metal, with many metal thresholds featuring a flexible vinyl insert that creates a tight seal when the door closes against it. Other thresholds consist of two parts, one on the floor and a mating piece on the bottom of the door, that interlock to form a weather-tight barrier.

•A threshold with a flexible vinyl insert is the best one for a novice weather stripper to install, since it adapts itself easily to most door bottoms. Interlock systems are effective when properly installed, but they require a perfect fit.

Wooden thresholds often wear down to the point where they must be replaced. This is an easy installation, and there are replacement thresholds from which to choose. Most are aluminum and come in standard door widths, but if your door is not standard width, trim the aluminum threshold with a hacksaw.

To install a replacement threshold, remove the old threshold. If it is wood, you can pry it up after removing the door stops with a small flat pry bar or putty knife, but you must work carefully and slowly.

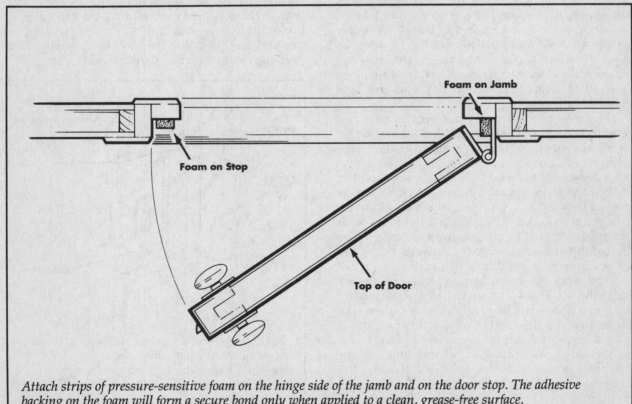

Attach strips of pressure-sensitive foam on the hinge side of the jamb and on the door stop. The adhesive backing on the foam will form a secure bond only when applied to a clean, grease-free surface.

In some installations the jamb rests on the threshold. If this is what you find, then it is best to saw through the old threshold at each end. Use a backsaw placed against the jamb, and saw down through the threshold, being careful not to scar the floor. Once you make the cuts, the threshold should be easy to pry up. If prying fails to do the job, use a chisel and hammer to split the piece.

Metal thresholds are frequently held down by screws concealed under the vinyl inserts. Remove the insert and the screws, and the threshold will come up easily.

Install the replacement threshold by driving screws through the metal unit and into the floor. If the idea of an aluminum threshold doesn't appeal to you, you can cut a replacement from wood, using the original one as a pattern. Then install a door sweep to seal the gap.

•If a gap exists between the door and the threshold, add a door sweep. Most sweeps are attached with nails or screws to the inside of the door. Just cut the sweep to size and close the door. Then tack both ends of the sweep to the door, installing the remaining nails or screws. If you are using screws, drill pilot holes first.

Some sweeps slip under the door and wrap around the bottom. Others fit on the outside, with a section of it flipping upward to miss the threshold when the door is opened. When the door is closed, this section flips back down to provide a seal against the threshold. You can adjust this door sweep to get a snug fit.

INSULATING

Inadequate insulation lets heating or cooling energy escape through your walls and ceilings. To keep this energy in, wrap the entire living area of your house in the proper amount of insulating material.

Insulation should go between the floor and either a crawl space or unfinished basement, between the ceiling and an unfinished attic or between the attic and the roof if the attic is finished, and inside all exterior walls, including those next to an unheated garage.

A material's R-value means its resistance to heat passing through it. The higher its R-value, the greater the material's insulating qualities. The insulation materials available to homeowners include a variety of R-values. Since these materials also vary in terms of installation ease and flammability, selection of the right one for a particular application is not merely a matter of picking the one with the highest R-value. You must be familiar with all the properties of the most common insulating materials.

Insulation. Here are some things to consider about the different materials commonly used for residential insulation:

Most door sweeps are attached to the inside of the door with nails or screws. You cut the sweep to size, close the door and install the sweep.

Another kind of door sweep is attached to the outside and flips up to pass over the threshold when the door is opened.

•Vermiculite is low in cost, widely distributed, and easy to install. A loose-fill material, vermiculite can be poured and then raked, or it can be blown into place. It is an expanded mineral material that is easily introduced into hollow spaces, but it has the disadvantage of packing down from its own weight after several years. As it packs down, it loses thickness, and its R-value is diminished. In addition, vermiculite absorbs moisture, causing even more packing, and the water itself greatly reduces the insulating qualities of the material. Vermiculite is not well suited to wall applications, where its settling tendency would leave uninsulated voids at the top of the wall space. Vermiculite is fire resistant.

•Perlite shares almost all the qualities outlined for vermiculite but has a slightly higher R-value.

•Fiberglass comes in batts, in rolls (blankets), and in pellets for loose-fill applications. It is inex-

293

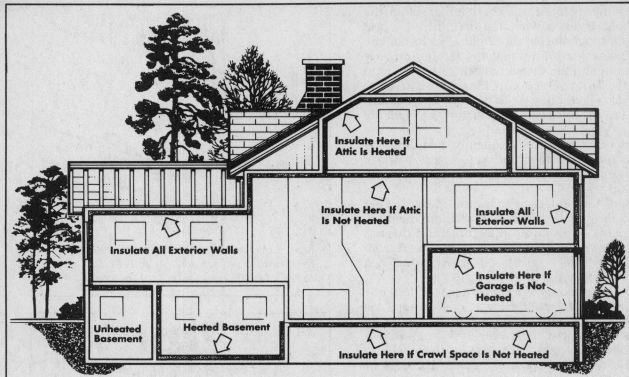

Insulation should go between the floor and either the unheated crawl space or basement, between the ceiling and unheated attic or between the attic and roof if the attic is heated, and inside all exterior walls, including those adjacent to an unheated garage.

pensive and usually easy to apply. Fiberglass itself is fire resistant, although the heavy paper facing frequently found on fiberglass batts and rolls is not fireproof. Fiberglass also can be faced with materials that form a good vapor barrier, and it is available in an unfaced version for addition on top of existing insulation. Its few disadvantages are that fiberglass is a skin irritant when handled and that it develops an odor when damp.

•Rock wool offers almost the identical qualities as fiberglass; even its cost and R-value are nearly the same. Like fiberglass, rock wool can irritate the skin when handled. About the only difference is the fact that rock wool does not develop an odor when wet.

•Polystyrene, popularly known as Styrofoam, is a kind of rigid board insulation that is an excellent material to use in new construction. Because it is combustible, polystyrene cannot be exposed in its finished state. It must be covered with wallboard, exterior siding, or other material as specified by local codes. Since it is moisture resistant, it can be used below grade; it is often used around slab foundations and can be used as a base to provide extra insulation under a poured concrete slab. Polystyrene boards, which are susceptible to gouges and dents, generally are attached to the studs of new construction during the framing.

•Cellulose has been much maligned as a fire hazard and is often called newspaper insulation. When properly treated, cellulose is as fire resistant as fiberglass or rock wool. It offers a higher R-value than either fiberglass or rock wool, and it does not irritate the skin as some insulation materials do. Cellulose comes in rolls (blankets), batts, or loose fill. In its loose-fill version, cellulose has a fine consistency, permitting blow-in installation through small access holes. Make sure that the cellulose you purchase carries the brand name and treatment certification of a reputable manufacturer.

•Urethane is foam insulation that is effective when installed properly. Its R-value is high, and it offers excellent fire resistance. Urethane foam has excellent sound-absorbing qualities. A foam-in material has the advantage of completely filling any cavity in which it is injected, but it has the disadvantage of requiring installation equipment that is too expensive for the homeowner. Some insulation professionals lack the knowledge and experience to do a competent job. If you elect to use this kind of insulation, be sure to hire a qualified contractor to install it.

You need to know the kind and quantity of insulation already in your house before buying additional material. You can easily check the attic insulation. With an unfloored attic, merely measure the thickness of the insulation with a ruler. If

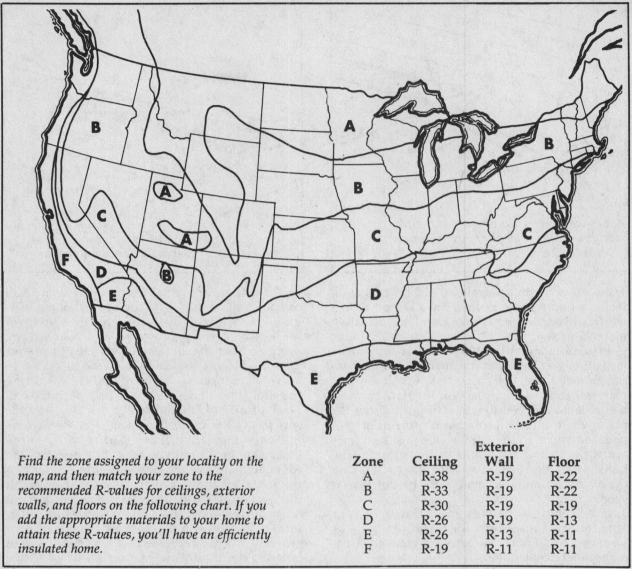

		Exterior	
Zone	Ceiling	Wall	Floor
A	R-38	R-19	R-22
B	R-33	R-19	R-22
C	R-30	R-19	R-19
D	R-26	R-19	R-13
E	R-26	R-13	R-11
F	R-19	R-11	R-11

Find the zone assigned to your locality on the map, and then match your zone to the recommended R-values for ceilings, exterior walls, and floors on the following chart. If you add the appropriate materials to your home to attain these R-values, you'll have an efficiently insulated home.

you know what the material is, you can estimate its R-value. If you don't know the kind of material, take a sample of it to an insulation dealer.

A floored attic presents a slightly different problem. If the boards are just butted together and nailed down, you can pry up a board to check. The easiest place to start is at an exposed end at the attic entrance.

If the flooring is tongue and groove, you can drill a hole (1/2 inch or larger) through the floor in an obscure corner. Be sure the hole is not over a joist and that you have a dowel to plug the hole when you're finished checking the insulation. Use a flashlight to peer into the hole. If you can see that the insulation comes up to the flooring, you need only to find out what kind of material it is; the hook portion of a wire coat hanger works well in retrieving a bit of the material.

If the insulation doesn't come up to the flooring, lower a probe into the hole until it touches the top of the insulation. Mark the probe at that point and then withdraw it. If you know the

depth of the cavity and the thickness of the flooring, you can figure out how many inches of insulation are presently under your attic floor. If you don't know the depth of the cavity, you must push the probe through the insulation until it strikes the solid surface below. Mark the probe at that point and then compute the depth of the cavity by subtracting the thickness of the flooring from the total depth indicted on the probe.

To measure the insulation inside a wall, you must again find an opening. If possible, use existing openings, such as those around electrical outlets. Before you start probing, turn off the electric current to the outlet that you have selected.

Take the cover plate off the outlet and see if there is enough space to the side of the junction box to allow you to inspect the insulation with a flashlight. If not, widen the crack on the side opposite the side where the metal box is attached to the stud. Use a utility knife to widen a crack in wallboard; use a cold chisel if the wall is plaster. Widen only as much as the cover plate can hide.

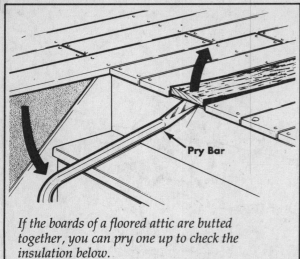

If the boards of a floored attic are butted together, you can pry one up to check the insulation below.

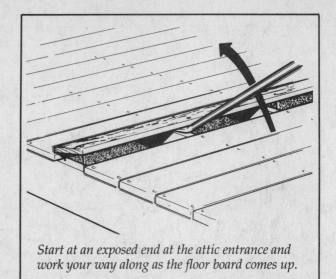

Start at an exposed end at the attic entrance and work your way along as the floor board comes up.

Then inspect with a flashlight and probe as you would a floored attic, pulling out a sample with a wire coat hanger if you don't know the insulating material used.

Insulating an Attic. Now that you know what insulation you have and the quantity of the material already there, you're ready to install the new material. The easiest place to insulate in most homes is the attic. Fortunately, the attic also is the place where proper insulation has the most pronounced effect. In the winter most lost heat goes out through the attic, and in the summer the uninsulated attic acts as a heat collector, making the air conditioning system work harder than it should.

If you find that there is no insulation in your attic, follow these steps for installing batts or blankets. You'll find that batts are generally easier to install than blankets.

To decide how much insulation you need, measure the length and width of the attic and multiply the length by the width to arrive at the total square footage. Measure the distance between the joists. Most are on 16-inch centers (16 inches from the center of one to the center of the next), but some are on 24-inch centers. Buy batts or blankets of the correct width to fit between joists. For 16-inch centers, multiply the square footage by .90; that computation will give you the number of square feet of insulation required. With 24-inch centers, multiply by .94. You must install a vapor barrier in attics having no insulation. The easiest way to lay down a vapor barrier is to install batts or blankets of insulation with a vapor barrier attached.

Before you begin the installation, cut pieces of plywood to use as movable flooring, and carry up wide planks to serve as walkways. If you were to step onto the ceiling material, you would likely break right through it, but the joists will support your weight. If the attic is inadequately lighted, rig up a lighting system so that you can see what you're doing. A drop light suspended from a nail or hook will do the job. If you are installing fiberglass or rock wool, you must protect yourself with gloves, safety goggles, and a breathing mask. A hard hat also is a good idea to protect your head from protruding nails and low rafters.

Now you're ready to lay down the insulating material. Start under the eaves and push the end of the blanket or batt in place with a long stick. Be sure to put the vapor barrier side on the bottom. Press the insulation down firmly between the joists. Continue until you reach the center of the room, and then work from the opposite end of the joists out to the center. When you must cut the insulating material to fit around pipes and other obstructions, use a sharp knife with a serrated edge. You will find that the material is easier to cut when compressed with a scrap piece of board. Trim the insulation to fit around vents, recessed lighting fixtures, exhaust fan motors, or any heat-producing equipment that protrudes into the attic. Allow 3 inches of clearance. Do not pull on any electrical wiring in order to move it out of the way.

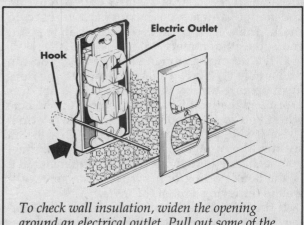

To check wall insulation, widen the opening around an electrical outlet. Pull out some of the insulation with a wire hook.

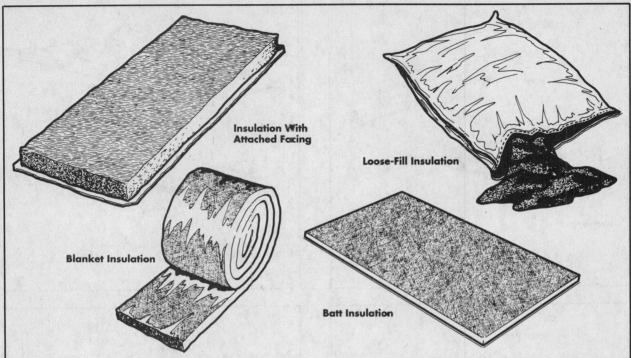

Insulation is available in blankets, batts, and loose fill. Batts and blankets can have an attached facing that serves as a vapor barrier, or they can come unfaced. Batts are easier to install in attics than blankets.

If you choose to insulate your uninsulated attic with loose fill, first staple polyethylene between joists to serve as a vapor barrier. To calculate your total material needs, measure the square footage of the attic and then consult an insulation dealer. The dealer has a chart showing the maximum net coverage per bag at various thicknesses and the R-value for each thickness. The bags in which the loose fill is packaged also supply the same information.

Be careful not to cover vents and heat-producing gadgets sticking up in the attic. Strips of insulating batts do a good job of guarding vents, while metal retainers made from tin cans will keep loose fill away from the other areas. Pour the insulation into the spaces between the joists, and then spread and level the material with a garden rake. If you want the joists to be covered with the loose fill, work from all sides back toward the attic access hole. Finally, staple a batt of insulation material to the access cover.

You can use either batts or blankets, or loose fill to add material to existing but inadequate insulation. Follow the same application procedure outlined for an uninsulated attic, but lay down unfaced batts or blankets instead of batts or blankets with a vapor barrier attached. If you add loose fill, do not apply a vapor barrier over the existing insulation.

If your access to the attic consists of a disappearing section of stairs, you must construct a box in the attic over the folded-up stairs. Add a plywood door to the top of the box, and then sta-

ple batts to all sides of the box and to the door. Hand pack insulation around pipes and wires that come up through the floor of the attic, closing the holes around these elements.

If you decide to heat your attic to provide extra living space, you should remove the existing insulation from between the joists before installing the finished attic floor. Leave out insulation under the eaves, or add insulation there as needed. Remember that insulation should only go between heated and unheated areas, and keep in mind that the vapor barrier always faces the heated area.

Staple insulation blankets between knee wall studs and rafters before you cover them with paneling or wallboard. You might choose to use loose fill in sloping sections of the ceiling.

Insulating Walls. The next most important places to insulate after the attic are the exterior walls. If you live in an older home in which you have access from the attic to the cavities between the wall studs, you can merely pour loose fill in the holes; just make sure that the cavities are closed at the bottom.

If you don't have this kind of construction, you must cut holes in the walls about every 16 inches and blow the insulation in with a special machine, which you are able to rent. If your exterior walls have fire stops (2 x 4s nailed horizontally between the studs), you'll need a second row of holes below the fire stops.

Many exterior walls are built without fire stops, but you'll have to cut extra holes beneath

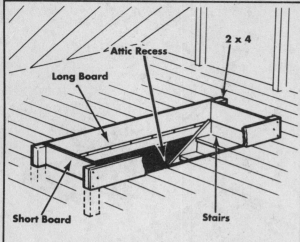

To insulate a disappearing stairway, first build a box over the stairs.

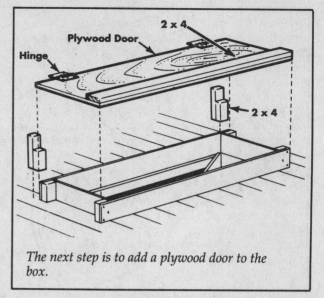

The next step is to add a plywood door to the box.

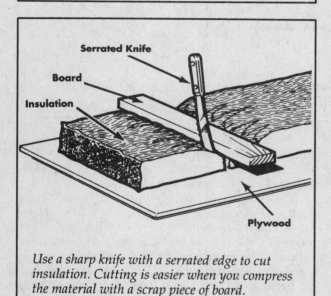

Use a sharp knife with a serrated edge to cut insulation. Cutting is easier when you compress the material with a scrap piece of board.

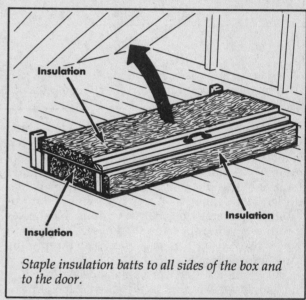

Staple insulation batts to all sides of the box and to the door.

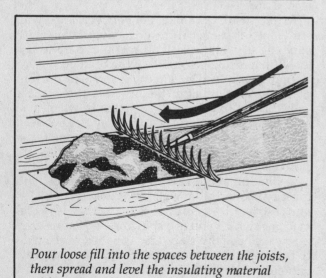

Pour loose fill into the spaces between the joists, then spread and level the insulating material with a rake.

windows and any other obstructions. A two-story house needs holes at the top of each floor in addition to all the other locations mentioned.

You can drill from the inside or from the outside. If the inside walls have decorative molding, you may be able to remove the molding, make holes behind it, and then cover the holes with the molding. If you have a brick home or one with metal siding, then you should drill from inside, but most other exteriors can be cut into and patched. Clapboard siding often can be pried up without damage and replaced after the insulating is done.

To remove clapboard siding, insert a piece of sheet metal or a flat wide-blade scraper under the piece of siding to be removed. The sheet metal or scraper will protect the siding from the pry bar that is wedged in under the siding. Pry gently until the siding comes up about 1/2 inch. Then remove the pry bar and push the siding back in place; use a mallet if the siding won't go down. Pull out the nails you find sticking up, then repeat the prying every 16 inches to remove all the nails. If a piece of siding does not come out, look for a nail you missed or a paint seal holding the siding from above.

Wood shingles have hidden nails except at the top, although the top row may have some sort of overlap. If it does, pry away the overlap. Now that the top row of shingles is exposed, you can usually pry them up without breaking any shingles. A flat spade slipped under the shingles provides good prying leverage. After the shingles are pried up slightly, the nail heads will be up far enough so that you can pull them out.

You may have to remove more than one row of shingles to find the right spots for the insulation access holes. For prying up shingles from the lower areas under obstructions, you might want to invest in a specialized tool called a shingle nail remover.

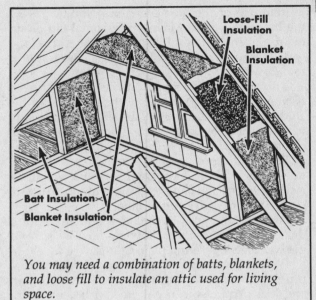

You may need a combination of batts, blankets, and loose fill to insulate an attic used for living space.

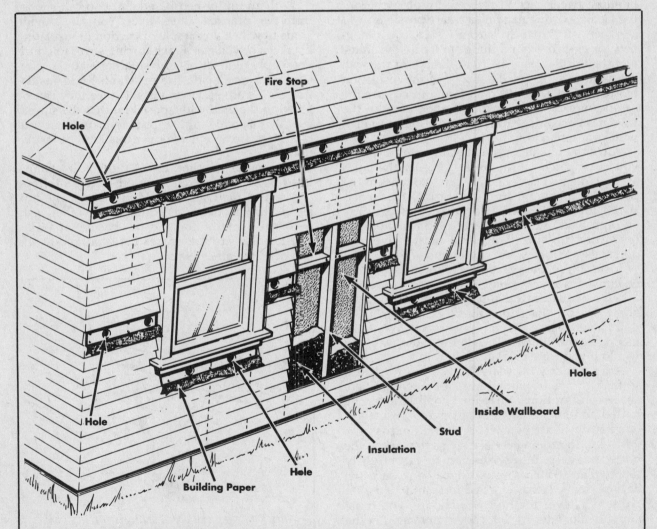

To insulate your home from the outside, cut holes in the walls about every 16 inches and blow in the insulation. If the walls have fire stops, you'll need a second row of holes below these horizontal 2 x 4s. There also must be holes beneath windows and other obstructions, and at the top of each floor level.

Removal of the facing material should reveal the building paper. Make a horizontal cut along the top of the paper, going all the way across the wall. Then make vertical cuts at each end, and fold down the building paper.

You are ready to position the holes between each pair of studs. You should be able to spot the studs by noting the nails in the sheathing. Be sure to make the holes large enough to hold the nozzle of the insulation blower.

Before filling each cavity, make sure that the hole is open all the way down. Lower a weight on a string to check. If you encounter an obstruction, you'll need to drill another hole.

Large tool rental companies and insulation dealers rent insulation blower units. Be sure to get complete operating instructions.

When all cavities are filled with insulation, plug the holes with plastic inserts that snap in and lock. You also can nail tin-can lids or sheet-metal squares over the holes. Then staple the building paper back in place and replace the siding, using existing nail holes where possible.

When you must drill from inside, use a magnetic or electronic stud finder to locate the studs, and then drill or saw holes at the top of the wall big enough to accept the nozzle of the insulation blower. Drop a weight on a string to be sure the cavities are unobstructed, and then blow in the insulation according to the instructions supplied with your rental unit.

After the insulation has been blown in place, you must patch all the holes. Usually the holes are so large that they need backing to prevent the patching compound from falling into the cavity. If the loose-fill insulation does not provide enough backing, cram scraps from insulation batts into the holes, and then plaster over the openings with spackling compound.

Insulating Floors. Exposed joists in an unheated crawl space or basement allow you to provide a layer of insulation under the floor of your home. The best insulation for this kind of installation is batts, since they are the easiest to handle. Estimate your material needs the same way you would if you were insulating the attic.

After you buy the material, you must install it so that it stays in place between the joists. There are several options: Strips of wood lath can be nailed across the joists about every 16 inches; chicken wire strips can be stapled across the joists, leaving room between strips to work in the batts; heavy-gauge wires can be cut slightly longer than 16 inches and wedged between joists; or wire can be laced back and forth and held with nails. Whatever method you choose, you must support the batts so that they don't sag. On the other hand, don't worry about an air space between the batts and the subflooring. If the batts are snug, the dead air space will contribute to the R-value.

If you detect ground moisture, provide a ground vapor barrier. If the moisture problem still exists after you install the vapor barrier or if the crawl space is open, cover the bottom of the joists with low-grade plywood or staple a plastic vapor barrier in place.

Some homes have an insulated basement or insulation on the foundation to provide what is called a heated crawl space. The heated crawl space doesn't necessarily mean that heat is piped there. The insulation around the foundation is designed to prevent heated air that reaches the crawl space from escaping.

The basement or crawl space with insulation around the foundation does not provide as effective a barrier to heat loss as does insulation under the floor. A heated basement, on the other hand, should be insulated around the foundation, while its ceiling should not. The warm air that rises from the heated basement will help warm the house.

With an unfinished basement, you can choose from two practical alternatives: You can provide studs to which you staple or friction fit insulating blankets, or you can attach furring strips to which you apply rigid sheets of insulating material, covered over and made fire resistant. Rigid insulation sheets are easier to install, since they can be glued to the wall with special mastics. Be sure to check your local building code to learn what wall coverings are acceptable over this kind of insulation.

With either method cover the box joists and headers with blankets stapled to the subfloor above and the framing added below. The box joist is the joist that runs parallel to all other joists between the subfloor and the basement walls. The headers are the spaces between and at the end of all the other joists.

When removing clapboard siding, use a pry bar against a flat piece of metal to lift the siding up gently. Repeat the prying every 16 inches, pulling out the nails holding the siding as you go.

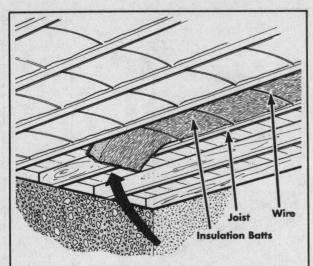

Insulation batts are easy to install between the exposed joists of an unheated crawl space or basement; heavy-gauge wire will hold the batts in place. You also can support the batts with strips of wood lath or chicken wire.

With a heated crawl space in which the walls will never be finished, you need only fasten insulating blankets at the top and pile bricks to hold the blankets against the wall at the floor. Wider blankets make the installation quicker, but a narrow crawl space is never going to be easy to insulate. Here is the what to do:

Start on a box joist side of the wall. Lay a plastic vapor barrier strip on the ground along that wall, leaving about 2 inches at each end to run up the wall. Use duct tape to secure the ends. Starting at a corner, staple the blankets to the box joist, trimming the blankets at ground level. Butt the next strip to the first and trim it, working all the way across. Trim the last panel to fit. Lay the next strip of vapor barrier, letting the two overlap by 6 inches. Attach a blanket strip in the corner of the wall with headers. Trim to fit the joists, but don't trim at ground level; place a brick on the ground to hold the blanket. Then run the blanket out to the middle of the room. Now go to the opposite corner, attach another strip, and run it out to meet the first strip. Trim both at the center and use bricks to hold each end down. Work your way down each wall, overlapping vapor barrier strips as you go and trimming and attaching the blankets at the top. At floor level extend the blankets toward the center no more than about 2 feet. When you reach the other box joist side, finish the wall and run corner blankets to the center.

A home built on a slab should have rigid insulation attached to the foundation around its perimeter. Such insulation will make a significant difference in the temperature of the slab floor.

Since the insulating material should extend down below the frost line, the installation generally involves considerable digging. After the rigid insulating sheets are attached to the foundation with the specific mastic recommended by the insulation manufacturer, they should then be finished with stucco, plaster, asbestos board, or another material that is code approved.

When converting a garage or porch to living space, you can insulate the concrete floors with rigid sheets. If there was no vapor barrier installed under the slab when it was poured, you should apply a vapor-repellent coating.

Apply rigid sheets to the floor using the recommended mastic. Nail furring strips on top of the rigid insulation sheets, using masonry nails. Be sure to wear safety goggles. Lay the furring strips on 16-inch centers to hold the subflooring. Finally, nail 1/2-inch exterior grade plywood to the furring strips, and then apply your desired flooring.

INSTALLING A WOOD-BURNING STOVE

Wood-burning stoves are alternate sources of energy. If you're planning to purchase one to heat part or all of your home, there are many safety and installation considerations of which you should be aware.

Most stove manufacturers supply instructions for installation with their products. You should be wary of buying a stove that doesn't have complete instructions. It's also recommended that the product be certified by a recognized testing organization, such as Underwriters Laboratories. Before installing a stove, obtain a building permit, if one is required in your area, to put in a chimney. After it is installed, have building code officials inspect it.

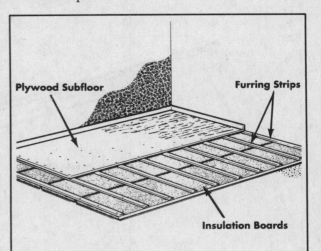

Nail furring strips on top of the rigid insulation sheets, laying the furring strips on 16-inch centers to accommodate the subflooring. If there is no vapor barrier under the slab, you should apply a vapor-repellent coating to the slab before attaching the rigid insulating sheets.

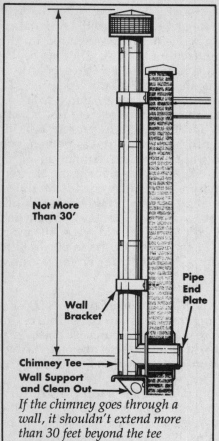

Not More Than 30'

Wall Bracket

Pipe End Plate

Chimney Tee

Wall Support and Clean Out

If the chimney goes through a wall, it shouldn't extend more than 30 feet beyond the tee section through the wall.

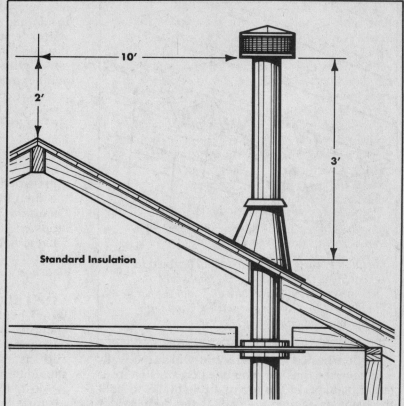

Standard Insulation

10'

2'

3'

The top of the chimney should be at least 3 feet above the point where it goes through the roof. It also should be 2 feet higher than the house at any point within 10 feet.

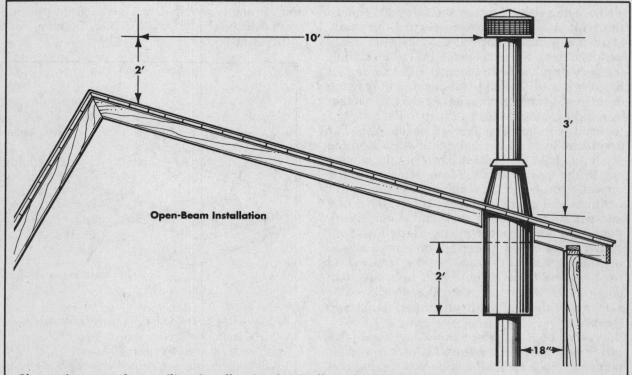

10'

2'

3'

2'

18"

Open-Beam Installation

If yours is an open-beam ceiling, install an insulated collar at least 24 inches in length. Exposed pipe must be three times its diameter from anything that will burn.

If you are shopping for a new stove, here are some basic requirements for installation that you should check with the retailer before you buy:

•The top of the chimney should be at least 3 feet above the point where it goes through the roof. It also should be 2 feet higher than the house at any point within 10 feet.

•The chimney should not extend more than 90 feet for 6-inch, 7-inch, or 8-inch pipe sizes, and it should not go beyond 50 feet for 10-inch and 12-inch pipe sizes. If the chimney goes through a wall, it should not extend more than 30 feet beyond the tee section that goes through the wall.

•The chimney, which can act like a lightning rod, should be grounded; ground the stove as you would any electrical appliance.

•If the chimney pipe goes through a closet or built-in storage area, such as kitchen cabinets, it must be in an enclosed space. Enclosures for chimney pipes are available from many manufacturers.

•If more than one stove will be connected to a pipe chimney, the chimney should be equal in size to the combined area of the connector pipes. Never connect additional wood-burning appliances or fireplaces to a fireplace chimney.

•Floor protection should consist of an approved stove mat, such as fiberglass batts covered with sheet metal, mortared bricks, stone, or concrete with at least 4 inches of clearance from the stove to the floor. The protection should extend at least 18 inches around the stove so that embers don't fall on an unprotected floor.

•Minimum wall clearance, where combustible materials, such as paneling, gypsum wallboard, and wood studs, are involved, is 3 feet. If the walls are protected with mineral wool paddings and have a 28-gauge sheet-metal covering with a 1-inch air space between the back of the shield and the wall, the stove may be moved to within 18 inches of the wall.

•Exposed stovepipe must be three times its diameter away from anything that will burn: for example, an 8-inch pipe would have to be at least 24 inches away from combustible material. If a heat shield is used, this distance may be reduced to a minimum of 9 inches, but always check your local codes.

•A spark screen should be installed over the outside opening of the chimney to prevent sparks from escaping and causing a roof fire.

INSTALLING A CEILING FAN

If you've ever installed a light fixture, you already know most of what's involved in hanging a ceiling fan. You turn off the power, connect the fan's black lead to the black wire in the ceiling box, its white lead to the white wire, then slip a canopy up around the fan's shaft and secure it to the box. The main differences are that a fan is much heavier than a light fixture, and its motor

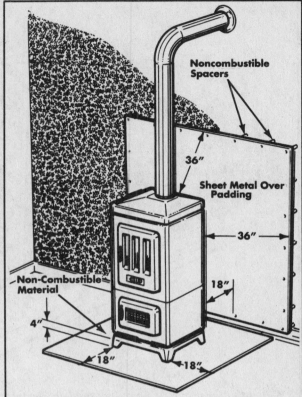

There are minimum clearances for stove installations. For example, floor protection should include a stove mat with at least 4 inches of clearance from stove to floor. The protection should extend at least 18 inches around the stove.

produces torque that could cause annoying, even destructive, vibration. A fan must be hung from a securely mounted ceiling box that can support at least 50 pounds. The box should be firmly attached to a piece of wood that is in turn nailed to joists on either side. If the box you're thinking of using is not mounted in this way, you or an electrician must remount the box.

Fan mounting systems vary, but most hang from a hook, with a doughnut-shaped bushing that absorbs vibration by letting the entire unit wobble slightly as the fan blades rotate. Here are the steps to follow in installing a ceiling fan:

•Turn off power to the ceiling box from a circuit breaker or fuse panel. If the box is controlled by a switch, don't assume that merely turning off the switch will de-energize the box. The box may still be live and you could receive a serious shock.

•Prepare the fan according to the manufacturer's instructions. Connect the motor to the shaft it hangs from, then slip a canopy over the shaft so that it loosely rests on top of the motor. If your ceiling is extremely tall, you can buy a longer shaft. But a fan always should be more than 7 feet above the floor. Don't attach the blades until you've hung the motor.

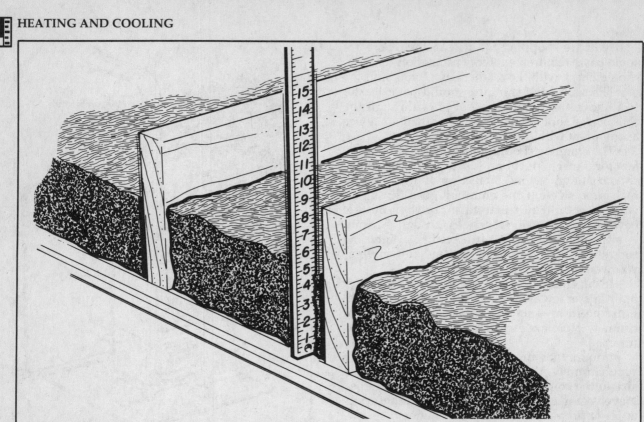

With an unfinished attic floor, just measure the thickness of the insulation with a ruler. If you know what the material is, you can estimate its R-value. If you don't know the kind of material, take a sample of it to an insulation dealer.

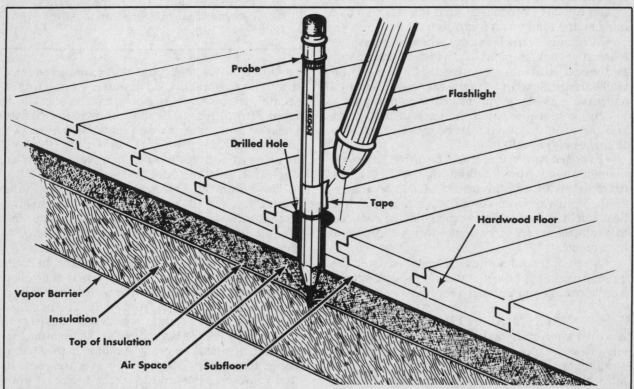

Probe

Flashlight

Drilled Hole

Tape

Hardwood Floor

Vapor Barrier

Insulation

Top of Insulation

Air Space   Subfloor

If the boards of a floored attic are tongue and groove, drill a hole through an obscure portion (not over a joist) and use a flashlight to see whether the insulation comes up to the flooring. If it doesn't, lower a probe into the hole until it touches the material.

•Exactly how you install the ceiling hook depends on what's up there. Most fans come with a simple screw eye. You drill a hole through the center of the box (if there is not one there already) and into solid wood above, then thread the hook into the wood until it extends 1 1/4 inches below the ceiling surface. If your box has an integral fixture stud, screw a machine-threaded hook into the stud.

•Slip the rubber bushing into the hook and push a pivot pin through the bushing. The pin should project an equal distance from either side of the bushing.

•Lift the fan and hang it from the pivot pin. You may need a helper for this step. Secure the fan's hanger hook with retaining rings that clip onto each end of the pivot pin.

•Make the electrical connections with twist-on wirenuts, connecting the fan's black lead to the outlet box's black wire, its white lead to the white wire. If the box has a green or bare grounding wire, connect it to the grounding screw in the fan's hanger hook. If the box doesn't have a grounding wire, run a short piece of wire from the grounding screw to a screw threaded into one side of the outlet box. Carefully tuck all wires into the box, then pull up the fan's ceiling canopy and attach it with long screws into the box's ears.

•Install the blades by slipping each into position in the motor hub, aligning its threaded holes with holes in the hub, then threading in screws to secure the blade.

•With some fans you control the speed with a pull chain that hangs from the fan; with others you need to install a wall-mounted rheostat that lets you adjust the amount of current flowing to the motor. Make sure that any rheostat you buy will be compatible with your fan; ordinary light-dimmer rheostats shouldn't be used with motors. Before you install a rheostat, turn off power to the ceiling box and the wall switch that controls it.

DETERMINING R-VALUES

Basic Material	Approximate R-value Per Inch of Thickness*
Vermiculite	2.1
Perlite	2.7
Fiberglass	3.3
Rock Wool	3.3
Polystyrene	3.5
Cellulose	3.7
Urethane	5.3

*Unfortunately, the per inch figure, when multiplied by thickness, is not a certain guide to discovering the material's R-value. Therefore, companies marketing insulation indicate the exact R-value on the product itself or on its package. Federal law also requires that bags of loose-fill insulation show the R-valve yield inch by inch.

VAPOR BARRIERS

A vapor barrier doesn't actually save energy, but it should always be included when insulation is installed for the first time. Since proper insulation increases the difference between the temperature on the inside and the temperature on the outside of a wall surface, it leads to increased condensation. Warm moist air passes through walls and ceilings and condenses when it reaches the colder surfaces. Moisture left on wall surfaces can cause paint failure, mildew, and rotting, while moisture left inside the wall renders the insulating material almost worthless.

The key to stopping condensation is a vapor barrier. It keeps warm moist air from passing through the walls or ceiling to the cold surfaces, preventing condensation from forming on walls and ceilings.

Adding a vapor barrier to an attic is simple when you are starting an insulation installation from scratch. You can buy batts or blankets with the vapor barrier facing attached, or you can put down a layer of special plastic material before pouring or blowing loose-fill insulation in place. Wide duct tape is useful in patching any tears or holes in the plastic and for taping two sections together.

A vapor barrier is difficult to add to existing insulation or to wall insulation. If moisture is a problem, you can create an effective vapor barrier by applying an oil-base enamel with an alkyd-base top coat to walls. A penetrating floor sealer or several coats of varnish can provide a satisfactory vapor barrier on existing floors. Even floor wax and wax coats on wood-paneled walls help stop vapor-laden air from passing through.

Vinyl wall coverings and resilient flooring act as a vapor barrier, but tile squares are not as effective as sheet goods; the cracks between the tiles, small as they are, allow moisture to pass through. Although these materials can help when no proper vapor barriers can be installed, the conventional vapor barrier materials, including 4-mil polyethylene sheeting, aluminum foil, and impregnated papers, provide the best protection against the harmful effects of condensation.

REMODELING A KITCHEN

A kitchen, like a car, eventually wears out, and when that happens, you're faced with spending about as much as you would for a new automobile. You can't do much about the way cars are designed, but you can plan a kitchen suited exactly to your family's needs. A kitchen's design makes the difference between a facility that is adequate and one that works well.

Planning and Design

Designing a kitchen is a game of inches. Since you will be buying and installing many cabinets and appliances, all of which have specific sizes, there is no room for error. The first step in planning and designing a kitchen is to measure the available space and to record your measurements.

Use a 6-foot folding carpenter's rule or 3/4-inch steel measuring tape. A household yardstick is too short, and a narrow retractable steel tape measure can sag or slip.

Measure all room dimensions to within 1/16 inch, and record each measurement accurately. Even a slight error can mean significant difficulties later. For example, if the space you think can fit 120 inches of cabinets and appliances turns out to be no more than 119 1/2 inches, your original plan may prove unfeasible.

Before you start taking measurements, make a rough outline of the entire room on a grid sheet where each square equals 6 inches. Then begin at one corner and measure the distance from the corner to a window's trim at a height of 36 inches above the floor (the height of a countertop). Proceed by measuring from the outside of the window trim on one side of the window to the outside of the trim on the other side, then from that trim edge to the door trim, recording each measurement on your grid sheet. Write each measurement as you go along without trying to add them up. Adding them as you go diverts your

attention and can lead to error. Note obstacles, such as the chimney, offsets, and radiators, on the grid sheet. Also show the locations of electrical outlets, light switches, and fixtures.

When you finish measuring a wall, total the figures. Then make another overall measurement to check your addition. If you discover any discrepancy, start over.

Now indicate on the sketch where doors lead, door and windowsill heights, and the height from the windowsill to the top of window trim. Also measure and record the height of the ceilings, from floor to ceiling, and the height and depth of the existing soffit (the wall area above the upper cabinets). Soffit height should be measured from the floor to the soffit.

Mark the locations for the sink drain and the incoming water supply on the grid sheet, but you can move the sink to one side or the other; all you have to do is turn and extend the drain trap (it need not go straight into the wall) and extend the supply lines to the faucets.

You must check the angle of the room's corners because they are seldom square. Such discrepancies must be considered. To check the corners, mark a point 36 inches from the corner along one wall at a height of 36 inches above the floor. Do the same for the other corner wall, but at a distance of 48 inches from the corner. Now measure the direct distance between the two points (the hypotenuse of what is supposed to be a right triangle). This distance should be exactly 60 inches. If it is less, the angle between the two walls is less than 90 degrees; if it is more, the angle is more than 90 degrees. Note any lack of squareness so that your countertop can be cut to match the actual shape of the corner.

Draw the entire room on your grid sheet, not just the walls that will be in your kitchen installation. The distances to other walls or parts of the room are important. Where you find corners out of square, note both the distance along the wall and the distance 24 inches out from the wall; you

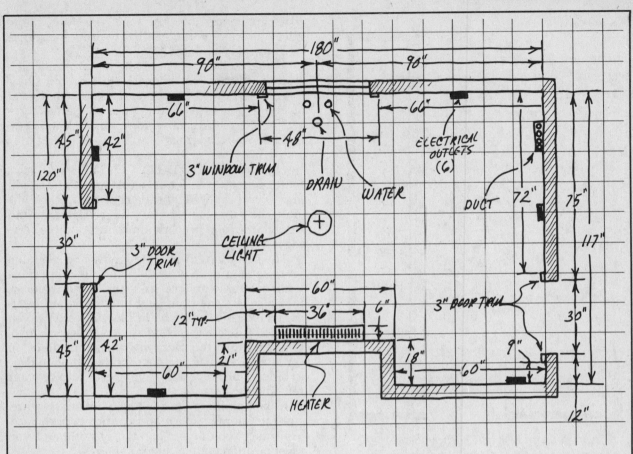

Before measuring, make a rough outline of the entire room on a grid sheet. Then measure all room dimensions to within 1/16 inch.

must plan your kitchen for the shorter measurement because the cabinets will not fit if sized for the longer measurement.

SAFETY FIRST

Many potentially hazardous activities take place in the kitchen. Besides cutting, chopping, grinding, and slicing, people are often handling hot items, probing into drawers and cabinets, and operating electrical appliances.

This means that the kitchen is a place where accidents can happen. Although most accidents are caused by carelessness, a kitchen can be designed to make the probability of accidents less likely.

The key to kitchen safety is to maximize efficiency and to minimize potential hazards. Here are some guidelines:

• Make sure your kitchen offers an efficient and effective work triangle. This means that the total distance from sink to range to refrigerator should not be less than 12 feet nor more than 22 feet. The work areas should not be closer than 4 feet nor farther than 9 feet from one another. Shorter distances mean you are too cramped; longer ones mean you must take tiring extra steps.

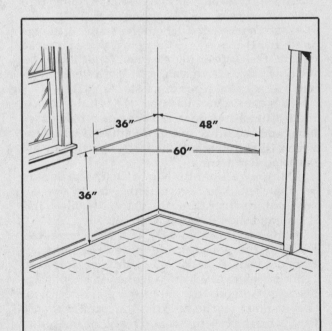

To check for squareness, measure 36 inches from the corner along one wall and 48 inches along the other. The distance between the two points (if the walls are square) should be 60 inches.

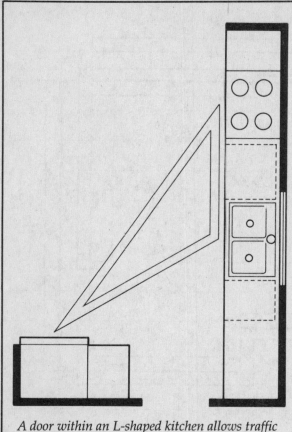

A door within an L-shaped kitchen allows traffic to cross the work triangle, creating a safety hazard.

•Make sure your kitchen is well lit, with sufficient general and "task" lighting.

•Make sure your kitchen offers ample storage space and that access to the items stored poses no danger. Shelf space higher than 72 inches above the floor presents a hazard, because a stool or ladder is required to reach items stored there.

•Make sure you have ample counter space, including the proper amount of work space alongside the range and refrigerator. Otherwise, you will be doing too much transporting of hot pans and cold foods.

•Minimize the number of sharp corners in your kitchen. Square corners on island or peninsula countertops are hazardous to hips and hands, and should be rounded.

•Vent hoods should be at least 56 inches above the floor and not protrude more than 18 inches from the wall. A hood that protrudes more than 18 inches should be moved higher. If a vent hood needs to be more than 60 inches above the floor (for instance, if the cook is much taller than 6 feet), a more powerful vent fan will be needed to compensate for the greater distance.

•Avoid the exasperation of a refrigerator door that does not open into the work triangle. Avoid oven or other appliance doors that block doorways or bump each other when opened. Do not place appliances too close together or so close to either a wall or corner so that the action of doors or drawers is inhibited.

•When selecting a new range and positioning it in the kitchen, consider the fire and burn hazard. You should not be forced to reach over steaming pots to get to the controls, and the burners should not be near window curtains and combustible wall coverings.

THE ACTIVITY CENTERS

Storage areas, countertop work space, and appliances form the activity centers of the kitchen: the sink, the range or cooktop, the refrigerator and freezer, the food preparation center, and the serving center.

The best place to start designing and planning your kitchen usually is the window. Since most homeowners want the sink under the window, that is where the plumbing lines often are located. One element may be in place already. If you want to reserve the window for an eating area, you can move the plumbing lines, but doing so can get expensive and complicated. It should be avoided unless you are willing to add to your remodeling costs.

If the plumbing lines will stay where they are, consider storage space and counter work space. You must provide for enough of both, and you must position both in the right places.

Efficient storage means storing everything at the point of first use. For example, dinner dishes should be stored as close as possible to the dining area where they are first used. If this is impractical, they should be stored near the dishwasher and sink, where they are last used.

When considering the things you must store, think about basic activity centers of the kitchen. The following list of items to be stored and the best locations for storing them should help you to begin planning a kitchen for maximum storage efficiency.

•**Utensils.** The tools of the kitchen include pots and pans, cutlery, baking dishes, spoons, and spatulas. They are best stored near the range.

•**Dinnerware.** Store fine china in or near a separate dining room; store everyday dishes near the kitchen eating area.

•**Food.** Place packaged, canned, and bottled groceries (plan on a week's supply) in cabinets, ideally in a tall pantry cabinet with revolving or swing-out shelves. Fresh perishables go in a refrigerator, except potatoes and onions, which should be stored in bins or drawers. Food storage areas should be near the food preparation center.

•**Cleaning supplies.** Soaps, detergents, and cleaning implements go in an under-the-sink cabinet. Bigger items, such as mops and brooms, can be concealed in a tall utility cabinet; the utility cabinet need not be located in the kitchen as long as it is handy.

This represents faulty planning. There should be at least 15 inches of counter space on the working side of the oven.

Don't make sink cabinet and dishwasher doors fight each other. Note the space doors will need when you draw plans.

Don't let room and refrigerator doors fight each other. Include arcs that represent door swings on your plan.

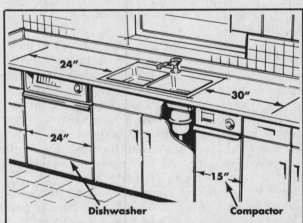

Here's the recommended minimum counter space for the cleanup center and sink. A double-bowl sink is essential.

For safety's sake don't position the range next to the sink. This situation also results in a loss of storage space in the corner.

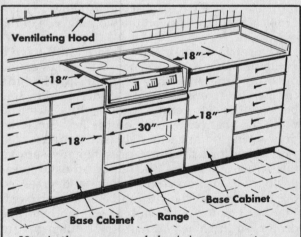

Here's the recommended minimum counter space for the cooking center. If the oven is separate, allow 15 inches of counter on its working side.

•**Linens, paper goods, and place mats.** Get these items out of the way. A paper caddy with paper towels, aluminum foil, and plastic wrap can be recessed into a wall near the food preparation or cleanup center. Linens should be placed in a drawer. These items should be stored near the point of first use.

•**Small appliances.** Countertop clutter is undesirable. One answer is to build in as many small appliances as you can. There are toasters and electric can openers that can be recessed into the wall. An appliance garage with a door to conceal mixers and food processors is another option.

•**Trash.** You must plan a temporary storage place for trash and recyclables. A trash compactor can be valuable for a large family, especially if the unit can be built in where a cabinet would otherwise go. Most compactors take up the space of a 15-inch base cabinet, although at least one brand can fit in a 12-inch space. A series of bins for sorting trash is a more ecologically sound solution to kitchen trash.

The sink area includes a minimum of 30 inches of counter space to the right of the sink and 24 inches to the left (for right-handed persons), dishwasher adjacent (usually on the left), disposer under the sink, and compactor on the right. A double-bowl sink is essential, even when the sink area includes a dishwasher. This area should contain storage facilities for foods that need washing and for fruits and vegetables that do not go into the refrigerator. Cabinets with bins or shelves are ideal for such purposes. While most cooking pots and pans belong near the range, saucepans and the coffeepot go best in the sink center.

The range or cooktop area should include at least 18 inches of counter space on either side; a ventilating hood and fan above; and storage for pots, pans, seasonings, and cooking utensils. If the cooktop and oven are separate, allow 15 inches of countertop space on the working side of the oven.

The refrigerator-freezer area should have a minimum counter work space of 18 inches on the door-opening side. The popular side-by-side refrigerator-freezers defeat this design principle because the refrigerator side is always on the right and the freezer side on the left. Since the door swing on such models is a short arc, the side-by-side unit seldom presents any serious interference problems. The refrigerator and freezer doors should open more than 90 degrees, so that crispers and shelves can be easily removed. The refrigerator is the hub of the food storage center, so kitchen planners try to incorporate other food storage facilities, such as base cabinets or a pantry cabinet, close by.

The food preparation center requires at least 36 inches of counter space, between the sink and range or between the sink and refrigerator.

Refrigerator and wall oven need adjacent counter space and should not be placed next to each other.

The serving center usually is positioned near the cooking center; it should be between the cooking center and the eating area. It requires 30 inches of counter space for serving and for storing trays, platters, serving dishes, napkins, and table linens.

Note that you can combine many counter space requirements. For example, the 30 inches needed to the right of the sink can be part of the 36 inches of space needed for a food preparation center.

LAYING OUT A KITCHEN

Up to now, we have been talking in averages and minimums. You might need more countertop or more storage space. In your kitchen you have to make compromises between what you need, what you would like, and the space available. The way you resolve these opposing factors is what makes the kitchen unique.

You want a work triangle of not less than 12 feet and not more than 22 feet. The work triangle is the straight-line distance between the center fronts of the sink and range, range and refrigerator, and refrigerator and sink. No two of the basic activity centers in a kitchen should be less than 4 feet apart or more than 9 feet apart. The following distances are ideal: sink to range—4 to 6 feet; range to refrigerator—4 to 9 feet; refrigerator to sink—4 to 7 feet. There are several kitchen layouts that fulfill these requirements.

•**The one-wall kitchen** is the simplest possible layout. There will be no work triangle when the entire kitchen is along one wall. The one-wall layout can provide ample storage and work space, but it usually puts too much distance between the work centers on the flanks. A single person or a couple might be able to tolerate a one-wall kitchen, but it is not efficient.

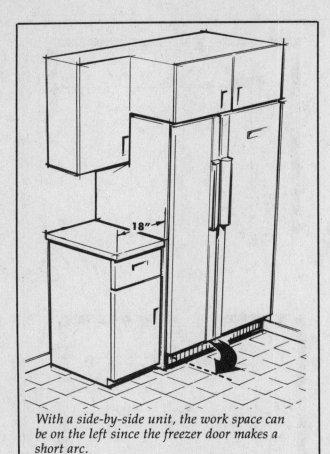

With a side-by-side unit, the work space can be on the left since the freezer door makes a short arc.

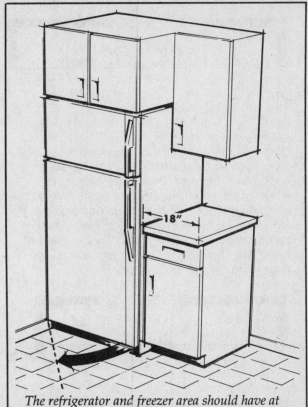

The refrigerator and freezer area should have at least 18 inches of counter space on the door-opening side.

•The corridor kitchen that is open on both ends, permitting traffic to cross two legs of the work triangle, is another kitchen layout to be avoided. A closed corridor can be efficient. Often called a "Pullman" kitchen, the corridor has two work centers on one side, one on the other, and a minimum of 48 inches clearance in between. Since cabinets and appliances project about two feet from either wall, a corridor layout requires a kitchen that is at least 8 feet wide.

•The L-shaped kitchen is quite common and makes for an efficient work triangle that is open to other activities, such as eating and recreation. The two legs of the L are on adjacent walls with no intervening doorways. This layout works well where space is limited; where there is a great deal of space, an island can be added or a peninsula extended inward on either leg to maximize efficiency.

•The U-shaped kitchen is the most efficient, provides the most storage, and is the most desirable. The kitchen is arranged on three adjacent walls with a work center on each wall; the U often can open onto eating or recreation areas or areas to be used for other activities. If an island or peninsula is added to an L-shaped kitchen, the layout becomes the preferable U-shaped design.

A door within an L- or U-shaped layout transforms them into what is called a broken L or a broken U. Such broken layouts suffer a loss of efficiency because of through traffic.

One-Wall Kitchen. In a one-wall kitchen, you do not have many choices for appliance placement, but you can put some flair into the layout. The room should be a minimum of 14 3/4 feet long and 5 feet wide to conform with basic planning principles on counter space and appliance placement. A kitchen with at least those minimum dimensions allows for a sink area of 33 inches in the center; 36 inches of counter to the right of the sink as a food preparation area; 36 inches to the right of that area for the refrigerator; 24 inches for the dishwasher to the left of the sink; 30 inches for the range to the left of the dishwasher; and 18 inches of counter for work space and safety to the left of the range. The counters and appliances will protrude 24 inches from the wall, and you should allow at least another 36 inches for movement.

The work triangle in this one-wall kitchen consists of a straight line measuring from the refrigerator at one end to the range at the other. This distance should not be extended any more than necessary even if the kitchen is longer than the one described. Extending the work triangle adds extra steps, and the amount of counter space provided in our example is ample.

If the room is wider than 5 feet but narrower than the 8 feet required for a corridor kitchen,

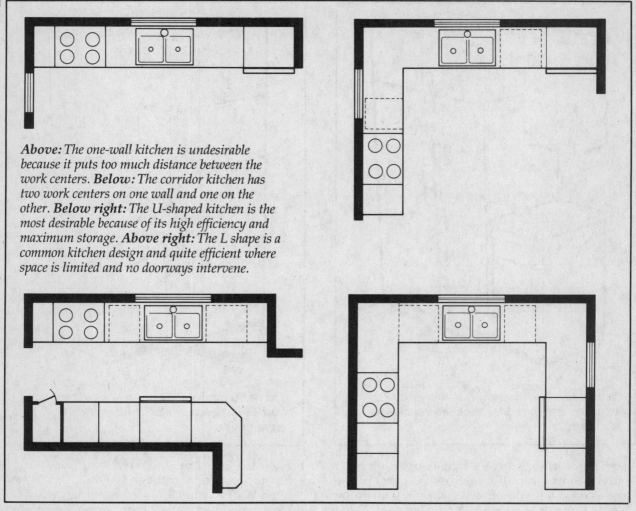

Above: The one-wall kitchen is undesirable because it puts too much distance between the work centers. *Below:* The corridor kitchen has two work centers on one wall and one on the other. *Below right:* The U-shaped kitchen is the most desirable because of its high efficiency and maximum storage. *Above right:* The L shape is a common kitchen design and quite efficient where space is limited and no doorways intervene.

you can consider several options for increasing counter and storage space. Since wall cabinets are only 12 inches deep compared with 24-inch-deep base cabinets, you could install a run of wall cabinets along the opposite wall in a room that is, say, 6 feet wide. Such cabinets can be ordered with the toe-kick, or they can be set on 2 x 4s recessed 4 inches. If additional work space is required, this run of wall cabinets can be topped with a countertop that is 13 or more inches deep. If you need additional storage space, you can either stack the standard wall cabinets to reach to the ceiling or put in 84-inch utility and pantry cabinets that are no deeper than the wall cabinets.

Corridor Kitchen. The corridor kitchen uses two opposing walls. It is easy to install because there are no corners. Because it results in a maximum of counter space with a minimum of floor space, it is an efficient use of space. It requires at least 8 feet of space between opposing walls, which leaves 4 feet of maneuvering space after the cabinets and appliances are installed.

If the corridor is positioned between other living areas of the home, a problem will exist with through traffic. Traffic will cut through two legs of the work triangle.

If the corridor is a cul-de-sac, the traffic problem will be lessened. With an eating or hobby area at the closed end, the traffic problem will appear again.

If the corridor is more than 10 feet wide, you can solve any traffic problems by creating an island kitchen. The sink, refrigerator, and their countertop work spaces would go on one wall, the range would be placed in an island (generally opposite the sink), and approximately 4 feet of maneuvering area would remain between. With such an arrangement, it would be best to have at least 2 feet of counter space on either side of the range. If you choose a 30-inch range or stovetop, the island should be 78 inches long and 26 to 38 inches deep. Standard base cabinets on either side of the range would provide valuable storage space. Extending utility lines to the range-equipped island could prove costly.

In any corridor kitchen, you should avoid placing the range and the refrigerator opposite each other. Situations in which it is necessary to have the oven door and the refrigerator door open simultaneously could prove annoying.

L-Shaped Kitchen. An L-shaped kitchen involves turning a corner and will be more

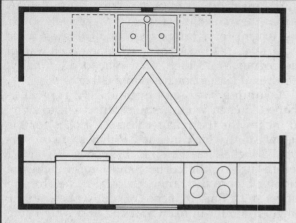

Traffic will cut through two legs of the work triangle when a corridor kitchen is positioned between other living areas.

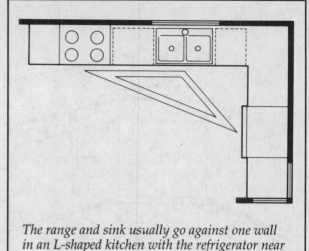

The range and sink usually go against one wall in an L-shaped kitchen with the refrigerator near the end of the other wall.

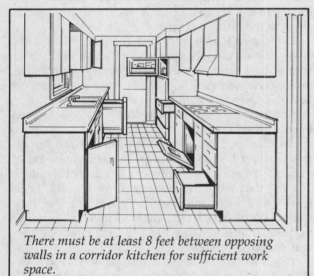

There must be at least 8 feet between opposing walls in a corridor kitchen for sufficient work space.

Lazy Susan corner cabinet

expensive than a corridor design. It can be efficient and gives considerable latitude in appliance placement. Although an L shape will not necessarily provide any more storage or work space than a corridor design, it protects the work triangle from through traffic.

The L shape can be derived from two adjacent walls, or it can be formed by extending a peninsula out from a wall. A peninsula is often used when the room is large and when it also can separate the kitchen area from an eating or family activity area.

For efficiency and saving many thousands of steps, plan the appliances and work spaces so that they run sequentially from refrigerator to sink to range to serving area. The refrigerator usually goes against a wall at one end of the L.

The problem of turning the corner introduces opportunities for different design elements, some of which can waste space. The easy and cheapest way to turn the corner is with a blind base cabinet

and a blind wall cabinet; a blind cabinet is one that has an unfinished part that butts against the side of the cabinet already in place. The butted area can vary by several inches; this is helpful in compensating for measuring mistakes. There always will be a blind corner walled off from you by the cabinet walls. In a blind base cabinet, you can get semicircular shelves that are attached to the cabinet door.

A better answer is a lazy-Susan corner cabinet, available for base or wall. Some of these units have a corner door that opens to expose lazy Susan shelves, while others have pie-shaped shelving to which doors are attached to form the corner. A push on the door in either direction spins the entire assembly around.

Another way to turn a corner is to design the sink or one appliance into the corner at an angle. Some double-bowl sinks are made in a pie-cut corner configuration, with one bowl placed on either side of the corner.

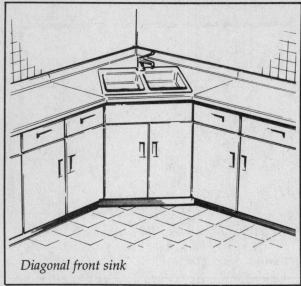

Diagonal front sink

Pie-cut corner sink

Diagonal corner oven

The main disadvantage of corner installations is that they consume a great deal of wall space. For example, a range that is 30 inches wide requires 45 1/4 inches of space along each wall of the corner. A 33-inch sink, placed diagonally, requires at least 42 inches along either wall.

Assuming average appliances, a typical L-shaped kitchen would require, from left to right, 30 inches for the refrigerator; 24 inches for the dishwasher, which means 24 inches of counter-top; 33 inches for the sink; 18 inches of counter before turning the corner; another 18 inches of counter before the range, then 30 inches for the range; and a final 18 inches of counter beyond the range. If a built-in oven and cooktop were being used, the cooktop could go in the same place as the complete range, but there would be no good place for the wall oven until after the full run was complete. The wall oven would go at the opposite end from the refrigerator, adding another 24 to 30 inches to the layout. Try not to crowd appliances close to the interior corner.

U-Shaped Kitchen. A U shape is the most efficient kitchen design. It adapts to large and small rooms, and with the basic appliances distributed on its base and two legs, it shortens the distance between the work centers.

The kitchen must be at least 8 feet wide at the base of the U, but 10 or 12 feet is preferable to avoid cramped working conditions. Each leg of the U must be long enough to accommodate a major appliance and the associated work space. The leg that will hold a refrigerator should be at least 4 1/2 feet long. You'll need a leg that is a minimum of 5 1/2 feet for a 30-inch range, and no less than 6 feet for the leg that contains the sink and dishwasher.

These dimensions are minimums. While a U-shaped kitchen of minimum dimensions permits unrestricted operation of the appliances, it results in a cramped working area. For an efficient work triangle, try to have a minimum of 4 feet up to a maximum of 8 feet between the centers of the fronts of any two appliances. Since the U shape works well in large kitchens without making the work triangle too long, kitchen designers often install a diagonal sink, a range, or a wall oven at interior corners.

Many U-shaped kitchens have long legs, often flaring out into an eating area and with one leg serving as a divider from another living area. An eating counter can be incorporated into one side of a long leg.

When one leg serves as a divider between kitchen and dining or living room, the cabinets along that leg often open from both sides to give access from both rooms. Double-opening cabinets are available through home centers as well as from custom kitchen specialists. While the home center may not carry these cabinets as stock items, they can be ordered.

Island and Peninsula Kitchens. Islands can be designed into a kitchen to add countertop work space, to provide a place for sink or range with work space, to provide an eating area, or to provide a place for a built-in barbecue or a bar and hospitality center. An island also can change a one-wall kitchen into a corridor kitchen.

A peninsula can serve as one leg of an L-shaped kitchen, one or two legs of a U-shaped kitchen, or create added counter space or eating area for any kitchen.

Both islands and peninsulas function well in large kitchens to make the work triangle more compact. The entire kitchen might be an island, with wall cabinets suspended from the ceiling. Two islands can be used to form a corridor kitchen in a large room, and one island might even form a one-wall kitchen in a large, open area.

When the only purpose of an island or peninsula is to increase countertop space, either only needs to be 18 inches deep from front to back. To add cabinets under an island or peninsula of this depth, you can put 12-inch-deep wall cabinets on a kick-rail; base cabinets are 24 inches deep and would not fit.

Normal island countertop depth is 26 inches. When a sink or range is to be installed in an island, this depth should be extended to 36 or even 38 inches to allow for spatter and splash.

Eat-In Kitchens. Most people like to have an eating area in the kitchen. For family dining you must allow about 12 to 15 square feet per person to fit table, chair, and person. A family of four, for example, requires at least 48 square feet of floor space to accommodate a table and four chairs. Each person needs 21 to 24 inches of table space, and you should allow a minimum of 36 inches of clearance between the table and a wall to edge around a seated person. A minimum of 32 inches is needed for a seated person to rise from a table, and serving around a table requires clearance of 44 inches from table to wall.

Snack counters along peninsulas or islands generally have the same clearance requirements for movement behind the chairs, and you still should allow 21 inches of space along the counter for each person. By multiplying the number of people who will eat at the counter by 21 inches, you will arrive at the counter length you need.

The height of a counter used for eating need not be the same height as the kitchen work surface. A table-height counter will be 28 to 32 inches high; an eating counter the same height as the kitchen work counter will be 36 inches high. For the lower counter, a person will need 20 inches of legroom when sitting on a chair 18 inches high. For the higher counter, a person will require a bar stool with the seat 24 inches from the floor. With this higher stool, required knee space decreases to 14 inches.

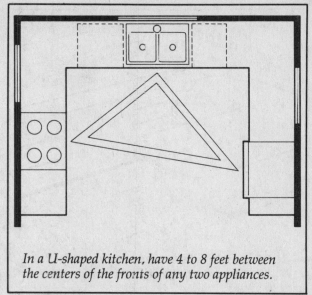

In a U-shaped kitchen, have 4 to 8 feet between the centers of the fronts of any two appliances.

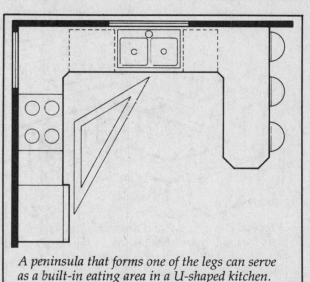

A peninsula that forms one of the legs can serve as a built-in eating area in a U-shaped kitchen.

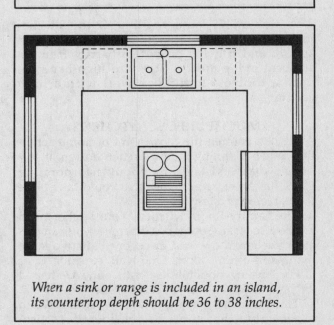

When a sink or range is included in an island, its countertop depth should be 36 to 38 inches.

Allow 21 inches of space along a peninsula counter for each adult who will be eating there.

A typical kitchen installation showing some storage possibilities: shelf storage in the closet, lazy Susan shelves in a corner cabinet, and bread and produce drawers.

A high eating counter will be 42 to 45 inches high. The height protects diners from spatter and splash, and it helps provide a barrier from an adjacent living area. A standard high bar stool with a footrest will work well with a high counter.

MULTIPURPOSE KITCHENS

A kitchen is often the focal point of home activities. When planning a new kitchen design, if sufficient space exists, think about incorporating space for the extra activities that could take place there. Here are a few ideas:

The Family-Room Kitchen. Your kitchen need not be a separate room. For example, you can create a kitchen at one end or on one side of a large living-and-dining room. One-wall, corridor, L, or U kitchens are possibilities, but L- and U-shaped kitchens require plenty of open space.

The problems with the family-room kitchen are few, but they must be considered. House-keeping should be impeccable. Many people do not like to see open shelving or pot racks in a family-room kitchen. A family-room kitchen means more noise and odors in the living area of the home than does a closed-room kitchen. The dishwasher, disposer, ventilating fan, and refrigerator are sources of noise.

The Home Office. The kitchen can be a convenient place for a home office, and facilities for an office easily can be designed into a kitchen.

An office in the kitchen calls for a dropped desk area with a counter about 6 inches below the regular 36-inch counter height. A desk should be at least 24 inches wide, with its depth matching the cabinet depth at that point. A single apron (shallow) drawer can be placed beneath the desk top, but the drawer should not interfere with knee space. A drawer unit or a two-drawer file can be placed beside the open knee space underneath the desk top.

The Communication Center. A complete intercom system, one that includes a two-way communication system between the kitchen and the bedrooms, recreation room, and basement, smoke and intruder alarms; radio and tape music facilities; and even a closed-circuit TV for supervision of the children's play area, can be installed in the kitchen. Such an installation should be located away from the work triangle.

The Craft and Hobby Center. The kitchen can provide a well-lighted area for working on crafts and hobbies. Like the home office, the craft and hobby center that is incorporated in the kitchen may require little more than a cabinet or two suited to the activity, but if the hobby is one that requires a kiln or soldering or otherwise produces heat and fumes, install an extra ventilating hood over the area.

The Greenhouse Center. There are greenhouses made to fit in kitchen windows, and grow lights help plants thrive almost anywhere. Such lights can provide a pleasant lighting effect in the kitchen. Since kitchens develop special heat and humidity conditions that differ from other home areas, it is essential to consult an expert on the kind of plants to buy for a kitchen greenhouse. Be sure to tell the expert whether your kitchen appliances are gas or electric; the difference is important when it comes to plant selection and care.

The Laundry Center. The best place for laundry facilities is not in the kitchen itself, but rather in a separate room next to the kitchen. Washer and dryer units require about 5 feet of wall space, and they extend 27 to 33 inches from the wall, with space allowed for ducts and hoses. If possible, the dryer should be positioned against an outside wall for outdoor venting of moist air.

Cabinets for laundry supplies must be close. A deep utility sink, at least 48 inches of counter space, and at least 5 feet for ironing space also must be designed into the laundry center.

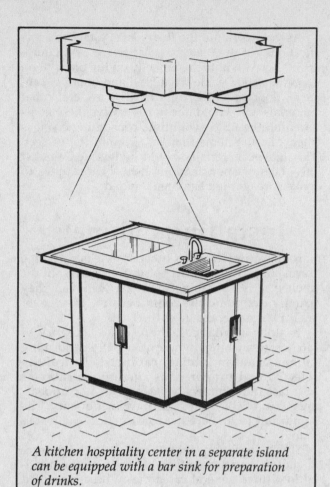

A kitchen hospitality center in a separate island can be equipped with a bar sink for preparation of drinks.

The Hospitality Center. The kitchen is frequently the place where drinks are prepared, and there is no reason for not installing a bar. Since the bar should be well removed from the work triangle, the ideal place would be a peninsula separating the kitchen and living area. On the living area side, the peninsula could be equipped with a bar sink, under-counter refrigerator, ice maker, liquor cabinet, and an overhead or side wine rack. It also could contain an indoor barbecue unit.

LIGHTING AND COLOR

Kitchen lighting must be planned from both the decorative and functional points of view. General daytime illumination usually is provided by windows. Some houses are built with interior kitchens, where little daylight is available. A skylight could be added to bring in daylight.

Artificial light can be used to supplement daylight and to provide lighting at night. Incandescent light is "warmer" and more pleasing to skin tones, natural woods, and the color of food. The light always comes on immediately, can be hooked to a dimmer switch to control its brightness, and the bulbs and fixtures are less expensive. Incandescent bulbs generate more heat and consume more electricity, while putting out less

actual light per watt than a comparably sized fluorescent tube. This kind of lighting source is best for the general dining area of the kitchen and for areas where food is prepared.

Fluorescent light is "cooler" in heat output and in color rendition. Compared to incandescent bulbs, fluorescent lighting is more energy efficient and produces about 250 percent more light for the current used; service life is about seven times that of incandescent bulbs. Color rendition is "flatter" in the standard bulbs, but this can be eliminated by using warm white tubes that are designed to simulate the warmer tones of incandescent bulbs. As a specific lighting source, fluorescent lights serve well as a general overall light in the kitchen and as specific "task" lighting over countertops and other areas.

One of the best ways to provide general illumination in the kitchen is to install a full luminous ceiling. This kind of ceiling simulates natural daylight because it comes from above and in a broad source. It is important when such ceilings are installed that they are situated along the centerline of the room, with the tubes spaced at least 10 inches apart, and covered by diffusers, which spread the light. Unless installed during new construction, luminous ceilings will drop the height of the ceiling.

Square or rectangular ceiling boxes with either tubes or bulbs that are surface mounted on the ceiling also are available. These boxes come in various sizes and are intended to replace a single fixture.

Besides a good source of general illumination, the well-planned kitchen should have directional or task lighting over work surfaces. Counter areas can be well lit by under-cabinet fluorescent fixtures. Sinks that are beneath or near a window usually are lit by two 40-watt tubes mounted over a diffuser placed in the soffit or a 75-watt incandescent down-light centered over the sink.

Lighting requirements over a range usually are covered by the fixture built into the range hood. Such fixtures take a 25-watt incandescent bulb or a 15-watt fluorescent tube that is warm white for the best color rendition. An alternative would be to use a recessed ceiling or soffit down-light with a 75-watt incandescent bulb focused on top of the range.

STORAGE IDEAS

There are times when a kitchen is too small for the things you want to put into it. A kitchen cabinet can make very efficient use of space, but cabinets come in certain sizes that may not fit every situation. There are other ways to take advantage of the smaller spaces in the kitchen.

One answer is open shelving. A wall cabinet is normally 12 inches deep, but you can get good use from shelving that is only 6 to 10 inches deep. One disadvantage to open shelving is that it requires good housekeeping; dishes and other items that are on display must be kept clean and orderly.

Pot racks are another space-saver. They are suspended from the ceiling and can be used to hang pots, utensils, plants, and other objects. Once hung, these things are on constant display and will demand housekeeping.

Cabinet organizers are commercially available in many housewares departments. They fit inside cabinets and increase their storage capacity, making the space even more efficient.

A peninsula or island in the center of the kitchen can sometimes be added for extra storage or counter space. This can be useful in a one-wall kitchen where there is one long wall covered with cabinets. If all you need is more counter space, it can consist of a countertop only. Other alternatives include putting one or more wall cabinets beneath this or, if you have the room, base cabinets below. There should be at least 1 inch of overlap of the countertops on all free sides.

Between-the-Stud Storage. Between-stud cabinets, which are designed to fit between standard wall studs, are available in different heights. Before installing them, check for pipes or electrical wiring behind the wallboard so that you have enough room to install the stud-cabinet.

You can cut out the wallboard in the area where the cabinet will fit with a keyhole saw. The cabinet usually will have a flange that will conceal any cut marks in the wallboard after installation. The cabinet is simply inserted into the wall and nailed from the inside into the two standing studs. If you cannot find room to insert the cabinet into the wall, many units can be surface-mounted.

FINAL PLANS AND DRAWINGS
Before you begin remodeling, prepare a series of rough sketches that show all measurements and details. These can be refined sketches or informal drawings, but they should be done in considerable detail and to scale. The larger the drawings, the easier they will be to work with. Include the principal elements of the remodeling project, including wall placement; locations, kinds, and sizes of doors and windows; built-in furnishings, such as cabinets, counters, and shelves; and placement of plumbing fixtures and appliances. Note dimensions wherever necessary.

The plans can be prepared in many ways. A floor plan is the first requirement so you can work out proper placement and proportions of various elements. Interior elevations, which are detailed drawings of a single plane of the room as viewed head on, are helpful. Utilities drawings, such as those showing electrical and plumbing extensions, usually are drawn symbolically on a basic floor plan.

As you work out the final plans, establish specifications for the materials, hardware, and equipment. You can note this directly on the plans or on separate lists. Decide what kind and brand of cabinets, floor covering, lighting fixtures, and other materials you would like to have. Give these items careful thought to avoid time-consuming changes later. List the items that will go into the project. This bill of materials should be checked against the plans or specifications lists several times to make sure nothing has been omitted.

Installing Cabinets
In rooms other than the kitchen, style is set by the furnishings, wall coverings, and draperies. In the kitchen, it is the cabinets that set the style. They usually dominate the room because they cover such a large percentage of the walls.

Besides appliances, there is no category of kitchen furnishings where you will spend more money than on kitchen cabinets. If carefully selected and properly installed, good cabinets will last indefinitely. Neither price nor appearance is a reliable indicator of cabinet quality. The significant factors are the construction and installation.

Style and design factors are a matter of personal choice. Apart from that, cabinets can be divided into three general categories. These are called stock, special-order, and custom. The main difference between the three is in cabinet construction. Price is not a good criterion. A top-line stock cabinet can cost more than a cheap custom model, and their appearance may be the same.

Stock cabinets are what their name implies: mass manufactured cabinets in a variety of standard sizes. Size is based on 3-inch standard modules. The smallest is 9 inches wide, and each cabinet will be wider by 3 inches until the maximum width of 48 inches. Stock also means that they are kept in a warehouse for immediate delivery. What you are getting in stock cabinets is delivery convenience, a name-brand manufacturer, and many choices within preset limits. If a run of cabinets will not fit the available space, stock filler strips can be used to make up the difference.

Special-order cabinets can be any standard size, shape, or finish. They are available with a wider choice of accessories than stock cabinets. A large manufacturer makes the cabinets to your order in the sense that the whole kitchen is made at once. They will still be a standard size box cabinet, but the finishes are sure to match. For this service you will pay a premium of 20 percent or more and there will be some delay in delivery. You will get a set of cabinets that will last, in the finish you want, and with a precise fit to the kitchen. Their general appearance will not differ substantially from stock cabinets.

Custom cabinets usually are made by local craftspeople. The construction may be different because the entire face frame of a run of cabinets can be made in one piece and then the box built around that. You will get an exact fit to your kitchen and the spacing between the doors will be even for a uniform appearance. You may not get as wide a choice of additional accessories. What you are paying for is that built-on-the-job look that only custom work can give you.

The difference between a good cabinet and a poor one is materials, structure, and design. Here are some things to look for:

•Hardware. Drawer slides are important because they are the main wearing parts of the system. Quality cabinets have metal slides; cheap cabinets have drawers sliding directly on the wood frame. The best drawer systems will feature double metal tracking with nylon and ball bearing rollers. Shelves should be removable, attached by clips, and carefully constructed. Hinges should be strong, swing freely without binding, and be silent in their operation.

•Joinery. Look for tight joints where stiles and rails (the vertical and horizontal framing) come together. The corners should be braced for dimensional stability. Drawers and shelves should be carefully put together with mortised joints. The whole box of the cabinet should look and feel sturdy.

•Materials. Solid wood is not the best material for case construction because large pieces are subject to warping. Plywood should be a good grade and thick enough for stability. Cabinets with unfinished plywood shelves or flimsy backs are not recommended. Wide shelves should have support in the center to bear any expected weight.

•Style and finish are less important, unless you choose a cabinet with a laminated surface. Laminates can splinter and their wearing qualities are only as good as the substructure beneath them. Molded or plastic drawers, for example, can break if a heavy weight is dropped on them. Any edges on laminated cabinets should be clean and neat, and the laminated surface as thick as possible.

•Steel cabinets are durable and easy to clean. They can be purchased with a laminated or wood finish. One drawback is that they weigh more than some wood cabinets, and this may be a difficulty if you choose to put them up yourself.

Here are some buying tips you should look for when purchasing kitchen cabinets:

Take note of whether the manufacturer is domestic or foreign. Some dealers carry foreign-built cabinets. These are high quality and expensive. Most are in a contemporary style and finished in bright plastic laminates. Delivery time could be a problem, particularly if you choose unusual fittings. Warranty service is generally good, but service is a definite question when buying imported cabinets.

Know something about quality cabinet construction when you make your selection. It may be better to spend a few dollars more on a special-order cabinet rather than on a special offer the dealer may be having. Good cabinets are built to last and their price will reflect this.

Both knock-down and unfinished cabinets are available. The price differential in either case is only about 10 percent. With a knock-down cabinet what you are saving on is the shipping and assembly cost. For uniformity of finish, large manufacturers offer more consistent quality control than either in stock or special-order work.

Check the warranty on cabinets you plan to buy. While it is a federal requirement that dealers give you a set of installation instructions if you choose to do the work yourself, this may void the guarantee. Look for as long a warranty period as possible.

No matter what kind of cabinets you buy, they must be installed correctly. The best cabinets will show racking or other flaws if they are not set right. If you have any doubts about tackling this job, have it done by a professional.

CABINET DESIGNS AND SIZES

Kitchen cabinets come in a variety of designs and sizes to suit various storage needs. Wall cabinets are generally mounted on the walls, although they can be hung from the ceiling over a peninsula or island; they can even be put on a toe-kick and used as base cabinets.

Although wall cabinets are a standard 12 inches in depth (with the doors projecting an extra 3/8 to 3/4 inch), they can differ in height. Those 12 to 15 inches high are usually mounted above high refrigerators and high oven ranges, while 18-inch models are used over standard ranges, over the sink, and over smaller refrigerators. Wall cabinets that are 30 inches high are the basic storage units for dishes, glasses, and foods. Custom manufacturers offer wall cabinets in models reaching 32 or 33 inches high.

Diagonal corner cabinets are 30 inches high, as are the blind corner wall cabinets that are useful in turning corners in an L- or U-shaped kitchen. Diagonal corner cabinets can be fitted with regular or revolving shelves.

Peninsular wall cabinets for use over the range or sink generally are 18 inches high, while those for storage are 30 inches high and frequently open on both sides for easy access to stored items. They are usually hung from a soffit.

The other basic kitchen cabinet is the base cabinet. Base cabinets are 24 inches deep and 34 1/2 inches high, including the toe-kick, which measures 4 inches deep and 4 inches high. Base cabinets are used for storage.

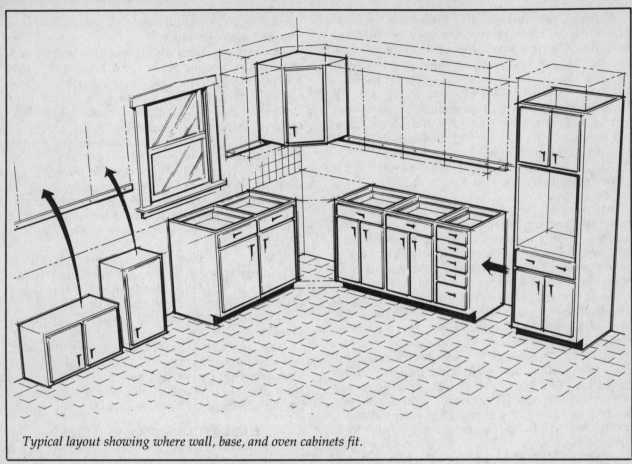

Typical layout showing where wall, base, and oven cabinets fit.

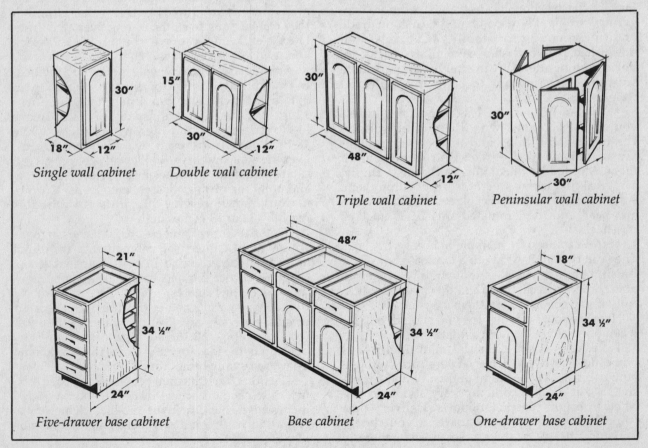

30"

18" 12"

Single wall cabinet

15"

30" 12"

Double wall cabinet

30"

48" 12"

Triple wall cabinet

30"

30"

Peninsular wall cabinet

21"

34 ½"

24"

Five-drawer base cabinet

48"

34 ½"

24"

Base cabinet

18"

34 ½"

24"

One-drawer base cabinet

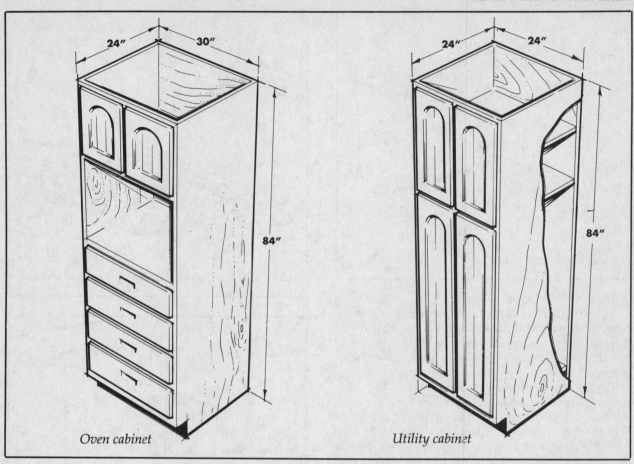

Oven cabinet

Utility cabinet

As with wall cabinets, base cabinets are available in diagonal corner, blind corner, and lazy-Susan corner units for turning corners in L- and U-shaped kitchens. Peninsula base cabinets may have doors that open on both sides.

While the usual base cabinet has one drawer at the top, some consist entirely of drawers (called base drawer units); they are usually placed near the sink and range. Under the sink itself is either a sink front or a sink cabinet. The sink cabinet is a complete box with a floor and back; the sink front has no back and sometimes no floor.

Oven cabinets are tall cabinets used for installing wall ovens. Available in stock sizes of 24 or 27 inches wide and 84 inches high, oven cabinets are designed for either a single-cavity oven or a double oven.

Tall utility cabinets reach up to 84 inches high. Usually 18 or 24 inches wide, they can be used for various storage needs (mops, brooms, cleaning supplies, etc.). Fitted with adjustable, revolving, or fold-out shelves, these cabinets can function as pantries for bulk food storage.

When a run of cabinets fails to fill a given space, manufacturers offer wall and base fillers to fill the odd dimensions. Fillers also provide clearance for drawers in a corner and give a decorative termination to a cabinet run. Just how many and what kind of fillers are needed depend on the size and style of the kitchen.

HOW TO INSTALL KITCHEN CABINETS

Kitchen cabinets must be installed with painstaking care. Cabinets usually are installed before final finishing of the floors and walls and laying of finish floor material. They are permanently installed by securing them to the structural framework. The floor must be prepared so it is level, and the walls where the cabinets will be mounted must be made so that they are as close to plumb as possible. Any high or unshimmed low spot on the wall or floor can cause racking of the cabinet, which will force the drawers and doors out of alignment.

The most expensive cabinets cannot compensate for improper installation. If poorly installed, the best cabinets will work no better than the cheapest.

Before you start, equip yourself with the following: one or two helpers; a 1 x 2-inch strip of wood (to use as a temporary cleat to help support wall cabinets); an electric drill with a 1/8-inch bit and a 90-degree drilling adapter; a 4-foot level; a screwdriver; a T-brace (made from a 54-inch length of 2 x 4 topped by a 1-foot piece of 2 x 4 mounted at right angles and covered with carpeting); a box of 2 1/2 inch Number 10 wood screws; a couple of C-clamps; wood shingles for shims; and a box of toggle or molly bolts.

When you have everything you need, follow these instructions:

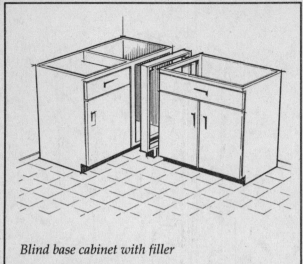

Blind base cabinet with filler

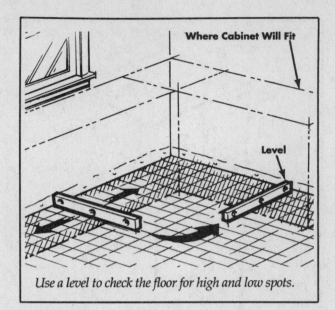

Use a level to check the floor for high and low spots.

Make sure your electrical and plumbing roughing in is complete. Then examine your design drawings, familiarizing yourself with just how the base and wall cabinets are supposed to run. Prepare the room. Shave or sand down obvious high spots in the walls.

Locate the wall studs behind where the cabinets will be and mark their location on the wall. Although the distance between studs, center to center, should be 16 inches, you cannot rely on that standard distance, especially in older homes. Be sure to mark the location of every stud along the run, placing the marks both above and below where the cabinets will be; you will want to be able to see the marks after the cabinets are in position.

Move the cabinets, still in their boxes, to an adjacent room where they will be handy but will not interfere with your work. Check your drawings again, and then number the boxes and the appropriate wall locations to make sure you get the cabinets in the right places. You should start installing from a corner, and you should mount the wall cabinets first to avoid damaging the base cabinets. Arrange the cabinets in the adjacent room in a way that makes for an easy and orderly flow into the kitchen.

Attach the 1 x 2-inch strip to the wall precisely so you can rest the bottom back of each wall cabinet on it when you move the cabinet into position. For standard 30-inch wall cabinets, the top of the cleat should be 54 inches above the floor. Nail the cleat to the wall studs securely, and make sure it is level.

Line up wall cabinets in a run together on the floor. Use a drill to make pilot holes for screws in the outside stiles of each adjacent cabinet; make two for each pair of cabinets. Clamp the stiles with two C-clamps and screw them together securely. The purpose is to line up the faces in one level, straight run, making the cabinets a unit when you move them.

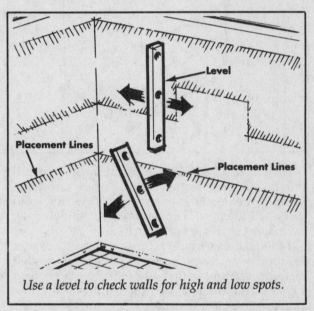

Use a level to check walls for high and low spots.

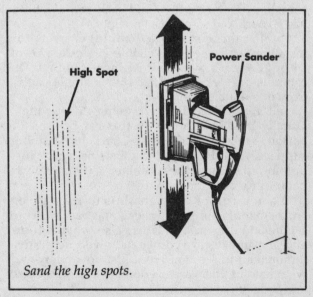

Sand the high spots.

Use a hammer to locate the studs.

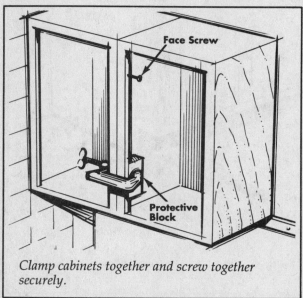

Clamp cabinets together and screw together securely.

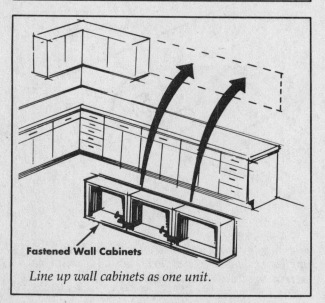

Line up wall cabinets as one unit.

Have your helpers hold up the whole unit into the correct position on the wall, resting the backs on the cleat and using the T-brace to help hold it. Drill 1/8-inch holes through the mounting rail at the top back of the cabinet and into the studs. Then screw the cabinet to the wall with the Number 10 screws, four per cabinet. You may have to use the toggle bolts if there are not enough available studs. Check the assembly with a level to make sure it is plumb, and do whatever shimming is needed before tightening the mounting screws and removing the cleat.

Follow the same basic procedure with the base cabinets, fastening them together as a unit and then moving them against the wall. You will not need a cleat or T-brace for the base cabinets; make certain the whole unit is shimmed level so that a countertop will rest securely. When you finish installing the wall and base cabinets, insert the drawers, hang the doors, and attach appropriate hardware.

Installing Countertops

You have a choice of four basic materials for your new countertop: high-pressure plastic laminate, Corian, ceramic tile, and laminated hardwood.

•High-pressure plastic laminate is the least expensive and by far the most popular kitchen countertop material. It comes in a large range of patterns, colors, and woodgrains. As countertop material, it usually is 1/16 inch thick, although identical material 1/32 inch thick is available for use on vertical surfaces; thinner laminate should not be used on kitchen countertops. You can buy high-pressure plastic in sheets and laminate it yourself to plywood or particle board, but it is far easier to buy laminated boards ready for countertop installation.

•Corian is a synthetic marble that differs from other artificial marbles in that it is can be cut, drilled, and shaped like wood. It is heavy and care must be taken because it chips. More expensive than laminates, Corian is a superb material for a kitchen countertop. You can even buy a Corian top with an integral sink of the same material. If you install it yourself, put in 3/4-inch-thick Corian.

•Ceramic tile is the most expensive countertop material. It is elegant and durable, but it has some disadvantages. Its hard surface reflects noise, and the grout between the tiles can pose a cleaning problem if it is not sealed properly. Tiles range in thickness from 1/4 to 3/8 inch and in size from 1/2-inch to a 6-inch square.

•Laminated hardwood is the familiar butcher block material. Always popular for the food preparation section of the countertop, butcher block has been used throughout many kitchens. The hardwood usually is maple; the thickness can

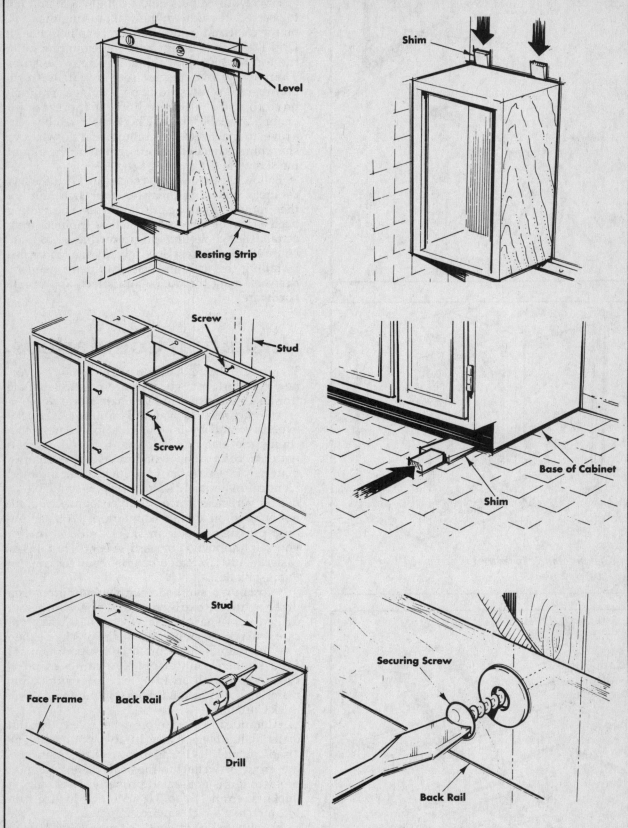

Use a level to make sure each cabinet is level and plumb, shimming it if necessary. Fasten wall and base cabinets together and attach them to the wall as a unit. Shim base cabinets to level them. Drill 1/8-inch holes through the mounting rail into the studs. Use Number 10 screws to secure the cabinets to the wall.

vary, but 1 1/2-inch material is quite common. The wood must be well sealed to prevent excessive staining, and it requires a good deal of care and attention to look its best.

To enhance the flexibility of your new countertop, consider including special-purpose inserts. The inserts most often used are butcher block, but an alternative material is Pyroceram, a tempered glass ceramic that will not cut, stain, or scratch. Stainless steel inserts are sometimes used, but stainless steel dents, dulls knives, scratches, and shows water spots.

HOW TO INSTALL PLASTIC LAMINATED COUNTERTOPS

Plastic laminated countertops can be self-edged or post-formed. Self-edged tops have a square front and are faced with a separate strip of the same material found on the top. The back splash is a separate piece joined at right angles to the top. A post-formed countertop is rounded over the front edge and coved at the back splash and over the top to the wall.

Plastic laminated countertops are available in 6-, 8-, 10-, 12-foot, and custom lengths. If two lengths are to be joined to form an L, they must be joined with a 45-degree miter joint. Your dealer can cut the miter for you, and you can put the two pieces together in your kitchen.

To install a plastic laminated countertop, you will need the following tools: a screwdriver, hammer, small wedge, level, tape measure, some 3/4-inch stock nails, adhesive caulking, a pencil, wood screws, a drill and drill bits, transparent tape, and if there is a miter joint, an adjustable wrench to tighten bolts.

To replace an existing countertop with a plastic laminated post-formed one, follow these instructions:

Remove the old countertop. Since it is probably fastened to the base cabinets with screws, check inside the base cabinets for screws or nails. Remove the fasteners and lift off the old top. Besides screws or nails, the countertop may be glued down and pulling it up sharply could damage the base cabinets. A hammer and wedge may be necessary to free a glued countertop. Level the base cabinets by shimming them at the floor.

Place the new top in position, and then measure up from the floor. The top surface should be 36 inches from the floor to provide clearance for undercounter appliances and drawers. Most countertops need to be raised to this height. Turn the top over and nail 3/4-inch-thick, 2-inch-square riser blocks along the front and back, spacing them about every 8 inches. Use nails no longer than 1 1/8 inches; longer nails could penetrate the top.

Assemble the miter joints by placing the sections together, bottom side up, on a soft surface

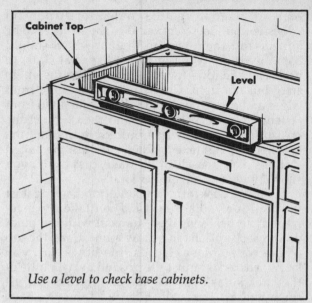
Use a level to check base cabinets.

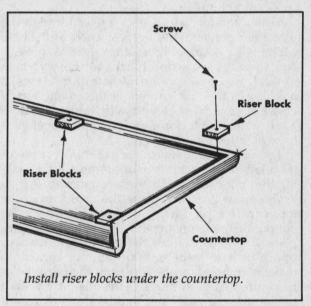
Install riser blocks under the countertop.

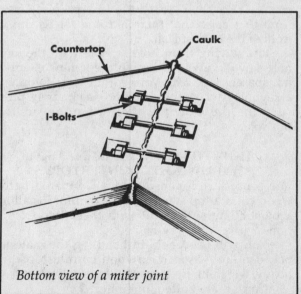
Bottom view of a miter joint

325

that will not damage the countertop. Apply an adhesive caulking compound to the surfaces to be joined, and then use the I-bolts, which should come with the top and fit into special slots, to hold the sections together. Turn the fasteners snug but not tight. Check alignment of the front edges and top surfaces, and then tighten the front fastener. Now check again, and then tighten the next fastener. Follow this procedure until all the fasteners are tightened. When you turn the bolted sections over and clean off the excess caulk, you should have a perfect miter joint.

Push the post-formed countertop back against the wall (or walls if an L). Then take a pencil, place it vertically against the wall with the point on the back splash, and draw a line along the top of the back splash. If this line bows out, you know where you must file or sand away a little of the back splash so that the countertop will fit flush against the wall. File and sand the back splash until it fits flush.

Fasten the top with wood screws through the triangular gusset plates in the corners of the base cabinets. If your cabinets do not have gussets, you should have wood blocks in those corners through which you can drill holes for screws to hold down the four corners of the countertop. If you are certain that you will never want to remove the countertop, you can apply panel mastic to hold the top in place.

For a sink installation, check the sink carton for installation instructions and a template for making the sink cutout in the new countertop. With a keyhole saw, you can make the cutout from the top; with a saber saw, you have to cut from the bottom or the laminate will chip. Using the template, draw the line for the cutout. Use a sharp punch or nail inside each of the four corners to make pilot holes for the drill, and then drill holes through at each corner. Be sure the bit does not cut outside the guideline, and be sure before you cut that you have spaced the sink properly from front to rear so that there is room for its rim in front of the back splash.

Start sawing from hole to hole with the keyhole saw. To avoid chipping the laminate, apply transparent tape over your cutout line. If you use a keyhole saw, do not saw too hard; apply pressure on the downstroke and none on the upstroke.

HOW TO INSTALL LAMINATED HARDWOOD COUNTERTOPS

The procedure for installing a laminated hardwood countertop is the same as that for installing a plastic laminated unit with these two exceptions:

• You will need help in handling the material because laminated hardwood countertops are heavy, weighing up to several hundred pounds.

• Corners are butted, not mitered.

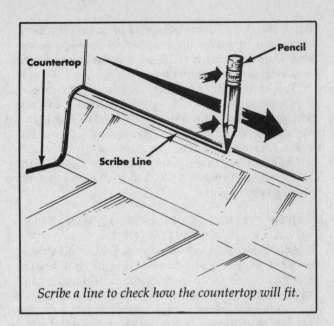

Scribe a line to check how the countertop will fit.

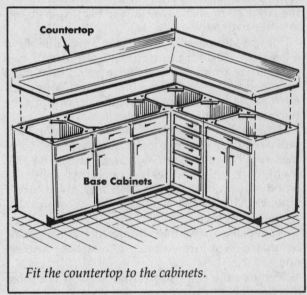

Fit the countertop to the cabinets.

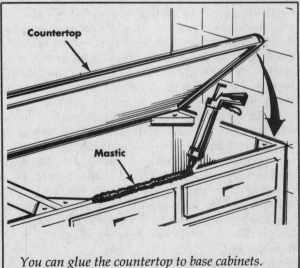

You can glue the countertop to base cabinets.

HOW TO INSTALL CORIAN COUNTERTOPS

Corian can be worked just like wood, although it looks like marble; care must be used in cutting this material. It is heavy (you will need a helper), and it will chip or break unless care is taken with it. You should be careful with this expensive material. If you lack the time or skill to do the work, have the top and cutout made by a professional.

You will need the following tools and materials: a screwdriver, hammer and wedge, level, circular saw (with a carbide-tooth blade), router, C-clamps, neoprene adhesive, turnbuckles and screws, scrap lumber, and sandpaper. To install a Corian countertop, follow these steps:

Remove the old countertop and level the base cabinets. If your kitchen has just a sink front instead of a sink cabinet, you must provide extra support for the new countertop. Corian is very heavy, and it needs support behind the sink. A wooden cleat nailed to the wall can provide support here and at other places, such as to the corners, where there may not be adequate support.

If you ordered a Corian top with an integral sink, the piece will be cut 25 inches front to back. But if you ordered a sheet of 3/4-inch Corian, you must cut the Corian to the correct 25-inch depth as well as to the proper length. The best way to cut Corian is to go slowly with a circular saw equipped with a sharp carbide blade. The blade must be sharp to avoid chipping. Since cutting will produce a "storm" of dust and Corian bits, plan to size it outdoors if possible and wear protective eyeglasses or goggles.

To raise the Corian countertop so that the top surface will be 36 inches off the floor, cut a strip 3 inches wide from the scrap to run the entire length of the top. Turn the Corian over and glue the strip along the bottom front, recessed about 1/8 inch, using neoprene adhesive. Be sure to glue so that the factory-finished edge will face the front. Then do the same along all sides. A ready-made top will already have this done for you.

If you must turn a corner for an L shape, make a butt joint rather than the miter joint. Seal the butt joint with neoprene adhesive. If you wish to draw the two sections of Corian snugger (never tight), you can install a turnbuckle underneath attached to a recessed screw on either side of the joint. Ready-made tops will already have turnbuckles.

You can make a sink cutout in the same manner as in a plastic laminate top, except that a router will do the job faster and better than a keyhole or saber saw. If you use a router, first make a jig to guide the router, and fasten it to the slab with C-clamps. Once the cutout has been made, do not move the top without help. Corian fractures easily. Cutting Corian leaves sharp edges; sand cut edges until they are smooth.

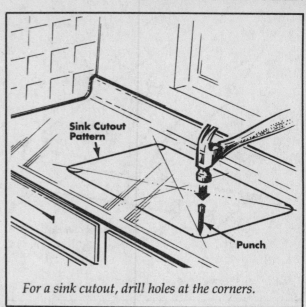

For a sink cutout, drill holes at the corners.

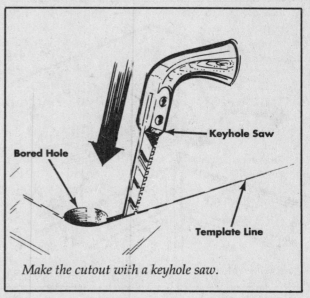

Make the cutout with a keyhole saw.

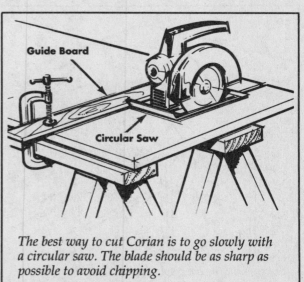

The best way to cut Corian is to go slowly with a circular saw. The blade should be as sharp as possible to avoid chipping.

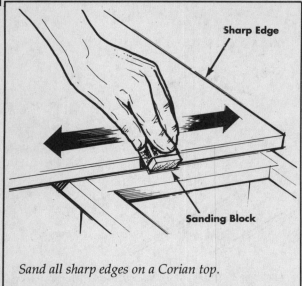

Sharp Edge

Sanding Block

Sand all sharp edges on a Corian top.

Bullnose Caps

Face Tiles

Here's how to handle the front edges.

Trowel

Spread adhesive on the countertop.

Apply grout with a rubber trowel.

Set tiles on the back splash.

HOW TO INSTALL CERAMIC-TILE COUNTERTOPS

Installing ceramic tile is the messiest approach to installing a new kitchen countertop, but it could prove to be the most durable. You will need the following tools and materials: hammer, keyhole saw, notched trowel, tile cutter or glass cutter and tile nippers (both a tile cutter and tile nippers can be rented where you buy the tile), rubber trowel, and a pencil. A plywood sheet (if a new under-surface is required, 3/4-inch CDX is best), epoxy or organic adhesive, grout, and a silicone sealer also are required. Follow these directions:

Make sure the cabinets are level; shim at the floor, if necessary. Use a 3/4-inch sheet of exterior plywood as the base for the tile countertop. Place blocks as necessary under the perimeter of the plywood so that the top surface of the tile will be 36 inches above the floor. If more than one sheet of plywood is required to form the base, leave a 1/4-inch gap between the sheets and fill the gap(s) with epoxy. Make the sink cutout in the plywood (and any other cutouts such as those for a built-in cooktop or counter inserts).

You can lay tile "wet," which means in mortar, or you can fasten it down with an epoxy or organic adhesive. The manufacturer of the tile usually recommends a specific brand (or brands) of adhesive. Since the adhesive method is easier and faster, it is the method used here.

Determine the width of the grout line. With sheets of mosaic tile, the width of the grout line is already determined; with larger tiles, a small tab provides the correct spacing. If not, you must make the decision. To minimize cleaning problems, keep the grout lines narrow. The determination of grout width helps you calculate how much tile to buy. When buying tile, be sure to buy bullnose cap or cove pieces for the back splash and edge pieces for the sink and front edge of the countertop. Buy a few extra because some are certain to break. Lay the tile out on the counter and plan the grout gaps; then draw the pattern you will follow on the plywood.

Spread the adhesive evenly on the base with a notched trowel. Then lay in the tile, working on just a couple of rows at a time. Put each tile down flat and avoid sliding it; sliding thins the adhesive. Let the adhesive dry overnight before applying the grout.

Apply the grout with the rubber trowel according to the manufacturer's directions. Hold the trowel at an angle to force the grout down between the tiles. When the grout begins to dry, run the eraser end of a pencil down the grout lines to give them an even depth. Wipe off any excess grout with a damp rag. When the grout is completely dry, spray it with a silicone sealer to prevent oil or dirt from discoloring the grout.

Installing Major Components

With cabinets and countertops in place, you're ready to install the sink and major appliances. Some appliances, such as ranges, refrigerators, and trash compactors, slide into the niches you've provided for them. Hookups generally amount to nothing more than plugging in a power cord or attaching to the gas supply line. The sink, the disposer, and the dishwasher require minor plumbing work.

HOW TO INSTALL A KITCHEN SINK

When you set out to shop for a kitchen sink, you'll find four basic models: stainless steel, pressed steel, cast iron, and an integral bowl(s) molded into a Corian countertop. If your dealer has a large inventory, he or she may have the cultured marble or the vitreous china sinks. Both have maintenance problems, and they are not recommended for use in the kitchen.

The stainless steel sink that you see in the showroom is not really "stain"-less. All will show marks, and the durability of the finish depends on the composition of the steel. Stainless steel sinks have some chrome added to preserve the finish and a nickel content that helps to withstand corrosion. You will want to get the largest percentage of each you can find. Cheaper models of stainless steel sinks are constructed of 20-gauge stainless, while more expensive ones are 18-gauge. The heavier ones will take more punishment and are less noisy during use.

Cast iron and pressed steel, which may be called enameled ware, enameled steel, or porcelain-on-steel, have a surface material that is baked on after the sink shape is made. Porcelain will chip, but you can buy porcelain sinks in many colors. Cast-iron and pressed-steel sinks are easy to care for and will last a long time if you do not use an abrasive on them.

Corian sinks are molded into the countertop. The price is high and that is a reason why they have not been installed in many kitchens. They are available in either single- or double-bowl models. Corian will scratch and nick, and while such marks can be sanded out, they require more care than other surfaces.

You can purchase any of these sinks in a variety of shapes and sizes. The standard size is one that is 22 inches deep (front to rear), 33 inches wide (in a double bowl), and 7 1/2 inches in depth. Variations are available, as are corner models to fit in the countertops used in L- or U-shaped kitchens.

On the back of all sinks is the deck or a mounting platform with three or four openings. These are for the faucet-and-spout assembly with its incoming hot and cold lines, a sprayer, and other appliances. If you choose to install an instant-hot-water device and there is no room, an extra hole can be cut into the deck. Integral drain boards are another optional feature with any kind of sink. When purchasing a sink, consider the following:

Be sure any sink you buy is coated with a sound-deadener, especially if you plan to install a disposer. A sink can act as a sounding board and create many unwanted echoes.

If you want stainless steel, buy the heaviest gauge sink you can afford. The literature should say 18-8 (the respective percentage of chrome and nickel) or series 302 or 304 (industry designations). A satin or brushed chrome finish is the easiest to care for.

Cast-iron sinks are heavy, so there is less noise from water splashing. These sinks can chip, and while they can be touched up, it will show. Check the length of the warranty period. The finish on porcelain will wear well if it is not abraded; you should not use abrasives on porcelain sinks.

Sinks come with a separate steel rim or are self rimming. Both are connected to the countertop with clamps provided with the sink; you must follow the specific instructions that come with the sink. All kinds require that a sealant be placed under the rim to provide a watertight seal between the countertop and the sink's edge. New sinks come with specific installation instructions, so use the following procedure as a guide:

If you are installing the new sink in an old countertop, first turn off the water supply and remove the old sink. In a new countertop, cut out the opening, using the template provided, or have it done wherever the top is made. Be careful to go slowly and use a router or saber saw. There will be a slight clearance for the sink to fit in, but it is not much. Try the rim after the cutout is made to make sure.

Install the faucet-and-spout assembly on the sink. It is secured by large locknuts on the threaded stems of the hot and cold water faucets. Make sure the rubber gasket is in place around the rim of the assembly so water will not leak under the sink.

Place a 1/8-inch bead of plumber's putty around the underside rim of the strainer body and set it in the drain opening. Attach the metal and rubber washers over the screw threads, followed by the large locknut. Slide on the strainer sieve, tighten the next locknut, and insert the tailpiece that connects the strainer body with the drainpipe. Tighten the nuts with a large pipe wrench, but be careful that you do not tighten them so hard as to chip the porcelain on the sink.

Apply a 1/4-inch-thick bead of plumber's putty around the rim of the countertop opening. If using an old countertop, make sure all old putty has been removed.

Lift up the sink and put it into the countertop opening. Slide the clips into the grooves or channels underneath. If the sink requires fasteners to be located on the counter rim, do this before dropping in the sink (the installation instructions will specify this). Tighten the fasteners firmly; over-tightened fasteners may crimp or bow the sink top. Check for a tight fit between sink and countertop on all sides before proceeding.

There should be shutoff valves on the water supply pipes coming from the wall. If not, now is the time to install them.

Galvanized steel pipe requires tightening of the unions and pipe sections after liberal application of pipe joint compound. Work from the wall pipe union to the faucet stems.

Copper pipe requires that all joints be made with compression fittings. Compression fittings have to be tightened, but be careful not to over-tighten them because the metal is soft and can twist out of shape.

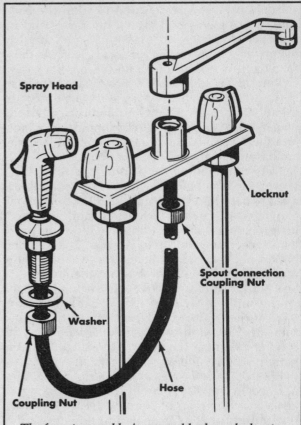

The faucet assembly is secured by large locknuts on the faucet bodies.

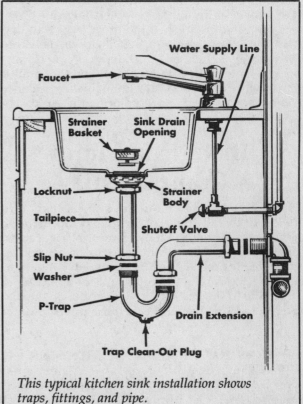

This typical kitchen sink installation shows traps, fittings, and pipe.

Then install a P-trap from the tailpiece of the strainer body to the drainpipe. Tighten all sections of the assembly, then turn on the water supply and check for leaks.

HOW TO INSTALL A DISPOSER

A disposer can be an important aid in kitchen cleanup. An in-the-sink food waste disposer will help you keep your kitchen free of odors caused by wet garbage.

Better units can handle soft foods, stringy foods, rinds, and even corn cobs. Unlike many other products, better disposers are quite different from inexpensive units. Quality units have stainless steel grind-impeller assemblies, sink flanges, and drain housings. They also have heavy-duty motors. Inexpensive units may not stand up well to tough food wastes. Overloading and jamming can be the troublesome result of a unit not built to handle a tough job.

There also is the matter of safety. Heavy-duty models have an antijam system. Such systems reverse the grinding direction or use another mechanism to clear obstructions. Sound insulation is another primary difference between inexpensive units and quality disposers.

Disposers come in batch-feed and continuous-feed models. Both have advantages, also specific modes of operation.

Batch-feed units are more expensive to purchase, because the "wiring" is already done on these models. They have the "on/off" switch control in the cover and are less expensive to have installed. You load it, put in the cover, and turn it to the "on" position to activate the unit. You cannot add additional wastes without stopping the unit.

Continuous-feed units are wired through a wall switch. These units require an additional cost to install. The units are less expensive to buy. With a continuous-feed model, you load, put in a cover that prevents garbage from flying out yet allows water into the unit, and turn on the wall switch. Additional wastes can be added while the unit is running. Consumers replacing a disposer should stick to the existing type to keep installation simple. Any home with a standard kitchen sink can accommodate a disposer. If you have a septic system, check with a local expert before installing a unit.

Disposers are equipped with a sink flange to fit the disposer to the sink at the drain and come with full instructions on how to install the unit. Models vary, but the procedure here is typical.

Check the code to find out if the unit is permitted in your area and if you are permitted to install it. If you are, get the necessary permit. This installation calls for plumbing and electrical work. **Caution:** *Whenever you propose to tackle an appliance maintenance task, repair, or new installation, be sure that you first disconnect the appliance*

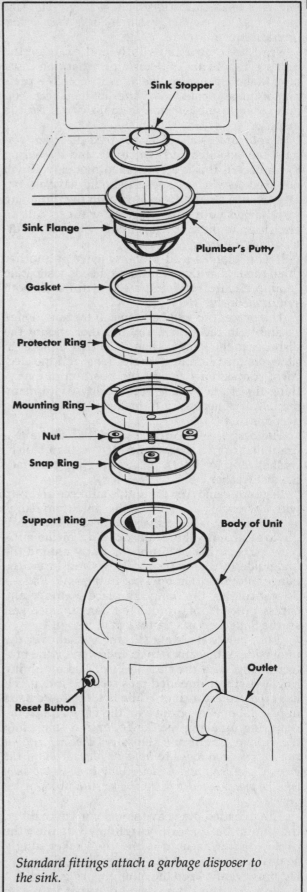

Standard fittings attach a garbage disposer to the sink.

from its power source. Either pull the plug, remove the proper fuse, or trip the correct circuit breaker for the electrical circuit involved.

Read the instructions fully and examine the unit's components to determine what you must buy. Make all measurements, and note the position of hot and cold water lines to the faucet. You may have to move them to make room for the disposer.

If your unit is a continuous-feed disposer, you must buy a switch and switch box and the wiring to connect it. If it is a batch-feed model, you will not need a switch. Disposers should have a separate 15-amp circuit. Even if you do the plumbing installation yourself, you may want to call an electrician to put a special circuit with a wall outlet under the sink.

If you plan to add a dishwasher at another time, remember the dishwasher needs a separate 20-amp circuit. Have the electrician install both simultaneously.

The procedure will be to install the sink flange assembly to the sink drain and then mount the disposer to the flange. Then cut the pipe pieces to fit, make the plumbing connections, and the electrical connections. Study the position of everything first to determine accessibility. With many models, it is necessary to make all electrical connections first.

The disposer also has a plug that can take a drain line from a dishwasher. If you plan a dishwasher now (or later), this drain plug must face the dishwasher.

Begin by removing the sink's tailpiece and trap with a wrench. Also remove the sink drain flange as well as any sealing material or gaskets. Clean the area around the drain opening in the sink. Now place a ring of plumber's putty around the underside of the new sink flange and insert the flange into the drain opening in the sink. Press—do not rotate—the flange in place. Remove any excess putty from around the flange. Once you set the flange, do not try to turn it.

From below the sink, slip the gasket over the underside of the sink flange, followed by the protector ring with the flat side up. The mounting ring, with three threaded pins screwed into it, follows the protector ring. While holding these parts in place above the groove on the flange, push the snap ring up along the flange, until it snaps into the groove. **Caution:** *If you spread the snap ring, it can become too loose to hold in place around the groove. You may find it slow going to push the snap ring in place, but it will go. Make sure it fits in the groove.*

The threaded pins have slots for a screwdriver; they must be uniformly tightened against the protector ring to hold it and the gasket snugly against the bottom of the flange. Tighten the slotted pins evenly; keep the mounting ring level.

Now lift the disposer and put it in place.

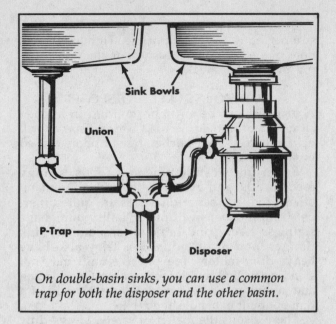

On double-basin sinks, you can use a common trap for both the disposer and the other basin.

Match the holes in the top of the disposer with the threaded pins, but before tightening the nuts that hold the disposer in place, make sure that its outlet pipe faces in the right direction for its connection to the drainpipe outlet. Tighten the nuts.

Now you are ready to hook up the trap to the disposer's outlet pipe. Use a P-trap if the drain goes into the wall or an S-trap if it goes down into the floor. Do not allow the upsweep of the trap to get as high as the outlet from the disposer. The P-trap entry into the wall also must be lower than the drain from the disposer or it will malfunction or back up. Use the slip nuts and washers; remember that the tailpiece, trap, and drain extension usually can be maneuvered so that they will fit together. You may have to buy and install some extra or replacement drain sections to complete a proper trap assembly. On double-basin sinks, a common trap for both the disposer and the other basin is acceptable.

For a continuous-feed disposer, you must install a switch. The most convenient place is on the bottom of the top rail of the sink cabinet, so when you open the cabinet door, the switch is at your fingertips. You also can mount the switch up in the back splash area more than an arm's length from the disposer, so it cannot be turned on when a hand is in the disposer.

Check the disposer to see if any tools, screws, or other materials have been dropped inside. Plug in the unit or install the switch and other wiring, following the manufacturer's directions and your local electrical code. Then test the disposer and check for leaks.

HOW TO INSTALL A DISHWASHER

Dishwashers are available as built-ins or portable units. The latter include convertible models, sometimes called convertible-portables, which

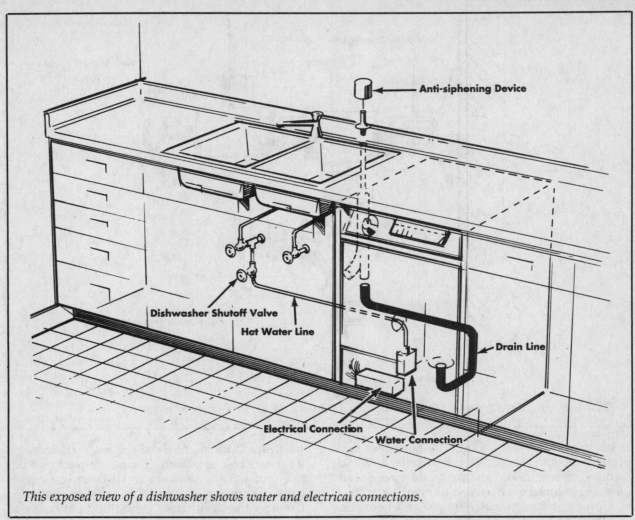

This exposed view of a dishwasher shows water and electrical connections.

can be first used as portables and then later be installed under a counter.

When you shop for a dishwasher, consider one that has an energy-saver switch to eliminate the powered drying cycle. The dishes can air dry instead, and you will save about 10 percent on energy. Soft food disposers and screens that keep scraps from jamming a dishwasher pump are standard features. The number of cycles varies widely, but most consumers can get by with short wash, normal, and pots and pans. Select added cycles to suit your requirements. For example, a rinse-and-hold feature is handy if you have just a few dishes to wash. Sanitizing, plate-warming, and china-crystal are among other settings.

Installing a new dishwasher is easier than putting in other fixtures because you must hook up only the hot water supply line; cold water is not needed. To install a dishwasher, use the following general procedure:

If the dishwasher is to fit where you presently have a 24-inch cabinet, look for screws fastening the cabinet through the face frame to cabinets on either side. Remove them. Check for screws fastening the cabinet to the wall and take them out. There also may be screws through the corner gus-

sets that fasten it to the countertop; these must be removed.

The cabinet will be fitted tightly and you may have to take up the floor covering to slide it out. In pulling it out, be very careful not to chip or mar the cabinets on either side. You may find that the cabinet rests on a kick rail, rather than the kick rail being a part of the cabinet; the cabinet will come out more easily and will not disturb the floor covering, and you can simply saw out the piece of kick rail, flush at either side.

If you are going to slide the dishwasher into place under a tiled countertop, do not remove any wood strips supporting the tile. Check the floor and wall first for any cracks that should be sealed to prevent insects from entering the house. Make sure you have a solid wood base under the countertop for fastening the dishwasher at the front. There usually is ample room and screws will go directly through the tabs on the dishwasher into the countertop. If your countertop is Corian, holes must be drilled for the screws. Now check your space and measure the dishwasher to make sure it will fit.

You will need a separate 20-amp circuit for the dishwasher. It may be best to have a professional

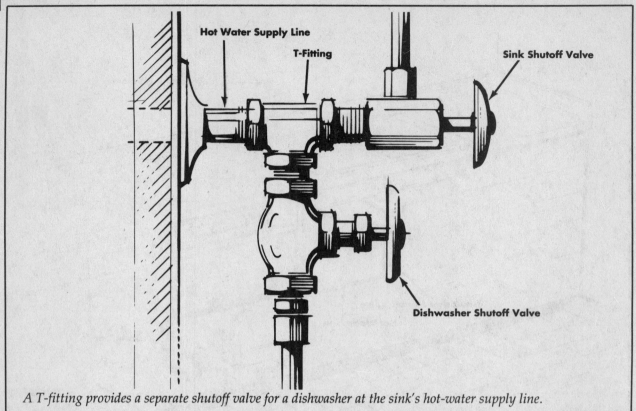

A T-fitting provides a separate shutoff valve for a dishwasher at the sink's hot-water supply line.

electrician put in this circuit. The hot water supply line to your dishwasher should be 1/2-inch flexible copper tubing, and it should have a shutoff valve in a place where you can reach it.

Turn off the main water supply and hot water valve at your water heater. Open all house faucets and drain the pipes. Remove the hot water shutoff valve under the kitchen sink and install a T-fitting to the hot water supply stubout. Reinstall the old shutoff valve that goes to the faucet, and install a new shutoff valve for the dishwasher line directly to the T-fitting. Now run flexible copper tubing from the T-fitting to the inlet valve on the dishwasher and connect it according to the manufacturer's instructions. Apply plumber's joint compound or tape to all threaded connections.

The drain line from the dishwasher can feed directly into your sink's food waste disposer, attaching to a plug designed for that purpose, or into the sink drainpipe. If you plan to connect the drain line into the sink drain, insert a waste T-fitting in the sink drainpipe between the tailpiece and the trap, or a new tailpiece with a T-fitting for this purpose. If the dishwasher drain hose has a threaded coupling, obtain a waste T-fitting with a threaded connection on its side; otherwise, the drain hose can be connected to a smooth side connection on the T-fitting by means of a hose clamp.

To connect the dishwasher's drain hose to a food waste disposer that has a short inlet pipe on its side, remove the knockout plug blocking the

inlet pipe from inside the disposer. You can angle a screwdriver or punch against the plug and tap the tool with a hammer until the plug comes loose. Remove the plug from the disposer. Connect the drain hose from the dishwasher to the disposer's inlet pipe according to the manufacturer's instructions.

The dishwasher's drain hose must be routed up to above the highest level of water in the sink to prevent siphoning. Hand screw a hook into the bottom rear of the countertop, loop the hose over it, then drill a 1-inch hole in the side of the sink cabinet for the drain hose to enter. You might prefer to install an "air gap" antisiphon device on the sink, routing the dishwasher drain up to it and then down to the disposer or drain. For this, you need an opening in the deck of the sink. This device can be mounted in the countertop. While plumbers recommended this device, kitchen installers usually find looping the drain will do the job. Behind the rear of the dishwasher, there will be room to run the loop up to the countertop and then down to the hole in the sink cabinet.

With all electrical and plumbing connections made, slide the dishwasher into place and screw it to the countertop through the two front tabs. Adjust the leveling legs at the base to make sure the unit is level.

Turn on the main water supply, and the hot water at the shutoff valve, and check all fittings for leaks. Run the dishwasher through a full cycle, again checking for leaks.

REMODELING A BATHROOM

Baths last longer than kitchens before an overhaul is needed, and even if a bath at your house has seen better days, it may require only a simple fixing up. Fresh paint or vinyl wall covering, new tile, better lighting, a new lavatory and toilet, and improved storage can update all but the most hopeless facility. If your bath wasn't well planned to begin with, or you'd like to alleviate morning traffic jams by adding another bath, prepare for a major job. The most important part of the project is to work it out on paper beforehand.

Planning and Design

The major problem in planning a bathroom is space. The bathroom usually is the smallest room in the house. But compared with other rooms, it must accommodate a disproportionate amount of activity. The bathroom also must contain certain immovable and large fixtures. Getting the greatest possible convenience out of this small space is the goal of bathroom planning.

You must decide how your bathroom is going to be used. Function, not size, should be the guiding factor in planning a new bathroom or remodeling an existing one. In terms of function, there are four basic bathrooms.

Single Bathroom. A single bathroom is one that has a toilet, lavatory, and tub or shower, and is designed for use by only one person at a time. Such a bathroom can be as small as 30 square feet or as large as you wish. The "standard" single bathroom is 5 by 8 feet, because the most popular tub size is 30 inches wide and 5 feet long, and the tub is usually installed across one end of the room.

Family Bathroom. Besides having at least the same facilities as a single bathroom, a family bathroom also is compartmented to allow it to be used by two or more people at a time. Although it's a great convenience to have two lavatory basins for scrubbing kids before meals or at bedtime, this is a task that doesn't require privacy. A bathroom with twin lavatories but no privacy compartments is a single-function bathroom.

Master Bathroom. This kind of bathroom is intended for the exclusive use of the heads of the household. A master bathroom usually is entered from the master bedroom and is an integral part of the master bedroom suite. It need not be the largest bathroom in the house, but it often is the most luxurious. If there is to be an extra-special fixture anywhere in the house, the master bathroom is the likely place for it.

To fulfill its function, a master bathroom should be compartmented in the same way that a family bathroom is. Because a house with a master bathroom also will have at least one other bathroom, this is not a rigid rule. The ultimate master bathroom provides for full and private use by two people simultaneously. This kind of bathroom is possible only where there is plenty of space. Its layout is two full bathrooms divided for privacy, but entered from the bedroom through the same door. Each half of the bathroom contains its own toilet and lavatory, often with a bidet. The bathing facilities may be in a shared area of the room, but many couples prefer to have a separate bathtub and shower.

Half Bathroom. Also called a powder room, a half bathroom contains only lavatory and toilet facilities. A half bathroom is almost a necessity in two-story homes in which the only full bathroom is on the second floor. A half bathroom can be incorporated into any area of the house where plumbing lines are nearby. The minimum comfortable floor space for such a facility is 3 by 3 1/2 feet, although half bathrooms have been squeezed into spaces only 2 feet wide.

LIMITATIONS
Before you become committed to a particular bathroom plan, be aware of some factors that can impose limitations on bathroom planning.

Plumbing. Changing the location of an existing toilet requires extensive plumbing work. It's wise not to change the toilet location. Plan to install a new toilet in the old location.

If your home is built atop a concrete slab, any change in drain lines will be expensive because the existing drains are buried in the concrete slab.

Wherever floor joists must be cut for new drain or supply lines, the cut joists must be reinforced before the floor is closed. This job is not particularly difficult or expensive, but it must be done to avoid seriously weakening the floor structure.

Another important consideration is whether the water supply pipes are located within one, two, or three walls of the bathroom. You can learn the plumbing layout simply by looking at the fixtures. If the toilet and the faucets for the lavatory and tub or the shower are all along one wall, you can be sure that the room has one-wall plumbing; if these elements are distributed on two walls, the room has two-wall plumbing.

If your bathroom has one-wall plumbing, you cannot plan to place a fixture on a wall that presently has no water supply pipes without also planning for major and expensive changes in the entire plumbing layout. Changing from one-wall to two-wall plumbing or from two-wall to three-wall not only requires new supply pipes but also necessitates changes in the drain lines. In view of these potential problems, you may decide to settle for new fixtures in the old locations.

Clearance. Plumbing codes and human comfort require minimum separations between fixtures. Clearances are definite limitations to planning. There is just so much that can be put into an existing space and be functional.

The most important clearances usually are governed by plumbing codes. All codes are not in agreement, so you'll have to find out what is required in your community. The clearances required by most codes are minimums; you'll want greater separation between fixtures wherever it's possible. For example, some codes require 15 inches between the centerline of a toilet and a wall or tub, while other codes set this minimum at 18 inches. For cleaning you'll appreciate having at least 6 inches between the side of a toilet tank and any object alongside it. The centerline of a lavatory bowl must be 14 to 18 inches from an adjacent wall, but convenience demands at least 6 inches between the side of a lavatory and an adjacent wall. To enter and leave a shower stall, you'll need a minimum of 18 inches between the shower door and a facing wall. If you want to avoid walking sideways to get into that shower, allow at least a 28-inch-wide space. For knee room you'll want at least 28 inches between the front of a toilet and a facing wall, although codes often require a 30-inch separation if the toilet faces the side of a bathtub. When you plan for twin lavatory basins, be sure to allow space for elbow room. The minimums are 30 inches between bowl centers and at least 14 inches between the center of a bowl and the adjacent wall. These are minimums, and comfort requires more room. Try to make counters at least 20 inches deep with at least 6 inches between the edge of the bowl and the end of the counter to minimize splashing on the floor.

Fixtures and Floor Space. There is more to consider when selecting fixtures than aesthetic appeal. Tubs, toilets, lavatories, and showers are all available in a variety of sizes and styles. These differences can be significant when you are attempting to design the greatest efficiency into a small space. They also can have an impact on the structure and plumbing of your house.

If a standard tub exists, it is rectangular, 5 feet long and 30 inches wide. It is not essential to plan your bathroom around a standard tub. As an alternative to a rectangular tub, a square shower receptor tub can be a good space saver. Even the so-called standard tub is available in 29-to-32-inch widths and in lengths from 4 to 6 feet.

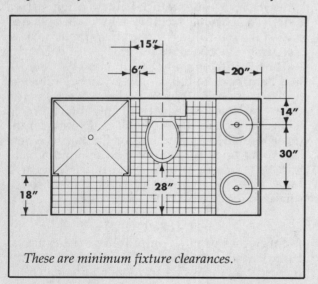
These are minimum fixture clearances.

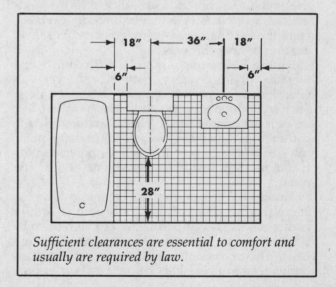
Sufficient clearances are essential to comfort and usually are required by law.

Styles of toilets and lavatories also can be selected for their space-saving advantages. A round-seated toilet takes up less space than an elongated one, although you'll have to trade a bit of comfort for that space. A triangular wall-mounted lavatory can help increase useful floor space in a very small bathroom. To choose the best fixtures in relation to floor space, you'll have to investigate the varieties of fixtures available.

You'll see a corner shower in some bathroom plans in this chapter. The dimensions given for this shower are those of a molded shower floor, not a modular shower stall. Some modular units of the same size are too big to get into an existing home.

Heating. No one likes to leave a warm bed on a cold morning for the discomfort of a chilly bathroom. Providing adequate heating is an essential part of bathroom planning. If you are planning to add a bathroom, your furnace must have the heating capacity to handle an extra room. If it will, new ducts are all you'll need. If the furnace cannot supply the needed extra heat, supplemental heaters might offer the solution.

Supplemental heaters can either be electric or gas. Products and installation are strictly regulated by building codes. The code in your area might require all electrical hookups to be made by a licensed electrician. Check code requirements before choosing a heater.

A wall heater requires thoughtful planning. It must be located where it won't pose a burn hazard and can't ignite towels or curtains. Portable electric heaters can be hazardous in the humid environment of a bathroom. Do not use one. Electrical heaters and the electrical controls of gas heaters must be grounded to prevent creation of a shock hazard. Safety demands a thermostatic control with automatic shutoff when the temperature reaches a preset level. Good venting and a pilot light shutoff are essential with a gas heater.

Radiant ceilings should definitely be considered for supplemental heating. When wired into the house circuit, the system provides clean, comfortable, and low-cost heat. Installation is not for the do-it-yourselfer; consult an electrician and plastering contractor for more information.

LIGHTING

For most bathrooms good lighting means a blend of natural and artificial light. In a bathroom, windows are not the only means for admitting natural light.

Skylights. If yours is a single-story home or if the bathroom is to be on the second floor of a two-story home, you should consider a skylight for your bathroom. For a first-floor bathroom in a two-story home, the cost of a skylight can be high. Although skylights have been installed in house walls, it's not a good solution. Mounting a skylight vertically and in a way that allows it to be opened for ventilation is tricky. Screening such an opening may destroy the visual appeal of the skylight. About the only way to bring skylight benefits to a first-floor bathroom is to build a small extension with a sloping roof.

Commercial skylights are available in both glass and plastic. Translucent plastic is the best choice. Clear plastic or glass is not good for a skylight on the south or west side of a sloped roof. These sides of the house receive direct sunlight for much of the day, even during winter, and so much direct light can have a "greenhouse effect" in the bathroom, making the room very hot. If you must place a skylight on the south or west side, it should be glazed with translucent, rather than clear, glass or plastic, which will filter part of the sun's rays.

Most skylights available to the home market are complete units with integral mounting flanges for ease of installation. A double-glazed dome is essential in cold climates to minimize condensation. Even a double-glazed skylight needs the help of a good ventilating system to keep the inside of the dome clear of condensation.

Windows. Correct placement of a window is important for both light and ventilation. The window must open and close easily, and it must be screened. Choosing and placing a window for an all-new bathroom is easy. For a remodeling project, there are limitations. Moving or relocating a window in an existing bathroom requires removal of outside surfacing, cutting load-bearing studs, and patching the outside surface. It's easier to replace an existing window with a new window of a different size or style than to install a new window in a new location.

Replacing an old window with a new one can bring improvement. If the old window is double hung (vertical sliding), a new casement window (side hinged) can make life more pleasant. In cold climates, wood or plastic-clad wood windows are warmer to the touch than metal windows and retain heat better.

A variety of glass and plastic panes are possible. Clear panes transmit the most light, but translucent panes add privacy. Reflective glass prevents people from looking in while you can look out. Thermal windows having two sheets of glass with air or gas sealed between them can cut heat loss up to 50 percent, a definite plus in areas with a cold climate.

Artificial Lighting. Lighting engineers recommend about 30 footcandles of illumination for bathrooms. That translates to about 150 watts of incandescent lighting for a standard 5-by-8-foot bathroom, which is 3 3/4 watts per square foot of floor area. The same level of illumination is provided by 70 watts of fluorescent lighting, which is 1 3/4 watts of fluorescent lighting per square foot of floor area.

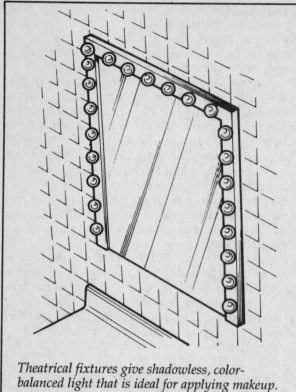

Theatrical fixtures give shadowless, color-balanced light that is ideal for applying makeup.

Incandescent light looks more natural than fluorescent. Two fixtures help avoid shadows.

The first aspect of lighting to consider is safety. The safest location for your bathroom light switch is outside your bathroom door. Your complete wiring plan must be drawn and submitted to your local code official for approval. Learn code requirements before planning.

Luminous ceiling lighting provides the most even illumination and is not difficult to install. Because the suspension grid that supports the luminous panels must be 6 to 12 inches below the bulbs or tubes that provide light, an 8-foot-high ceiling makes installation impractical. If your home has high ceilings, a luminous ceiling can be the ideal solution to the problem of lighting the bathroom.

Localized lighting is most often chosen for bathrooms. A prime requirement is that no single fixture be too bright. Strive for balance.

Mirrors require good lighting. Fluorescent tubes or incandescent bulbs behind a diffusing panel can be placed across the top and along each side of a mirror. Fluorescent tubes, because of the color of light emitted, are not well-suited to makeup areas. Theatrical lighting, which is rows of incandescent bulbs around three sides of a mirror, provides shadowless, color-balanced light that is ideal for applying makeup or for shaving. Single light fixtures installed at each side of a mirror can provide good light if they are properly placed. A good height for side lights is 62 inches above the floor. Do not install a single bulb fixture above the center of a mirror; the result is harsh, unpleasant light. Lights need not be just lights. There are combination units that also incorporate ventilating fans and heating elements.

For compartmented bathrooms light in toilet compartments does not need to be as bright as in washing and bathing areas. A single 60- or 75-watt incandescent fixture is enough. The switch for this fixture should be located outside the compartment door.

VENTILATION

Nothing contributes more to an efficiently functioning bathroom than effective ventilation. Nothing is more offensive than the dank, musty smell of a bathroom in which nothing ever gets completely dry. Windows and doors traditionally have provided bathroom ventilation. During warm weather they still can, but in cold climates and in windowless baths, mechanical ventilation is essential. It not only prevents condensation from forming on walls, ceilings, and mirrors but also preserves and extends the life of the bathroom.

Exhaust fans can either be wired into the lighting circuit switch or switched independently. Some codes require that in windowless bathrooms, exhaust fans must be controlled by the light switch.

Bathroom ventilators should handle eight complete changes of air every hour. Exhaust fans are rated according to the number of cubic feet of air they can move each minute: the CFM capacity.

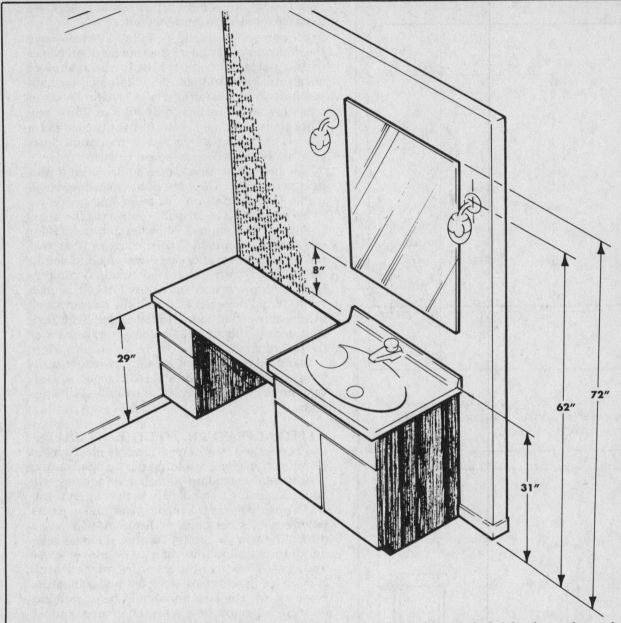

These dimensions and clearances can be altered to suit the user's height. Although the height of manufactured vanities is standard, lower or higher vanities can be custom made.

For example, if you have a 5-by-8-foot bathroom, there are 40 square feet of floor area. If the ceiling is 8 feet high, the bath has a volume of 320 cubic feet. To change that volume of air eight times each hour means moving 2,560 cubic feet of air. Divide that volume of air by 60, and you need an exhaust fan that can move 42.67 CFM. Apply similar calculations to your own bath.

ACCESSORY FIXTURES

The location of the toilet-tissue holder, the number of towel bars, and the height of the shower head are matters of personal preference. But there are established standards. For example, members of your family might want a lower or higher

shower head than is standard. That may be fine for now, but should you ever want to sell your home, nonstandard features could hamper its sale. Consider that fact in deciding whether to depart from standards.

A towel bar installed above a tub should be 48 inches above the floor. Install soap dishes and grab bars 24 inches above the floor. If there is a shower head above the tub, allow 74 inches under the head for clearance, install a second soap dish at a 54-inch height and a second grab bar slightly higher. If you intend to use a shower curtain, install the rod 78 inches above the floor.

The top of the mirror above the lavatory should be 72 to 78 inches above the floor. Allow

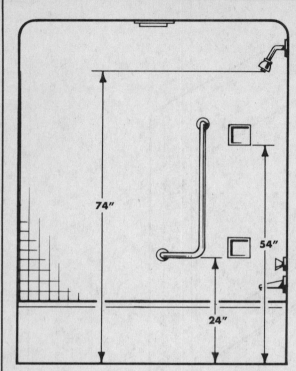

Positioning accessory fixtures can be a matter of preference, but standard clearances are based on comfort and convenience.

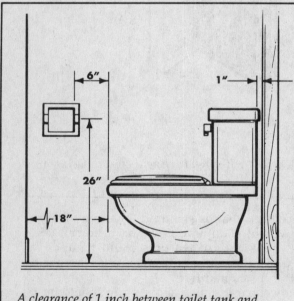

A clearance of 1 inch between toilet tank and wall will avoid the problem of condensation soaking into the wall.

about 8 inches between the top of the lavatory or counter and the bottom of a cabinet or mirror.

A medicine cabinet should be within easy reach of the lavatory. If there are children in the household, the medicine cabinet should be placed high enough to be out of their reach. A separate lockable cabinet can be a good idea.

Shower valves should be 48 to 54 inches above the floor and always near the shower door. Never install valves in the back wall of the shower enclosure, because you'll have to reach through running water to adjust them. A shower head can be as low as 60 inches or as high as 75 inches. Since there is no need to step over the side of a tub to enter a shower enclosure, minimum clearance under the shower head isn't a factor.

The best place for a tissue holder is on a wall next to the toilet. The edge of the roll should be 6 inches from the front of the toilet, and the center of the roll should be 26 inches above the floor.

Allow a minimum of 24 inches of towel bar for each family member. A 24-inch towel bar will hold a bath towel and face towel, each folded in thirds, and a washcloth folded in half. If you prefer to fold towels only once, it will take a 30-inch bar to fit the three items. Install the bars about 40 inches above the floor. If wall space is limited, consider installing one 24-inch bar on the back of the bathroom door.

Standard height for a lavatory, whether wall-hung or as a part of a vanity, is 31 inches. A vanity counter, without basin, is usually 29 inches high.

SPECIAL FEATURES FOR THE DISABLED

Old people and handicapped people need special consideration when a bathroom is being planned.

Although a standard 30-inch door opening will allow access for a standard wheelchair, an extra-wide opening, say 34 inches, can make access much easier. A person in a wheelchair will have a difficultly using a vanity, because the base cabinet does not allow the chair to be moved close enough. A wall-hung lavatory placed high enough for the chair arms to pass under the front edge is best. The lavatory should be extra wide, because a person in a wheelchair needs more elbow room. Plumbing under the lavatory should be placed so as not to obstruct the approach of the wheelchair.

Push-button or lever water controls are easier to use than are twist faucets. A temperature regulator also will help avoid scalding for people with impaired sensation in their hands.

Extra-high toilets and showers with seats, rather than tubs, can be a boon to the elderly. Grab bars located both at the toilet and in the shower or tub are essential.

LAYING OUT A BATHROOM

To experiment with different bathroom floor plans, you'll save time by making cutouts for tracing fixture outlines on graph paper. You'll find it useful to make cutouts for fixtures of various sizes. Then test each layout to see how it works with large fixtures, then again with smaller

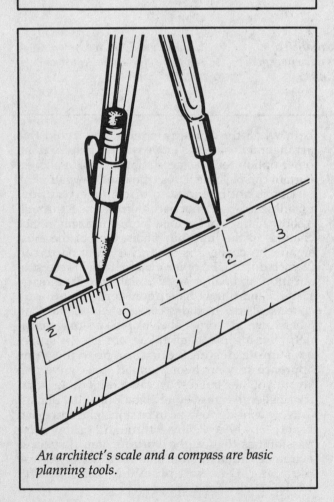

These silhouettes are 1/4-inch scale. Use them to make cutouts for planning. The tub is 5 feet by 30 inches; the shower base is 36 by 36 inches.

An architect's scale and a compass are basic planning tools.

fixtures. Having adequate clearance between fixtures is more important than having large fixtures.

You'll quickly discover that planning a new bathroom, or rearranging an old one, involves experimentation. The best place for trial and error is on paper. Use graph paper ruled in 1/2-inch squares, and let 1/2 inch equal 1 foot when you draw your plans.

Especially useful tools are an inexpensive architect's scale, which is a special ruler that has markings for many different scales, and a pencil compass. The scale you'll use is the one on which 1/2 inch equals 1 foot. One 1/2-inch space on this scale is divided to represent 12 inches. By combining feet and inch marks, you can draw any dimension to scale.

You'll have only one use for the compass, but it's a very important use. The final test of a plan is to draw the arc through which the bathroom door will swing. You don't want a bathroom in which the door strikes the toilet or lavatory, and can't be fully opened.

Begin by measuring the inside dimensions of your bathroom, or the space in which you'd like to add a bath, down to the smallest fraction of an inch that you can accurately measure. Use these measurements to make your scale drawing. If you intend to remodel an existing bathroom, measure and locate positions for electrical outlets, drains, windows, and doors. Be precise in locating drain positions; measure from two walls to find the exact centerline of each drain.

FLOOR PLAN POSSIBILITIES

Study floor plans 1 through 4 on the next page. All four plans may appear to be workable layouts. Although they use large fixtures that seem to fit, each example shows something you'll want to avoid in your own plans.

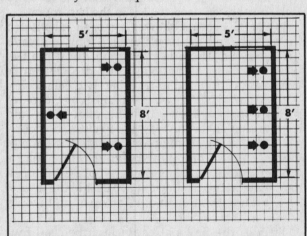

Measure your bathroom and make a scale drawing on graph paper. Mark drain locations. The drawing at left shows two-wall plumbing; the one on the right is one-wall plumbing.

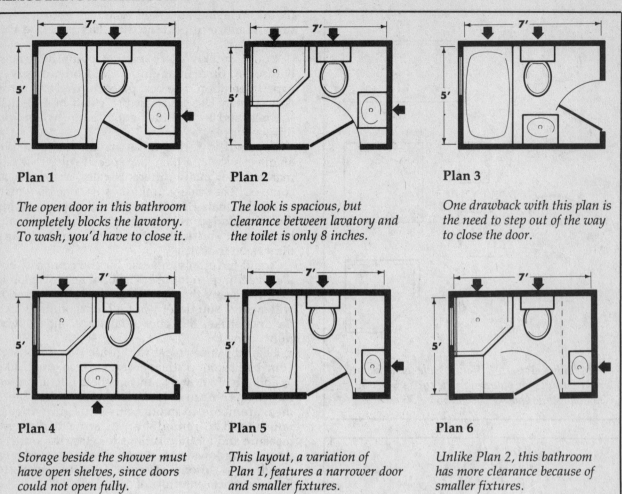

Plan 1

The open door in this bathroom completely blocks the lavatory. To wash, you'd have to close it.

Plan 2

The look is spacious, but clearance between lavatory and the toilet is only 8 inches.

Plan 3

One drawback with this plan is the need to step out of the way to close the door.

Plan 4

Storage beside the shower must have open shelves, since doors could not open fully.

Plan 5

This layout, a variation of Plan 1, features a narrower door and smaller fixtures.

Plan 6

Unlike Plan 2, this bathroom has more clearance because of smaller fixtures.

In Plan 1 the open door completely blocks the lavatory. To wash your hands, you'd have to enter and close the door behind you. This is hardly practical when you consider that the lavatory is the most often used fixture in the bathroom.

In Plan 2 a corner shower has been substituted for the tub, and the result gives a look of greater spaciousness. There is even room for a built-in linen cabinet or shelving, but the clearance between lavatory and toilet is barely 8 inches.

Plan 3 shows the same sort of door-clearance problem that ruins Plan 1. In this plan you would have to step out of the way just to close the door.

In Plan 4 the storage area beside the shower would have to be open shelving rather than a cabinet, because cabinet doors would be difficult to operate in the confined space beside the lavatory. Even the lower shelves of an open unit would be almost inaccessible.

Besides the flaws already described, all four plans have another undesirable feature: Each has a window located within a tub or shower enclosure. Many existing bathrooms have a window over a tub/shower because no other arrangement was possible within the space allocated for the

bath when the home was built. But avoid this arrangement whenever possible. If there is no other option for placing a shower stall, a shower curtain can be hung across the window wall.

This is not intended to discourage you from planning a 5-by-7-foot bathroom. Plans 5 through 8 show that it can be done by making only minor changes in the first four plans. One of the most significant changes is the inclusion of narrower, 28-inch doors. The other major change is the substitution of smaller-sized toilets and lavatories. Plans 5 and 6 now have room for a wall-to-wall counter. Plan 7 includes corner shelves, and Plan 8 has room for corner shelves plus a storage cabinet. Nothing has been taken out except space-consuming design features. Apply the same approach to your own plans. If you arrive at a layout you like but discover it doesn't quite work, try smaller fixtures before abandoning the plan.

Now consider what can be done in a space that is only 5 by 6 feet. Plans 9 through 11 show some possibilities that might work for you if space is extremely limited. Note that each uses two-wall plumbing. One-wall plumbing simply won't work in such a small space.

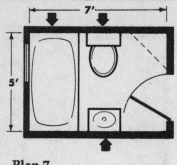

Plan 7

Smaller fixtures permit corner shelves that were not possible in Plan 3.

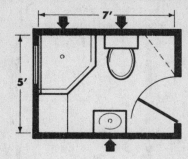

Plan 8

Use of a smaller toilet and lavatory allows corner shelves and storage.

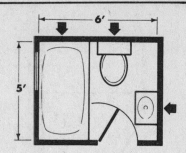

Plan 9

This small bathroom, only 5 by 6 feet, uses a 24-inch-wide door.

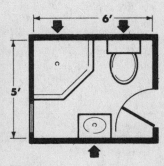

Plan 10

The 24-inch-wide door is not an ideal solution, but it may work for you.

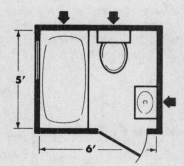

Plan 11

If a narrow door is not feasible, an outward-opening door may work.

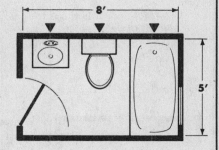

Plan 12

A typical 5-by-8-foot bathroom with one-wall plumbing.

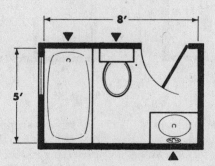

Plan 13

Two-wall plumbing allows more options for fixture arrangement.

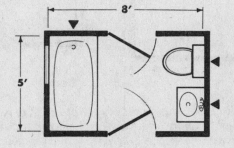

Plan 14

A 5-by-8-foot room can serve as a bathroom between two bedrooms.

Note the door arrangements in these plans. Plans 9 and 10 show 24-inch doors. That is not an ideal size, but there is no room for a wider door if it has to swing into the bathroom. Some building codes might prohibit the use of a narrow door.

Plan 11 shows how to solve the door problem by hinging 30-inch doors to swing outward. If you elect to install an outward-opening door, be sure to install it in a way that is compatible with traffic in your home. Most bathroom traffic will come from the direction of your living room, family room, and kitchen. Hinge the door to swing open to receive, not block, this traffic.

Single Bathroom. You've already seen some ways to make 5-by-6-foot and 5-by-7-foot spaces function efficiently as single bathrooms. The more space you have to work with, the more options you have. It is difficult to remodel a bath-

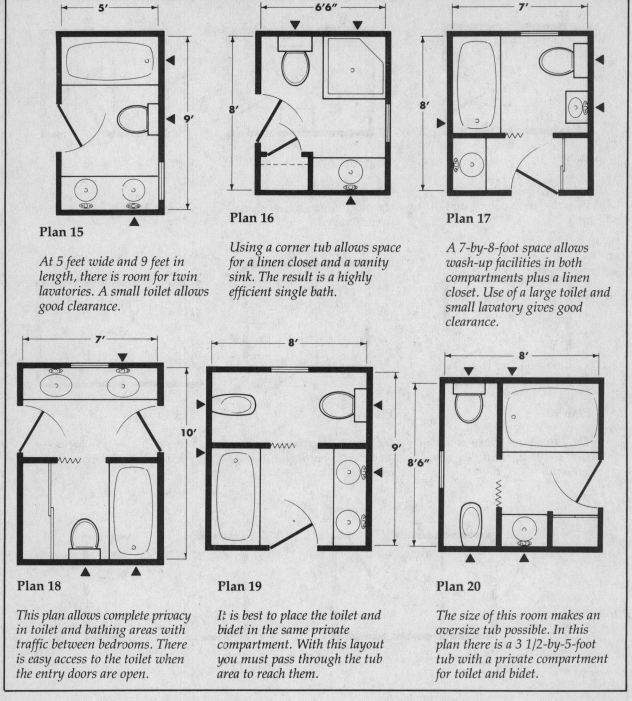

Plan 15

At 5 feet wide and 9 feet in length, there is room for twin lavatories. A small toilet allows good clearance.

Plan 16

Using a corner tub allows space for a linen closet and a vanity sink. The result is a highly efficient single bath.

Plan 17

A 7-by-8-foot space allows wash-up facilities in both compartments plus a linen closet. Use of a large toilet and small lavatory gives good clearance.

Plan 18

This plan allows complete privacy in toilet and bathing areas with traffic between bedrooms. There is easy access to the toilet when the entry doors are open.

Plan 19

It is best to place the toilet and bidet in the same private compartment. With this layout you must pass through the tub area to reach them.

Plan 20

The size of this room makes an oversize tub possible. In this plan there is a 3 1/2-by-5-foot tub with a private compartment for toilet and bidet.

room of 5 by 8 feet or less without capturing space from an adjacent room or adding onto the house.

Family Bathroom. Compartments for privacy characterize a family bathroom. The following plans suggest ways in which you can provide compartments in your new bath. A 6 1/2-by-8-foot space is about the smallest room that can be compartmented. That doesn't mean that a small family bathroom can't have many desirable features.

When laying out a compartmented bathroom, try to locate the lavatory in the compartment nearest the door; washing is not usually the function that requires privacy. Folding doors are less likely to warp and become stuck than pocket doors (doors that slide into the wall).

Master Bathroom. A master bathroom can be single, compartmented, or even a half bathroom. The factor that sets it apart from other bathrooms is that access is from the master bedroom. A master bedroom and an adjoining bathroom comprise a master bedroom suite.

The benefit of a master bathroom, even if only a half bathroom, isn't limited to a master suite. If your family includes an elderly or handicapped

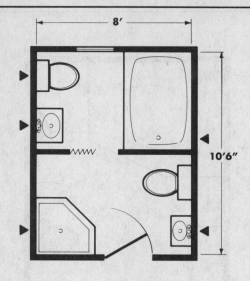

Plan 21

With this much space, there is room for a separate tub and shower.

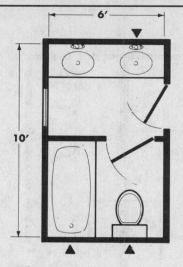

Plan 22

A double lavatory, compartmented for privacy, and plenty of clearance between fixtures make an efficient master bathroom.

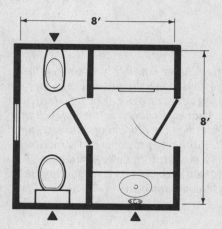

Plan 23

If your home already has an adequate and conveniently located family bathroom, a well-planned half bathroom can be compartmented as a master bathroom.

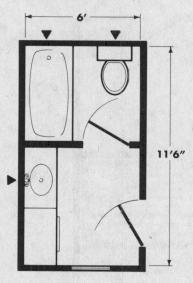

Plan 24

A long, narrow bathroom could be constructed across one end of a large bathroom.

person, bathroom facilities connected to that person's bedroom can be a blessing.

Compartmented Master Bathroom. It will have privacy compartments for toilets and lavatories but may have a single, shared bathing area. Such a bathroom may include a double tub. While one plan in this section includes such a tub, it is offered with a warning: Installation of a double tub is not recommended for a do-it-yourselfer. That same warning applies to installation of a sunken tub. The weight of water needed to fill a double tub or bathing pool to soaking depth can exceed 1,000 pounds, and it's likely that your floor framing would need reinforcement to support that much weight.

The hazards are even greater with the installation of a sunken tub. To install a sunken tub, sections of the floor joists have to be cut out and the opening framed to receive the tub. Extensive reinforcement is needed to replace the load-carrying

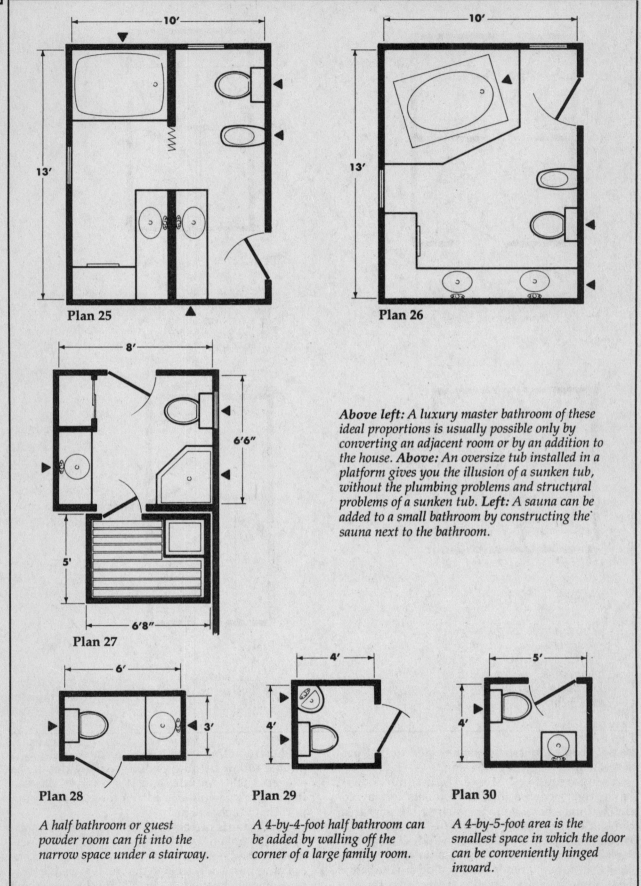

Plan 25

Plan 26

Plan 27

Above left: A luxury master bathroom of these ideal proportions is usually possible only by converting an adjacent room or by an addition to the house. Above: An oversize tub installed in a platform gives you the illusion of a sunken tub, without the plumbing problems and structural problems of a sunken tub. Left: A sauna can be added to a small bathroom by constructing the sauna next to the bathroom.

Plan 28

A half bathroom or guest powder room can fit into the narrow space under a stairway.

Plan 29

A 4-by-4-foot half bathroom can be added by walling off the corner of a large family room.

Plan 30

A 4-by-5-foot area is the smallest space in which the door can be conveniently hinged inward.

capacity of the cut joists. The bottoms of these bathing pools are so wide they need support. A boxlike receptacle usually is built in the opening below floor level and then partially filled with a lightweight, slow-setting plaster. Before the plaster has hardened, the tub is pressed down into it. When the plaster hardens, it provides support for the tub bottom. You can see that installation of a large sunken tub requires special expertise. If you still want to install one yourself, there is only one safe way to go about the job: Find an architect who's willing to accept small jobs and have plans drawn for the floor framing in your home.

Combination Bathroom. A combination bathroom is just what the name implies. It combines a bathroom with another different function within the same space. Such extra facilities depend on your personal needs and the available space. Typical special functions include laundry, exercise, or sauna facilities. For laundry and exercise facilities, all that is required is space that can be designed into a new bathroom. A sauna requires special planning.

Sauna planners have many options. These options range from a do-it-yourself project to having the complete installation done by a contractor. Between these extremes are sauna kits designed for homeowner installation. Kits are either precut or modular. Precut kits include all framing materials as well as some internal fixtures. All lumber is cut to size, and detailed instructions describe every construction step. Some kits include a prehung door. Modular saunas are factory-built panels that fit together. These kits are as complete as precut kits, go up faster, but cost more.

Some kit manufacturers include benches and duckboards (floor boards) in kit prices; others offer them as optional extras.

Building your own sauna from sticks and boards bought from a local lumber dealer might not be the bargain it appears to be. Cutting waste and the time needed for this method can quickly outweigh the potential cost savings.

Cost can't be cut by using two walls and the ceiling of an existing room partially to enclose a sauna. A sauna is a self-contained unit. Ceiling and walls must be insulated and contain a good vapor barrier. To conserve energy with the high heat required, sauna ceilings are never more than 7 feet high. The sauna floor also needs consideration. Some kit manufacturers say that a sauna can be built over any flooring except carpeting. The reason for that exception is that sweat generated by sauna heat drips onto the floor, and carpeting would soon take on a foul odor. Sauna literature also tells you that a floor drain isn't needed, claiming that water can be carefully poured over the heated rocks to make steam whether there is a floor drain or not. This may be true, but a floor drain makes cleaning much easier. Have a con-

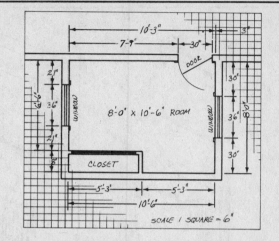

Before measuring, make a rough outline of the entire room on a grid sheet. Then measure all room dimensions to within 1/16 inch.

tractor install a properly sloped floor with a drain. Then erect a sauna kit over that floor.

Half Bathroom. Possible spaces for a half bath include a large closet, space under a stairway, or a pantry. Even the corner of a room should be considered.

If yours is a two-story home with its only bathroom on the second floor, a new half bathroom should be located on the first floor. If yours is a ranch home, you'll reduce costs if you can locate the half bathroom next to the existing bathroom. There are benefits from having a half bathroom just off the kitchen or near the kitchen or backdoor. Where space is available near the front entry, you might prefer to plan a half bathroom that functions as a powder room.

FINAL PLANS AND DRAWINGS

Before you begin remodeling, prepare a series of sketches that show all measurements and details. These can be refined sketches or informal drawings, but they should be done in considerable detail and to scale. The larger the drawings, the easier they will be to work with. Be sure to include the principal elements of the remodeling project, including wall placement; locations, styles, and sizes of doors and windows; built-in furnishings, such as cabinets, tub, and toilet; and placement of plumbing fixtures and appliances.

The plans can be prepared in many ways. A floor plan is the first requirement to work out proper placement and proportions of various elements. Interior elevations, which are detailed drawings of a single plane of the room as viewed head on, are also helpful. Utilities drawings, such as those showing electrical and plumbing extensions, are usually drawn symbolically on a basic floor plan.

Do not skimp on details or specifications. The plans are designed to help you work out prob-

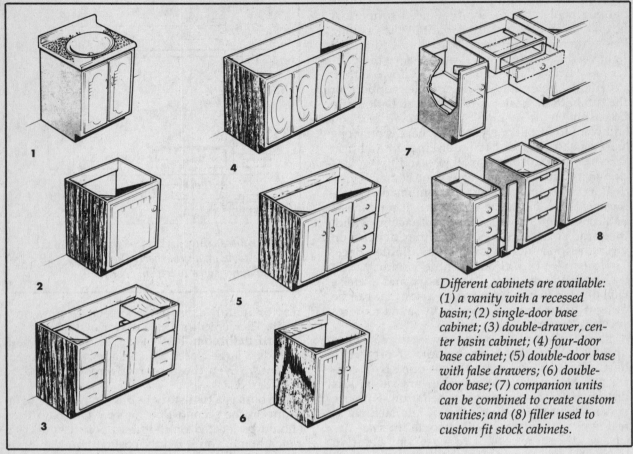

Different cabinets are available: (1) a vanity with a recessed basin; (2) single-door base cabinet; (3) double-drawer, center basin cabinet; (4) four-door base cabinet; (5) double-door base with false drawers; (6) double-door base; (7) companion units can be combined to create custom vanities; and (8) filler used to custom fit stock cabinets.

lems in advance and to serve as references as the job progresses.

As you work out the final plans, establish specifications for the materials, hardware, and equipment needed. You can note this directly on the plans or on separate lists. Give these items careful thought. List the items that will go into the project. This bill of materials should be checked against the plans or specifications lists several times to make sure nothing has been omitted.

Installing a Vanity Cabinet

Cabinets are an essential part of every complete bathroom. They might consist of built-ins, custom-built cabinets fabricated at the job site or in a custom cabinet shop, antique or new furniture that either serves as is or has been adapted for particular bathroom use, or commercially made bathroom cabinets and accessory furnishings. Along with the medicine cabinet and the vanity cabinet, other bathroom cabinets might include linen and towel storage, base cabinets not used as vanities, general storage cabinets, cupboards or shelving sections, and hampers.

With cabinets, you usually get what you pay for. Top-grade cabinets are expensive. Cheap cab-

inets are cheap in quality and in the long run, not a good buy. Cabinets built and installed on the job site are expensive. A well-skilled do-it-yourselfer who is an amateur cabinetmaker can build his or her own cabinets and save hundreds of dollars. But factory-made cabinets are likely to be more satisfactory.

When purchasing commercially made cabinets for the bathroom, there are several points to consider. Cabinets made of solid wood or with solid wood face frames and trims applied to hardwood veneer plywood are the best. Thin plywood, hardboard, particle board, pressed wood, or heavy cardboard do not hold up well and are unsatisfactory. Look for a tough, durable, well-applied finish; most cabinets are plasticized for longevity and easy cleaning. Styles with few cracks, indentations, joint lines, or deep patterns in the design are easiest to clean. Construction should be sturdy and solid, with moisture-proof glue, screws, and glue blocks at stress points. Units slapped together with a daub of glue and a handful of staples are not sturdy enough for use in the bathroom. Hardware should be well-machined or cast, nicely finished, properly aligned, and solidly anchored. Mounting strips for wall-hung cabinets or base cabinets that will be secured to the house structure should be rugged and solidly attached to the cabinet body.

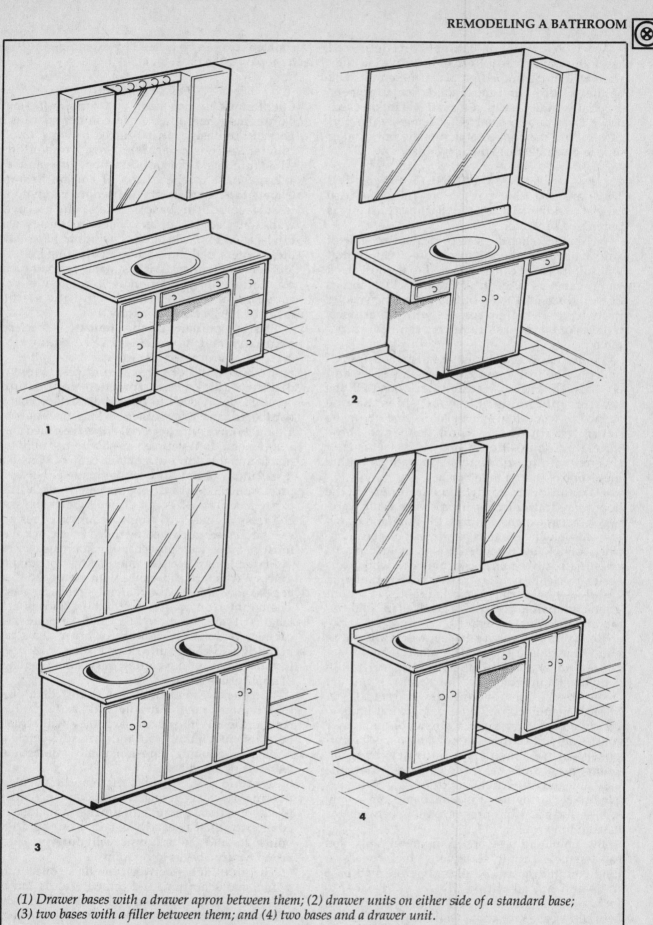

(1) Drawer bases with a drawer apron between them; (2) drawer units on either side of a standard base; (3) two bases with a filler between them; and (4) two bases and a drawer unit.

Most factory-made cabinets are delivered assembled and ready to install; provided they were well made in the first place, these units will be the sturdiest and most solid. Some cabinets, especially vanity bases, are available in knocked-down form to be assembled at home by the purchaser. You may save some money, but it takes time to assemble this kind of cabinet.

VANITY CABINETS

There are two basic parts to a vanity: the base cabinet and the lavatory top. Each part usually is purchased separately.

No matter what the size or decorative style of your bathroom, there is probably a vanity that will suit it or that can be adapted to it. Most stock vanity cabinets range in size from 16 to 20 inches deep and from 24 to 60 inches wide. The smaller units have a single door. As width increases, more doors or banks of drawers can be incorporated.

Vanity bases usually have hardwood frames and plywood or composition-board sides and bottoms. The backs of the units are open to fit the lavatory plumbing. Plywood sides may be stained in wood tones or in colors that allow the natural grain of the wood veneer to show through. Composition-board sides are usually covered with plastic laminate or painted with a tough epoxy or urethane finish.

Oak and other hardwoods are used for the doors and drawer fronts of expensive vanity cabinets. On less expensive units, the door and drawer fronts may be molded plastic that has been finished to look like wood. Although molded plastic does not really equal the richness of wood, it is easier to clean, is more resistant to scratching, and does not warp. Plastic laminates in wood-grain and marble patterns, as well as in solid colors, are also widely used.

Ready-made vanity bases are available in many decorative styles. The most common are contemporary, traditional, French or Italian provincial, and colonial. The various styles are created by the doors and the drawer fronts.

Most manufacturers offer companion units to match stock vanity bases. Companion units may consist only of drawers or contain a special purpose feature, such as a laundry hamper. Companion units have the same depth as the base unit and range in width from 12 to 18 inches. Wood filler strips also are available to join a vanity base and accessory unit or to fill in between the base and the wall.

By combining base and companion units, you can assemble a vanity to fit your precise needs. A long countertop can be placed across two base units and braced with a drawer skirt panel to form a dressing table. A bank of drawers inserted between a base unit and a wall can put otherwise wasted space to use for storage. Additional counter area can be created by extending the vanity top over the toilet tank.

COUNTERTOPS

Countertops are not much of a concern in small bathrooms where little or no counter space is a part of the design. In larger bathrooms ample counter space is a valuable asset. Countertops, while fulfilling a practical function, also can play a large part in the decor of the bathroom. Countertop materials can be used for vanity tops, to surface built-in base cabinets, and to cover wall-hung ledge counters. These materials also can be used for backsplashes, windowsills, shelving, planters, bathtub edging, and seating ledges.

There are four materials suitable for bathroom countertops: plastic laminate, ceramic tile, cultured marble, and Corian, a synthetic marble made by the DuPont Company.

Plastic Laminate. Plastic laminate is the least expensive and most widely used countertop material. Laminated plastic can be applied to many horizontal or vertical surfaces; there are different thicknesses for each application. Laminate is attached to plywood, particle board, hardboard, and a few other backing materials by gluing it down with a special adhesive called contact cement; do-it-yourselfers should use only the nonflammable kind of contact cement. Custom installations of any sort can be made either by a professional or by a do-it-yourselfer with a little experience. The job is not difficult, but some special tools are needed. Angled counter edges are easy to make but curved or rolled edges or coves must be made with post-forming laminate.

Plastic laminate also comes already bonded to a heavy countertop backing with factory-formed edges and with or without an integral backsplash. The countertop comes in standard widths and lengths. It must be cut to fit a vanity or other base cabinet. Washbasins, faucets, or other items can be added to the countertop after it has been installed by carefully cutting or drilling openings of appropriate sizes.

Whether prebonded or custom installed, plastic laminates make durable and easily cleaned countertops. With proper care, they will remain attractive indefinitely, but they are susceptible to scratching, gouging, abrasion, some staining, and extreme localized heat.

Ceramic Tile. All tiles that can be used for flooring or wall covering are suitable for countertop application. Ceramic tile makes a handsome countertop that is easily installed by the do-it-yourselfer and will last practically forever. There are a few drawbacks to ceramic tile.

The grout joints between the tiles collect dirt, grime, and soap film, and cement grouts can be difficult to keep clean and stain easily. Resin and epoxy grouts overcome this problem somewhat, but polyurethane grouts are best.

Ceramic tile is extremely hard, and glass objects dropped on it probably will break. Heavy objects dropped on the tile can crack or break the tile itself. Glazed tile in a bright finish is preferable but highly reflective; matte finish is comfortable on the eyes but more difficult to clean.

Cultured Marble. Cultured marble vanity tops are cast from a mixture of ground marble and epoxy. Cultured marble is cast both in flat sheets and with lavatory basins as part of the unit. These tops are available in single- or double-basin units of standard dimensions from about 20 inches to 5 feet in length and in varying depths. Cultured marble tops can be applied to cabinets of any kind that are the appropriate size. Some manufacturers also offer matching blank sheets of cultured marble for plain countertops.

Although cultured marble is easy to clean, it is susceptible to scratches and abrasion and must be well cared for. Gel-coated surfaces are less durable than acrylic finishes.

Corian. DuPont Corian synthetic marble, available in several sheet sizes and thicknesses, makes an excellent countertop. Since the color and pattern go entirely through the material, scratches or abrasions can be repolished easily. The material also can be custom cut, routed, edged, or even carved.

Other Materials. There are several other materials that can be used for countertops. Wood, such as veneer plywood, glued-up solid planks, or butcher block, is one alternative. Wood countertops should have smooth surfaces with no open cracks or joints, and should be finished with several coats of a tough, waterproof finish, such as polyurethane. Another possibility, using wood or other material as a base, is to pour a thick surface layer of casting resin. This material is hard, glossy, and practically indestructible. It can be used to cover decoupage and collage materials, or to embed seashells, wildflowers, leaves, or anything else that might provide a decorative design.

Sheet vinyl flooring also makes a good countertop material. It is easily cut, fitted, and glued down with mastic adhesive, and the counter edges can be trimmed with metal edging strips, wood strips, or ceramic bullnose tile. The surface is tough, durable, easily cleaned, inexpensive, and readily replaceable. For unusual treatments, marble, soapstone, polished granite or slate, plate glass over a shadow or diorama box-shelf, or a glass-topped aquarium or terrarium arrangement are further possibilities.

HOW TO INSTALL A VANITY BASE CABINET

A vanity base cabinet must be firmly attached to the wall, and the top must be level. If the floor is not level, place shims under the cabinet so that it rests plumb against the wall. Any high spots in the wall must be scraped or sanded smooth for

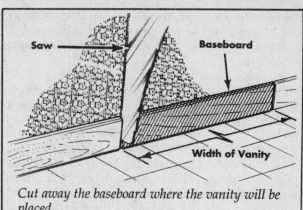

Cut away the baseboard where the vanity will be placed.

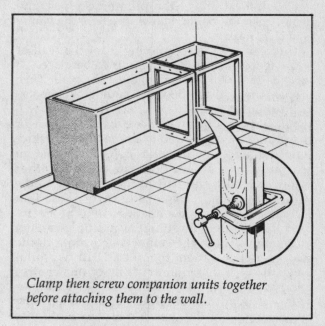

Clamp then screw companion units together before attaching them to the wall.

Shim the base of the cabinet to level it.

the countertop to fit flush. For proper drainage and to ensure that the drawers and doors will operate smoothly, take care to install the base unit correctly.

If your bathroom is small, consider putting off the vanity installation until the painting, wallpapering, and installation of floor covering have been completed. You'll eliminate the problem of having to work around the vanity.

To install a vanity cabinet, you'll need the following tools and materials: pencil, saw, carpenter's level, drill and bits, screwdriver, 2 1/2-inch Number 10 wood screws, toggle or Molly bolts, two clamps, and wood shingles for shims. Be sure you have everything you need before you start.

Check locations of the plumbing pipes, and draw a plan on paper, showing where the vanity is to be placed.

Cut away the base molding from the wall or walls against which the vanity is to be placed so that the unit will fit flush against the wall. Then prepare the wall and floor by sanding high spots.

Locate the wall studs where the vanity will stand, and mark them. Remove the vanity base or bases from the boxes and examine them for shipping damage. If your plan calls for a custom assembly, you should join the parts together before attaching any part of the assembly to the wall. Long double lavatory units or those that include a dressing table might have to be assembled inside the bathroom. On multiple-cabinet installations, align the cabinets according to the plan and clamp them together. Drill two pilot holes through the adjoining stile of one cabinet and partially into the stile of the other for two screws, one in the upper quarter and one in the lower quarter of the unit. Move the vanity into the bathroom and put it into position according to your plan. Place wooden shims under or behind the cabinet to level it. This will be easier if you have someone hold the cabinet level and plumb as you place the shims.

Drill a 1/8-inch hole through the top rail in the back of the cabinet and into the wall at each marked stud location. Place the Number 10 wood screws into the pilot holes and tighten them until they start to pull the cabinet against the wall. Before tightening them all the way, recheck the vanity; if it's level and plumb, secure everything in place. Two screws (or bolts) per unit are necessary. If there aren't enough studs behind the vanity, drill a 1/4-inch hole in the wall at the side without a stud behind it. Fasten this side of the cabinet with a Molly bolt.

HOW TO INSTALL A COUNTERTOP

A custom countertop is not difficult to construct from 3/4-inch plywood or particle board, and plastic laminate or ceramic tile. The plywood or particle board is used for the core onto which the laminate or tile is glued.

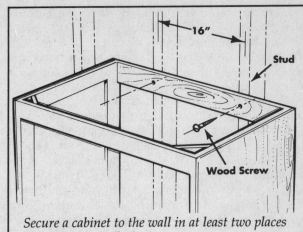

Secure a cabinet to the wall in at least two places along the rear rail.

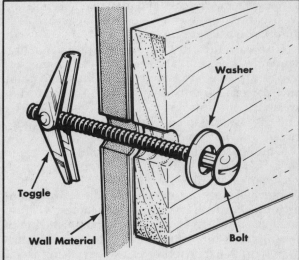

Use a toggle bolt to secure the vanity to the wall if there is no stud.

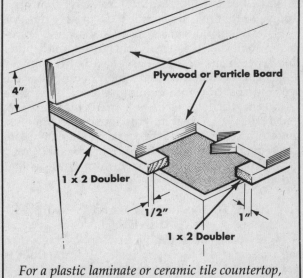

For a plastic laminate or ceramic tile countertop, first construct a plywood or particle board core.

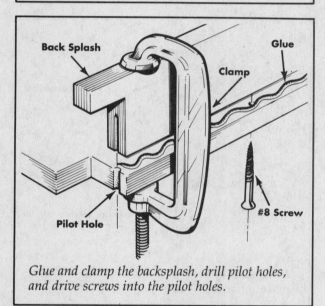

Attach doubler strips under edges of the top with nails and glue.

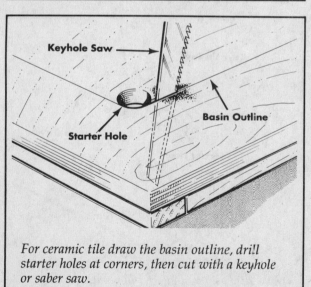

Glue and clamp the backsplash, drill pilot holes, and drive screws into the pilot holes.

For ceramic tile draw the basin outline, drill starter holes at corners, then cut with a keyhole or saber saw.

The first step is to plan your countertop carefully and prepare an accurate drawing. The dimensions for the top should be 1 inch larger in both length and width than the base. This will give your top a 1/2-inch overhang on both sides of the base cabinet, and when the cabinet is fitted flush to the wall, a 1-inch overhang in front. A 4-inch-high backsplash should be planned to run against the wall if you are using plastic laminate. If you are using ceramic tile, the height of the backsplash should be the height of one tile.

If the vanity is in a corner, add only an extra 1/2 inch to the width and plan a backsplash for the side, so that the top will fit flush against both walls. A recessed installation with walls at both ends calls for a wraparound backsplash and no overlap on the sides.

A 3/4-by-1 1/2-inch doubling strip should be installed around the entire underside of the top to increase the edge thickness to 1 1/2 inches. Strips of the core material or inexpensive 1 x 2 stock can be used for this doubler. After you have completed your plan, you can determine how much core material to purchase.

To construct the countertop core, you'll need the following tools and materials: pencil, tape measure, straightedge, screwdriver, hammer, drill and bits, keyhole or saber saw, sanding block and sandpaper, hard-setting wood filler, white glue, 2 1/4-inch Number 8 flat-head screws, and 2d box nails.

Cut the core material to size, including the backsplash and doubler strips. Using white glue and 2d box nails, attach the doubling strips under the edges of the top. Space the nails about 6 inches apart.

After the glue has set, use wood filler to fill any voids in the edges of the counter and backsplash. When the filler has dried completely, sand the edges smooth. This is especially important if you plan to use a router to trim the plastic laminate. Unless the edges are smooth, the cutter will give a rough cut.

Drill 1/8-inch pilot holes for attaching the backsplash to the countertop. To do this, position the bottom edge of the backsplash on the back of the countertop, flush with the edge. Clamp the backsplash to the countertop so it cannot shift position. Drill pilot holes from the underside of the countertop. Drill holes 2 inches from either end and space the remaining holes about 6 inches apart. Use at least five screws per backsplash.

If you plan to cover the top with ceramic tile, attach the backsplash to the top piece with Number 8 flat-head screws. Apply a bead of white glue along the backsplash and countertop joint, tightening it in place with screws through the pilot holes. If you're going to cover the counter with plastic laminate, set the backsplash aside for now; the backsplash will be attached after the laminate has been applied.

If you are going to apply ceramic tile, carefully lay out the opening for the lavatory basin at this time. (If you are going to use plastic laminate, the lavatory cutout will be made after the laminate has been glued down.) Most lavatory manufacturers give you a template for the basin opening, but you can use the basin itself. Use a pencil to outline the opening for the basin. Bore a starting hole in each corner of the outline if the pattern is for a rectangular lavatory basin. You'll need only one starting hole if the basin is round or oval. Be careful to bore the holes inside the outline. Use a keyhole saw or a saber saw and cut along the outline. Remove the center and sand split edges smooth.

Check for imperfections. Test fit the countertop to the base and check the fit of the backsplash against the wall. It's easy to adjust the fit now before the tile or the plastic laminate is applied. When you're satisfied, you can begin to start laminating.

Applying Plastic Laminate. To apply plastic laminate, you'll need all the tools you used in constructing the core, as well as the following tools and materials: block of wood, hacksaw (or metal-cutting blade for a saber saw), safety glasses, small block plane, fine file, inexpensive paintbrush, contact cement, several 1/2-inch dowels, caulking compound, and a rolling pin. The following additional power tools and special-purpose tools will make the job go faster and produce professional results: saber saw, sander, router with a carbide bit designed to trim laminate, and a J roller. After you've completed the countertop, you'll need a cartridge caulking gun and a tube of mastic to attach the top to the vanity base. To apply the plastic laminate to the core, follow this procedure:

Using a hacksaw or a saber saw equipped with a metal-cutting blade, cut oversize strips of laminate for the countertop edges and the top edge of the backsplash. Allow at least a 1/8-inch overlap on all sides. If you cut the laminate with a saber saw, keep the laminate face down and well supported as you cut it. A hacksaw cuts best with the material face up.

Use a brush to apply an even coat of contact cement to the back of the strips of laminate and to the edges of the countertop. Allow the cement to set according to the manufacturer's directions.

Start on one side of the countertop and carefully apply the laminate to the edge. Make the first contact at the center of the strip for better control. Work carefully, because contact cement will adhere instantly; you will not be able to slide the laminate once the two adhesive surfaces have made contact. Work your way around the countertop, applying the laminate first to a side, then to the front, and finally to the remaining side if there is one. Do the same with all exposed edges of the backsplash.

Apply contact cement to both surfaces, allow them to dry, then press laminate in place.

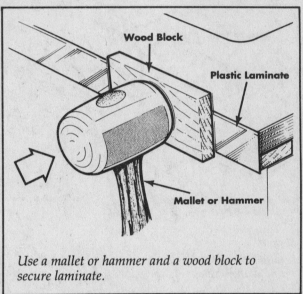

Use a mallet or hammer and a wood block to secure laminate.

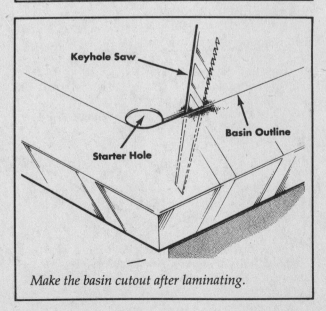

Make the basin cutout after laminating.

As you finish each side, apply pressure using a hammer and wood block. Heavy blows are not necessary; use a tapping motion and slide the block along the edge for even and complete distribution of pressure. Using a block plane or a router with a carbide cutter, trim the overhang. Use a fine file to smooth and bevel the joints on the corners. Remove any excess cement by using a scrap piece of laminate as a scraper.

Carefully measure the countertop and backsplash. The countertop laminate must overlap the side edge pieces, so make sure you allow for an overhang of at least 1/8 inch. Mark the laminate and cut it as before. When you've finished cutting, test the laminate for fit.

Apply an even coat of contact cement both to the countertop and to the back of the laminate and let it set as before. After the cement has set, lay the dowels across the surface of the underlayment. Place the sheet of laminate in position on top of the dowels. Slide the dowels from between the two pieces, pressing the laminate in place as you do so. When the cemented surfaces are in full contact, use a hammer and wood block or a roller to apply pressure over the entire surface. Give special attention to the edges; they must bond tightly. Apply laminate to the face of the backsplash in the same manner.

Use a block plane or router to trim the laminate. Hold the plane at a slight angle to avoid scuffing the laminate on the edges of the assembly. Use a fine file to smooth and bevel the joints. The router has a special bevel cutter for this, but test it for proper adjustment before using it on a conspicuous place on the vanity top.

Using the template or lavatory basin as a pattern, mark the location of the cutout on the countertop. Double check its position for drawer clearance inside the vanity base.

At the corners of the cutout, use a nail or punch to make a dent in the laminate, so that when you drill the starter holes for sawing, the drill will not skid. Bore a hole in each corner if the basin is square; make one hole on the perimeter if the basin is round. Drill the holes inside the outline. Carefully cut along the outline with a keyhole or saber saw, and smooth the rough edges with a file.

Turn the vanity countertop over and drill through the laminate for the backsplash screws. The holes are already there; all you have to drill through is the laminate, so use very little pressure.

Apply a generous bead of caulk between the bottom of the backsplash and countertop, and fasten, using 2 1/4-inch Number 8 flat-head screws. Immediately clean up the excess caulk with water and a rag.

Set the top onto the base and use a carpenter's level to make sure it does not slant from side to side and from front to back. Remove the top and apply a bead of mastic along the top edges of the base. Position the top on the base and press it in place. If leveling is necessary, use wooden shims between the top and the edge of the base, setting them in place with mastic.

How to Apply Ceramic Tile. This project is more involved than laminating plastic because you're dealing with many pieces of tile that must fit together to form the top. The extra effort can be well worth it, because you'll have a beautiful, long-lasting vanity top.

Planning is half the job. You'll need face tiles for the front edge of the counter; if they're not available, they can be cut from full tiles. Bullnose tiles, or tiles with a rounded leading edge, are then placed along the top edge as a starter row to give the edge a finished appearance. Then the regular field of tiles is laid with the last row cut to fit against the backsplash. Tiles are then set on the backsplash to hide the rough-cut edges of the last countertop row. Bullnose tiles are then cut to cap off the top of the backsplash.

Keeping this general scheme in mind, prepare a plan that you can follow for laying the tile. Here is a list of tools and supplies you'll need besides those you used for making the core top: saber saw with carbide blade, carpenter's level, epoxy or organic tile adhesive, grout, silicone sealer, caulking compound, wood shims, rubber grout trowel, notched trowel, and an old toothbrush or paint stick. You'll also need a tile cutter and tile nippers, which you can rent from a tile supplier.

Install the countertop core on the vanity and make sure it's level. Lay out a test area of tiles. Most tiles have small tabs attached to their sides for proper grout spacing, but if they don't, you'll have to decide the width of the grout line—about 1/16 inch wide usually looks best and is easy to keep clean. When you're satisfied that your plan will work, use a notched trowel to spread an even coat of adhesive over as much of the counter as you can cover with tile in the suggested time given by the manufacturer of the adhesive.

Lay in the tile starting at the front edge. Set a bullnose and face tile together and fill in behind with field tiles. Press them in place; don't slide them. Sliding the tiles will force the glue from under the tile and up through the grout lines. If necessary, insert a finishing nail between the tiles to maintain even spacing as you lay them. Cut the tiles to fit in the last row against the backsplash and continue up the backsplash. Finish by cutting bullnose tiles to cap off the backsplash.

Don't worry about the lavatory basin cutout. Place the tile to overhang the edge of the opening. After the glue has set, they can be trimmed off with a saber saw equipped with a carbide blade, thus avoiding the tiresome task of nipping and cutting each tile. When you're finished, clean off the excess glue and let the installation dry overnight.

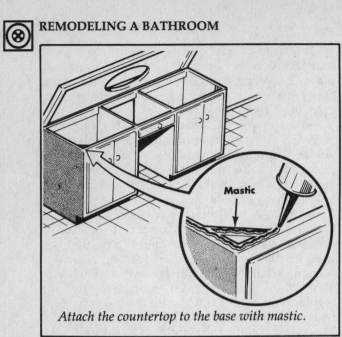

Attach the countertop to the base with mastic.

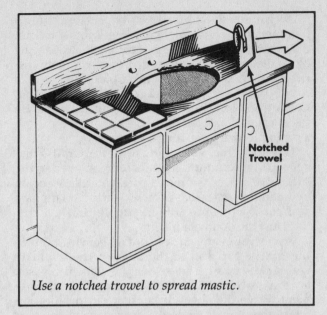

Use a notched trowel to spread mastic.

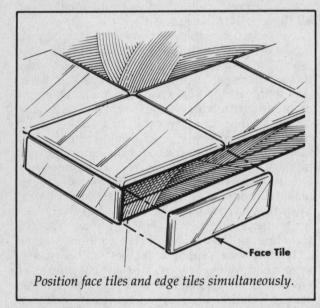

Position face tiles and edge tiles simultaneously.

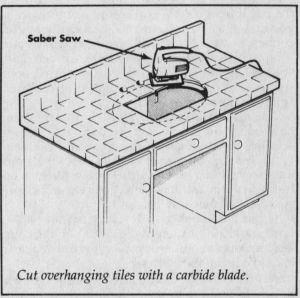

Cut overhanging tiles with a carbide blade.

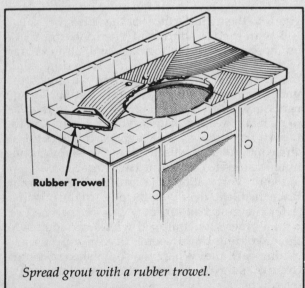

Spread grout with a rubber trowel.

Remove dried grout film with a soft rag.

Use a carbide blade in a saber saw to cut the overhanging tiles of the basin cutout. Move slowly with light pressure; don't force the blade.

Apply the grout according to the manufacturer's directions, using a rubber trowel to force it between tiles. Use the end of a toothbrush or a thin piece of wood, such as a paint stick, to force the grout deep into the grooves.

When the grout is completely dry, a light polishing with a rag will remove the light film of grout left on the tiles. Seal the grout with a silicone sealer to prevent dirt from discoloring it.

How to Install a Corian Vanity Top. Corian, a synthetic marble manufactured by the DuPont Company, may be worked like wood using power tools equipped with carbide-tipped blades. Planning and construction methods are the same as for a wooden-core countertop. Corian synthetic marble is available in sheets 25 or 30 inches wide and up to 145 inches long. A 25-by-98-inch sheet is the smallest available.

The first step is to measure the base cabinet accurately. Plan for the countertop to overhang the base by 1/2 inch on each side and by 1 inch along the front. If neither side of the cabinet is to be placed against a wall, the length of the counter should be 1 inch greater than the width of the base. If one side of the cabinet is to be against a wall, the length of the counter should be 1/2 inch greater than the width of the cabinet. If the cabinet is to be enclosed by walls on all three sides, the length of the top must be the same as the width of the base.

Plan for a backsplash along the wall or walls against which the vanity is placed. The backsplash should be about 4 inches high, although the actual height can be varied to make the most economical use of material.

Plan to cut the Corian sheet crosswise, to length, first. Then trim it lengthwise, to width. The lengthwise cutoff can be used for the backsplash. The side backsplash, if needed, can be cut to the same height from leftover stock.

Before you start, assemble the following tools: pencil, tape measure, straightedge, electric drill and bits, circular and saber saws with carbide blades, 400-grit sandpaper and sanding block, router and carbide-tipped bits, caulk, and neoprene adhesive. Follow these steps:

Accurately lay out the dimensions on the sheet of Corian material. Using the circular saw and a sharp carbide blade, cut the top to length first. Corian is heavy and always must be solidly supported. Then trim for width by cutting off the long section that will be used for the backsplash.

Smooth the cut edges with sandpaper. A fancy edge can be cut using a router equipped with a carbide bit. Apply a bead of sealing caulk along the top edge of the base cabinet and set the Corian top in place. Outline the opening for the lavatory basin using the template provided by the

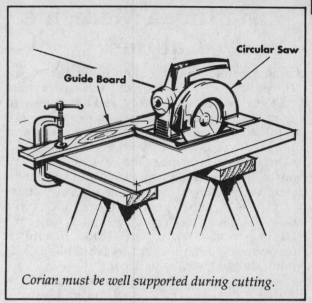

Corian must be well supported during cutting.

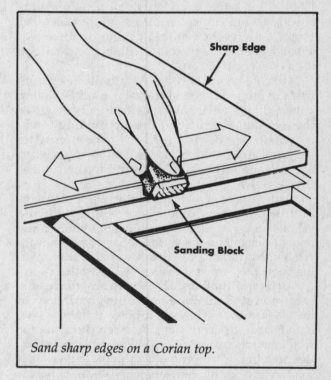

Sand sharp edges on a Corian top.

manufacturer or use the basin as a pattern. Check to be sure that the basin will be properly located in relation to the plumbing hookup.

Bore a hole just inside each corner of the basin outline if the lavatory is rectangular; if the lavatory is round, drill one hole just inside the perimeter of the outline. Using a saber saw with a carbide-edged blade, cut out the basin opening along the outline.

Install the backsplash by applying a bead of neoprene glue along the bottom of the backsplash. Press the backsplash in place by caulking the small gaps between the wall and the backsplash, and wipe off any excess glue and caulk.

Installing a Medicine Cabinet

Storage space is at a premium in the bathroom. Although most of the floor and wall space must be allotted to the tub, lavatory, and toilet, creative use of shelving and medicine cabinets can make useful storage out of hard-to-reach corners and put space over toilets and lavatories to good use.

Installing a new medicine cabinet is an easy way to increase the storage capacity of your bathroom. Wall-mounted units come in many attractive styles and shapes. Different looks are achieved by varying the mirror frames. Any style ranging from deeply carved and ornate to streamlined contemporary is available to suit your taste and match your decor.

Single medicine cabinet units are available to fit above a small vanity or wall-hung lavatory. Double and triple units provide maximum storage space and can cover up unsightly walls that might be left when an old cabinet is removed. Corner cabinets are also available and can be used over the toilet.

Multiple cabinets come with built-in mirrors that are hung on hinged doors or used as sliding panels. Triple units have the added advantage of the two outside mirror panels providing three-dimensional viewing for easy grooming. The swing of most cabinet doors can be adjusted to open to the right or left by turning the cabinet upside down.

Many medicine cabinets come equipped with built-in lighting. Some custom-built medicine cabinets are recessed into the wall. Others come ready to install on the surface of any smooth wall. A few screws hold them securely in place, making these medicine cabinets easy to install.

Surface-Mounted Cabinets. Ready-made surface-mounted cabinets are quick and easy to install. Removal of the old cabinet, if there is one, is the hardest part of the job. When shopping for a cabinet, choose one that will completely cover the opening left by the old cabinet. If there is a light over or in the old cabinet, you can choose a style with a built-in light or select a new matching fixture.

Before you begin, gather the following tools and supplies: pencil, hammer, screwdriver, level, drill and bits, tape measure, and wall anchors (not necessary if you use existing wall studs). If you plan to install a light in the cabinet, the following tools also will be needed: small pry bar, wire cutters, pliers, and wire nuts (if not supplied with the cabinet). After you've read the installation instructions supplied by the manufacturer and have everything on hand, follow these general directions:

Turn off the electricity by tripping the main circuit breaker or removing the proper fuse. This is necessary only if a light is close to or part of the old cabinet. Remove the old cabinet. If it's a metal unit, it will come out in one piece. Remove the hold-down screws in the back or sides of the cabinet and force the pry bar under the front flange. If the cabinet is made of wood, remove the door and dismantle it, starting with the trim moldings.

Disconnect any electrical wires leading to the old cabinet, and remove the cabinet. Lay out the location of the hanging fasteners for the new cabinet according to the manufacturer's specifications, and drill small pilot holes where these mounting screws will go. If you feel resistance as you drill into the wall, you're on a stud and a screw will hold; but if there is resistance for only an inch or so, you'll need a Molly bolt, toggle bolt, or plastic wall anchor.

Secure the top two fasteners and hang the cabinet on them. Make sure the cabinet is correctly centered and level; then mark the location of the two bottom fasteners using the cabinet as a guide. Remove the cabinet and drill pilot holes for the bottom fasteners and install wall anchors, if needed. If your cabinet is equipped with a light fixture, carefully read the wiring instructions. Two or three wires usually are all that have to be connected. The cabinet back is equipped with knock-out holes close to where the wires should enter the fixture. Remove the most convenient knock-out by prying it open and twisting it off with pliers. Attach the end of the armored cable to this opening and fasten it securely in place with a cable connector.

Attach the same color wires together. Take the two black wires and remove about 1/2 inch of insulation from the ends; grip the bare ends with the pliers and twist the ends of two wires tightly together. When they are completely twisted, turn on a wire nut and tighten. Do the same for the white wires. If you're using a nonmetallic cable, attach the green ground wires in the same way.

Push the wires carefully into the enclosure and put the cover on. Install the cabinet on the wall. Tighten the top mounting screws; then tighten the bottom screws. Install the light bulbs and trim, put in the shelves, and turn on the electricity.

Recessed Cabinets. Space can be saved by recessing the medicine cabinet into the wall. It's easiest if you remove the old cabinet and install a new one that is the same size in the recess. If you want a larger cabinet or there was no recessed cabinet, you'll have to enlarge or cut a hole. Use the instructions that apply to your situation.

Before you begin, the following tools and supplies are necessary: pencil, tape measure, hammer, screwdriver, keyhole saw, saber saw, level, extension cord, drill and bits, putty knife, patching plaster, wallboard tape, wallboard taping compound, Number 8 nails, 2 x 4s, 1/2-inch wallboard, wire cutter, pliers, and wire nuts.

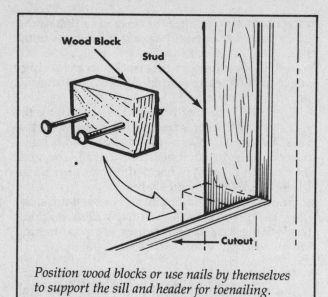

Position wood blocks or use nails by themselves to support the sill and header for toenailing.

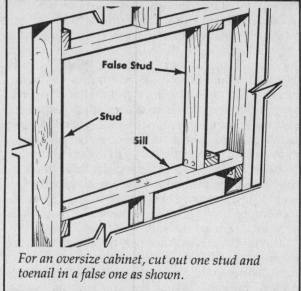

For an oversize cabinet, cut out one stud and toenail in a false one as shown.

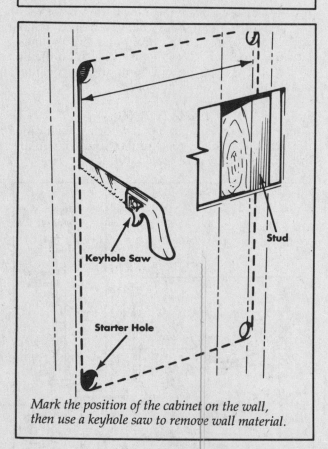

Mark the position of the cabinet on the wall, then use a keyhole saw to remove wall material.

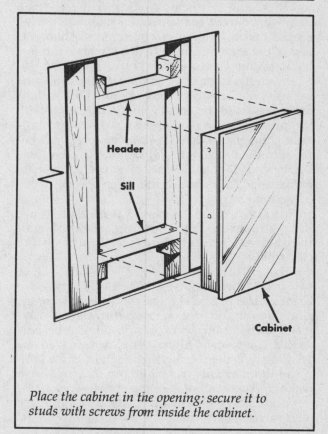

Place the cabinet in the opening; secure it to studs with screws from inside the cabinet.

Turn off the electricity to the bathroom. Remove the old cabinet. Lay out the dimensions of the new cabinet on the wall. You must cut away the plaster and studs in this area and install a 2 x 4 sill and header to frame the cabinet. Using a keyhole saw or saber saw, cut the wall opening along the outline. Go slowly and watch for electrical or plumbing lines. Then remove the plaster. The 2 x 4 header and sill pieces have to be nailed into a stud, so you'll probably need to widen the opening to the next full stud on each side. Cut two 2 x 4s to fit the top and bottom opening and toenail them into place by driving Number 8 common nails at 45-degree angles through the base of the 2 x 4 into the stud. To hold the 2 x 4 pieces in place while nailing, drive two nails into the vertical wall studs on both sides about 1 1/2 inches below where you want the sill and 1 1/2 inches above the header. Be sure the nails are level across.

Cut two 2 x 4s to fit vertically between the header and sill and toenail them in place to frame the opening for the cabinet. Then cut pieces of wallboard to surround the opening. Shim out and nail these flush with the existing wall and patch the cracks between the wallboard and the plaster with patching plaster. When the plaster is dry, sand the joint smooth. If the wall is wallboard, apply a coat of joint compound and then drywall tape. After the tape is in place, apply a thin second coat and let it dry. Apply a top coat, feathering the edges 3 or 4 inches on each side of the tape and let it dry; sand the surface smooth.

Paint the wall and patch area, and when it's dry, install the cabinet in the recess. Place the cabinet in position and check that it's level. Mark the location of the placement screws and remove the cabinet and drill pilot holes for these screws.

If your cabinet is equipped with a light fixture, carefully read the wiring instructions. Two or three wires usually are all that have to be connected. The cabinet back has knockout holes close to where the wires should enter the fixture. Remove the most convenient knockout by prying it open and twisting it off with pliers. Attach the end of the armored cable to this opening and fasten it securely in place with a cable connector.

Attach the same color wires together. Take the two black wires and remove about 1/2 inch of insulation from the ends; grip the bare ends with the pliers and twist the ends of the two wires tightly together. When they are completely twisted, turn on a wire nut and tighten. Do the same for the ends of the white wires. If you are using a nonmetallic cable, attach the green ground wires in the same way.

Install the cabinet into the wall, and secure it by tightening the mounting screws. Install the shelves and light bulbs, and turn on the electricity.

ADDITIONAL STORAGE

Creative use of shelving can solve some storage problems found in a small bathroom. Ready-made shelving that is easy to install can be purchased wherever hardware products are sold. By painting or wallpapering construction-grade lumber to complement your bathroom decor, you can make custom-made shelves inexpensively.

Locate the shelves in the "dead" wall space next to vanities, over toilets, and behind doors. These areas are out of the way and will not obstruct movement.

Added storage may be created by making a shelving unit to fit the space between the vanity and the toilet. By extending this unit to the ceiling, you receive increased privacy for the toilet area.

Narrow shelves also can be mounted on the backs of doors. This shelving will allow storage of cleaning equipment, soaps, and shampoos. The backs of vanity cabinet doors and linen cabinet doors are naturals for this kind of shelving. Don't forget to provide a lip for the shelves; otherwise, every time you open the door, the contents of the shelves will spill out.

Recessed shelving offers the same storage space as surface-mounted shelves, but doesn't project into the room.

The "wet" wall of most baths containing the soil stack is thicker than the standard wall. Use this added depth to advantage and plan a recessed shelving unit against the wall. The soffit over a bath or shower enclosure is another possible location for recessed shelving.

The wall has to be cut away between the studs for this type of shelving to be installed, so check that wiring or plumbing does not pass behind where you plan to cut.

Installing Fixtures

If you're installing a brand-new bathroom or relocating fixtures in an older one, you'll need to hire a plumber to "rough in" drain and supply lines. Hooking up the fixtures themselves isn't difficult, so if you're replacing old components consider installing the fixtures yourself.

LAVATORIES

There are many shapes for lavatories, including round, oval, square, rectangular, and triangular. But there are only three basic styles.

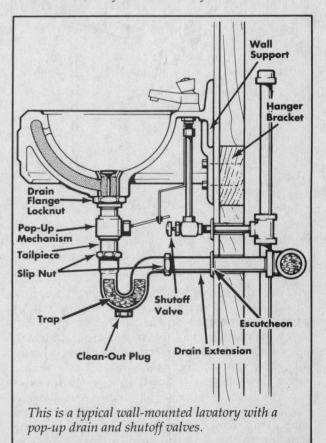

This is a typical wall-mounted lavatory with a pop-up drain and shutoff valves.

Wall-Hung Basin. A wall-hung basin is a complete unit that includes provisions for faucets, designed to be mounted directly to a structural member embedded in the wall frame. Some of these hang free, while others have added front support legs.

Pedestal Basin. A pedestal basin consists of a washbowl and faucets mounted on top of a free-standing column. It also can include a small countertop attached to the basin.

Countertop Basin. Countertop basins consist of only the basin, with or without faucets, and sometimes a separate rim and special mounting hardware. They can be inset singly or multiply in countertops.

Countertop basins are offered in many varieties and are divided into four groups.

•The surface-mounted, or self-rimming, basin has an integral lip that overlaps the countertop when the basin is lowered into position from above. The integral rim provides the basin seal and bears the entire weight of the basin against the countertop.

•The flush-mounted basin is recessed into the countertop, and a separate metal rim is fitted around the basin and against the countertop. The rim provides the seal, and special hardware locks the basin and rim in place beneath the countertop for support.

•The recessed basin is installed from beneath the countertop, flush against the underside with the edge of the countertop overlapping the basin by a small amount.

•The integral basin is molded in one piece with a countertop and is available in single- or double-basin styles in various countertop widths and lengths. The countertop may be installed upon vanities or built-in cabinets, or mounted on the wall like a shelf.

The plumbing usually is hidden in countertop basin installations, but is readily accessible. Pedestal lavatories also hide the plumbing, but the connections are much less accessible and trap removal is difficult. The plumbing is exposed to view in wall-hung lavatories and has to be kept clean and polished. Installation of countertop lavatories is not difficult; the integral and self-rimming kinds are easiest. Pedestal basins are also simple to install. Wall-hung basins are easy to put in if the wall support members exist, but they are problematic if new supports must be built into the wall.

HOW TO INSTALL A WALL-MOUNTED LAVATORY

A wall-mounted lavatory is supported by a metal hanger that is anchored by screws to a wood support in the wall. Although the lavatory may have metal legs at the front corners, these legs provide only additional support and do not carry the entire weight of the fixture. If you are replacing an old lavatory with the same style, the existing hanger bracket will serve. If your new lavatory is of a different style, you may need a bracket specifically designed for it. When you buy the new fixture, ask the dealer if you will need a new mounting bracket.

To remove the old lavatory and install a new one, follow this general procedure: Shut off the water supply. If there are no shutoff valves at the fixture, turn off the main shutoff valve. Place a bucket under the lavatory's trap and unscrew the clean-out plug if the trap has one. The water in the trap will pour into the bucket. If the trap does not have a plug, proceed carefully with the next step. Loosen the two slip nuts that hold the trap in place. If you intend to reuse these fittings, wrap tape around them and use a smooth-jawed adjustable wrench to remove them; a pipe wrench will damage their surfaces. When the nuts have been loosened, pull down on the trap to free it. If the trap has no drain plug, remove the trap carefully and empty the water in the trap into the bucket.

Use a basin wrench to loosen the supply-line coupling nuts from the faucet studs, or shanks, if you cannot reach the nuts with another type of wrench. If the nuts are too rusted or corroded to turn, use a hacksaw to cut the supply pipes. With an adjustable wrench, loosen the nuts that couple the fixture supply pipes to the shutoff valves or to the wall supply pipes. Then, remove the fixture supply pipes.

When all supply and drain lines are disconnected, lift the lavatory straight up from the mounting bracket and place it on the floor, face down, on a rug or other padding.

You can now remove the nuts that hold the faucets in place and remove the faucet assembly. Be sure to keep the washers. (If you are also replacing the faucets, there is no need to remove the old ones.) Disconnect the pop-up drain linkage, if present. Then loosen the slip nut that holds the drain flange and the tailpiece of the drainpipe in place and remove both.

Now install your new wall-mounted lavatory. If necessary, remove the old hanger bracket from the wall and attach a new bracket to the wall. If you need to install shutoff valves, do so.

Place the new lavatory on the floor on its side on top of the padding to avoid damaging it. Apply plumber's putty (or the gasket supplied with a new faucet and spout assembly) around the base of the faucet and spout assembly, and put it in place. On the underside of the lavatory, screw the retaining nuts onto the faucet shanks. Install the drain flange and tailpiece. Tighten all nuts with a wrench. Attach the pop-up drain linkage. Connect the supply line sections to the faucet shanks and tighten their coupling nuts with a wrench.

Lift the lavatory and slide it straight down over the mounting bracket. Connect the supply lines to the stop valves or wall supply pipes. Then install the trap. Turn on the water supply and check all connections for leaks.

HOW TO INSTALL A COUNTERTOP LAVATORY

Countertop lavatories may be surface-mounted or frame-mounted. Both have identical plumbing hookups. A surface-mounted lavatory supports itself by a lip around the edge of the basin. To remove such a fixture, disconnect all the plumbing lines. Use a thin knife to break the seal around the lip, and then lift out the lavatory. To install a surface-mounted lavatory, obtain the proper mounting sealant from your plumbing supply dealer, apply it liberally under the lip of the lavatory, then lower the lavatory gently into place. Do not press it down tightly. Using a damp cloth, immediately wipe up any sealant that squeezes out from under the lip. The plumbing lines may be reconnected after the sealant has cured for about four hours.

A frame-mounted lavatory is held in place by clips and a metal frame that circles the edge of the lavatory. During removal and installation of a frame-mounted lavatory, take care that it does not fall through the opening in the countertop. To replace a frame-mounted lavatory, remove the trap and disconnect the faucets, then follow this procedure:

Drop a loop of lightweight rope, such as clothesline rope, through the lavatory's drain hole. Insert a length of wood through the top end of the loop so that the ends of the wooden piece rest on the countertop. Insert a small wood block through the bottom end of the loop and twist the block until it is wedged tightly against the bottom of the drain tailpiece. This arrangement will hold the lavatory in place as you remove the supporting clips.

Unscrew the bolts that hold the supporting clips in place under the lavatory and remove the clips. As you support the lavatory from below with one hand, turn the wood block with the other hand to untwist the rope. When the rope is loose enough, remove the block and let it drop. Then lower and remove the lavatory.

If you plan to use the lavatory's faucet and spout assembly again, use a pair of pliers or a wrench to loosen the retaining nuts on the faucet shanks. Remove the nuts and lift off the assembly. Then insert a thin knife blade between the edge of the metal support rim and the countertop to break the putty seal, and remove the rim.

You may install shutoff valves for the fixture at this time. Then install the faucet and spout assembly on the new lavatory. Apply plumber's putty or a gasket to the base of the faucet and spout assembly, and press the assembly into place. Screw the retaining nuts onto the faucet

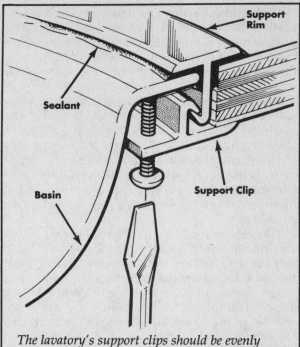

The lavatory's support clips should be evenly spaced around the perimeter of the lavatory. The bolts should then be turned down firmly.

shanks and tighten them with a wrench. Attach the water supply pipes to the faucet shanks, install the drain flange and drain tailpiece, and connect the pop-up drain linkage.

Then put a continuous bead of plumber's putty around the inside and outside lips of the mounting rim. Position the rim on the edge of the hole in the counter and press the rim firmly in place. Use a damp cloth to wipe away any excess putty.

Use the rope-and-block technique to support the new lavatory. Put the mounting clips in place, spacing them evenly around the perimeter of the lavatory, and turn the bolts firmly. Remove the rope-and-block support apparatus.

Connect the water supply lines to the shutoff valves and replace the trap assembly. Then restore the water supply.

LAVATORY FAUCETS AND CONTROLS

Lavatory faucet sets are available in two basic designs: two valves and a separate spout, all individually mounted; or the three elements as a single-piece unit. In either case, the pop-up drain control is at the back of the spout.

Mounting arrangements follow standard dimensions, so that most faucet assemblies will fit most lavatories. The assembly can be mounted directly upon the fixture in holes provided or deck-mounted upon the countertop; a few models are designed for mounting on the wall behind the basin.

Most faucet assemblies are made of a metal alloy. Solid brass is best because it is the most durable and the least subject to corrosion. The inner workings of a faucet, the valve assembly itself, can be either compression or noncompression. Compression faucets are mounted in pairs; one faucet for the hot water and another for the cold. When you turn down the handle of a compression faucet, a shaft in the faucet housing presses a washer over the water inlet, cutting off the water supply. Turning the faucet in the other direction lifts the washer and allows water to pass through the valve and to flow on to the spout. The trouble with compression faucets is that they drip. The washer wears out or the seat upon which the washer presses becomes worn, allowing water to seep between the washer and the seat. Although replacing a washer is neither complicated nor difficult, it is a nuisance to be expected with a compression faucet.

In a noncompression faucet, also called a washerless mixer or single-handle faucet, the water flow is controlled by a sliding gatelike mechanism inside the faucet housing. This is a more reliable valve design than the compression valve. There are several ways in which noncompression valve assemblies are made, but the kind in which the valve is enclosed in a replaceable cartridge is the most trouble free.

BATHTUBS

Bathtubs are made in many sizes, shapes, styles, and colors. Some bathtubs are custom made, or a bathtub installation is custom designed to fit particular requirements.

Bathtubs are usually made of cast iron, stamped steel, or fiberglass-reinforced plastic. Cast-iron and stamped-steel tubs have enamel finishes. The enamel coating used on cast iron is thicker than that used on steel. Cast iron is far more rigid than stamped steel, making the finish on a cast-iron tub more resistant to cracking and chipping. Cast iron also retains heat longer than steel. Most cast-iron tubs weigh between 300 and 500 pounds, while most steel tubs weigh between 125 and 250 pounds. A cast-iron tub costs more than a steel one. If you're remodeling on a tight budget, a steel tub is worth considering, both for its lower initial cost and because its lighter weight makes it more amenable to do-it-yourself installation.

Fiberglass tubs are lighter in weight than either cast-iron or steel tubs, which can be a deciding factor when choosing a tub for do-it-yourself installation. Fiberglass tubs are more expensive than steel tubs, but they are not as costly as cast-iron tubs. The major drawback to a fiberglass tub is that its surface is not as durable as the enamel finish of either a cast-iron or steel tub; the surface scratches easily. A damaged enamel-coated tub can be reglazed, but a damaged fiberglass tub cannot.

Almost all modern tubs are designed to be built in. Most are manufactured with a skirt along the long side that faces into the room. Tubs made for installation in a corner are skirted both on a side and on one end.

Standard bathtub size is 29 to 32 inches wide, 5 feet long, and 16 inches high. These rectangular tubs can be joined to the walls along one, two, or three sides. They are also available in 4-, 4 1/2-, 5 1/2-, and 6-foot sizes. Rectangular tubs can include such safety and convenience features as built-in grab rails or handles, skid-free bottoms, headrests, and integral "grooming seats."

If you can't find a bathtub that completely fulfills your needs, consider having one custom designed and made for you. A bathtub is nothing more than a large, watertight container. The key word is "watertight." The unit must be able to withstand a certain amount of hydrostatic pressure over an indefinite period, with no leaks or seepage.

The installation of a bathtub in new construction is not a difficult job. All that is involved is setting the unit in place, making the necessary plumbing connections, and then continuing the construction, finish, and trim work around the tub site.

HOW TO REPLACE A BATHTUB

The bathtub is the most difficult of the basic bathroom fixtures to replace. If you have a recessed tub, there are certain circumstances under which it is inadvisable to attempt to replace it yourself. A recessed tub has a flange, or lip, that is usually attached directly to the wall studs. The wall finishing material is applied over the flange. If your present recessed tub extends the full width of your bathroom, the tub may be longer than the bathroom is wide. Such circumstances may require that part of the wall be cut away so the tub can be removed through an adjacent room. Before deciding to replace your recessed tub, find out what removal and replacement may entail. You may decide to leave the work to a professional plumber. If you do decide that you can handle the situation yourself, remember that the existing drain is plumbed for a tub of a specific width. Installing a wider or narrower tub will require some relocation of the drain. Removing a tub on legs is usually much simpler than removing a recessed tub, because the drain connections are exposed. Replacing it with a recessed tub will require matching the drain opening to the new tub. You also must remove the wall material below the edge of the new tub to attach the tub flange to the studs.

The following general procedures are for removing and installing a recessed tub. You must adapt them to the design of your new tub. If you are removing a tub on legs, removal of the drain connections is the same as for a recessed tub.

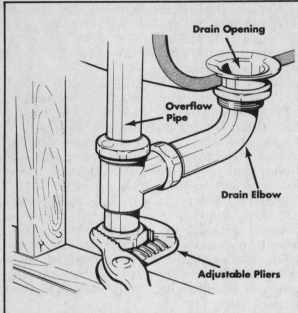

If you are able to reach the drain connections through an access panel, loosen the slip nuts that join the overflow pipe and the drain elbow to the main drainpipe.

Turn off the water at the main shutoff valve. Remove the screws that hold the tub's overflow plate in place. Remove the overflow plate and pull out the stopper control mechanism. Then remove the access panel in the opposite side of the wall at the drain end of the tub. If there is no such panel, you have two options. You can cut into the wall where the access panel should be. (After you have replaced the tub, you can install a removable panel in place over the opening.) Or you can disconnect the tub from the drainpipe through the drain opening in the tub itself.

If you are able to reach the drain connections through an access opening, use a wrench or adjustable pliers to loosen the slip nuts that join the overflow pipe and the drain elbow to the main drainpipe. Remove the overflow pipe.

If there is no access opening, unscrew and remove the drain flange from inside the tub. Then use pliers to remove the sleeve inside the tub drain opening. That will disconnect the tub from the drain elbow.

Remove the faucets and tub spout from the wall. Remove the nipples (short lengths of pipe) to which the faucets and spout were attached, and remove anything else that projects beyond the face of the studs and might interfere with removal of the tub.

Free the tub flanges. Using a cold chisel and a hammer, cut away a 4-inch-high section of the wall surface all the way around the tub. Some tubs are anchored to the studs with nails or screws. If your tub is so anchored, remove all the fasteners.

Insert a pry bar under the tub skirt at one end of the tub. Raise the end of the tub and place a small wedge under it. Repeat this process until a 1 x 2 wood strip can be placed under that end of the tub to hold it off the floor. Repeat the procedure at the other end of the tub.

At this point, you will need help. If your tub is cast iron, you probably will need two assistants to move the tub out safely. Two people can handle a steel tub. In either case, have a dolly handy to move the tub through the house to the outdoors.

Your helpers (or helper) should pull outward on the tub while you use a pry bar to force the tub away from the studs. Work the tub outward until there is space behind it for you to stand. Then get behind it and tilt the tub forward until it is standing on the front skirt. Continue to work the tub out of the recess until it can be lifted onto the dolly. You will find it easier to lift the tub onto a dolly that is lying flat than to stand the tub on end and get the foot of the dolly under the tub.

There is no standard tub installation method, so you must follow the specific instructions from the manufacturer.

Some enameled steel and fiberglass tubs come with foam padding cemented to the outside bottom. This padding supports the tub. When the tub is properly leveled (with the help of a carpenter's level), the padding supports the tub at a height that leaves about a 1/8-inch gap between the floor and the bottom of the tub apron or skirt. If one of these padded tubs cannot be leveled, it might be necessary to remove a section of the floor under the tub, place shims on the joists, and then replace the flooring. Under no circumstances should you attempt to put shims under the padding.

Some tubs are supported at the ends and along the back by wood supports nailed to the studs. These supports must be level and placed at the exact height required for the tub. Some plastic tubs have flange extensions that must be drilled at stud locations for nails or screws. Other tubs require special clips that fit over the tub flange and are nailed to the studs. Some tubs with thick flanges need shim strips nailed to the stud faces, so that there is a level base for the wallboard that has to extend down over the tub flange. The width of the offset below the flange on some tubs dictates the thickness of wallboard that can be installed over the flange. You must have the manufacturer's instructions to install your new tub properly. But there are general rules to consider before attempting to install a recessed or corner tub:

Use a carpenter's level to be sure the tub or the tub flange supports are level. Do not rely on "eyeball" leveling.

Place a mineral-fiber or glass-fiber insulation blanket under steel or plastic tubs that do not

Some tubs with thick flanges make it necessary to nail shim strips to the stud faces, so that there is a level base for wallboard that has to extend down over the tub flange.

come with padding. This insulation will reduce noise when the tub is filled. Use enough insulation to pack the space, but not enough to support the tub. Wallboard must be installed over the tub flange, but it must not touch the tub rim. If it does touch the rim, it will soak up water, which will damage the board's core. To avoid this problem, place 1/8-inch wood strips around the rim to ensure proper separation when you install the wallboard. When the wallboard is in place, pull out the strips and fill the gap with caulking or sealant material.

If your local building code requires water-resistive wallboard for tub and shower enclosures, be sure to get the special sealant that goes with it. Whenever this kind of wallboard is cut, the cut edge must be painted with the sealant to preserve the water-resistive properties of the core. You should be aware that this type of gypsum board is intended for walls only, not for ceilings. On ceilings in high-humidity areas, this board is less sag-resistant than conventional wallboard. You can replace the faucets and spout and connect the tub to the drain to put it into service

before you repair the walls around the rim of the tub. Because the rim of the tub will not yet be sealed, you must avoid splashing water into the wall cavity.

TOILETS

Toilets are available in a variety of designs, styles, and colors. The most obvious design distinction among toilets is the configuration of their bowls and tanks. The bowl and tank may be combined in a single molded unit, or they may be separate. Two-piece toilets are less expensive than one-piece toilets and are available in either floor-mounted or wall-hung models. The advantage of a wall-hung toilet is that it leaves the floor below it clear for easy cleaning. But special wall reinforcement and plumbing hookups are required to install a wall-hung toilet. One-piece toilets for residential use are available only in floor-mounted models. The advantage of a one-piece toilet is that there is no possibility of a leak developing between the tank and the bowl. One-piece toilets also can be designed with lower tank heights than two-piece toilets.

More important than whether the toilet is of one- or two-piece construction is the efficiency of its flushing action and the internal design of its bowl. A well-designed toilet should flush quietly and completely. The water in the bowl should be deep enough to keep the bowl surfaces clean. The water also should have a large exposed surface area to seal the bowl from the drain system. Each flushing should wash the entire inside surface of the bowl.

There are two standard bowl configurations: round and elongated. A variation is the sculptured or contour-styled bowl, which is an elongated bowl with a squared-off front. The seat of an elongated bowl is more comfortable than that of a round bowl. A round bowl does not project from the wall as far as an elongated one and should be considered when space is at a premium.

Toilets come as complete units ready for installation. Plumbing hookups are standardized, which means that toilets made by different manufacturers can be interchanged without altering your home's plumbing system. There are certain restrictions. If you are purchasing a floor-mounted toilet without the help of a plumber or designer, you must know the clearance between the center of the toilet drain pipe and the wall against which the toilet is to be placed. The standard clearance is 12 inches, although 10-inch and 14-inch clearances are common. A toilet that requires a clearance of 14 inches won't fit over a drain that is only 12 inches from the wall. A toilet requiring a clearance of 10 inches will leave an unsightly gap behind the tank if it is installed over a drain that is 14 inches from the wall.

APPENDIX

Success in any do-it-yourself project depends on knowing how to do the work and on having the tools and materials required to do the job. You don't need an elaborate workshop or power tools to accomplish the projects in this book. A 30-inch-long tool chest will hold just about everything you need. Team these basic tools with the proper abrasives, materials, and fasteners, and you'll get results you can be proud of.

Basic Tools

After you've acquired a hammer, pliers, screwdrivers, and wrenches, what other tools are essential? For most jobs you'll need measuring and marking tools, saws, and a drill; planes, files, and clamps are next. Add tools and accessories as your budget permits. Power tools do what hand tools do faster and usually easier.

There is only one rule about tools: Buy good ones. Quality tools are safer and easier to use, and most will last a lifetime if you take care of them. You can spot a quality tool by its machining: The metal parts are smooth and shiny, and the tool is well balanced. Inexpensive tools are often painted to hide the defects or roughness of the metal parts, and the machining is crude. You also can tell quality by the price tag: You'll pay more for quality equipment. Cheap tools are no economy; you get what you pay for.

MEASURING AND MARKING TOOLS
Almost every project calls for accurate measurements. Not only must you know precisely how many feet and inches are involved, you also usually have to assure that everything comes out plumb, level, and square. Here are the basic devices for measuring and marking.

Measuring Rule or Tape Measure. Flexible tape measures are available in lengths of up to 50 feet; a tape that is 16 to 24 feet is adequate. Buy a tape at least 5/8-inch wide, so it will stay rigid

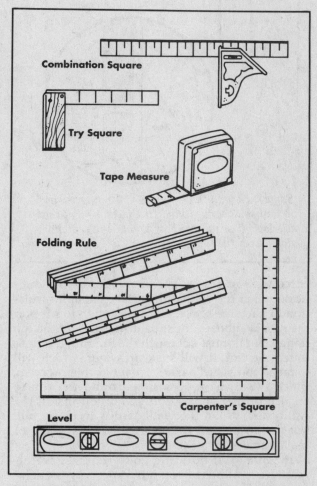

Combination Square

Try Square

Tape Measure

Folding Rule

Carpenter's Square

Level

when extended. Many rules have an automatic power return.

Folding Rule. Folding rules are available in 4-foot, 6-foot, and 8-foot lengths; they're used for laying out projects. The rules fold down to 6 inches; take care not to strain the metal joints at the folding points. Some rules have a metal insert in the first 6 inches. This insert is pulled out of the rule for use as a depth or marking gauge or for critical measurements. A folding rule also can be used for measurements inside door or window frames or between parallel surfaces.

Carpenter's Square. The standard sizes for carpenter's squares are 18 to 24 inches (body) by 12 or 18 inches (tongue); the size is important for laying out projects on plywood and hardboard. Carpenter's squares are steel or aluminum; they have multiple scales for figuring board-foot requirements, brace (rafter) height, stair-step stringer angles, and rafter cuts.

Combination Squares. For small jobs a combination square may be easier to use than a carpenter's square because the combination square is smaller; most are 12 inches long. The body of the square slides along the blade and can be fixed at any point with a thumbscrew. The body of the square may incorporate a small bubble level or a scratch awl, which can be used for leveling or marking. This square also can be used as a depth gauge, a miter square, and a straightedge and ruler.

Try Square. This tool looks like a small carpenter's square with a wood handle. The measurements go across the metal blade only (not the handle). The try square is generally used to test the squareness of edges in planing and sawing work. It also can be used to check right-angle layouts. The tongue usually is 12 inches or shorter, and it can be used as a straightedge, ruler, and depth gauge.

Level. Two- and three-bubble levels are standard for most leveling and plumbing (vertical level) projects. Some of the bubbles are in vials that can be moved for angle "leveling"; these vials sometimes can be replaced if they are damaged or broken. The edges of a level can be used as a straightedge. Laid flat against a vertical surface, the level can find both horizontal and vertical levels for installing cabinets, hanging wallpaper, or hanging pictures. Level frames are either wood, plastic, or lightweight metal, such as aluminum. Lengths range to 6 feet, but most do-it-yourselfers find a 30-inch level adequate.

Chalk Line. Chalk lines are heavy twine in a metal canister filled with powdered chalk. To use a chalk line, stretch it taut along a surface and snap the line; the chalk leaves a blue line along the work for measuring and cutting. A chalk line is also used to suspend plumb bobs, for vertical lines, and to lay out walks, driveways, and foundations.

HANDSAWS

Once you've made your measurements, you usually need to cut material to length and sometimes need to rip it to the right width. For these jobs you need one of five different handsaws.

Crosscut Saw. The crosscut saw cuts across the grain of the wood. Crosscut saws have from 5 to 10 or more teeth per inch to produce a smooth cut in the wood. They can be used for cutting ply-

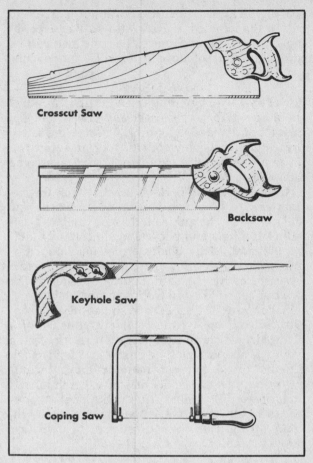

Crosscut Saw

Backsaw

Keyhole Saw

Coping Saw

wood and hardboard panels, and sometimes to cut miters.

Ripsaw. The ripsaw cuts along the grain of the wood; this is called "ripping." There are 3 to 5 teeth per inch. The ripsaw's teeth are wider set than those of the crosscut saw, so they slice through the wood like a chisel. The final cut of a ripsaw is rough, and the wood usually has to be planed or sanded to its final measurement.

Backsaw. A backsaw cuts through wood when you draw back the blade, not when you push it forward. It has a reinforced back to stiffen the blade; its teeth are closely spaced so the cut is smooth. A backsaw is used to make miter cuts and for trimming molding. It's designed for use in a miter box.

Keyhole Saw. This saw has a 10- to 12-inch tapered blade; it is used to cut openings for pipes and electrical boxes. Any straight or curved internal cuts that are too large for an auger bit, drill, or hole saw are made with a keyhole saw. Some keyhole saws have removable blades with a variety of tooth spacings, for use on different materials, such as wood, plastic, metal, and hardboard.

Coping Saw. This saw looks like a letter C with a handle. The blades are thin and replaceable; they are secured with two pins at the ends of the saw, and the handle turns to put the proper tension on the blade. Many different blades are available, with both ripsaw and crosscut tooth spacing. Blades can be inserted into the frame to cut on the forward or backward stroke, depending on the sawing project; the pins also can be turned to set the blade at an angle for special cuts.

POWER SAWS

Power saws can be intimidating at first, and they should be: Improperly used, any power tool can do a lot of damage in a hurry. Observe the safety precautions that come with the tool, and after you make a few practice cuts, you'll soon overcome your fears.

Circular Saw. A portable electric tool, the circular saw is the power version of a crosscut saw and a ripsaw. The guide on the saw can be adjusted to cut miters and pockets in almost any building material. Many blades are available, including crosscut, rip, masonry, metal, and plastic. Accessories for the saw include a table, so the saw can be mounted to work as a small table saw.

Saber Saw. The saber saw, sometimes improperly called a jigsaw or scrollsaw, consists of a blade, driven in an up-and-down reciprocating motion. This portable power tool can hold many different blades and cut many materials, including wood, metal, plastic, masonry, ceramic, and high-pressure laminate. This is the power counterpart to the keyhole and the coping saw; it will make straight or contour cuts either with or across the grain.

DRILLS

Hole-cutting tools have two parts: A drill or brace applies rotating force to a bit that makes the hole. Here are the main kinds of drills and bits and the jobs each does best.

Hand Drill. The hand drill is like an eggbeater; a drive handle moves bevel gears to turn a chuck in which a drill has been locked. This drill can't make large holes, but it can make small-diameter, shallow holes in wood and soft metals.

Push Drill. The push drill requires only one hand to use. As you push down on the handle, the shank turns a chuck into which a small bit fits. This is a limited-capacity tool, but it is excellent for making pilot holes and handy for setting hinges and similar jobs. The bits are usually stored in the handle of the drill; sizes are available up to 1/4 inch.

Brace. The hand brace has a rotating offset handle that turns a chuck with a ratcheting mechanism. Auger bits, countersinks, and screwdriver attachments are available, and the ratchet lets you work in restricted areas. The large-capacity chuck holds bits that will cut holes up to 1 1/2 inches in diameter. The brace is the counterpart of the electric drill, but a hand brace chuck isn't designed for twist drills, unless the drills have a square shank for brace use.

Electric Drill. Three sizes of chucks are available for power drills: 1/4-, 3/8-, and 1/2-inch

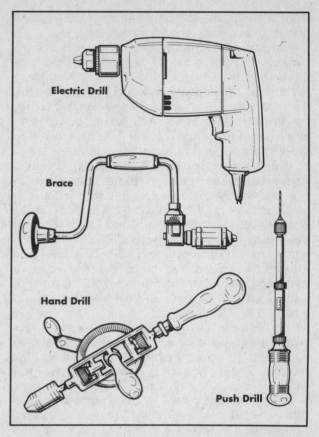

Electric Drill

Brace

Hand Drill

Push Drill

capacity. The 1/4-inch chuck can hold larger bits (up to 1/2-inch wood bits) if they have a 1/4-inch shank. This drill has a limited range of drilling operations, but it is the least expensive electric drill. It should not be used for prolonged hard jobs. Accessories are available.

The 3/8-inch drill can make 3/8-inch holes in metal and 3/4-inch holes in wood; a hole saw also can be used with this tool, to cut holes up to 3 inches in diameter. Many 3/8-inch drills can drill in concrete and have a reversing feature that is handy for removing screws. A variable-speed drill is recommended; this drill can be started slowly and then speeded up and can be used in a variety of materials. Many attachments and accessories are available, including wire brushes and paint mixers.

PLANES

When you need a flat surface or square edge, a plane is the tool to use. Planes also quickly remove large amounts of material.

Jack Plane. The jack plane removes excess wood and brings the surface of the wood to trueness and smoothness. The plane is 12 to 14 inches long. Depending on the job, it also can be used to true long edges for gluing.

Smoothing Plane. This plane, smaller than the jack plane, is used to bring wood to a final finish. The plane measures from 6 to 9 inches long.

Block Plane. The block plane is small and is designed to smooth and cut the end grain of

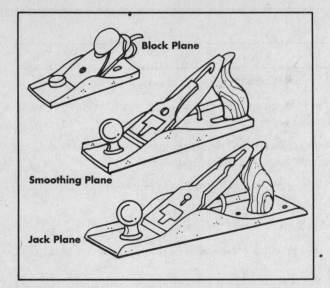

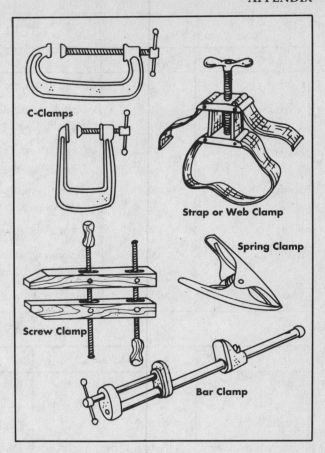

wood. The plane has a low blade angle that permits smooth cutting, and only one hand is needed to use it. Although the block plane is a cabinetmaker's tool, it can be used to smooth almost any soft material, even aluminum. For large jobs a longer and wider smoothing or jack plane should be used.

CLAMPS

Clamps are essential for many jobs. Start with several C-clamps and a set of bar clamps. If you plan to work on furniture, get strap clamps too.

C-Clamps. These clamps are made from cast iron or aluminum, and have a C-shaped body; a screw with a metal pad applies the tension on the material being clamped. Because C-clamps can exert lots of pressure, buffer blocks of scrap wood or other materials should be inserted between the jaws of the clamp and the material being clamped. A wide range of sizes is available.

Screw Clamps. These clamps have parallel wood jaws; they are the basic woodworking clamps. Tension is applied by hand with two threaded spindles; the clamps can be adjusted to angles by moving the spindles.

Bar Clamps. These clamps fit on metal rods or pieces of pipe; tension is applied by tightening a screw. Bar clamps are used for gluing boards together on surfaces where the throats of C-clamps are too shallow to accept the work. Fixtures and pipe can be purchased separately.

Strap or Web Clamps. These clamps are webbing straps, usually nylon, with a sliding tension clamp. The clamp is used for four-way tensioning on odd-shaped or four-cornered pieces. Because the clamps are fabric, the pressure won't damage the material being clamped.

Spring Clamps. These clamps look like large metal clothespins; they're used for clamping light jobs, such as veneers glued to core material. Spring clamps also come in handy as holding devices.

Abrasives

Choosing the proper abrasive for a given job usually means the difference between mediocre results and a professional appearance. There are four primary factors to be considered when selecting any coated abrasive, including sanding paper and emery cloth: the abrasive mineral, the type of rough material; the grade, the coarseness or fineness of the mineral; the backing, paper or cloth; and the coating, the nature and extent of the mineral on the surface.

The coating can either be "open" or "closed." Open means that the grains are spaced so as only to cover a portion of the surface; an open-coated abrasive is best used on gummy or soft woods, soft metals, or on painted surfaces. Closed means that the abrasive covers the entire area. Closed-coated abrasives provide maximum cutting, but they also clog faster; a closed-coated abrasive is best used on hard woods and on hard metals.

Other finishing abrasives include pumice, rottenstone, rouge, and steel wool. Pumice is a volcanic abrasive powder used for fine finishing; it is generally lubricated with water or oil, and comes in several grades. Rottenstone is a fine powder, finer even than pumice, that is used to render a high sheen. Rouge is an abrasive powder used primarily for polishing metal. Steel wool comes in many grades of coarseness, and you should be careful to apply the correct grade of steel wool.

STEEL WOOL

Grade	Number	Common Uses
Coarse	3	Paint and varnish removal; removing paint spots from resilient floors
Medium Coarse	2	Removing scratches from brass; removing paint spots from ceramic tile; rubbing floors between finish coats
Medium	1	Rust removal; cleaning glazed tiles; removing marks from wood floors, removing finishes with paint and varnish removers
Medium Fine	0	Brass finishing; cleaning tile; removing stubborn finishes with paint and varnish remover
Fine	00	Satinizing high-gloss finishes with linseed oil
Extra Fine	000	Removing paint spots or stains from wood; cleaning polished metals; rubbing between finish coats
Superfine	0000	Final rubbing of finish; stain removal

ABRASIVE CLOTHS

Type	Grades	Common Uses
Emery	Very coarse through fine	General light metal polishing; removing rust and corrosion from metal; wet or dry sanding
Crocus	Very fine	High-gloss finishing for metals
Aluminum Oxide	Very coarse through fine	Power sanding belts

ABRASIVE POWDERS

Type	Grades	Common Uses
Pumice	F through FFF	Rubbing between finish coats; final buffing; stain removal
Rottenstone	None	Buffing between finish coats; final buffing; stain removal
Rouge	None	Metal polishing

Plywood Grading

Knowing everything you can about plywood can save you money and mean the difference between a successful project and one that fails. For example, there is no reason for you to buy an expensive piece of plywood that is perfect on both sides if only one side will show. There is no sense in paying for 5/8-inch thickness when 1/4-inch plywood is all you need. Plywood also comes with different glues, different veneers, and different degrees of finish. By knowing these characteristics you may be able to save money, and you will improve your chances of getting the right material for the job.

Plywood is better than lumber for some jobs. It's strong, lightweight, and rigid. Its high impact resistance means that plywood doesn't split, chip, crack all the way through, or crumble. Its cross-laminated construction restricts expansion and contraction within the individual plies, and you never get "green" wood with plywood. Easy to work from cutting to fastening to finishing, plywood is available at home centers, hardware stores, and lumberyards.

When you buy a sheet of plywood, you know exactly what size you're getting. A 4-by-8-foot sheet of 3/4-inch plywood measures 4 by 8 feet and is exactly 3/4 inch thick. This contrasts with the distinction between nominal and actual measurements with lumber.

When you buy plywood, look for a back-stamp or edge-marking bearing the initials APA or DFPA. APA stands for American Plywood Association, while DFPA is the Douglas Fir Plywood Association. These two organizations represent most of the plywood manufacturers, and they inspect and test plywood quality and

SANDPAPER				
Grit	Number	Grade	Coating Available[1]	Common Uses
Very Coarse	30	2½	F,G,S	Rust removal on rough finished metal
	36	2	F,G,S	
Coarse	40	1½	F,G,S	Rough sanding of wood; paint removal
	50	1	F,G,S	
	60	½	F,G,A,S	
Medium	80	0 (1/0)	F,G,A,S	General wood sanding; plaster smoothing; preliminary smoothing of previously painted surfaces
	100	00 (2/0)	F,G,A,S	
	120	3/0	F,G,A,S	
Fine	150	4/0	F,G,A,S	Final sanding of bare wood or previously painted surfaces
	180	5/0	F,G,A,S	
Very Fine	220	6/0	F,G,A,S	Light sanding between finish coats; dry sanding
	240	7/0	F,A,S	
	280	8/0	F,A,S	
Extra Fine	320	9/0	F,A,S	High-satinized finish on lacquer, varnish, or shellac; wet sanding
	360	—[2]	S	
	400	10/0	S	
Superfine	500	—[2]	S	High-satinized finishes; wet sanding
	600	—[2]	S	

[1]F = flint; G = garnet; A = aluminum oxide; S = silicon carbide. Silicon carbide is used dry or wet, with water or oil.
[2]No grade designation.

grading accuracy. Their stamp is your assurance that what you see is what you get.

Plywood is categorized exterior or interior. Exterior plywood is made with nothing but waterproof glue, and you should always select exterior plywood for any exposed application. Interior plywood, made with highly resistant glues, can withstand some moisture. There is interior plywood made with IMG (intermediate glue), which is resistant to bacteria, mold, and moisture, but no interior plywood is made for use outdoors. The inner plies of most interior plywood are made of lower grade woods. The most critical plywood grading category for most home projects is the appearance grade of the panel faces.

Fasteners

Nails, screws, and bolts are fasteners that every do-it-yourselfer uses. The following are the most common fasteners and their uses.

NAILS

The easiest way to fasten two pieces of wood together is with nails, and nails are manufactured in a variety of shapes, sizes, and metals, to do almost any fastening job. Most nails are made of steel, but aluminum, brass, nickel, bronze, copper, and stainless-steel nails are available for use where corrosion could occur. Nails are also manufactured with coatings (galvanized, blued, or cemented) to prevent rusting and add holding power.

Nail size is designated by penny size, originally the price per hundred nails. Penny size, usually called d, ranges from 2 penny, or 2d (1 inch long), to 60 penny, or 60d (6 inches long). Nails shorter than 1 inch are called "brads"; nails longer than 6 inches are called "spikes."

The length of the nails is important; at least two thirds of the nail should be driven into the base, or thicker, material. For example, a 1 x 3 nailed to a 4 x 4 beam should be fastened with an 8-penny, or 8d, nail. An 8d nail is 2 1/2 inches long; 3/4 inch of its length will go through the 1 x 3, and the remaining 1 3/4 inches will go into the beam.

Bulk nails usually are sold by the pound; the smaller the nail, the more nails to the pound. You can buy bulk nails out of a nail keg; the nails are weighed and then priced by the retailer. You also can buy packaged nails, sold in boxes ranging from 1 pound to 50 pounds.

There are several different kinds of nails: common, box, casing. and finishing nails, brads, spikes, and nails for special applications.

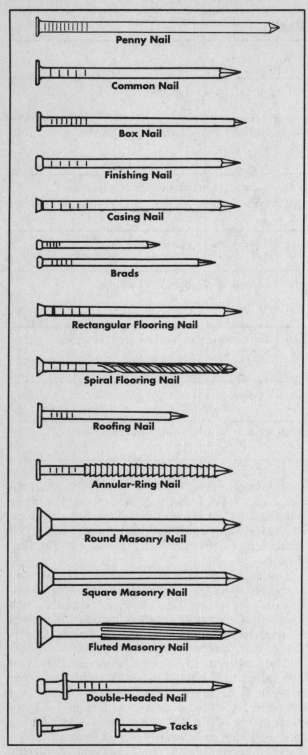

Penny Nail

Common Nail

Box Nail

Finishing Nail

Casing Nail

Brads

Rectangular Flooring Nail

Spiral Flooring Nail

Roofing Nail

Annular-Ring Nail

Round Masonry Nail

Square Masonry Nail

Fluted Masonry Nail

Double-Headed Nail

Tacks

Common Nails. Common nails are made from wire, cut to the proper length; they have thick heads and can be driven into tough materials. They're used for most medium-to-heavy construction work. Common nails are available in sizes from 2d to 60d.

Box Nails. Box nails are similar to common nails, but they are both lighter and smaller in diameter. Box nails are designed for light construction and household use.

Finishing Nails and Casing Nails. Finishing nails are lighter than common nails and have a small head. They're used primarily in building furniture. Casing nails are similar but heavier; they're used mostly for woodwork.

Brads. Nails less than 1 inch long are called brads; they're used to tack on trim and moldings. Brads are sold not by weight but in boxes, by size, from 3/16 inch to 1 inch.

Spikes. Nails longer than 6 inches are called spikes; they're used for heavy construction and are available in sizes from 6 to 12 inches. Spikes are sold individually.

Flooring Nails. Both rectangular-cut and spiral flooring nails are available. Spiral nails are recommended for secure attachment of floorboards.

Roofing Nails. Roofing nails, usually galvanized, have a much larger head than common nails, to prevent damage to shingles.

Annular-Ring Nails. These nails have sharp ridges all along the nail shaft; their holding power is much greater than regular nails. Nails made for drywall installation are often ringed.

Masonry Nails. Three types of nails are designed specifically for use with concrete and concrete block: round, square, and fluted. Masonry nails should not be used where high strength is required. Fastening to brick, stone, or reinforced concrete should be made with screws or lag bolts.

Double-Headed Nails. These nails are used for temporary fastening jobs. The nail is driven in as far as the first head; the second head sticks out for easy removal.

Tacks and Upholstery Tacks. Tacks, made in both round and cut forms, are used to hold carpet or fabric to wood; upholstery tacks have decorative heads.

Corrugated Nails. These fasteners, sometimes called "wiggly nails," are used for light-duty joints where strength isn't important. The fasteners are set at right angles to the joint.

SCREWS

Screws provide more strength and holding power than nails. If the work will ever be disassembled, screws can be removed and reinserted without damage. For these reasons screws should be used instead of nails for most woodworking.

Wood Screws. Most wood screws are made of steel, but brass, nickel, bronze, and copper are used where corrosion could occur. Like nails, screws are also made with coatings, including zinc, chromium, or cadmium, to deter rust.

Screws are manufactured with four basic heads and with different kinds of slots. Flathead screws are always countersunk into the material being fastened, so that the screw head is flush with the surface. Oval-head screws are partially countersunk; about half the screw head lies above the surface. Round-head screws are not counter-

DRILLING FOR WOOD SCREWS

Gauge Number	Decimal Diameter	Fractional Diameter	Shank Hole Twist Bit	Shank Hole Drill Gauge	PILOT HOLE HARDWOOD Twist Bit		HARDWOOD Drill Gauge		SOFTWOOD Twist Bit		SOFTWOOD Drill Gauge		Auger Bit Number	Threads per Inch
					s	p	s	p	s	p	s	p		
0	.060	1/16 −	1/16	52	1/32	—	70	—	1/64	—	75	—	—	32
1	.073	5/64 −	5/64	47	1/32	—	66	—	1/32	—	71	—	—	28
2	.086	5/64 +	3/32	42	3/64	1/32	56	70	1/32	1/64	65	75	3	26
3	.099	3/32 +	7/64	37	1/16	1/32	54	66	3/64	1/32	58	71	4	24
4	.112	7/64 +	7/64	32	1/16	3/64	52	56	3/64	1/32	55	65	4	22
5	.125	1/8 −	1/8	30	5/64	1/16	49	54	1/16	3/64	53	58	4	20
6	.138	9/64 −	9/64	27	5/64	1/16	47	52	1/16	3/64	52	55	5	18
7	.151	5/32 −	5/32	22	3/32	5/64	44	49	1/16	3/64	51	53	5	16
8	.164	5/32 +	11/64	18	3/32	5/64	40	47	5/64	1/16	48	52	6	15
9	.177	11/64 +	3/16	14	7/64	3/32	37	44	5/64	1/16	45	51	6	14
10	.190	3/16 +	3/16	10	7/64	3/32	33	40	3/32	5/64	43	48	6	13
11	.203	13/64 −	13/64	4	1/8	7/64	31	37	3/32	5/64	40	45	7	12
12	.216	7/32 −	7/32	2	1/8	7/64	30	33	7/64	3/32	38	43	7	11
14	.242	15/64 +	1/4	D	9/64	1/8	25	31	7/64	3/32	32	40	8	10
16	.268	17/64 +	17/64	I	5/32	1/8	18	30	9/64	7/64	29	38	9	9
18	.294	19/64 −	19/64	N	3/16	9/64	13	25	9/64	7/64	26	32	10	8
20	.320	21/64 −	21/64	P	13/64	5/32	4	18	11/64	9/64	19	29	11	8
24	.372	3/8	3/8	V	7/32	3/16	1	13	3/16	9/64	15	26	12	7

s = slotted head   p = Phillips head

sunk; the entire screw head lies above the surface. Fillister-head screws are raised above the surface on a flat base, to keep the screwdriver from damaging the surface as the screw is tightened.

Most screws have plain slots and are driven with blade screwdrivers. Phillips-head screws have crossed slots, and are driven with Phillips screwdrivers. Square-slot screws are driven with a special screwdriver.

Screw size is measured in two dimensions: length and diameter at the shank. Shank diameter is stated by gauge number, from 0 to 24. Length is measured in inches: in 1/8-inch increments from 1/4 to 1 inch, in 1/4-inch increments from 1 to 3 inches, and in 1/2-inch increments from 3 to 5 inches. Not all lengths are available for all gauges, but special sizes sometimes can be ordered.

The length of screws is important. At least half the length of the screw should extend into the base material. For example, if a piece of 3/4-inch plywood is being fastened, the screws that hold it should be 1 1/2 inches long.

To prevent the screws from splitting the materials being fastened, pilot holes must be made before the screws are driven. For small screws pilot holes can be punched with an awl or ice pick, or even with a nail. For larger screws drill pilot holes with a small drill or a combination drill and countersink.

Sheet-Metal Screws. Sheet-metal screws, used to fasten pieces of metal together, form threads in the metal as they are installed. There are several different types of sheet-metal screws. Pointed pan-head screws are coarse-threaded; they are available in gauges from 4 to 14 and lengths from

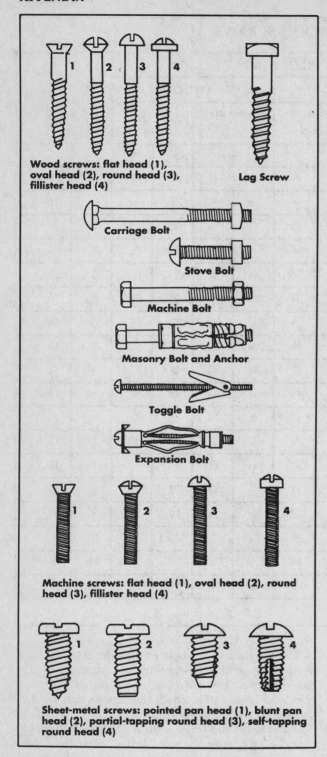

Wood screws: flat head (1), oval head (2), round head (3), fillister head (4)

Lag Screw

Carriage Bolt

Stove Bolt

Machine Bolt

Masonry Bolt and Anchor

Toggle Bolt

Expansion Bolt

Machine screws: flat head (1), oval head (2), round head (3), fillister head (4)

Sheet-metal screws: pointed pan head (1), blunt pan head (2), partial-tapping round head (3), self-tapping round head (4)

heavy-duty work with thick sheet metal. Both types of round-head screws are available with either plain or Phillips-head slots.

Nail-type sheet-metal screws are pounded, not screwed in; they have spiral thread-cutting shafts with pointed ends. The heads of these screws are not slotted. They are used for heavy-gauge sheet metal and for fastening other materials to metal.

Machine Screws. Machine screws are blunt-ended screws used to fasten metal parts together; they are commonly made of steel or brass. Like other fasteners, they are also made with coatings, including copper, nickel, zinc, cadmium, and galvanized, to deter rust. Machine screws are manufactured with flat, oval, round, and fillister heads, and with both plain and Phillips-head slots. They are available in gauges 2 to 12 and diameters from 1/4 inch to 1/2 inch, and in lengths from 1/4 inch to 3 inches.

Lag Screws. Lag screws are heavy-duty fasteners. They are driven with a wrench and used primarily for fastening to masonry. For light work lead, plastic, or fiber plugs can be used to hold large screws. For larger jobs and more holding power, lead expansion anchors and lag screws are used. The anchors are inserted into holes drilled in the masonry, and the lag screws driven firmly into the anchors.

BOLTS

Bolts are used with nuts or locknuts, and sometimes with washers. The three basic types are carriage bolts, stove bolts, and machine bolts. Other bolts include masonry bolts and anchors, and toggle and expansion bolts, used to distribute weight when fastening to hollow walls.

Machine bolts are manufactured in two gauges, fine-threaded and coarse; carriage and stove bolts are coarse-threaded. Bolt size is measured by shank diameter and by threads per inch, expressed as diameter by threads, for example, as 1/4 x 20. Carriage bolts are available up to 10 inches long, stove bolts up to 6 inches, and machine bolts up to 30 inches.

Carriage Bolts. Carriage bolts have a round head with a square collar; they are driven with a wrench. When the bolt is tightened, the collar fits into a prebored hole or twists into the wood, preventing the bolt from turning. Carriage bolts are used in making furniture; they are coarse-threaded, and are available in diameters from 3/16 to 3/4 inch and lengths from 1/2 inch to 10 inches.

Stove Bolts. Stove bolts are available in a wide range of sizes. They have a slotted head that is flat, oval, or round, and are driven with a screwdriver. Most stove bolts are completely threaded, but the larger ones may have a smooth shank near the bolt head. Stove bolts can be used for almost any fastening job; they are coarse-threaded and are available in diameters from 5/32 to 1/2 inch and lengths from 3/8 inch to 6 inches.

1/4 inch to 2 inches. Pointed pan-head screws are used in lightweight sheet metal. Blunt pan-head screws are used for heavier sheet metal; they are available in gauges from 4 to 14 and lengths from 1/4 inch to 2 inches. Both kinds of pan-head screws are available with either plain or Phillips-head slots.

Partial-tapping round-head screws have finer threads; they can be used in soft or hard metals. Self-tapping round-head screws are used for

Machine Bolts. Machine bolts have either a square head or a hexagonal head, and are fastened with square nuts or hex nuts; they are wrench-driven. Machine bolts are manufactured in large sizes; the bolt diameter increases with length. They are either coarse- or fine-threaded, and are available in diameters from 1/4 inch to 2 inches and lengths from 1/2 inch to 30 inches.

Masonry Bolts and Anchors. These bolts work on the same principle as the lag bolt or screw; a plastic sleeve expands inside a predrilled hole as the bolt is tightened.

Hollow-Wall Bolts. Toggle bolts and expansion bolts are used for fastening to hollow walls. Toggle bolt wings are opened inside the wall by a spring; the bolts are available in diameters from 1/8 to 1/2 inch and lengths up to 8 inches. Expansion bolts are inserted into an expansion jacket, which expands as the bolt is tightened; these bolts are available for walls as thick as 1 3/4 inches.

Adhesives

If you fail to use the right adhesive in the proper way, you'll end up with a poor joining job. Here is some information on adhesives do-it-yourselfers use most frequently.

MULTIPURPOSE ADHESIVES

Stock a small assortment of multipurpose adhesives, and you can make a variety of repairs.

White Glue (Polyvinyl Acetate). PVA glue is a white liquid, usually sold in plastic squeeze bottles; it's recommended for use on porous materials, including wood, paper, cloth, pottery, and nonstructural wood-to-wood bonds. It is not water resistant. Clamping is required for 30 minutes to one hour, until the glue sets; curing time is 18 to 24 hours. School glue, a type of white glue, dries more slowly. PVA glue dries clear. It is inexpensive and nonflammable.

Epoxy. Epoxies are sold in tubes or in cans. They consist of two parts, resin and hardener, which must be thoroughly mixed just before use. They are strong, durable, and water resistant, and are recommended for use on metal, ceramics, some plastics, and rubber. They aren't recommended for flexible surfaces. Clamping is required for about two hours for most epoxies. Drying time is about 12 hours; curing time is one to two days. Epoxy dries clear or amber.

Cyanoacrylate (Instant Glue). Cyanoacrylates are similar to epoxy but are one-part glues; they form a strong bond. They are recommended for use on metal, ceramics, glass, some plastics, and rubber; they aren't recommended for flexible surfaces. Apply sparingly. Clamping is not required; curing time is one to two days. Cyanoacrylates dry clear. They deteriorate gradually when exposed to weather and weaken in temperatures above 150°F.

Contact Cement. A rubber-based liquid sold in bottles and cans, contact cement is recommended for bonding laminates, veneers, and other large areas, and for repairs. It also can be used on paper, leather, cloth, rubber, metal, glass, and some plastics; it dries flexible. It isn't recommended for repairs where strength is necessary. Contact cement is applied to both surfaces and allowed to set; the surfaces are pressed together for an instant bond. No repositioning is possible once contact has been made. Clamping isn't required; curing is complete on drying. Some contact cement is flammable; read the label carefully to purchase nonflamable contact cement.

Polyurethane Glue. This high-strength glue is an amber paste, sold in tubes; it forms a strong bond, similar to epoxy. Polyurethane glue is recommended for use on wood, metal, ceramics, glass, most plastics, and fiberglass; it dries flexible and also can be used on leather, cloth, rubber, and vinyl. Clamping is required for about two hours; curing time is about 24 hours. Polyurethane glue dries translucent and can be painted or stained; its shelf life is short, and it is expensive.

Silicone Rubber Adhesive or Sealant. Silicone rubber glues and sealants are sold in tubes; they're similar to silicone rubber caulk. They form strong, durable, waterproof bonds, with excellent resistance to high and low temperatures. They're recommended for use on gutters and on building materials, including metal, glass, fiberglass, rubber, and wood; they also can be used on fabrics, some plastics, and ceramics. Clamping is usually not required; curing time is about 24 hours, but the adhesive skins over in less than one hour. They dry flexible and are available in clear, black, and metal-colored forms.

Household Cement. The various adhesives sold in tubes as household cement are fast-setting, low-strength glues. They are recommended for use on wood, ceramics, glass, paper, and some plastics; some dry flexible and can be used on fabric, leather, and vinyl. Clamping is usually not required. Setting time is 10 to 20 minutes; curing time is up to 24 hours.

Hot-Melt Adhesive. Hot-melt glues are sold in stick form and used with glue guns. A glue gun heats the adhesive above 200°F. For the best bond, the surfaces to be joined also should be preheated. Hot-melt adhesives are only moderately strong, and bonds will come apart if exposed to high temperatures. This glue is recommended for temporary bonds of wood, metal, paper, some plastics, and composition materials. Clamping isn't required; setting time is 10 to 45 seconds, and curing time is 24 hours.

WOOD GLUES

Yellow Glue (Aliphatic Resin, Carpenter's Glue). Aliphatic resin glue is a yellow liquid, usually sold in plastic squeeze bottles, and often labeled as carpenter's glue. Bulk quantities are available. Yellow glue is like white glue, but it is recommended specifically for general woodworking and forms a stronger bond. It is more water resistant than white glue. Clamping is required for about 30 minutes until the glue sets; curing time is 12 to 18 hours. Yellow glue dries clear; it doesn't accept wood stains.

Plastic Resin Glue (Urea Formaldehyde). Plastic resin glues are sold in powder form and mixed with water to the consistency of thick cream. They are recommended for laminating layers of wood and for gluing structural joints. Plastic resin glue is water-resistant but not waterproof, and it isn't recommended for use on outdoor furniture. It is resistant to paint and lacquer thinner. Clamping is required for up to eight hours; curing time is 18 to 24 hours. Use plastic resin glue only at temperatures above 70°F.

Resorcinol Glue. This two-part glue, consisting of a liquid and a powder, is sold in cans. It is waterproof and forms strong and durable bonds. Resorcinol glue is recommended for outdoor furniture, kitchen counters, structural bonding, boats, and sporting gear; it also can be used on concrete, cork, fabrics, leather, and some plastics. Resorcinol glue has excellent resistance to temperature extremes, chemicals, and fungus. Clamping is required; curing time is 8 to 24 hours, depending on humidity and temperature.

Hide Glue. Hide glue, the traditional woodworker's glue, is available in either liquid or flake form; the flake form must be soaked for about 12 hours in water, heated to 150°F, and applied hot. Hide glue forms a strong bond, but it isn't moisture-resistant. Clamping is required; curing time is about 12 hours. Hide glue dries to a clear amber; it doesn't accept wood stains.

Casein Glue. Casein glue is made from milk; it's sold in powder form and mixed with water to the consistency of thick cream. It forms strong bonds and is recommended for laminating resinous or oily woods; it is moisture-resistant but isn't recommended for outdoor use. Clamping is required for about 4 hours; curing time is about 12 hours. Casein glue must be stored tightly sealed.

ADHESIVES FOR GLASS AND CERAMICS

Most multipurpose adhesives will bond glass and ceramics, but specialized versions often bond more securely.

China and Glass Cement. Many cements are sold for mending china and glass, usually in tubes. Acrylic latex-based cements have good resistance to water and heat; other types are not recommended. Clamping is required.

Silicone Rubber Adhesives. Only silicone adhesives made specifically for glass and china are recommended. They form strong bonds, with excellent resistance to water and temperature extremes. Clamping is required.

METAL ADHESIVES AND FILLERS

Steel Epoxy. Steel epoxy is a two-part compound sold in tubes, similar to regular epoxy. It forms a strong, durable, heat- and water-resistant bond, and is recommended for patching gutters and gas tanks, sealing pipes, and filling rust holes. Drying time is about 12 hours; curing time is one to two days.

Steel Putty. This metal putty consists of two parts that are kneaded together before use. It forms a strong, water-resistant bond, and is recommended for patching and for sealing pipes that aren't under pressure; it also can be used for ceramic and masonry. Curing time is about 30 minutes. When dry, it can be sanded or painted.

Plastic Metal Cement. Plastic metal is a one-part adhesive and filler; it is moisture-resistant but cannot withstand temperature extremes. It is recommended for use on metal, glass, concrete, and wood, where strength is not required. Curing time is about four hours; when dry, it can be sanded or painted.

PLASTIC ADHESIVES

Plastics present a special problem for adhesives because solvents in the adhesives can dissolve plastic.

Model Cement. Model cements usually are sold in tubes. They form a strong bond on acrylics and polystyrenes, and can be used on most plastics, but don't use them on plastic foam. Clamping is usually required until the cement has set, about 10 minutes; curing time is about 24 hours. Model cement dries clear.

Vinyl Adhesive. Vinyl adhesives, sold in tubes, form a strong, waterproof bond on vinyl and on many plastics, but don't use them on plastic foam. Clamping is usually not required. Vinyl adhesive dries flexible and clear; curing time is 10 to 20 minutes.

Acrylic Solvent. Solvents are not adhesives as such; they act by melting the acrylic bonding surfaces, fusing them together at the joint. They are recommended for use on acrylics and polycarbonates. Clamping is required; the bonding surfaces are clamped or taped together and the solvent is injected into the joint with a syringe. Setting time is about five minutes.

INDEX